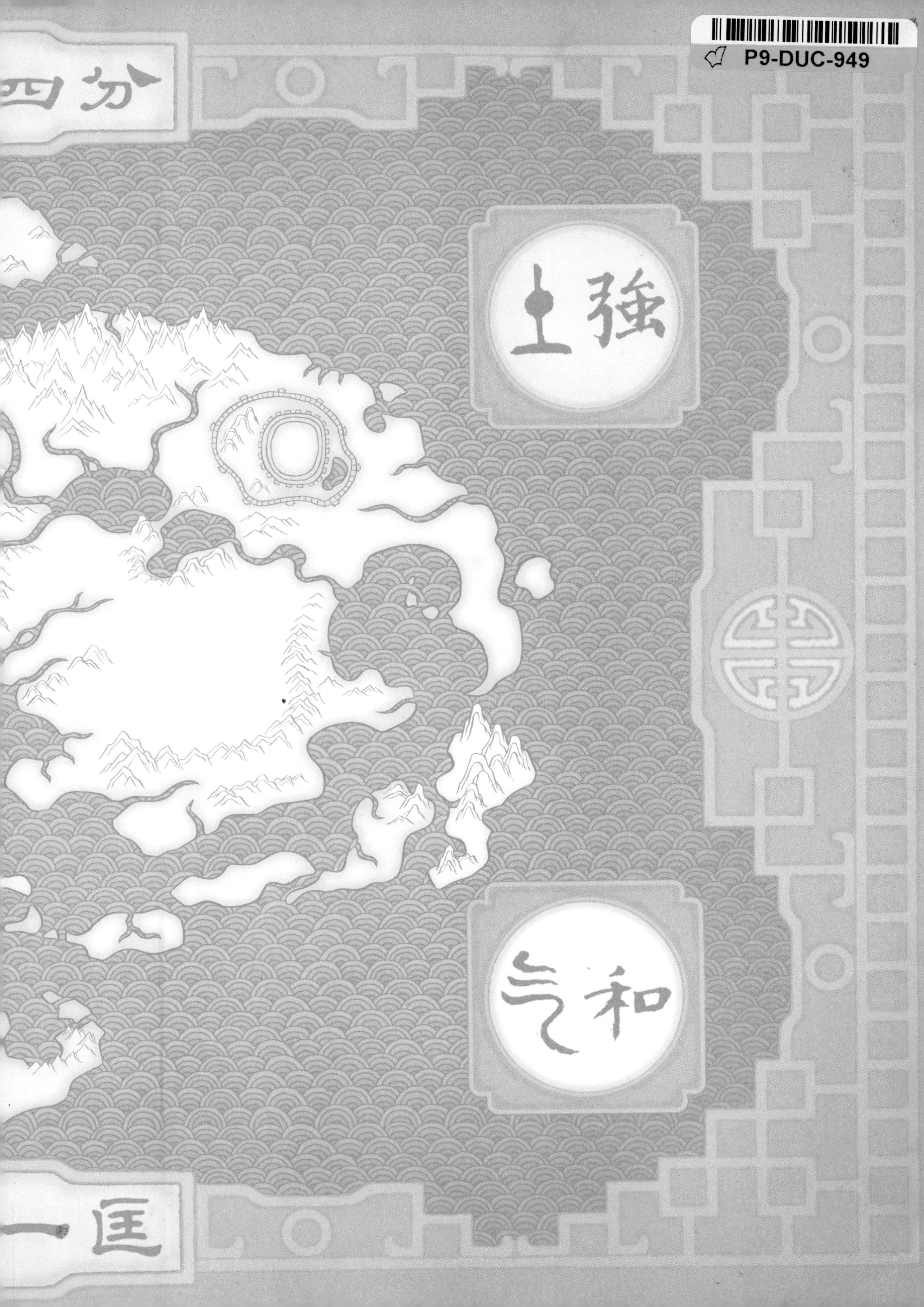
四分
土強
和
匡

AVATAR
THE LAST AIRBENDER

Created by

BRYAN KONIETZKO

**MICHAEL DANTE
DiMARTINO**

nickelodeon

降去神通

AVATAR

THE LAST AIRBENDER

THE SEARCH

GENE
LUEN YANG
Script

GURIHIRU
Art & Cover

MICHAEL
HEISLER
Lettering

DARK HORSE BOOKS

MIKE RICHARDSON
Publisher

DAVE MARSHALL
Editor

JUSTIN COUCH
Collection Designer

SHANTEL LaROCQUE, IAN TUCKER,
***and* AARON WALKER**
Assistant Editors

Translation by AKI YANAGI

Special thanks to LINDA LEE,
KAT VAN DAM, JAMES SALERNO, *and* JOAN HILTY
at Nickelodeon, and to BRYAN KONIETZKO *and*
MICHAEL DANTE DiMARTINO.

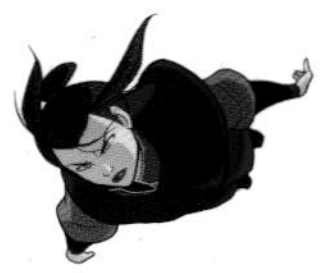

13 15 17 19 20 18 16 14 12

ISBN 978-1-61655-226-8 Nick.com DarkHorse.com First edition: February 2014

Published by **DARK HORSE BOOKS**, a division of Dark Horse Comics LLC, 10956 SE Main Street, Milwaukie, OR 97222

To find a comics shop in your area, visit comicshoplocator.com.

This book collects *Avatar: The Last Airbender—The Search* Parts 1 through 3.

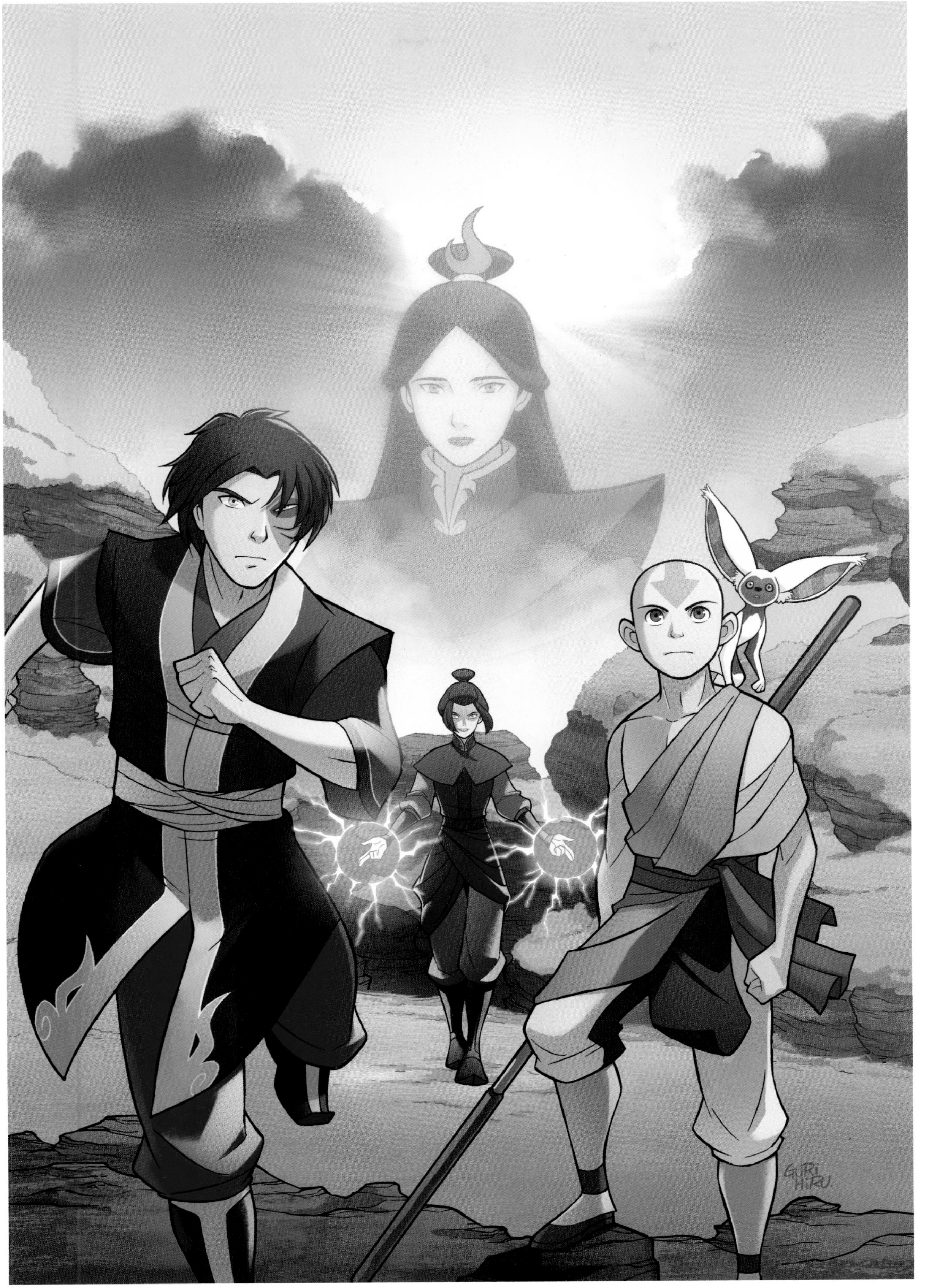
GURI HIRU.

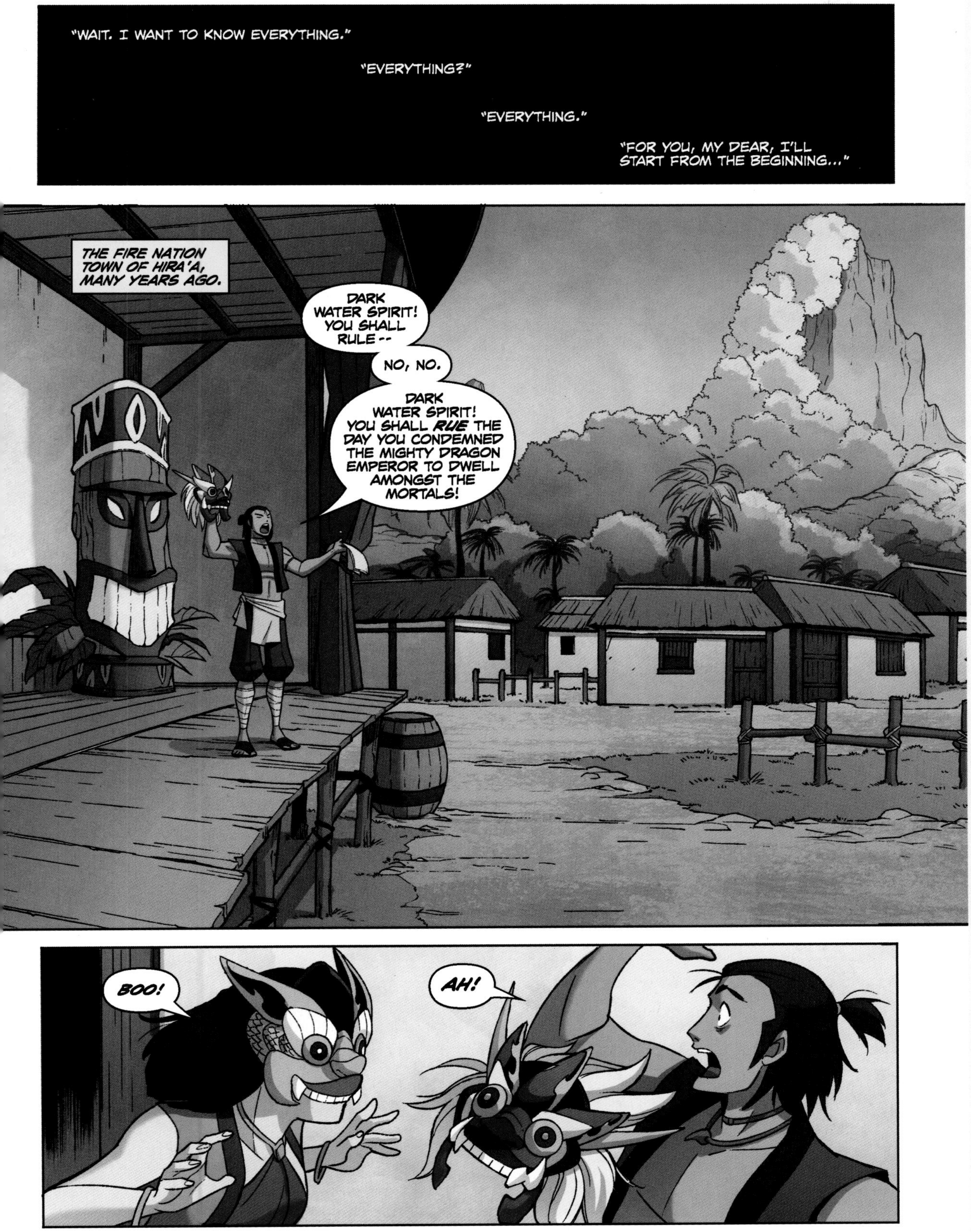
"WAIT. I WANT TO KNOW EVERYTHING."
"EVERYTHING?"
"EVERYTHING."
"FOR YOU, MY DEAR, I'LL START FROM THE BEGINNING..."
THE FIRE NATION TOWN OF HIRA'A, MANY YEARS AGO.
DARK WATER SPIRIT! YOU SHALL RULE --
NO, NO.
DARK WATER SPIRIT! YOU SHALL RUE THE DAY YOU CONDEMNED THE MIGHTY DRAGON EMPEROR TO DWELL AMONGST THE MORTALS!
BOO!
AH!

MICHAEL DANTE DIMARTINO: *Over the years, the number-one question fans asked Bryan and me was, "What happened to Zuko's mom?" It was a story we always wanted to tell, and once Gene was onboard to write the graphic novels, we knew this would be the time and place to tell it. After catching up with Team Avatar in* The Promise, *we all agreed the next story should focus on Zuko's search for Ursa.*

GENE LUEN YANG: *We wanted Ursa to be from someplace remote, far removed from the hustle and bustle of the Fire Nation capital city. Since the Fire Nation takes many of its cues from early twentieth-century Japan, why not base Ursa's hometown on a Hawaiian village? Many Japanese immigrants settled in Hawaii around the turn of the century. They created communities that combined the familiar with the foreign. Hira'a, the name of Ursa's hometown, is a contraction of the Japanese name Hirahara. Hirahara Zenmatsu was one of the first Japanese to set foot in Hawaii.*

GURIHIRU: *The model for Hira'a was a small, old-fashioned village of Japanese immigrants. Contemporary photos are rare, so finding visual references was a challenge. We combined Japanese imagery with that of an old, tropical Hawaiian settlement.*

M: *I never thought we'd see* Love amongst the Dragons *make a comeback. In "The Ember Island Players," Zuko tells his friends that his mom would drag him to see the play when he was younger. I love how Gene tied it into this story. Now we know why the play meant so much to Ursa!*

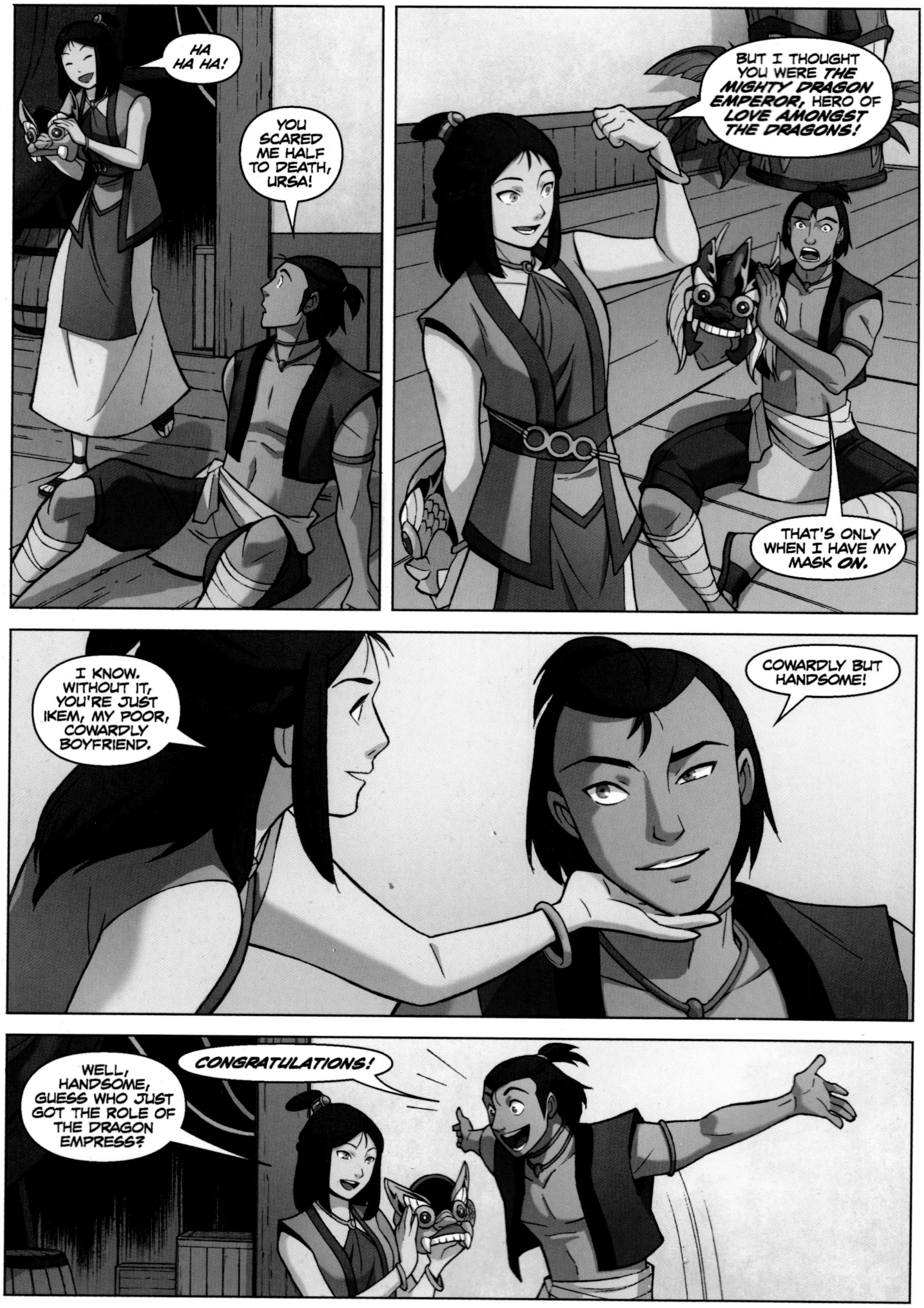
HA HA HA!
YOU SCARED ME HALF TO DEATH, URSA!
BUT I THOUGHT YOU WERE THE MIGHTY DRAGON EMPEROR, HERO OF LOVE AMONGST THE DRAGONS!
THAT'S ONLY WHEN I HAVE MY MASK ON.
I KNOW. WITHOUT IT, YOU'RE JUST IKEM, MY POOR, COWARDLY BOYFRIEND.
COWARDLY BUT HANDSOME!
WELL, HANDSOME, GUESS WHO JUST GOT THE ROLE OF THE DRAGON EMPRESS?
CONGRATULATIONS!

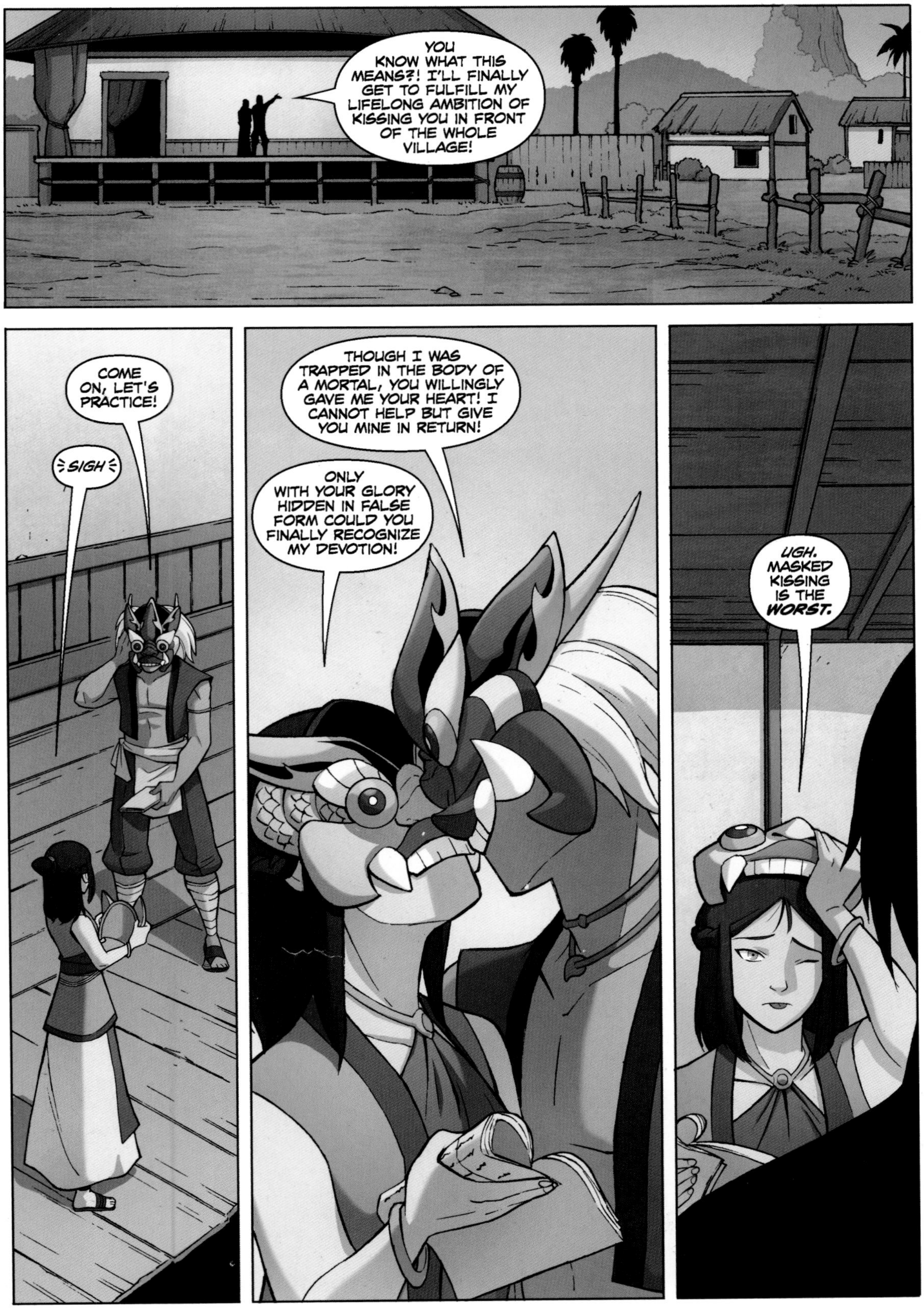
YOU KNOW WHAT THIS MEANS?! I'LL FINALLY GET TO FULFILL MY LIFELONG AMBITION OF KISSING YOU IN FRONT OF THE WHOLE VILLAGE!
COME ON, LET'S PRACTICE!
SIGH
THOUGH I WAS TRAPPED IN THE BODY OF A MORTAL, YOU WILLINGLY GAVE ME YOUR HEART! I CANNOT HELP BUT GIVE YOU MINE IN RETURN!
ONLY WITH YOUR GLORY HIDDEN IN FALSE FORM COULD YOU FINALLY RECOGNIZE MY DEVOTION!
UGH. MASKED KISSING IS THE WORST.

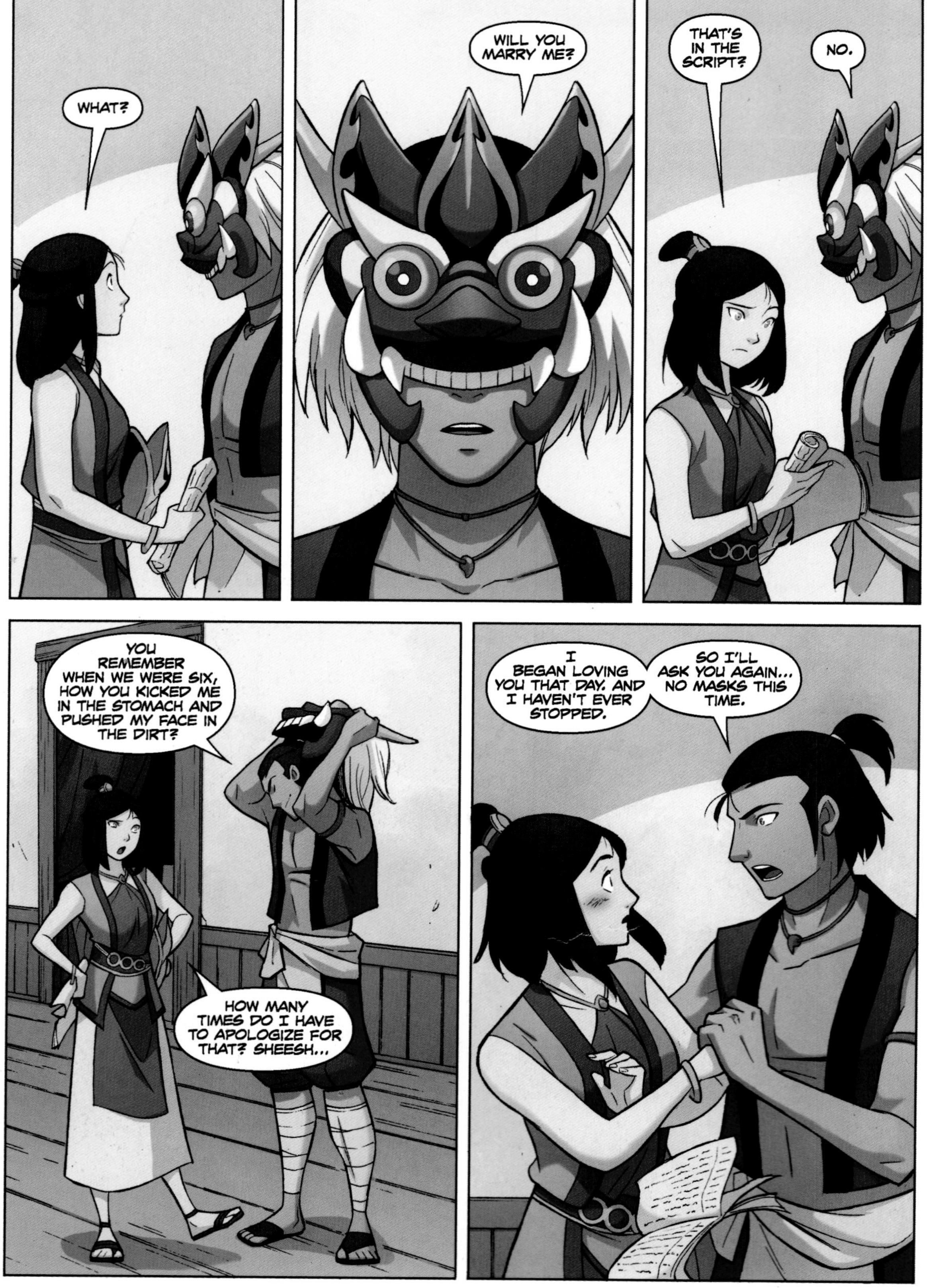
WHAT?
WILL YOU MARRY ME?
THAT'S IN THE SCRIPT?
NO.
YOU REMEMBER WHEN WE WERE SIX, HOW YOU KICKED ME IN THE STOMACH AND PUSHED MY FACE IN THE DIRT?
HOW MANY TIMES DO I HAVE TO APOLOGIZE FOR THAT? SHEESH...
I BEGAN LOVING YOU THAT DAY. AND I HAVEN'T EVER STOPPED.
SO I'LL ASK YOU AGAIN... NO MASKS THIS TIME.

G: *The dragon masks Ikem and Ursa wear were inspired by southeast Asian masks.*

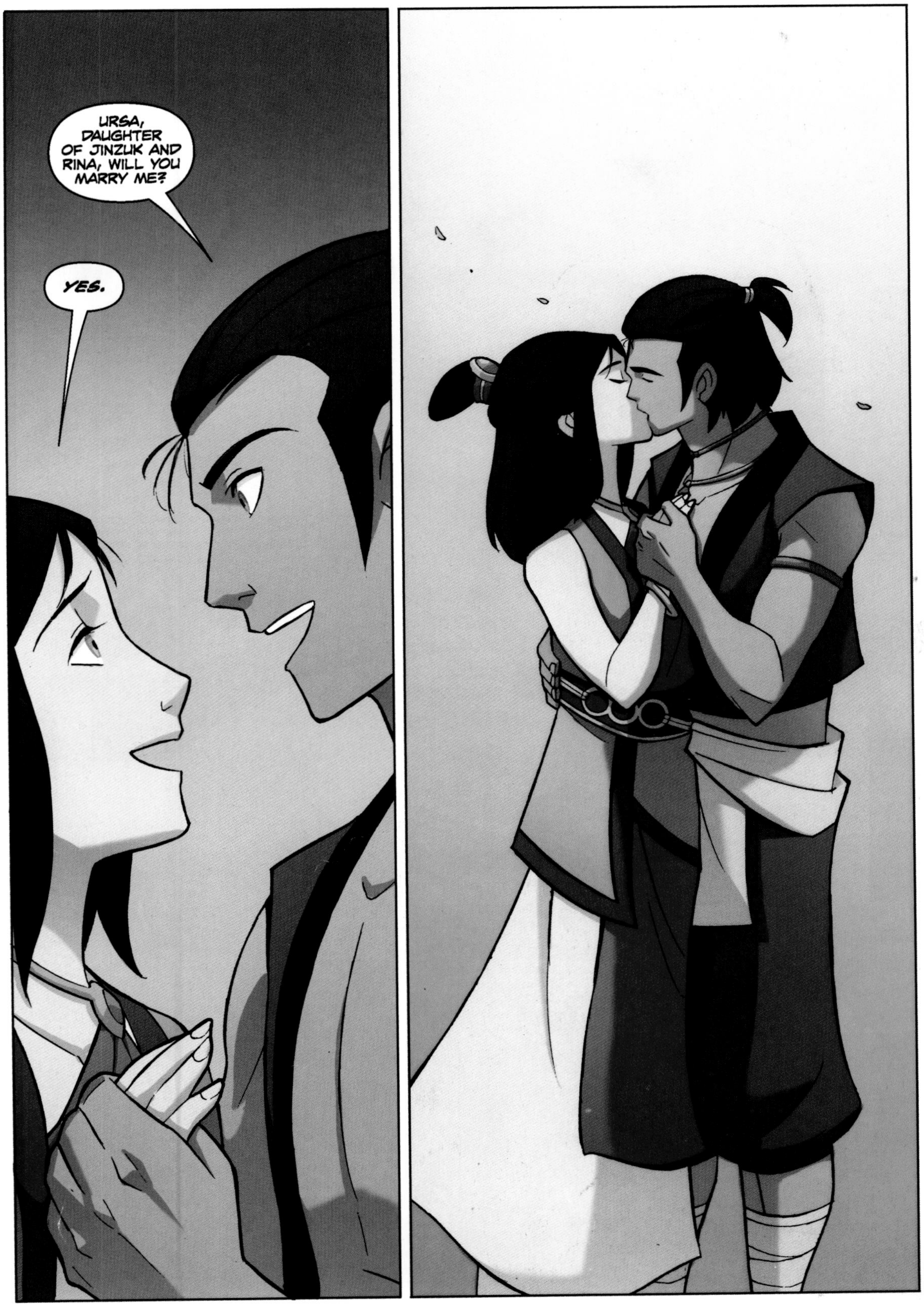
URSA, DAUGHTER OF JINZUK AND RINA, WILL YOU MARRY ME?
YES.

M: *Coming into* The Search, *Bryan and I had some ideas about what happened to Ursa, but nothing was really nailed down until my discussions with Gene, who added a ton to the story, including Ursa's backstory with Ikem.*

THE CITY OF YU DAO, NOW.

M: *Through the story of Yu Dao, the seeds are being planted in Aang and Zuko's minds for Republic City. Even the horseshoe shape of the meeting table is a precursor to the one seen in the United Council chambers in Legend of Korra.*

BLAH BLAH BLAH BLAH

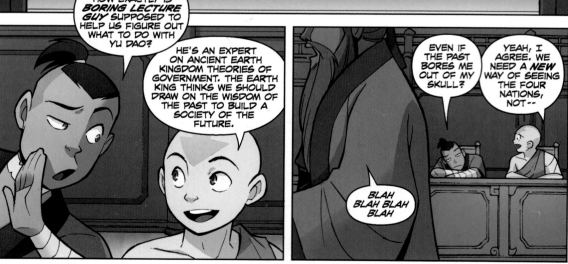

TELL ME AGAIN, HOW EXACTLY IS *BORING LECTURE GUY* SUPPOSED TO HELP US FIGURE OUT WHAT TO DO WITH YU DAO?

HE'S AN EXPERT ON ANCIENT EARTH KINGDOM THEORIES OF GOVERNMENT. THE EARTH KING THINKS WE SHOULD DRAW ON THE WISDOM OF THE PAST TO BUILD A SOCIETY OF THE FUTURE.

EVEN IF THE PAST BORES ME OUT OF MY SKULL?

YEAH, I AGREE. WE NEED A *NEW* WAY OF SEEING THE FOUR NATIONS, NOT--

BLAH BLAH BLAH BLAH

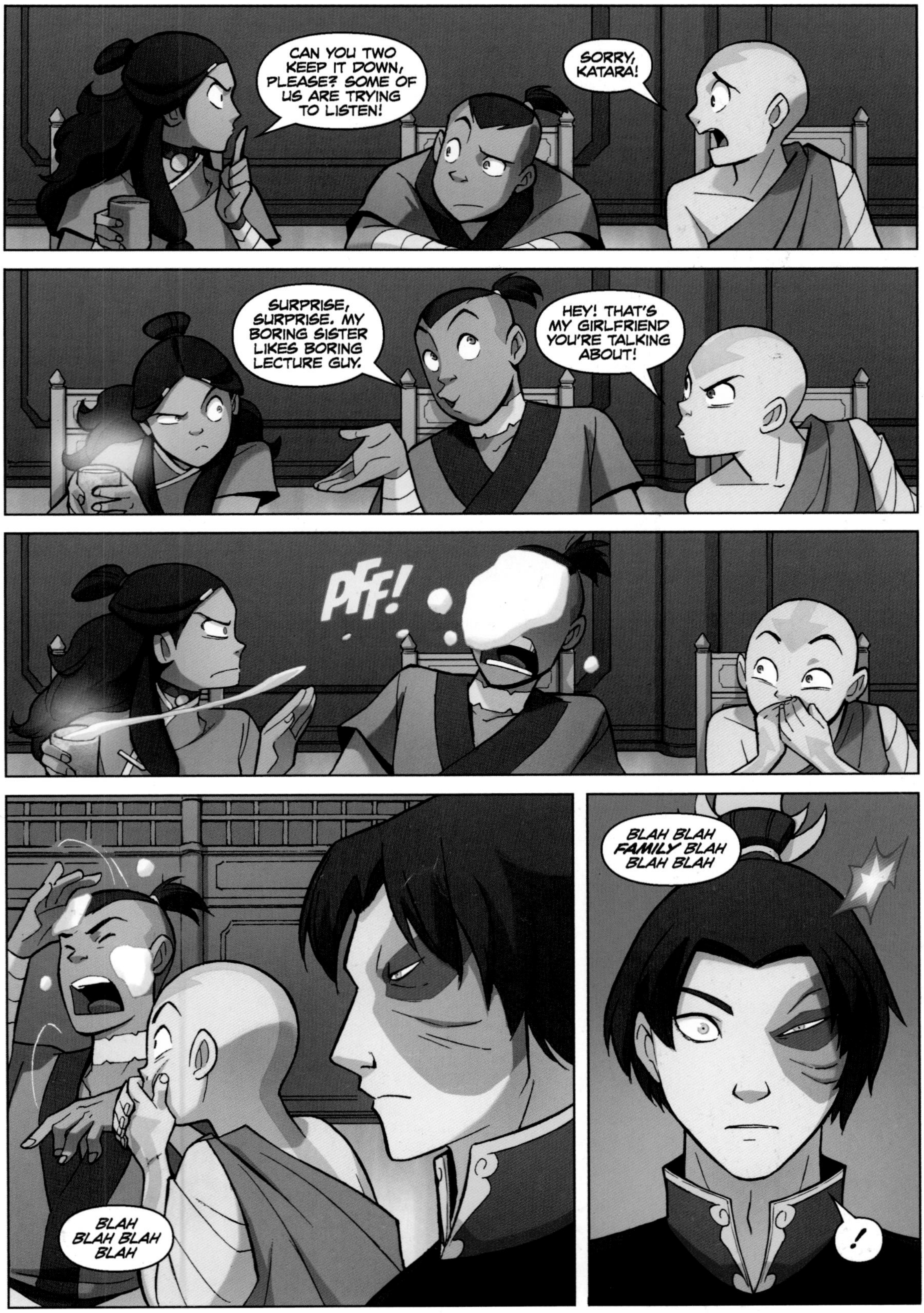
CAN YOU TWO KEEP IT DOWN, PLEASE? SOME OF US ARE TRYING TO LISTEN!
SORRY, KATARA!
SURPRISE, SURPRISE. MY BORING SISTER LIKES BORING LECTURE GUY.
HEY! THAT'S MY GIRLFRIEND YOU'RE TALKING ABOUT!
PFF!
BLAH BLAH BLAH BLAH
BLAH BLAH FAMILY BLAH BLAH BLAH
!

G: *The model for the professor was the Chinese philosopher Confucius, which was a request from Gene.*

GLY: *The unnamed Earth Kingdom scholar here is the Avatarverse version of Confucius. The philosophy he advocates, linking family to nation, is a loose paraphrase of a Confucian principle.*

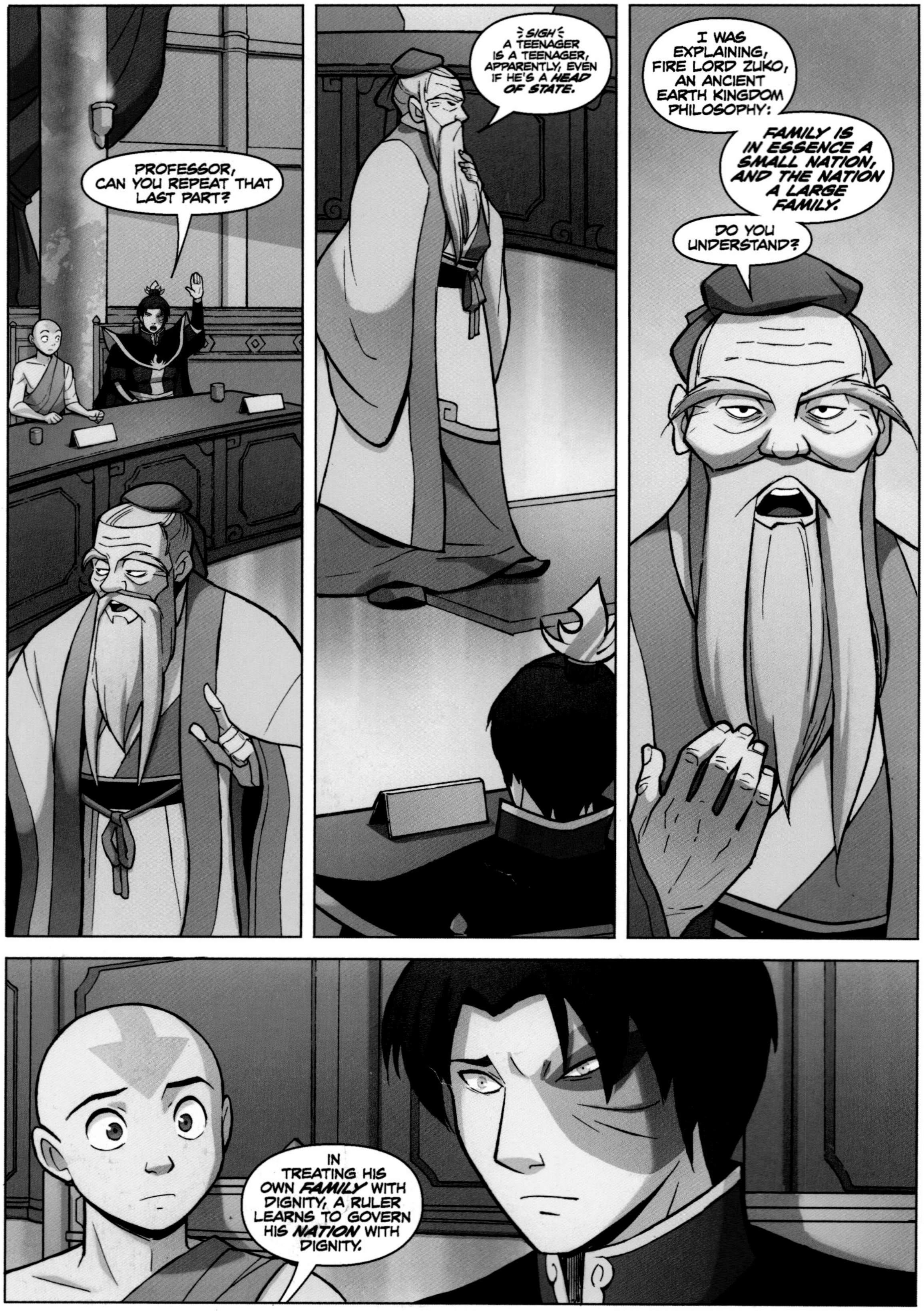
PROFESSOR, CAN YOU REPEAT THAT LAST PART?
SIGH A TEENAGER IS A TEENAGER, APPARENTLY, EVEN IF HE'S A HEAD OF STATE.
I WAS EXPLAINING, FIRE LORD ZUKO, AN ANCIENT EARTH KINGDOM PHILOSOPHY:
FAMILY IS IN ESSENCE A SMALL NATION, AND THE NATION A LARGE FAMILY.
DO YOU UNDERSTAND?
IN TREATING HIS OWN FAMILY WITH DIGNITY, A RULER LEARNS TO GOVERN HIS NATION WITH DIGNITY.

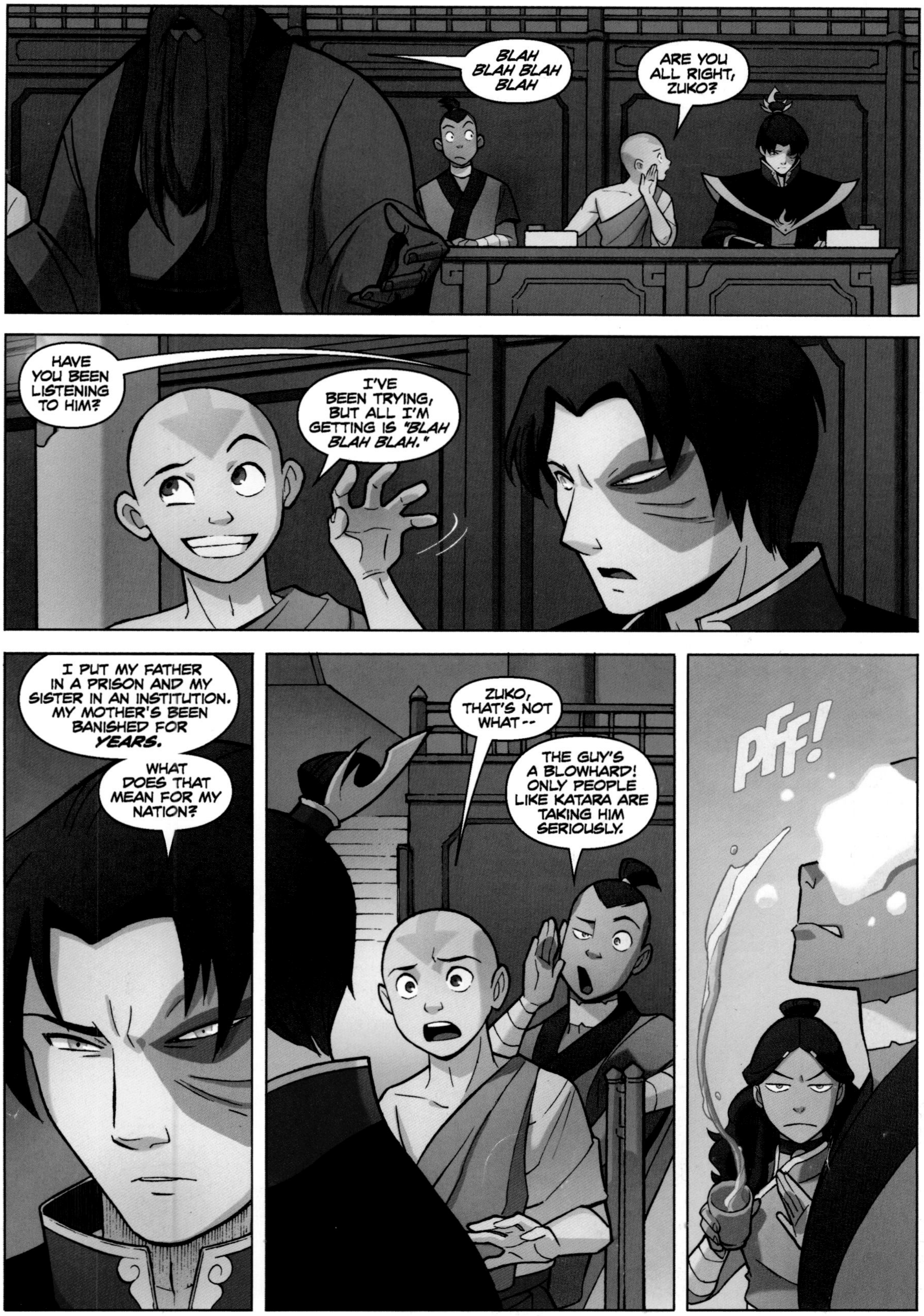
BLAH BLAH BLAH BLAH
ARE YOU ALL RIGHT, ZUKO?
HAVE YOU BEEN LISTENING TO HIM?
I'VE BEEN TRYING, BUT ALL I'M GETTING IS "BLAH BLAH BLAH."
I PUT MY FATHER IN A PRISON AND MY SISTER IN AN INSTITUTION. MY MOTHER'S BEEN BANISHED FOR *YEARS*.
WHAT DOES THAT MEAN FOR MY NATION?
ZUKO, THAT'S NOT WHAT--
THE GUY'S A BLOWHARD! ONLY PEOPLE LIKE KATARA ARE TAKING HIM SERIOUSLY.
PFF!

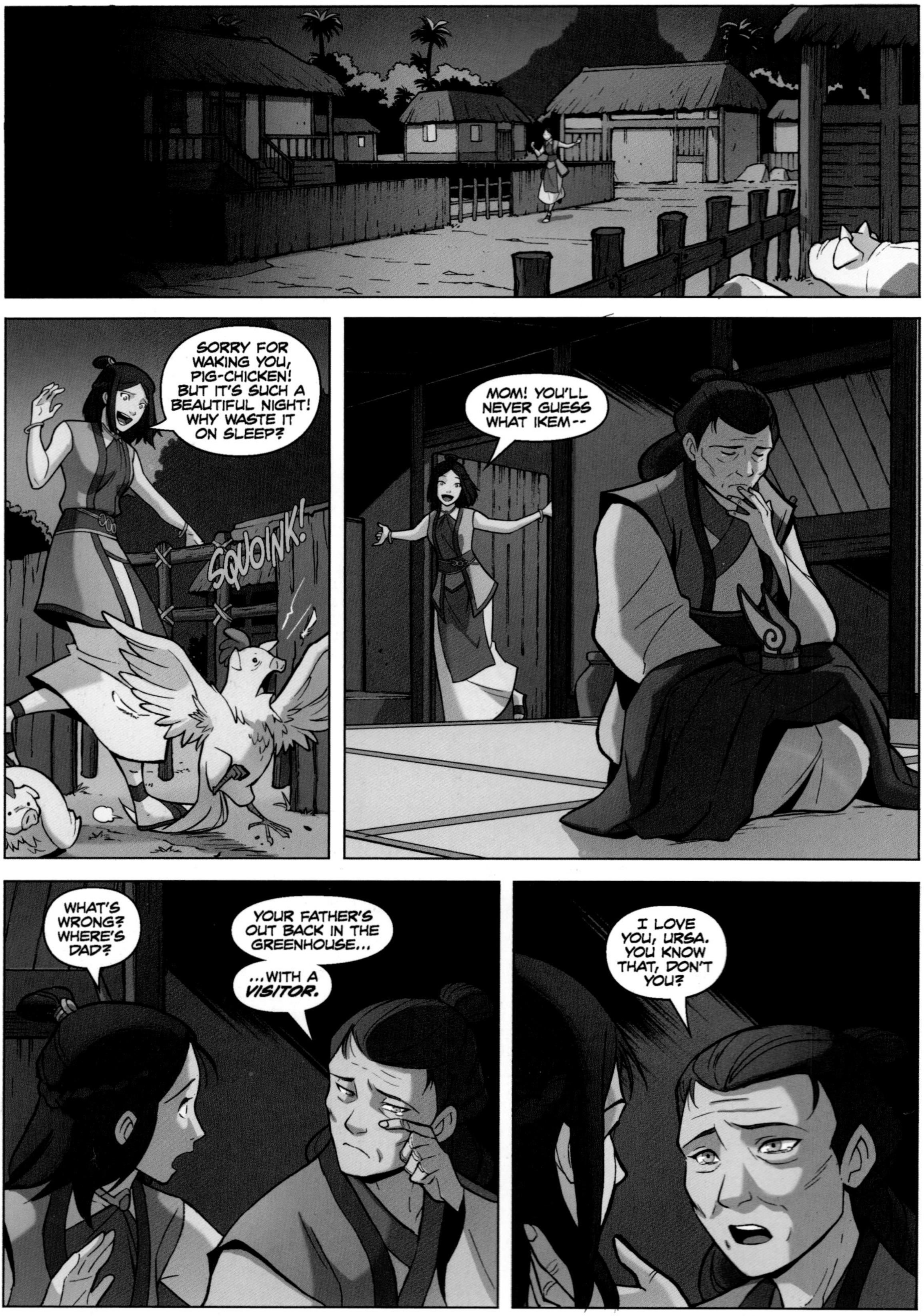
SORRY FOR WAKING YOU, PIG-CHICKEN! BUT IT'S SUCH A BEAUTIFUL NIGHT! WHY WASTE IT ON SLEEP?
SQUOINK!
MOM! YOU'LL NEVER GUESS WHAT IKEM--
WHAT'S WRONG? WHERE'S DAD?
YOUR FATHER'S OUT BACK IN THE GREENHOUSE...
...WITH A *VISITOR*.
I LOVE YOU, URSA. YOU KNOW THAT, DON'T YOU?

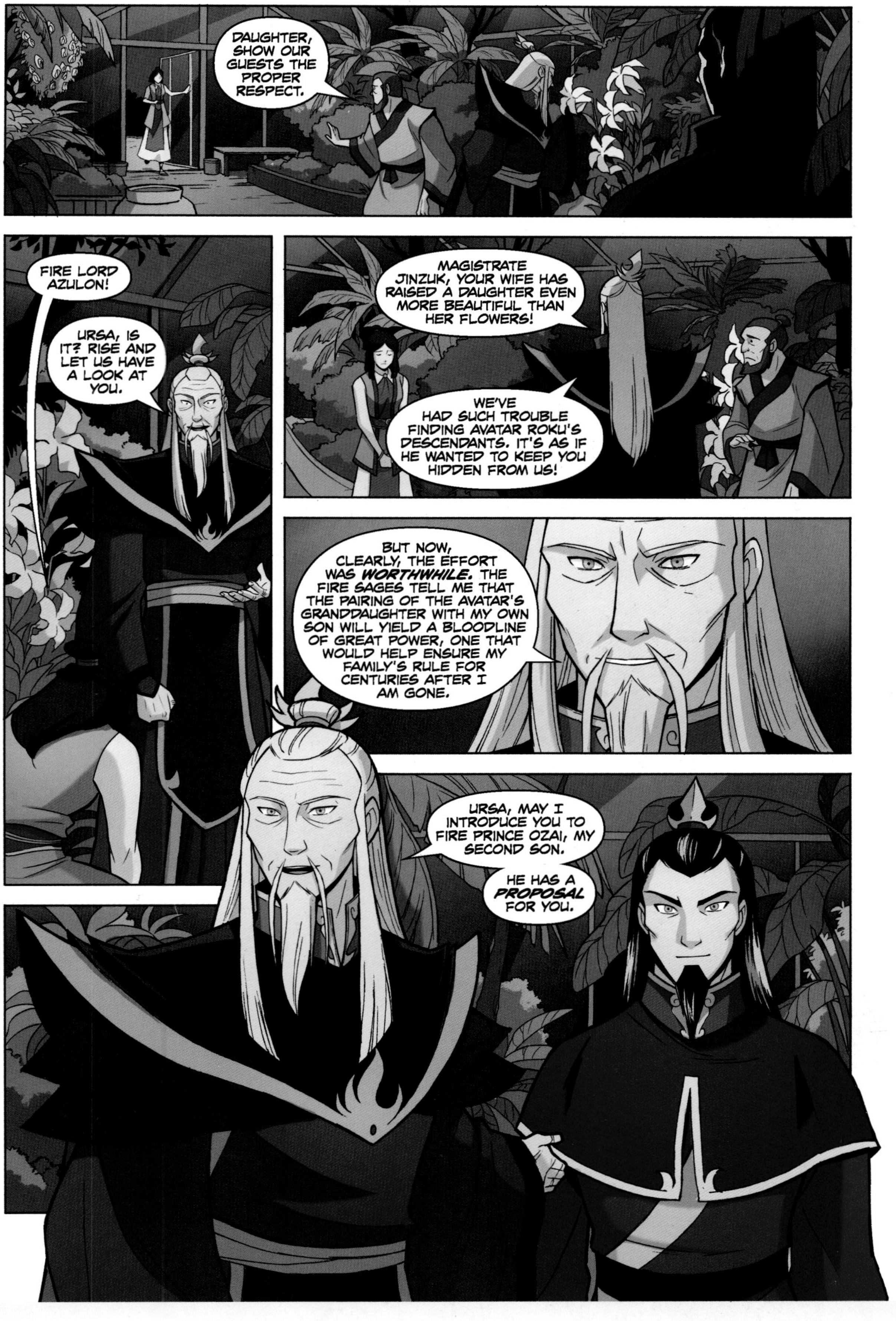
DAUGHTER, SHOW OUR GUESTS THE PROPER RESPECT.
FIRE LORD AZULON!
URSA, IS IT? RISE AND LET US HAVE A LOOK AT YOU.
MAGISTRATE JINZUK, YOUR WIFE HAS RAISED A DAUGHTER EVEN MORE BEAUTIFUL THAN HER FLOWERS!
WE'VE HAD SUCH TROUBLE FINDING AVATAR ROKU'S DESCENDANTS. IT'S AS IF HE WANTED TO KEEP YOU HIDDEN FROM US!
BUT NOW, CLEARLY, THE EFFORT WAS WORTHWHILE. THE FIRE SAGES TELL ME THAT THE PAIRING OF THE AVATAR'S GRANDDAUGHTER WITH MY OWN SON WILL YIELD A BLOODLINE OF GREAT POWER, ONE THAT WOULD HELP ENSURE MY FAMILY'S RULE FOR CENTURIES AFTER I AM GONE.
URSA, MAY I INTRODUCE YOU TO FIRE PRINCE OZAI, MY SECOND SON.
HE HAS A PROPOSAL FOR YOU.

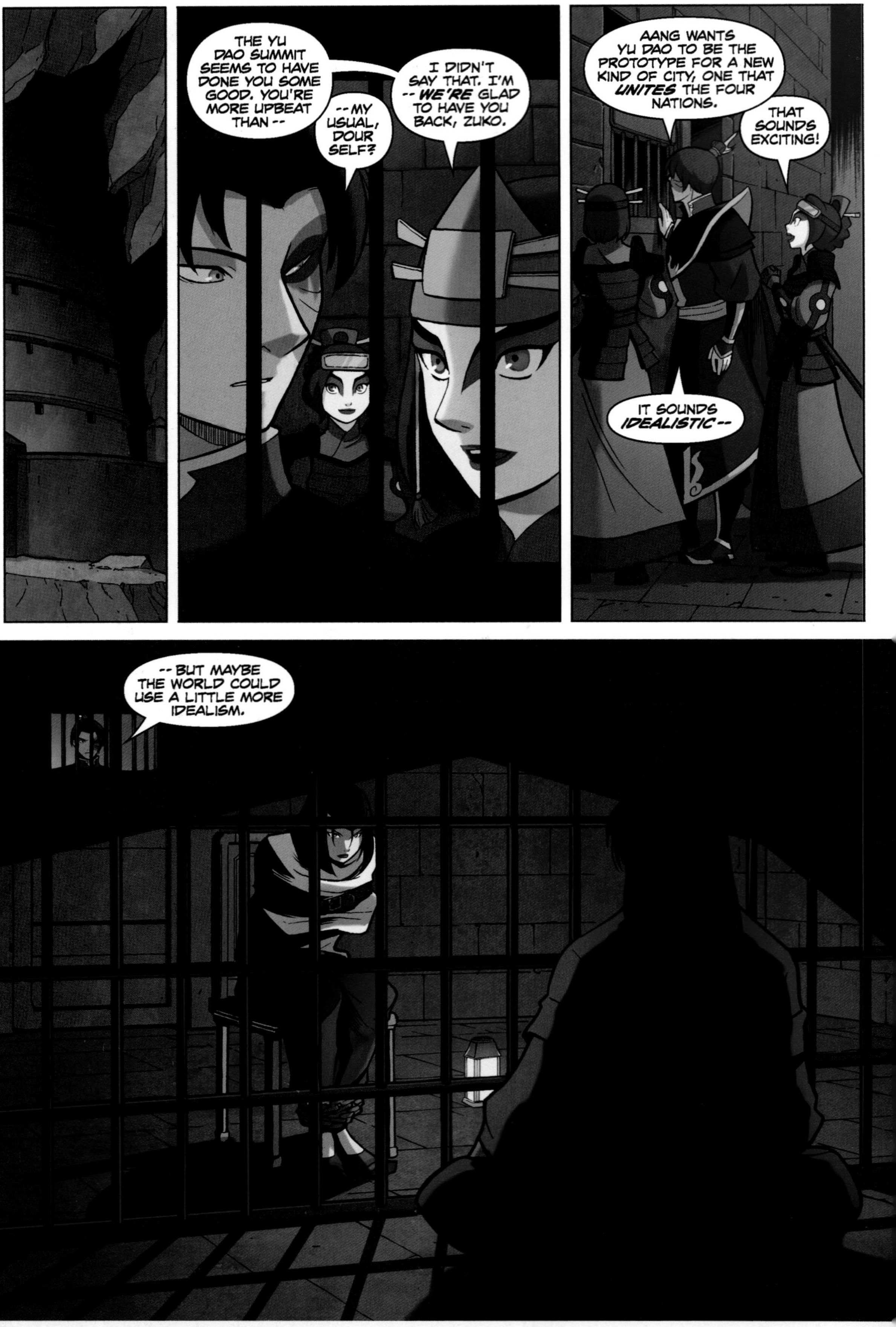
THE YU DAO SUMMIT SEEMS TO HAVE DONE YOU SOME GOOD. YOU'RE MORE UPBEAT THAN --
--MY USUAL, DOUR SELF?
I DIDN'T SAY THAT. I'M --*WE'RE* GLAD TO HAVE YOU BACK, ZUKO.
AANG WANTS YU DAO TO BE THE PROTOTYPE FOR A NEW KIND OF CITY, ONE THAT *UNITES* THE FOUR NATIONS.
THAT SOUNDS EXCITING!
IT SOUNDS *IDEALISTIC* --
--BUT MAYBE THE WORLD COULD USE A LITTLE MORE IDEALISM.

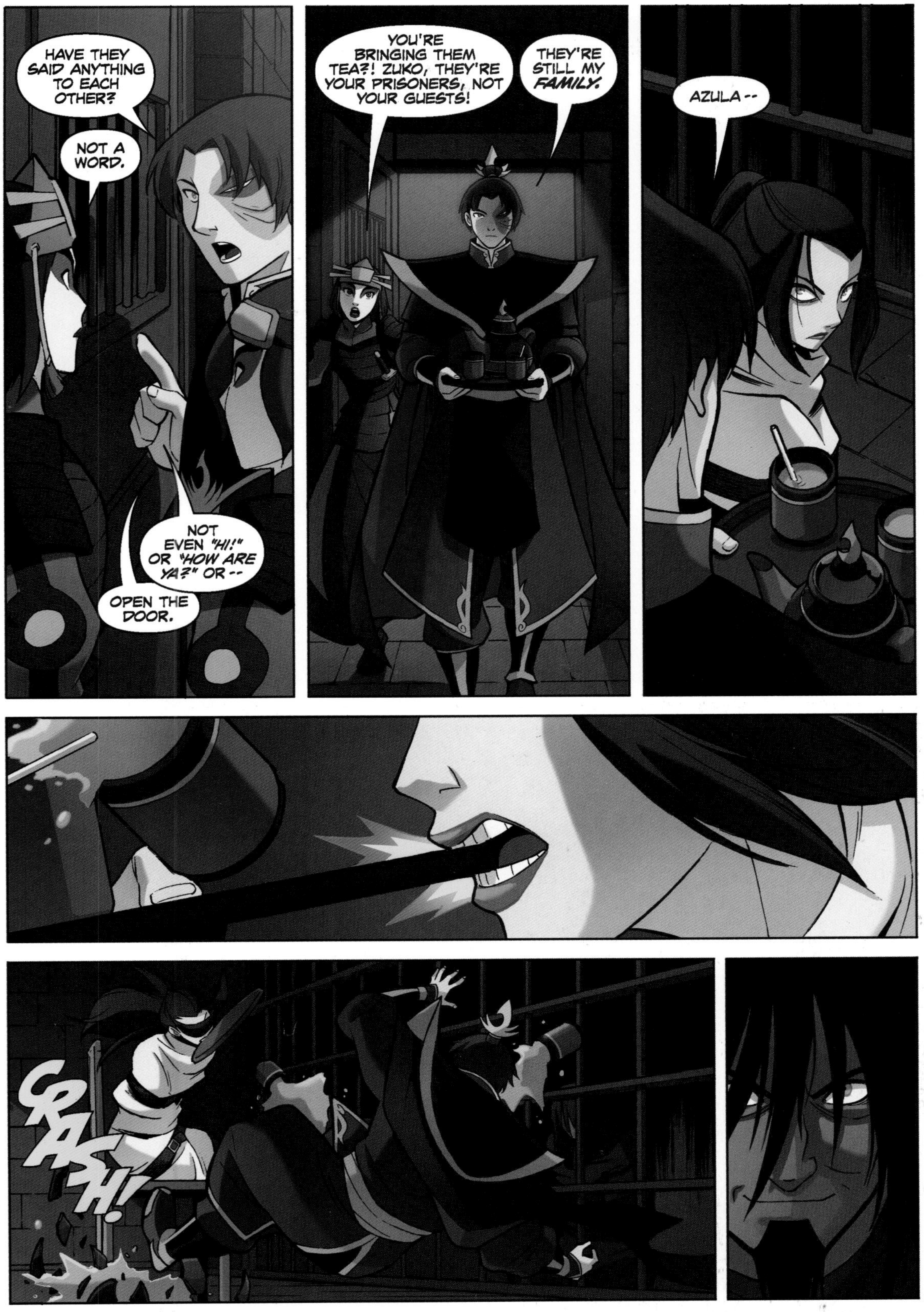
HAVE THEY SAID ANYTHING TO EACH OTHER?
NOT A WORD.
NOT EVEN "HI!" OR "HOW ARE YA?" OR --
OPEN THE DOOR.
YOU'RE BRINGING THEM TEA?! ZUKO, THEY'RE YOUR PRISONERS, NOT YOUR GUESTS!
THEY'RE STILL MY FAMILY.
AZULA --
CRASH!

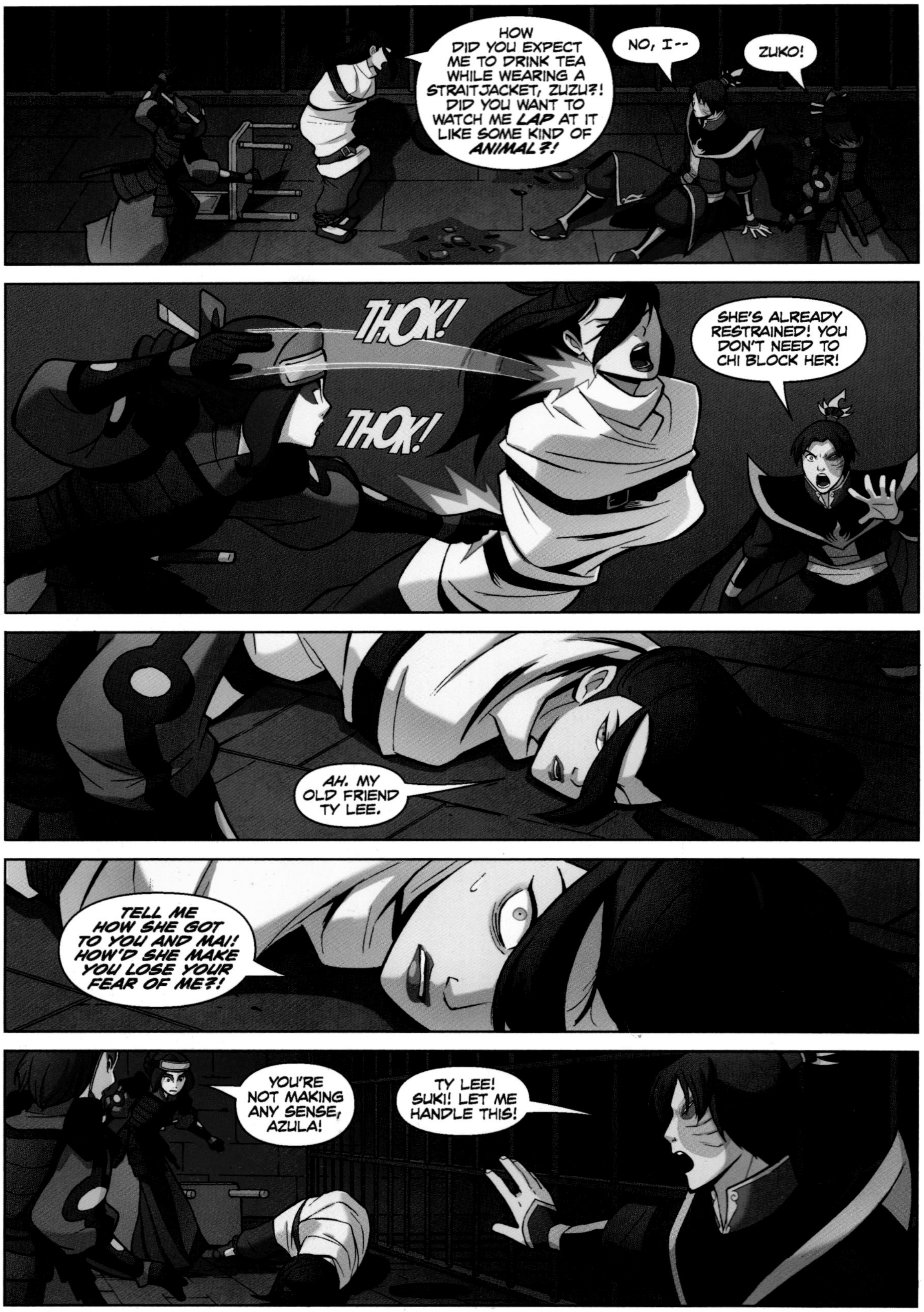
HOW DID YOU EXPECT ME TO DRINK TEA WHILE WEARING A STRAITJACKET, ZUZU?! DID YOU WANT TO WATCH ME LAP AT IT LIKE SOME KIND OF ANIMAL?!
NO, I--
ZUKO!
THOK!
THOK!
SHE'S ALREADY RESTRAINED! YOU DON'T NEED TO CHI BLOCK HER!
AH. MY OLD FRIEND TY LEE.
TELL ME HOW SHE GOT TO YOU AND MAI! HOW'D SHE MAKE YOU LOSE YOUR FEAR OF ME?!
YOU'RE NOT MAKING ANY SENSE, AZULA!
TY LEE! SUKI! LET ME HANDLE THIS!

YOU AND FATHER ARE MEETING FOR THE FIRST TIME IN OVER A YEAR, AND I KNOW THESE AREN'T THE BEST OF CIRCUMSTANCES.

I THOUGHT THE TEA MIGHT LEND A LITTLE... *DIGNITY.*

YOU WANT DIGNITY? LET FATHER AND ME TALK TO ONE ANOTHER LIKE TWO HUMAN BEINGS.

IN PRIVATE.

...

FINE.

WE'LL GIVE THEM HALF AN HOUR.

YOU SURE ABOUT THIS?

ONE IS CHI BLOCKED AND THE OTHER HAS COMPLETELY LOST HIS FIREBENDING. THEY CAN'T DO ANYTHING BUT TALK.

LIKE IT OR NOT, AZULA IS MY *BEST CHANCE* OF *FINDING MY MOTHER.*

SHE'S WRONG, YOU KNOW. I NEVER LOST MY FEAR OF HER.

M: *As with the series, we often use flashback stories to illuminate what is going on with the characters in the present. The ideas of karma, and how past actions influence the present, are big themes throughout both* The Last Airbender *and* Legend of Korra.

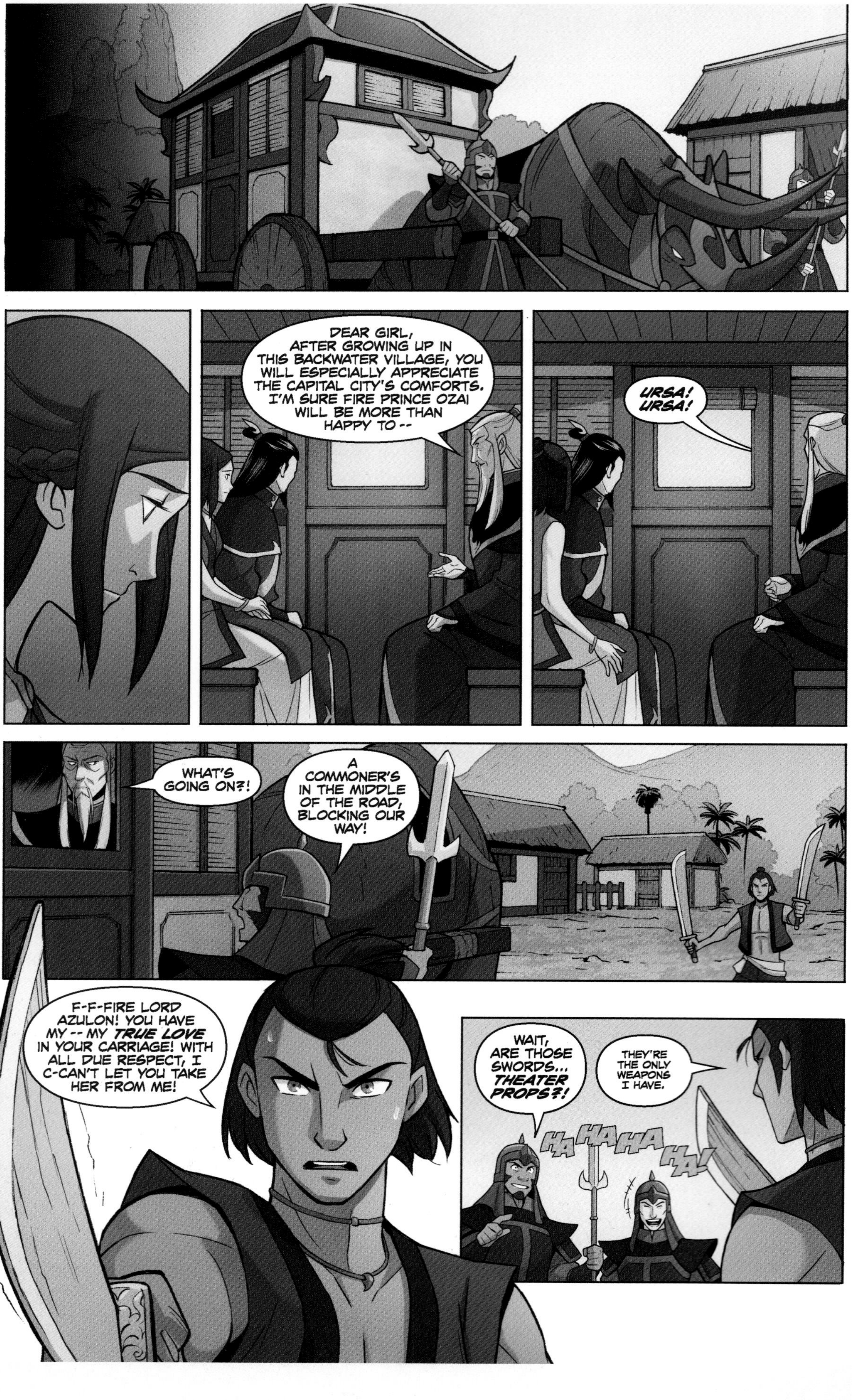
DEAR GIRL, AFTER GROWING UP IN THIS BACKWATER VILLAGE, YOU WILL ESPECIALLY APPRECIATE THE CAPITAL CITY'S COMFORTS. I'M SURE FIRE PRINCE OZAI WILL BE MORE THAN HAPPY TO --
URSA! URSA!
WHAT'S GOING ON?!
A COMMONER'S IN THE MIDDLE OF THE ROAD, BLOCKING OUR WAY!
F-F-FIRE LORD AZULON! YOU HAVE MY -- MY TRUE LOVE IN YOUR CARRIAGE! WITH ALL DUE RESPECT, I C-CAN'T LET YOU TAKE HER FROM ME!
WAIT, ARE THOSE SWORDS... THEATER PROPS?!
THEY'RE THE ONLY WEAPONS I HAVE.
HA HA HA HA HA!

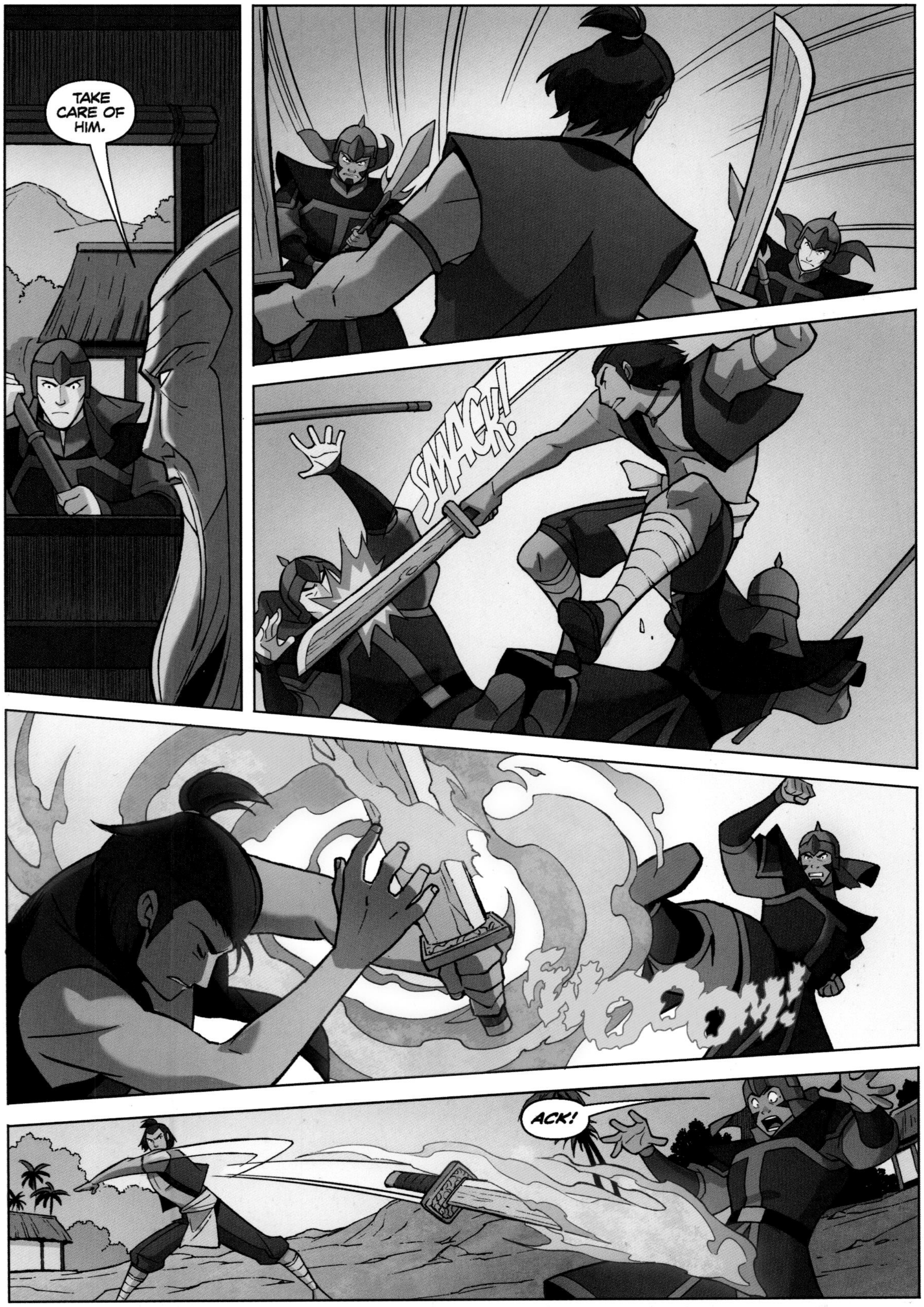
TAKE CARE OF HIM.
SMACK!
FWOOOM!
ACK!

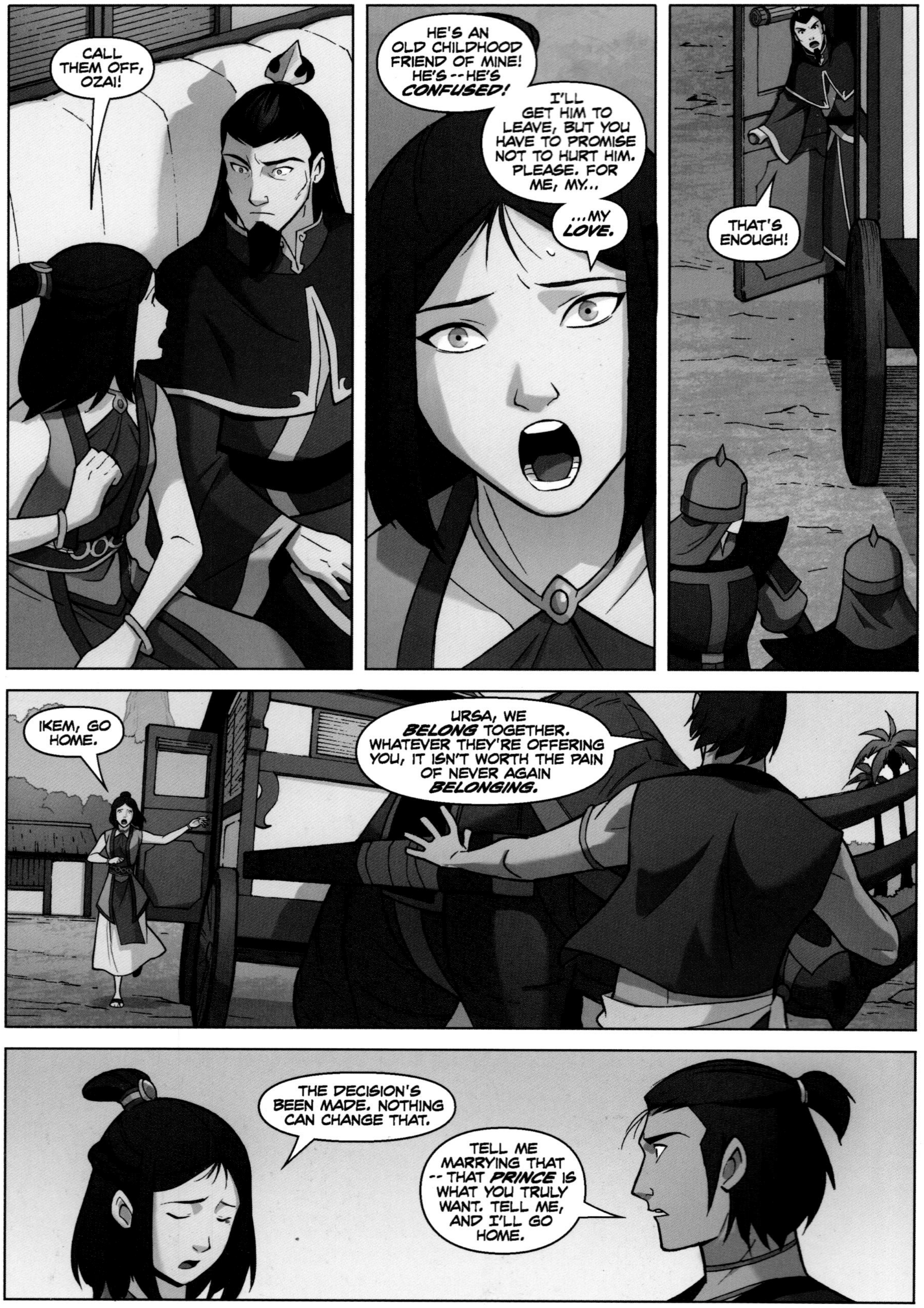
CALL THEM OFF, OZAI!
HE'S AN OLD CHILDHOOD FRIEND OF MINE! HE'S--HE'S CONFUSED!
I'LL GET HIM TO LEAVE, BUT YOU HAVE TO PROMISE NOT TO HURT HIM. PLEASE. FOR ME, MY...
...MY LOVE.
THAT'S ENOUGH!
IKEM, GO HOME.
URSA, WE BELONG TOGETHER. WHATEVER THEY'RE OFFERING YOU, IT ISN'T WORTH THE PAIN OF NEVER AGAIN BELONGING.
THE DECISION'S BEEN MADE. NOTHING CAN CHANGE THAT.
TELL ME MARRYING THAT --THAT PRINCE IS WHAT YOU TRULY WANT. TELL ME, AND I'LL GO HOME.

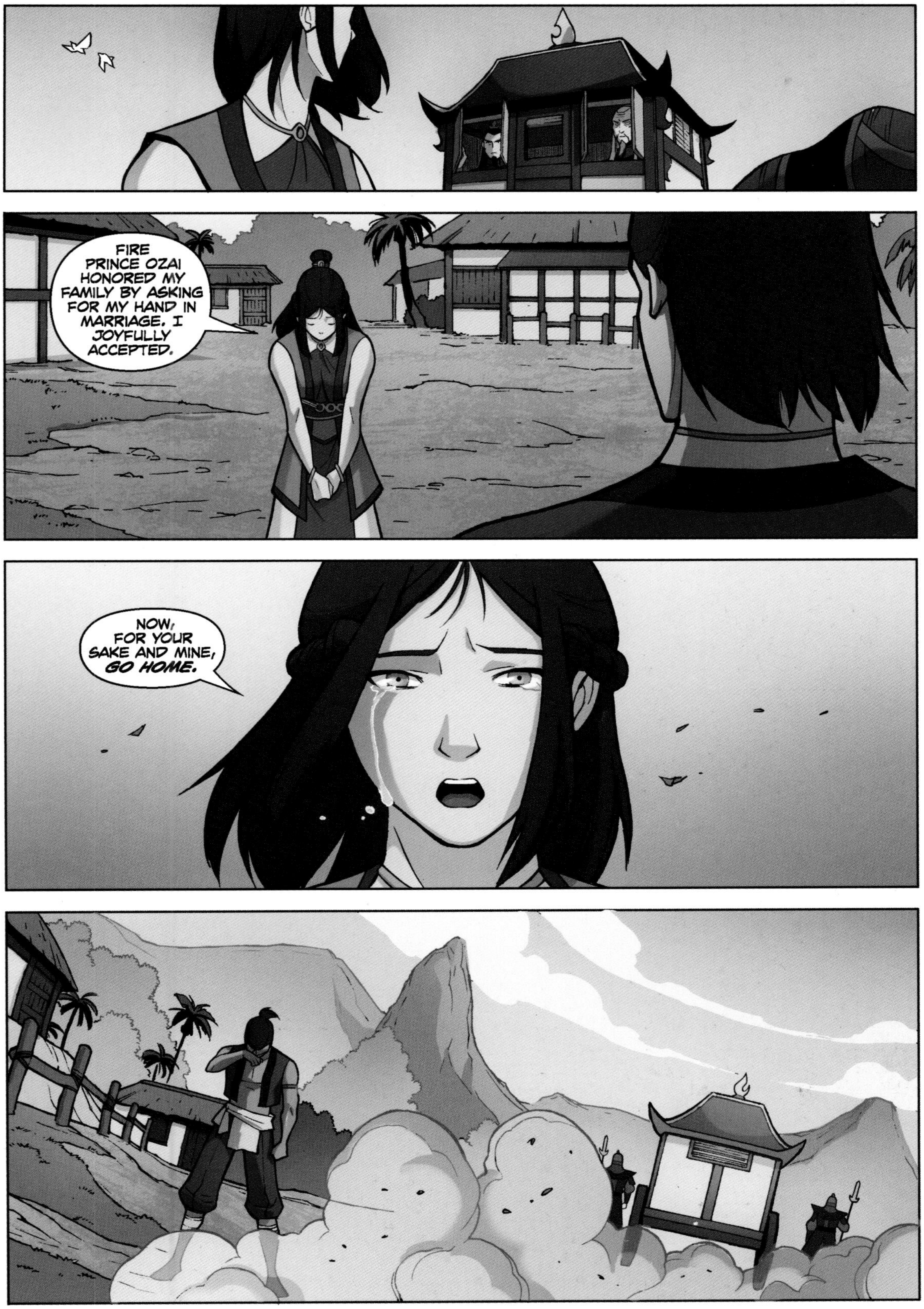
FIRE PRINCE OZAI HONORED MY FAMILY BY ASKING FOR MY HAND IN MARRIAGE. I JOYFULLY ACCEPTED.
NOW, FOR YOUR SAKE AND MINE, GO HOME.

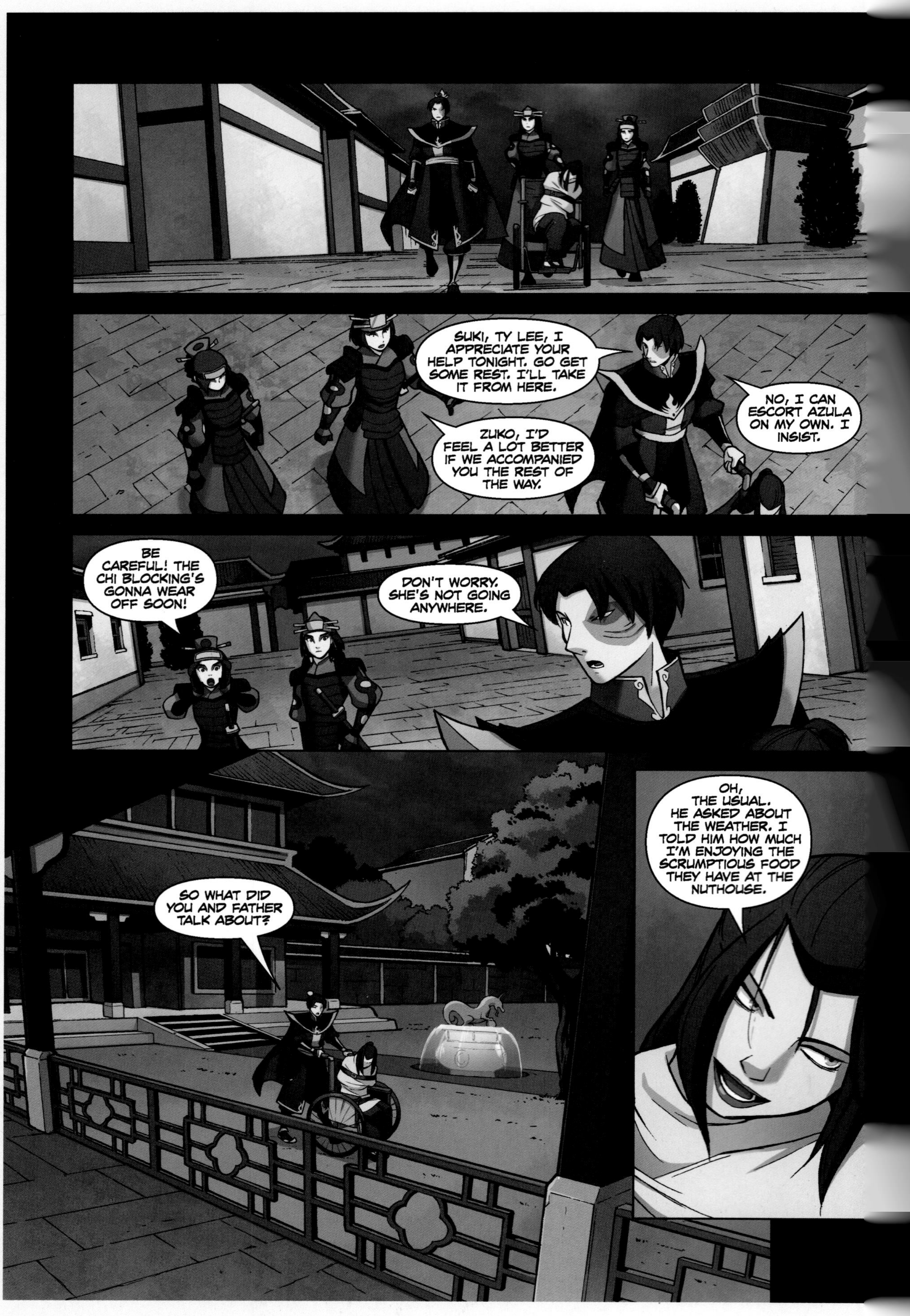
SUKI, TY LEE, I APPRECIATE YOUR HELP TONIGHT. GO GET SOME REST. I'LL TAKE IT FROM HERE.
ZUKO, I'D FEEL A LOT BETTER IF WE ACCOMPANIED YOU THE REST OF THE WAY.
NO, I CAN ESCORT AZULA ON MY OWN. I INSIST.
BE CAREFUL! THE CHI BLOCKING'S GONNA WEAR OFF SOON!
DON'T WORRY. SHE'S NOT GOING ANYWHERE.
SO WHAT DID YOU AND FATHER TALK ABOUT?
OH, THE USUAL. HE ASKED ABOUT THE WEATHER. I TOLD HIM HOW MUCH I'M ENJOYING THE SCRUMPTIOUS FOOD THEY HAVE AT THE NUTHOUSE.

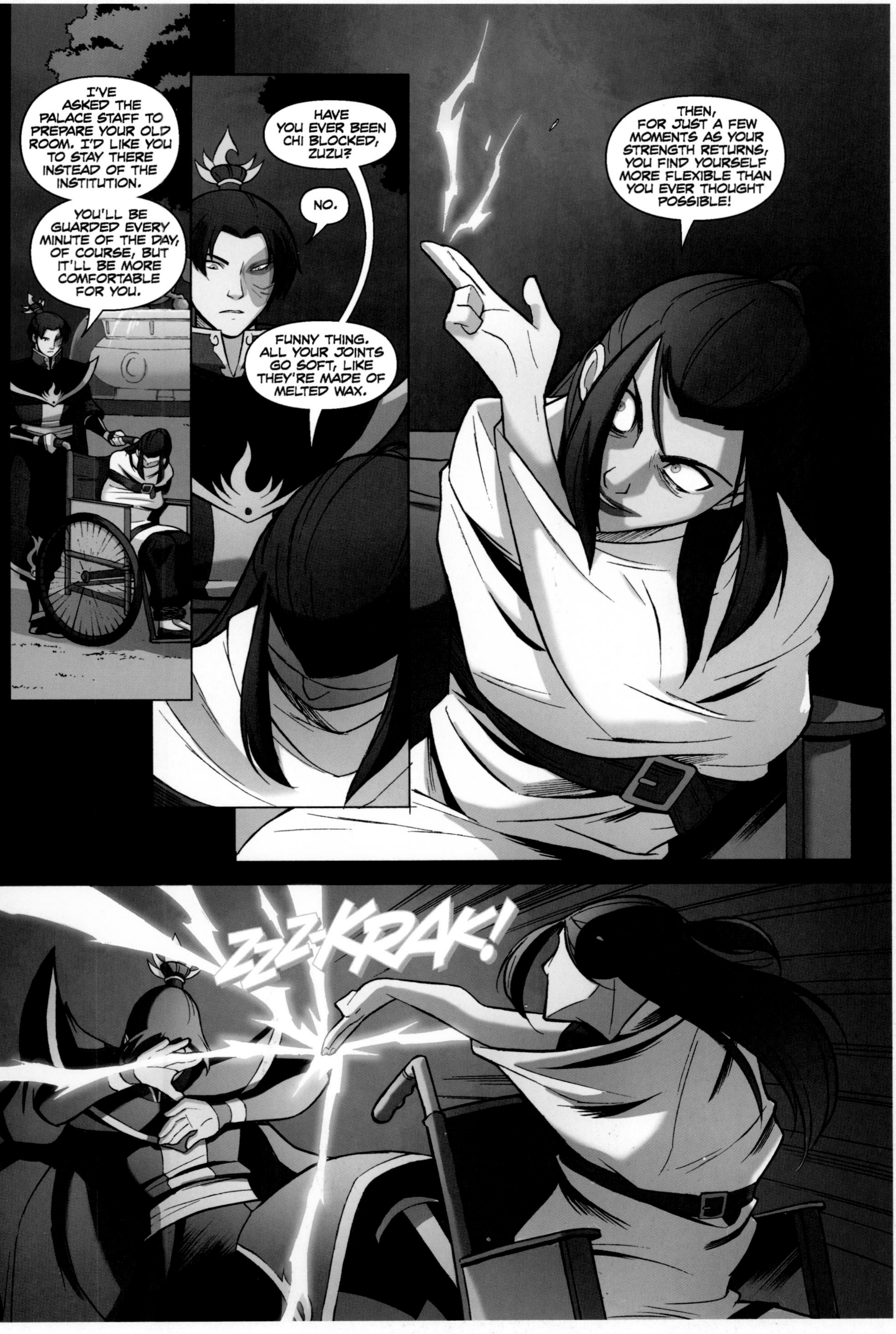
I'VE ASKED THE PALACE STAFF TO PREPARE YOUR OLD ROOM. I'D LIKE YOU TO STAY THERE INSTEAD OF THE INSTITUTION.
YOU'LL BE GUARDED EVERY MINUTE OF THE DAY, OF COURSE, BUT IT'LL BE MORE COMFORTABLE FOR YOU.
HAVE YOU EVER BEEN CHI BLOCKED, ZUZU?
NO.
FUNNY THING. ALL YOUR JOINTS GO SOFT, LIKE THEY'RE MADE OF MELTED WAX.
THEN, FOR JUST A FEW MOMENTS AS YOUR STRENGTH RETURNS, YOU FIND YOURSELF MORE FLEXIBLE THAN YOU EVER THOUGHT POSSIBLE!
ZZZ-KRAK!

G: *Azula has two modes—calm and crazy. We took particular care when illustrating the two. When she thinks about Ursa, she goes crazy: her pupils constrict, shadows appear under her eyes, and, when she is at her worst, even her hairstyle becomes chaotic.*

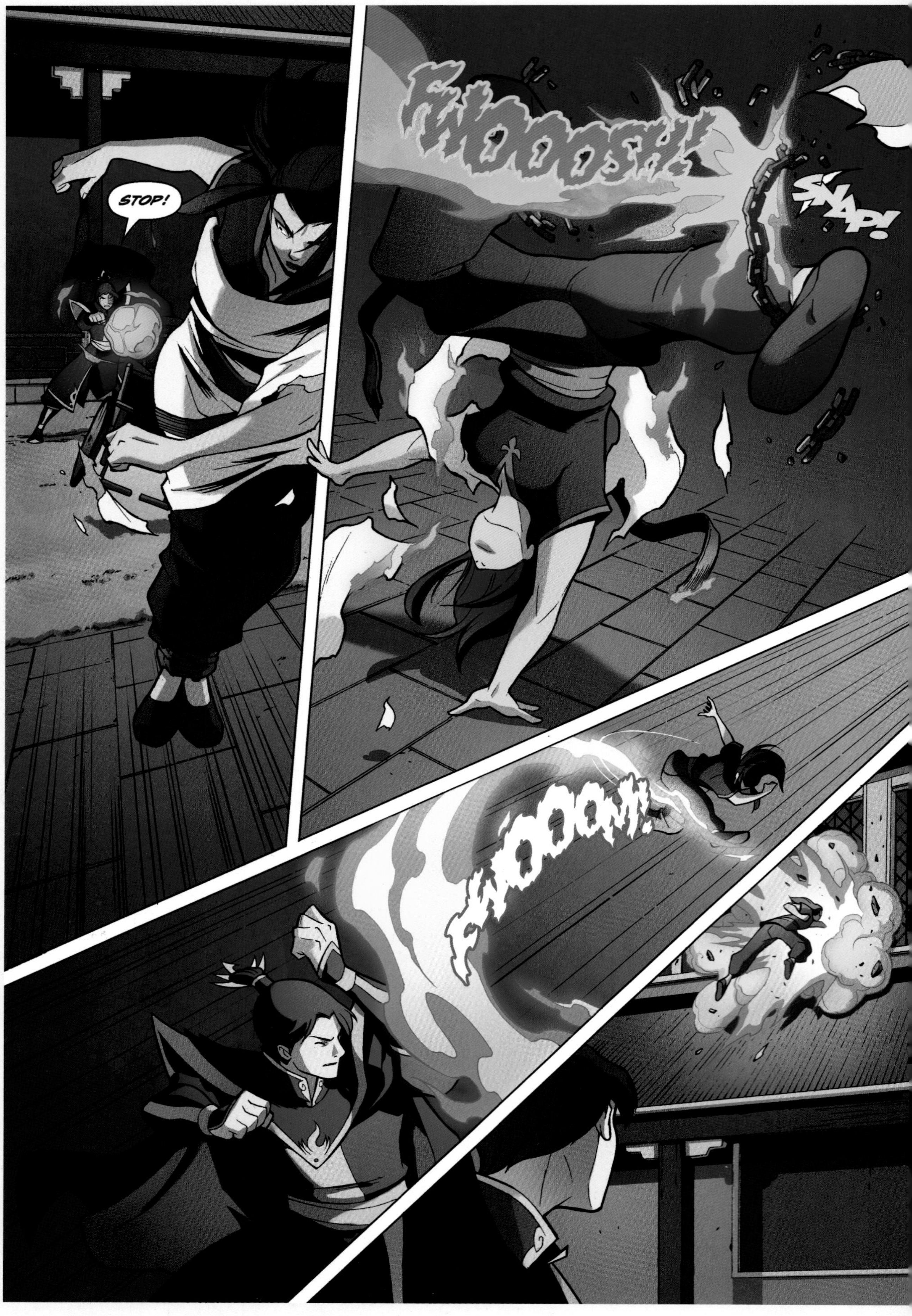
STOP!
FWOOOSH!
SNAP!
FWOOOM!

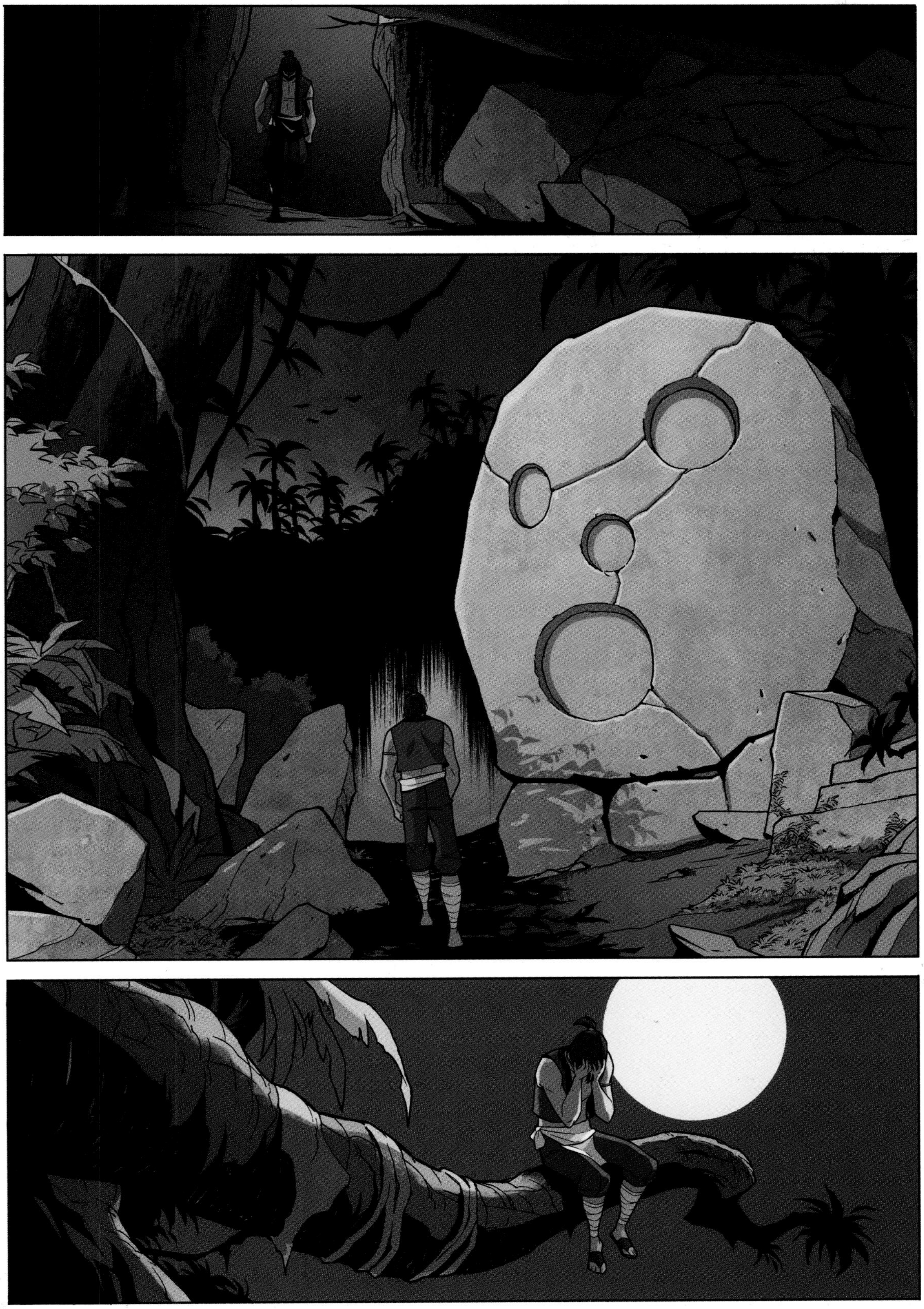

M: *Sometimes the best writing is the kind without dialogue. This wordless sequence of the heartbroken Ikem is both beautiful and powerful. In just a few panels, Gene and Gurihiru did a great job of showing the passage of time, as Ikem makes a life for himself out in the wilderness.*

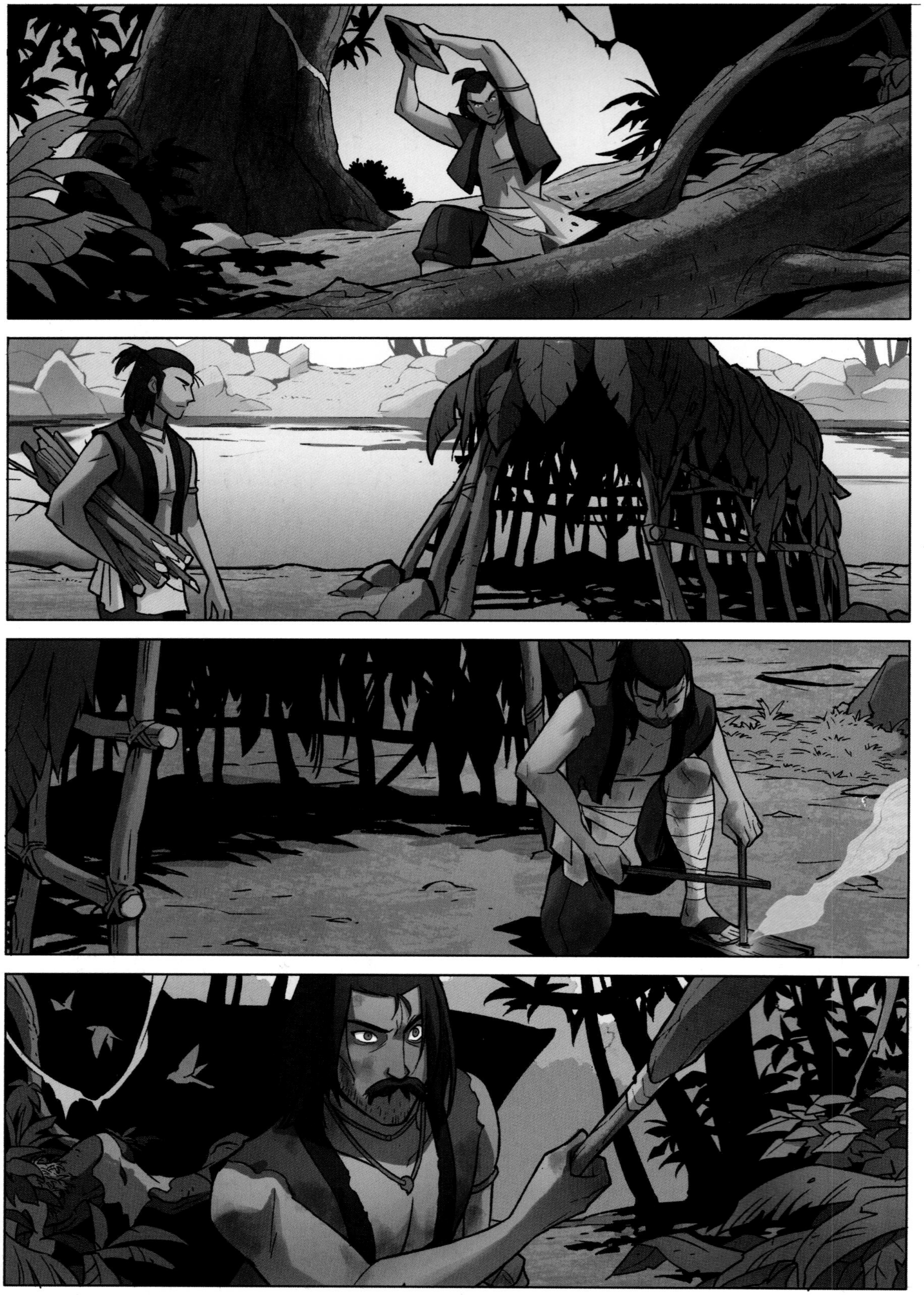

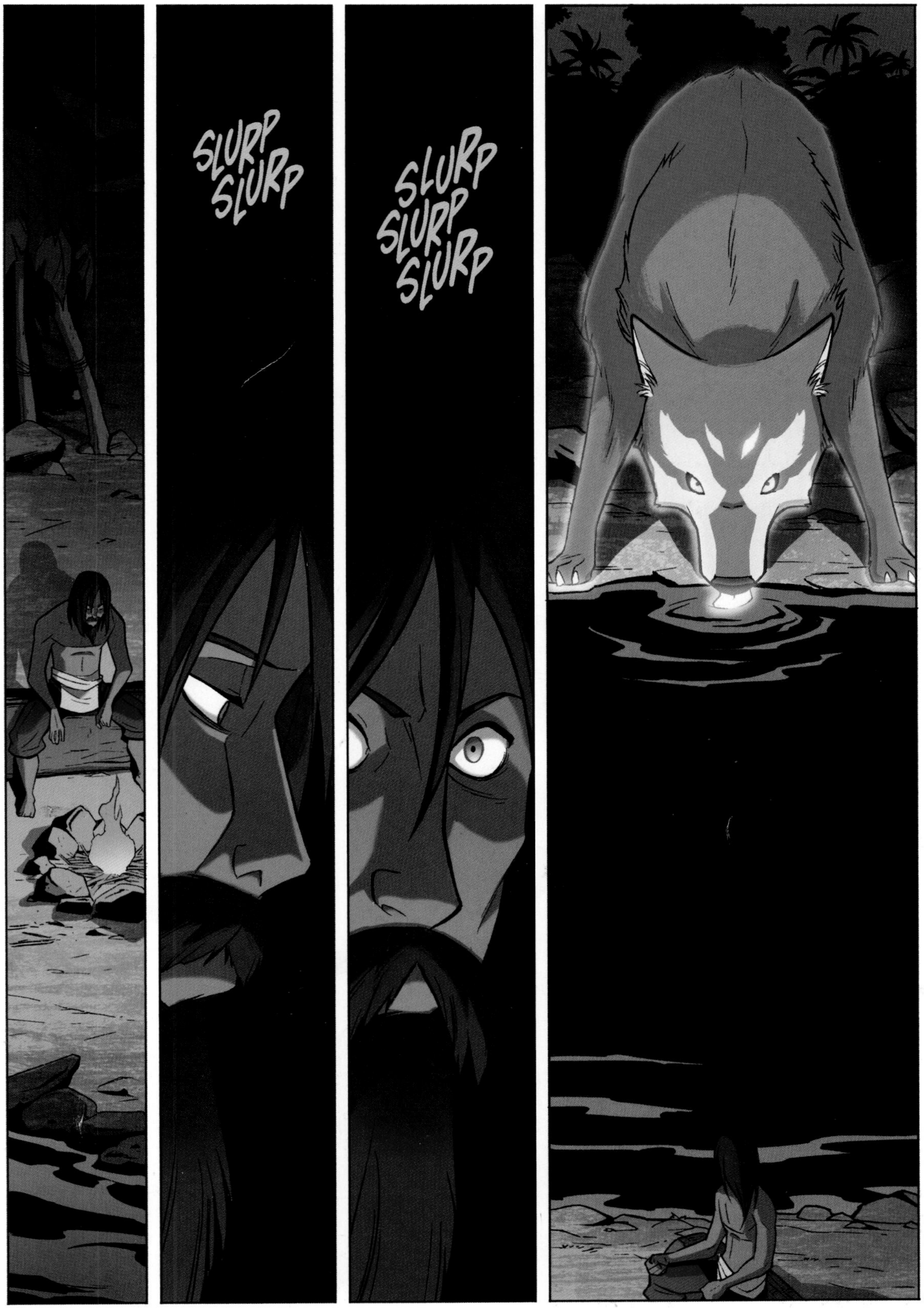
SLURP
SLURP
SLURP
SLURP
SLURP

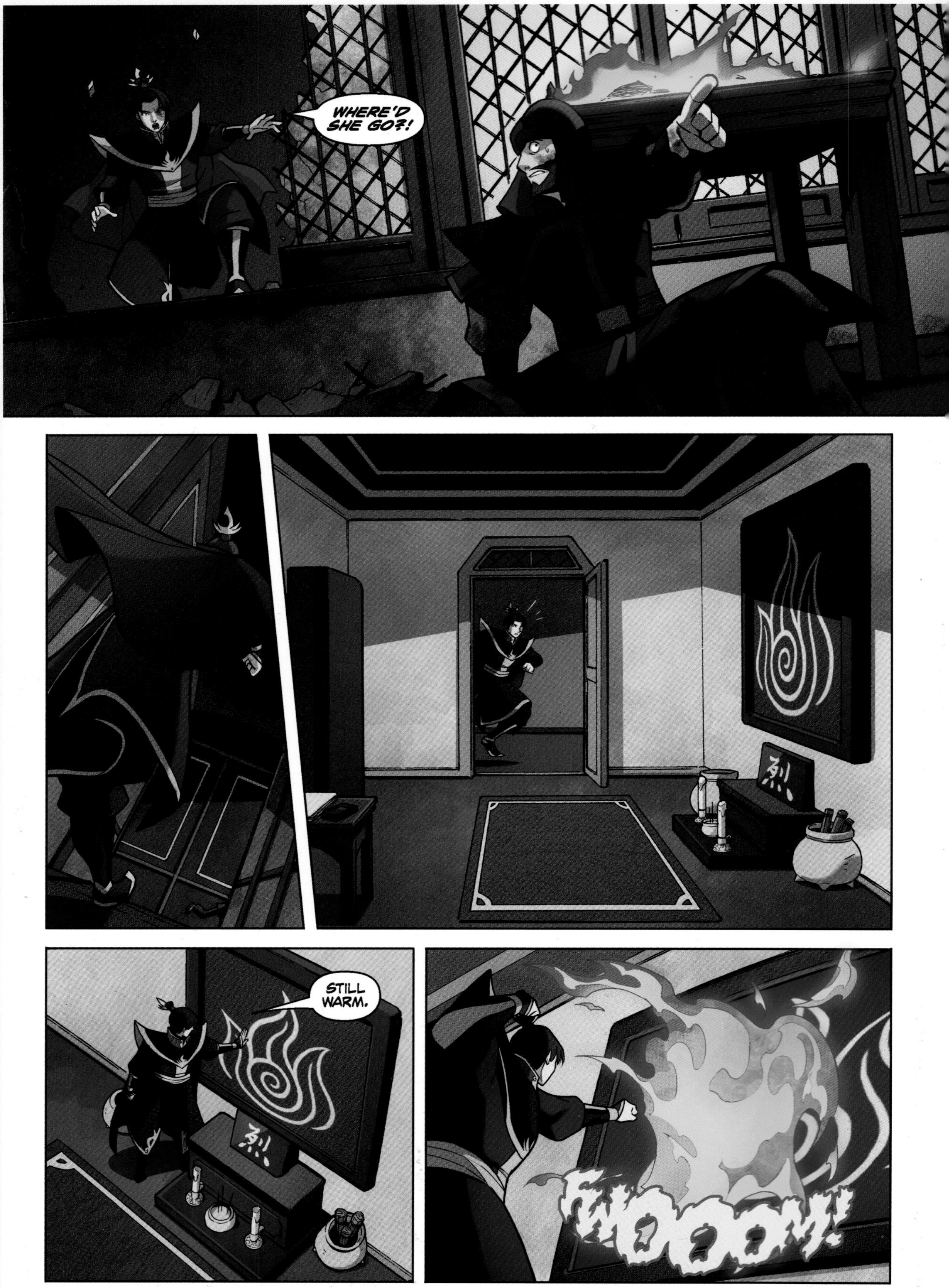
WHERE'D SHE GO?!
STILL WARM.
FWOOOM!

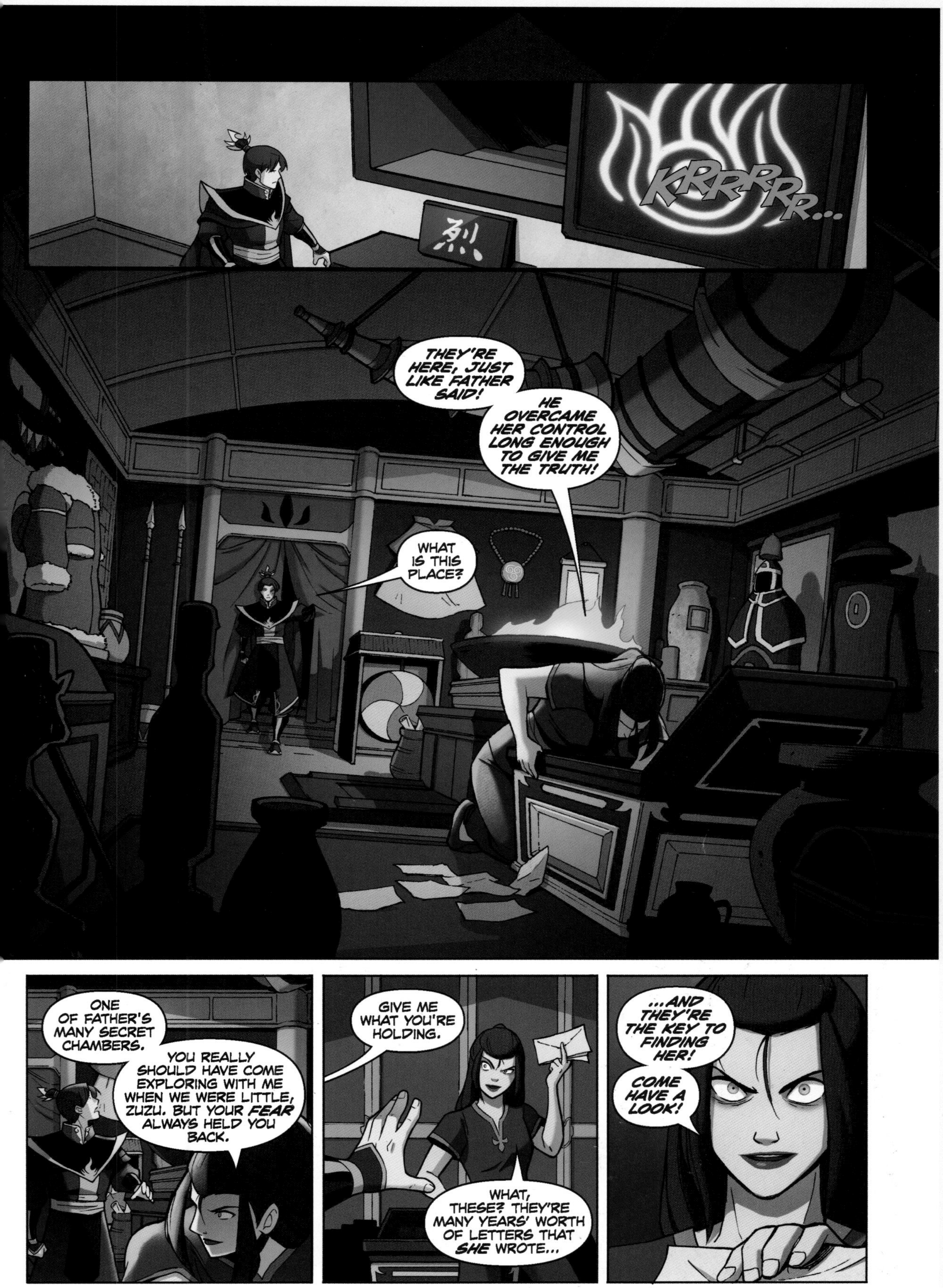
KRRRRR...
THEY'RE HERE, JUST LIKE FATHER SAID!
HE OVERCAME HER CONTROL LONG ENOUGH TO GIVE ME THE TRUTH!
WHAT IS THIS PLACE?
ONE OF FATHER'S MANY SECRET CHAMBERS.
YOU REALLY SHOULD HAVE COME EXPLORING WITH ME WHEN WE WERE LITTLE, ZUZU. BUT YOUR FEAR ALWAYS HELD YOU BACK.
GIVE ME WHAT YOU'RE HOLDING.
WHAT, THESE? THEY'RE MANY YEARS' WORTH OF LETTERS THAT SHE WROTE...
...AND THEY'RE THE KEY TO FINDING HER!
COME HAVE A LOOK!

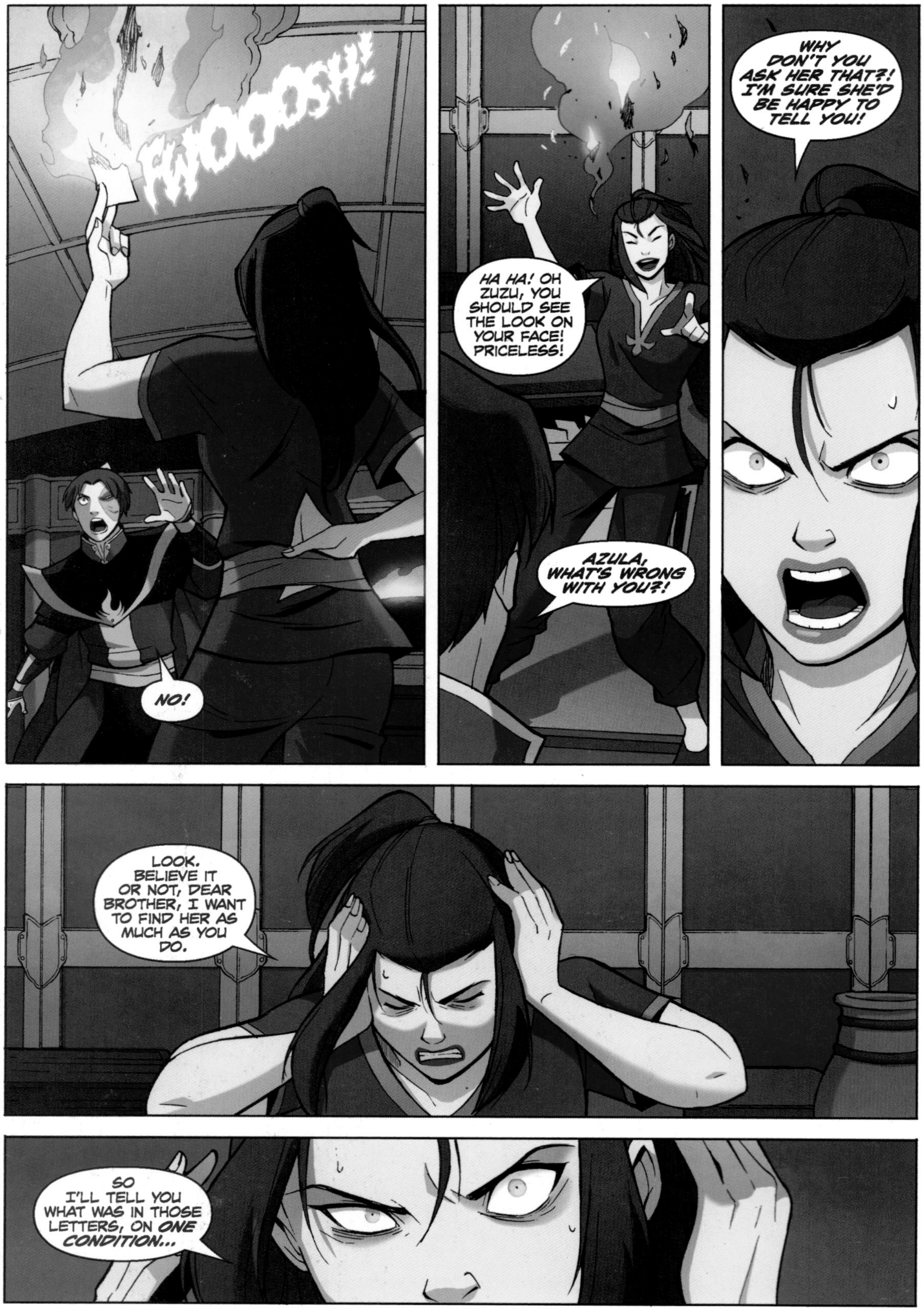
FWOOOSH!
NO!
HA HA! OH ZUZU, YOU SHOULD SEE THE LOOK ON YOUR FACE! PRICELESS!
AZULA, WHAT'S WRONG WITH YOU?!
WHY DON'T YOU ASK HER THAT?! I'M SURE SHE'D BE HAPPY TO TELL YOU!
LOOK. BELIEVE IT OR NOT, DEAR BROTHER, I WANT TO FIND HER AS MUCH AS YOU DO.
SO I'LL TELL YOU WHAT WAS IN THOSE LETTERS, ON ONE CONDITION...

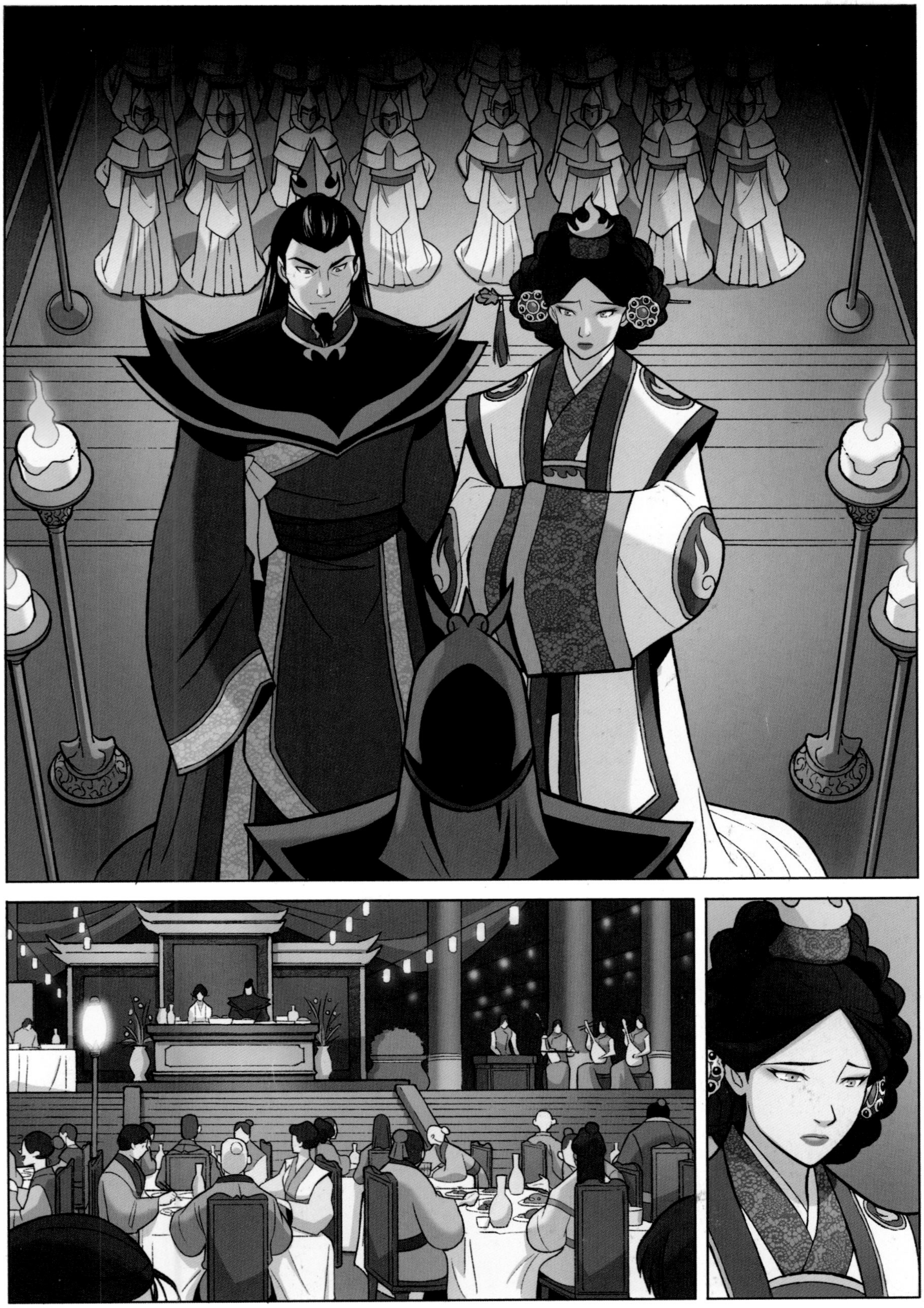

G: *The fashions of ancient Korean nobility inspired Ursa's wedding dress.*

M: *We added this detail of Ozai forbidding Ursa from speaking of her old life again as a way to explain why Ursa's hometown and relation to Avatar Roku was not common knowledge. (In "The Avatar and the Fire Lord," Iroh tells Zuko that Avatar Roku was his great-grandfather on his mother's side.) It also parallels the present story in a cool way: When Ursa married Ozai, she had to forget her past. Later, she makes a similar choice.*

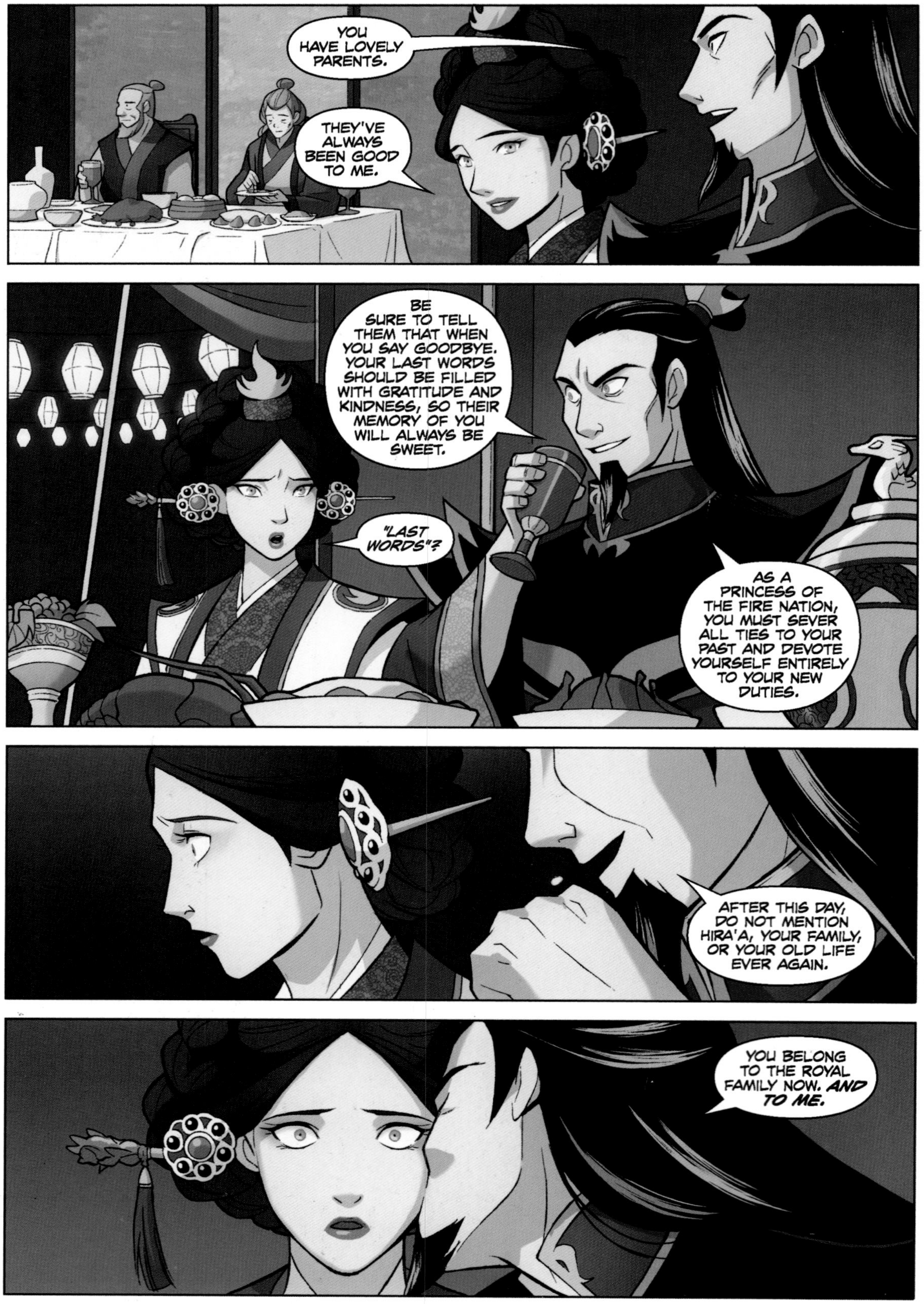
YOU HAVE LOVELY PARENTS.
THEY'VE ALWAYS BEEN GOOD TO ME.
BE SURE TO TELL THEM THAT WHEN YOU SAY GOODBYE. YOUR LAST WORDS SHOULD BE FILLED WITH GRATITUDE AND KINDNESS, SO THEIR MEMORY OF YOU WILL ALWAYS BE SWEET.
"LAST WORDS"?
AS A PRINCESS OF THE FIRE NATION, YOU MUST SEVER ALL TIES TO YOUR PAST AND DEVOTE YOURSELF ENTIRELY TO YOUR NEW DUTIES.
AFTER THIS DAY, DO NOT MENTION HIRA'A, YOUR FAMILY, OR YOUR OLD LIFE EVER AGAIN.
YOU BELONG TO THE ROYAL FAMILY NOW. AND TO ME.

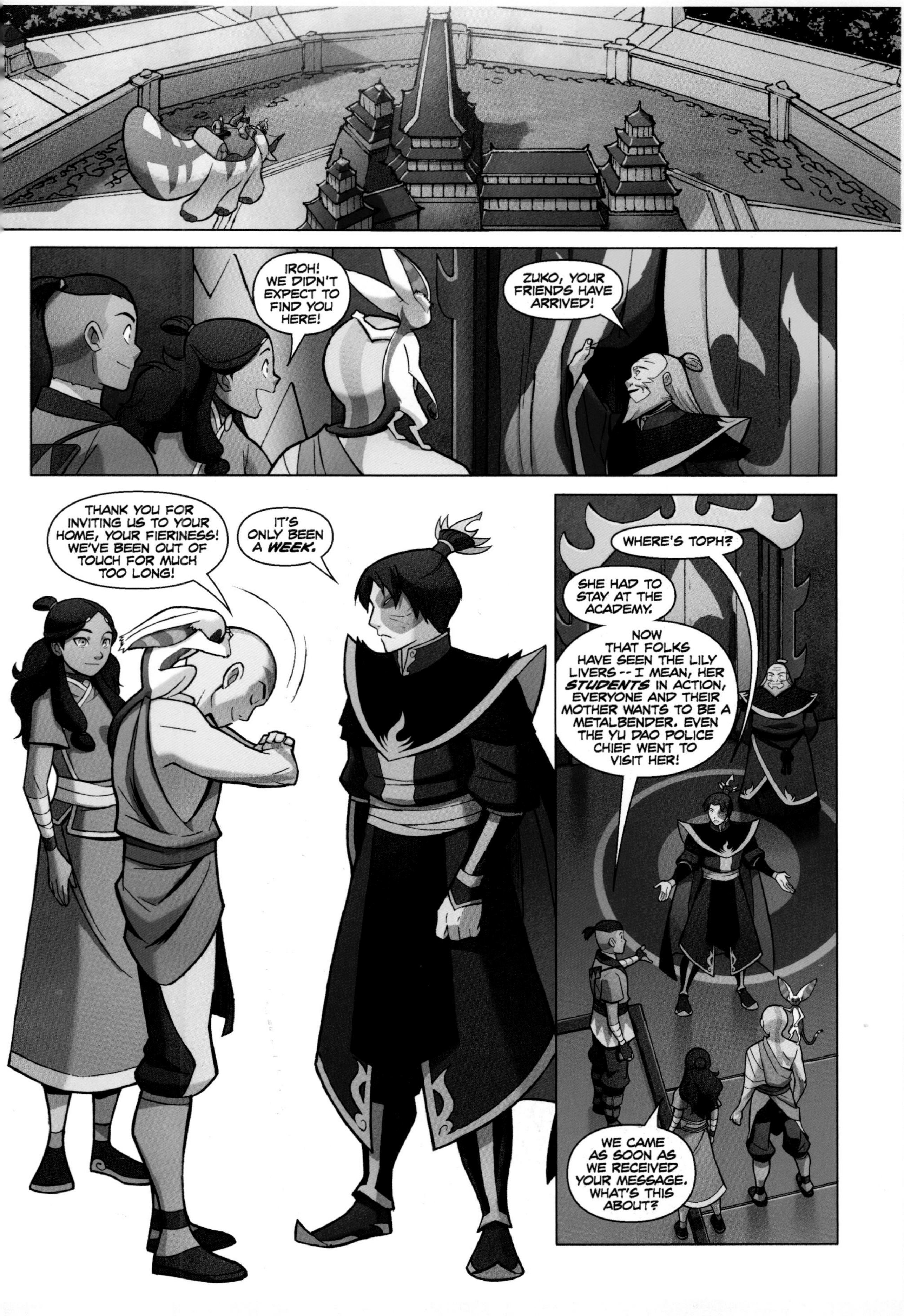
IROH! WE DIDN'T EXPECT TO FIND YOU HERE!
ZUKO, YOUR FRIENDS HAVE ARRIVED!
THANK YOU FOR INVITING US TO YOUR HOME, YOUR FIERINESS! WE'VE BEEN OUT OF TOUCH FOR MUCH TOO LONG!
IT'S ONLY BEEN A **WEEK.**
WHERE'S TOPH?
SHE HAD TO STAY AT THE ACADEMY.
NOW THAT FOLKS HAVE SEEN THE LILY LIVERS -- I MEAN, HER **STUDENTS** IN ACTION, EVERYONE AND THEIR MOTHER WANTS TO BE A METALBENDER. EVEN THE YU DAO POLICE CHIEF WENT TO VISIT HER!
WE CAME AS SOON AS WE RECEIVED YOUR MESSAGE. WHAT'S THIS ABOUT?

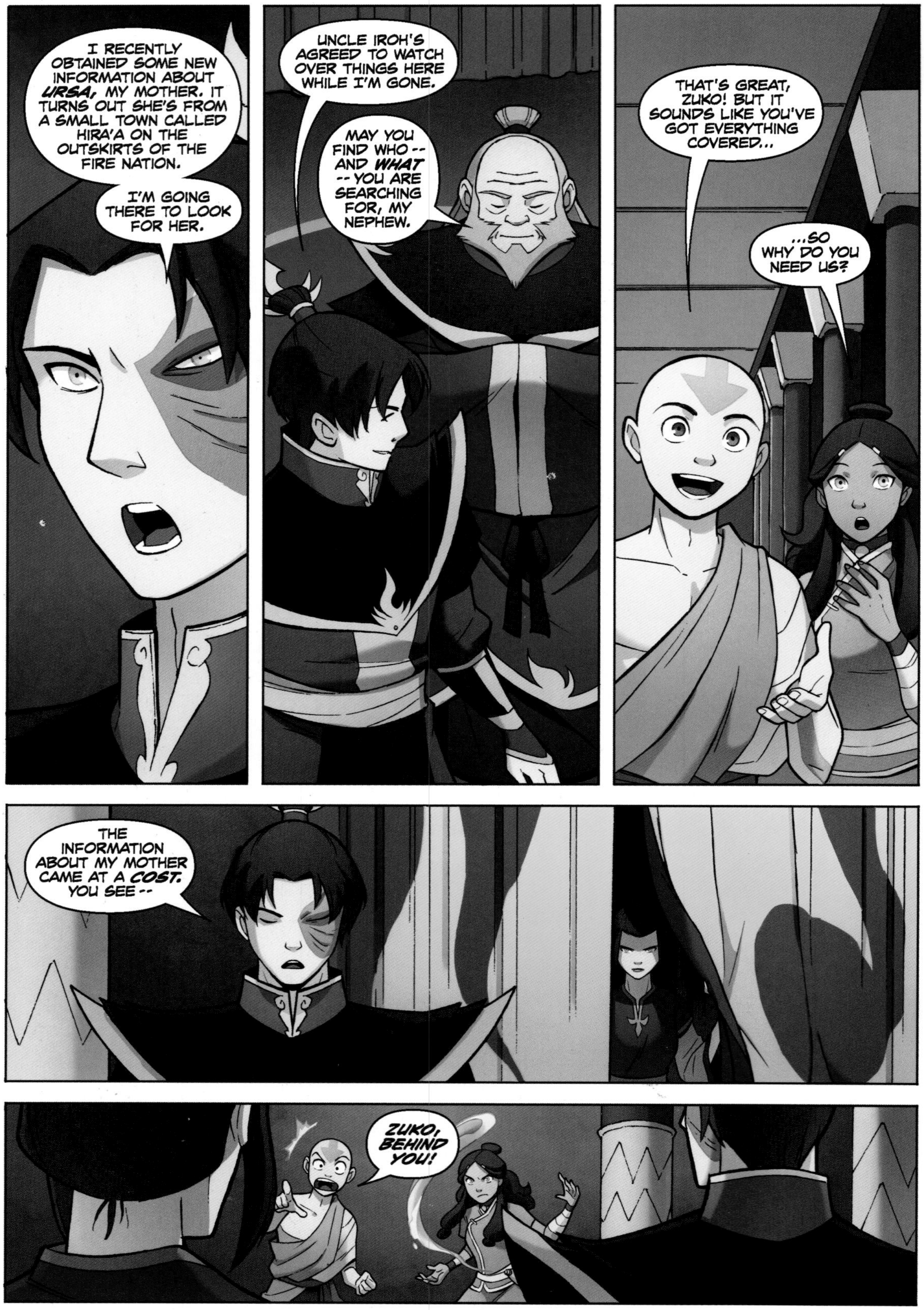
I RECENTLY OBTAINED SOME NEW INFORMATION ABOUT URSA, MY MOTHER. IT TURNS OUT SHE'S FROM A SMALL TOWN CALLED HIRA'A ON THE OUTSKIRTS OF THE FIRE NATION.
I'M GOING THERE TO LOOK FOR HER.
UNCLE IROH'S AGREED TO WATCH OVER THINGS HERE WHILE I'M GONE.
MAY YOU FIND WHO -- AND WHAT -- YOU ARE SEARCHING FOR, MY NEPHEW.
THAT'S GREAT, ZUKO! BUT IT SOUNDS LIKE YOU'VE GOT EVERYTHING COVERED...
...SO WHY DO YOU NEED US?
THE INFORMATION ABOUT MY MOTHER CAME AT A COST. YOU SEE --
ZUKO, BEHIND YOU!

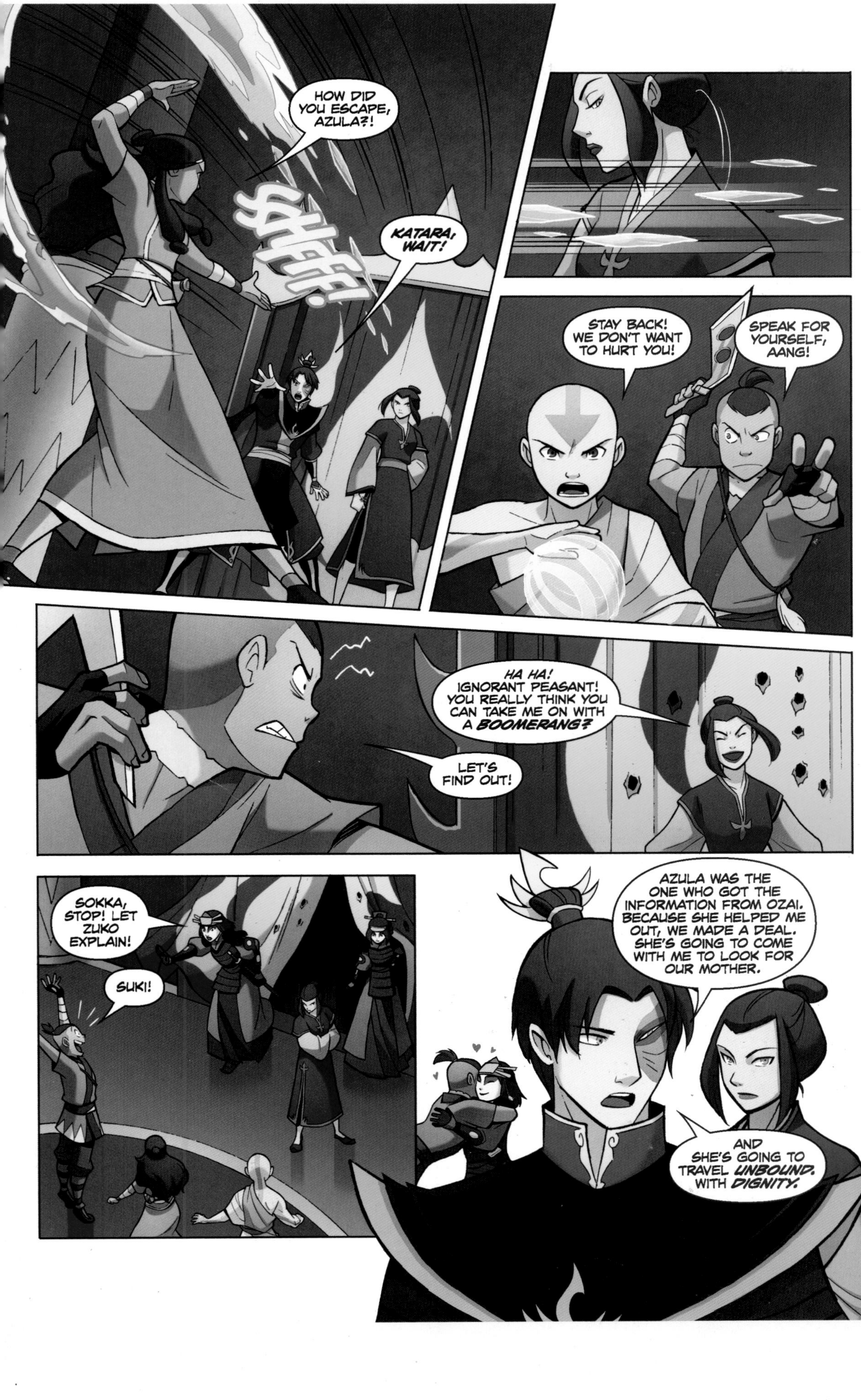
HOW DID YOU ESCAPE, AZULA?!
SHFF!
KATARA, WAIT!
STAY BACK! WE DON'T WANT TO HURT YOU!
SPEAK FOR YOURSELF, AANG!
HA HA! IGNORANT PEASANT! YOU REALLY THINK YOU CAN TAKE ME ON WITH A BOOMERANG?
LET'S FIND OUT!
SOKKA, STOP! LET ZUKO EXPLAIN!
SUKI!
AZULA WAS THE ONE WHO GOT THE INFORMATION FROM OZAI. BECAUSE SHE HELPED ME OUT, WE MADE A DEAL. SHE'S GOING TO COME WITH ME TO LOOK FOR OUR MOTHER.
AND SHE'S GOING TO TRAVEL UNBOUND. WITH DIGNITY.

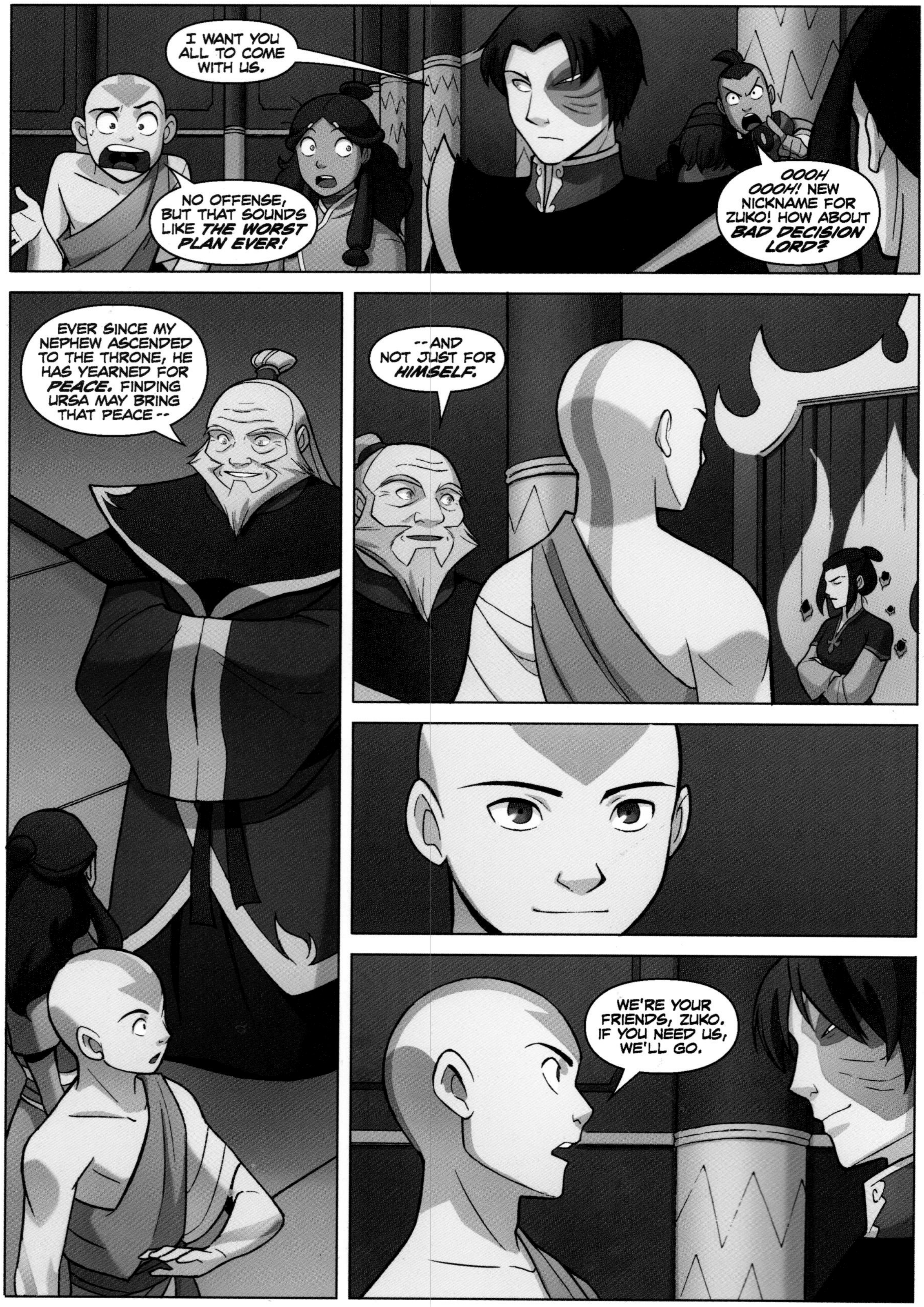
I WANT YOU ALL TO COME WITH US.
NO OFFENSE, BUT THAT SOUNDS LIKE THE WORST PLAN EVER!
OOOH OOOH! NEW NICKNAME FOR ZUKO! HOW ABOUT BAD DECISION LORD?
EVER SINCE MY NEPHEW ASCENDED TO THE THRONE, HE HAS YEARNED FOR PEACE. FINDING URSA MAY BRING THAT PEACE --
--AND NOT JUST FOR HIMSELF.
WE'RE YOUR FRIENDS, ZUKO. IF YOU NEED US, WE'LL GO.

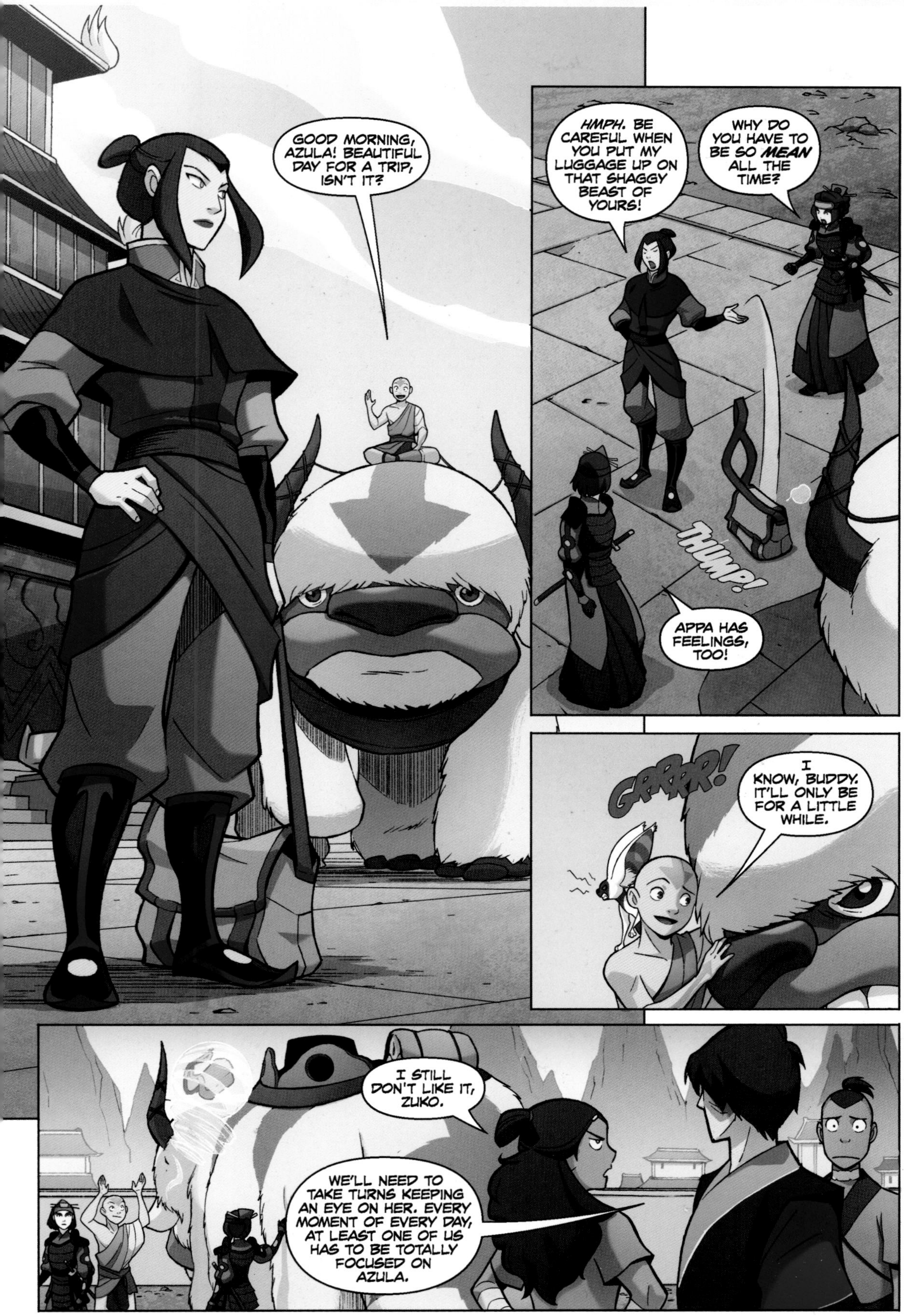
GOOD MORNING, AZULA! BEAUTIFUL DAY FOR A TRIP, ISN'T IT?
HMPH. BE CAREFUL WHEN YOU PUT MY LUGGAGE UP ON THAT SHAGGY BEAST OF YOURS!
WHY DO YOU HAVE TO BE SO MEAN ALL THE TIME?
THUMP!
APPA HAS FEELINGS, TOO!
GRRRR!
I KNOW, BUDDY. IT'LL ONLY BE FOR A LITTLE WHILE.
I STILL DON'T LIKE IT, ZUKO.
WE'LL NEED TO TAKE TURNS KEEPING AN EYE ON HER. EVERY MOMENT OF EVERY DAY, AT LEAST ONE OF US HAS TO BE TOTALLY FOCUSED ON AZULA.

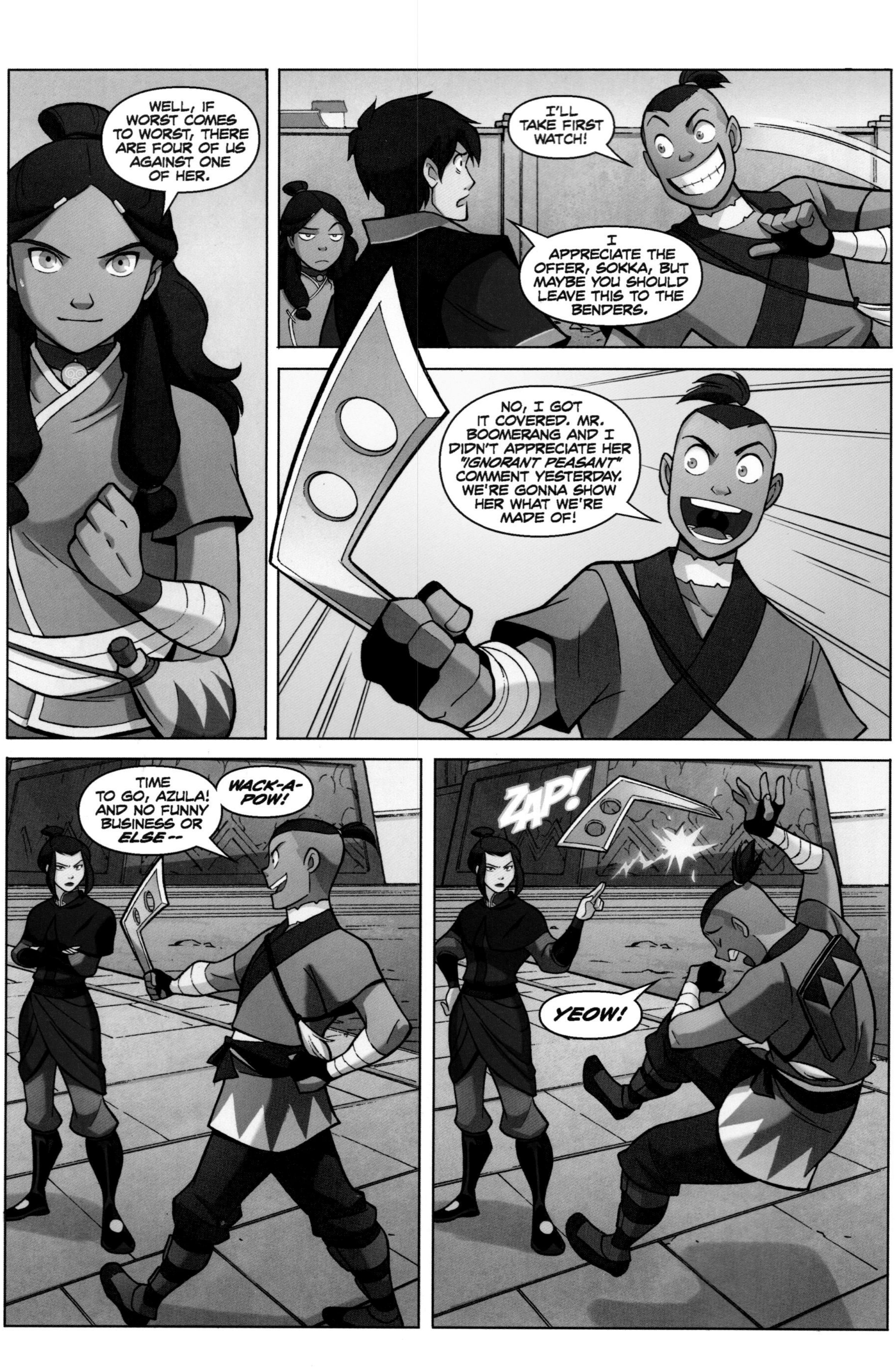
WELL, IF WORST COMES TO WORST, THERE ARE FOUR OF US AGAINST ONE OF HER.
I'LL TAKE FIRST WATCH!
I APPRECIATE THE OFFER, SOKKA, BUT MAYBE YOU SHOULD LEAVE THIS TO THE BENDERS.
NO, I GOT IT COVERED. MR. BOOMERANG AND I DIDN'T APPRECIATE HER *"IGNORANT PEASANT"* COMMENT YESTERDAY. WE'RE GONNA SHOW HER WHAT WE'RE MADE OF!
TIME TO GO, AZULA! AND NO FUNNY BUSINESS OR *ELSE* --
WACK-A-POW!
ZAP!
YEOW!

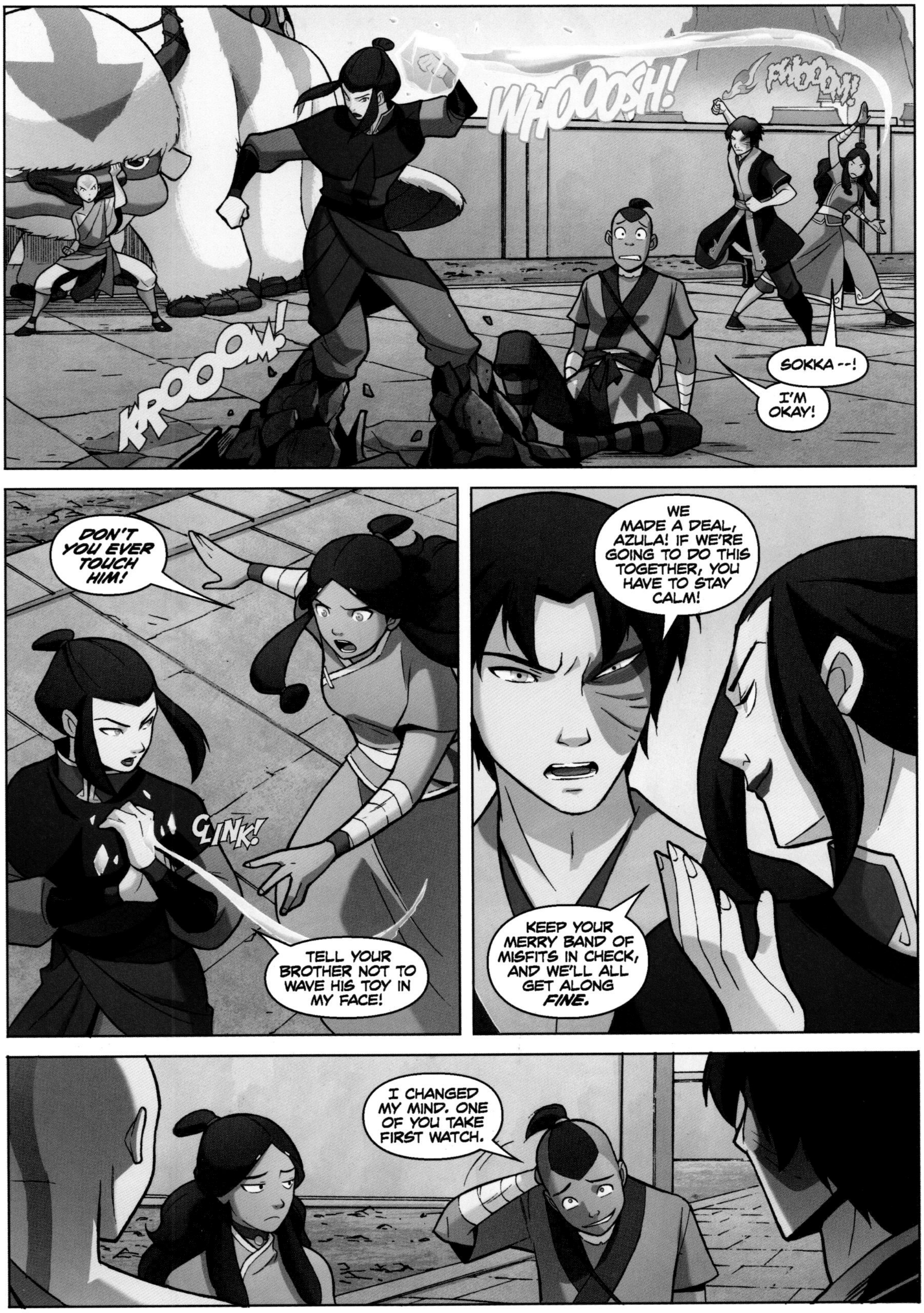
WHOOOSH!
FWOOOM!
KROOOM!
SOKKA--!
I'M OKAY!
DON'T YOU EVER TOUCH HIM!
CLINK!
TELL YOUR BROTHER NOT TO WAVE HIS TOY IN MY FACE!
WE MADE A DEAL, AZULA! IF WE'RE GOING TO DO THIS TOGETHER, YOU HAVE TO STAY CALM!
KEEP YOUR MERRY BAND OF MISFITS IN CHECK, AND WE'LL ALL GET ALONG *FINE.*
I CHANGED MY MIND. ONE OF YOU TAKE FIRST WATCH.

TO THINK THAT I EVER ASPIRED TO BECOME LORD OF THIS DREARY PALACE...

ANYTHING WE CAN DO TO MAKE YOU FEEL MORE AT HOME, IROH?

YOU SEE, THE PROBLEM WITH THE FIRE NATION IS EXACTLY THIS --

-- FOR THE PAST HUNDRED YEARS WE HAVE HAD TOO MANY *WEAPONS*, AND TOO LITTLE *TEA*.

THAT'S IT! I HAVE DISCOVERED MY FIRST ORDER OF BUSINESS AS INTERIM FIRE LORD! I WILL DECLARE A NATIONAL TEA APPRECIATION DAY!

DRINK UP, MY FRIEND!

SIP

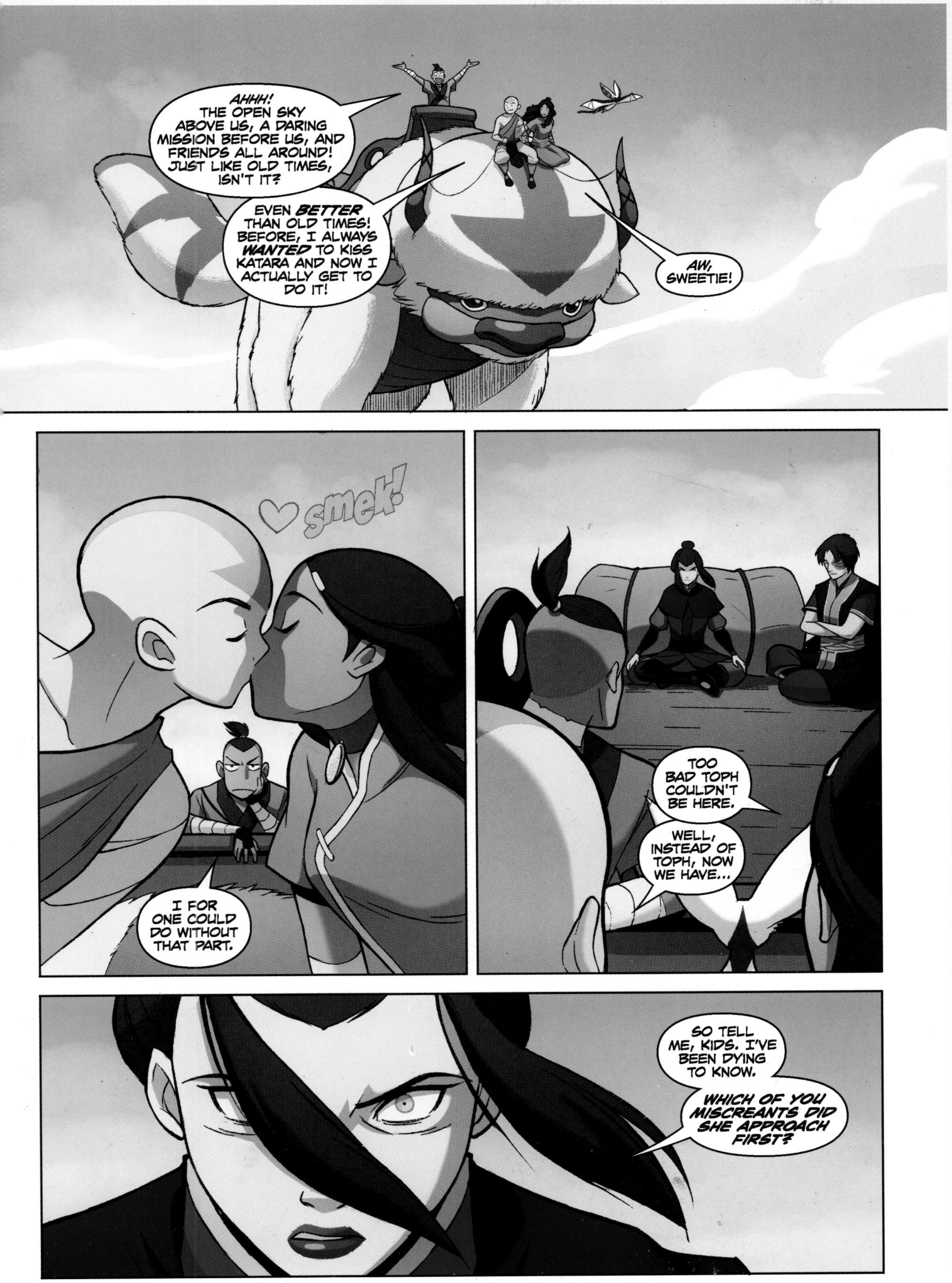
AHHH! THE OPEN SKY ABOVE US, A DARING MISSION BEFORE US, AND FRIENDS ALL AROUND! JUST LIKE OLD TIMES, ISN'T IT?
EVEN BETTER THAN OLD TIMES! BEFORE, I ALWAYS WANTED TO KISS KATARA AND NOW I ACTUALLY GET TO DO IT!
AW, SWEETIE!
smek!
I FOR ONE COULD DO WITHOUT THAT PART.
TOO BAD TOPH COULDN'T BE HERE.
WELL, INSTEAD OF TOPH, NOW WE HAVE...
SO TELL ME, KIDS. I'VE BEEN DYING TO KNOW.
WHICH OF YOU MISCREANTS DID SHE APPROACH FIRST?

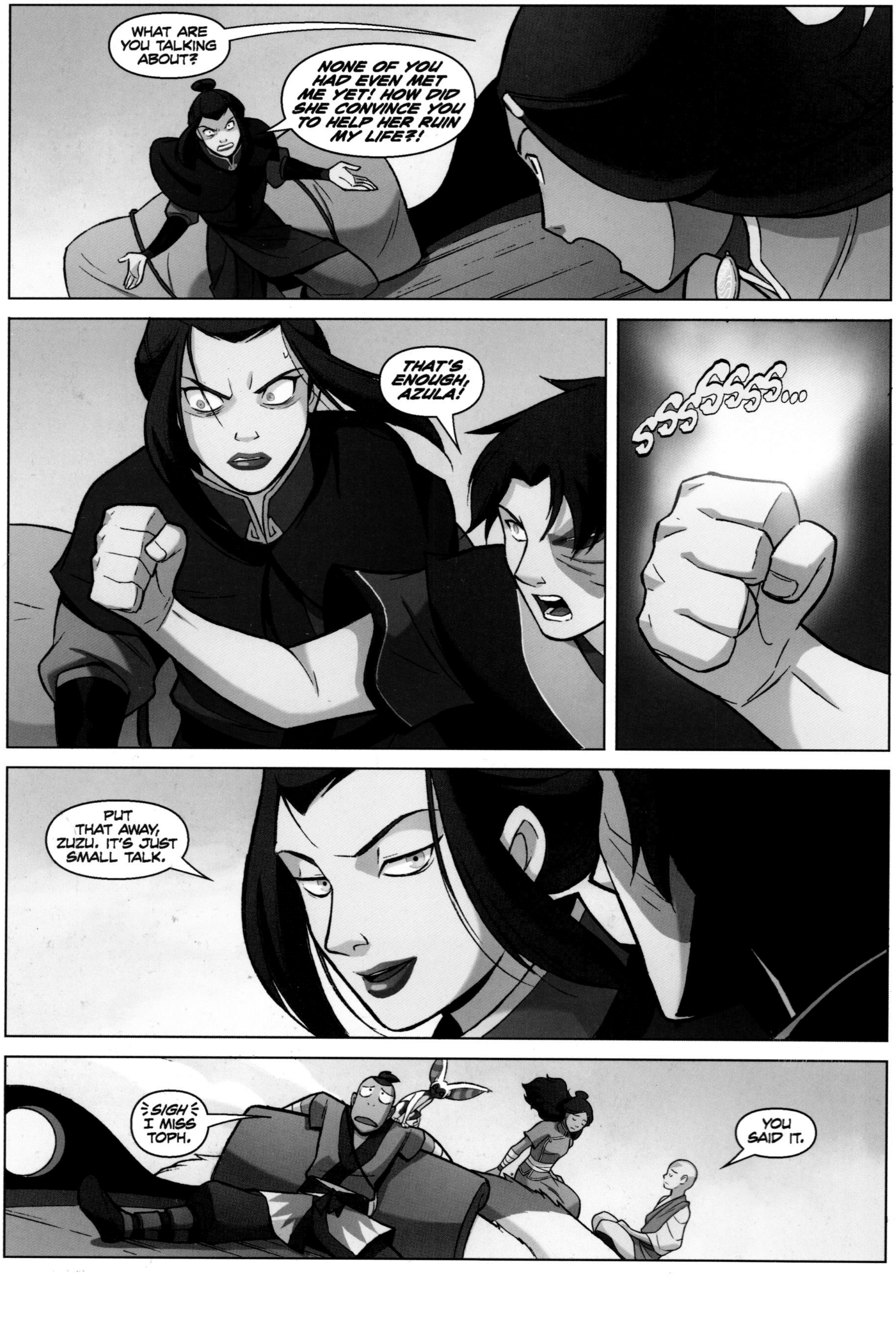
WHAT ARE YOU TALKING ABOUT?
NONE OF YOU HAD EVEN MET ME YET! HOW DID SHE CONVINCE YOU TO HELP HER RUIN MY LIFE?!
THAT'S ENOUGH, AZULA!
SSSSSSSS...
PUT THAT AWAY, ZUZU. IT'S JUST SMALL TALK.
SIGH
I MISS TOPH.
YOU SAID IT.

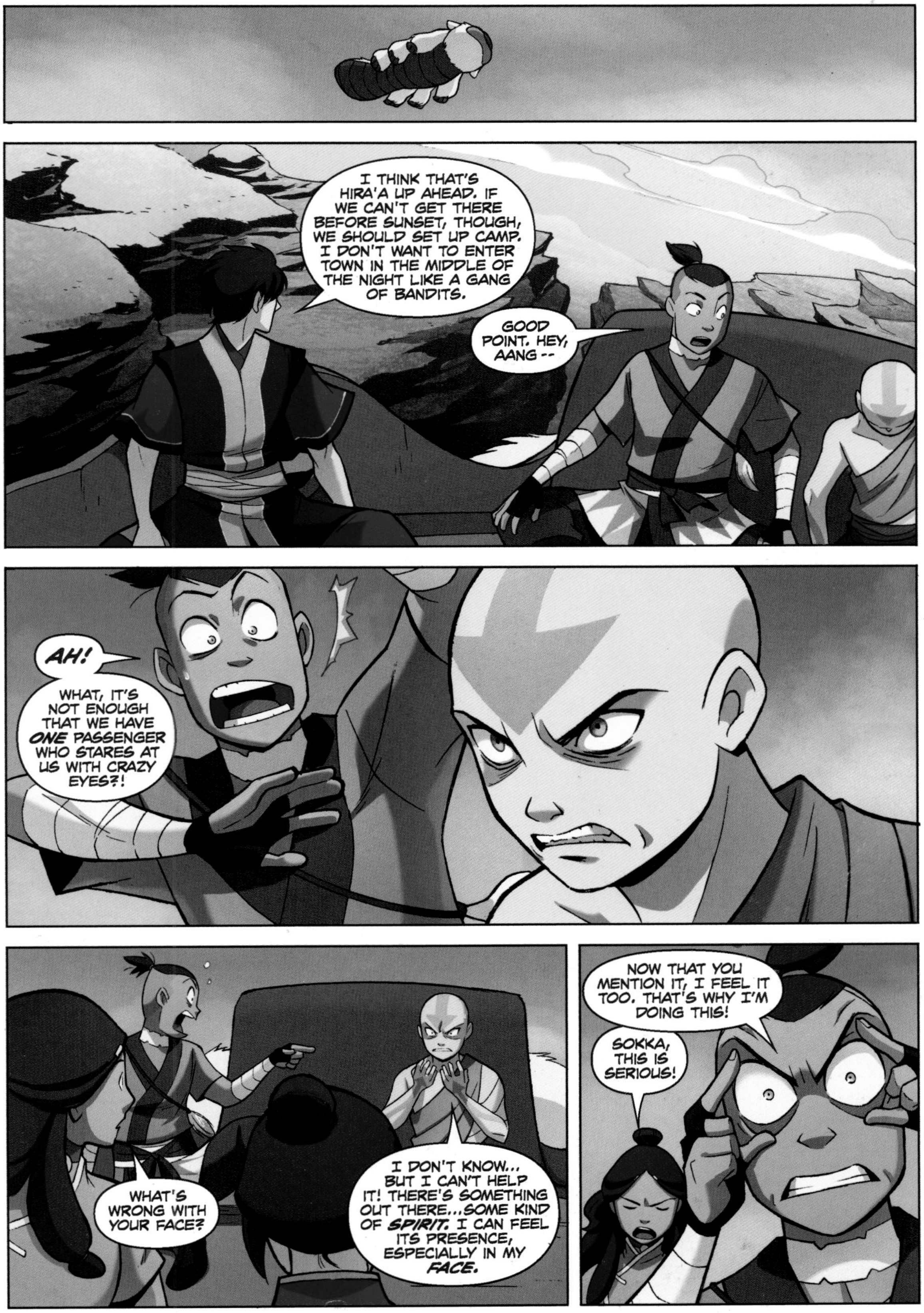
I THINK THAT'S HIRA'A UP AHEAD. IF WE CAN'T GET THERE BEFORE SUNSET, THOUGH, WE SHOULD SET UP CAMP. I DON'T WANT TO ENTER TOWN IN THE MIDDLE OF THE NIGHT LIKE A GANG OF BANDITS.
GOOD POINT. HEY, AANG --
AH!
WHAT, IT'S NOT ENOUGH THAT WE HAVE ONE PASSENGER WHO STARES AT US WITH CRAZY EYES?!
WHAT'S WRONG WITH YOUR FACE?
I DON'T KNOW... BUT I CAN'T HELP IT! THERE'S SOMETHING OUT THERE...SOME KIND OF SPIRIT. I CAN FEEL ITS PRESENCE, ESPECIALLY IN MY FACE.
NOW THAT YOU MENTION IT, I FEEL IT TOO. THAT'S WHY I'M DOING THIS!
SOKKA, THIS IS SERIOUS!

G: *We had a hard time with Aang's expression when his mind synchronized with the spirits. The script specified an angry face, and we wondered just how much we could change it.*

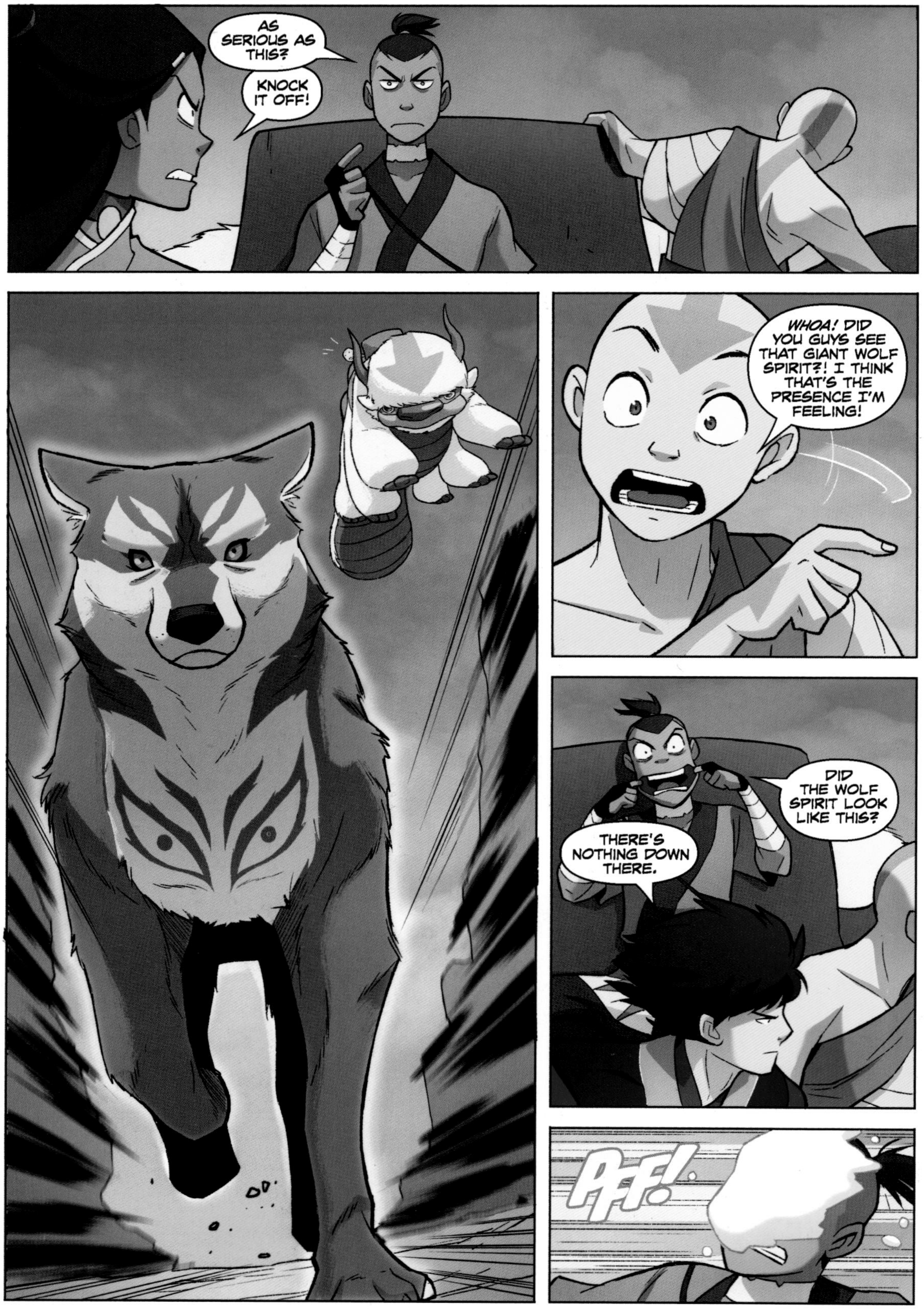
AS SERIOUS AS THIS?
KNOCK IT OFF!
WHOA! DID YOU GUYS SEE THAT GIANT WOLF SPIRIT?! I THINK THAT'S THE PRESENCE I'M FEELING!
DID THE WOLF SPIRIT LOOK LIKE THIS?
THERE'S NOTHING DOWN THERE.
PFF!

G: *Since this spirit is a wolf, we gave it a different color than real wolves to make it special.*

M: *As I recall, the wolf spirit was inspired by a similar spirit seen near Koh's lair in "The Siege of the North, Part 2." By the time Gene was writing* The Search, *we were already deep into writing book 2 of* Korra, *during which time we had developed more rules and ideas for how the spirit world worked. Those ideas directly influenced the human/spirit interactions in this story.*

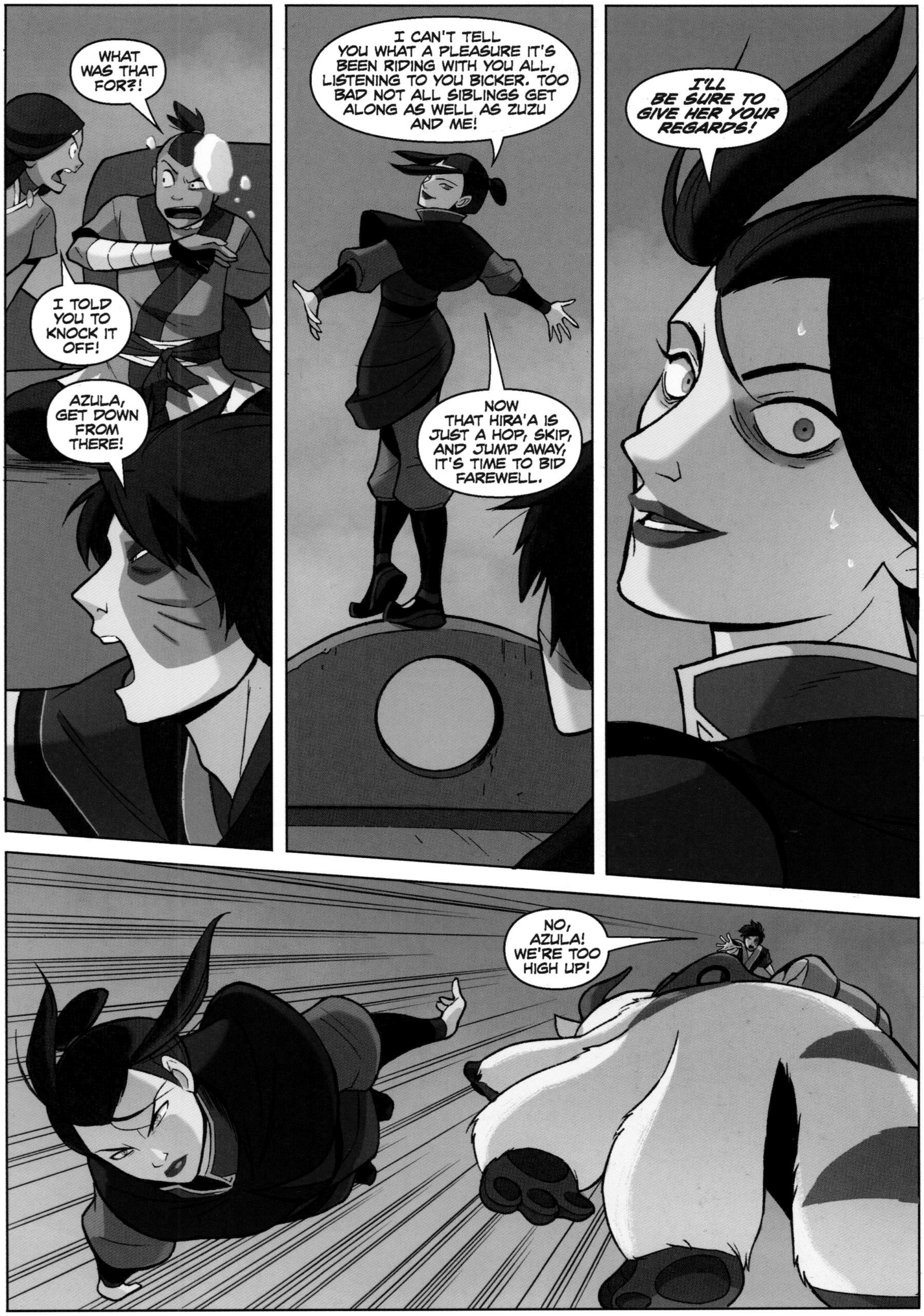
WHAT WAS THAT FOR?!
I TOLD YOU TO KNOCK IT OFF!
AZULA, GET DOWN FROM THERE!
I CAN'T TELL YOU WHAT A PLEASURE IT'S BEEN RIDING WITH YOU ALL, LISTENING TO YOU BICKER. TOO BAD NOT ALL SIBLINGS GET ALONG AS WELL AS ZUZU AND ME!
NOW THAT HIRA'A IS JUST A HOP, SKIP, AND JUMP AWAY, IT'S TIME TO BID FAREWELL.
I'LL BE SURE TO GIVE HER YOUR REGARDS!
NO, AZULA! WE'RE TOO HIGH UP!

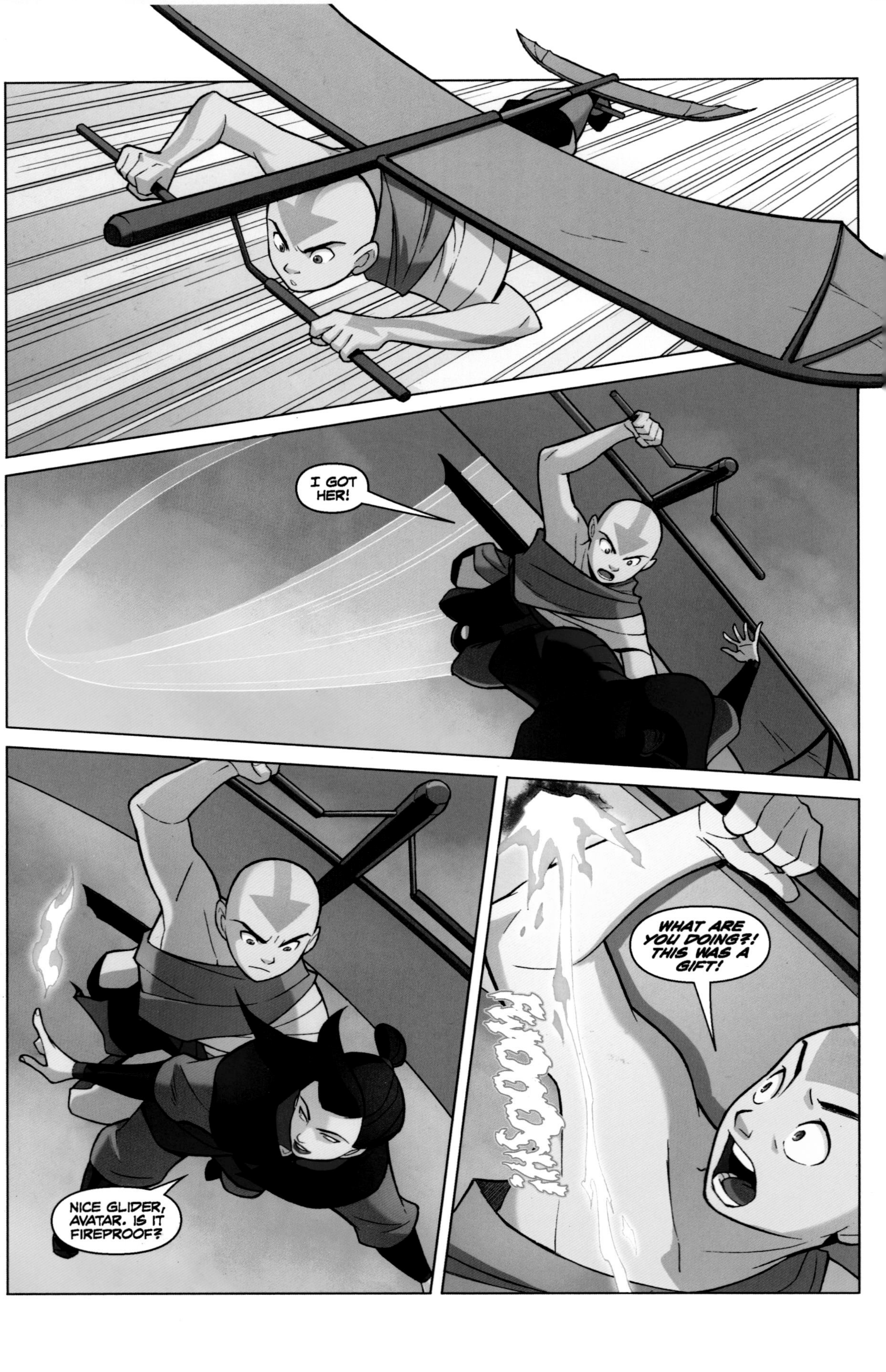
I GOT HER!
NICE GLIDER, AVATAR. IS IT FIREPROOF?
WHAT ARE YOU DOING?! THIS WAS A GIFT!

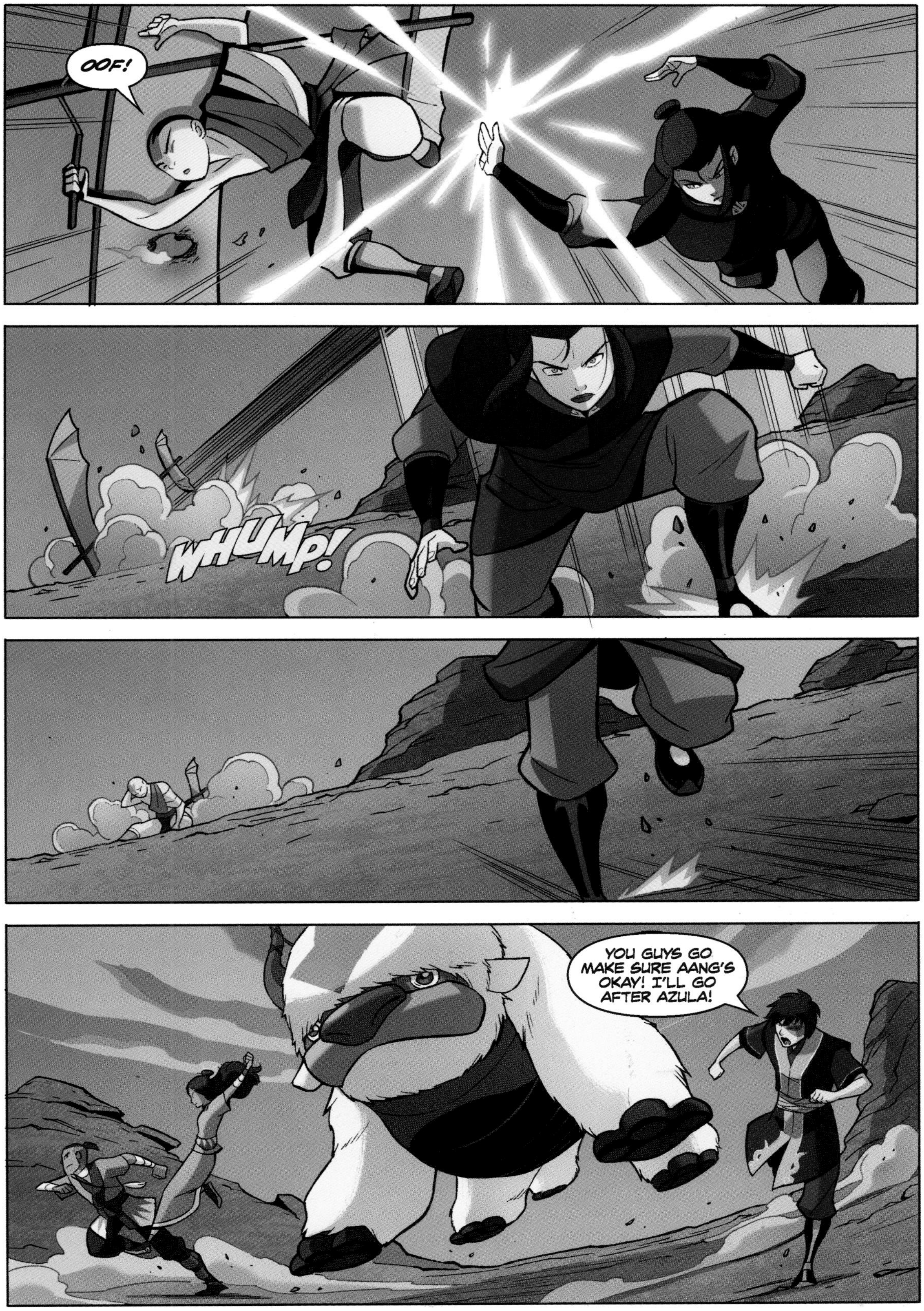
OOF!
WHUMP!
YOU GUYS GO MAKE SURE AANG'S OKAY! I'LL GO AFTER AZULA!

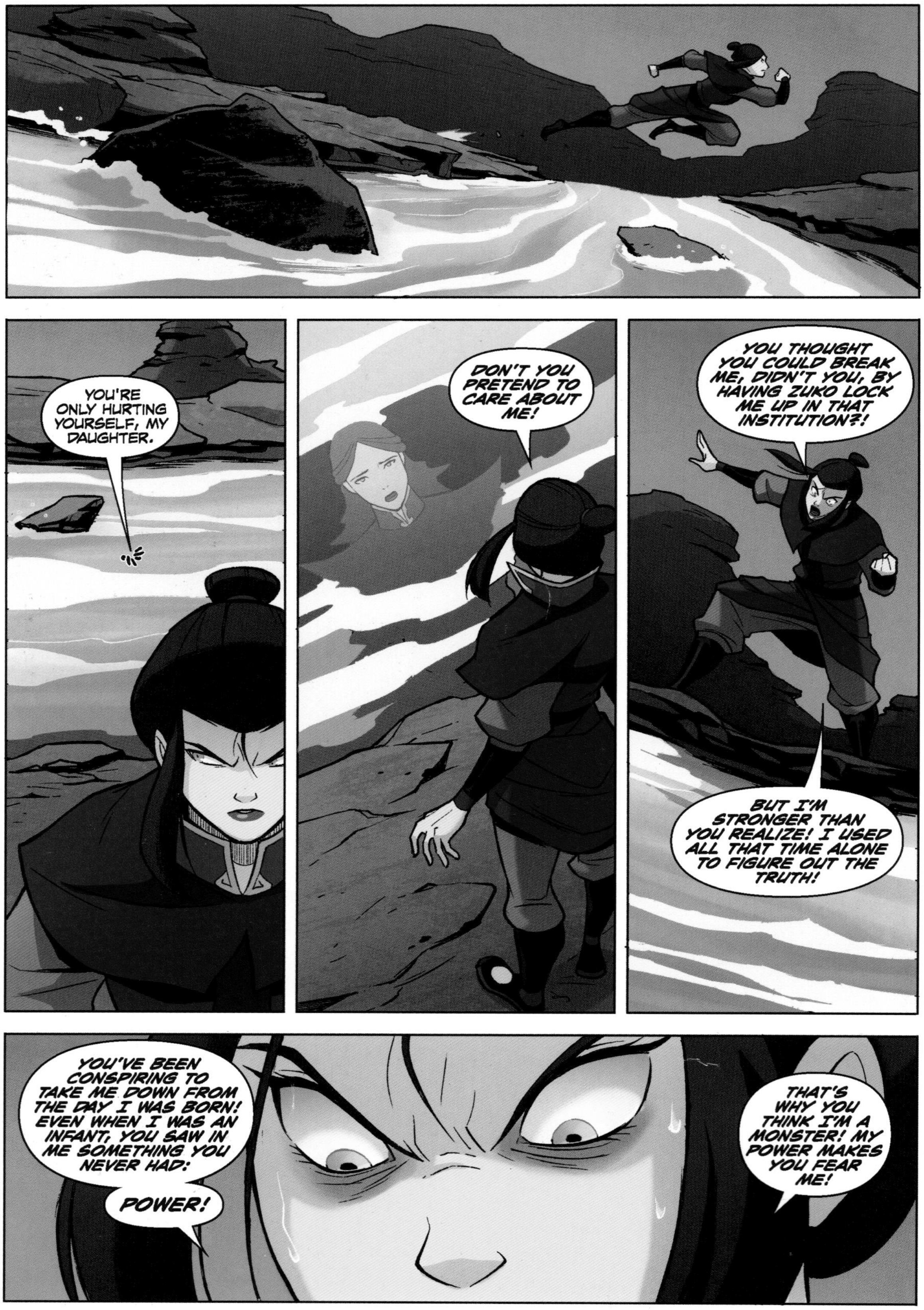
YOU'RE ONLY HURTING YOURSELF, MY DAUGHTER.
DON'T YOU PRETEND TO CARE ABOUT ME!
YOU THOUGHT YOU COULD BREAK ME, DIDN'T YOU, BY HAVING ZUKO LOCK ME UP IN THAT INSTITUTION?!
BUT I'M STRONGER THAN YOU REALIZE! I USED ALL THAT TIME ALONE TO FIGURE OUT THE TRUTH!
YOU'VE BEEN CONSPIRING TO TAKE ME DOWN FROM THE DAY I WAS BORN! EVEN WHEN I WAS AN INFANT, YOU SAW IN ME SOMETHING YOU NEVER HAD:
POWER!
THAT'S WHY YOU THINK I'M A MONSTER! MY POWER MAKES YOU FEAR ME!

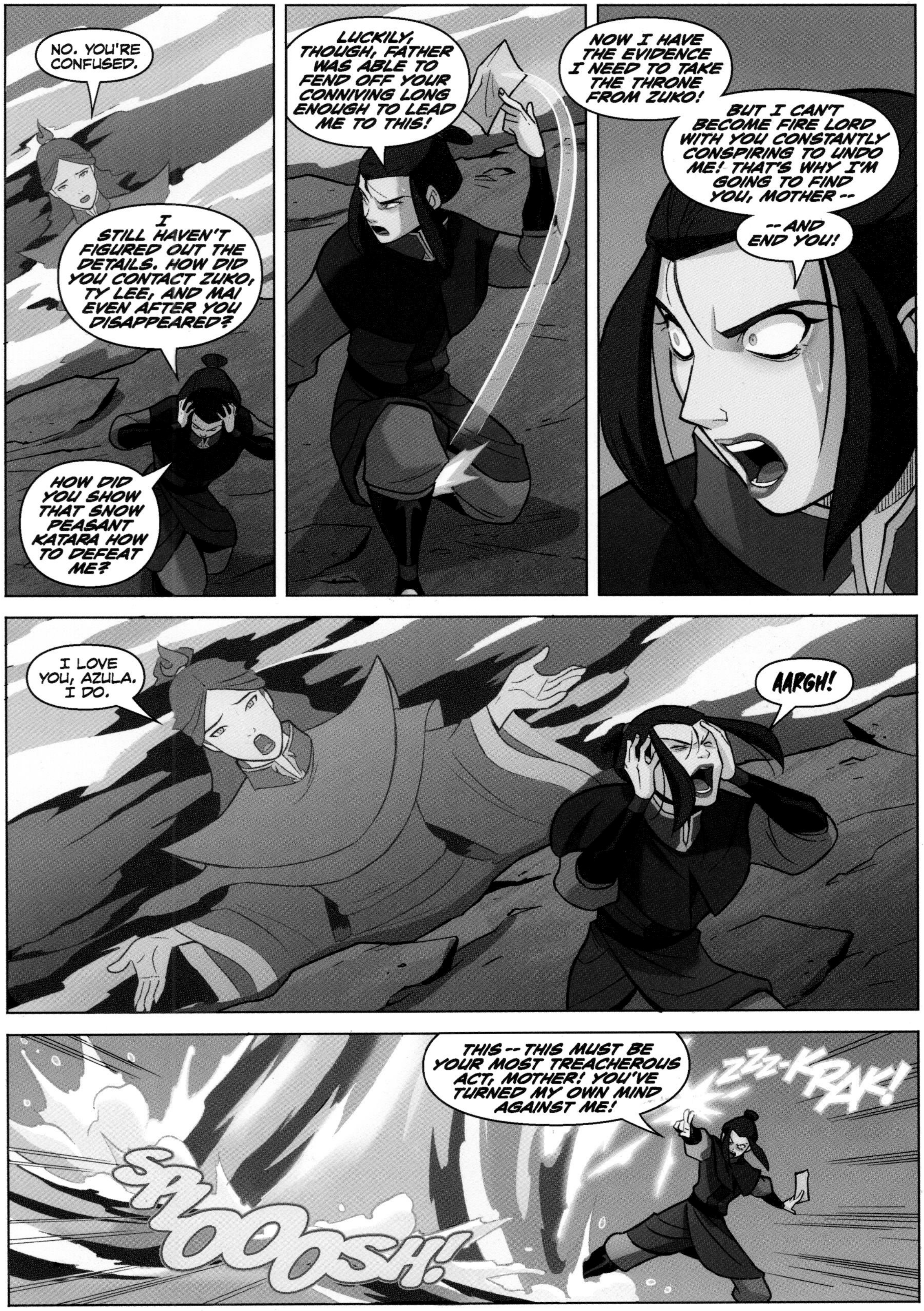
NO. YOU'RE CONFUSED.
I STILL HAVEN'T FIGURED OUT THE DETAILS. HOW DID YOU CONTACT ZUKO, TY LEE, AND MAI EVEN AFTER YOU DISAPPEARED?
HOW DID YOU SHOW THAT SNOW PEASANT KATARA HOW TO DEFEAT ME?
LUCKILY, THOUGH, FATHER WAS ABLE TO FEND OFF YOUR CONNIVING LONG ENOUGH TO LEAD ME TO THIS!
NOW I HAVE THE EVIDENCE I NEED TO TAKE THE THRONE FROM ZUKO!
BUT I CAN'T BECOME FIRE LORD WITH YOU CONSTANTLY CONSPIRING TO UNDO ME! THAT'S WHY I'M GOING TO FIND YOU, MOTHER --
-- AND END YOU!
I LOVE YOU, AZULA. I DO.
AARGH!
THIS -- THIS MUST BE YOUR MOST TREACHEROUS ACT, MOTHER! YOU'VE TURNED MY OWN MIND AGAINST ME!
ZZZ-KRAK!
SPLOOOSH!

GLY: *In the original series, Azula was all kinds of awesome. I found her tragic character arc incredibly compelling. She began as a master manipulator bent on power. But when she finally achieved her goals, her mind broke. We gave her a split personality in order to preserve both the manipulative and lunatic halves of her identity.*

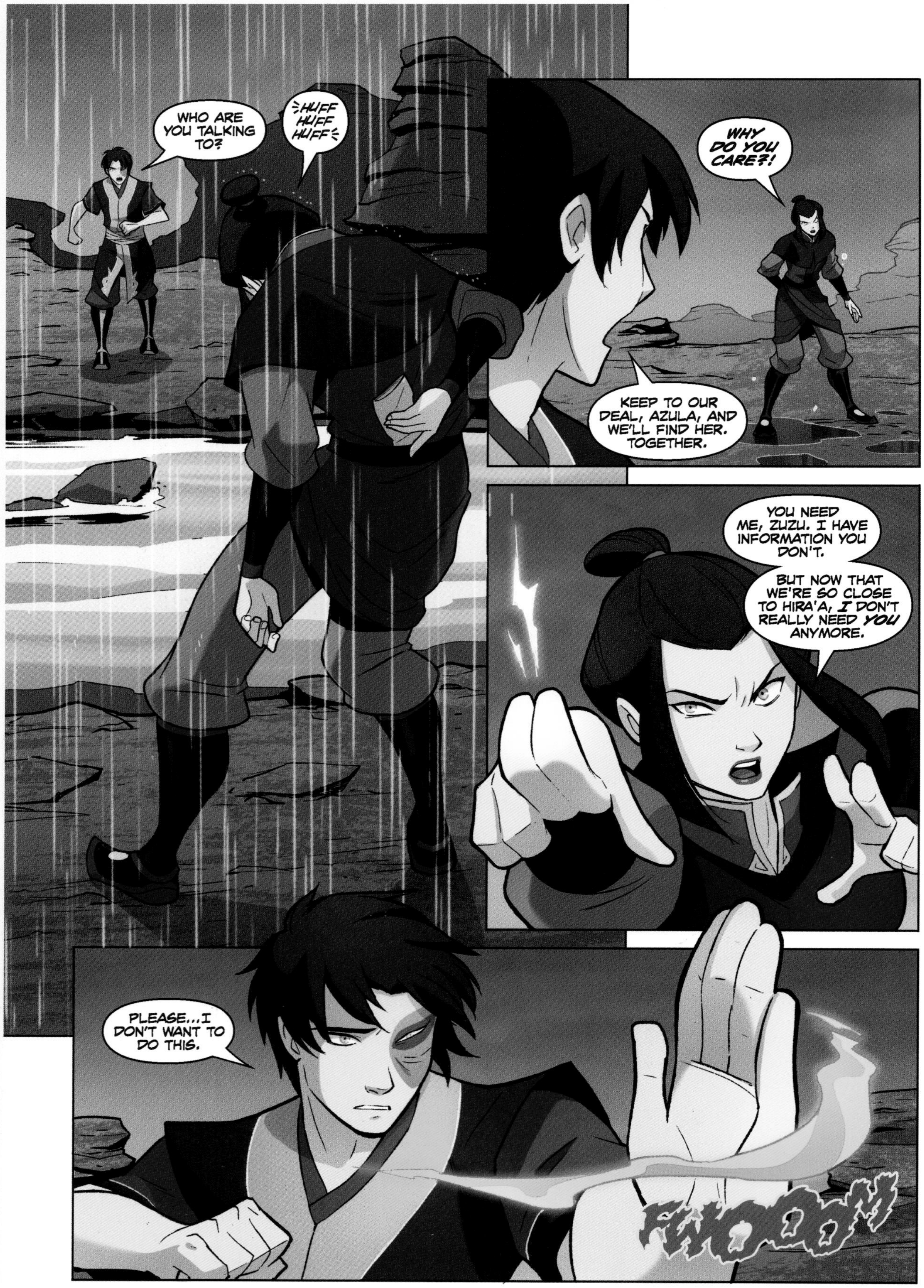
WHO ARE YOU TALKING TO?
HUFF HUFF HUFF
WHY DO YOU CARE?!
KEEP TO OUR DEAL, AZULA, AND WE'LL FIND HER. TOGETHER.
YOU NEED ME, ZUZU. I HAVE INFORMATION YOU DON'T.
BUT NOW THAT WE'RE SO CLOSE TO HIRA'A, I DON'T REALLY NEED YOU ANYMORE.
PLEASE...I DON'T WANT TO DO THIS.
FWOOM

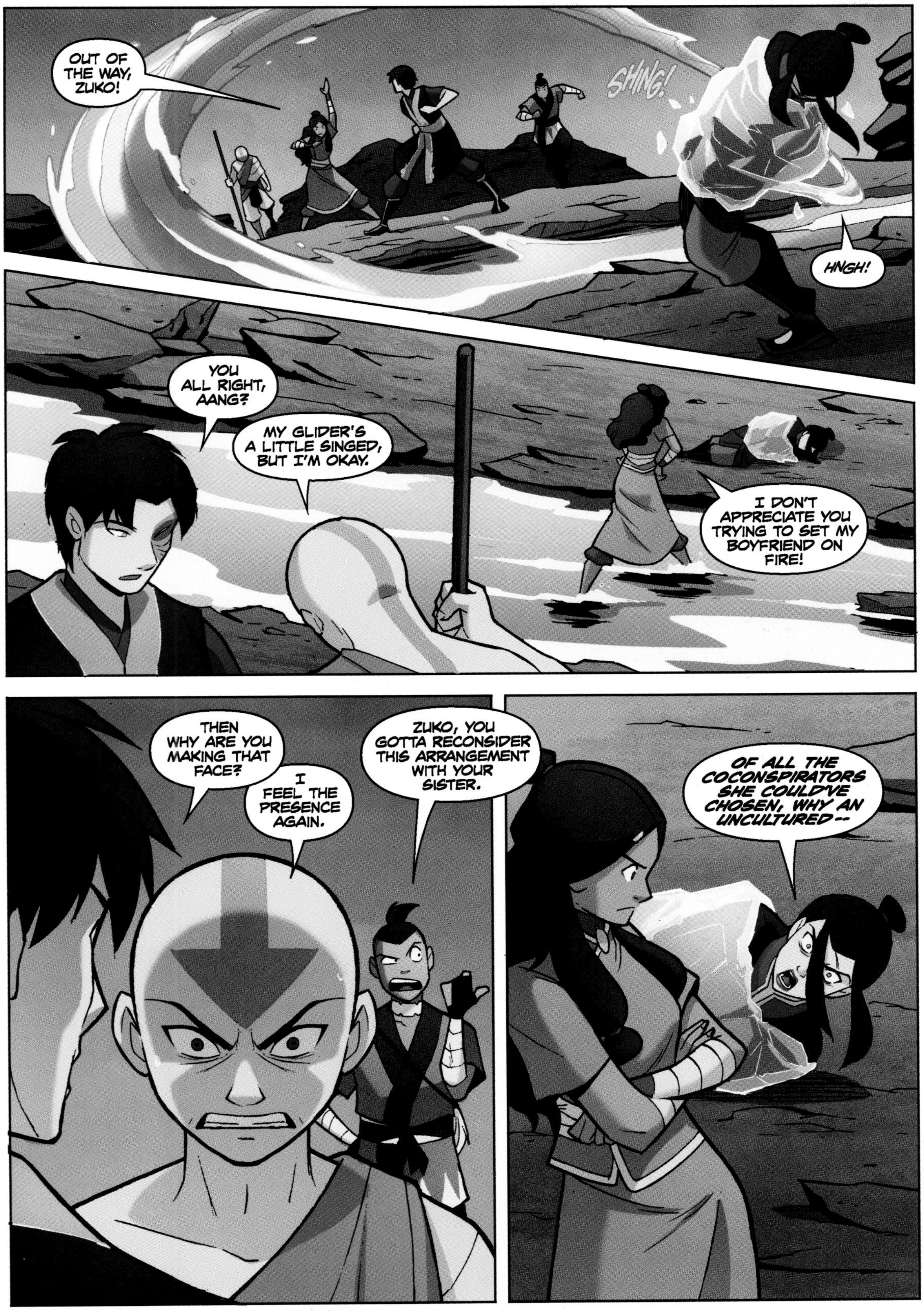
OUT OF THE WAY, ZUKO!
SHING!
HNGH!
YOU ALL RIGHT, AANG?
MY GLIDER'S A LITTLE SINGED, BUT I'M OKAY.
I DON'T APPRECIATE YOU TRYING TO SET MY BOYFRIEND ON FIRE!
THEN WHY ARE YOU MAKING THAT FACE?
I FEEL THE PRESENCE AGAIN.
ZUKO, YOU GOTTA RECONSIDER THIS ARRANGEMENT WITH YOUR SISTER.
OF ALL THE COCONSPIRATORS SHE COULD'VE CHOSEN, WHY AN UNCULTURED--

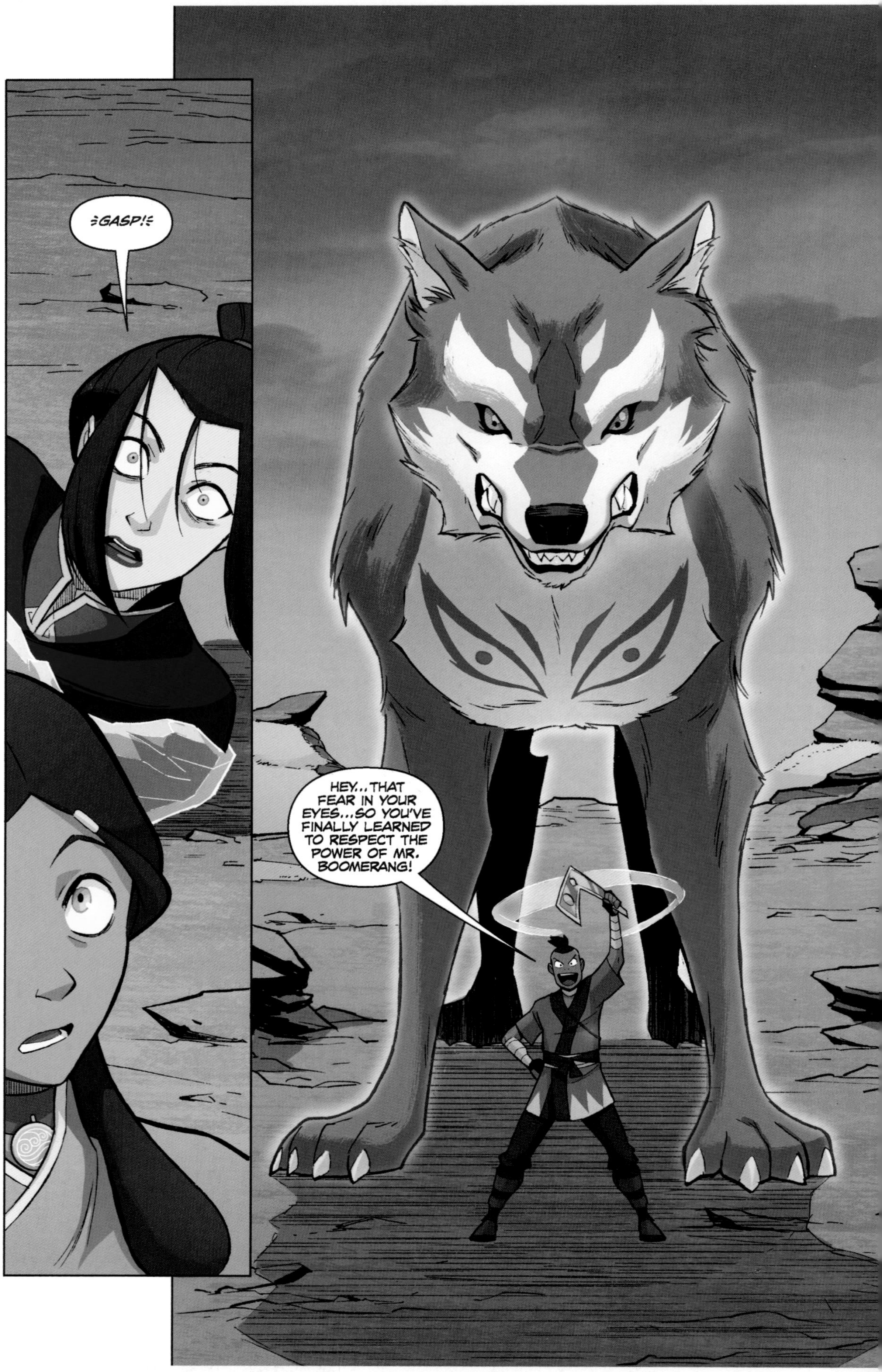

≑GASP!≑
HEY...THAT FEAR IN YOUR EYES...SO YOU'VE FINALLY LEARNED TO RESPECT THE POWER OF MR. BOOMERANG!

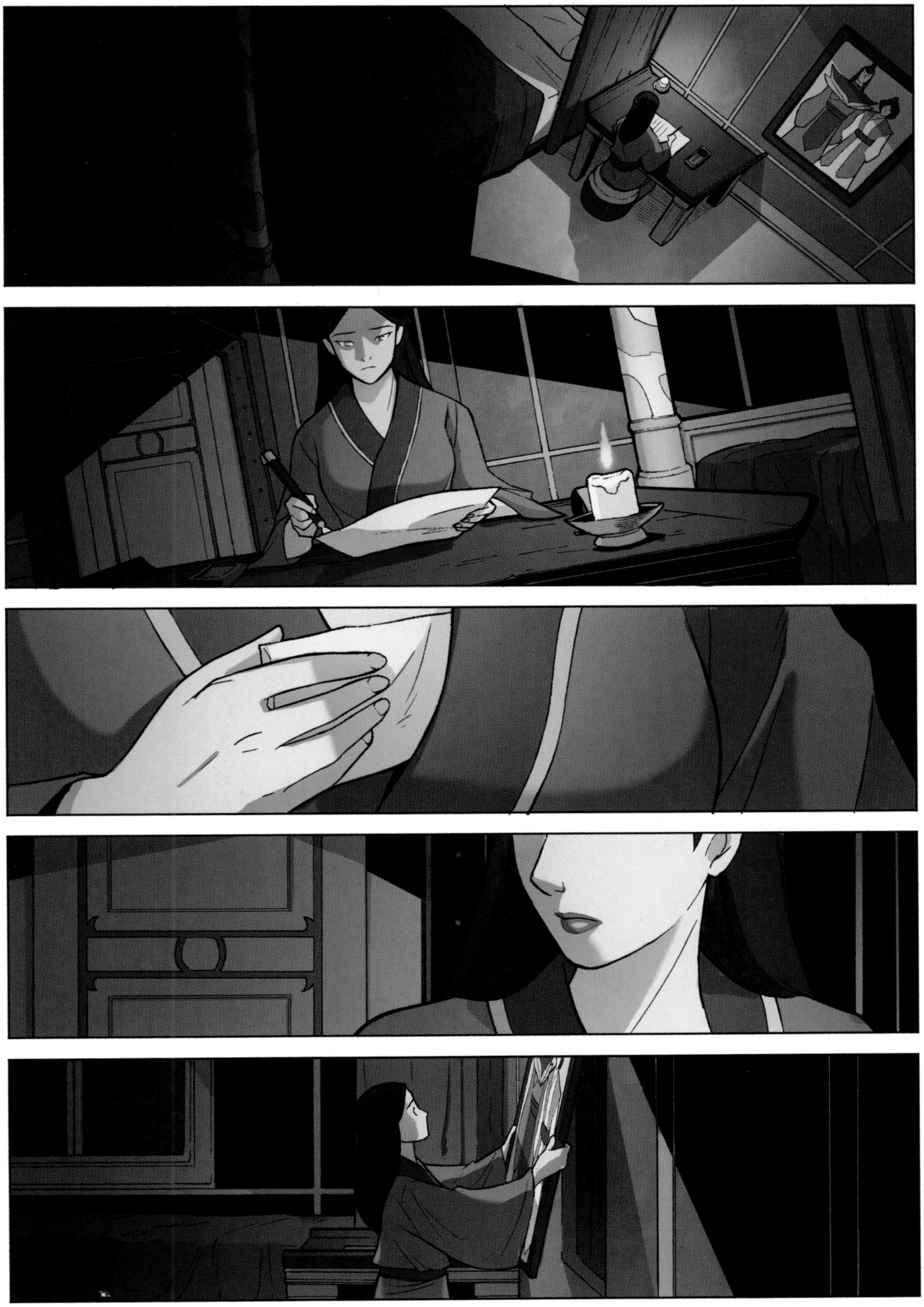

GLY: *When I was watching book 1 of the original series, I wondered where Zuko got his Blue Spirit mask. Masks are important in the dramatic traditions of various Asian cultures. Here, we make that connection explicit. We also imply that after Ursa left, young Zuko searched her stuff for clues about where she might have gone. He stumbled across her secret masks and used the blue one to become the Blue Spirit.*

M: *The origins of the Blue Spirit are revealed! In* Avatar: The Last Airbender, *Bryan based the Blue Spirit mask on the mask of Dragon King Nuo from Chinese drama, though we never detailed exactly why Zuko chose this particular mask. I like how Gene tied it into Ursa's backstory with the acting troupe.*

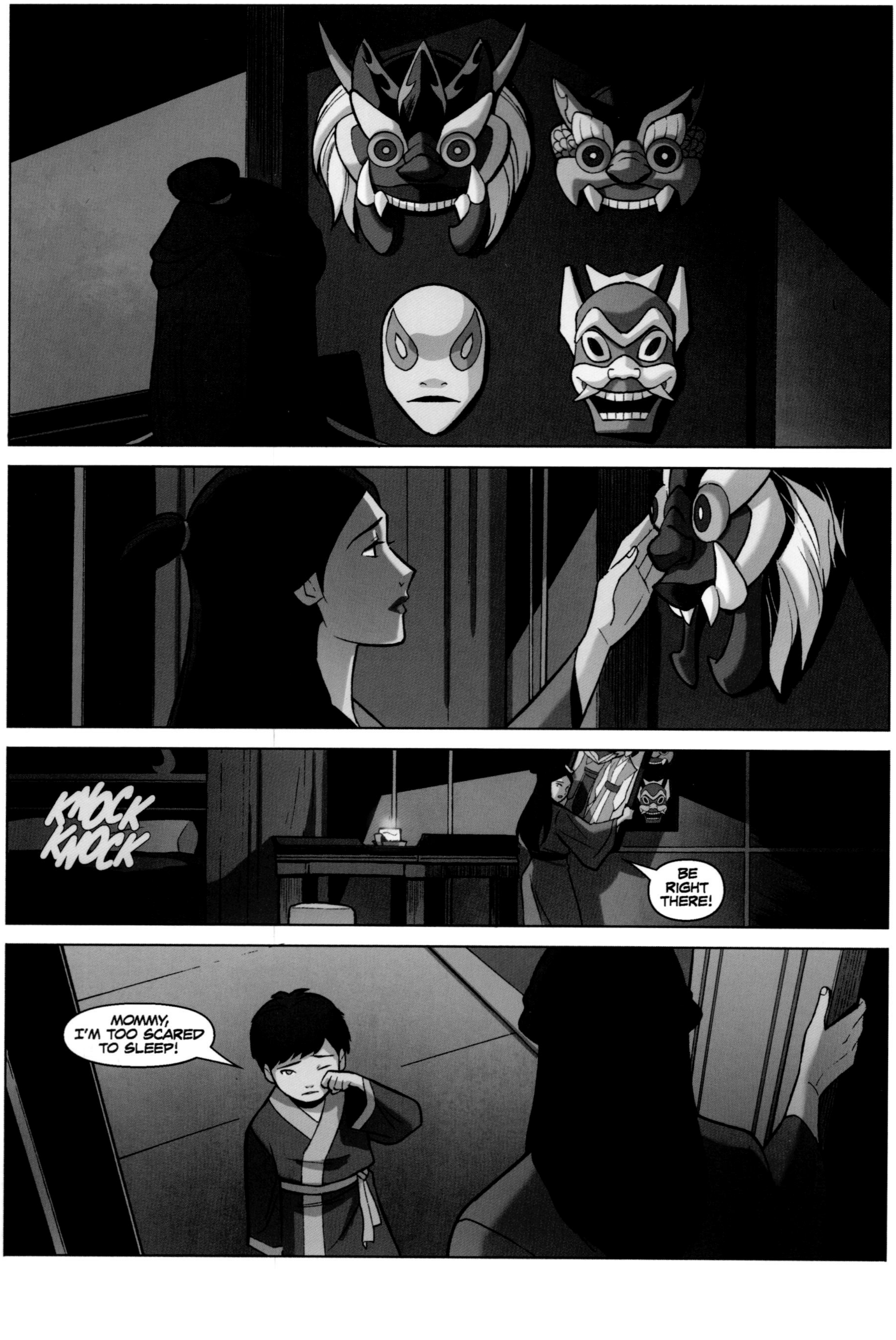
KNOCK KNOCK
BE RIGHT THERE!
MOMMY, I'M TOO SCARED TO SLEEP!

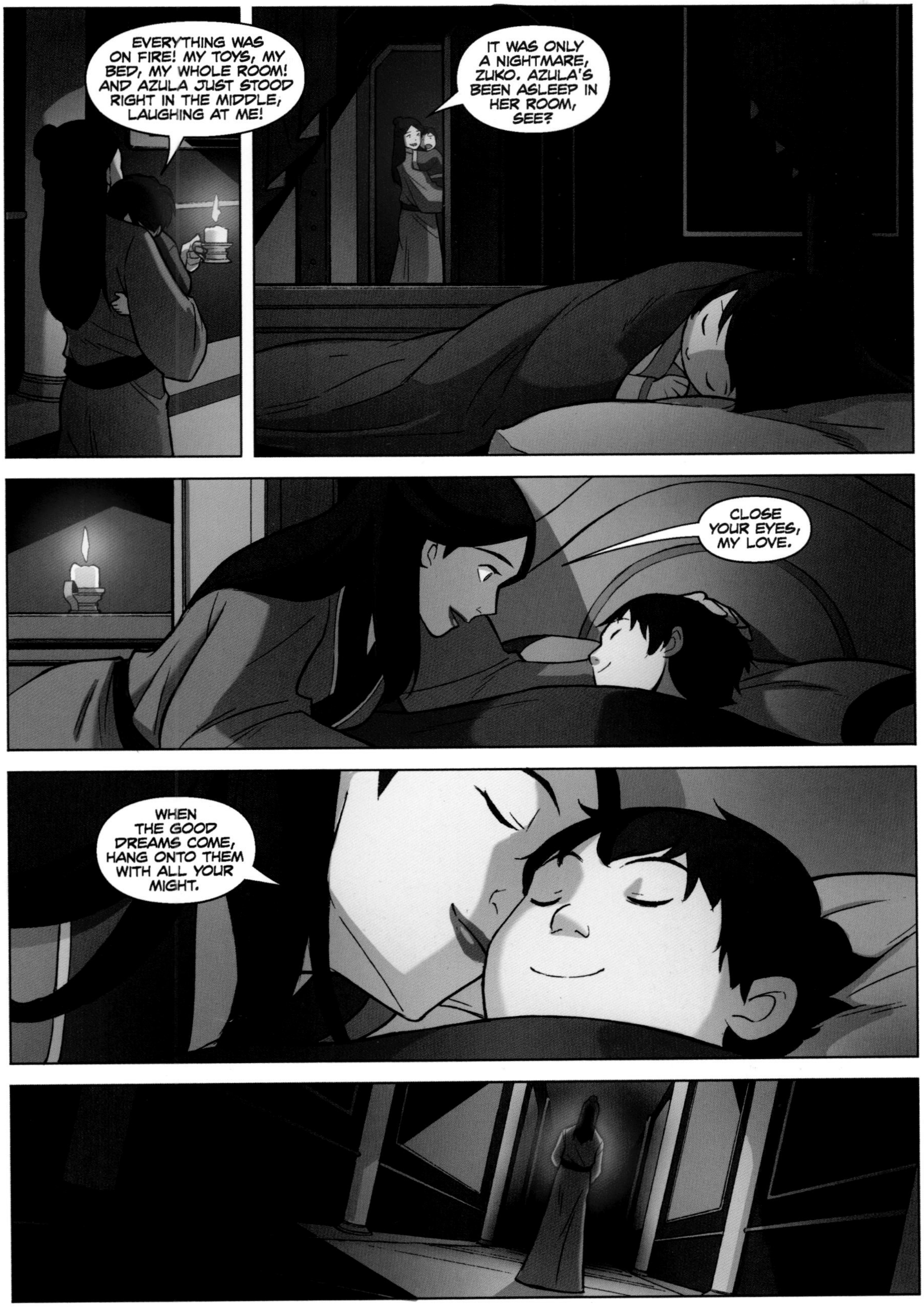
EVERYTHING WAS ON FIRE! MY TOYS, MY BED, MY WHOLE ROOM! AND AZULA JUST STOOD RIGHT IN THE MIDDLE, LAUGHING AT ME!
IT WAS ONLY A NIGHTMARE, ZUKO. AZULA'S BEEN ASLEEP IN HER ROOM, SEE?
CLOSE YOUR EYES, MY LOVE.
WHEN THE GOOD DREAMS COME, HANG ONTO THEM WITH ALL YOUR MIGHT.

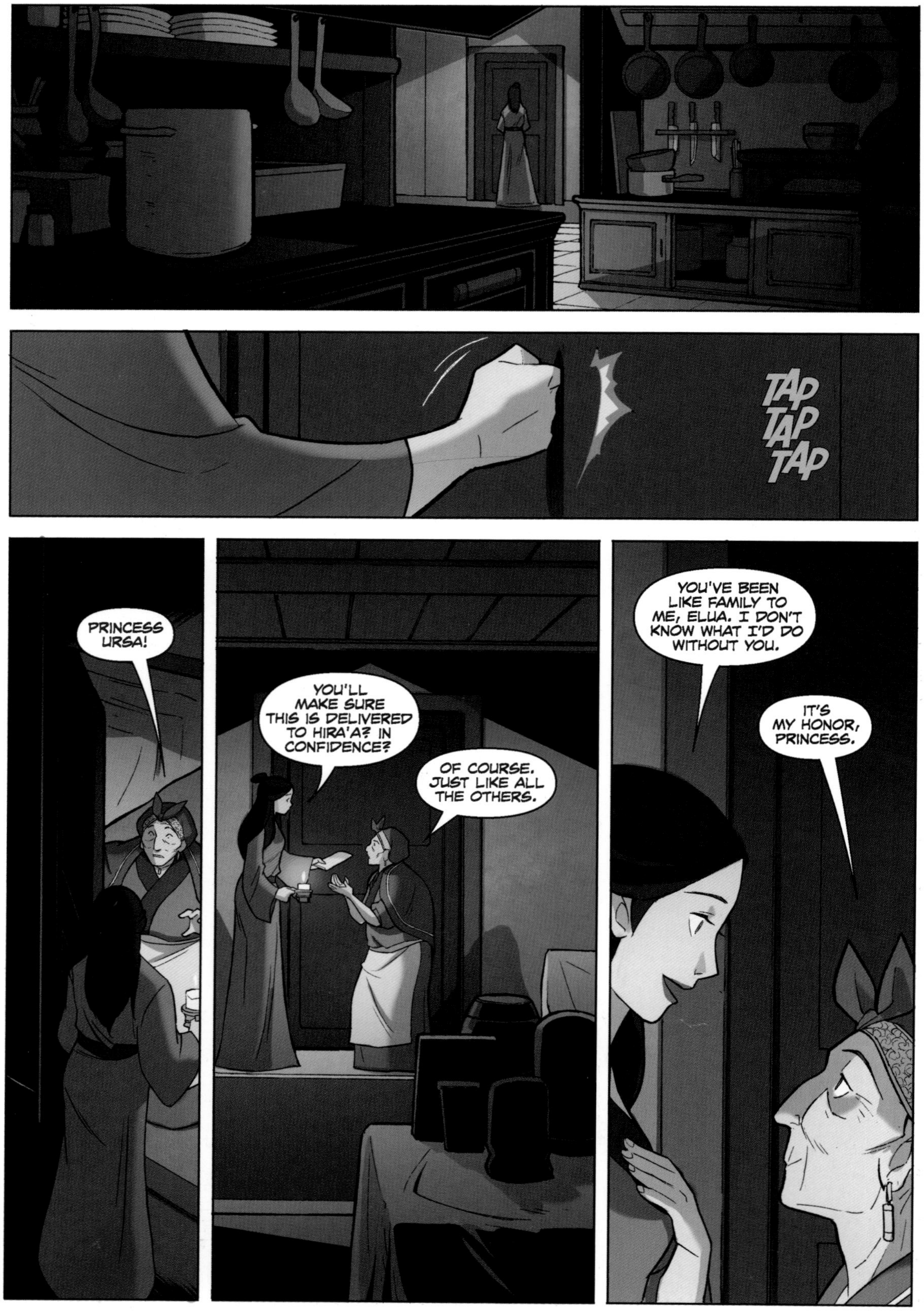
TAP
TAP
TAP
PRINCESS URSA!
YOU'LL MAKE SURE THIS IS DELIVERED TO HIRA'A? IN CONFIDENCE?
OF COURSE. JUST LIKE ALL THE OTHERS.
YOU'VE BEEN LIKE FAMILY TO ME, ELUA. I DON'T KNOW WHAT I'D DO WITHOUT YOU.
IT'S MY HONOR, PRINCESS.

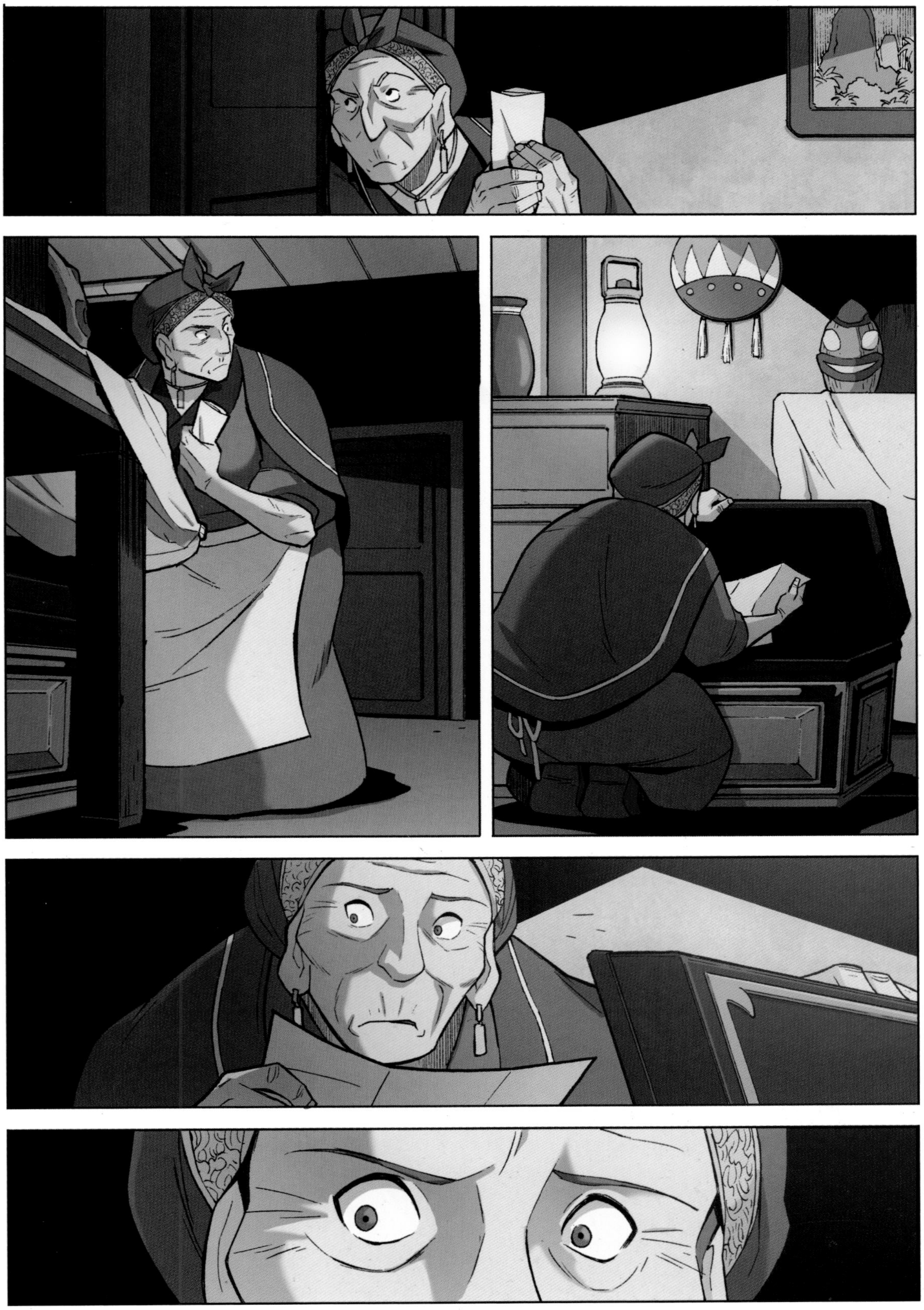

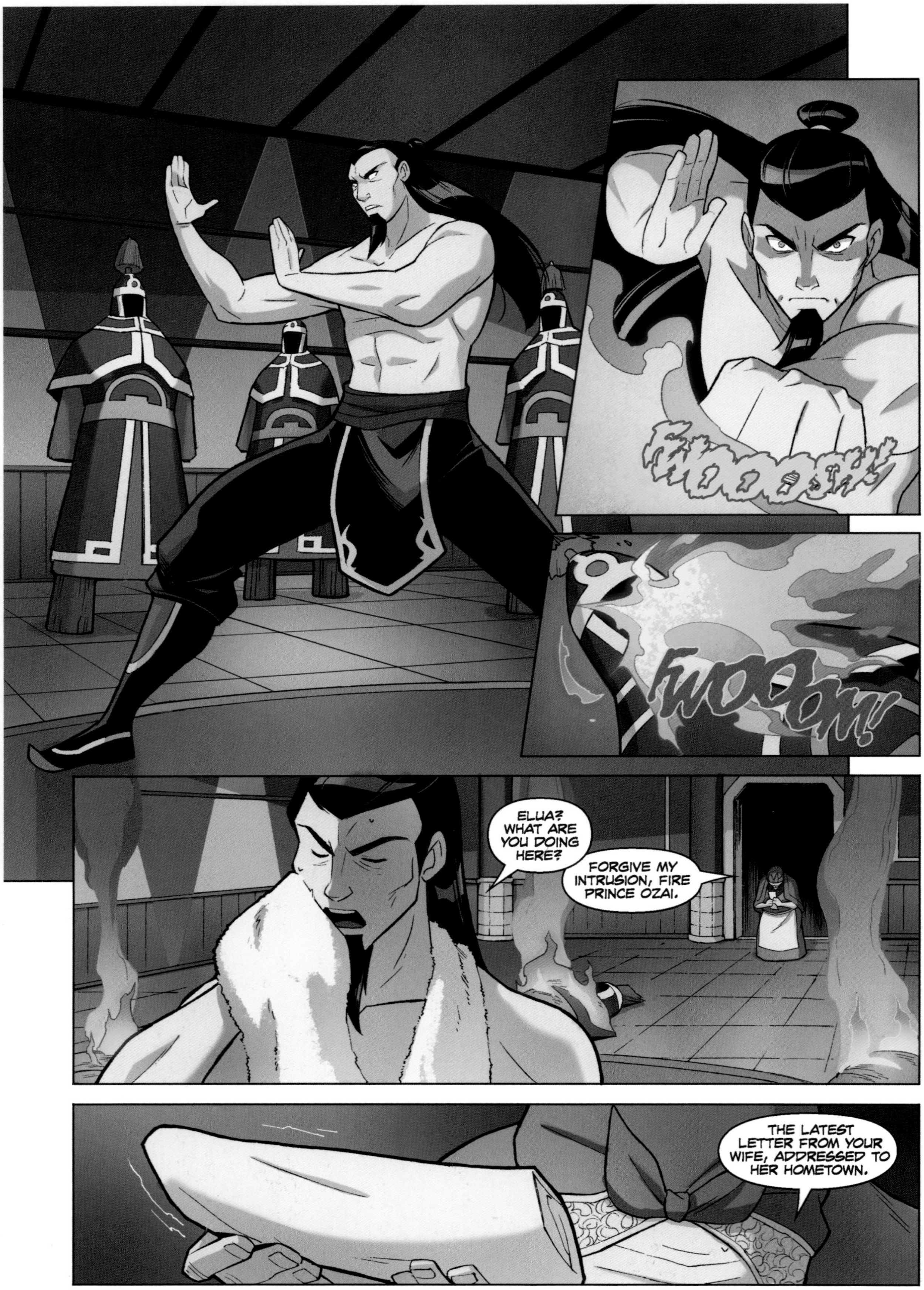
FWOOOSH!
FWOOOM!
ELUA? WHAT ARE YOU DOING HERE?
FORGIVE MY INTRUSION, FIRE PRINCE OZAI.
THE LATEST LETTER FROM YOUR WIFE, ADDRESSED TO HER HOMETOWN.

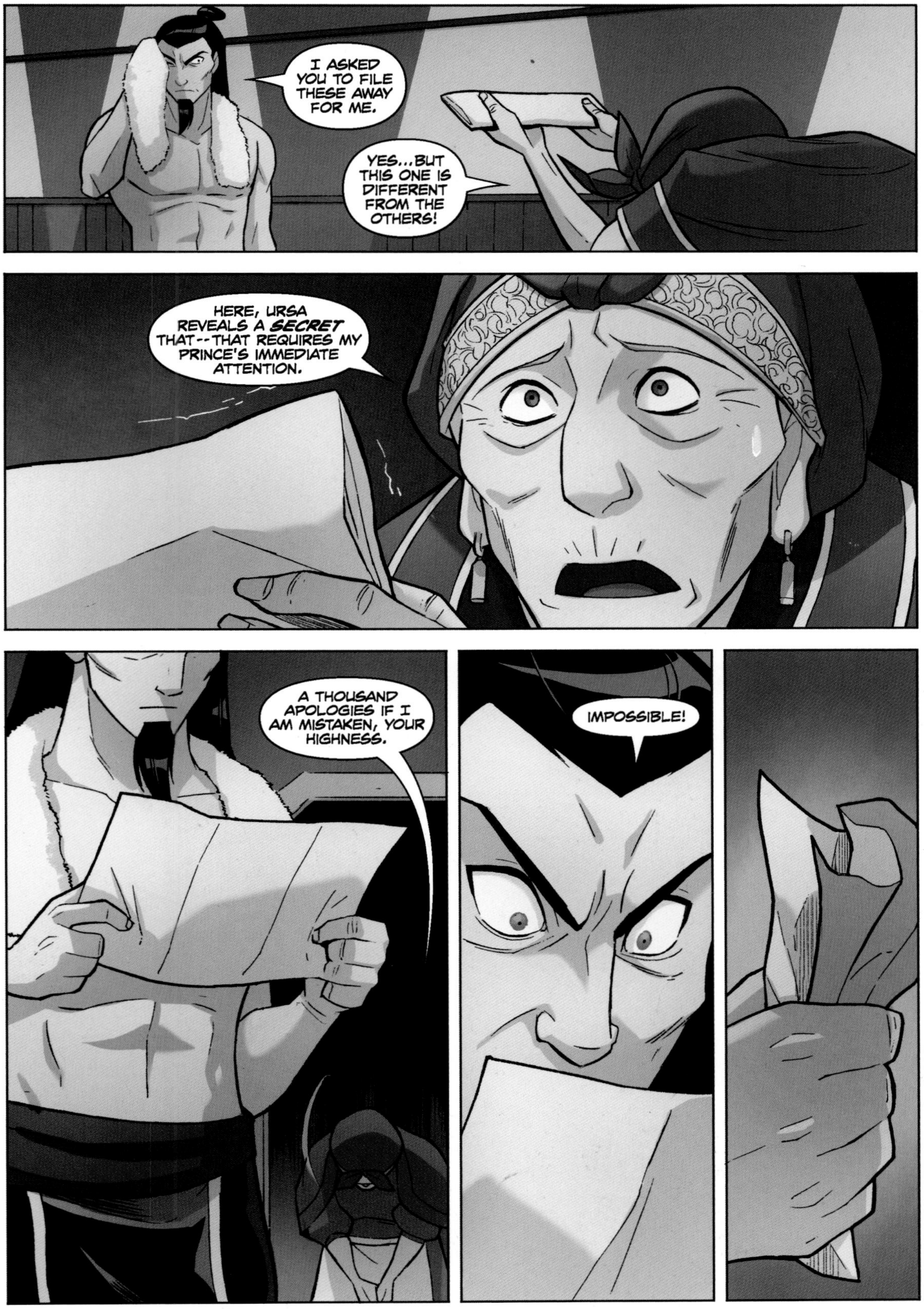
I ASKED YOU TO FILE THESE AWAY FOR ME.
YES...BUT THIS ONE IS DIFFERENT FROM THE OTHERS!
HERE, URSA REVEALS A SECRET THAT--THAT REQUIRES MY PRINCE'S IMMEDIATE ATTENTION.
A THOUSAND APOLOGIES IF I AM MISTAKEN, YOUR HIGHNESS.
IMPOSSIBLE!

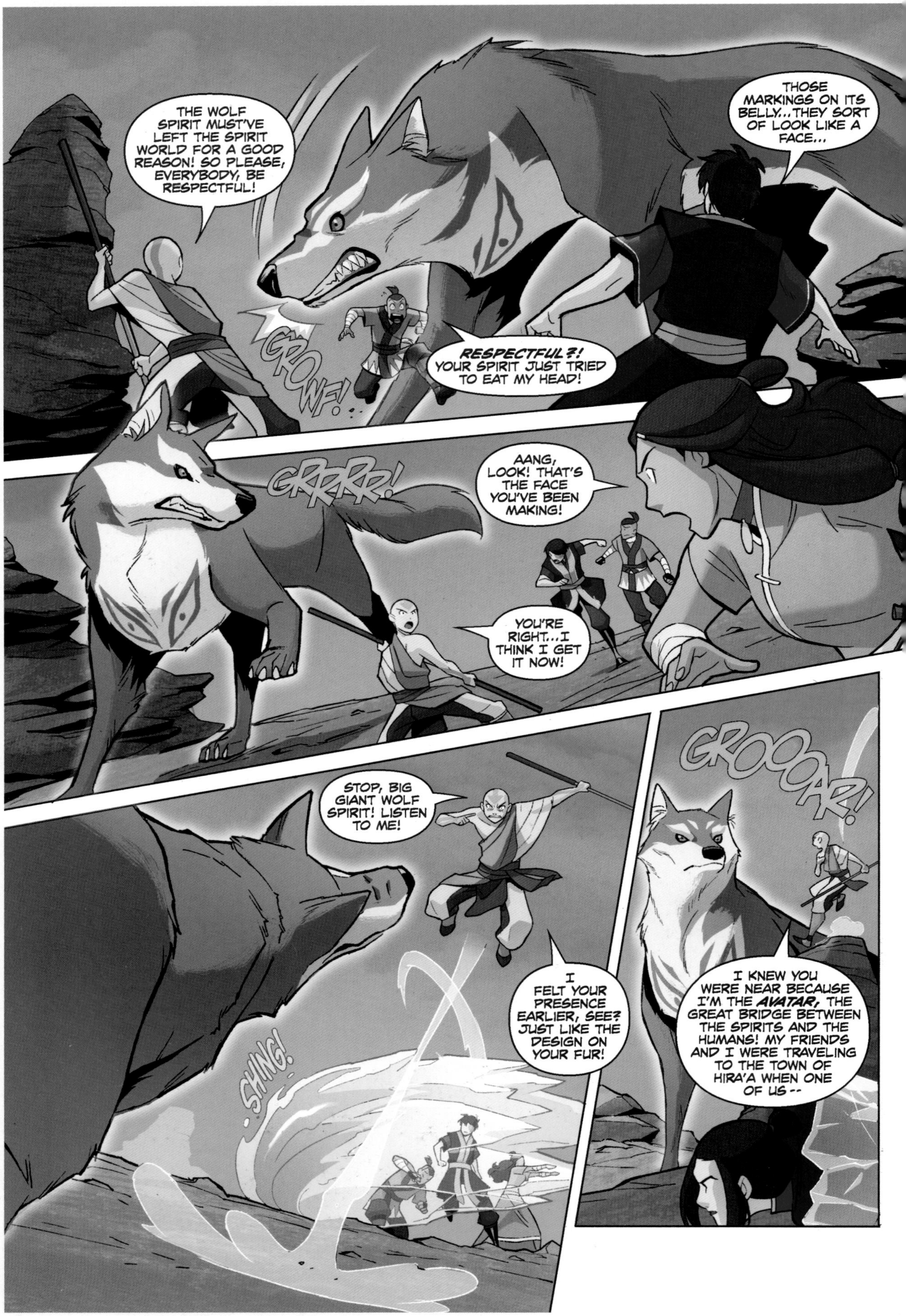
THE WOLF SPIRIT MUST'VE LEFT THE SPIRIT WORLD FOR A GOOD REASON! SO PLEASE, EVERYBODY, BE RESPECTFUL!
THOSE MARKINGS ON ITS BELLY...THEY SORT OF LOOK LIKE A FACE...
GROWF!
RESPECTFUL?! YOUR SPIRIT JUST TRIED TO EAT MY HEAD!
GRRRR!
AANG, LOOK! THAT'S THE FACE YOU'VE BEEN MAKING!
YOU'RE RIGHT...I THINK I GET IT NOW!
STOP, BIG GIANT WOLF SPIRIT! LISTEN TO ME!
I FELT YOUR PRESENCE EARLIER, SEE? JUST LIKE THE DESIGN ON YOUR FUR!
SHING!
GROOOAR!
I KNEW YOU WERE NEAR BECAUSE I'M THE AVATAR, THE GREAT BRIDGE BETWEEN THE SPIRITS AND THE HUMANS! MY FRIENDS AND I WERE TRAVELING TO THE TOWN OF HIRA'A WHEN ONE OF US --

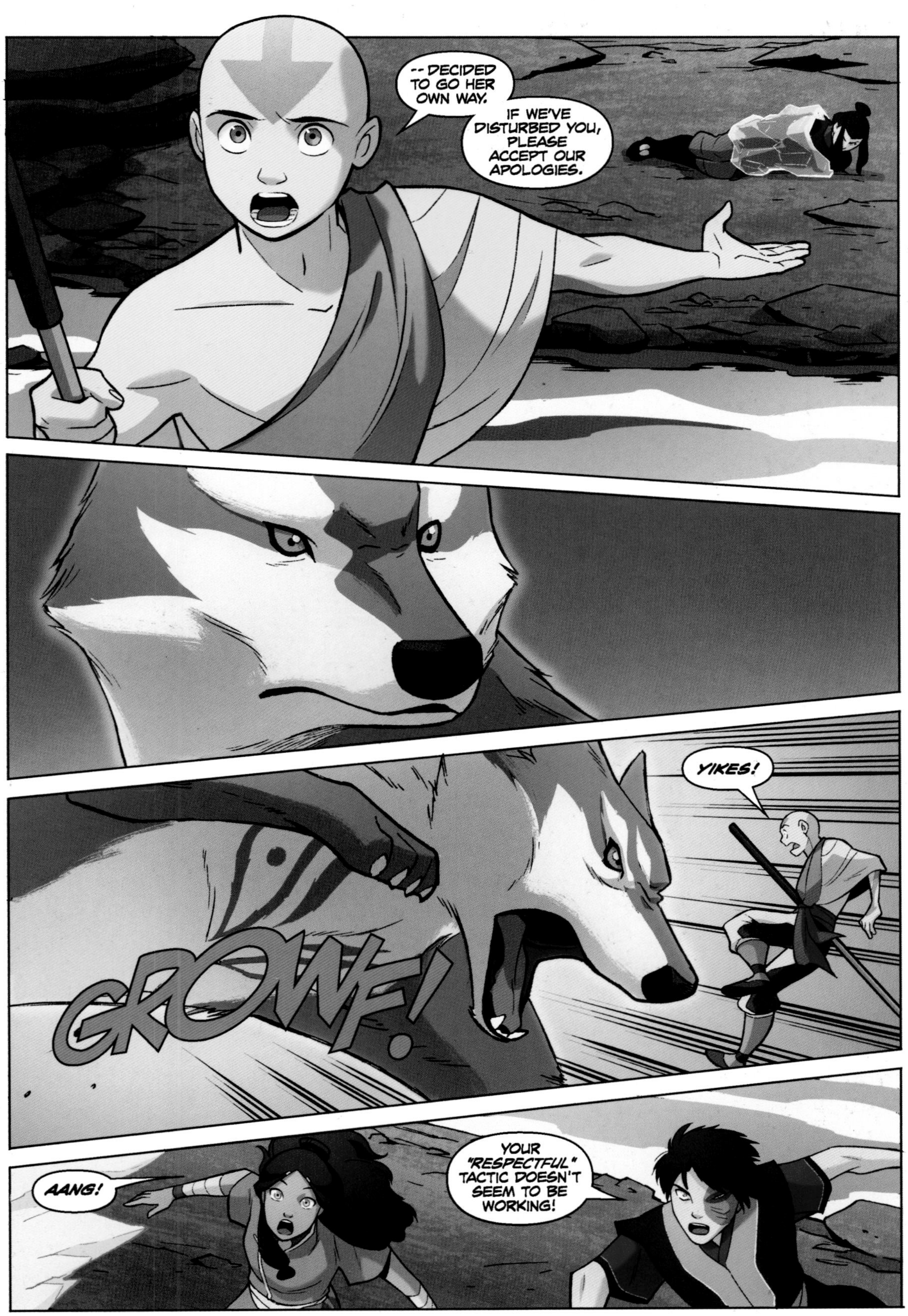
--DECIDED TO GO HER OWN WAY.
IF WE'VE DISTURBED YOU, PLEASE ACCEPT OUR APOLOGIES.
YIKES!
GROWF!
AANG!
YOUR "RESPECTFUL" TACTIC DOESN'T SEEM TO BE WORKING!

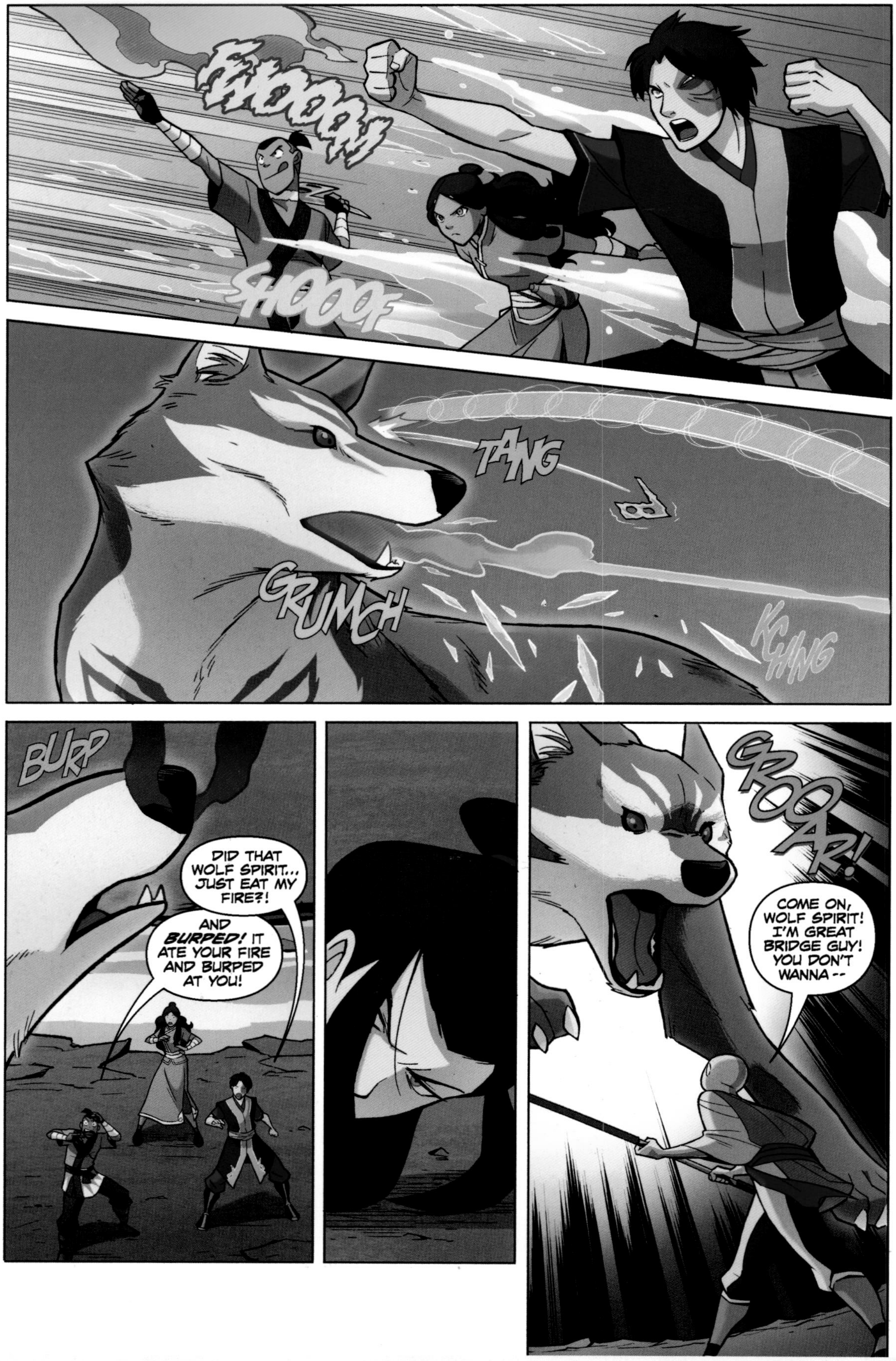
FWOOOM
SHOOOF
TANG
GRUMCH
KCHING
BURP
DID THAT WOLF SPIRIT... JUST EAT MY FIRE?!
AND BURPED! IT ATE YOUR FIRE AND BURPED AT YOU!
GROOOAR!
COME ON, WOLF SPIRIT! I'M GREAT BRIDGE GUY! YOU DON'T WANNA --

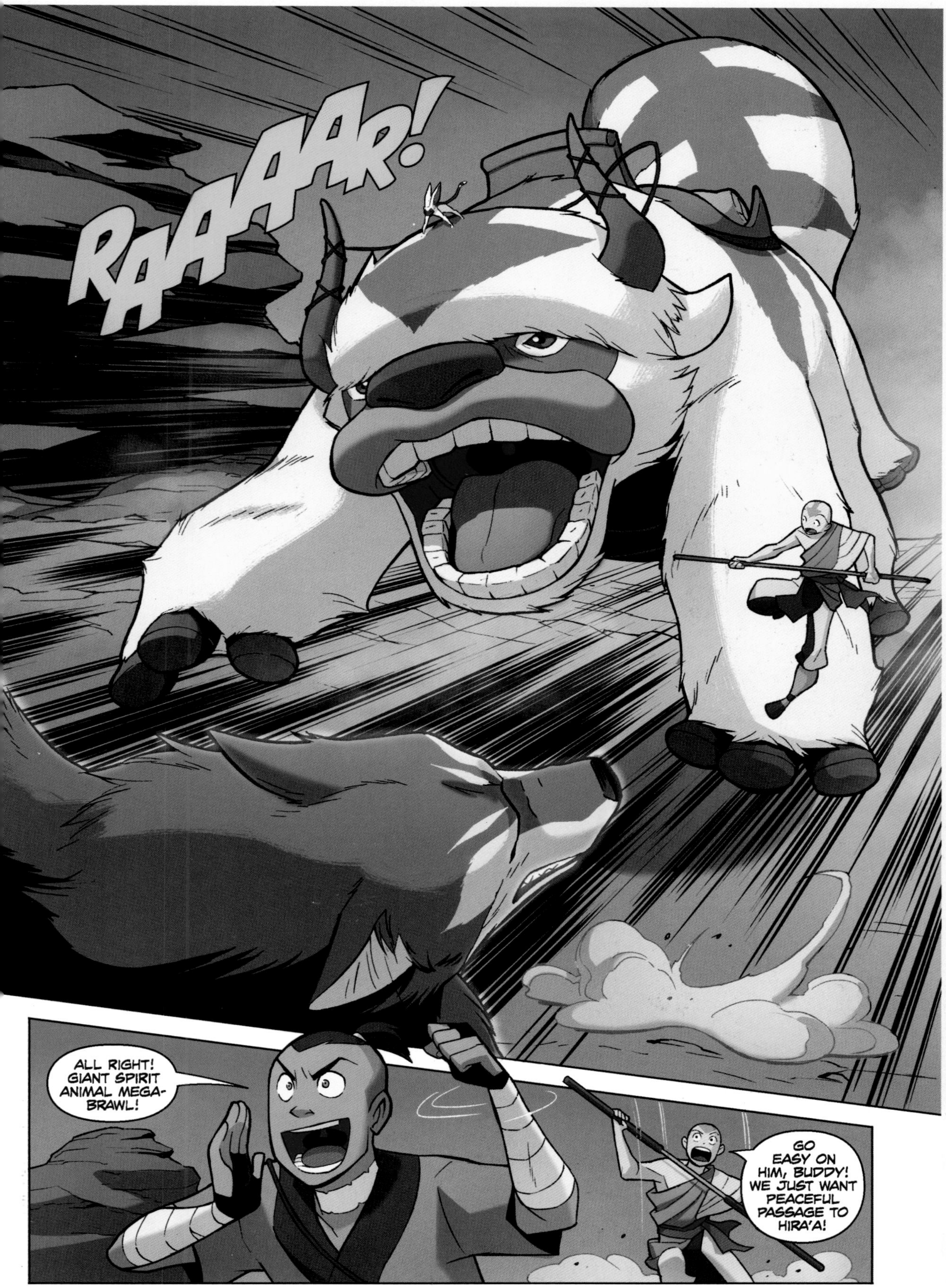
RAAAAAR!
ALL RIGHT! GIANT SPIRIT ANIMAL MEGA-BRAWL!
GO EASY ON HIM, BUDDY! WE JUST WANT PEACEFUL PASSAGE TO HIRA'A!

GLY: *At WonderCon 2013, I had the pleasure of meeting Dee Bradley Baker, the voice of Appa and Momo. He did an amazing reading of this section. He made the Giant Spirit Animal Megabrawl come alive. Look for clips of his performances on YouTube. You won't believe how many different voices and noises can come out of one man.*

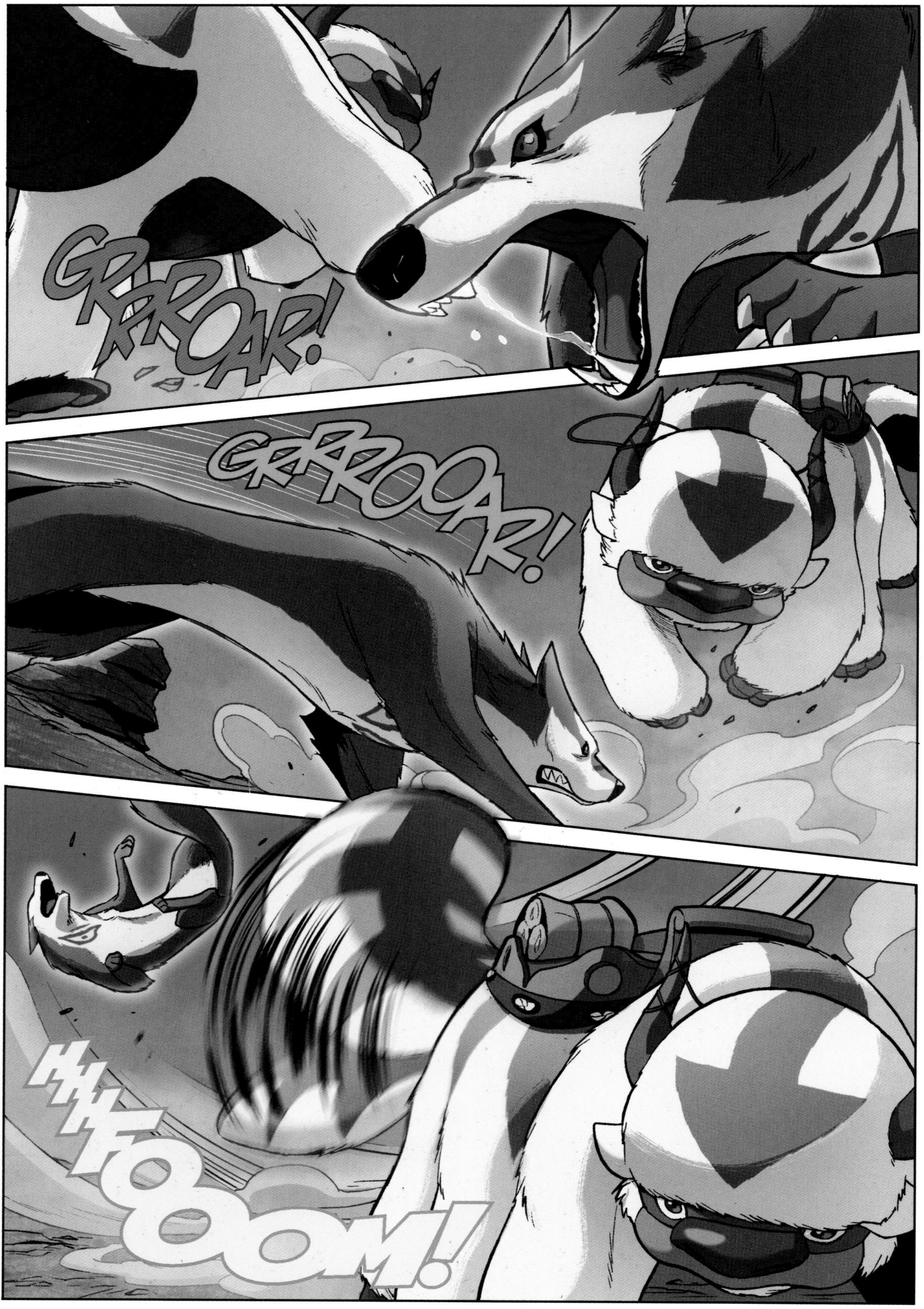
GRRROAR!
GRRROOAR!
HHHFOOOM!

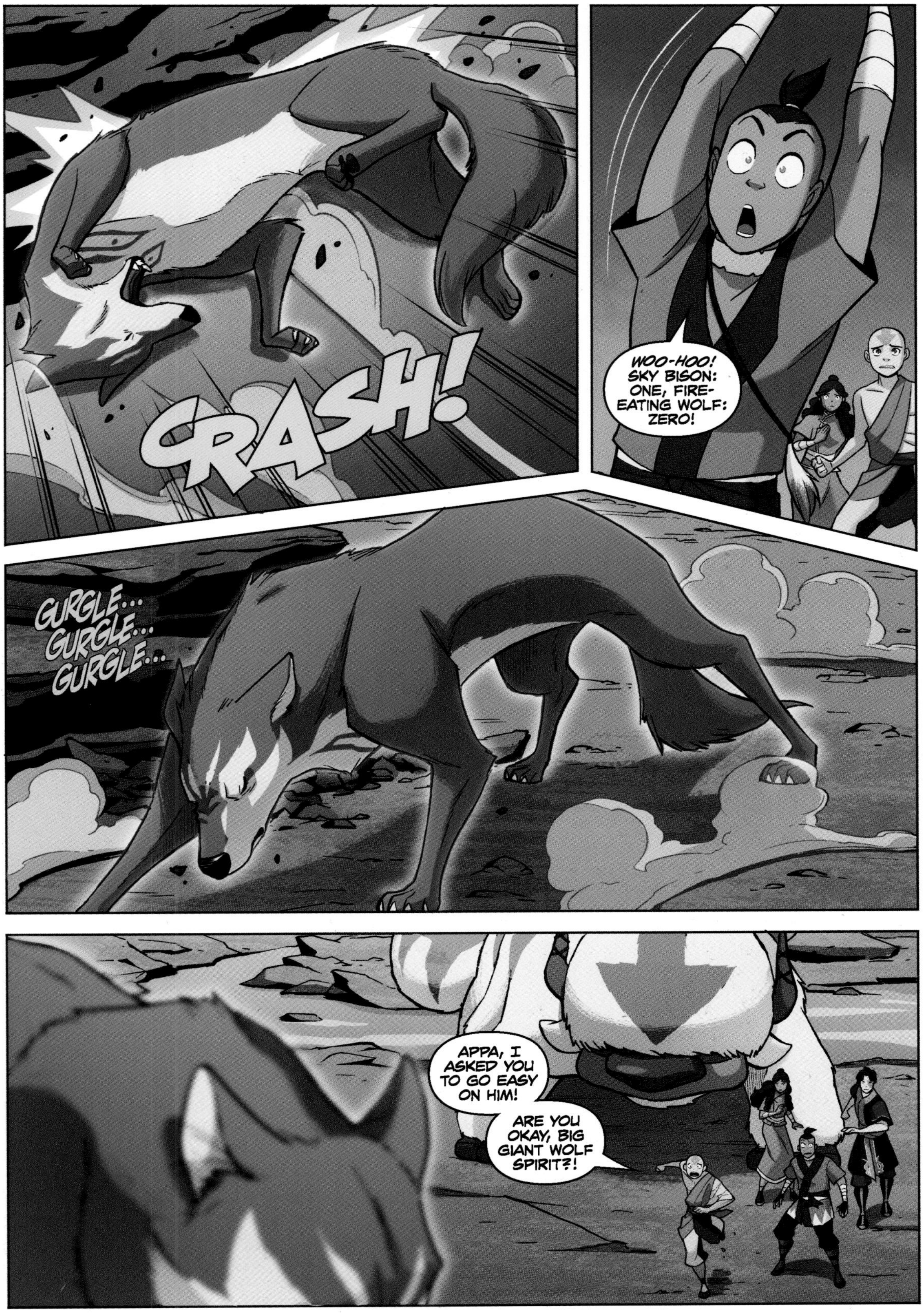
CRASH!
WOO-HOO! SKY BISON: ONE, FIRE-EATING WOLF: ZERO!
GURGLE... GURGLE... GURGLE...
APPA, I ASKED YOU TO GO EASY ON HIM!
ARE YOU OKAY, BIG GIANT WOLF SPIRIT?!

G: *We're actually afraid of moths, so it was really scary for us to look at photos of moths for reference. (Even though this is a moth-wasp, not really a moth . . .)*

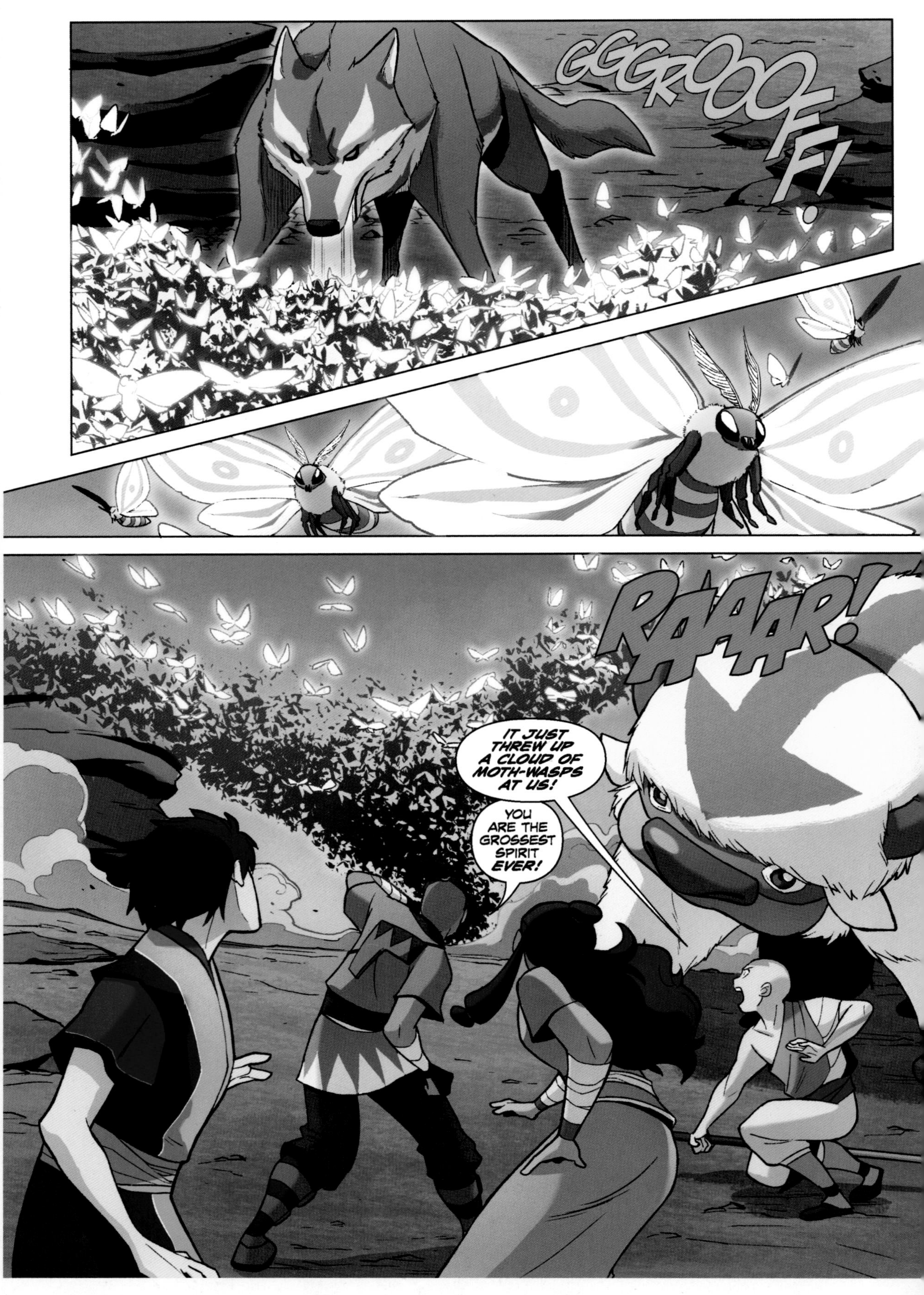
GGGROOOFF!
RAAAR!
IT JUST THREW UP A CLOUD OF MOTH-WASPS AT US!
YOU ARE THE GROSSEST SPIRIT EVER!

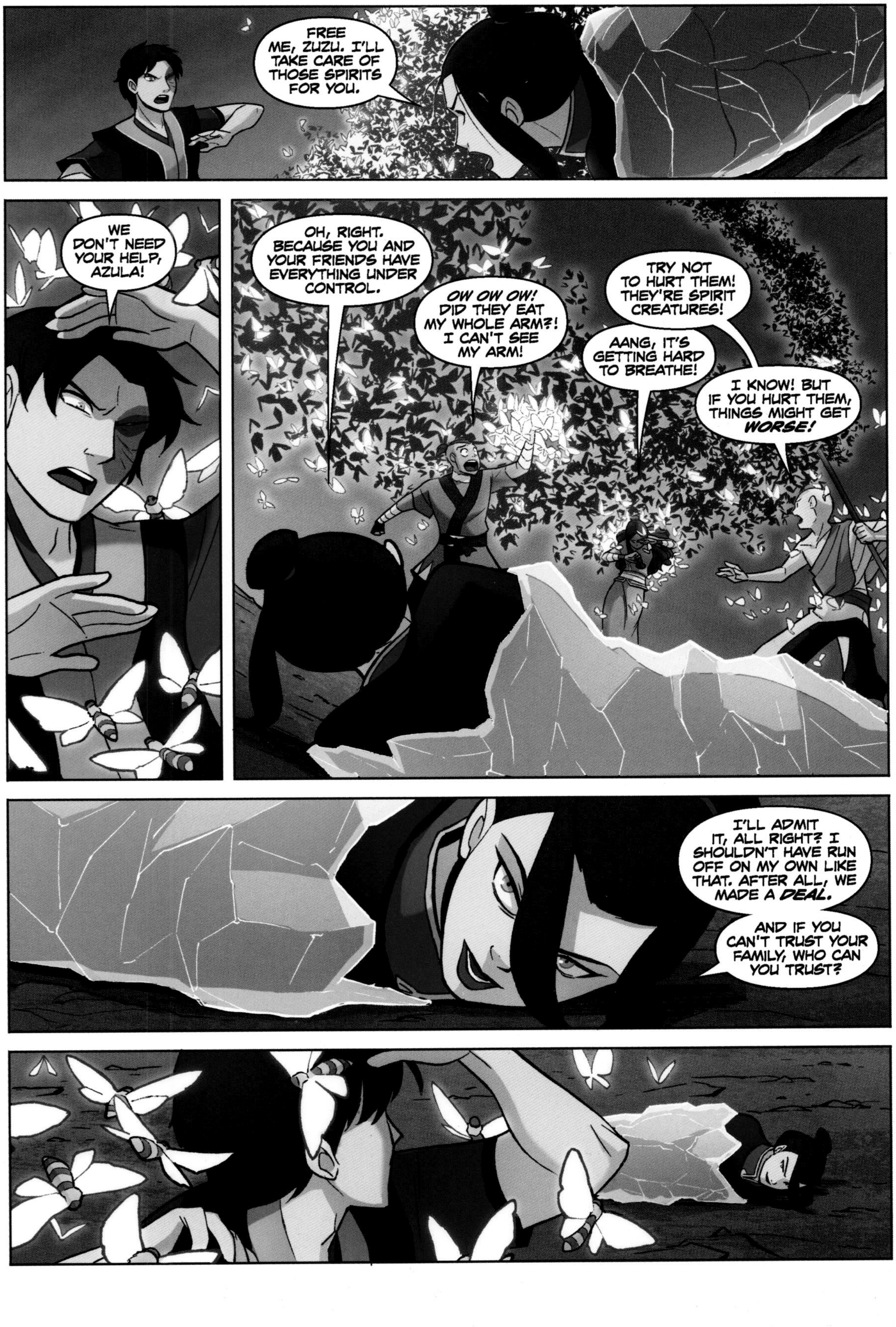
FREE ME, ZUZU. I'LL TAKE CARE OF THOSE SPIRITS FOR YOU.
WE DON'T NEED YOUR HELP, AZULA!
OH, RIGHT. BECAUSE YOU AND YOUR FRIENDS HAVE EVERYTHING UNDER CONTROL.
OW OW OW! DID THEY EAT MY WHOLE ARM?! I CAN'T SEE MY ARM!
TRY NOT TO HURT THEM! THEY'RE SPIRIT CREATURES!
AANG, IT'S GETTING HARD TO BREATHE!
I KNOW! BUT IF YOU HURT THEM, THINGS MIGHT GET WORSE!
I'LL ADMIT IT, ALL RIGHT? I SHOULDN'T HAVE RUN OFF ON MY OWN LIKE THAT. AFTER ALL, WE MADE A DEAL.
AND IF YOU CAN'T TRUST YOUR FAMILY, WHO CAN YOU TRUST?

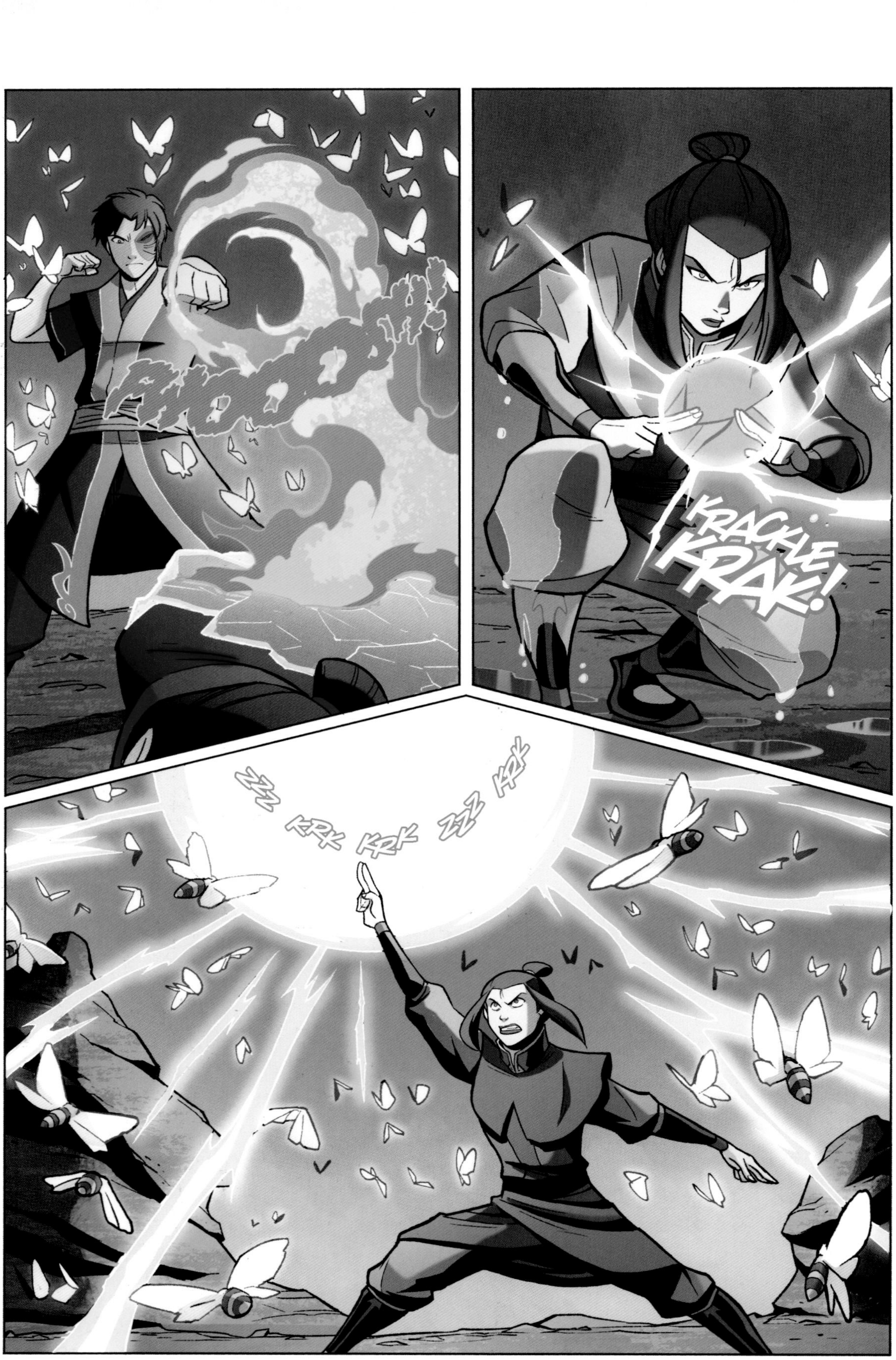
FWOOOSH!
KRACKLE KRAK!
ZZZ KRK KRK ZZZ KRK

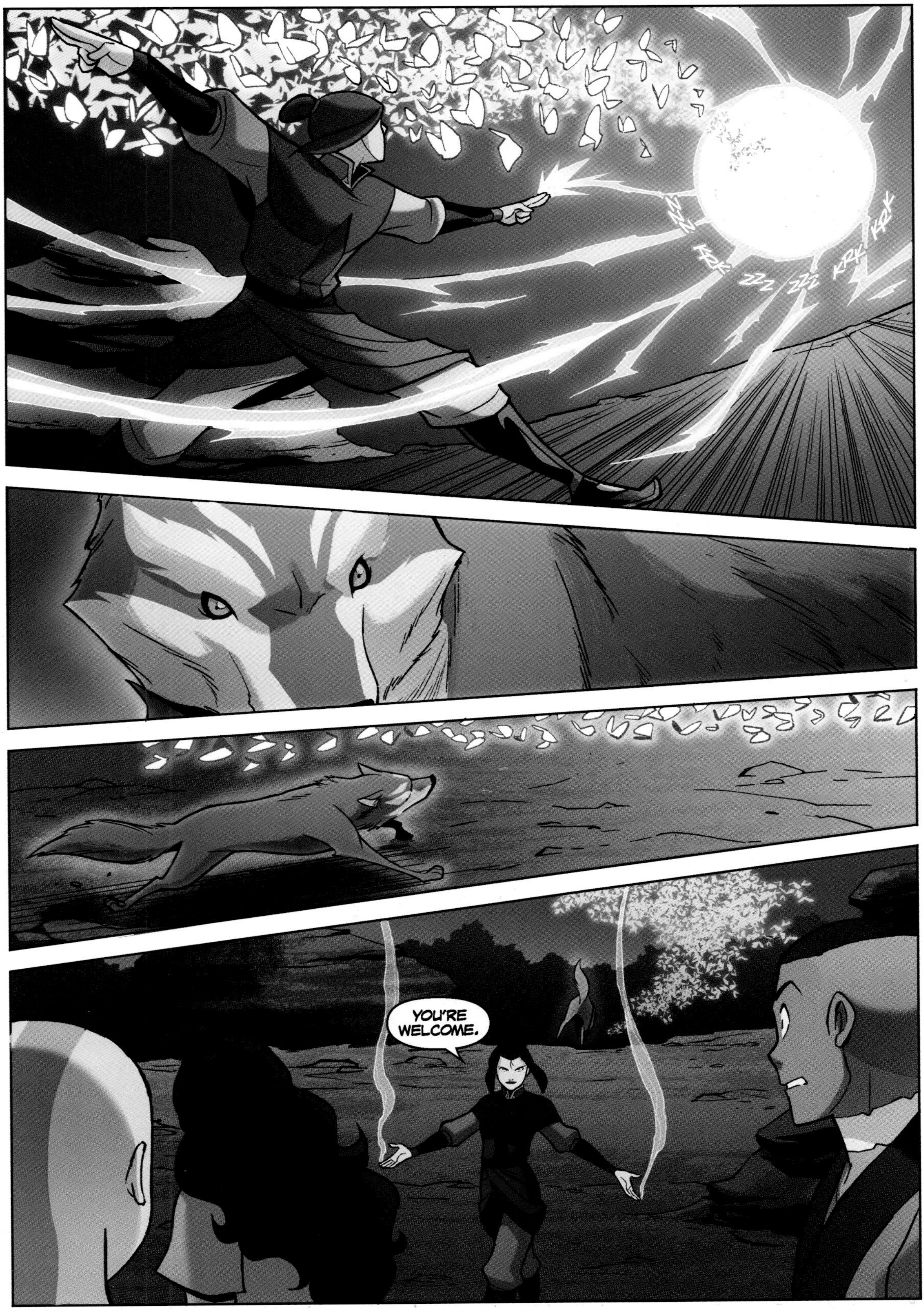
ZZZ
KRK
ZZZ
ZZZ
KRK
KRK
YOU'RE WELCOME.

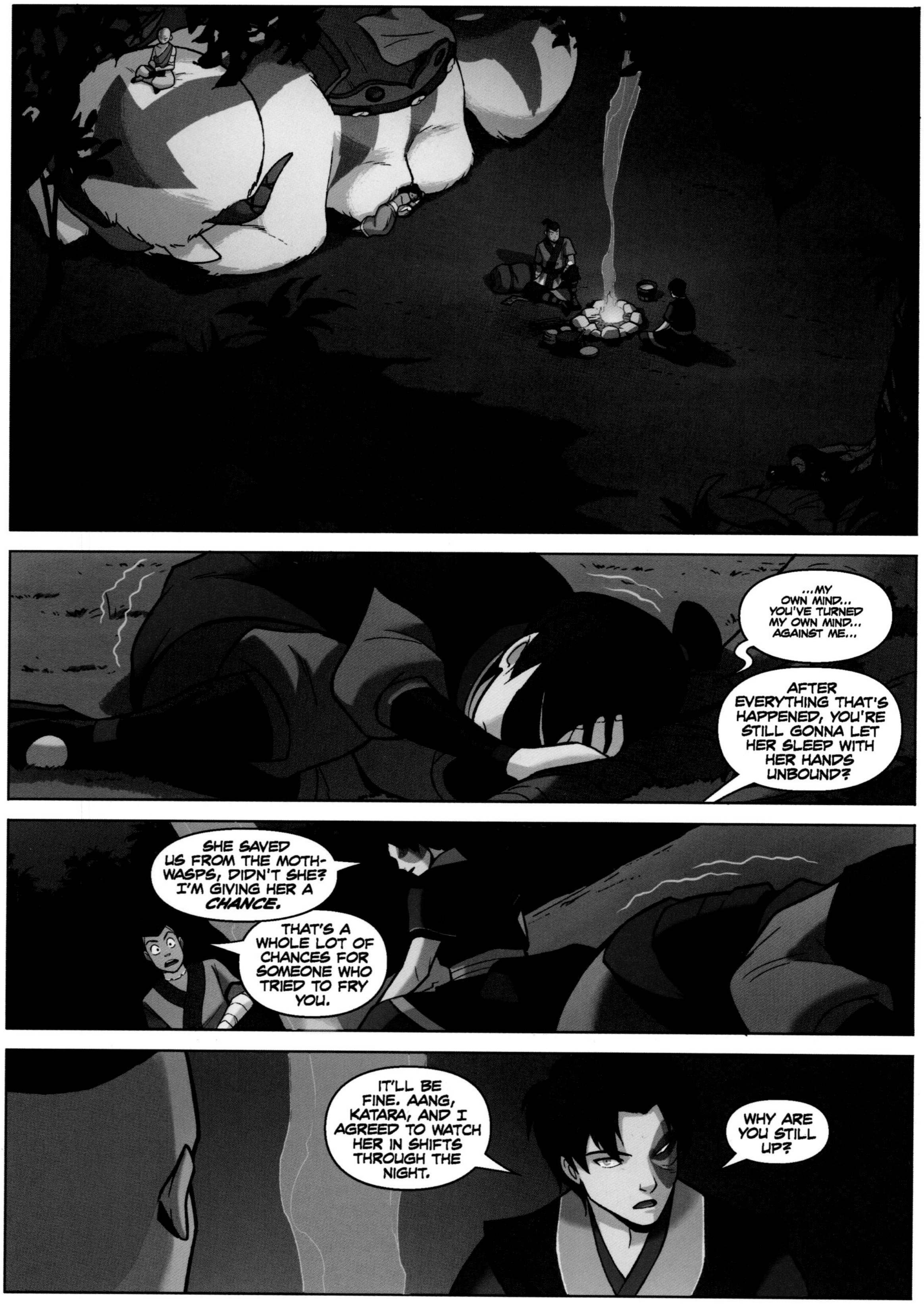
...MY OWN MIND... YOU'VE TURNED MY OWN MIND... AGAINST ME...
AFTER EVERYTHING THAT'S HAPPENED, YOU'RE STILL GONNA LET HER SLEEP WITH HER HANDS UNBOUND?
SHE SAVED US FROM THE MOTH-WASPS, DIDN'T SHE? I'M GIVING HER A *CHANCE*.
THAT'S A WHOLE LOT OF CHANCES FOR SOMEONE WHO TRIED TO FRY YOU.
IT'LL BE FINE. AANG, KATARA, AND I AGREED TO WATCH HER IN SHIFTS THROUGH THE NIGHT.
WHY ARE YOU STILL UP?

I DRANK A TON OF WATER TRYING TO GET THE TASTE OF MOTH-WASP OUT OF MY MOUTH. NOW MY BLADDER'S--

I GET THE PICTURE. THANKS.

LITTLE COLD TONIGHT, ISN'T IT?

I THOUGHT YOU WATER TRIBE FOLKS LIKED THE COLD.

YEAH. MAYBE WE'VE BEEN AWAY FROM HOME FOR TOO LONG.

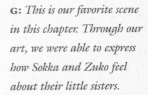

G: *This is our favorite scene in this chapter. Through our art, we were able to express how Sokka and Zuko feel about their little sisters.*

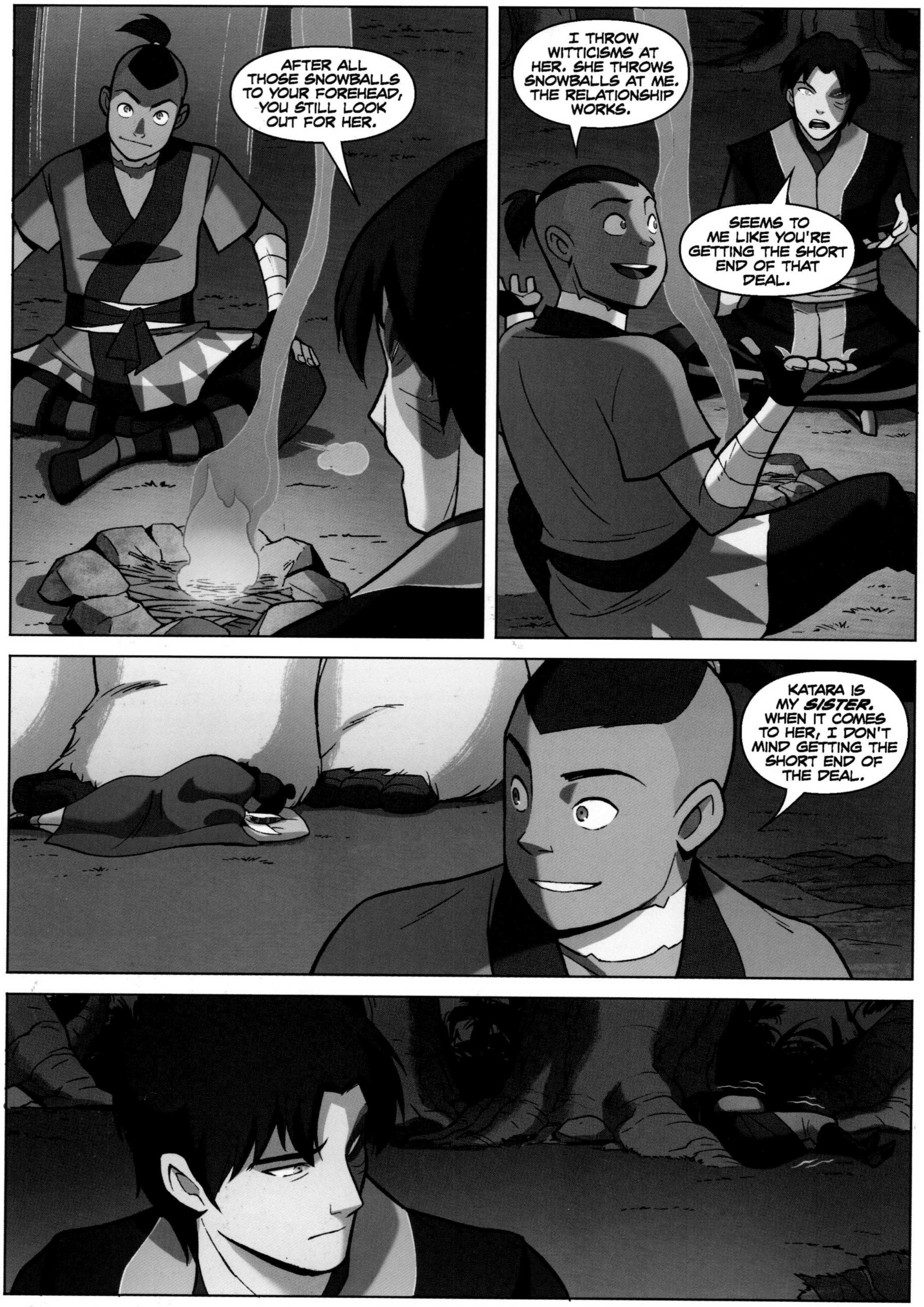
AFTER ALL THOSE SNOWBALLS TO YOUR FOREHEAD, YOU STILL LOOK OUT FOR HER.
I THROW WITTICISMS AT HER. SHE THROWS SNOWBALLS AT ME. THE RELATIONSHIP WORKS.
SEEMS TO ME LIKE YOU'RE GETTING THE SHORT END OF THAT DEAL.
KATARA IS MY *SISTER.* WHEN IT COMES TO HER, I DON'T MIND GETTING THE SHORT END OF THE DEAL.

GLY: *The original series developed Sokka and Katara's relationship into something special, something real. Anyone who has a sibling can relate to both their little tiffs and their deep love for one another.*

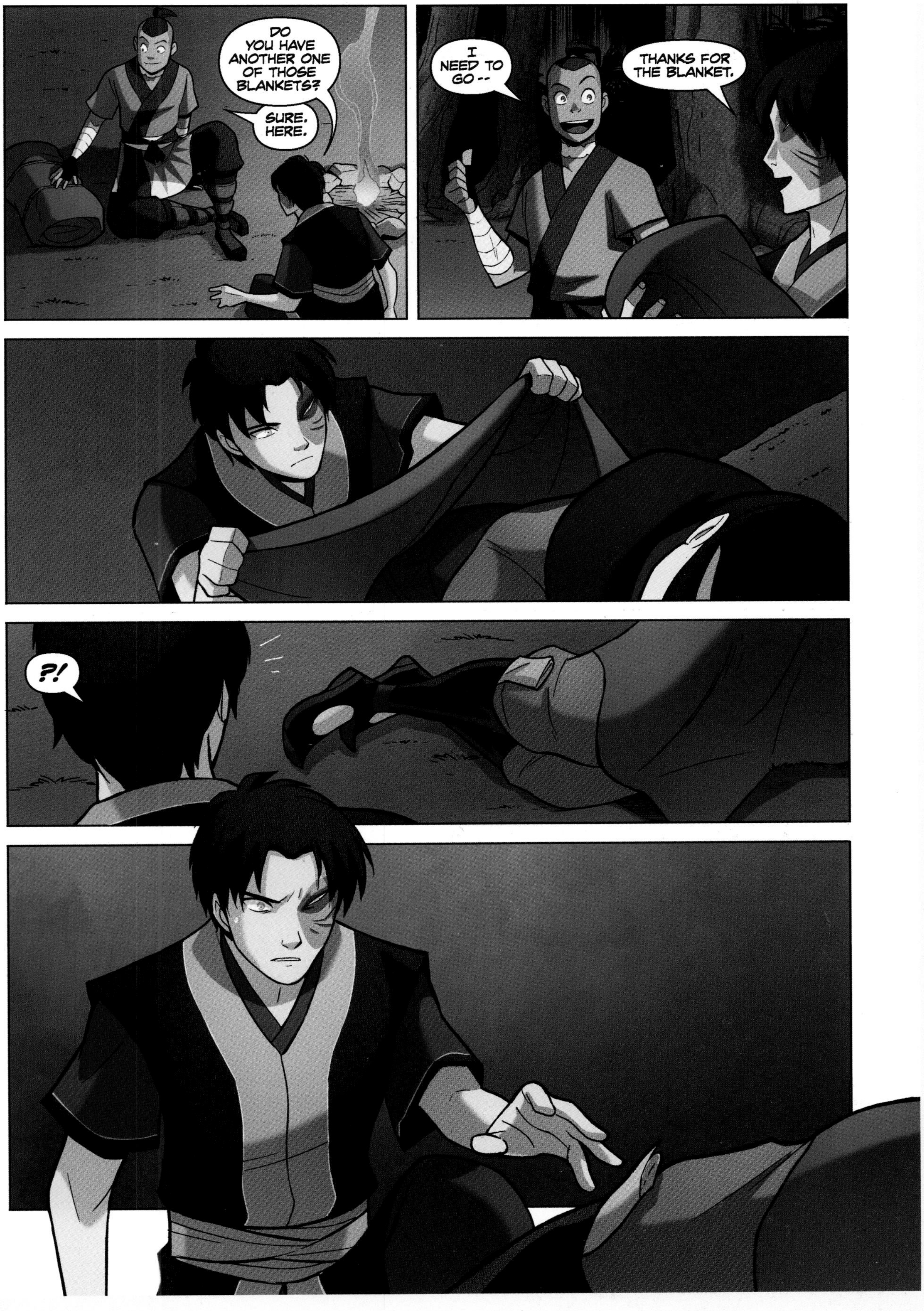
DO YOU HAVE ANOTHER ONE OF THOSE BLANKETS?
SURE. HERE.
I NEED TO GO--
THANKS FOR THE BLANKET.
?!

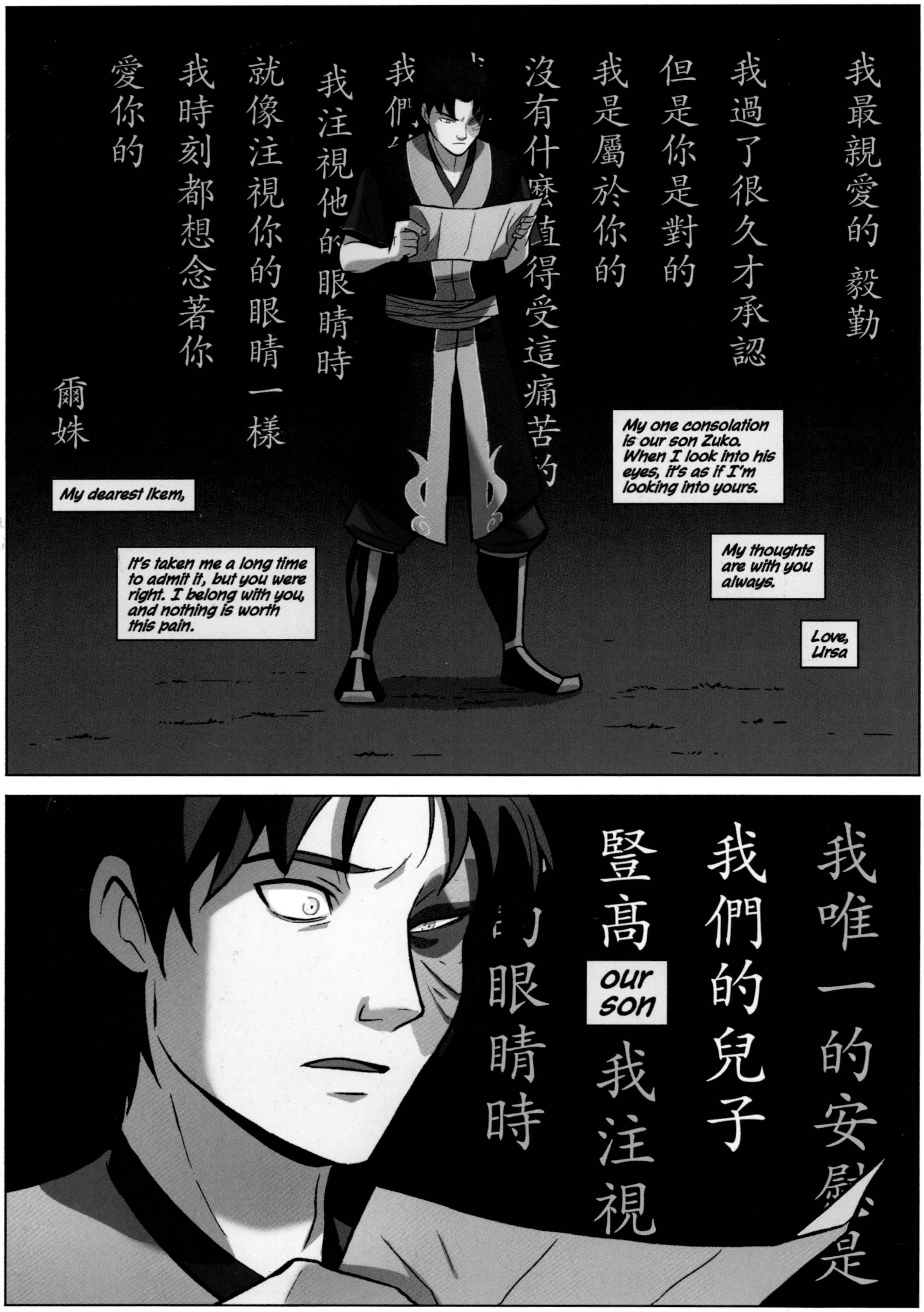
My dearest Ikem,
It's taken me a long time to admit it, but you were right. I belong with you, and nothing is worth this pain.
My one consolation is our son Zuko. When I look into his eyes, it's as if I'm looking into yours.
My thoughts are with you always.
Love, Ursa
our son

M: *This cliffhanger caused quite a stir when the first volume of* The Search *was released. It's a huge moment for Zuko, whose entire life and identity are now in question. This story is not only about Zuko's external search for his mother, but also his internal search for who he really is. And I love the way Gene and Gurihiru decided to depict this page, with the words of the letter becoming the backdrop. This is the kind of visual that might look odd in an animated version, but has such impact in a comic panel.*

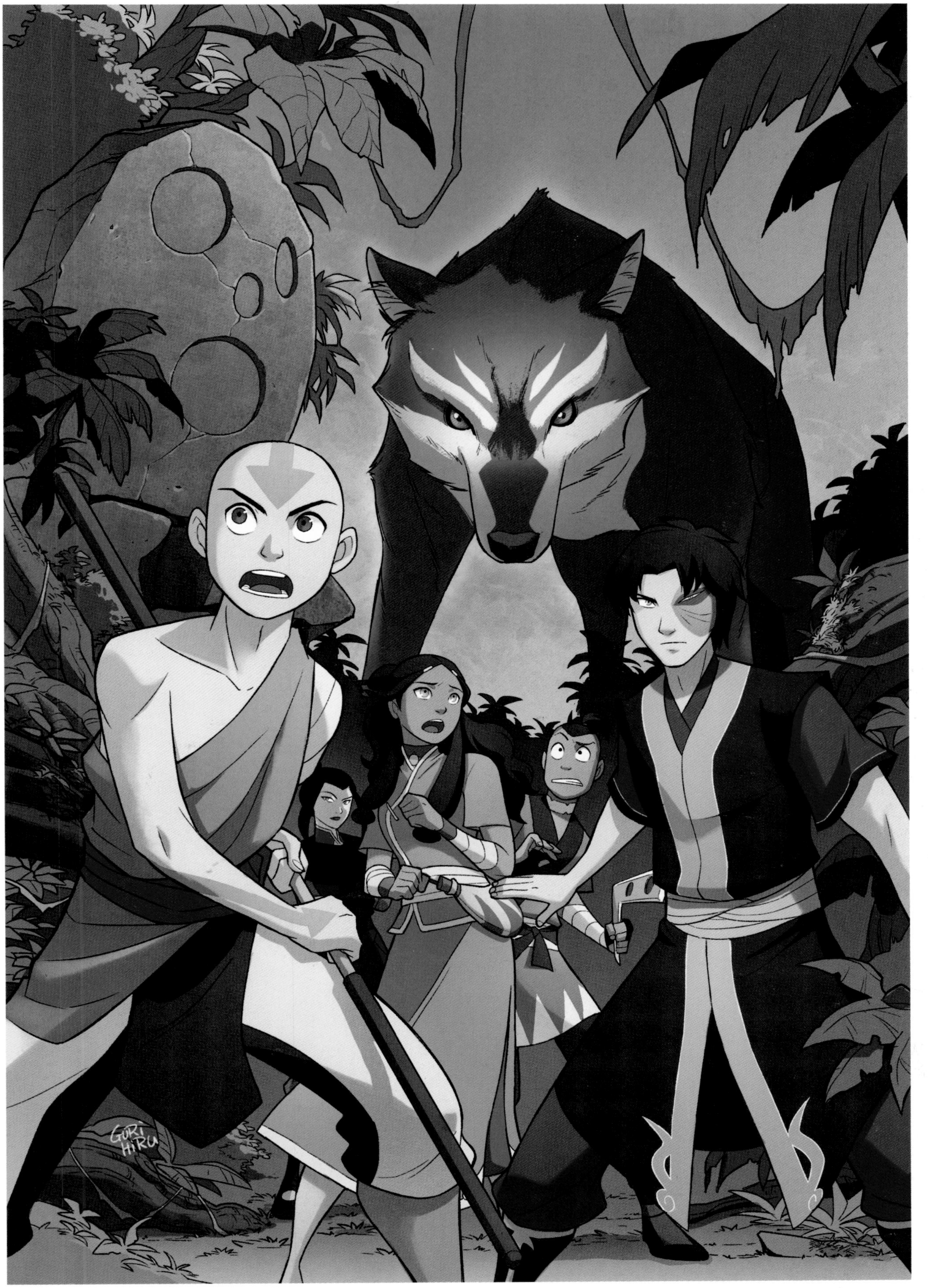
GURI HIRU

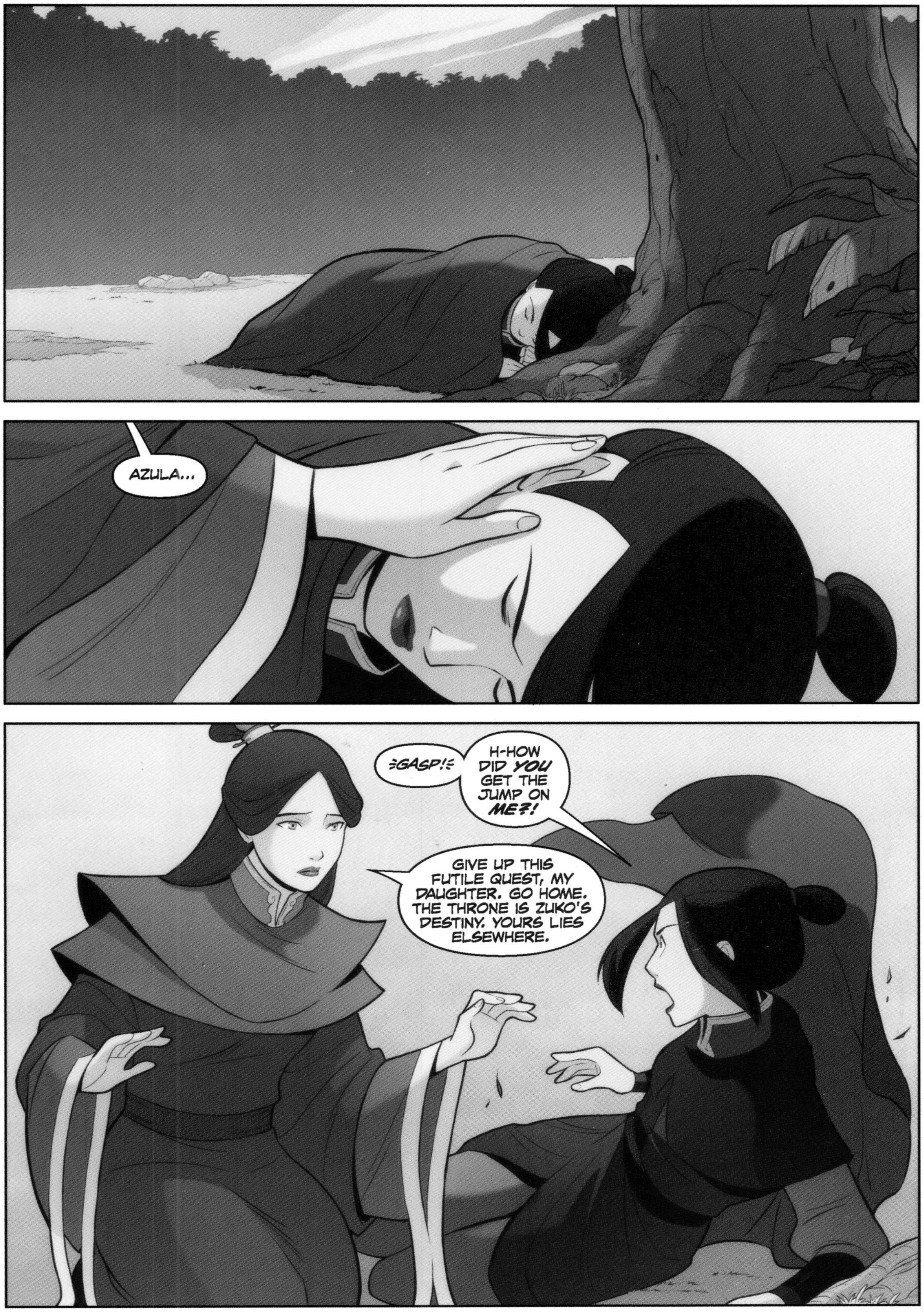
AZULA...
≥GASP!≤
H-HOW DID YOU GET THE JUMP ON ME?!
GIVE UP THIS FUTILE QUEST, MY DAUGHTER. GO HOME. THE THRONE IS ZUKO'S DESTINY. YOURS LIES ELSEWHERE.

G: *Starting with part 2, we began working fully digitally. We used to use pencils and inks, but by working digitally, our efficiency has grown. However, since we don't see the whole picture as we're working, we try to be more careful about catching small mistakes.*

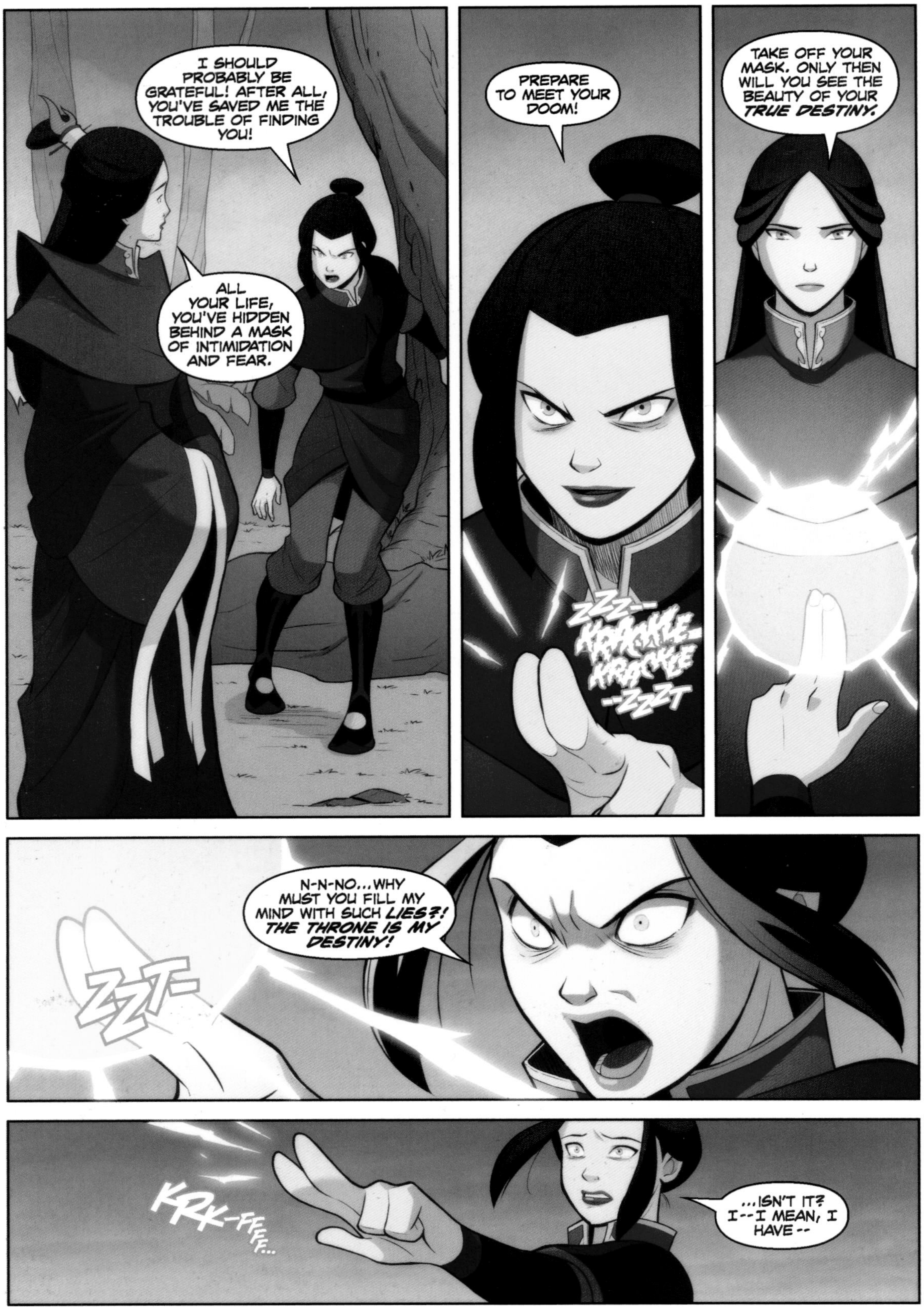
I SHOULD PROBABLY BE GRATEFUL! AFTER ALL, YOU'VE SAVED ME THE TROUBLE OF FINDING YOU!
ALL YOUR LIFE, YOU'VE HIDDEN BEHIND A MASK OF INTIMIDATION AND FEAR.
PREPARE TO MEET YOUR DOOM!
ZZZ-- KRAKKLE-KRAKKLE --ZZZT
TAKE OFF YOUR MASK. ONLY THEN WILL YOU SEE THE BEAUTY OF YOUR TRUE DESTINY.
N-N-NO...WHY MUST YOU FILL MY MIND WITH SUCH LIES?! THE THRONE IS MY DESTINY!
ZZT-
KRK-FFFF...
...ISN'T IT? I--I MEAN, I HAVE --

M: *I was concerned that depicting Azula's fragile mental state in comic form would be difficult, but the combination of Gene's writing and Gurihiru's art makes it very clear when Azula is becoming unhinged. Adding Azula to the mix provided a lot of great character interactions, as well as a ticking human time bomb, so to speak.*

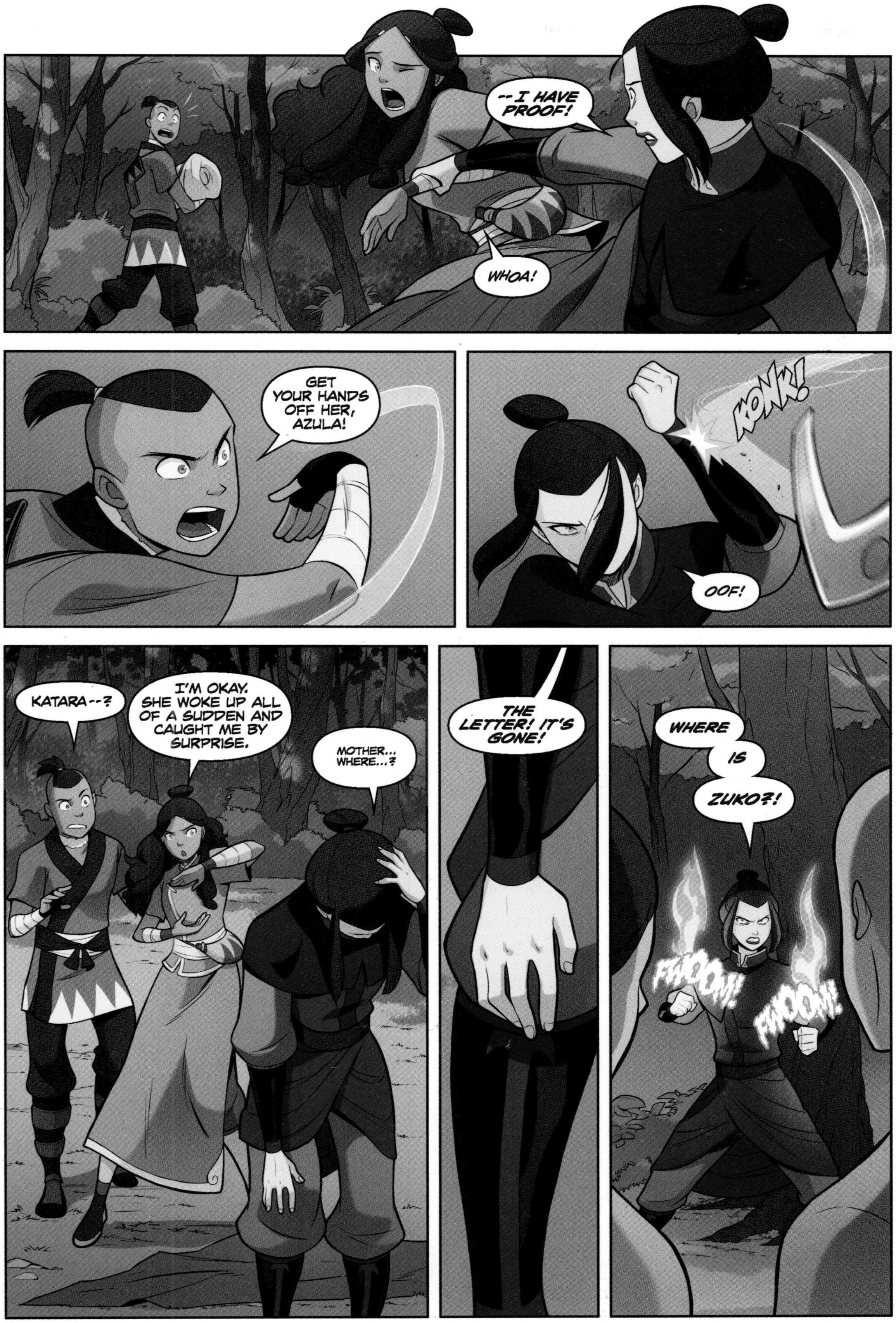
--I HAVE PROOF!
WHOA!
GET YOUR HANDS OFF HER, AZULA!
KONK!
OOF!
KATARA--?
I'M OKAY. SHE WOKE UP ALL OF A SUDDEN AND CAUGHT ME BY SURPRISE.
MOTHER... WHERE...?
THE LETTER! IT'S GONE!
WHERE IS ZUKO?!
FWOOM!
FWOOM!

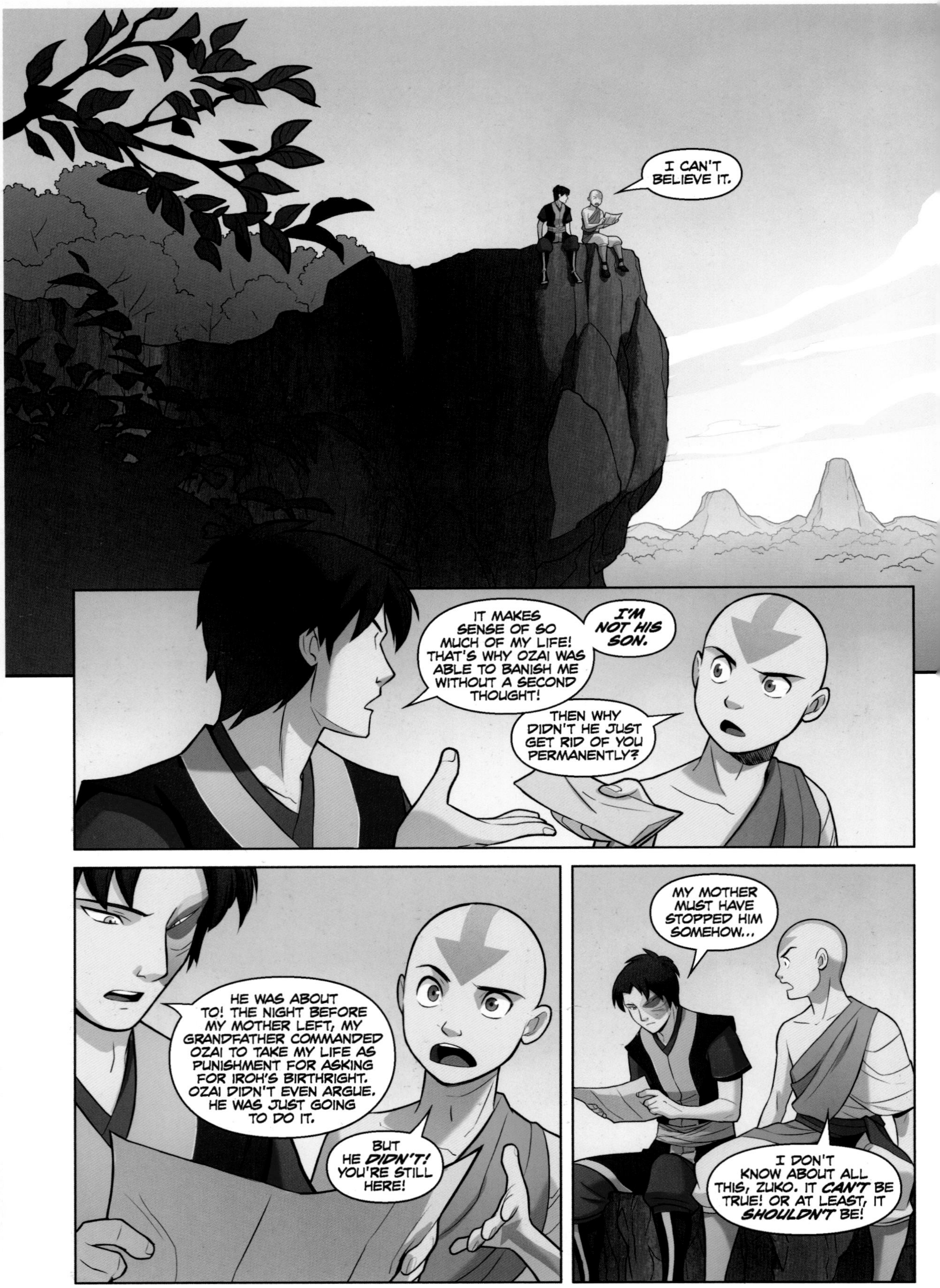
I CAN'T BELIEVE IT.
IT MAKES SENSE OF SO MUCH OF MY LIFE! THAT'S WHY OZAI WAS ABLE TO BANISH ME WITHOUT A SECOND THOUGHT!
I'M NOT HIS SON.
THEN WHY DIDN'T HE JUST GET RID OF YOU PERMANENTLY?
HE WAS ABOUT TO! THE NIGHT BEFORE MY MOTHER LEFT, MY GRANDFATHER COMMANDED OZAI TO TAKE MY LIFE AS PUNISHMENT FOR ASKING FOR IROH'S BIRTHRIGHT. OZAI DIDN'T EVEN ARGUE. HE WAS JUST GOING TO DO IT.
BUT HE DIDN'T! YOU'RE STILL HERE!
MY MOTHER MUST HAVE STOPPED HIM SOMEHOW...
I DON'T KNOW ABOUT ALL THIS, ZUKO. IT CAN'T BE TRUE! OR AT LEAST, IT SHOULDN'T BE!

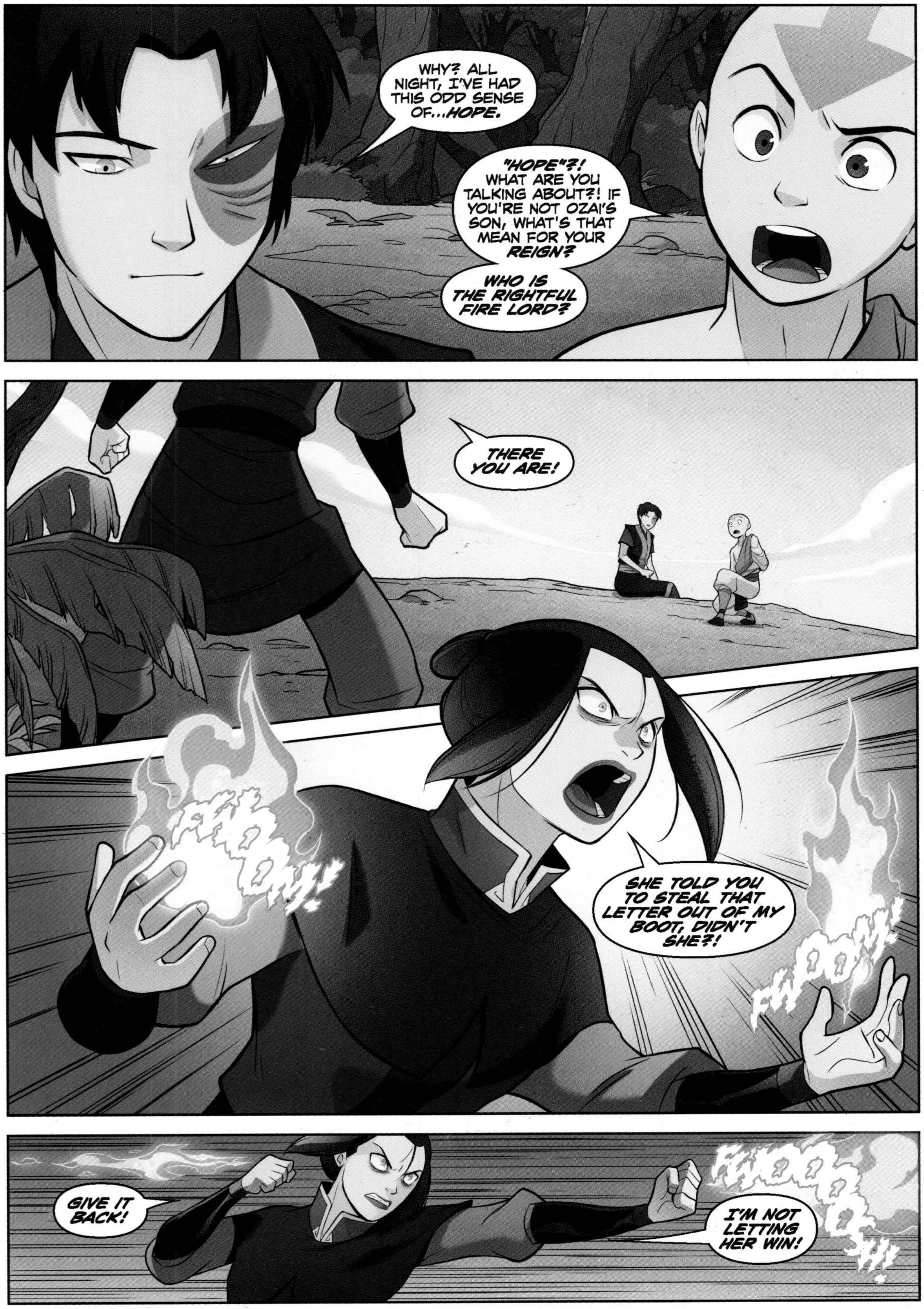
WHY? ALL NIGHT, I'VE HAD THIS ODD SENSE OF...HOPE.
"HOPE"?! WHAT ARE YOU TALKING ABOUT?! IF YOU'RE NOT OZAI'S SON, WHAT'S THAT MEAN FOR YOUR REIGN?
WHO IS THE RIGHTFUL FIRE LORD?
THERE YOU ARE!
FWOOM!
SHE TOLD YOU TO STEAL THAT LETTER OUT OF MY BOOT, DIDN'T SHE?!
FWOOM!
GIVE IT BACK!
FWOOOSH!
I'M NOT LETTING HER WIN!

M: *This first panel shows a rare role reversal, where Zuko is the calm one and Aang is frustrated and angry. I can totally understand why Zuko would feel hopeful about finding out Ikem may be his real father. If true, it would mean he could start over, and maybe be finally free of his past emotional scars.*

G: *We had fun drawing young Zuko and Azula.*

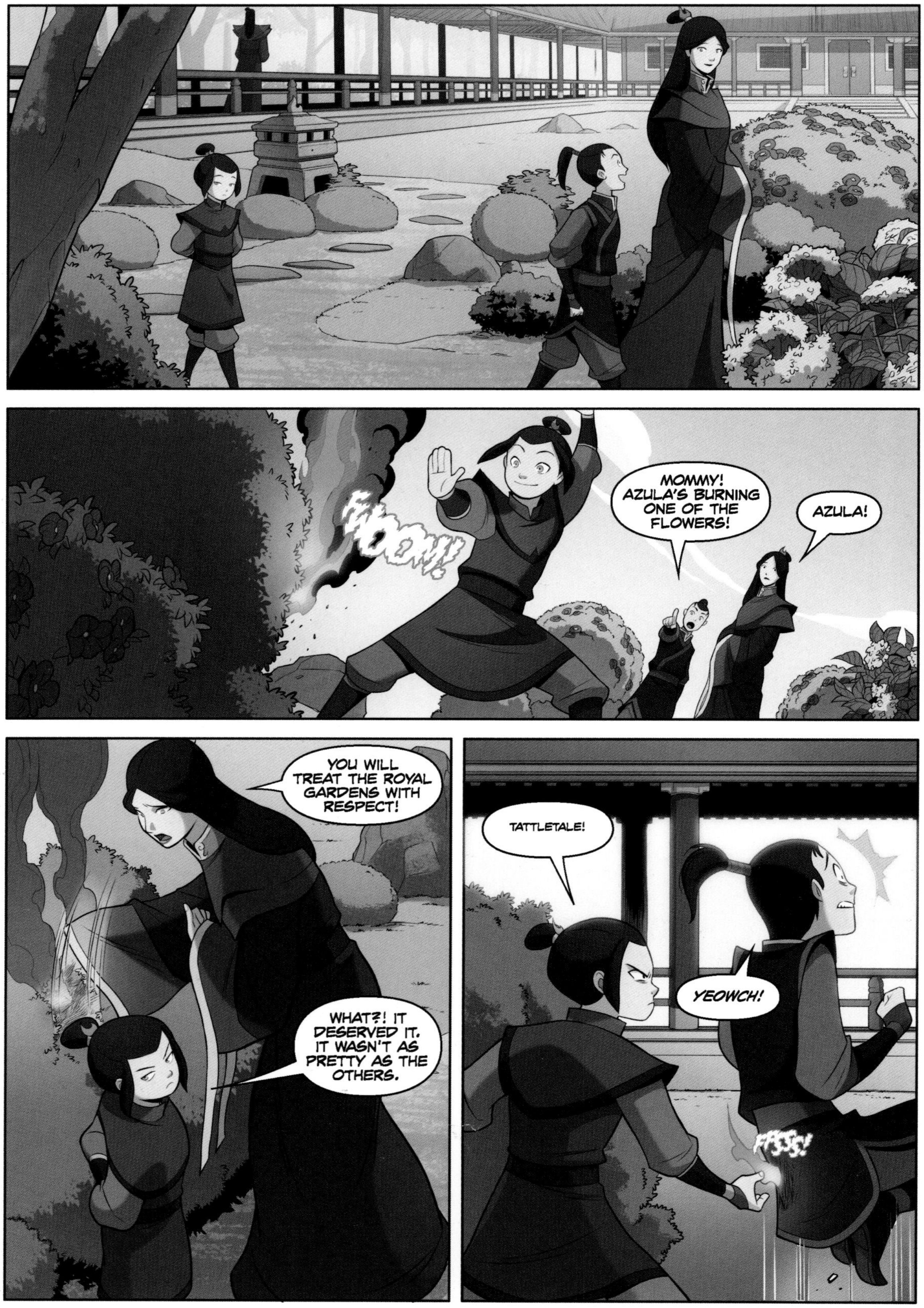
FWOOM!
MOMMY! AZULA'S BURNING ONE OF THE FLOWERS!
AZULA!
YOU WILL TREAT THE ROYAL GARDENS WITH RESPECT!
WHAT?! IT DESERVED IT. IT WASN'T AS PRETTY AS THE OTHERS.
TATTLETALE!
YEOWCH!
FFSSS!

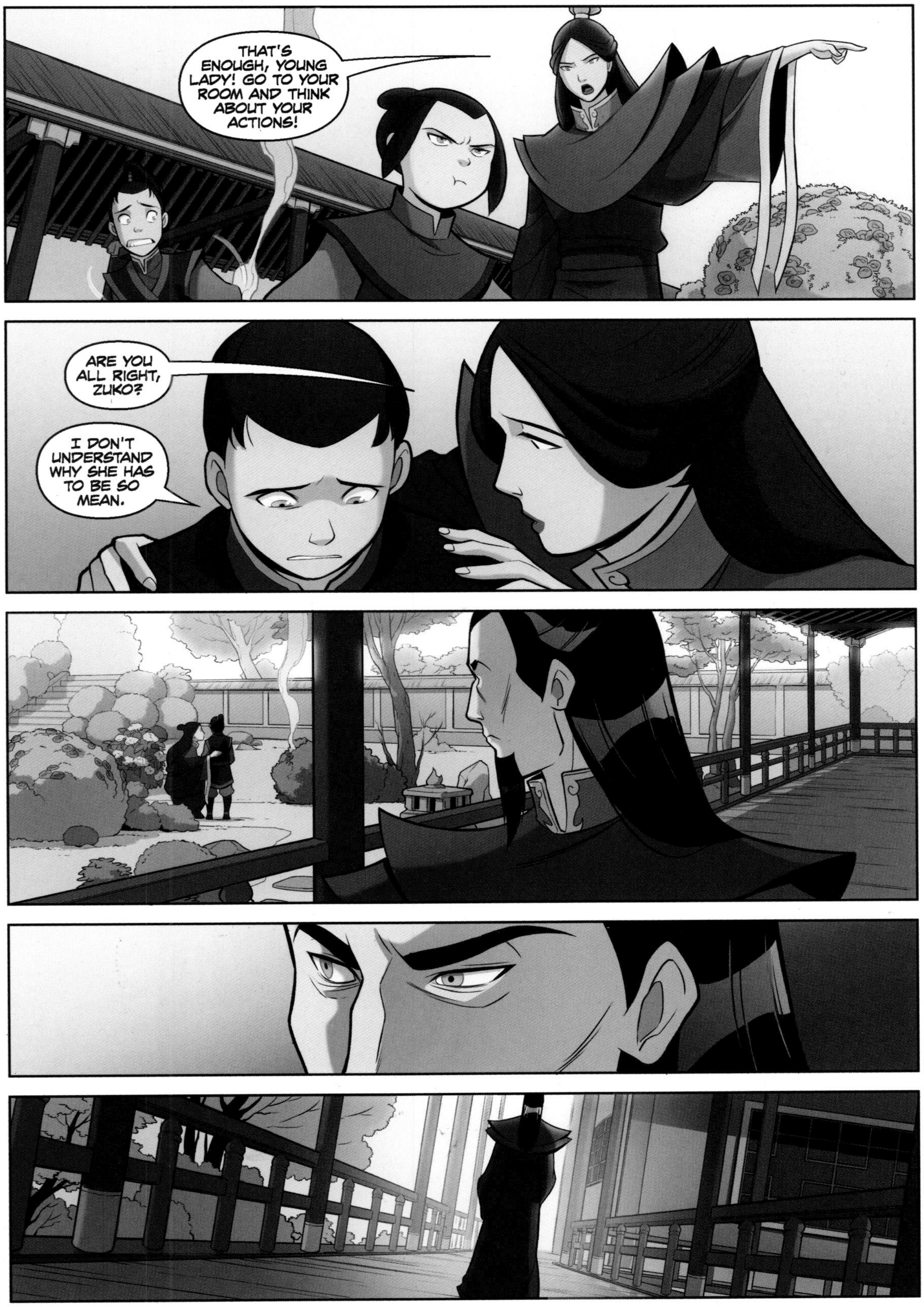
THAT'S ENOUGH, YOUNG LADY! GO TO YOUR ROOM AND THINK ABOUT YOUR ACTIONS!
ARE YOU ALL RIGHT, ZUKO?
I DON'T UNDERSTAND WHY SHE HAS TO BE SO MEAN.

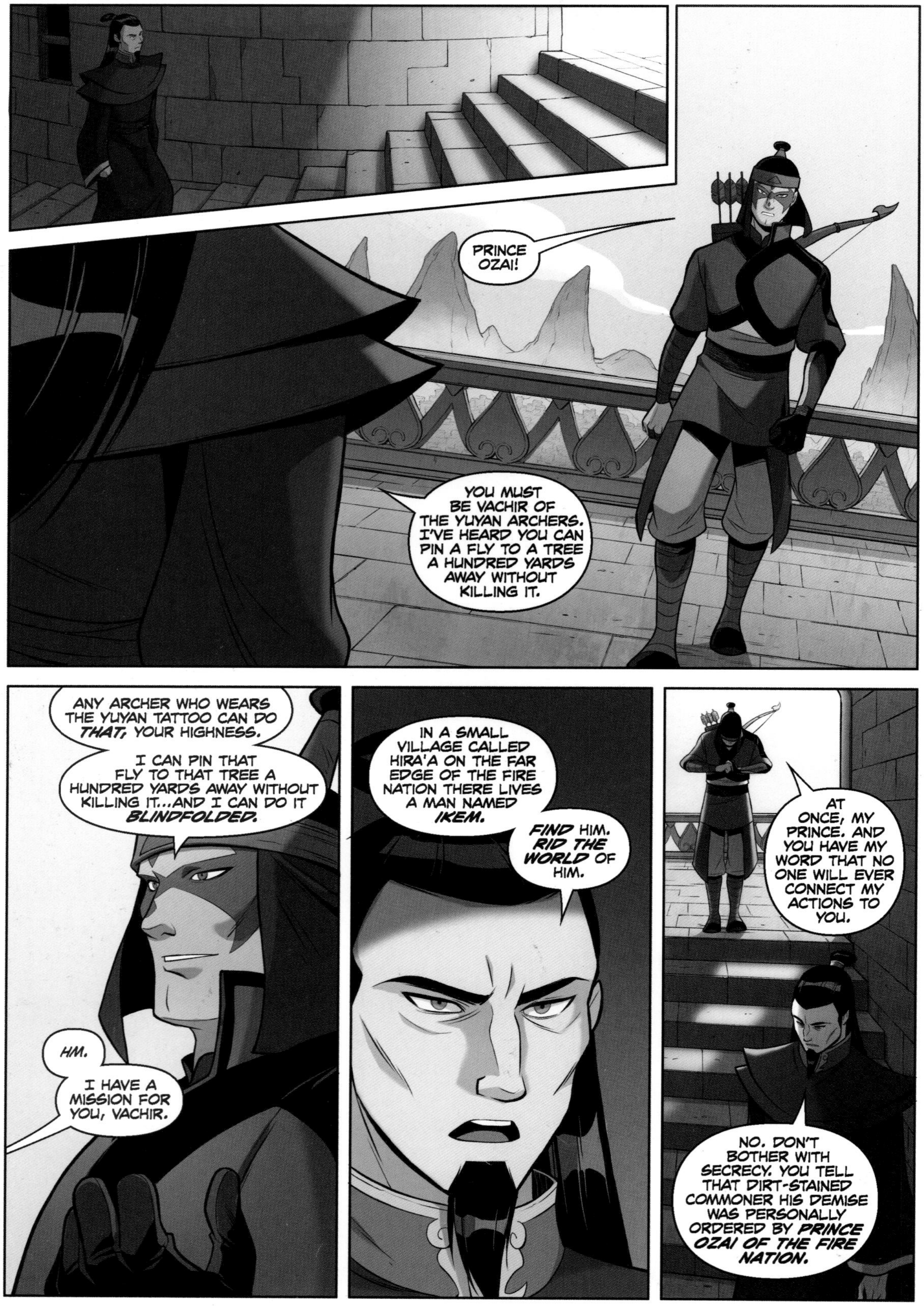
PRINCE OZAI!
YOU MUST BE VACHIR OF THE YUYAN ARCHERS. I'VE HEARD YOU CAN PIN A FLY TO A TREE A HUNDRED YARDS AWAY WITHOUT KILLING IT.
ANY ARCHER WHO WEARS THE YUYAN TATTOO CAN DO *THAT,* YOUR HIGHNESS.
I CAN PIN THAT FLY TO THAT TREE A HUNDRED YARDS AWAY WITHOUT KILLING IT...AND I CAN DO IT *BLINDFOLDED.*
HM.
I HAVE A MISSION FOR YOU, VACHIR.
IN A SMALL VILLAGE CALLED HIRA'A ON THE FAR EDGE OF THE FIRE NATION THERE LIVES A MAN NAMED *IKEM.*
FIND HIM. *RID THE WORLD* OF HIM.
AT ONCE, MY PRINCE. AND YOU HAVE MY WORD THAT NO ONE WILL EVER CONNECT MY ACTIONS TO YOU.
NO. DON'T BOTHER WITH SECRECY. YOU TELL THAT DIRT-STAINED COMMONER HIS DEMISE WAS PERSONALLY ORDERED BY *PRINCE OZAI OF THE FIRE NATION.*

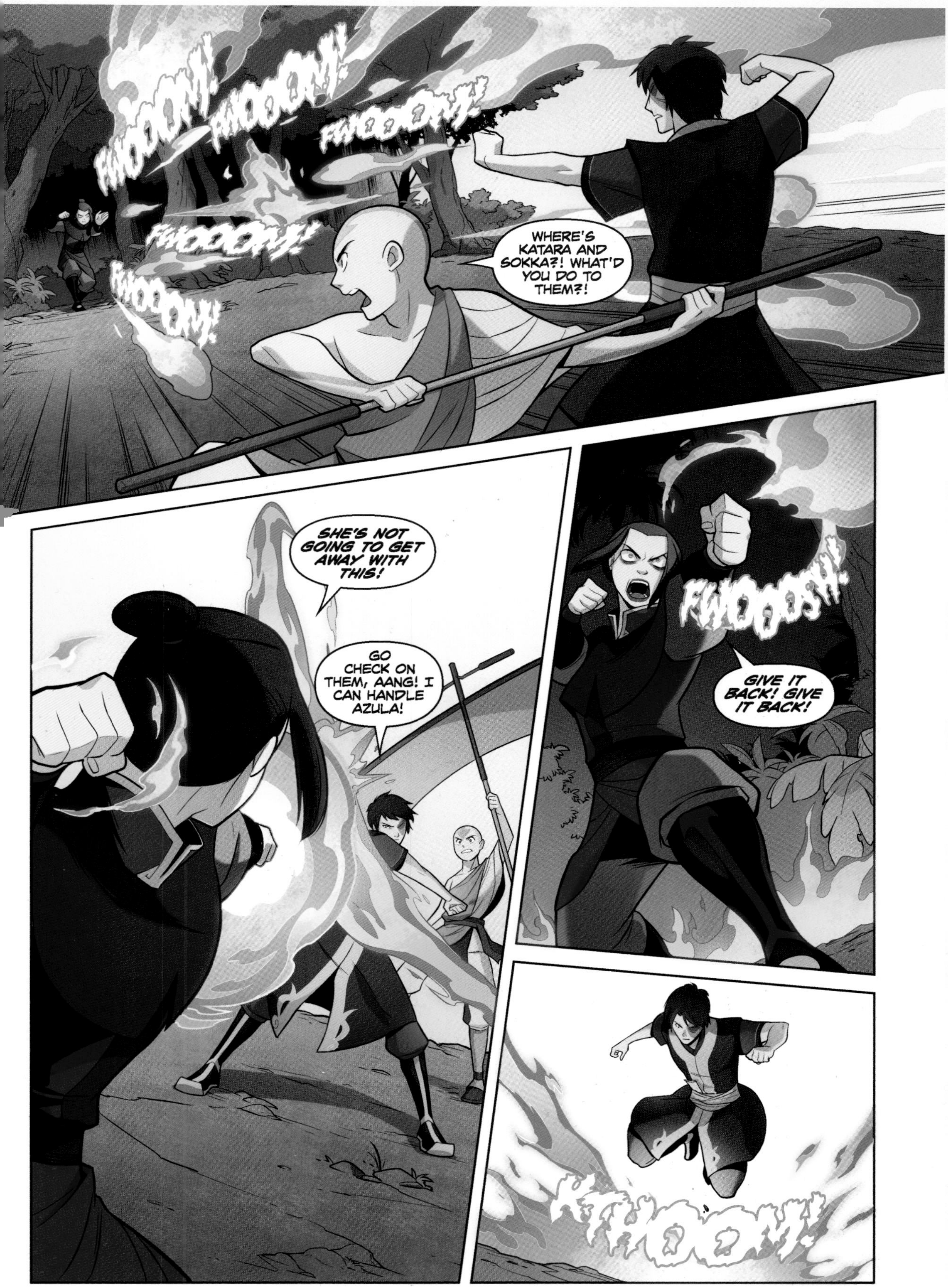
FWOOOM!
FWOOOM!
FWOOOM!
FWOOOM!
FWOOOM!
WHERE'S KATARA AND SOKKA?! WHAT'D YOU DO TO THEM?!
SHE'S NOT GOING TO GET AWAY WITH THIS!
GO CHECK ON THEM, AANG! I CAN HANDLE AZULA!
FWOOOSH!
GIVE IT BACK! GIVE IT BACK!
KTHOOOM!

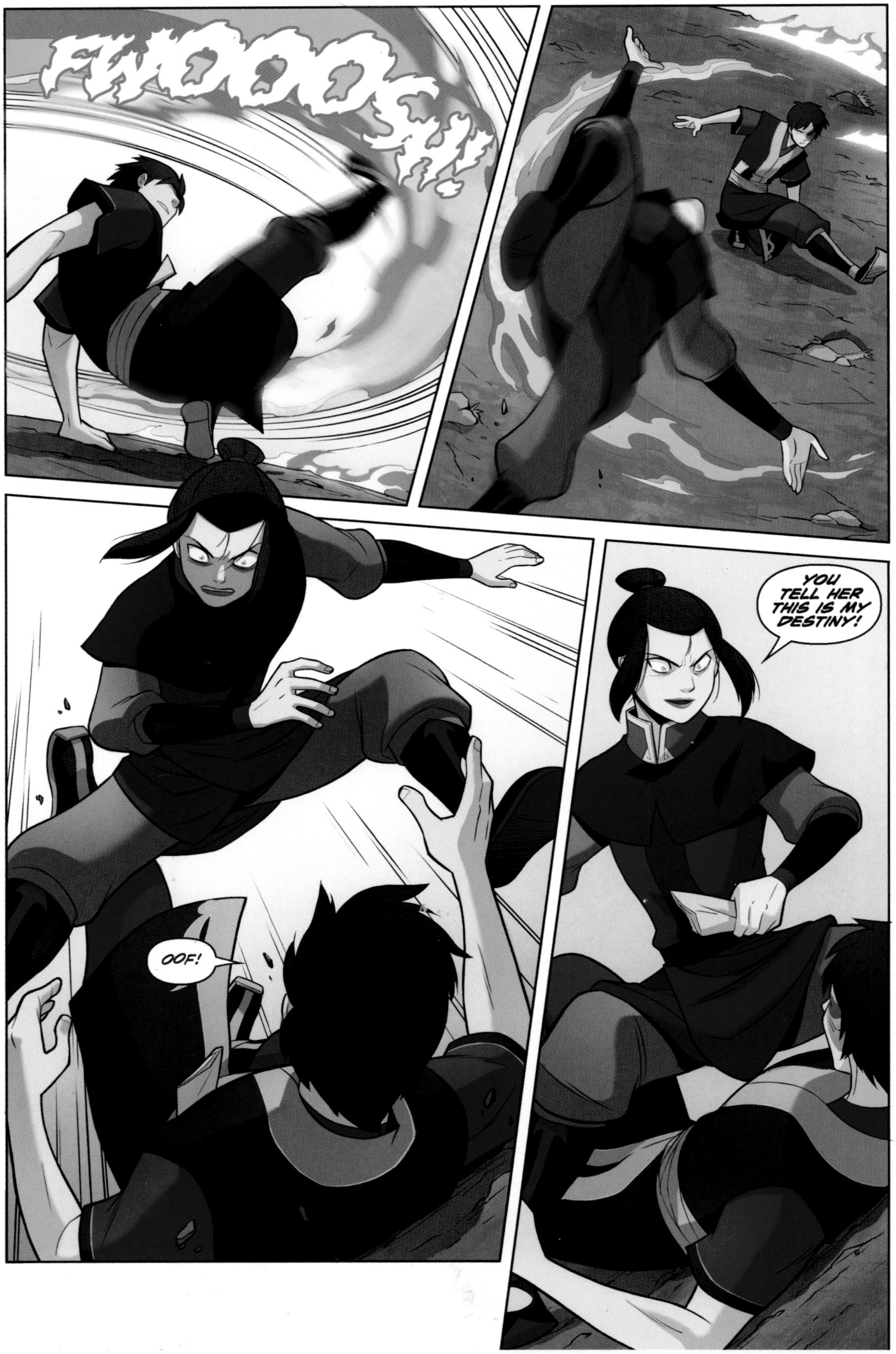
FWOOOSH!!
OOF!
YOU TELL HER THIS IS MY DESTINY!

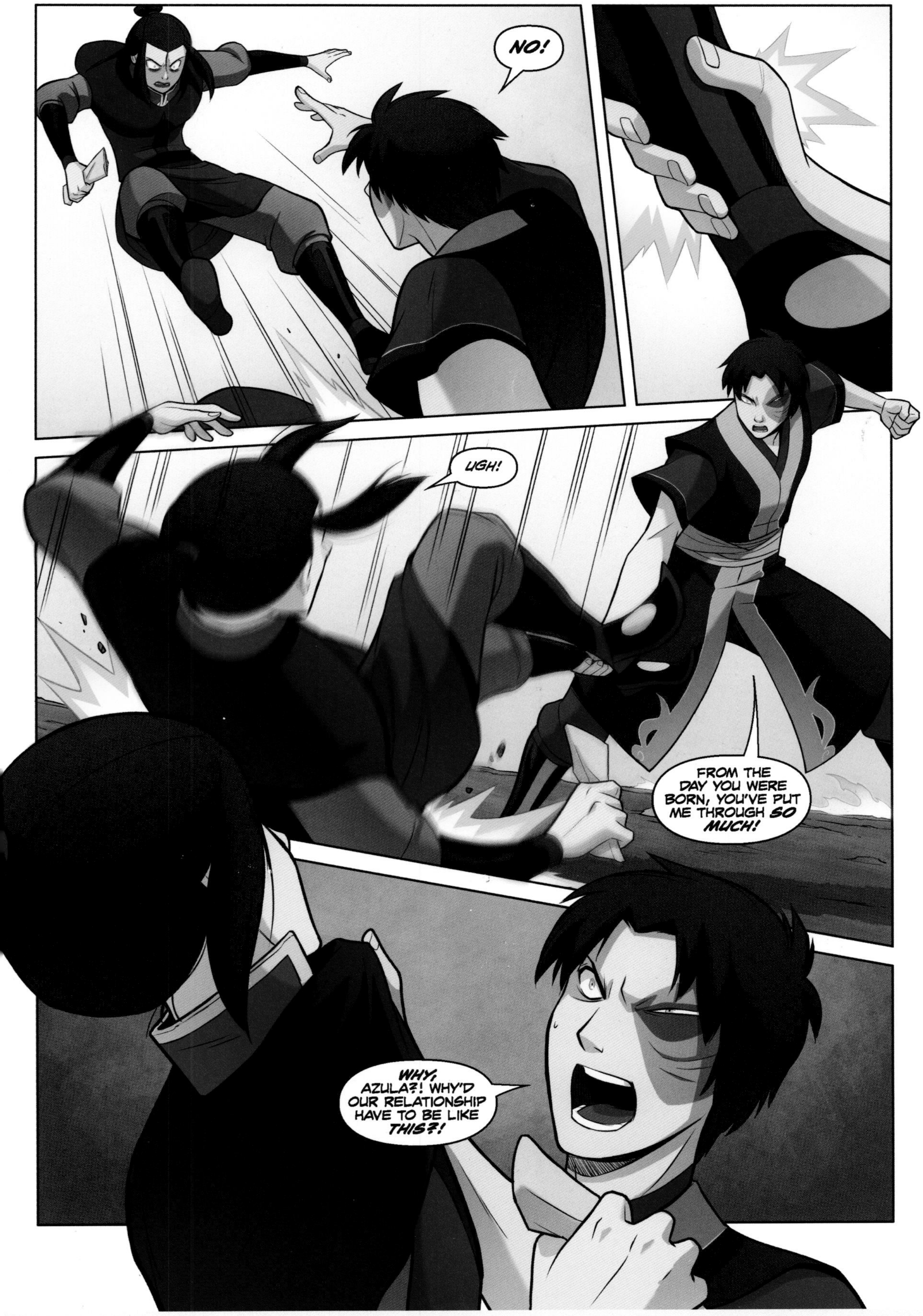
NO!
UGH!
FROM THE DAY YOU WERE BORN, YOU'VE PUT ME THROUGH SO MUCH!
WHY, AZULA?! WHY'D OUR RELATIONSHIP HAVE TO BE LIKE THIS?!

GLY: *Pretty much every one of Gurihiru's depictions of Azula is amazing, but panel 4 here is my favorite. It's a small drawing, but they perfectly capture her expression. You can almost hear the clicking gears of nuttiness in Azula's head.*

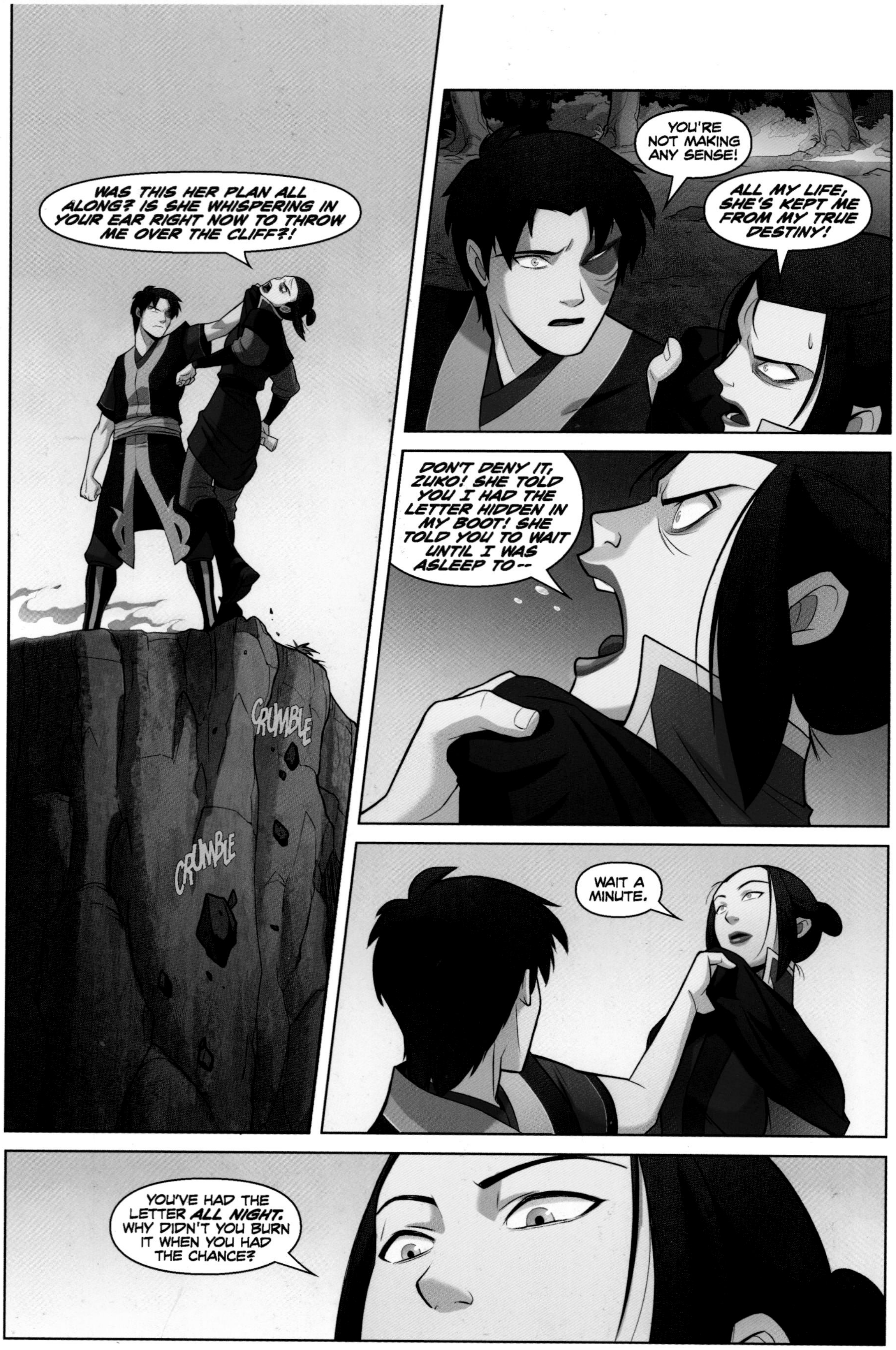
WAS THIS HER PLAN ALL ALONG? IS SHE WHISPERING IN YOUR EAR RIGHT NOW TO THROW ME OVER THE CLIFF?!
CRUMBLE
CRUMBLE
YOU'RE NOT MAKING ANY SENSE!
ALL MY LIFE, SHE'S KEPT ME FROM MY TRUE DESTINY!
DON'T DENY IT, ZUKO! SHE TOLD YOU I HAD THE LETTER HIDDEN IN MY BOOT! SHE TOLD YOU TO WAIT UNTIL I WAS ASLEEP TO--
WAIT A MINUTE.
YOU'VE HAD THE LETTER ALL NIGHT. WHY DIDN'T YOU BURN IT WHEN YOU HAD THE CHANCE?

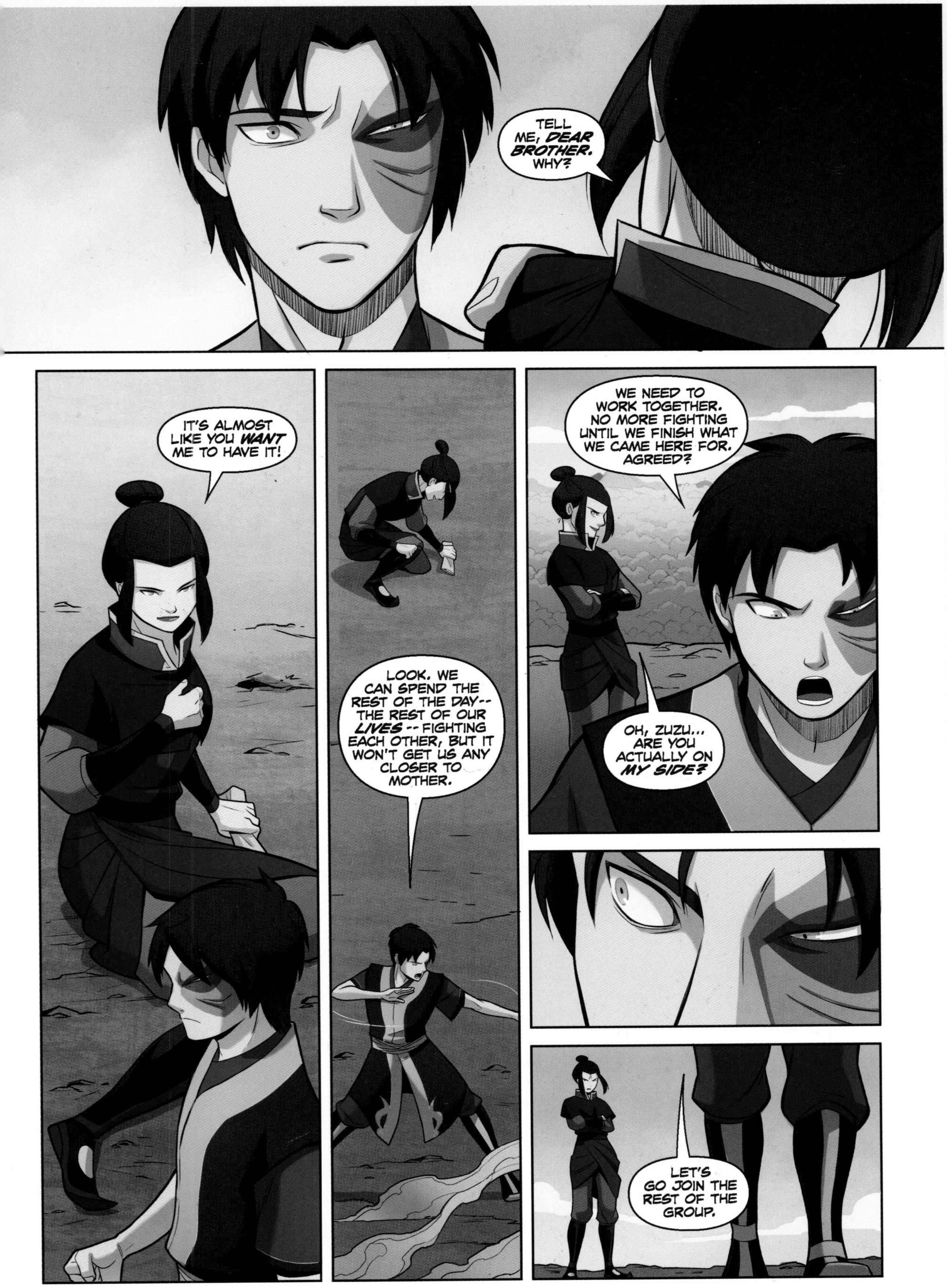
TELL ME, DEAR BROTHER. WHY?
IT'S ALMOST LIKE YOU WANT ME TO HAVE IT!
LOOK. WE CAN SPEND THE REST OF THE DAY-- THE REST OF OUR LIVES -- FIGHTING EACH OTHER, BUT IT WON'T GET US ANY CLOSER TO MOTHER.
WE NEED TO WORK TOGETHER. NO MORE FIGHTING UNTIL WE FINISH WHAT WE CAME HERE FOR. AGREED?
OH, ZUZU... ARE YOU ACTUALLY ON MY SIDE?
LET'S GO JOIN THE REST OF THE GROUP.

GLY: *Sokka's line in panel 4 is something a friend said to me when we were in college. I bought a single onion and asked the cashier for a plastic bag.*

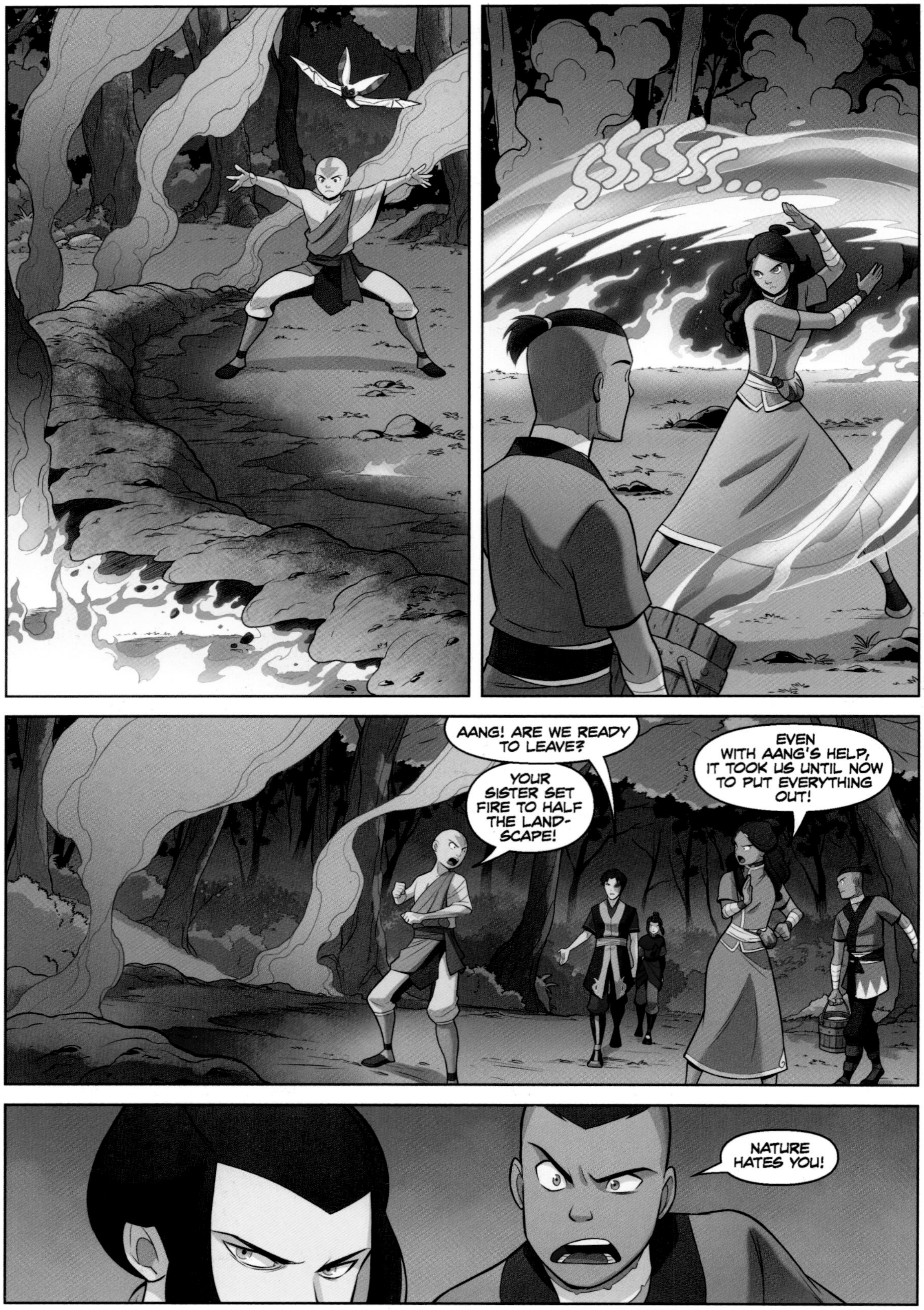
SSSSSS...
AANG! ARE WE READY TO LEAVE?
YOUR SISTER SET FIRE TO HALF THE LAND-SCAPE!
EVEN WITH AANG'S HELP, IT TOOK US UNTIL NOW TO PUT EVERYTHING OUT!
NATURE HATES YOU!

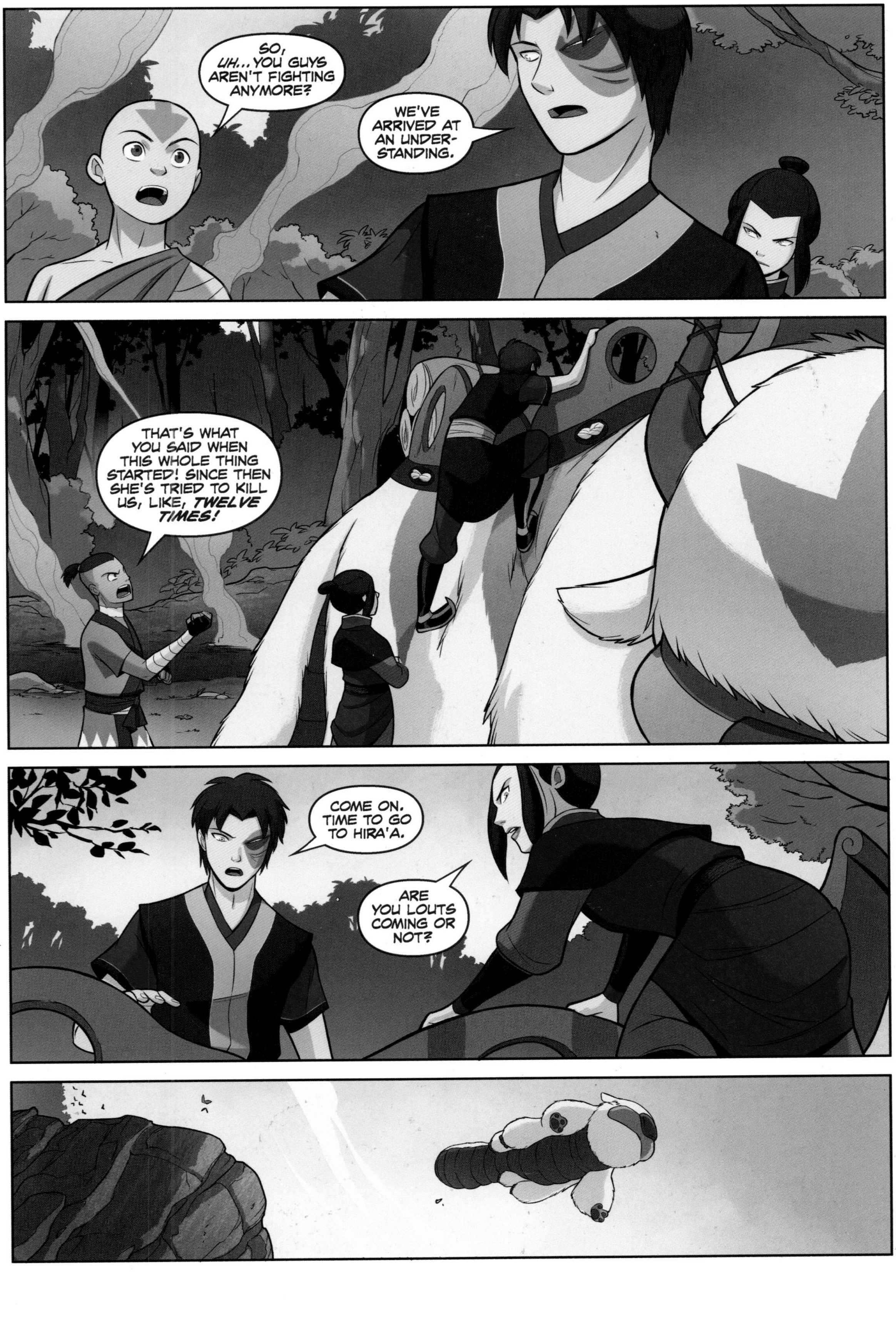
SO, UH... YOU GUYS AREN'T FIGHTING ANYMORE?
WE'VE ARRIVED AT AN UNDER-STANDING.
THAT'S WHAT YOU SAID WHEN THIS WHOLE THING STARTED! SINCE THEN SHE'S TRIED TO KILL US, LIKE, ***TWELVE TIMES!***
COME ON. TIME TO GO TO HIRA'A.
ARE YOU LOUTS COMING OR NOT?

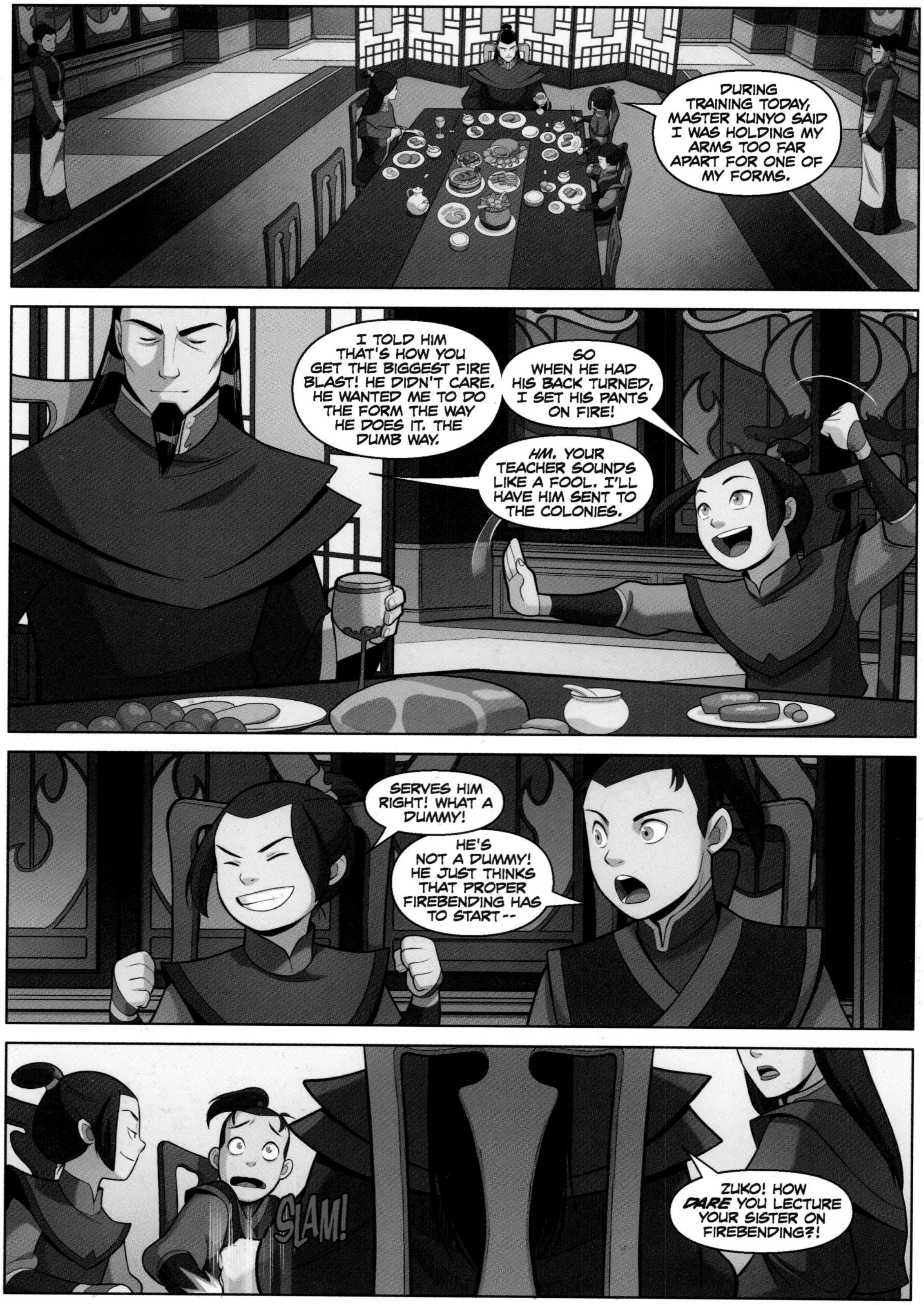
DURING TRAINING TODAY, MASTER KUNYO SAID I WAS HOLDING MY ARMS TOO FAR APART FOR ONE OF MY FORMS.
I TOLD HIM THAT'S HOW YOU GET THE BIGGEST FIRE BLAST! HE DIDN'T CARE. HE WANTED ME TO DO THE FORM THE WAY HE DOES IT. THE DUMB WAY.
SO WHEN HE HAD HIS BACK TURNED, I SET HIS PANTS ON FIRE!
HM. YOUR TEACHER SOUNDS LIKE A FOOL. I'LL HAVE HIM SENT TO THE COLONIES.
SERVES HIM RIGHT! WHAT A DUMMY!
HE'S NOT A DUMMY! HE JUST THINKS THAT PROPER FIREBENDING HAS TO START--
SLAM!
ZUKO! HOW DARE YOU LECTURE YOUR SISTER ON FIREBENDING?!

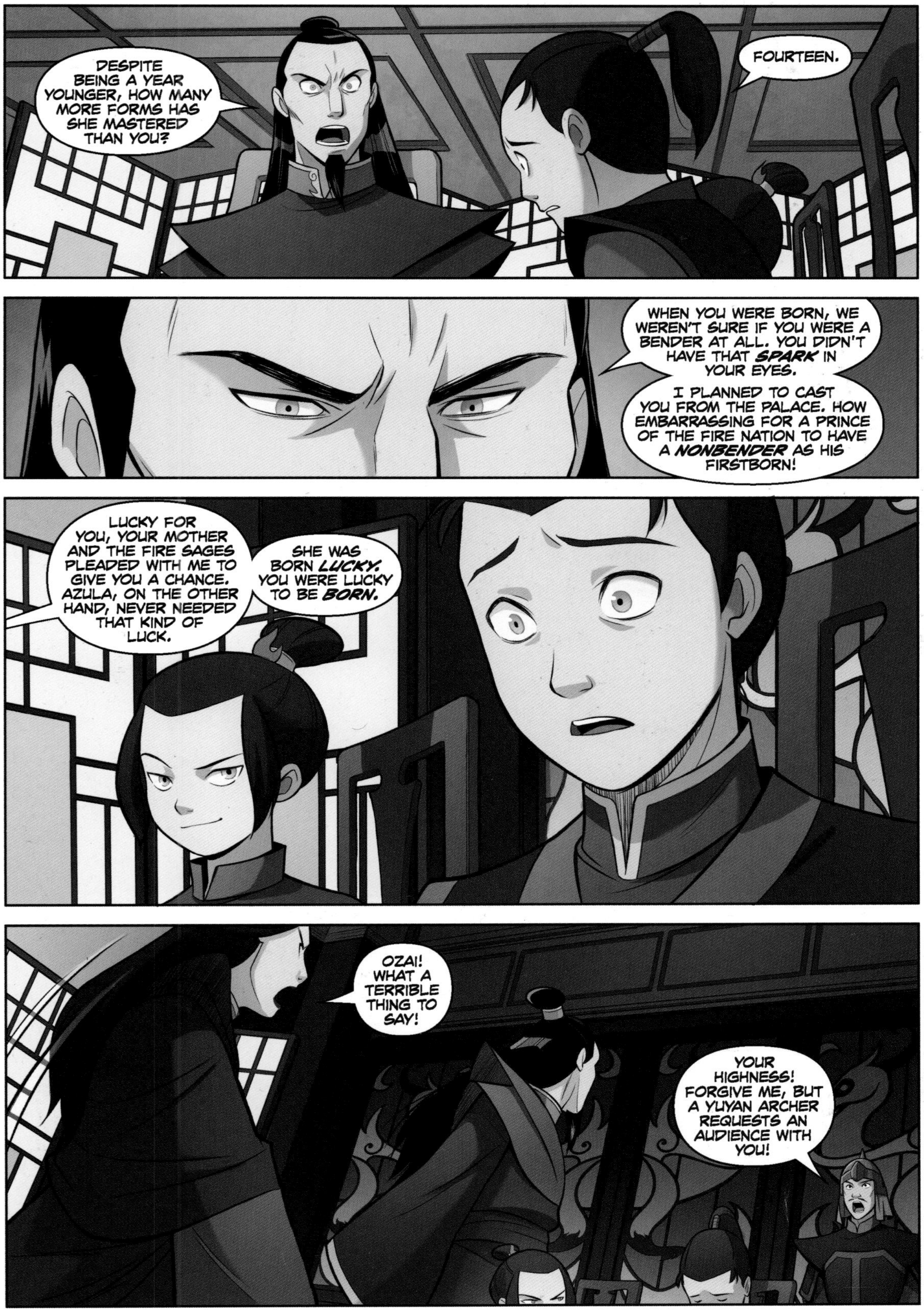
DESPITE BEING A YEAR YOUNGER, HOW MANY MORE FORMS HAS SHE MASTERED THAN YOU?
FOURTEEN.
WHEN YOU WERE BORN, WE WEREN'T SURE IF YOU WERE A BENDER AT ALL. YOU DIDN'T HAVE THAT SPARK IN YOUR EYES.
I PLANNED TO CAST YOU FROM THE PALACE. HOW EMBARRASSING FOR A PRINCE OF THE FIRE NATION TO HAVE A NONBENDER AS HIS FIRSTBORN!
LUCKY FOR YOU, YOUR MOTHER AND THE FIRE SAGES PLEADED WITH ME TO GIVE YOU A CHANCE. AZULA, ON THE OTHER HAND, NEVER NEEDED THAT KIND OF LUCK.
SHE WAS BORN LUCKY. YOU WERE LUCKY TO BE BORN.
OZAI! WHAT A TERRIBLE THING TO SAY!
YOUR HIGHNESS! FORGIVE ME, BUT A YUYAN ARCHER REQUESTS AN AUDIENCE WITH YOU!

M: *In "The Siege of the North, Part 2," Zuko tells Aang how his father always favored Azula over him, citing this particular line: "She was born lucky. You were lucky to be born." Tying in specific moments and characters from the series to the graphic novels really makes these new stories feel like an organic continuation of the* Avatar *universe.*

M: *Seeing Vachir's origins is a nice nod to the original series. Presumably, after Ozai forces Vachir to resign from the Yuyan Archers, he crosses paths with Colonel Mongke and joins the Rough Rhinos.*

FIRE PRINCE OZAI!

THE MAN NAMED IKEM NO LONGER LIVES IN HIRA'A.

THE LOCALS SAID HE'D RUN OFF TO A FOREST AT THE BOTTOM OF A NEARBY VALLEY.

I SEARCHED THAT FOREST FOR MANY MONTHS, BUT NEVER FOUND HIM.

THAT FOREST... YOUR HIGHNESS, I'VE NEVER BEEN ANYWHERE LIKE IT! THE TREES, THE ANIMALS, THE INSECTS...THEY'RE ALL OUT TO GET YOU! A COMMONER COULD NOT HAVE SURVIVED FOR LONG!

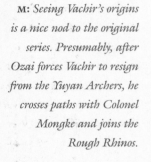

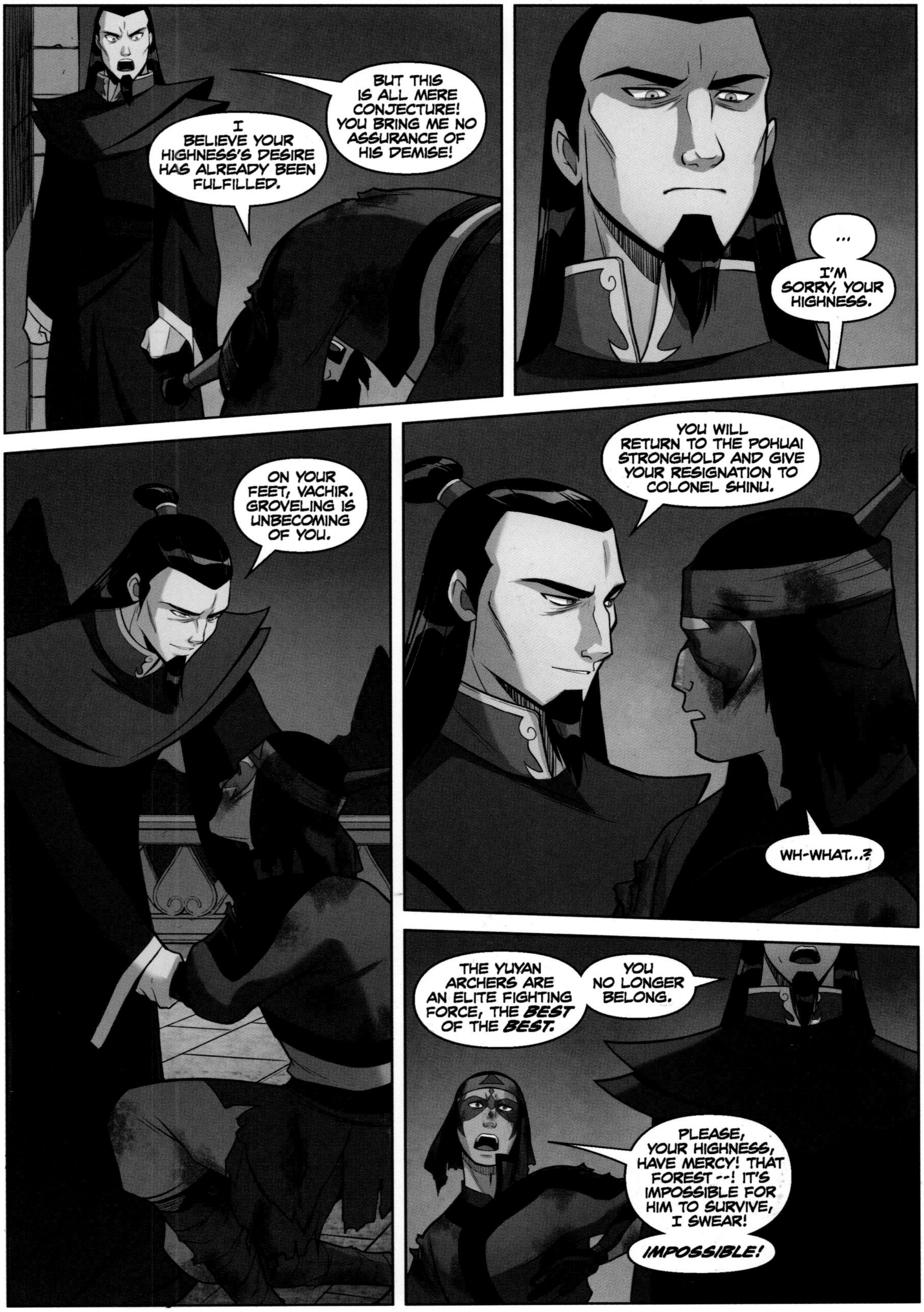
I BELIEVE YOUR HIGHNESS'S DESIRE HAS ALREADY BEEN FULFILLED.
BUT THIS IS ALL MERE CONJECTURE! YOU BRING ME NO ASSURANCE OF HIS DEMISE!
...
I'M SORRY, YOUR HIGHNESS.
ON YOUR FEET, VACHIR. GROVELING IS UNBECOMING OF YOU.
YOU WILL RETURN TO THE POHUAI STRONGHOLD AND GIVE YOUR RESIGNATION TO COLONEL SHINU.
WH-WHAT...?
THE YUYAN ARCHERS ARE AN ELITE FIGHTING FORCE, THE *BEST* OF THE *BEST.*
YOU NO LONGER BELONG.
PLEASE, YOUR HIGHNESS, HAVE MERCY! THAT FOREST --! IT'S IMPOSSIBLE FOR HIM TO SURVIVE, I SWEAR!
IMPOSSIBLE!

GLY: *I always found the character of Vachir intriguing. He's a member of the Rough Rhinos, yet he has the face tattoo of a Yuyan Archer. How did he go from being one of the elite warriors of the Fire Nation army to a mercenary? There had to be a good story there. I'm glad we got to explore it in* The Search.

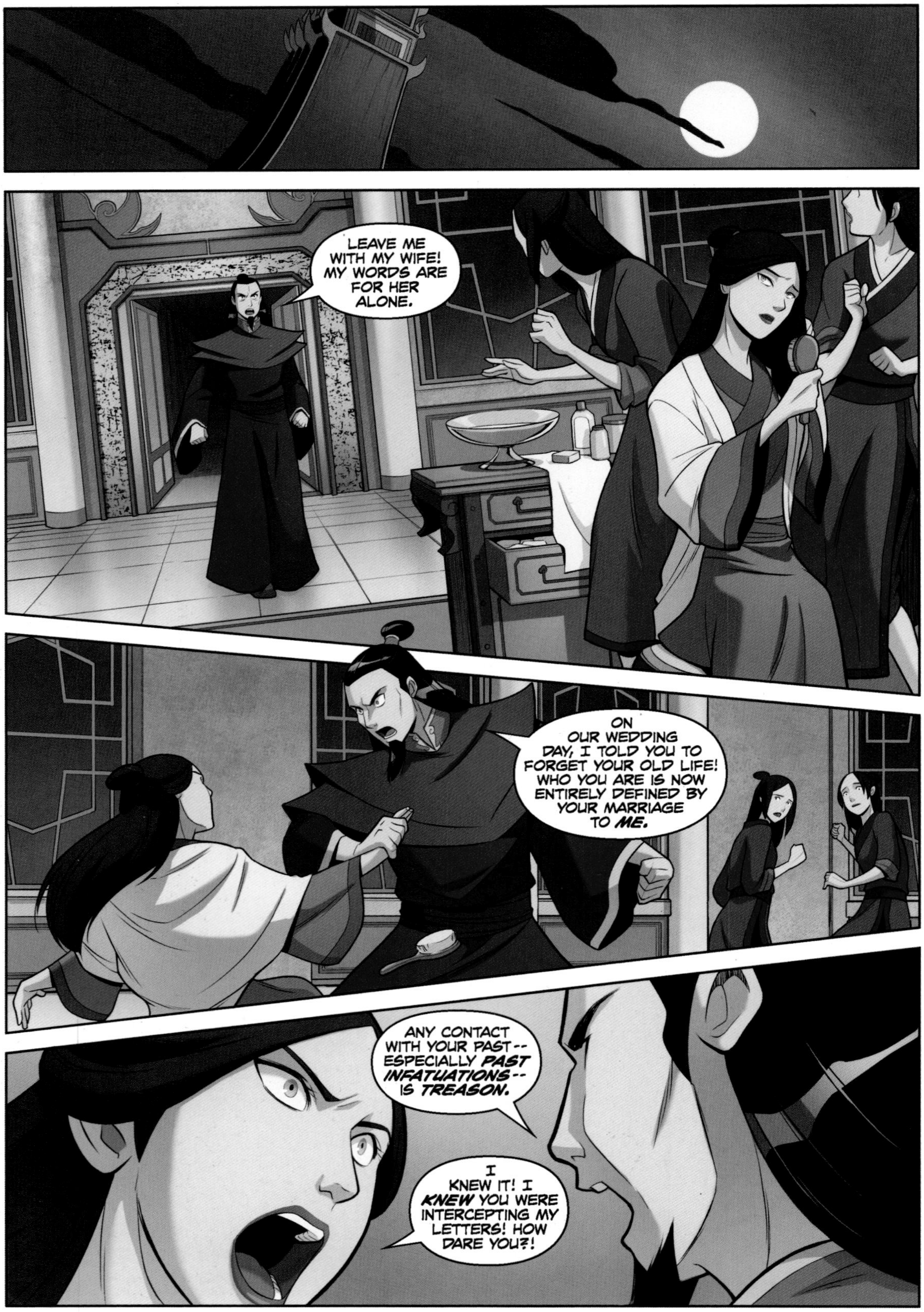
LEAVE ME WITH MY WIFE! MY WORDS ARE FOR HER ALONE.
ON OUR WEDDING DAY, I TOLD YOU TO FORGET YOUR OLD LIFE! WHO YOU ARE IS NOW ENTIRELY DEFINED BY YOUR MARRIAGE TO ME.
ANY CONTACT WITH YOUR PAST--ESPECIALLY PAST INFATUATIONS--IS TREASON.
I KNEW IT! I KNEW YOU WERE INTERCEPTING MY LETTERS! HOW DARE YOU?!

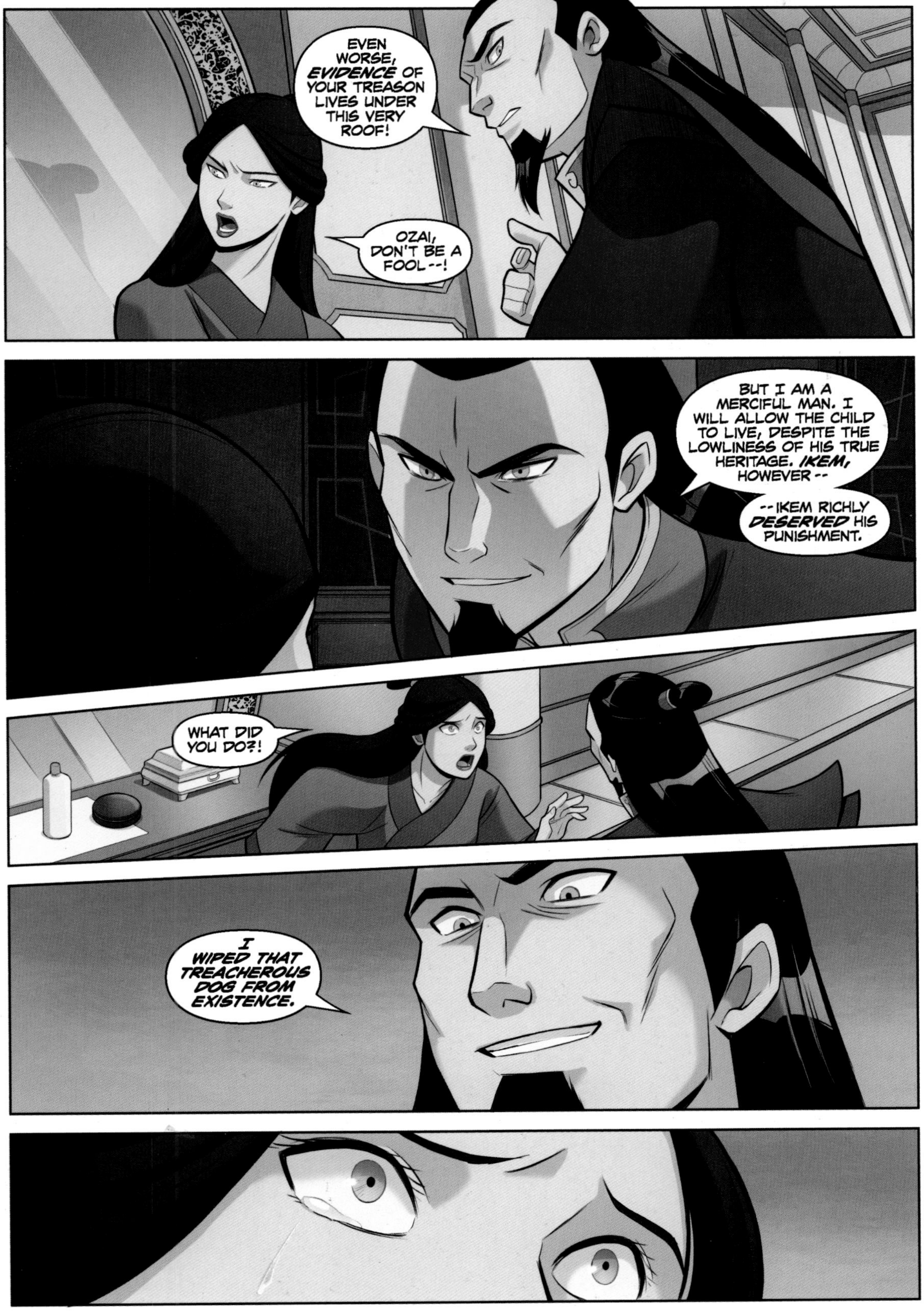
EVEN WORSE, *EVIDENCE* OF YOUR TREASON LIVES UNDER THIS VERY ROOF!
OZAI, DON'T BE A FOOL--!
BUT I AM A MERCIFUL MAN. I WILL ALLOW THE CHILD TO LIVE, DESPITE THE LOWLINESS OF HIS TRUE HERITAGE. *IKEM,* HOWEVER--
--IKEM RICHLY *DESERVED* HIS PUNISHMENT.
WHAT DID YOU DO?!
I WIPED THAT TREACHEROUS DOG FROM EXISTENCE.

WE NEED TO HIDE OUR IDENTITIES. WE'LL GET MOBBED IF PEOPLE FIGURE OUT WE'RE THE AVATAR AND THE FIRE LORD.

DON'T WORRY. AFTER HIDING FROM *YOU* FOR ALL THOSE MONTHS, WE'RE MASTERS OF DISGUISE!

AANG, THAT HEADBAND OF YOURS IS CUTE, BUT AS A DISGUISE IT WORKED A LOT BETTER WHEN YOU HAD HAIR.

SEE? A FAKE BEARD MADE OF SKY BISON FUR! A CLASSIC!

GET AWAY FROM ME! YOU SMELL LIKE A WET POSSUM-PIGEON!

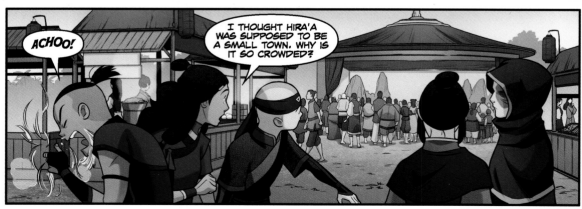

ACHOO!

I THOUGHT HIRA'A WAS SUPPOSED TO BE A SMALL TOWN. WHY IS IT SO CROWDED?

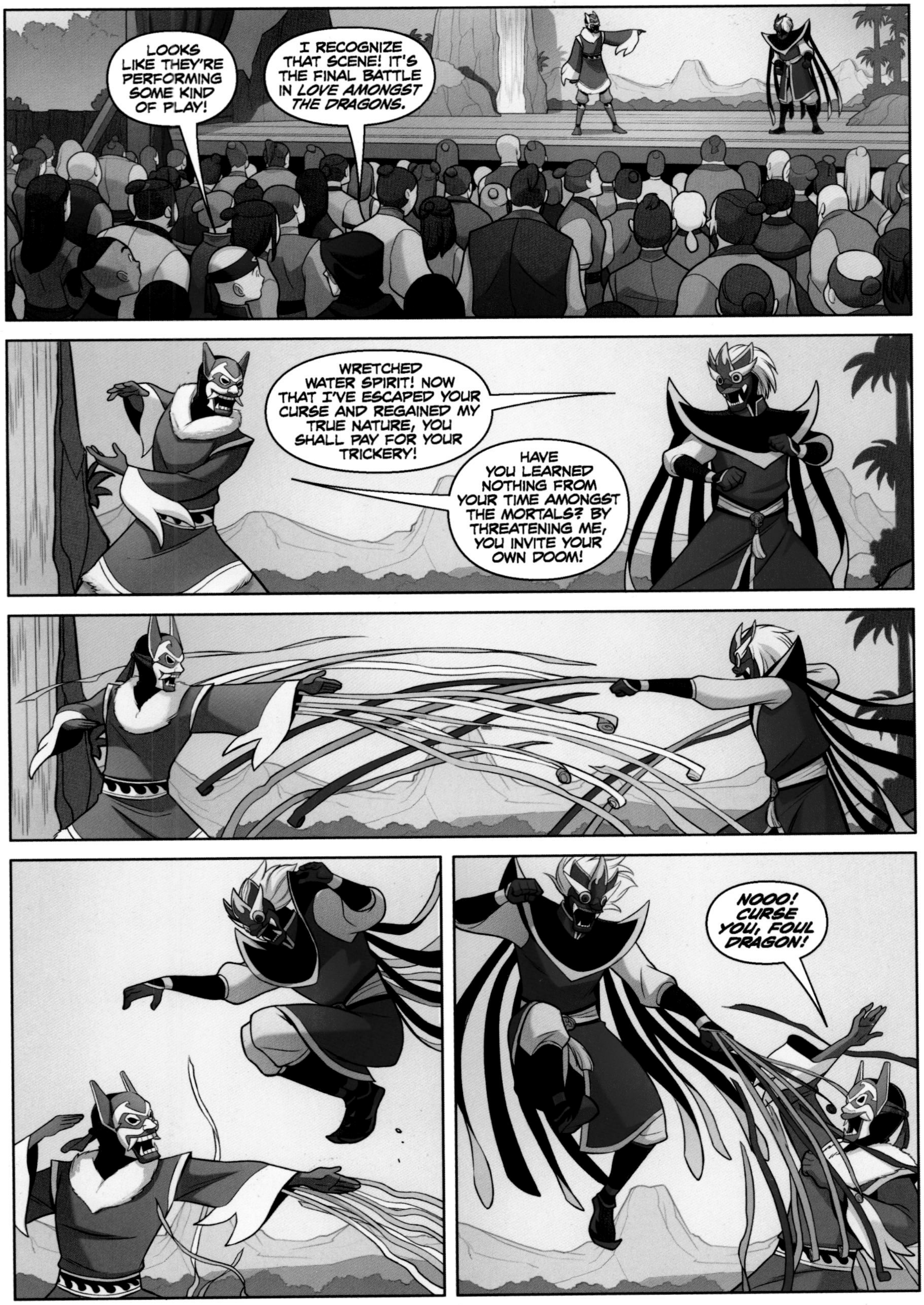
LOOKS LIKE THEY'RE PERFORMING SOME KIND OF PLAY!
I RECOGNIZE THAT SCENE! IT'S THE FINAL BATTLE IN *LOVE AMONGST THE DRAGONS*.
WRETCHED WATER SPIRIT! NOW THAT I'VE ESCAPED YOUR CURSE AND REGAINED MY TRUE NATURE, YOU SHALL PAY FOR YOUR TRICKERY!
HAVE YOU LEARNED NOTHING FROM YOUR TIME AMONGST THE MORTALS? BY THREATENING ME, YOU INVITE YOUR OWN DOOM!
NOOO! CURSE YOU, FOUL DRAGON!

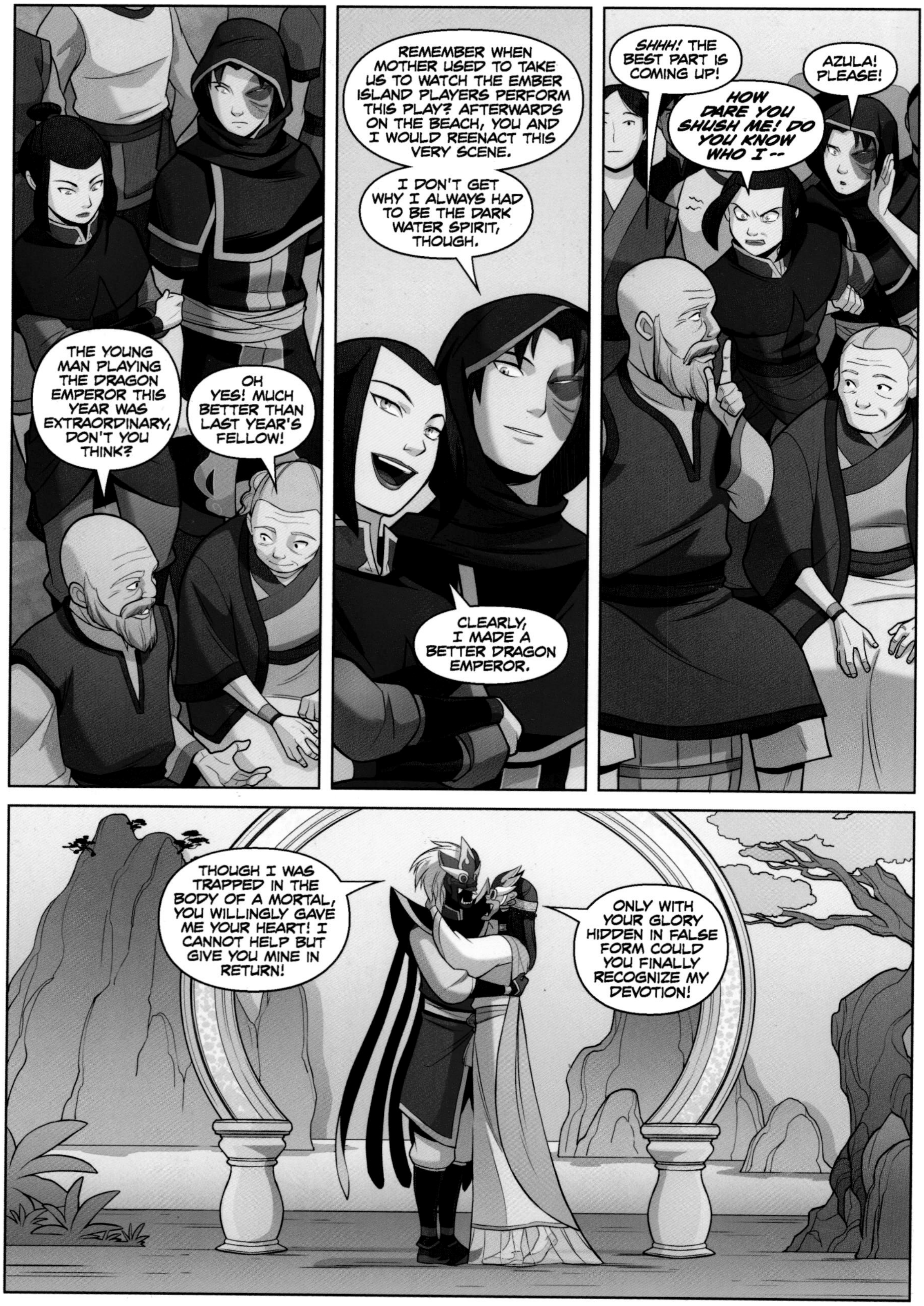
THE YOUNG MAN PLAYING THE DRAGON EMPEROR THIS YEAR WAS EXTRAORDINARY, DON'T YOU THINK?
OH YES! MUCH BETTER THAN LAST YEAR'S FELLOW!
REMEMBER WHEN MOTHER USED TO TAKE US TO WATCH THE EMBER ISLAND PLAYERS PERFORM THIS PLAY? AFTERWARDS ON THE BEACH, YOU AND I WOULD REENACT THIS VERY SCENE.
I DON'T GET WHY I ALWAYS HAD TO BE THE DARK WATER SPIRIT, THOUGH.
CLEARLY, I MADE A BETTER DRAGON EMPEROR.
SHHH! THE BEST PART IS COMING UP!
HOW DARE YOU SHUSH ME! DO YOU KNOW WHO I --
AZULA! PLEASE!
THOUGH I WAS TRAPPED IN THE BODY OF A MORTAL, YOU WILLINGLY GAVE ME YOUR HEART! I CANNOT HELP BUT GIVE YOU MINE IN RETURN!
ONLY WITH YOUR GLORY HIDDEN IN FALSE FORM COULD YOU FINALLY RECOGNIZE MY DEVOTION!

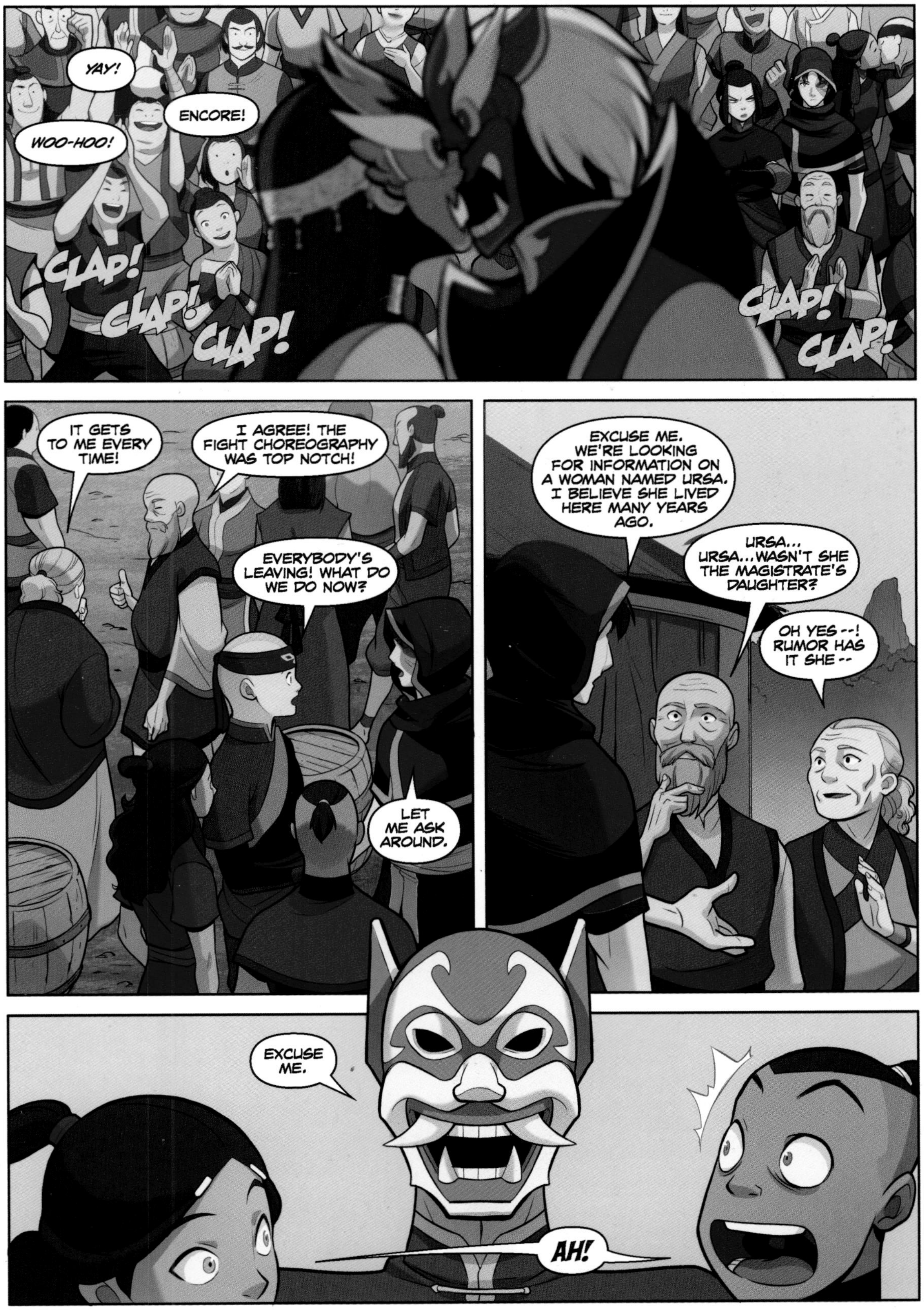
YAY!
ENCORE!
WOO-HOO!
CLAP! CLAP! CLAP!
CLAP! CLAP!
IT GETS TO ME EVERY TIME!
I AGREE! THE FIGHT CHOREOGRAPHY WAS TOP NOTCH!
EVERYBODY'S LEAVING! WHAT DO WE DO NOW?
LET ME ASK AROUND.
EXCUSE ME. WE'RE LOOKING FOR INFORMATION ON A WOMAN NAMED URSA. I BELIEVE SHE LIVED HERE MANY YEARS AGO.
URSA... URSA...WASN'T SHE THE MAGISTRATE'S DAUGHTER?
OH YES --! RUMOR HAS IT SHE --
EXCUSE ME.
AH!

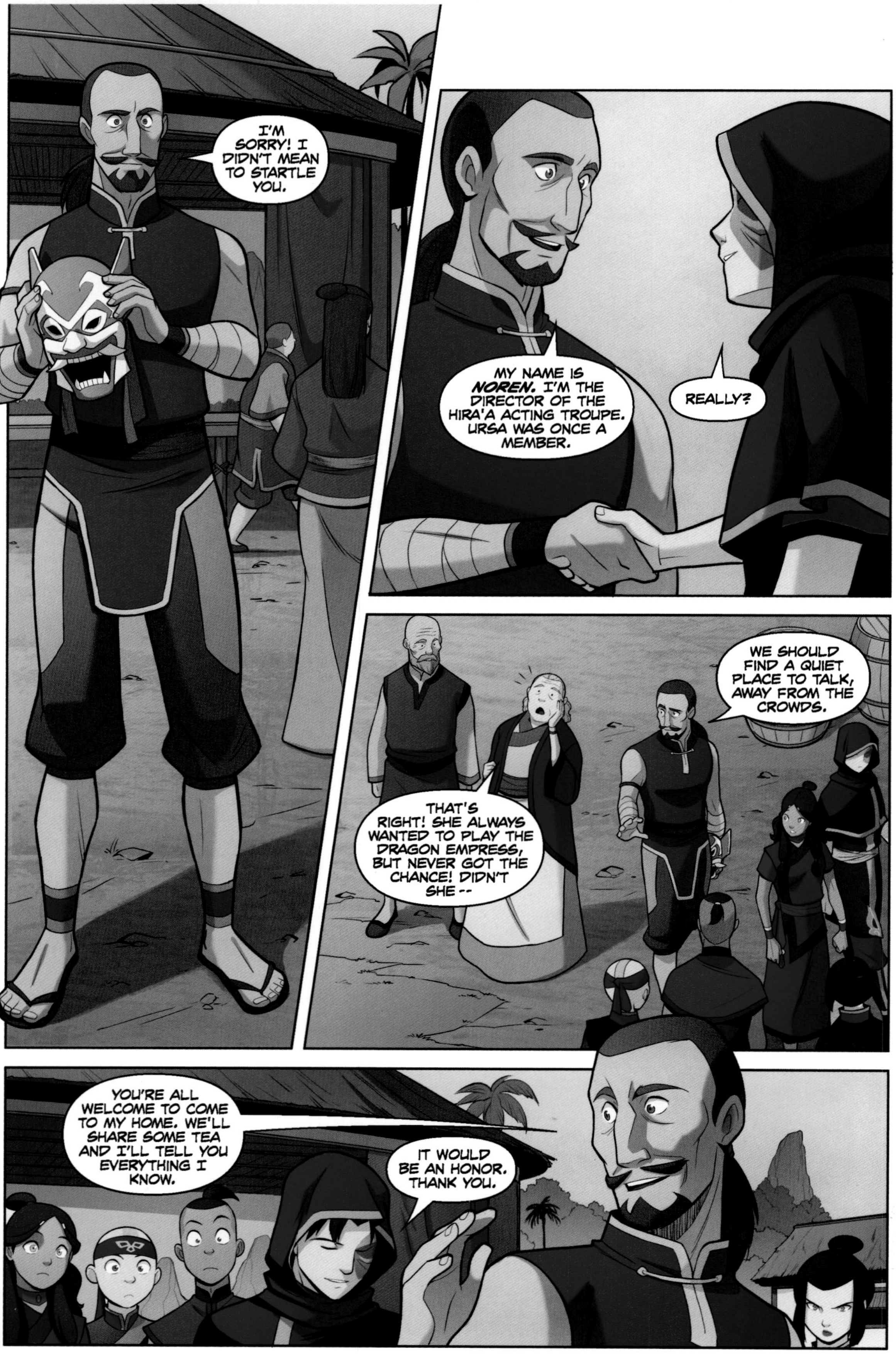
I'M SORRY! I DIDN'T MEAN TO STARTLE YOU.
MY NAME IS NOREN. I'M THE DIRECTOR OF THE HIRA'A ACTING TROUPE. URSA WAS ONCE A MEMBER.
REALLY?
THAT'S RIGHT! SHE ALWAYS WANTED TO PLAY THE DRAGON EMPRESS, BUT NEVER GOT THE CHANCE! DIDN'T SHE --
WE SHOULD FIND A QUIET PLACE TO TALK, AWAY FROM THE CROWDS.
YOU'RE ALL WELCOME TO COME TO MY HOME. WE'LL SHARE SOME TEA AND I'LL TELL YOU EVERYTHING I KNOW.
IT WOULD BE AN HONOR. THANK YOU.

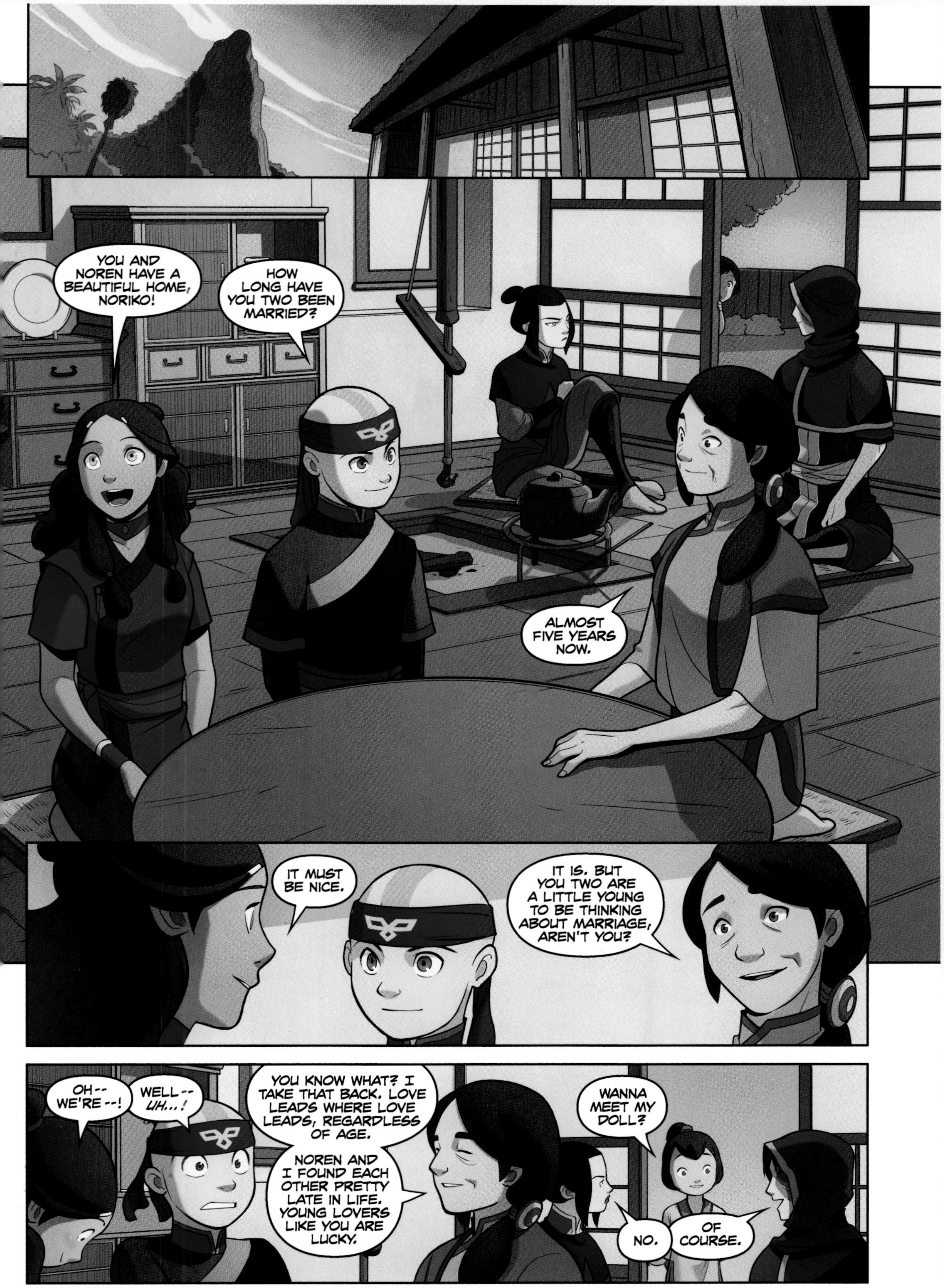
YOU AND NOREN HAVE A BEAUTIFUL HOME, NORIKO!
HOW LONG HAVE YOU TWO BEEN MARRIED?
ALMOST FIVE YEARS NOW.
IT MUST BE NICE.
IT IS. BUT YOU TWO ARE A LITTLE YOUNG TO BE THINKING ABOUT MARRIAGE, AREN'T YOU?
OH-- WE'RE--!
WELL-- UH...!
YOU KNOW WHAT? I TAKE THAT BACK. LOVE LEADS WHERE LOVE LEADS, REGARDLESS OF AGE.
NOREN AND I FOUND EACH OTHER PRETTY LATE IN LIFE. YOUNG LOVERS LIKE YOU ARE LUCKY.
WANNA MEET MY DOLL?
NO.
OF COURSE.

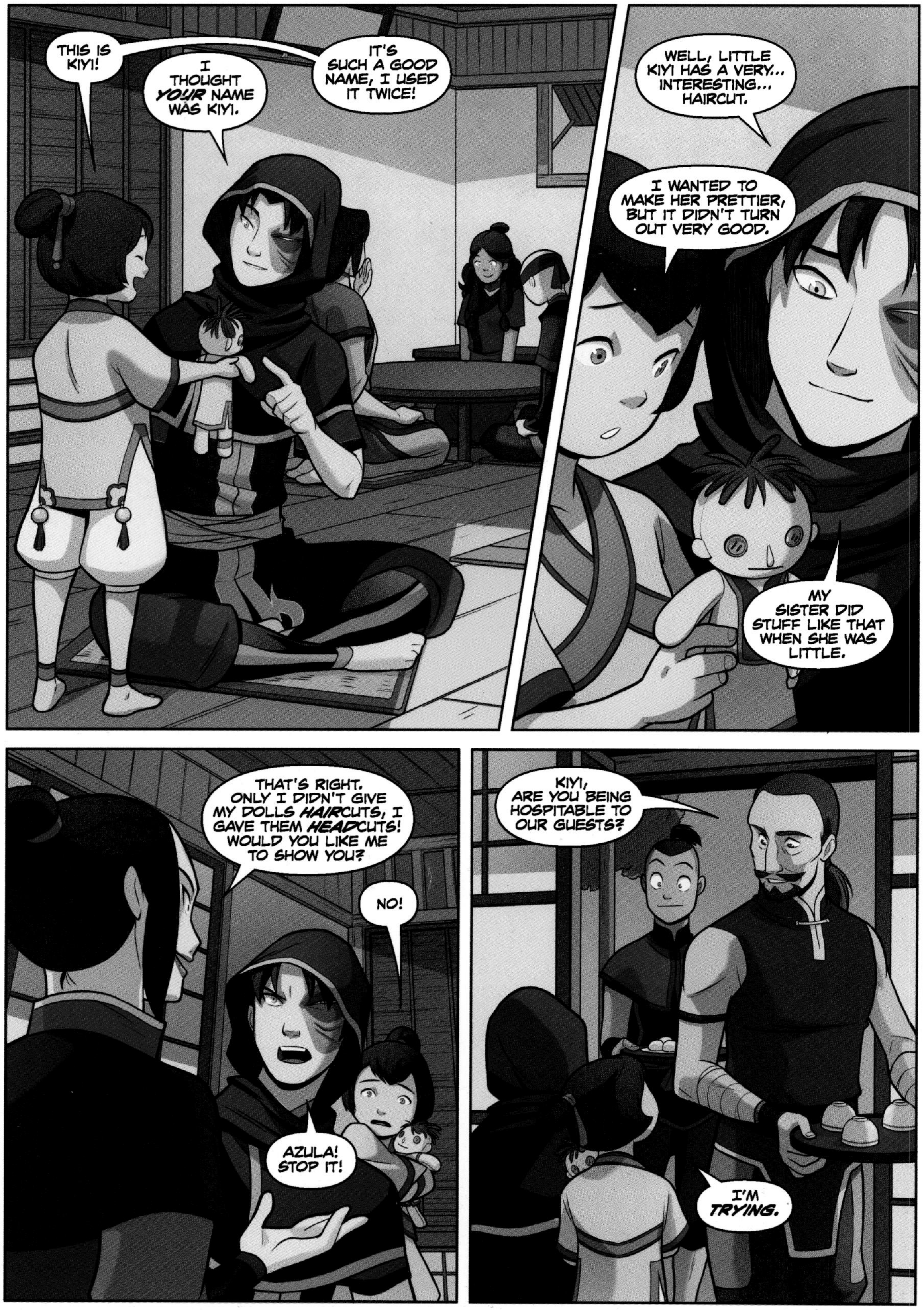
THIS IS KIYI!
I THOUGHT YOUR NAME WAS KIYI.
IT'S SUCH A GOOD NAME, I USED IT TWICE!
WELL, LITTLE KIYI HAS A VERY... INTERESTING... HAIRCUT.
I WANTED TO MAKE HER PRETTIER, BUT IT DIDN'T TURN OUT VERY GOOD.
MY SISTER DID STUFF LIKE THAT WHEN SHE WAS LITTLE.
THAT'S RIGHT. ONLY I DIDN'T GIVE MY DOLLS HAIRCUTS, I GAVE THEM HEADCUTS! WOULD YOU LIKE ME TO SHOW YOU?
NO!
AZULA! STOP IT!
KIYI, ARE YOU BEING HOSPITABLE TO OUR GUESTS?
I'M TRYING.

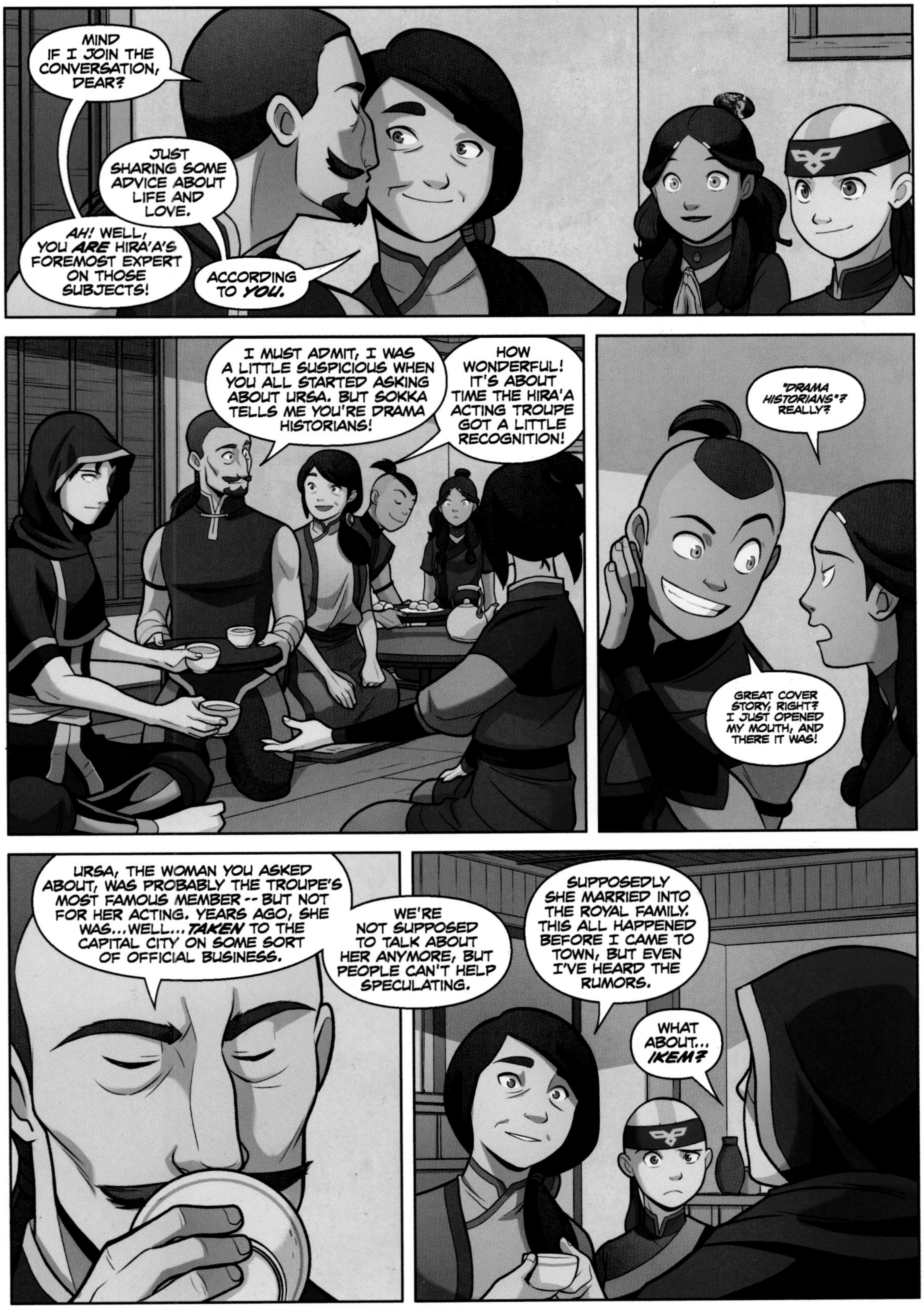
MIND IF I JOIN THE CONVERSATION, DEAR?
JUST SHARING SOME ADVICE ABOUT LIFE AND LOVE.
AH! WELL, YOU ARE HIRA'A'S FOREMOST EXPERT ON THOSE SUBJECTS!
ACCORDING TO YOU.
I MUST ADMIT, I WAS A LITTLE SUSPICIOUS WHEN YOU ALL STARTED ASKING ABOUT URSA. BUT SOKKA TELLS ME YOU'RE DRAMA HISTORIANS!
HOW WONDERFUL! IT'S ABOUT TIME THE HIRA'A ACTING TROUPE GOT A LITTLE RECOGNITION!
"DRAMA HISTORIANS"? REALLY?
GREAT COVER STORY, RIGHT? I JUST OPENED MY MOUTH, AND THERE IT WAS!
URSA, THE WOMAN YOU ASKED ABOUT, WAS PROBABLY THE TROUPE'S MOST FAMOUS MEMBER -- BUT NOT FOR HER ACTING. YEARS AGO, SHE WAS...WELL...TAKEN TO THE CAPITAL CITY ON SOME SORT OF OFFICIAL BUSINESS.
WE'RE NOT SUPPOSED TO TALK ABOUT HER ANYMORE, BUT PEOPLE CAN'T HELP SPECULATING.
SUPPOSEDLY SHE MARRIED INTO THE ROYAL FAMILY. THIS ALL HAPPENED BEFORE I CAME TO TOWN, BUT EVEN I'VE HEARD THE RUMORS.
WHAT ABOUT... IKEM?

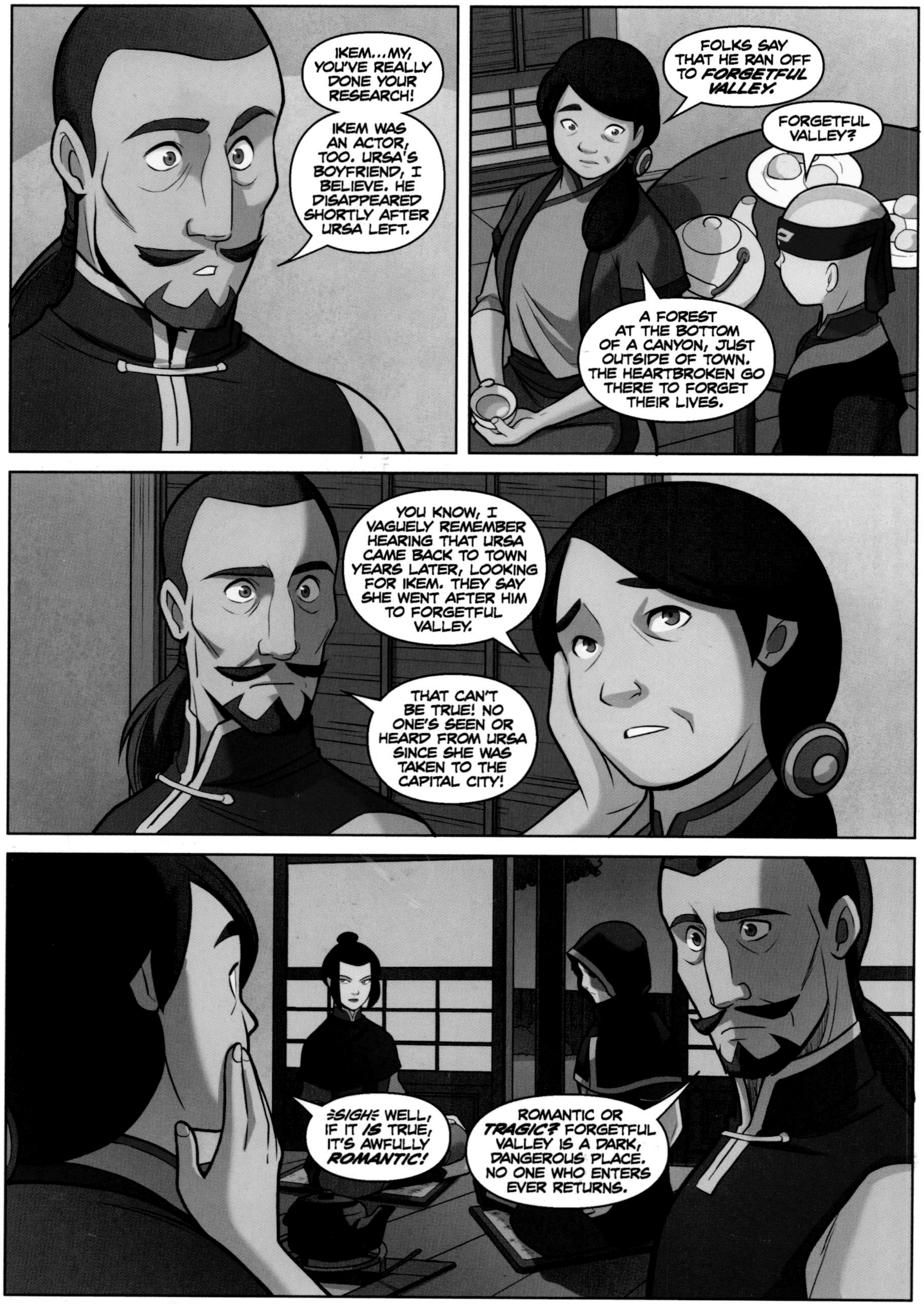
IKEM...MY, YOU'VE REALLY DONE YOUR RESEARCH!
IKEM WAS AN ACTOR, TOO. URSA'S BOYFRIEND, I BELIEVE. HE DISAPPEARED SHORTLY AFTER URSA LEFT.
FOLKS SAY THAT HE RAN OFF TO ***FORGETFUL VALLEY.***
FORGETFUL VALLEY?
A FOREST AT THE BOTTOM OF A CANYON, JUST OUTSIDE OF TOWN. THE HEARTBROKEN GO THERE TO FORGET THEIR LIVES.
YOU KNOW, I VAGUELY REMEMBER HEARING THAT URSA CAME BACK TO TOWN YEARS LATER, LOOKING FOR IKEM. THEY SAY SHE WENT AFTER HIM TO FORGETFUL VALLEY.
THAT CAN'T BE TRUE! NO ONE'S SEEN OR HEARD FROM URSA SINCE SHE WAS TAKEN TO THE CAPITAL CITY!
SIGH WELL, IF IT ***IS*** TRUE, IT'S AWFULLY ***ROMANTIC!***
ROMANTIC OR ***TRAGIC?*** FORGETFUL VALLEY IS A DARK, DANGEROUS PLACE. NO ONE WHO ENTERS EVER RETURNS.

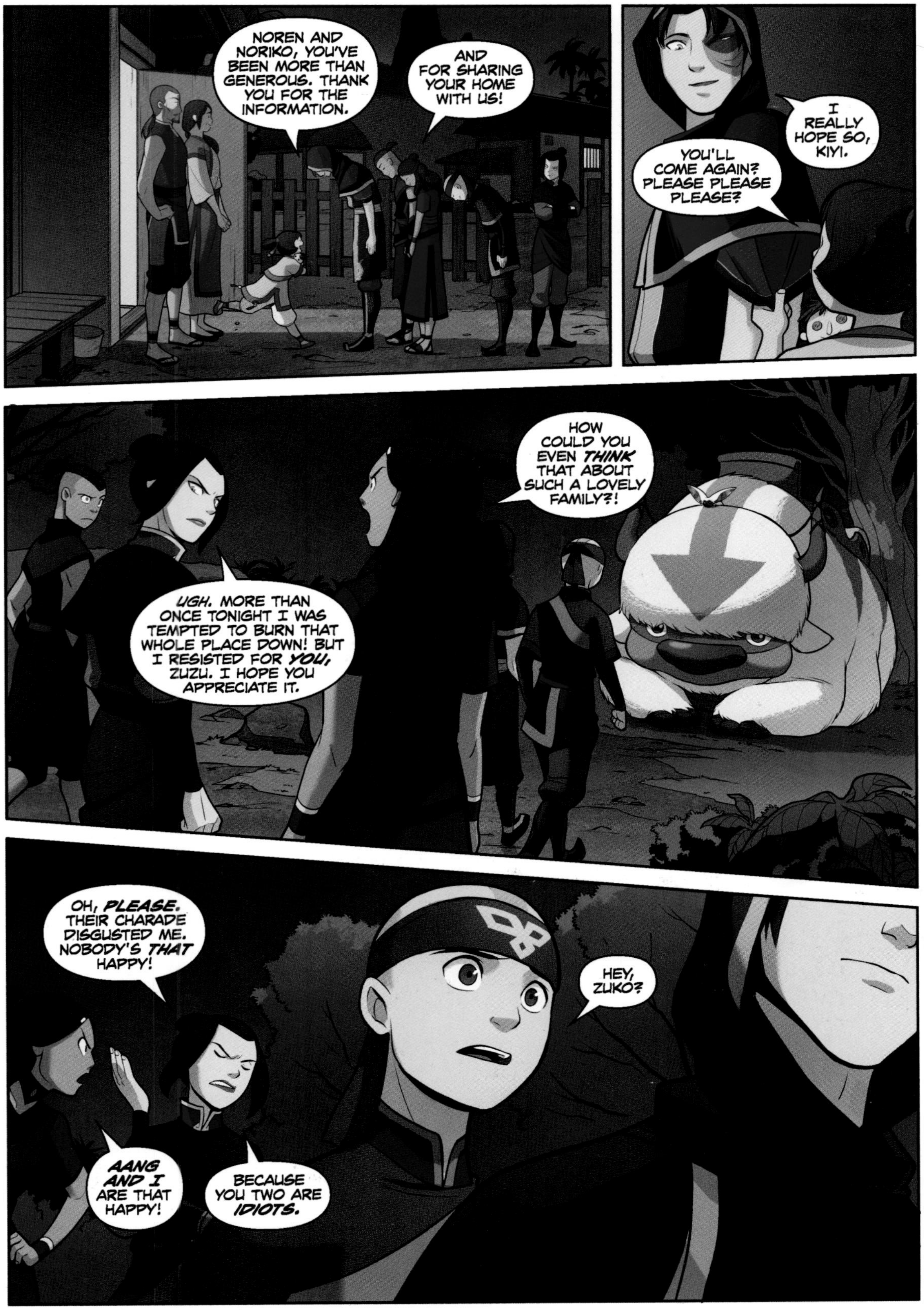
NOREN AND NORIKO, YOU'VE BEEN MORE THAN GENEROUS. THANK YOU FOR THE INFORMATION.
AND FOR SHARING YOUR HOME WITH US!
YOU'LL COME AGAIN? PLEASE PLEASE PLEASE?
I REALLY HOPE SO, KIYI.
HOW COULD YOU EVEN THINK THAT ABOUT SUCH A LOVELY FAMILY?!
UGH. MORE THAN ONCE TONIGHT I WAS TEMPTED TO BURN THAT WHOLE PLACE DOWN! BUT I RESISTED FOR YOU, ZUZU. I HOPE YOU APPRECIATE IT.
OH, PLEASE. THEIR CHARADE DISGUSTED ME. NOBODY'S THAT HAPPY!
AANG AND I ARE THAT HAPPY!
BECAUSE YOU TWO ARE IDIOTS.
HEY, ZUKO?

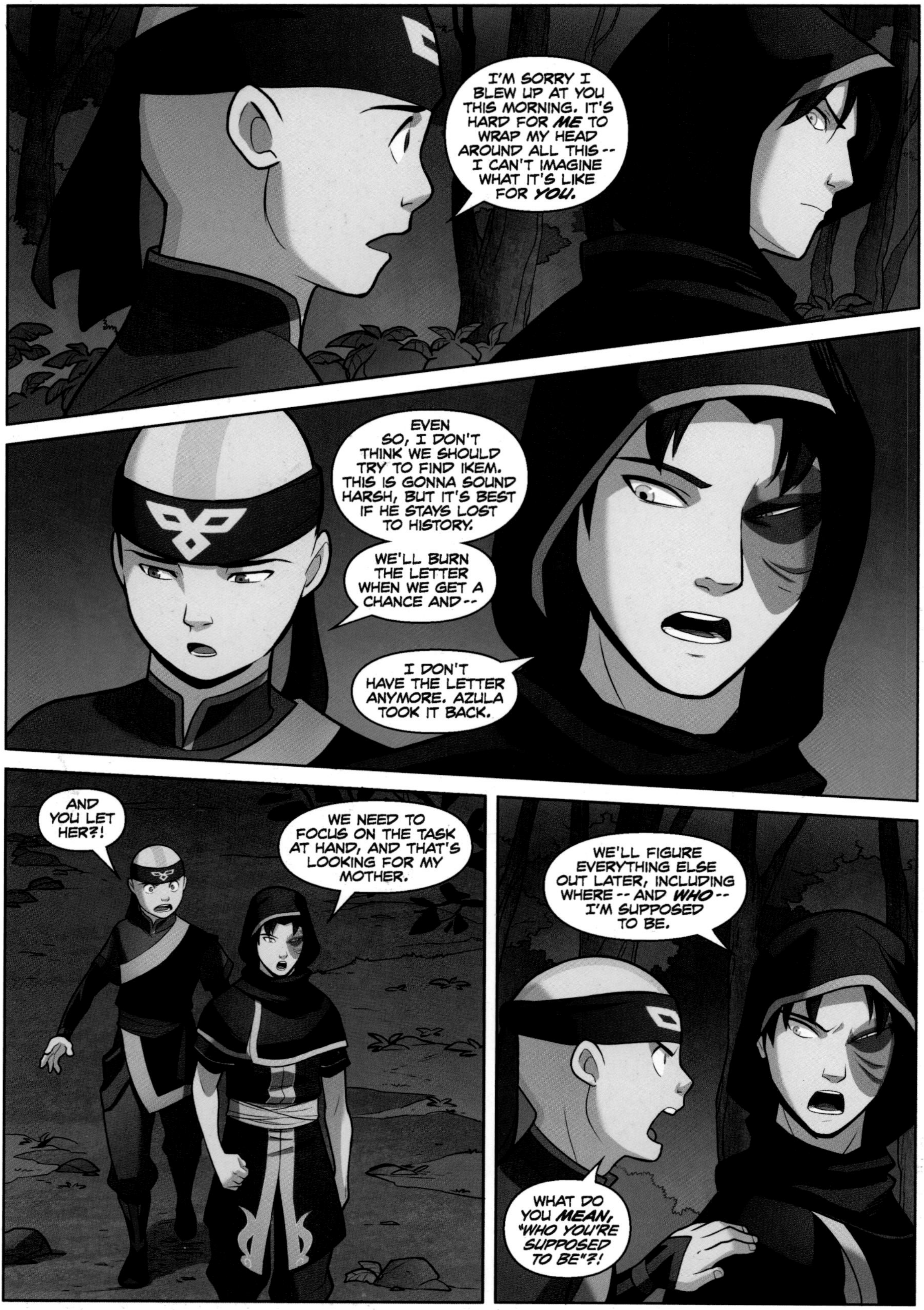
I'M SORRY I BLEW UP AT YOU THIS MORNING. IT'S HARD FOR *ME* TO WRAP MY HEAD AROUND ALL THIS -- I CAN'T IMAGINE WHAT IT'S LIKE FOR *YOU.*
EVEN SO, I DON'T THINK WE SHOULD TRY TO FIND IKEM. THIS IS GONNA SOUND HARSH, BUT IT'S BEST IF HE STAYS LOST TO HISTORY.
WE'LL BURN THE LETTER WHEN WE GET A CHANCE AND --
I DON'T HAVE THE LETTER ANYMORE. AZULA TOOK IT BACK.
AND YOU LET HER?!
WE NEED TO FOCUS ON THE TASK AT HAND, AND THAT'S LOOKING FOR MY MOTHER.
WE'LL FIGURE EVERYTHING ELSE OUT LATER, INCLUDING WHERE -- AND *WHO* -- I'M SUPPOSED TO BE.
WHAT DO YOU *MEAN,* "*WHO YOU'RE SUPPOSED TO BE*"?!

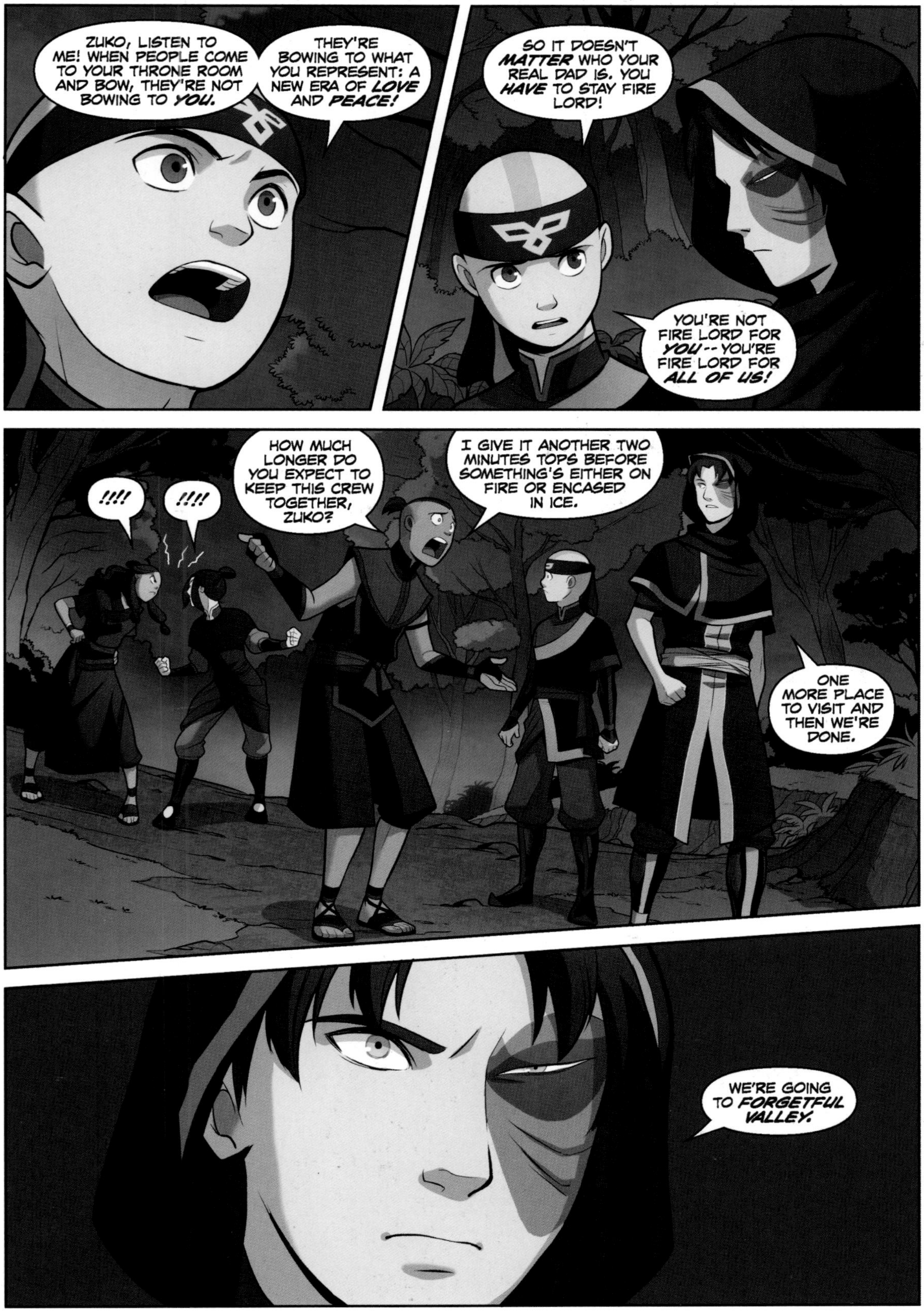
ZUKO, LISTEN TO ME! WHEN PEOPLE COME TO YOUR THRONE ROOM AND BOW, THEY'RE NOT BOWING TO YOU.
THEY'RE BOWING TO WHAT YOU REPRESENT: A NEW ERA OF LOVE AND PEACE!
SO IT DOESN'T MATTER WHO YOUR REAL DAD IS. YOU HAVE TO STAY FIRE LORD!
YOU'RE NOT FIRE LORD FOR YOU-- YOU'RE FIRE LORD FOR ALL OF US!
!!!!
!!!!
HOW MUCH LONGER DO YOU EXPECT TO KEEP THIS CREW TOGETHER, ZUKO?
I GIVE IT ANOTHER TWO MINUTES TOPS BEFORE SOMETHING'S EITHER ON FIRE OR ENCASED IN ICE.
ONE MORE PLACE TO VISIT AND THEN WE'RE DONE.
WE'RE GOING TO FORGETFUL VALLEY.

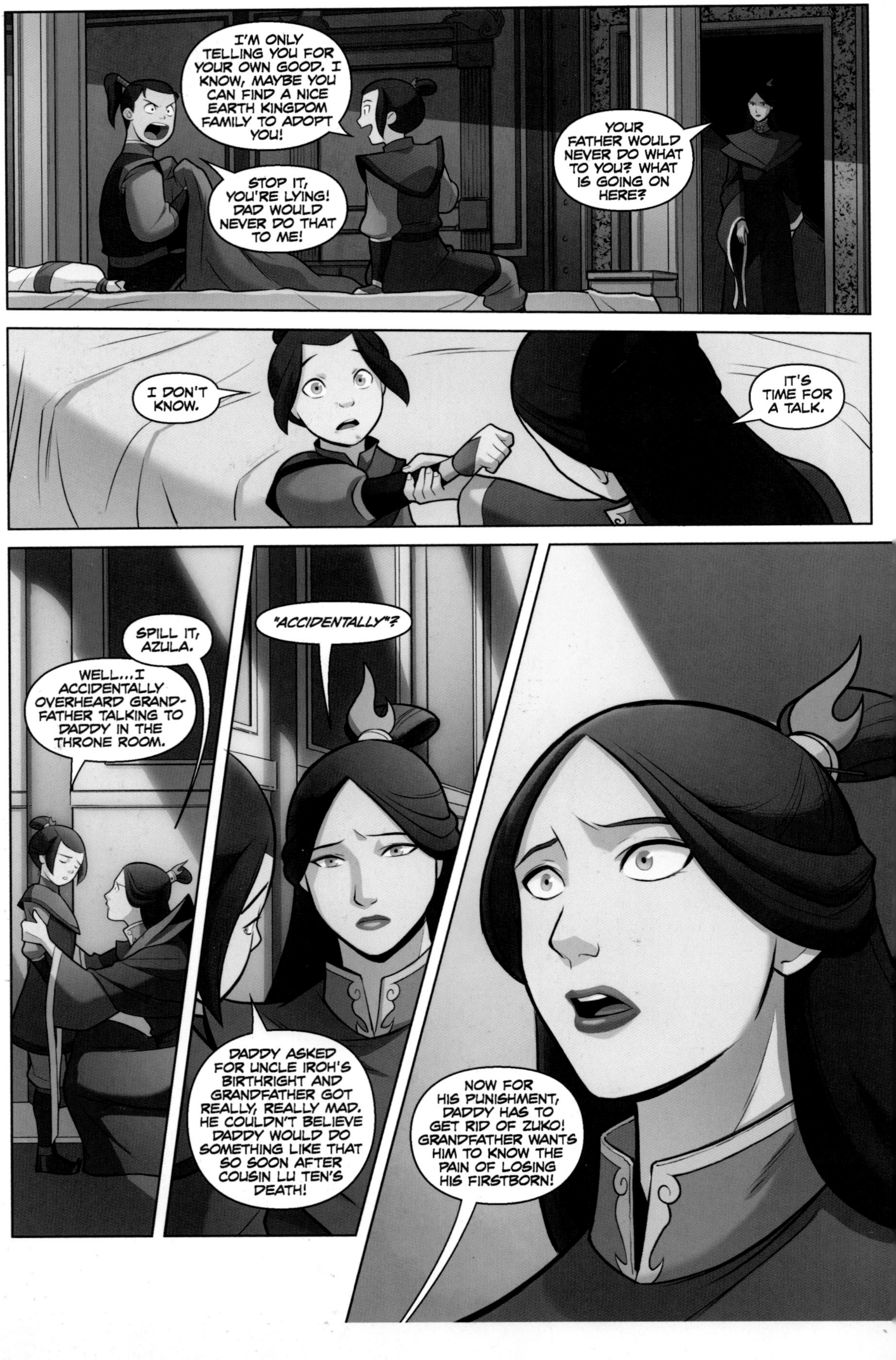
I'M ONLY TELLING YOU FOR YOUR OWN GOOD. I KNOW, MAYBE YOU CAN FIND A NICE EARTH KINGDOM FAMILY TO ADOPT YOU!
STOP IT, YOU'RE LYING! DAD WOULD NEVER DO THAT TO ME!
YOUR FATHER WOULD NEVER DO WHAT TO YOU? WHAT IS GOING ON HERE?
I DON'T KNOW.
IT'S TIME FOR A TALK.
SPILL IT, AZULA.
WELL...I ACCIDENTALLY OVERHEARD GRAND-FATHER TALKING TO DADDY IN THE THRONE ROOM.
"ACCIDENTALLY"?
DADDY ASKED FOR UNCLE IROH'S BIRTHRIGHT AND GRANDFATHER GOT REALLY, REALLY MAD. HE COULDN'T BELIEVE DADDY WOULD DO SOMETHING LIKE THAT SO SOON AFTER COUSIN LU TEN'S DEATH!
NOW FOR HIS PUNISHMENT, DADDY HAS TO GET RID OF ZUKO! GRANDFATHER WANTS HIM TO KNOW THE PAIN OF LOSING HIS FIRSTBORN!

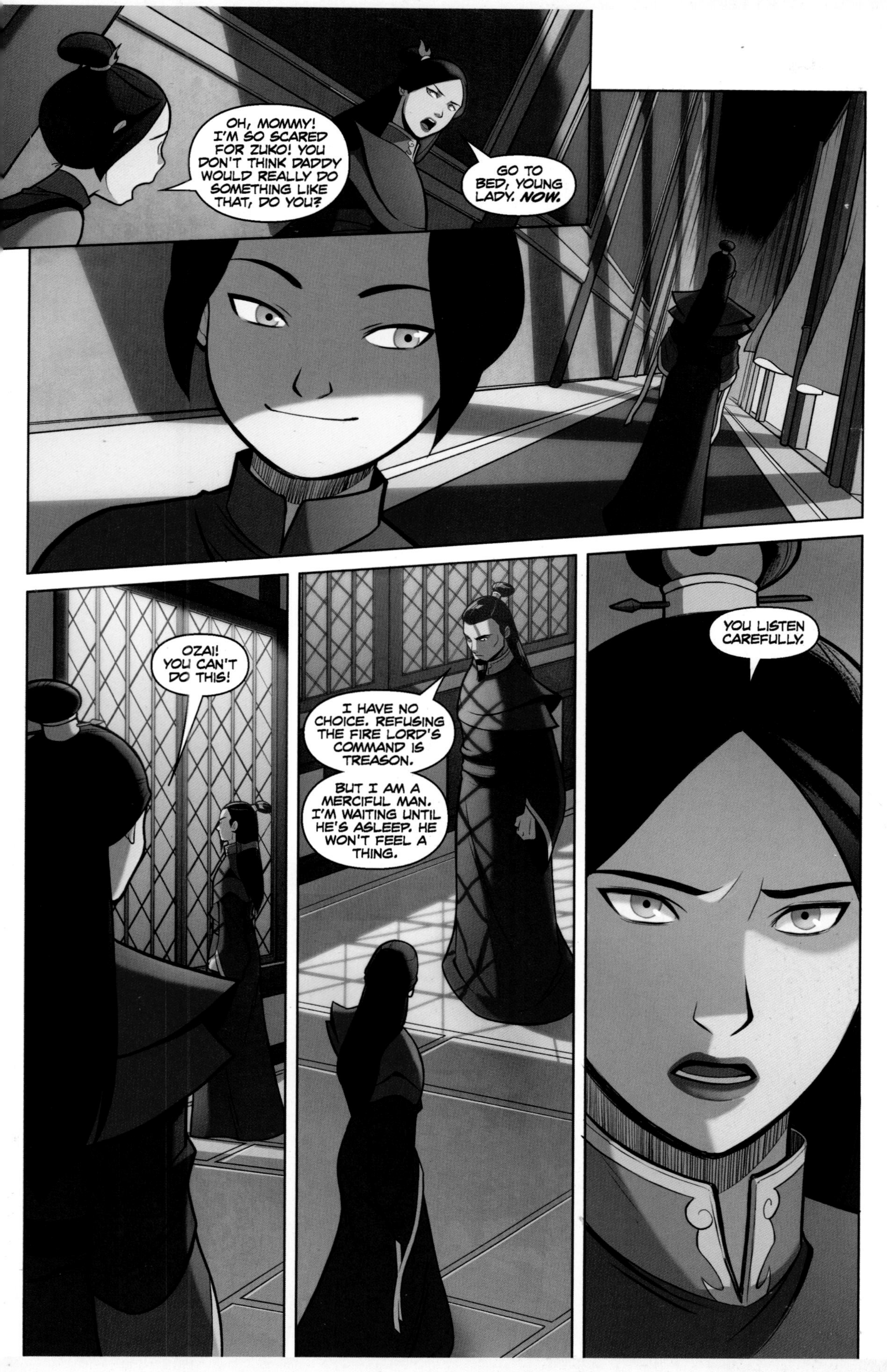
OH, MOMMY! I'M SO SCARED FOR ZUKO! YOU DON'T THINK DADDY WOULD REALLY DO SOMETHING LIKE THAT, DO YOU?
GO TO BED, YOUNG LADY. *NOW.*
OZAI! YOU CAN'T DO THIS!
I HAVE NO CHOICE. REFUSING THE FIRE LORD'S COMMAND IS TREASON.
BUT I AM A MERCIFUL MAN. I'M WAITING UNTIL HE'S ASLEEP. HE WON'T FEEL A THING.
YOU LISTEN CAREFULLY.

G: *This is the corridor that was shown in the TV show. Here we can see the origins of Azula's cruelty in her childhood. We think we were able to use light and shadow effectively in this scene.*

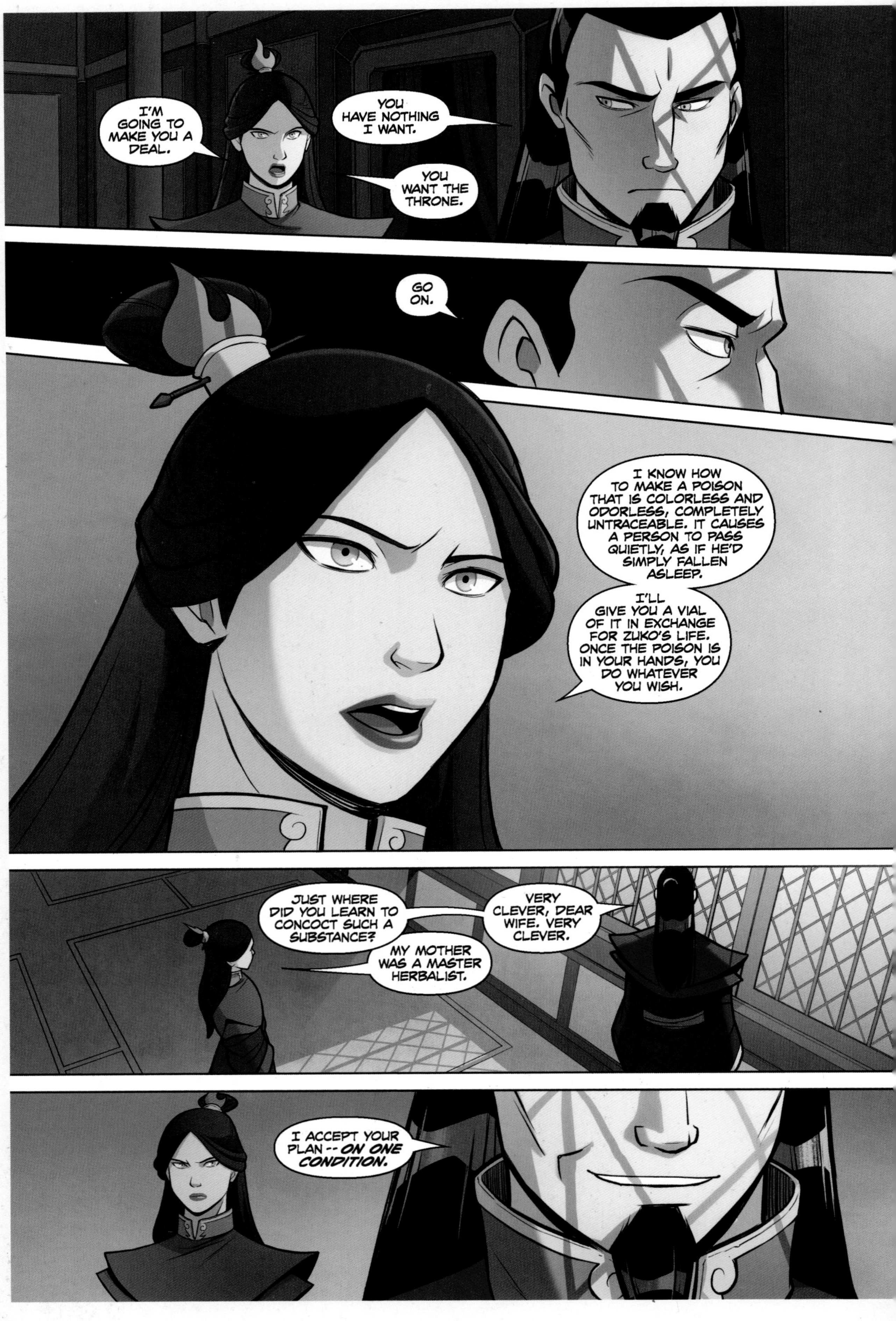
I'M GOING TO MAKE YOU A DEAL.
YOU HAVE NOTHING I WANT.
YOU WANT THE THRONE.
GO ON.
I KNOW HOW TO MAKE A POISON THAT IS COLORLESS AND ODORLESS, COMPLETELY UNTRACEABLE. IT CAUSES A PERSON TO PASS QUIETLY, AS IF HE'D SIMPLY FALLEN ASLEEP.
I'LL GIVE YOU A VIAL OF IT IN EXCHANGE FOR ZUKO'S LIFE. ONCE THE POISON IS IN YOUR HANDS, YOU DO WHATEVER YOU WISH.
VERY CLEVER, DEAR WIFE. VERY CLEVER.
JUST WHERE DID YOU LEARN TO CONCOCT SUCH A SUBSTANCE?
MY MOTHER WAS A MASTER HERBALIST.
I ACCEPT YOUR PLAN--ON ONE CONDITION.

G: *The dark deal between Ursa and Ozai is conducted with very little movement, so we concentrated on adding impact with the panel design.*

M: *This flashback is one of my favorites in* The Search, *where moments from "Zuko Alone" bookend a new scene in which we discover what was really said behind closed doors. Gene and I talked a lot about how complicit Ursa was in Azulon's death. We decided that what Ozai told Zuko in "The Eclipse" was essentially the truth—that Ursa did do "treasonous things" that night. But it was Ozai who delivered the poison.*

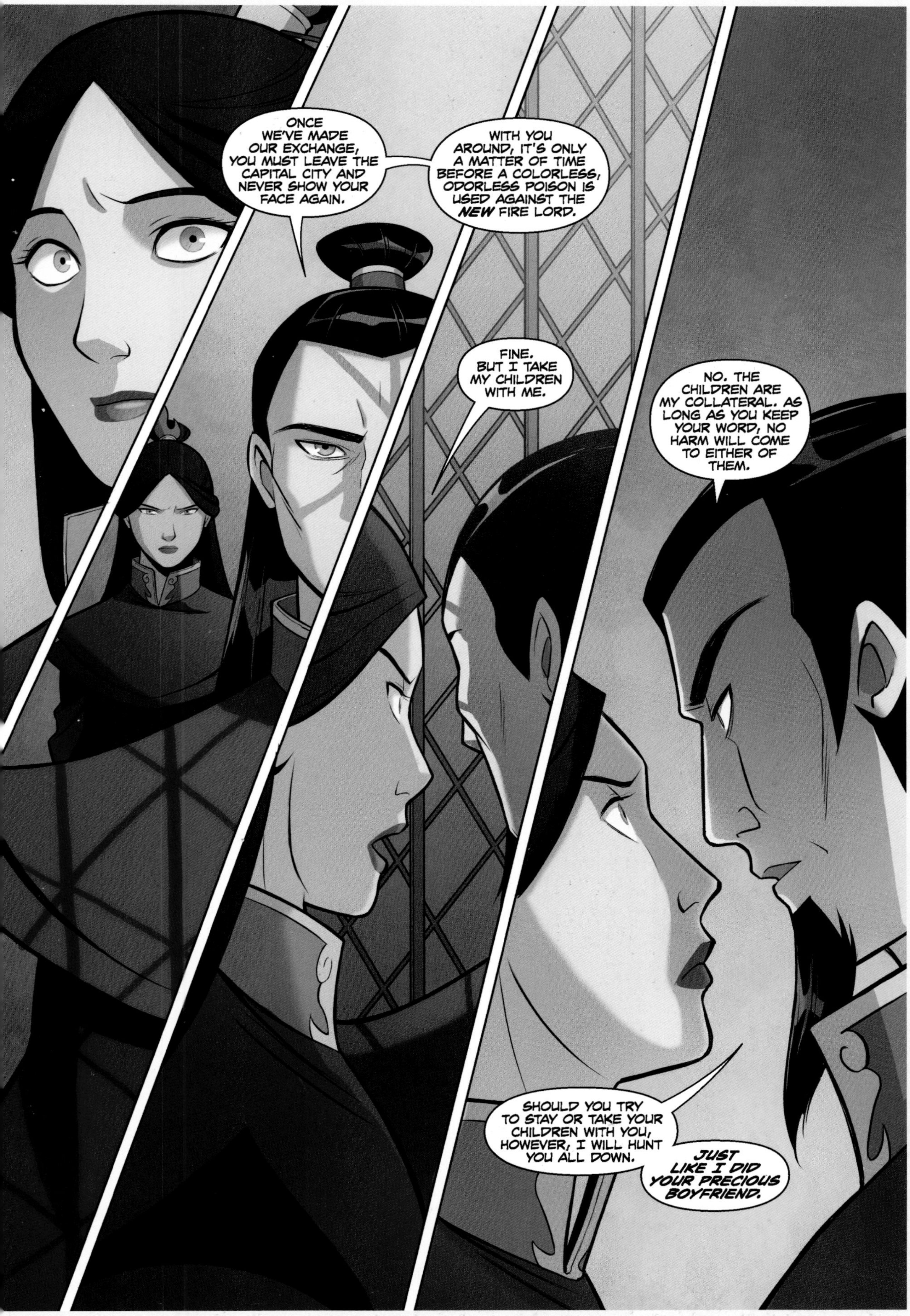
ONCE WE'VE MADE OUR EXCHANGE, YOU MUST LEAVE THE CAPITAL CITY AND NEVER SHOW YOUR FACE AGAIN.
WITH YOU AROUND, IT'S ONLY A MATTER OF TIME BEFORE A COLORLESS, ODORLESS POISON IS USED AGAINST THE *NEW* FIRE LORD.
FINE. BUT I TAKE MY CHILDREN WITH ME.
NO. THE CHILDREN ARE MY COLLATERAL. AS LONG AS YOU KEEP YOUR WORD, NO HARM WILL COME TO EITHER OF THEM.
SHOULD YOU TRY TO STAY OR TAKE YOUR CHILDREN WITH YOU, HOWEVER, I WILL HUNT YOU ALL DOWN.
JUST LIKE I DID YOUR PRECIOUS BOYFRIEND.

M: *Gurihiru's use of panel layout to heighten the emotion of a scene always amazes me, especially here. This layout is visually arresting, and the diagonal panels remind me of shards of glass—perfect for this emotionally charged moment.*

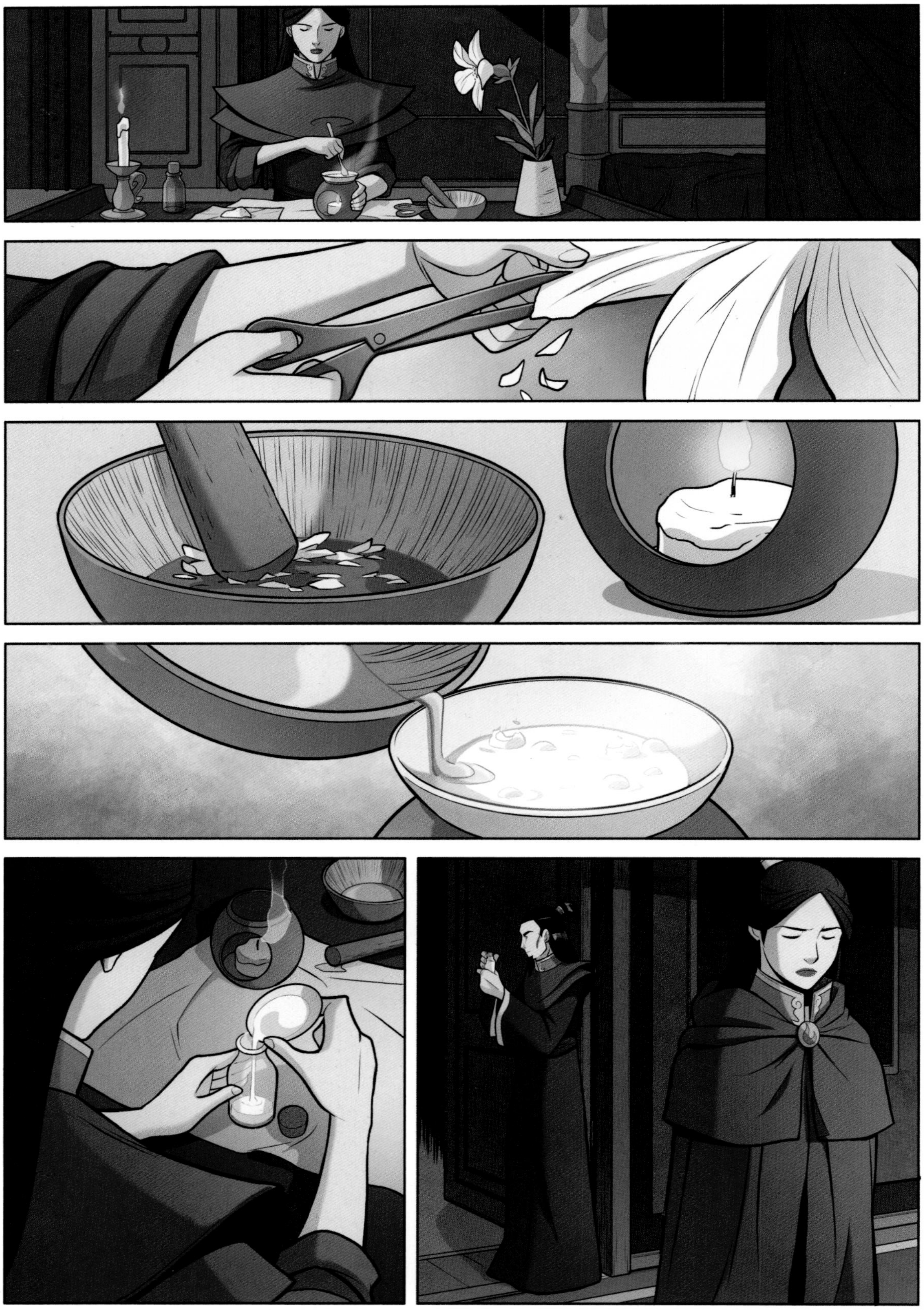

G: *Here, Ursa makes the poison from the same kind of flowers Azulon admired in Ursa's greenhouse in part 1.*

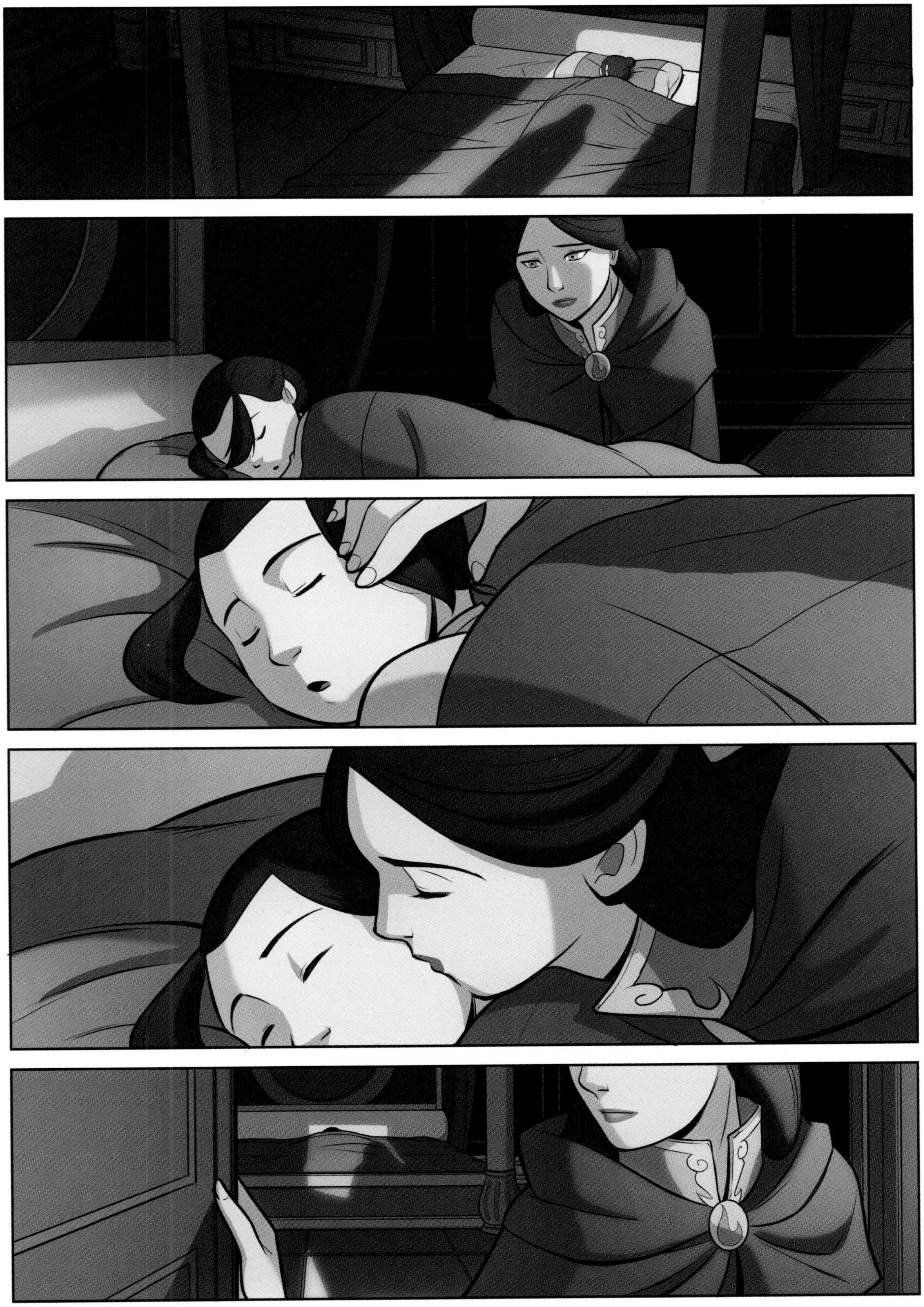

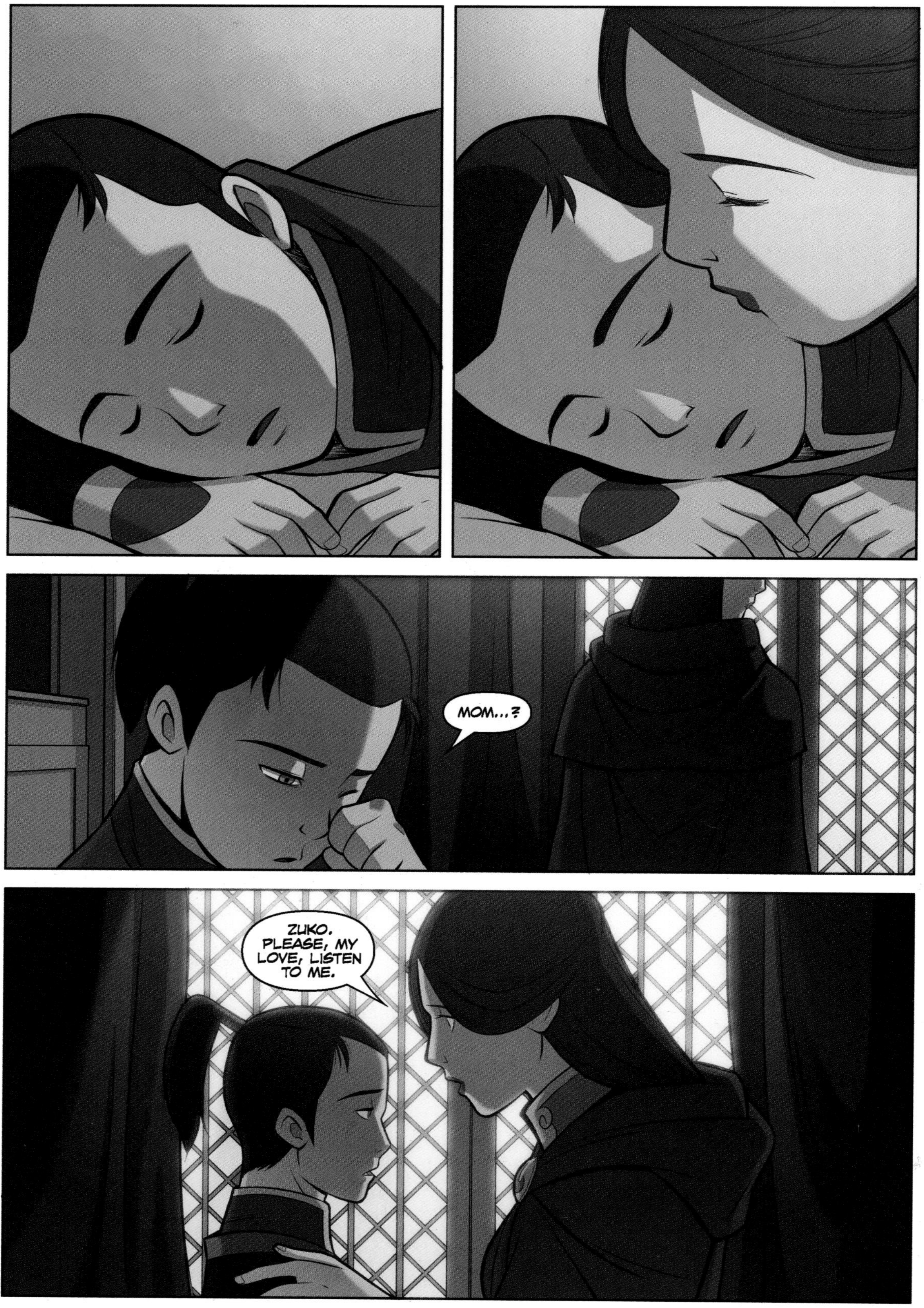
MOM...?
ZUKO. PLEASE, MY LOVE, LISTEN TO ME.

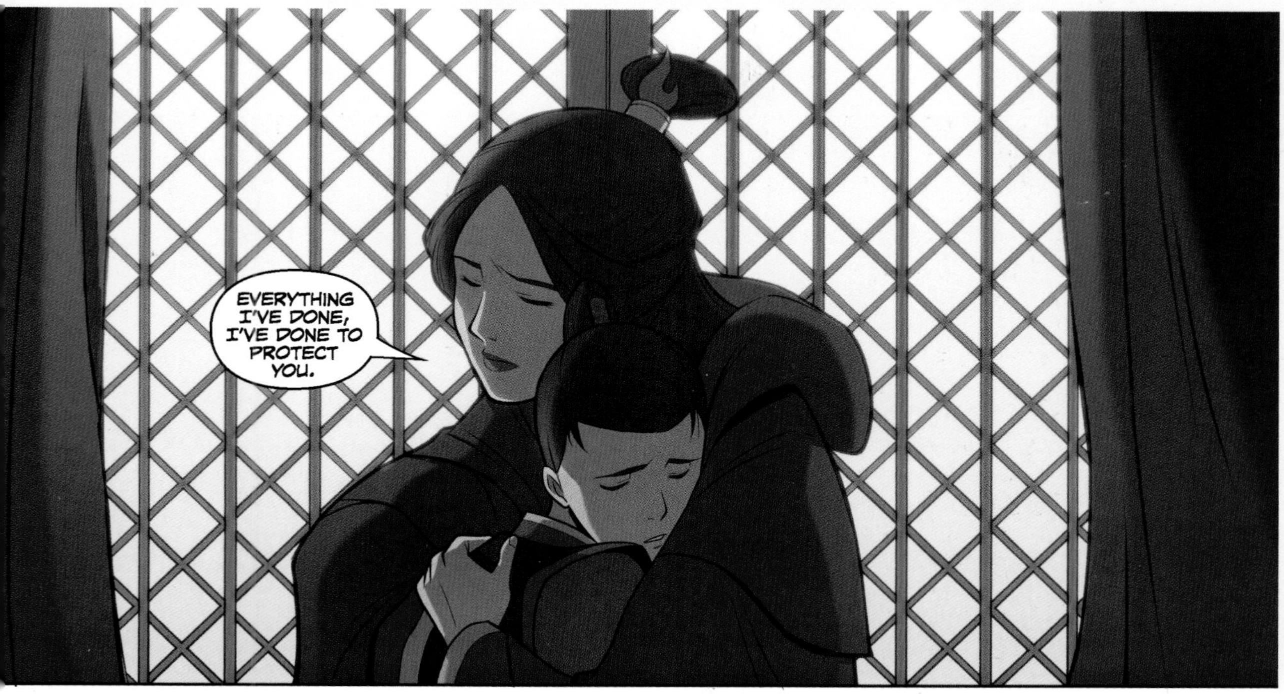
EVERYTHING I'VE DONE, I'VE DONE TO PROTECT YOU.

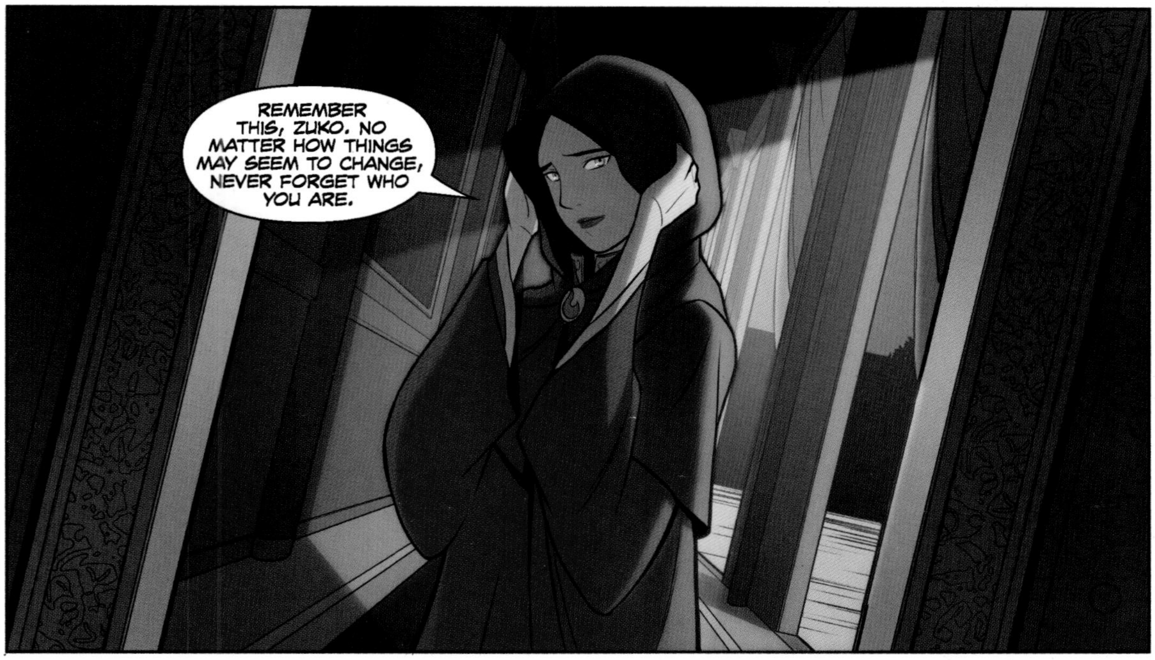
REMEMBER THIS, ZUKO. NO MATTER HOW THINGS MAY SEEM TO CHANGE, NEVER FORGET WHO YOU ARE.

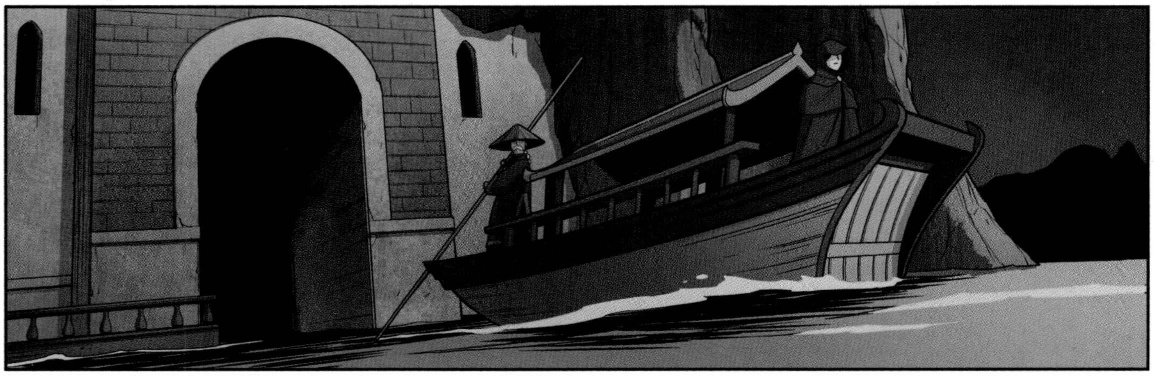

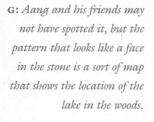

G: *Aang and his friends may not have spotted it, but the pattern that looks like a face in the stone is a sort of map that shows the location of the lake in the woods.*

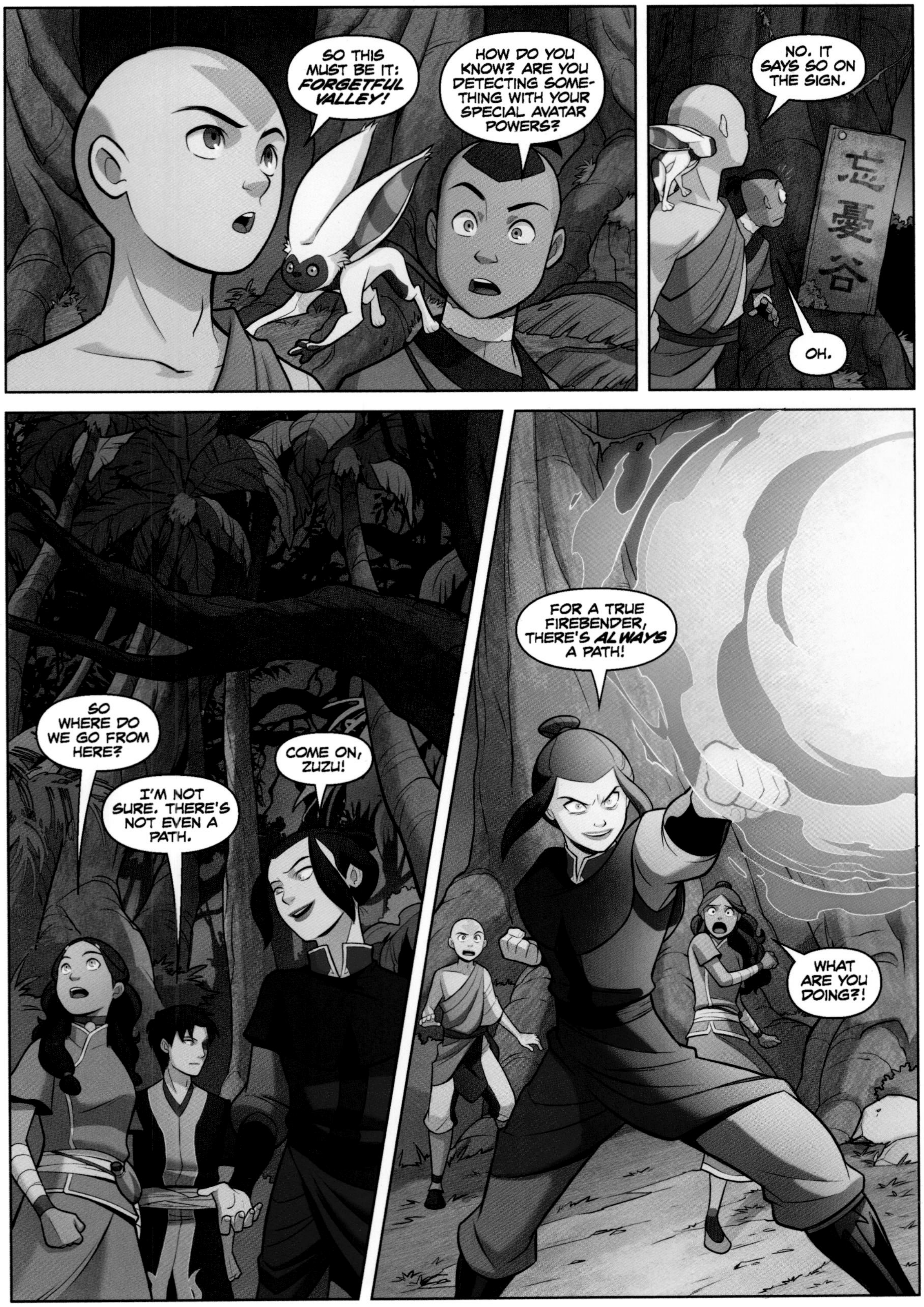
SO THIS MUST BE IT: FORGETFUL VALLEY!
HOW DO YOU KNOW? ARE YOU DETECTING SOMETHING WITH YOUR SPECIAL AVATAR POWERS?
NO. IT SAYS SO ON THE SIGN.
忘憂谷
OH.
SO WHERE DO WE GO FROM HERE?
I'M NOT SURE. THERE'S NOT EVEN A PATH.
COME ON, ZUZU!
FOR A TRUE FIREBENDER, THERE'S ALWAYS A PATH!
WHAT ARE YOU DOING?!

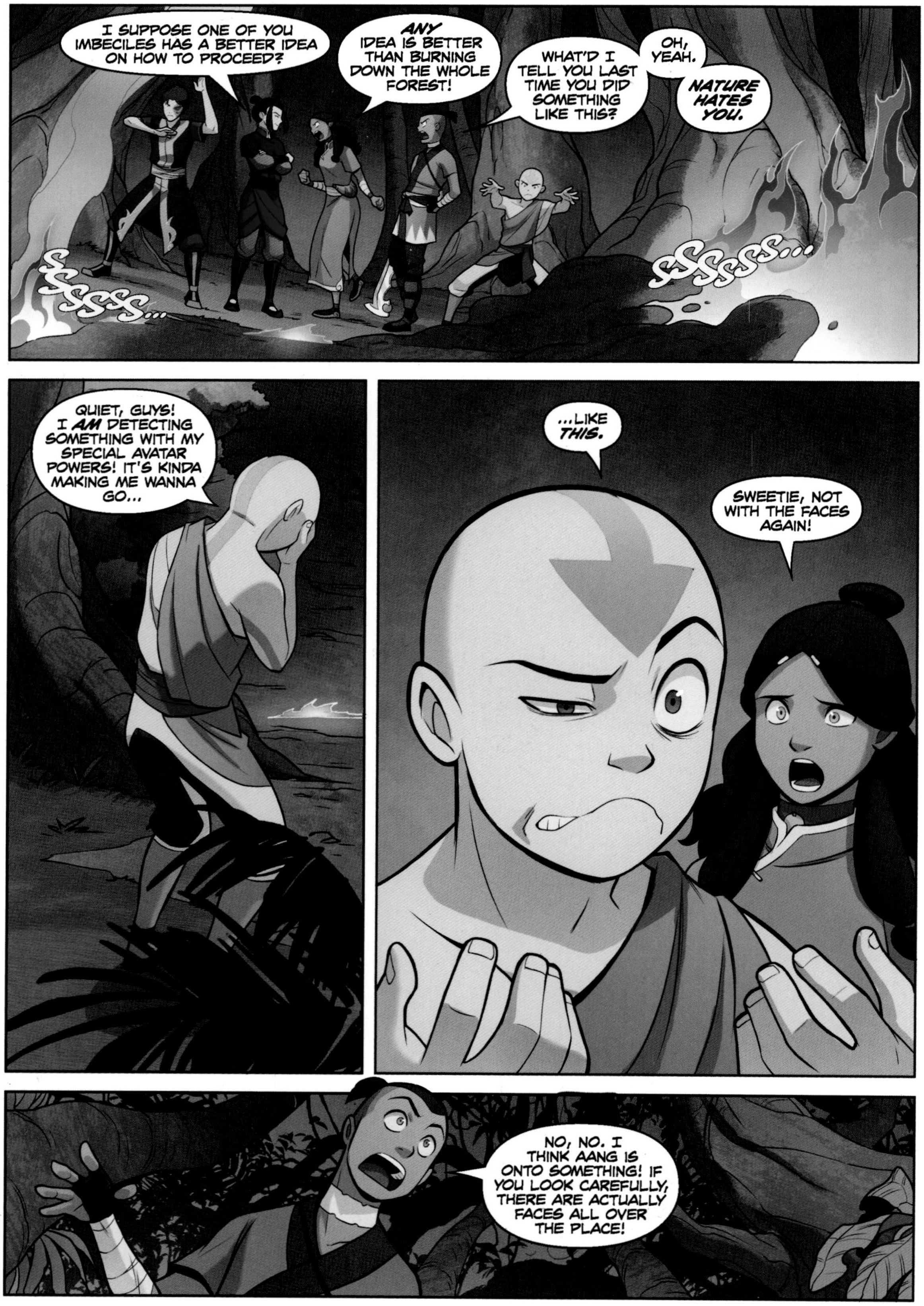
I SUPPOSE ONE OF YOU IMBECILES HAS A BETTER IDEA ON HOW TO PROCEED?
ANY IDEA IS BETTER THAN BURNING DOWN THE WHOLE FOREST!
WHAT'D I TELL YOU LAST TIME YOU DID SOMETHING LIKE THIS?
OH, YEAH.
NATURE HATES YOU.
SSSSSS...
SSSSSS...
QUIET, GUYS! I AM DETECTING SOMETHING WITH MY SPECIAL AVATAR POWERS! IT'S KINDA MAKING ME WANNA GO...
...LIKE THIS.
SWEETIE, NOT WITH THE FACES AGAIN!
NO, NO. I THINK AANG IS ONTO SOMETHING! IF YOU LOOK CAREFULLY, THERE ARE ACTUALLY FACES ALL OVER THE PLACE!

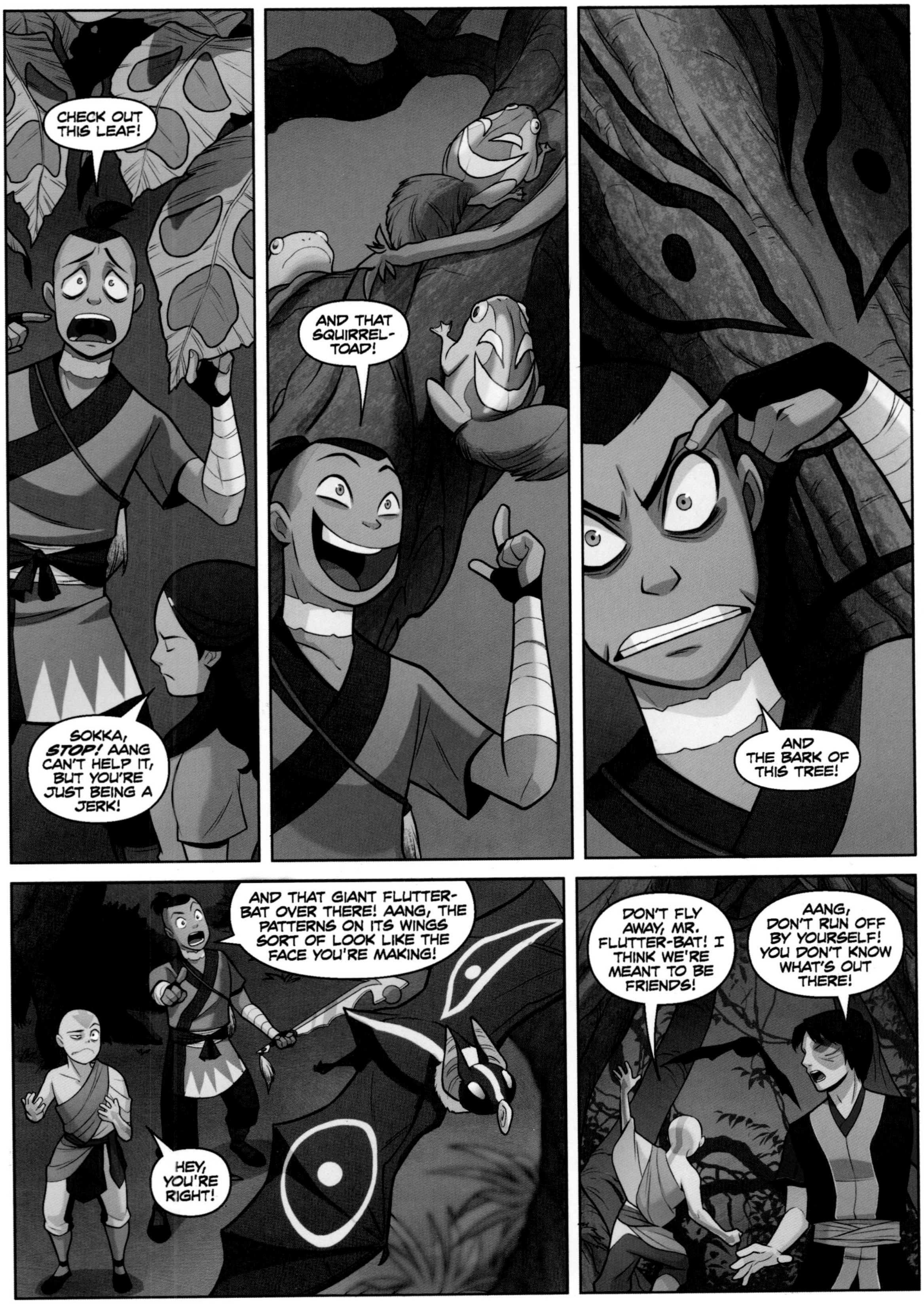
CHECK OUT THIS LEAF!
SOKKA, STOP! AANG CAN'T HELP IT, BUT YOU'RE JUST BEING A JERK!
AND THAT SQUIRREL-TOAD!
AND THE BARK OF THIS TREE!
AND THAT GIANT FLUTTER-BAT OVER THERE! AANG, THE PATTERNS ON ITS WINGS SORT OF LOOK LIKE THE FACE YOU'RE MAKING!
HEY, YOU'RE RIGHT!
DON'T FLY AWAY, MR. FLUTTER-BAT! I THINK WE'RE MEANT TO BE FRIENDS!
AANG, DON'T RUN OFF BY YOURSELF! YOU DON'T KNOW WHAT'S OUT THERE!

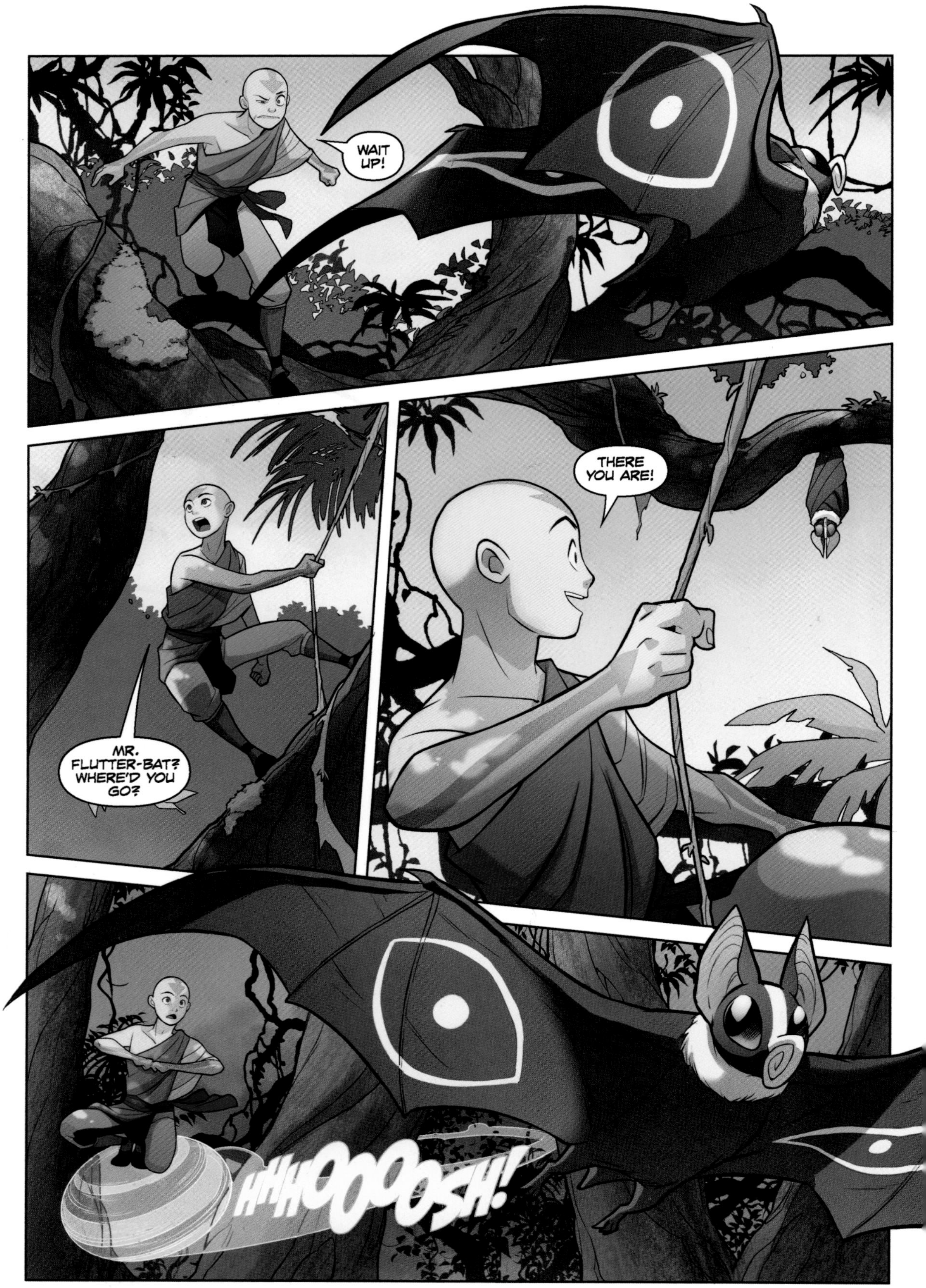
WAIT UP!
MR. FLUTTER-BAT? WHERE'D YOU GO?
THERE YOU ARE!
HHHOOOOOSH!

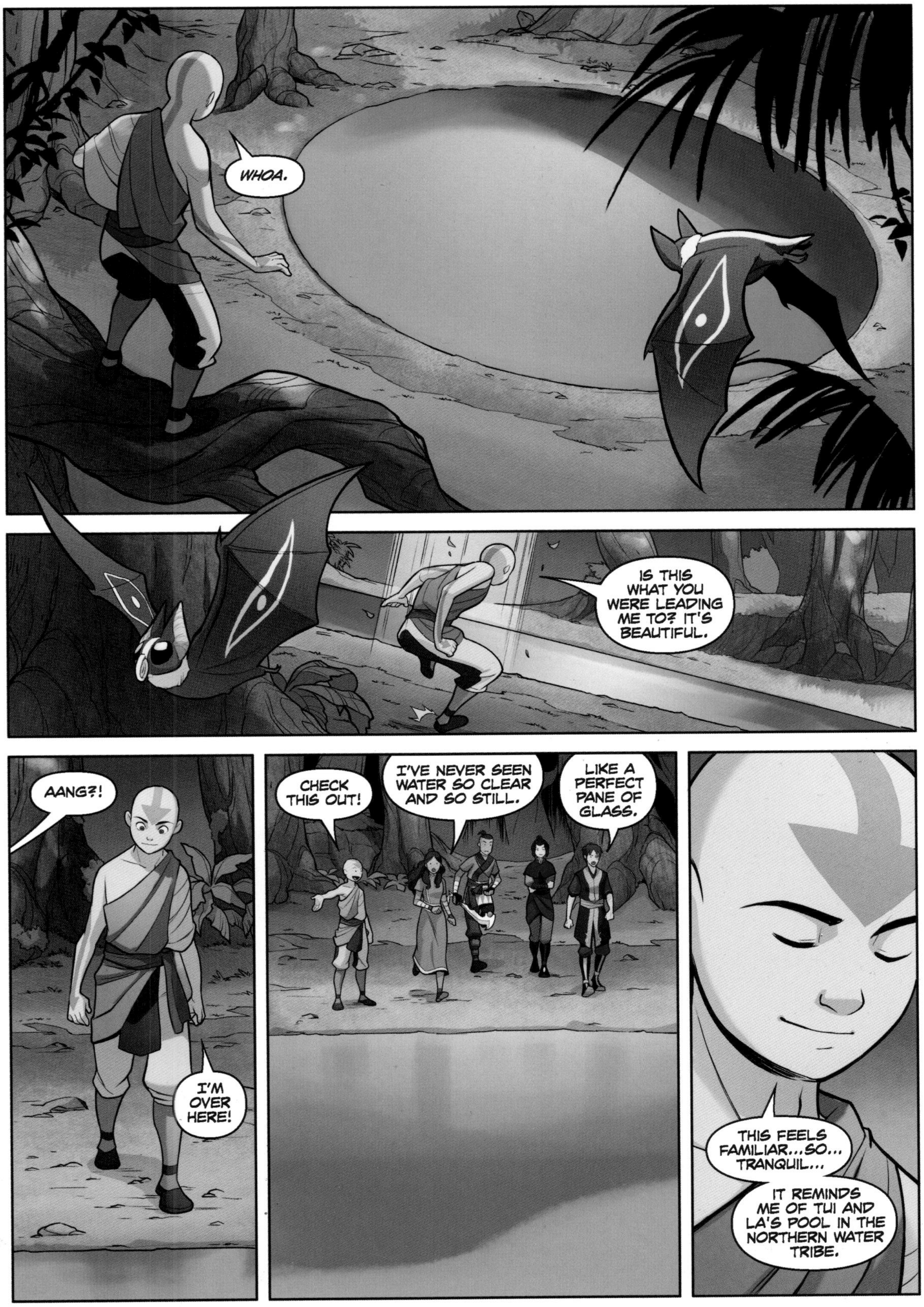
WHOA.
IS THIS WHAT YOU WERE LEADING ME TO? IT'S BEAUTIFUL.
AANG?!
I'M OVER HERE!
CHECK THIS OUT!
I'VE NEVER SEEN WATER SO CLEAR AND SO STILL.
LIKE A PERFECT PANE OF GLASS.
THIS FEELS FAMILIAR...SO... TRANQUIL...
IT REMINDS ME OF TUI AND LA'S POOL IN THE NORTHERN WATER TRIBE.

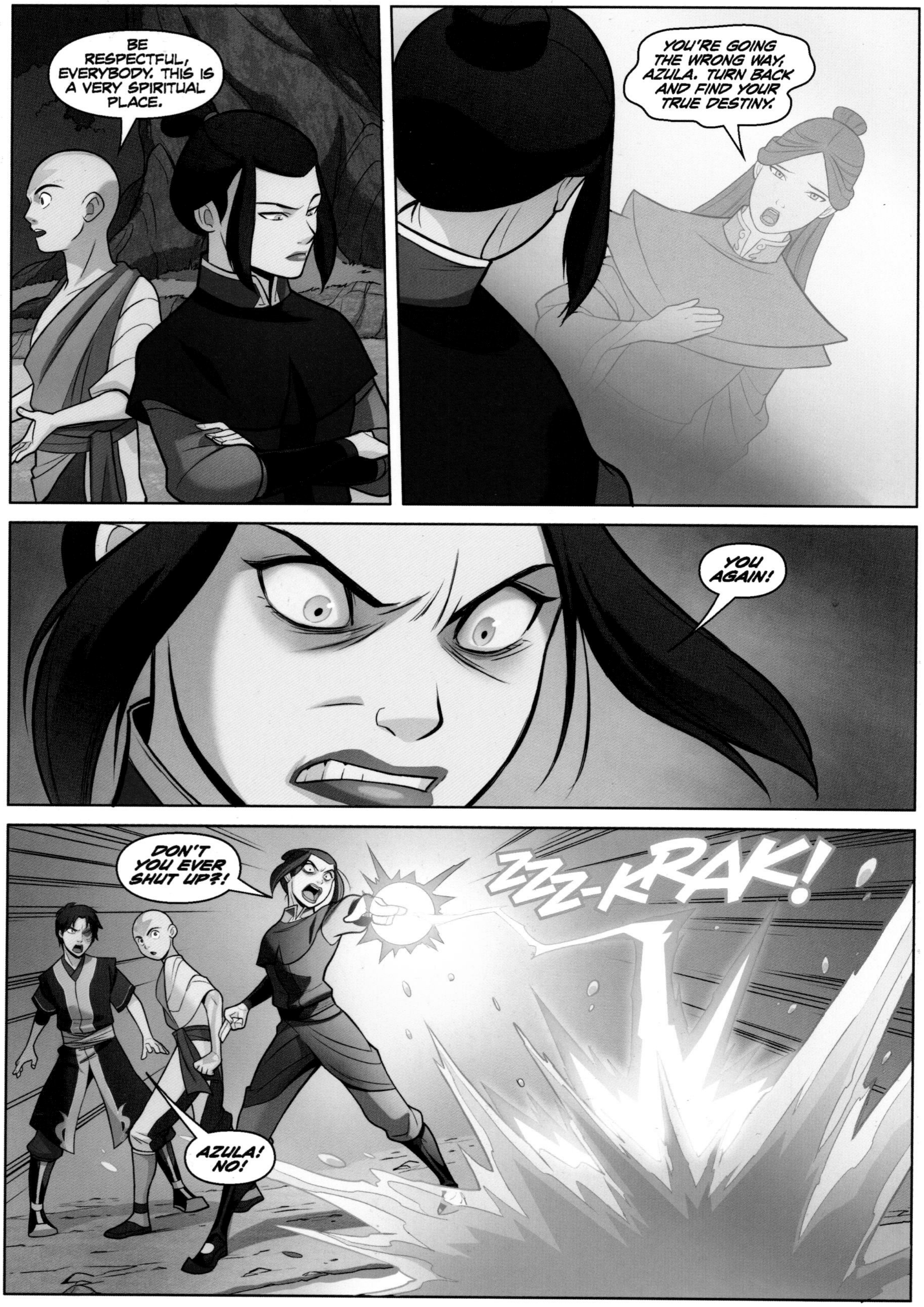
BE RESPECTFUL, EVERYBODY. THIS IS A VERY SPIRITUAL PLACE.
YOU'RE GOING THE WRONG WAY, AZULA. TURN BACK AND FIND YOUR TRUE DESTINY.
YOU AGAIN!
DON'T YOU EVER SHUT UP?!
ZZZ-KRAK!
AZULA! NO!

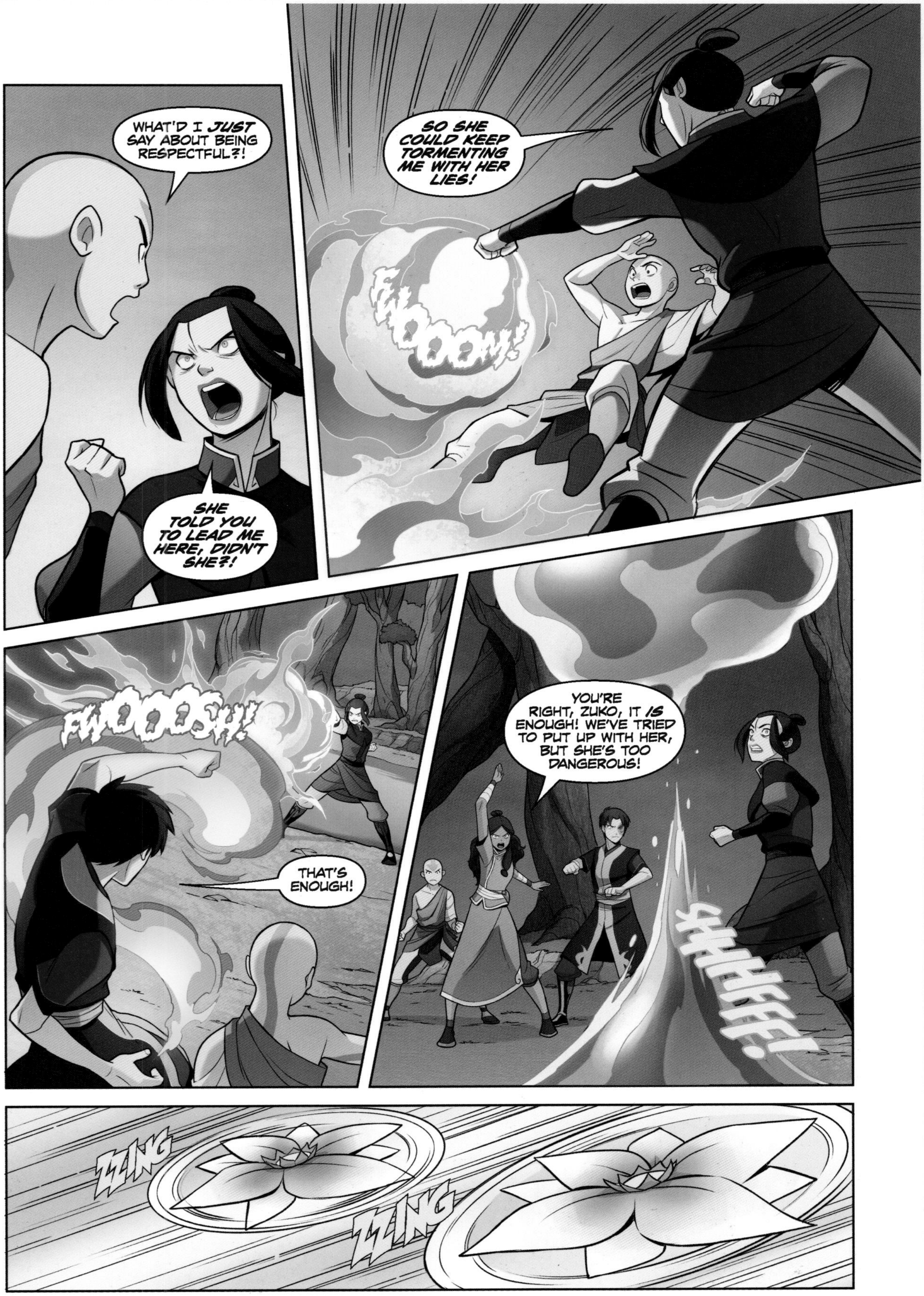
WHAT'D I JUST SAY ABOUT BEING RESPECTFUL?!
SHE TOLD YOU TO LEAD ME HERE, DIDN'T SHE?!
SO SHE COULD KEEP TORMENTING ME WITH HER LIES!
FWOOOM!
FWOOOSH!
THAT'S ENOUGH!
YOU'RE RIGHT, ZUKO, IT IS ENOUGH! WE'VE TRIED TO PUT UP WITH HER, BUT SHE'S TOO DANGEROUS!
SHHHFFF!
ZZING
ZZING

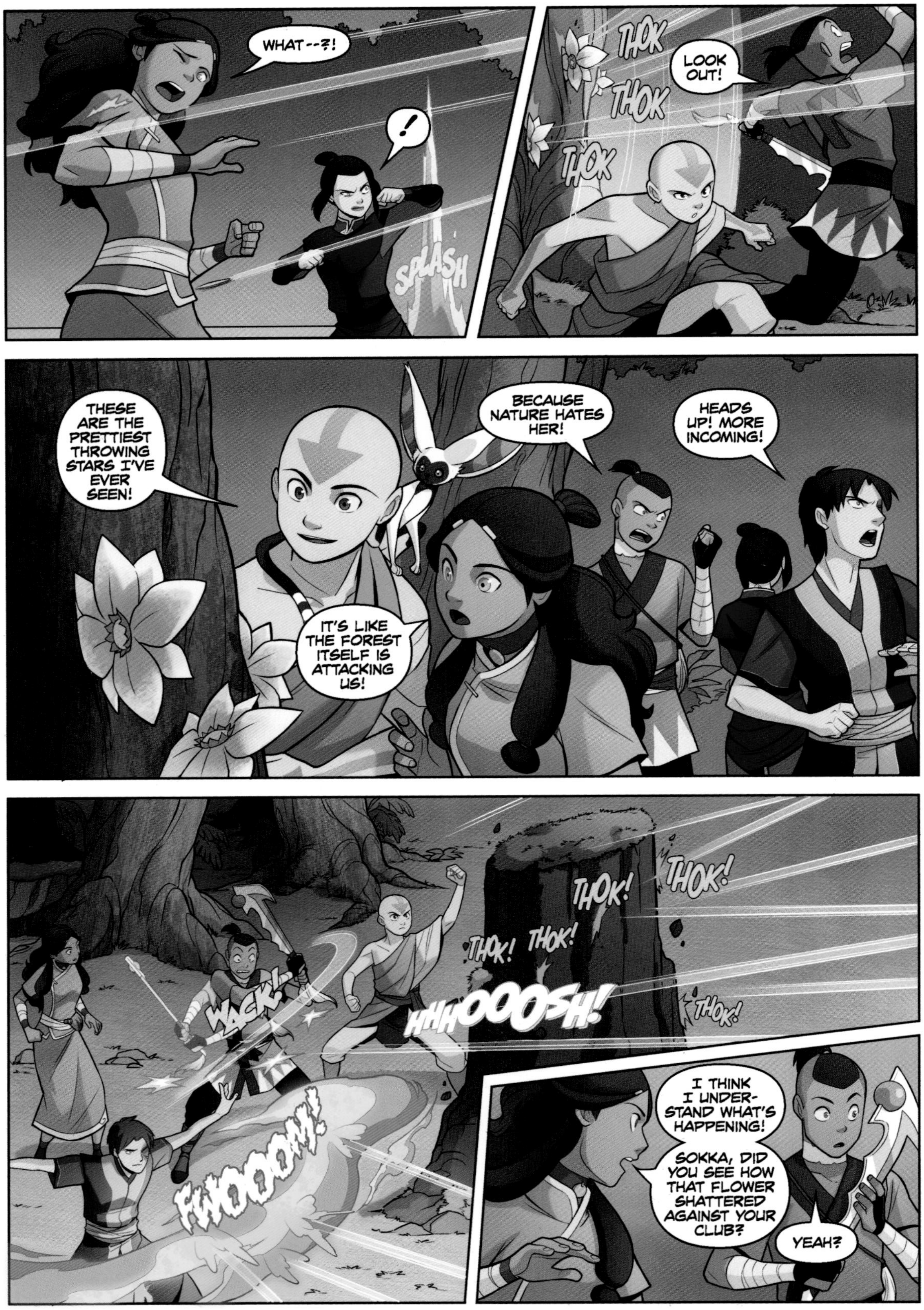
WHAT--?!
!
SPLASH
THOK
THOK
THOK
LOOK OUT!
THESE ARE THE PRETTIEST THROWING STARS I'VE EVER SEEN!
IT'S LIKE THE FOREST ITSELF IS ATTACKING US!
BECAUSE NATURE HATES HER!
HEADS UP! MORE INCOMING!
THOK!
THOK!
THOK!
THOK!
THOK!
WACK!
HHHOOOOSH!
FWOOOM!
I THINK I UNDERSTAND WHAT'S HAPPENING!
SOKKA, DID YOU SEE HOW THAT FLOWER SHATTERED AGAINST YOUR CLUB?
YEAH?

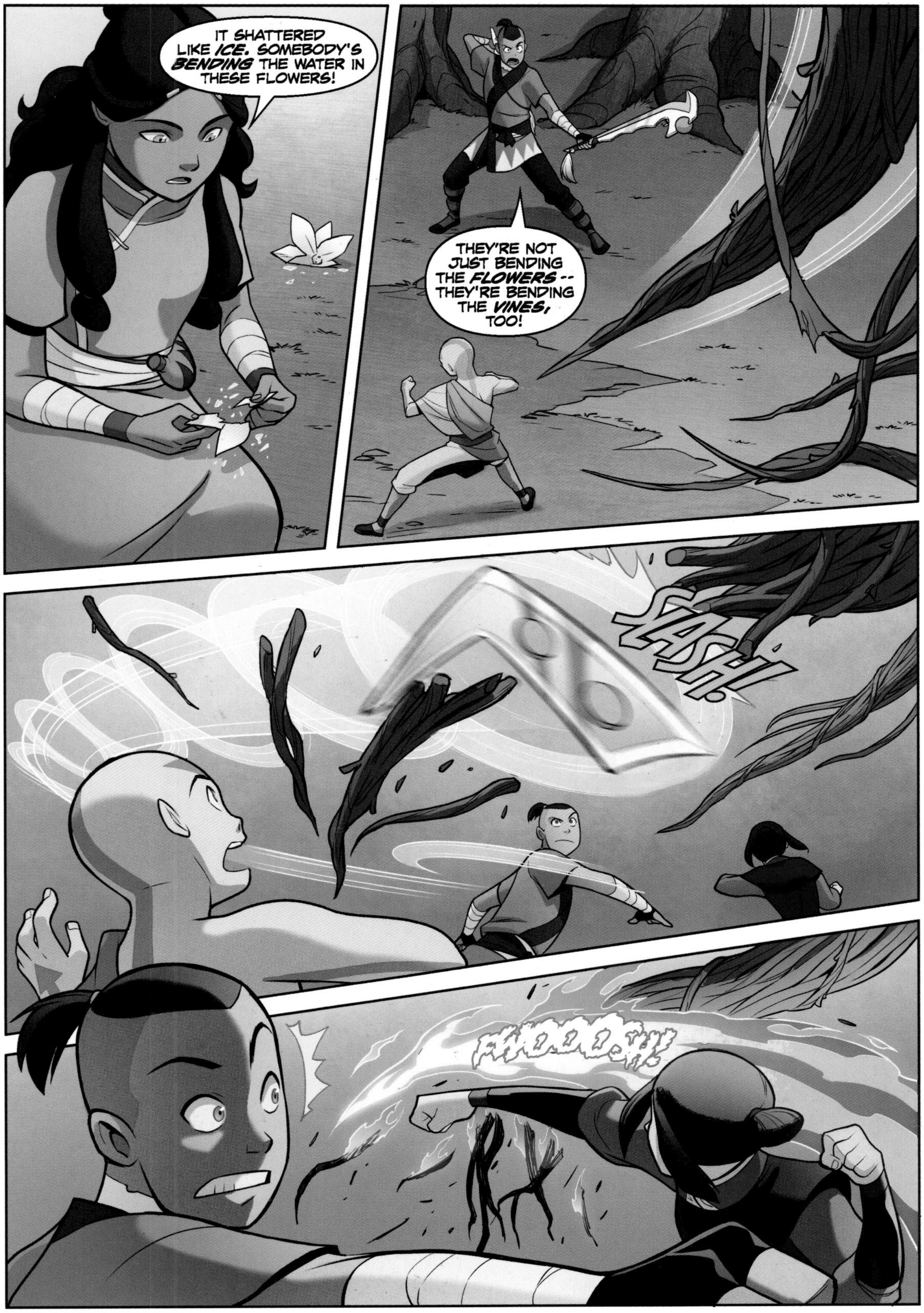
IT SHATTERED LIKE ICE. SOMEBODY'S BENDING THE WATER IN THESE FLOWERS!
THEY'RE NOT JUST BENDING THE FLOWERS -- THEY'RE BENDING THE VINES, TOO!
SHASH!
FWOOOSH!

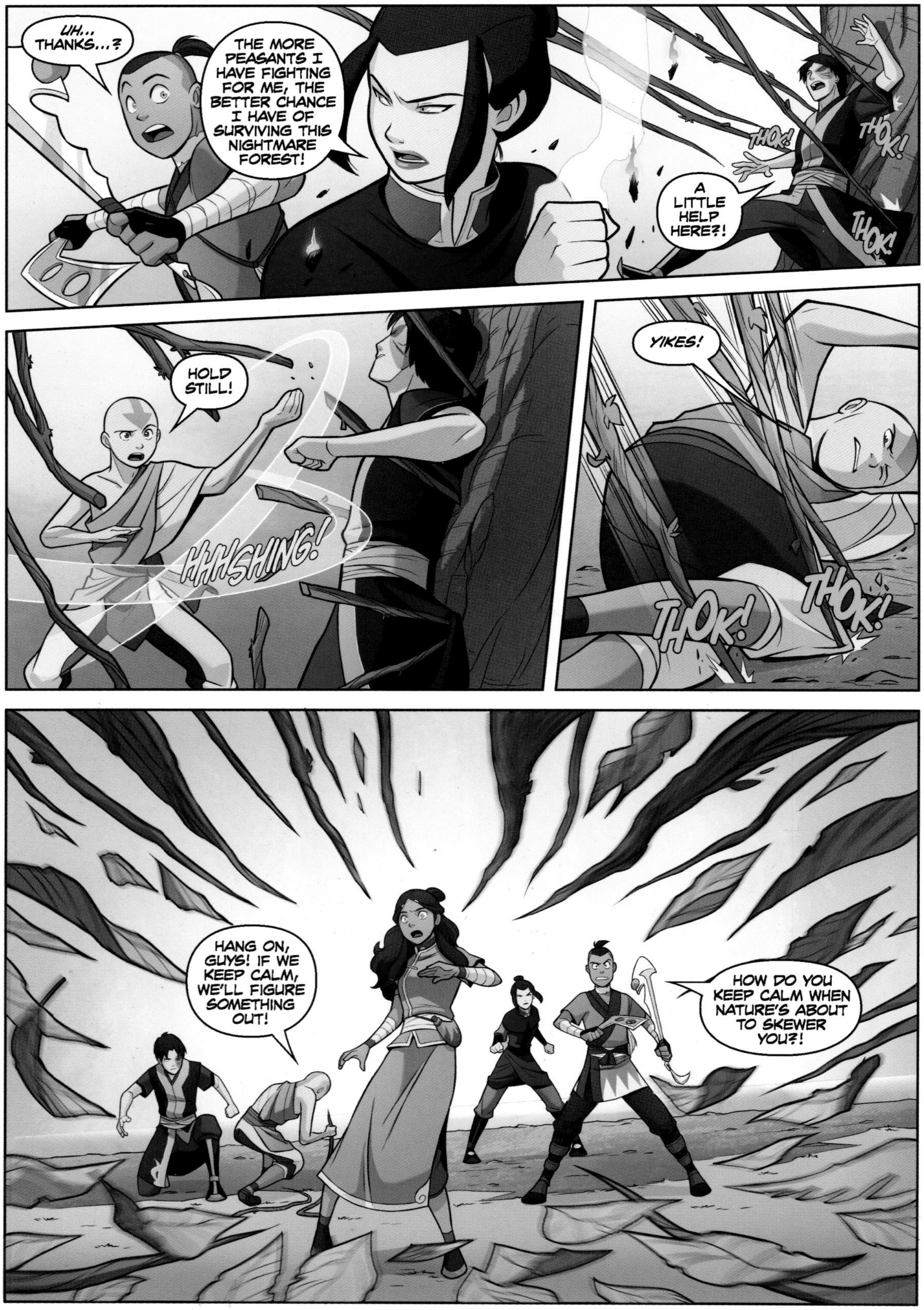
UH... THANKS...?
THE MORE PEASANTS I HAVE FIGHTING FOR ME, THE BETTER CHANCE I HAVE OF SURVIVING THIS NIGHTMARE FOREST!
THOK!
THOK!
A LITTLE HELP HERE?!
THOK!
HOLD STILL!
HHHSHING!
YIKES!
THOK!
THOK!
HANG ON, GUYS! IF WE KEEP CALM, WE'LL FIGURE SOMETHING OUT!
HOW DO YOU KEEP CALM WHEN NATURE'S ABOUT TO SKEWER YOU?!

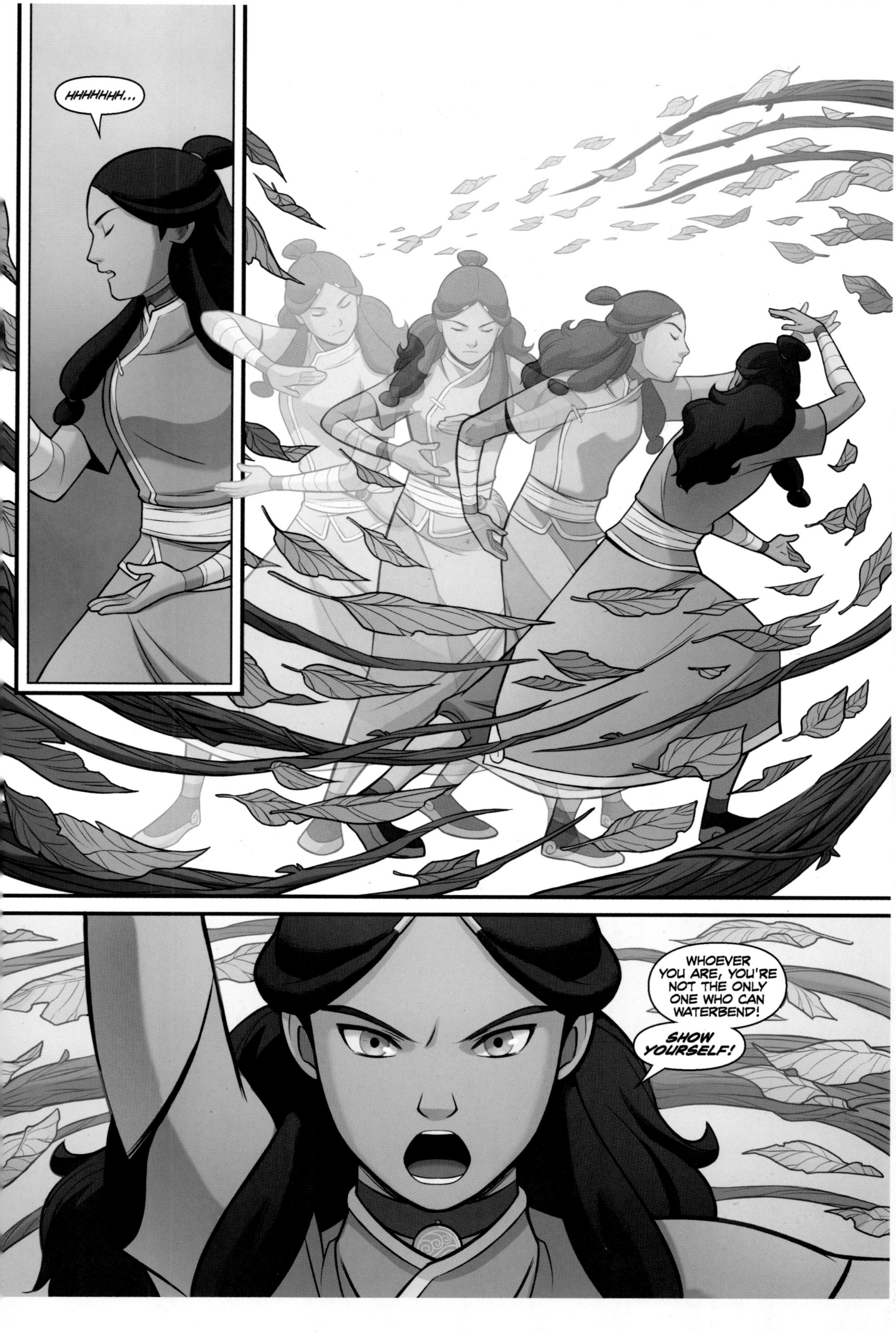
HHHHHHH...
WHOEVER YOU ARE, YOU'RE NOT THE ONLY ONE WHO CAN WATERBEND!
SHOW YOURSELF!

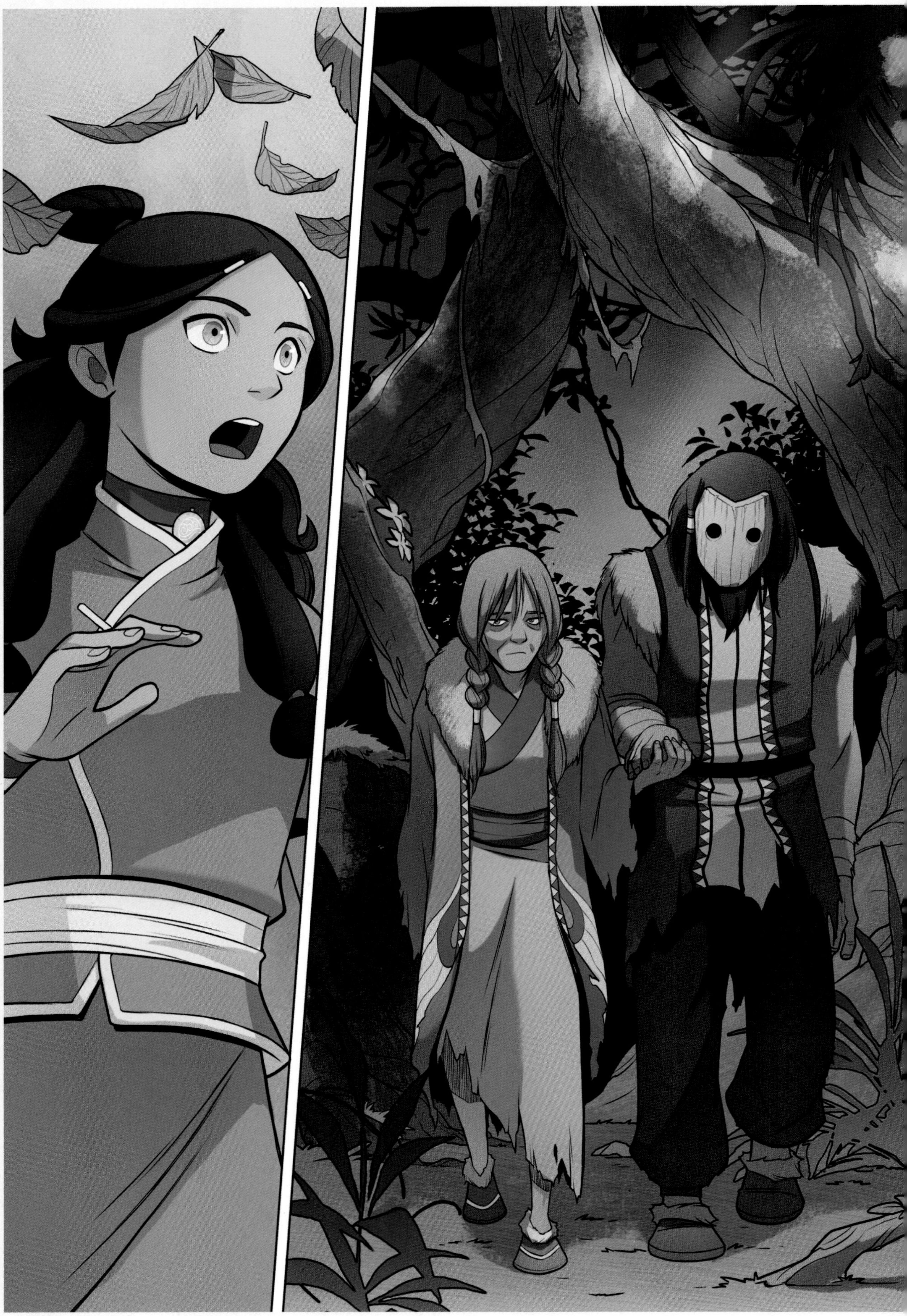

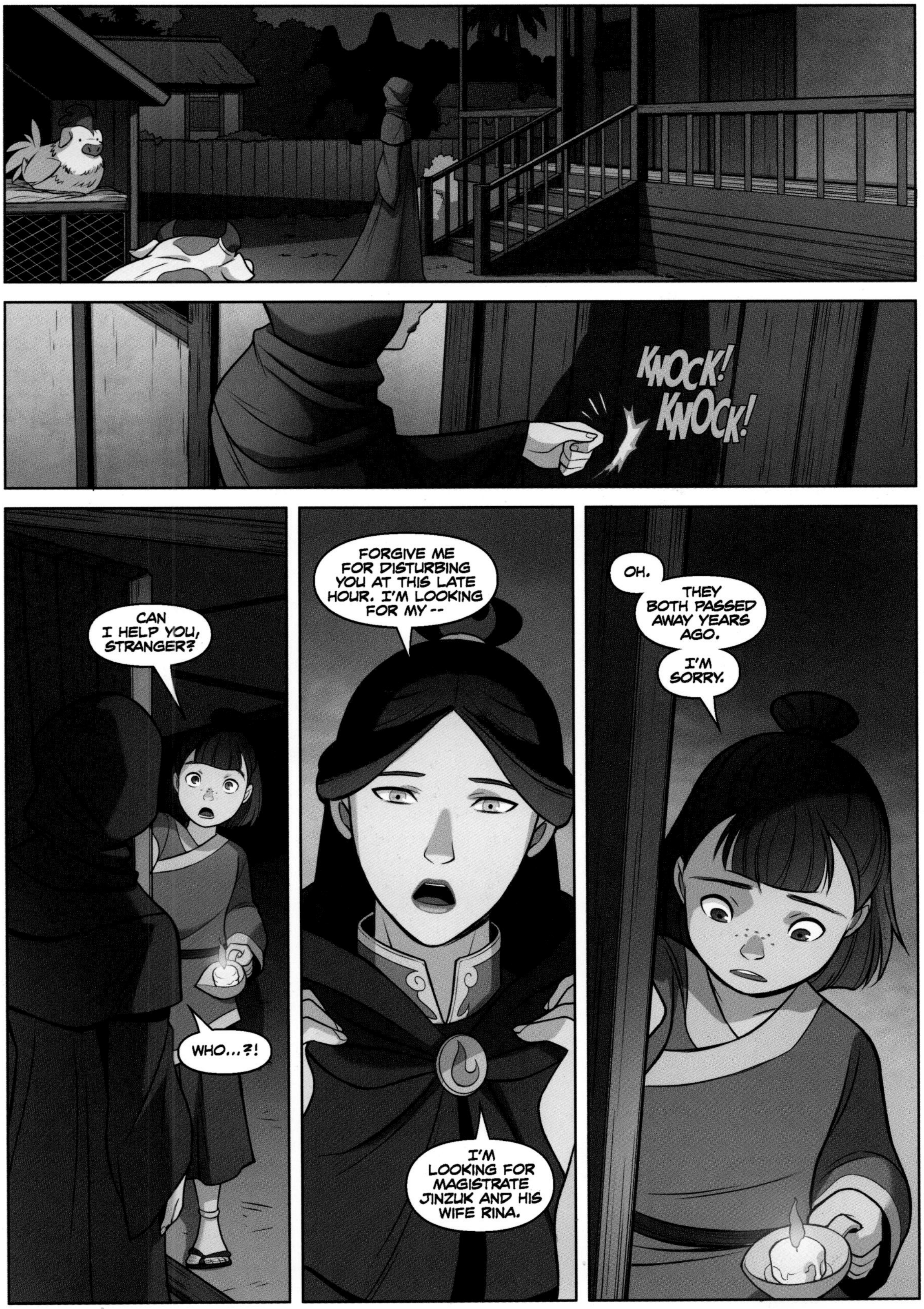
KNOCK! KNOCK!
CAN I HELP YOU, STRANGER?
WHO...?!
FORGIVE ME FOR DISTURBING YOU AT THIS LATE HOUR. I'M LOOKING FOR MY --
I'M LOOKING FOR MAGISTRATE JINZUK AND HIS WIFE RINA.
OH.
THEY BOTH PASSED AWAY YEARS AGO.
I'M SORRY.

IF YOU'RE LOOKING FOR A ROLE IN THIS YEAR'S PRODUCTION, I HAVE BAD NEWS FOR YOU. TRYOUTS ENDED WEEKS AGO.

OH, NO... I DIDN'T KNOW WHERE ELSE--

I'M JUST... VISITING *OLD MEMORIES*.

OH, I'M SORRY! I DIDN'T REALIZE--

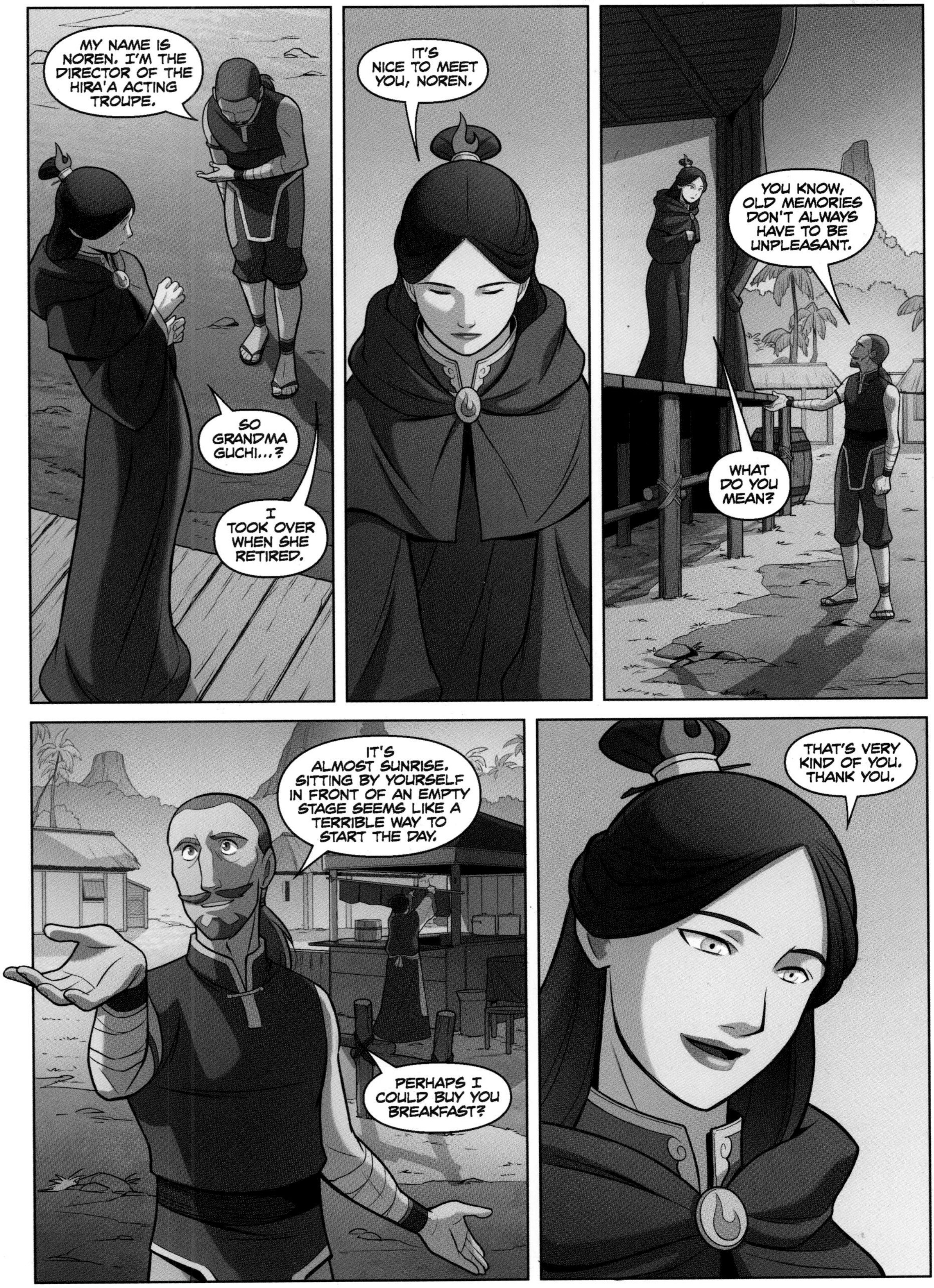
MY NAME IS NOREN. I'M THE DIRECTOR OF THE HIRA'A ACTING TROUPE.
SO GRANDMA GUCHI...?
I TOOK OVER WHEN SHE RETIRED.
IT'S NICE TO MEET YOU, NOREN.
YOU KNOW, OLD MEMORIES DON'T ALWAYS HAVE TO BE UNPLEASANT.
WHAT DO YOU MEAN?
IT'S ALMOST SUNRISE. SITTING BY YOURSELF IN FRONT OF AN EMPTY STAGE SEEMS LIKE A TERRIBLE WAY TO START THE DAY.
PERHAPS I COULD BUY YOU BREAKFAST?
THAT'S VERY KIND OF YOU. THANK YOU.

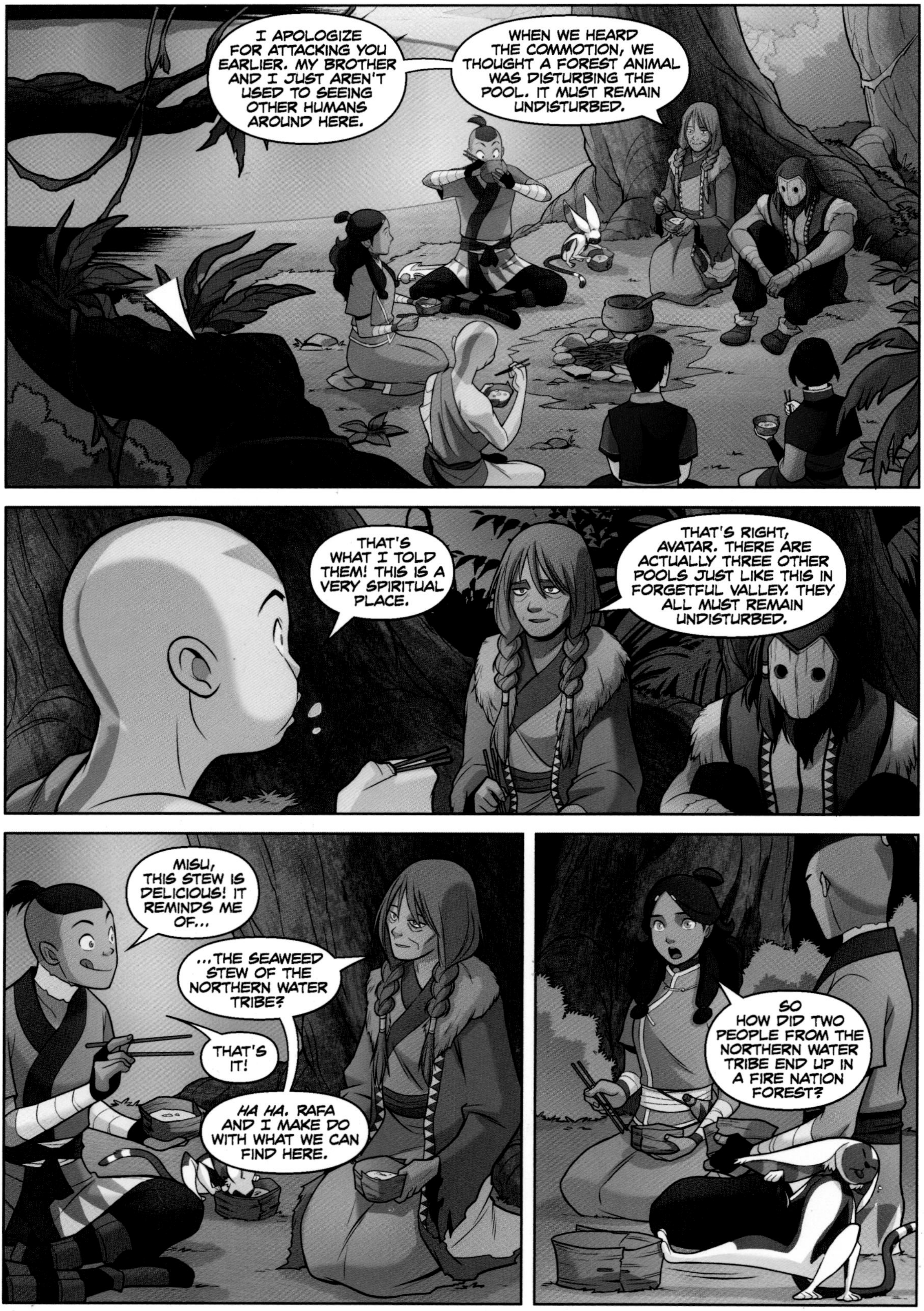
I APOLOGIZE FOR ATTACKING YOU EARLIER. MY BROTHER AND I JUST AREN'T USED TO SEEING OTHER HUMANS AROUND HERE.
WHEN WE HEARD THE COMMOTION, WE THOUGHT A FOREST ANIMAL WAS DISTURBING THE POOL. IT MUST REMAIN UNDISTURBED.
THAT'S WHAT I TOLD THEM! THIS IS A VERY SPIRITUAL PLACE.
THAT'S RIGHT, AVATAR. THERE ARE ACTUALLY THREE OTHER POOLS JUST LIKE THIS IN FORGETFUL VALLEY. THEY ALL MUST REMAIN UNDISTURBED.
MISU, THIS STEW IS DELICIOUS! IT REMINDS ME OF...
...THE SEAWEED STEW OF THE NORTHERN WATER TRIBE?
THAT'S IT!
HA HA. RAFA AND I MAKE DO WITH WHAT WE CAN FIND HERE.
SO HOW DID TWO PEOPLE FROM THE NORTHERN WATER TRIBE END UP IN A FIRE NATION FOREST?

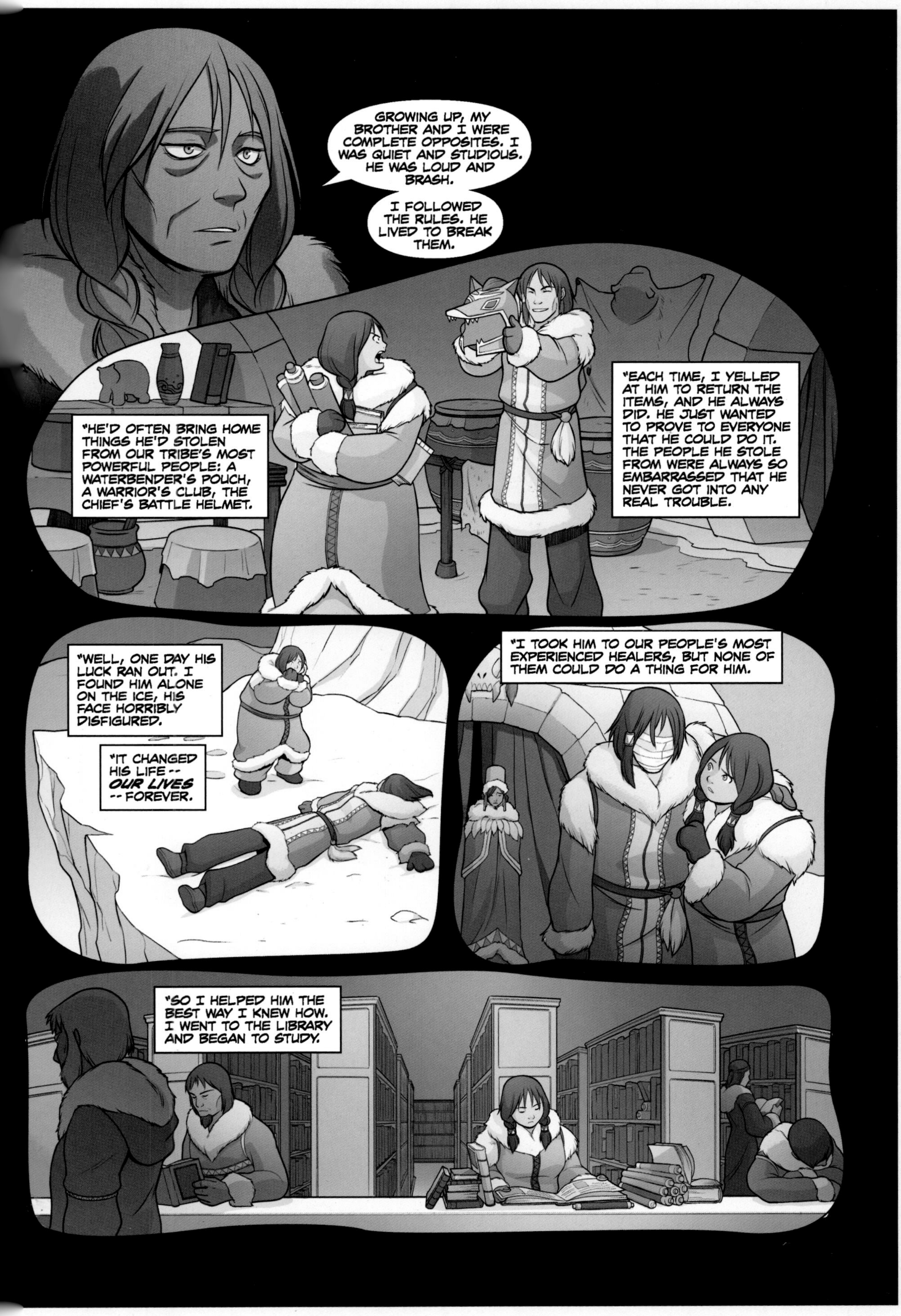
GROWING UP, MY BROTHER AND I WERE COMPLETE OPPOSITES. I WAS QUIET AND STUDIOUS. HE WAS LOUD AND BRASH.
I FOLLOWED THE RULES. HE LIVED TO BREAK THEM.
"HE'D OFTEN BRING HOME THINGS HE'D STOLEN FROM OUR TRIBE'S MOST POWERFUL PEOPLE: A WATERBENDER'S POUCH, A WARRIOR'S CLUB, THE CHIEF'S BATTLE HELMET.
"EACH TIME, I YELLED AT HIM TO RETURN THE ITEMS, AND HE ALWAYS DID. HE JUST WANTED TO PROVE TO EVERYONE THAT HE COULD DO IT. THE PEOPLE HE STOLE FROM WERE ALWAYS SO EMBARRASSED THAT HE NEVER GOT INTO ANY REAL TROUBLE.
"WELL, ONE DAY HIS LUCK RAN OUT. I FOUND HIM ALONE ON THE ICE, HIS FACE HORRIBLY DISFIGURED.
"IT CHANGED HIS LIFE-- *OUR LIVES* --FOREVER.
"I TOOK HIM TO OUR PEOPLE'S MOST EXPERIENCED HEALERS, BUT NONE OF THEM COULD DO A THING FOR HIM.
"SO I HELPED HIM THE BEST WAY I KNEW HOW. I WENT TO THE LIBRARY AND BEGAN TO STUDY.

GLY: *Rafa and Misu illustrate the extremes that family bonds can ask of us. As I was writing them, I thought about Sokka and Katara's relationship, only with more years and more tragedy.*

"IN AN ANCIENT FIRE NATION SCROLL, I LEARNED ABOUT A POWERFUL SPIRIT WHO WOULD VISIT A CERTAIN FIRE NATION FOREST FROM TIME TO TIME.
"THIS SPIRIT HAD THE POWER TO GIVE PEOPLE NEW FACES -- THE POWER TO HEAL RAFA."
I MADE IT MY LIFE'S MISSION TO BRING MY BROTHER HERE. I KNEW IT WOULD BE DANGEROUS FOR TWO WATER TRIBE FOLK TO SNEAK INTO THE FIRE NATION, SO I SPENT YEARS FIGURING OUT HOW TO USE WATERBENDING TO FIGHT.
I HAD TO LEARN SECRETLY, ON MY OWN, SINCE --
-- IN THE NORTHERN WATER TRIBE, WOMEN WATERBENDERS WERE ONLY ALLOWED TO HEAL. THINGS ARE DIFFERENT NOW.
AFTER MANY FAILED ATTEMPTS, WE FINALLY MADE IT TO FORGETFUL VALLEY. WE'VE LIVED HERE EVER SINCE, HOPING TO ENCOUNTER THE SPIRIT.
HOW COME RAFA HASN'T EATEN ANYTHING?

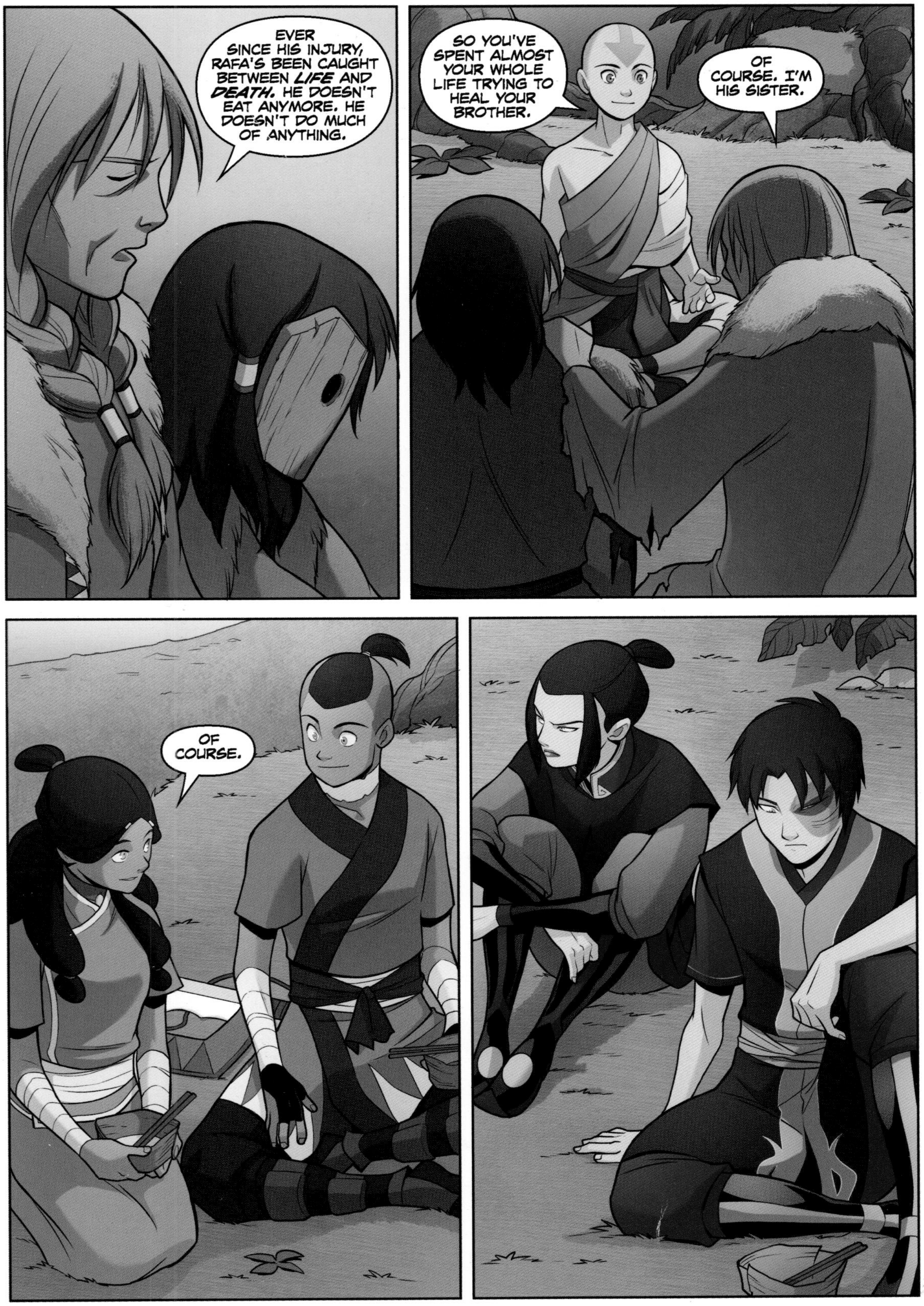
EVER SINCE HIS INJURY, RAFA'S BEEN CAUGHT BETWEEN *LIFE* AND *DEATH*. HE DOESN'T EAT ANYMORE. HE DOESN'T DO MUCH OF ANYTHING.
SO YOU'VE SPENT ALMOST YOUR WHOLE LIFE TRYING TO HEAL YOUR BROTHER.
OF COURSE. I'M HIS SISTER.
OF COURSE.

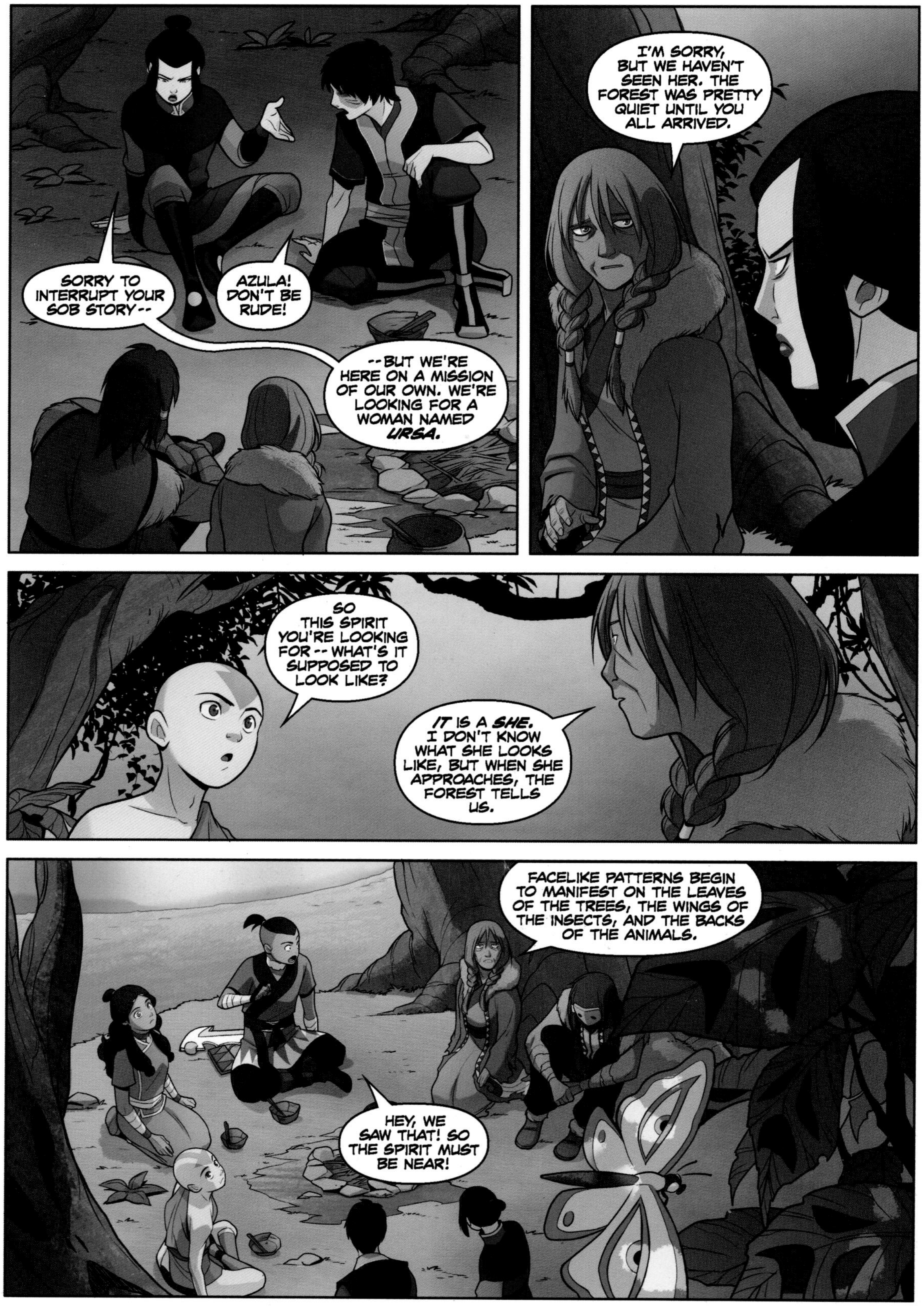
SORRY TO INTERRUPT YOUR SOB STORY--
AZULA! DON'T BE RUDE!
--BUT WE'RE HERE ON A MISSION OF OUR OWN. WE'RE LOOKING FOR A WOMAN NAMED *URSA.*
I'M SORRY, BUT WE HAVEN'T SEEN HER. THE FOREST WAS PRETTY QUIET UNTIL YOU ALL ARRIVED.
SO THIS SPIRIT YOU'RE LOOKING FOR--WHAT'S IT SUPPOSED TO LOOK LIKE?
IT IS A *SHE.* I DON'T KNOW WHAT SHE LOOKS LIKE, BUT WHEN SHE APPROACHES, THE FOREST TELLS US.
FACELIKE PATTERNS BEGIN TO MANIFEST ON THE LEAVES OF THE TREES, THE WINGS OF THE INSECTS, AND THE BACKS OF THE ANIMALS.
HEY, WE SAW THAT! SO THE SPIRIT MUST BE NEAR!

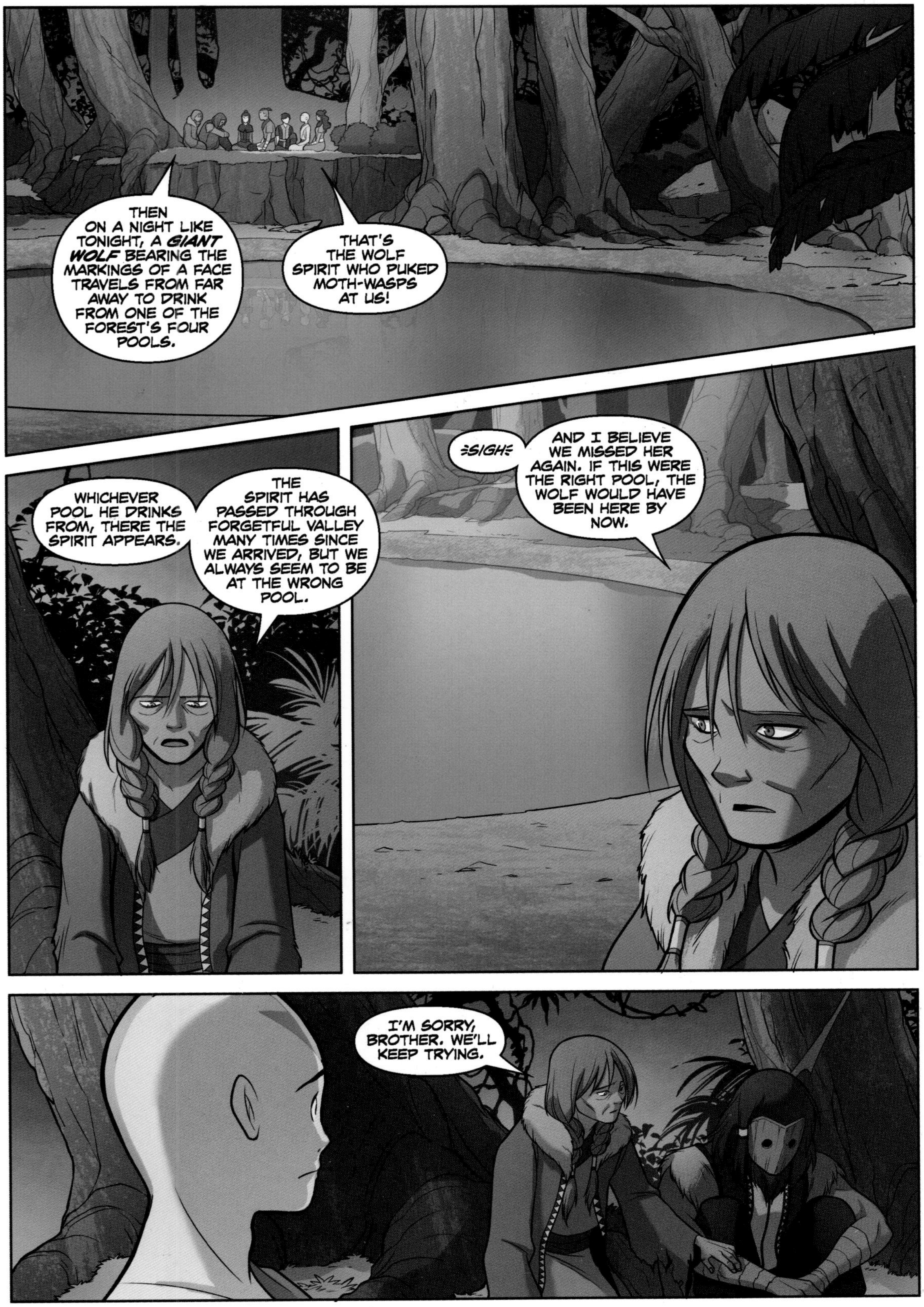
THEN ON A NIGHT LIKE TONIGHT, A GIANT WOLF BEARING THE MARKINGS OF A FACE TRAVELS FROM FAR AWAY TO DRINK FROM ONE OF THE FOREST'S FOUR POOLS.
THAT'S THE WOLF SPIRIT WHO PUKED MOTH-WASPS AT US!
WHICHEVER POOL HE DRINKS FROM, THERE THE SPIRIT APPEARS.
THE SPIRIT HAS PASSED THROUGH FORGETFUL VALLEY MANY TIMES SINCE WE ARRIVED, BUT WE ALWAYS SEEM TO BE AT THE WRONG POOL.
SIGH
AND I BELIEVE WE MISSED HER AGAIN. IF THIS WERE THE RIGHT POOL, THE WOLF WOULD HAVE BEEN HERE BY NOW.
I'M SORRY, BROTHER. WE'LL KEEP TRYING.

-- THE GREAT BRIDGE BETWEEN THE SPIRITS AND THE HUMANS. WE KNOW, WE KNOW!

NO! THERE'S GOTTA BE SOMETHING I CAN DO! AFTER ALL, I'M THE AVATAR, THE GREAT --

I'M GONNA CROSS OVER TO THE SPIRIT WORLD AND TRY TO GET THAT GIANT WOLF SPIRIT TO COME HERE.

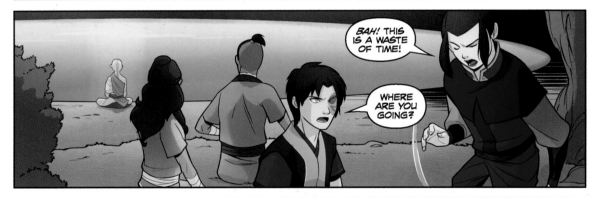

BAH! THIS IS A WASTE OF TIME!

WHERE ARE YOU GOING?

AZULA!

DID WE TRAVEL ALL THIS WAY TO HELP A COUPLE OF DIRTY VAGRANTS, OR TO FIND MOTHER?

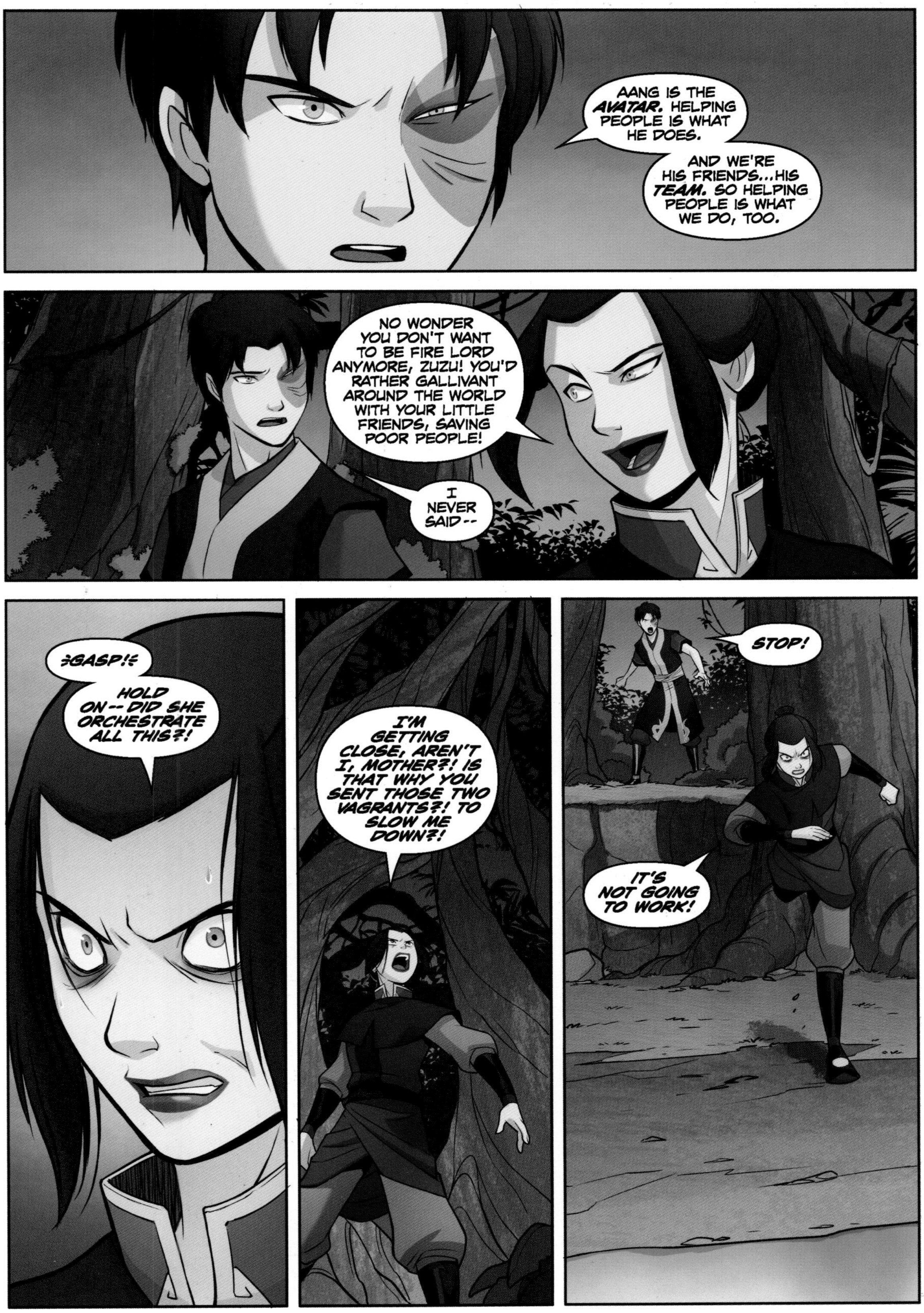
AANG IS THE AVATAR. HELPING PEOPLE IS WHAT HE DOES.
AND WE'RE HIS FRIENDS...HIS TEAM. SO HELPING PEOPLE IS WHAT WE DO, TOO.
NO WONDER YOU DON'T WANT TO BE FIRE LORD ANYMORE, ZUZU! YOU'D RATHER GALLIVANT AROUND THE WORLD WITH YOUR LITTLE FRIENDS, SAVING POOR PEOPLE!
I NEVER SAID--
GASP!
HOLD ON--DID SHE ORCHESTRATE ALL THIS?!
I'M GETTING CLOSE, AREN'T I, MOTHER?! IS THAT WHY YOU SENT THOSE TWO VAGRANTS?! TO SLOW ME DOWN?!
STOP!
IT'S NOT GOING TO WORK!

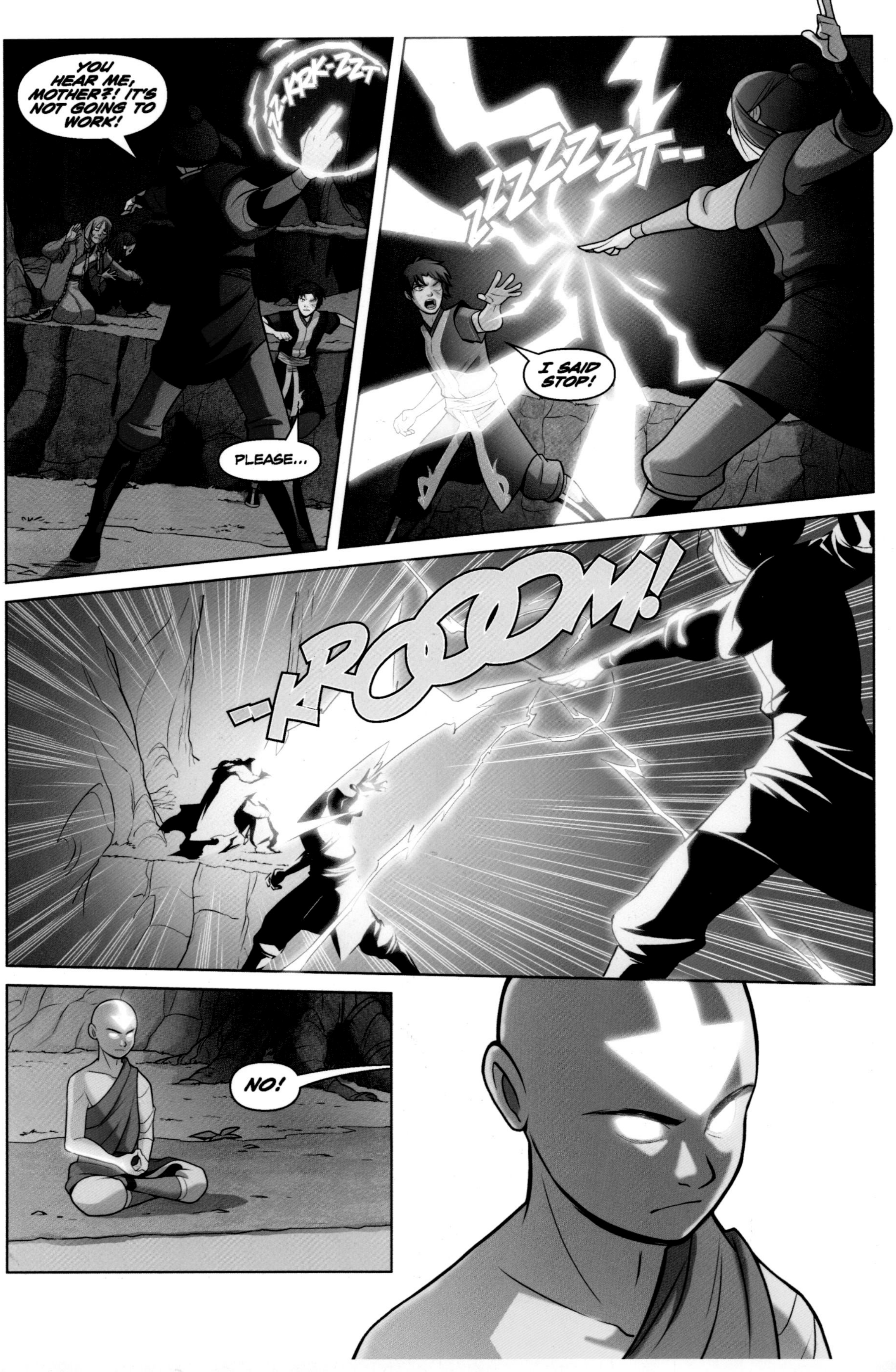
YOU HEAR ME, MOTHER?! IT'S NOT GOING TO WORK!
ZZ-KRK-ZZT
PLEASE...
ZZZZZZZT--
I SAID STOP!
--KROOOOM!
NO!

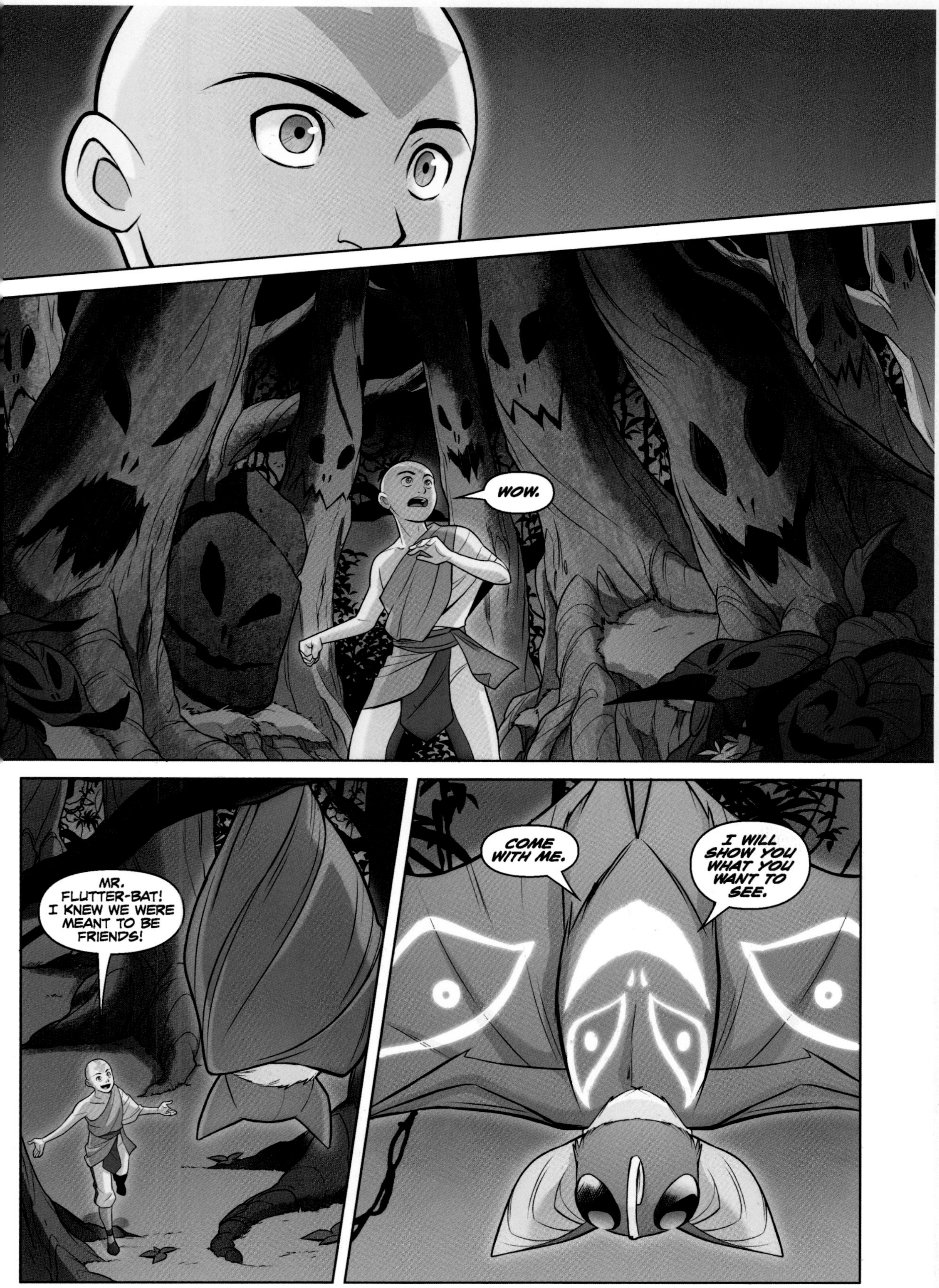
WOW.
MR. FLUTTER-BAT! I KNEW WE WERE MEANT TO BE FRIENDS!
COME WITH ME.
I WILL SHOW YOU WHAT YOU WANT TO SEE.

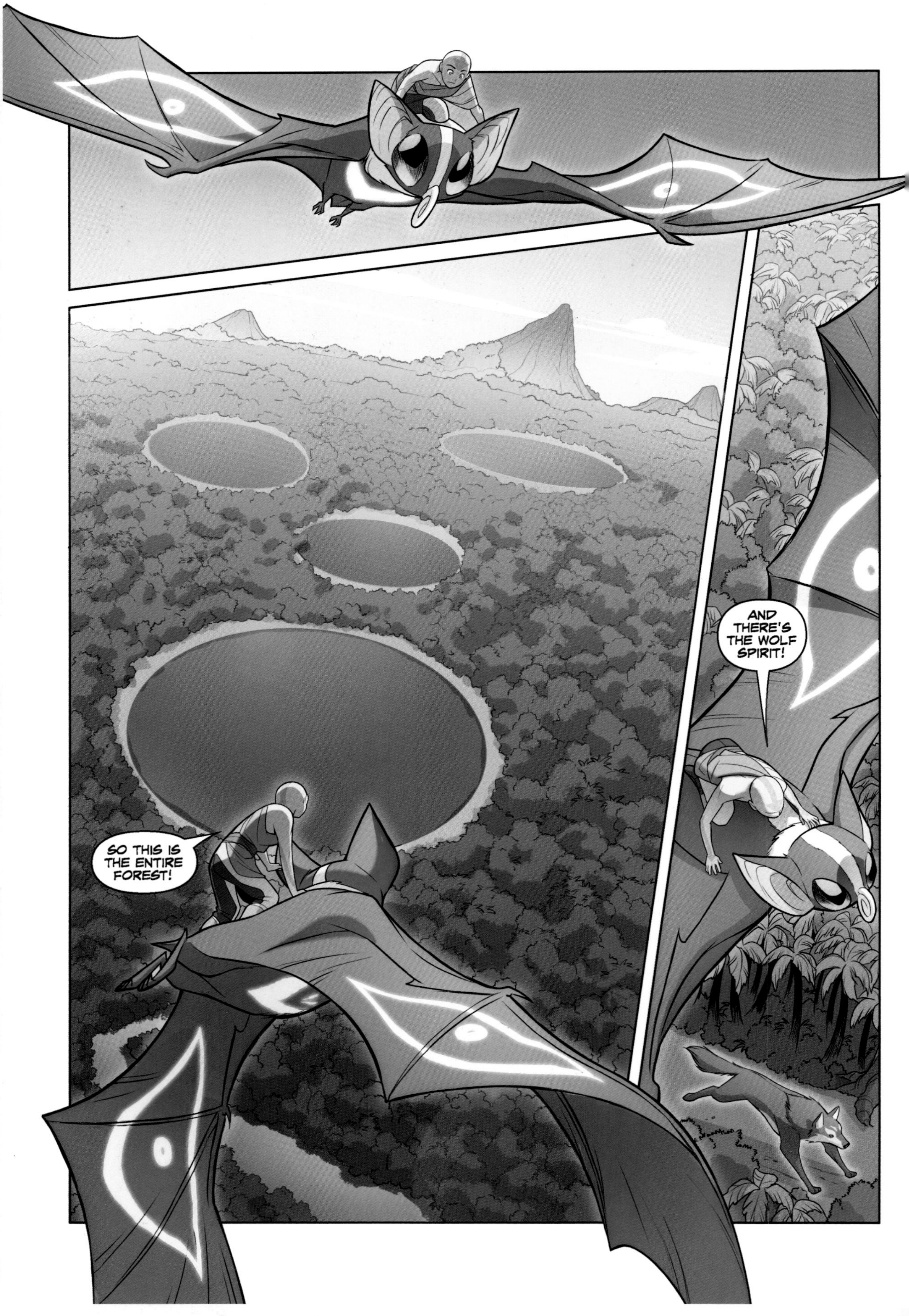
SO THIS IS THE ENTIRE FOREST!
AND THERE'S THE WOLF SPIRIT!

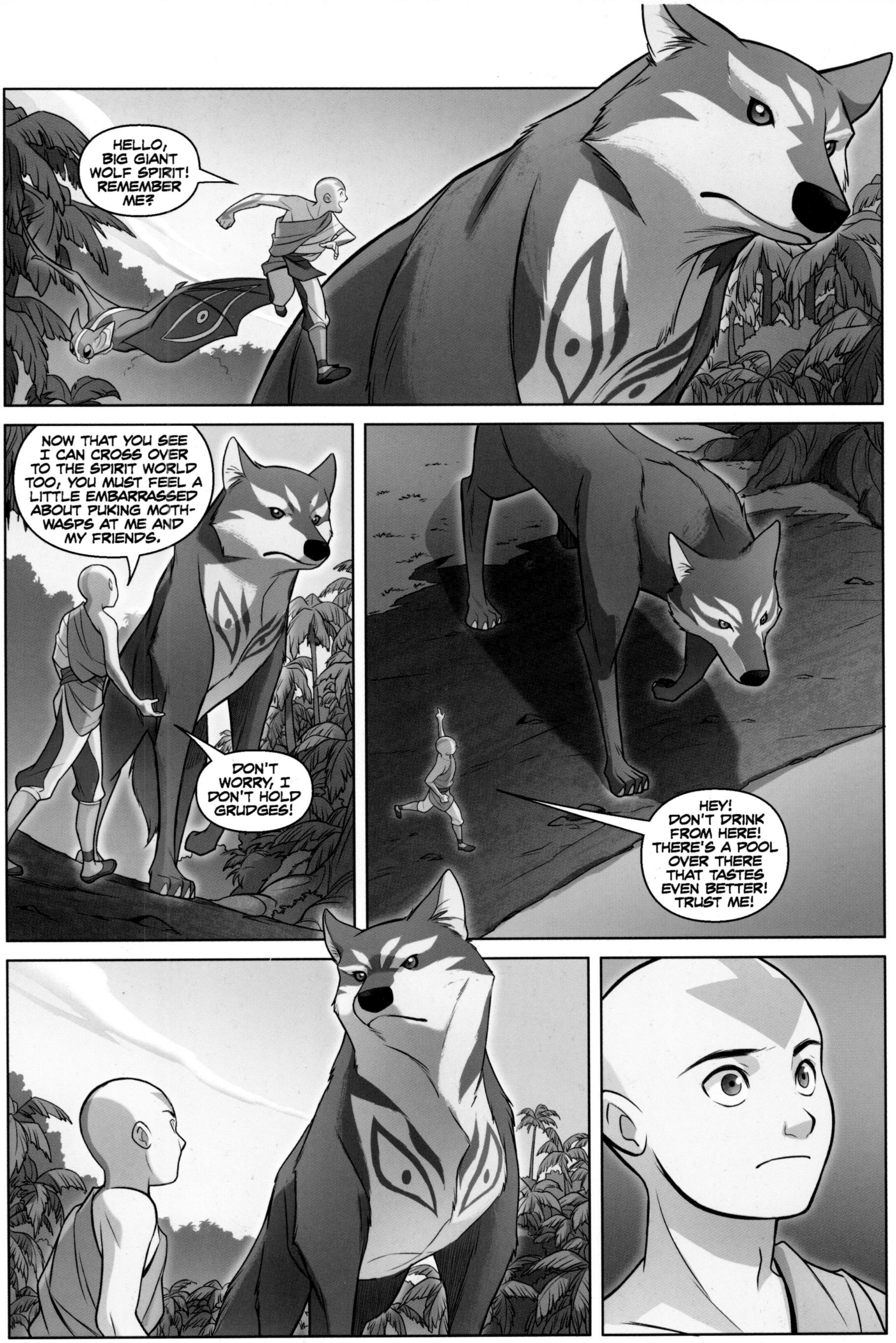
HELLO, BIG GIANT WOLF SPIRIT! REMEMBER ME?
NOW THAT YOU SEE I CAN CROSS OVER TO THE SPIRIT WORLD TOO, YOU MUST FEEL A LITTLE EMBARRASSED ABOUT PUKING MOTH-WASPS AT ME AND MY FRIENDS.
DON'T WORRY, I DON'T HOLD GRUDGES!
HEY! DON'T DRINK FROM HERE! THERE'S A POOL OVER THERE THAT TASTES EVEN BETTER! TRUST ME!

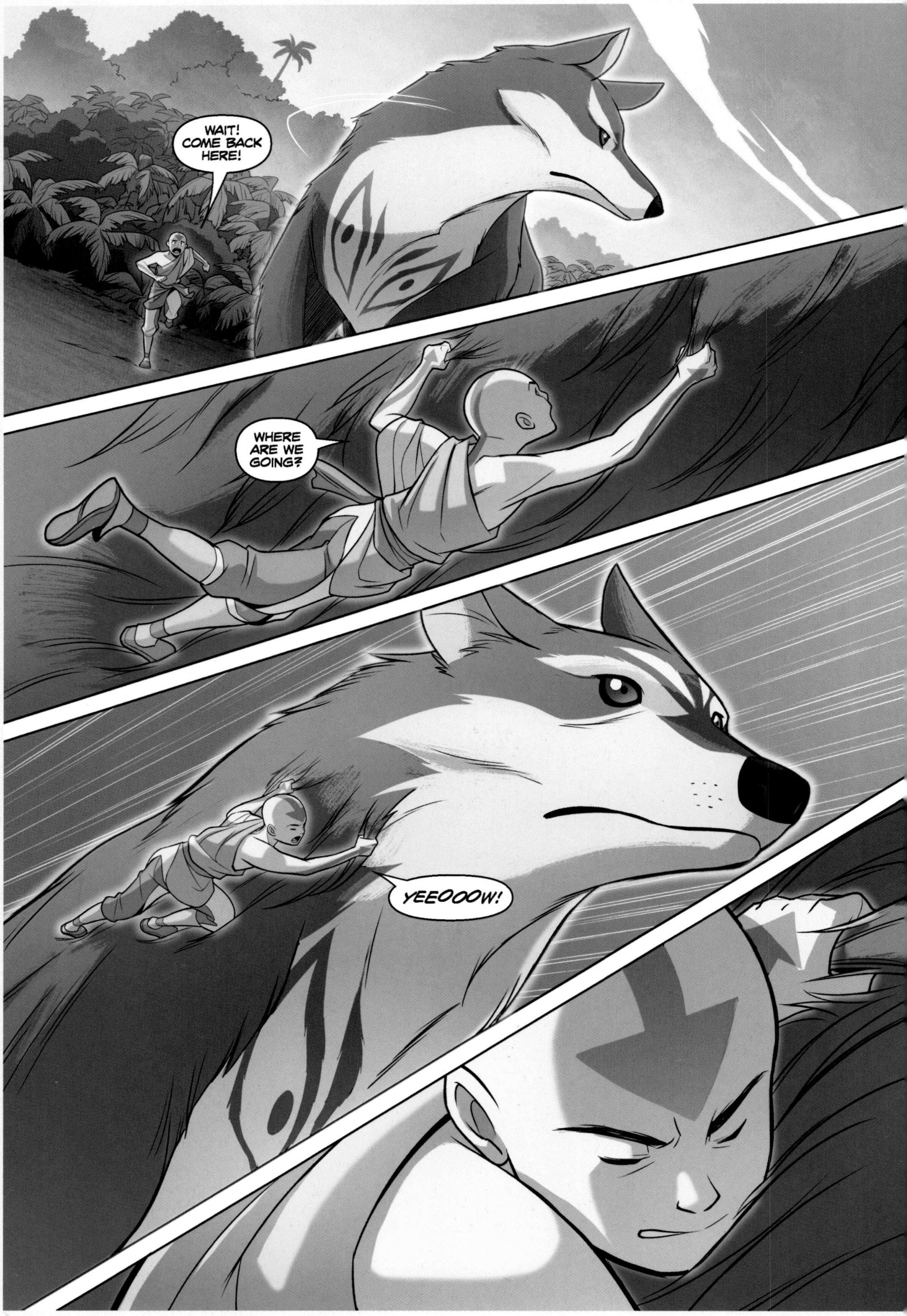
WAIT! COME BACK HERE!
WHERE ARE WE GOING?
YEEOOOW!

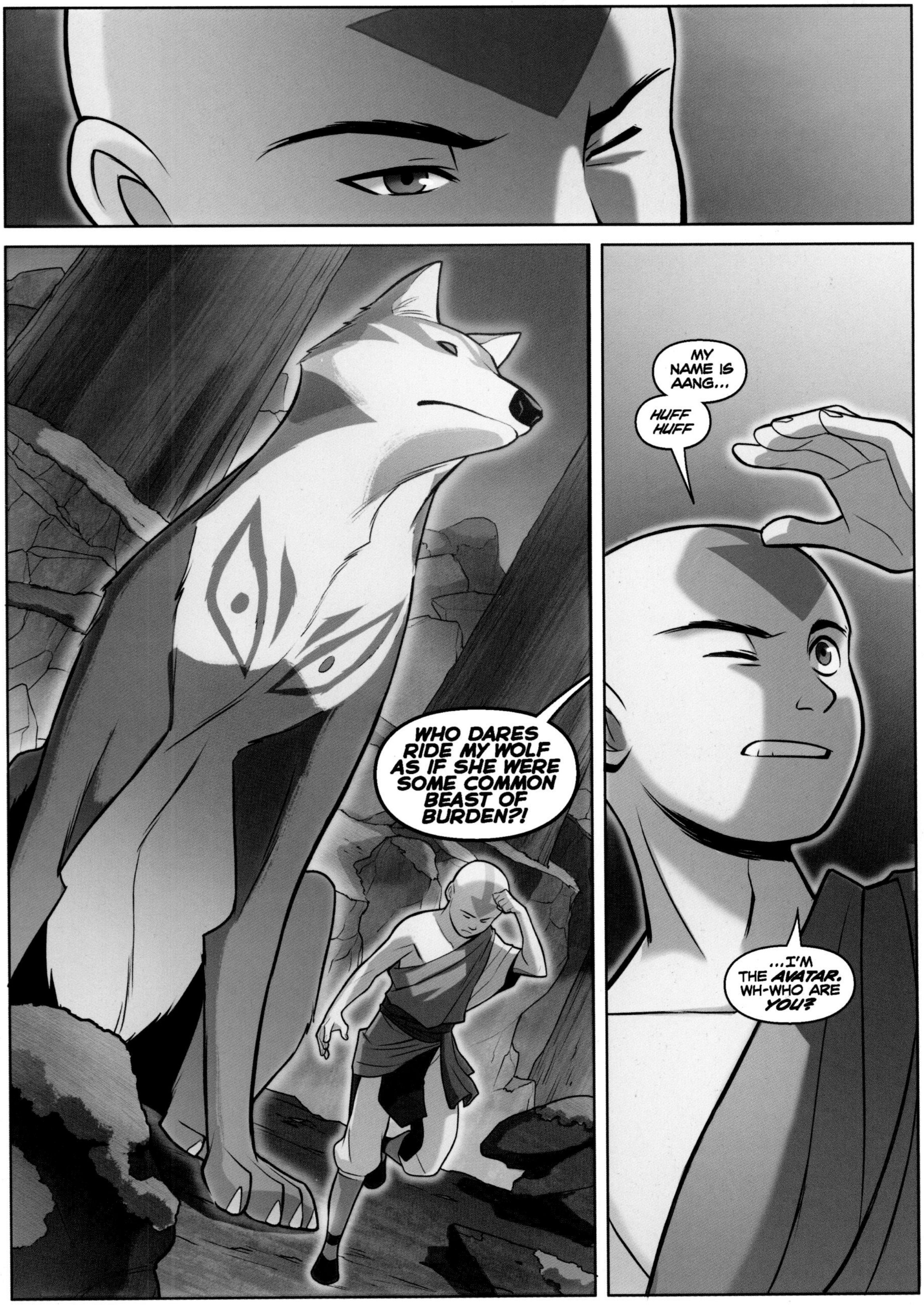
WHO DARES RIDE MY WOLF AS IF SHE WERE SOME COMMON BEAST OF BURDEN?!
MY NAME IS AANG...
HUFF HUFF
...I'M THE AVATAR. WH-WHO ARE YOU?

G: We really had a hard time designing Mother of Faces. There were many discussions about her among Mike, Bryan, and Gene. We think we came up with a very unique design. We're happy to know that the readers seem to like it.

GLY: *Faces and masks—fake faces—are such an important theme in Zuko's life story. His scarred face is a physical manifestation of his internal struggle between good and evil. He spent much of book 1 of the show behind the mask of the Blue Spirit. And one of the few things we know about his mother from the original series is that she was a fan of the theater, the art form where actors take on fake faces and fake identities. Since* The Search *is all about Zuko and his family, we wanted to continue that theme.*

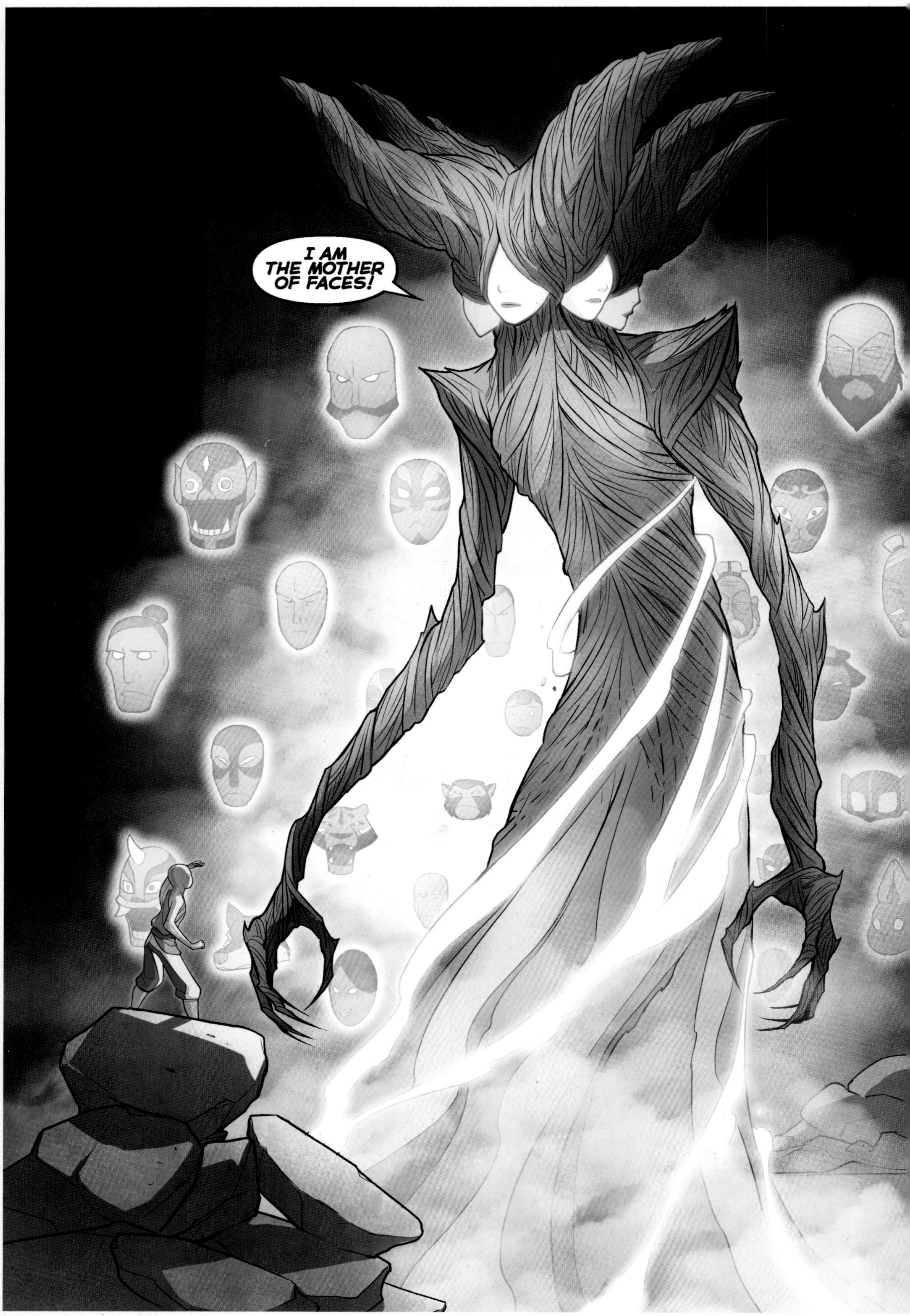
I AM THE MOTHER OF FACES!

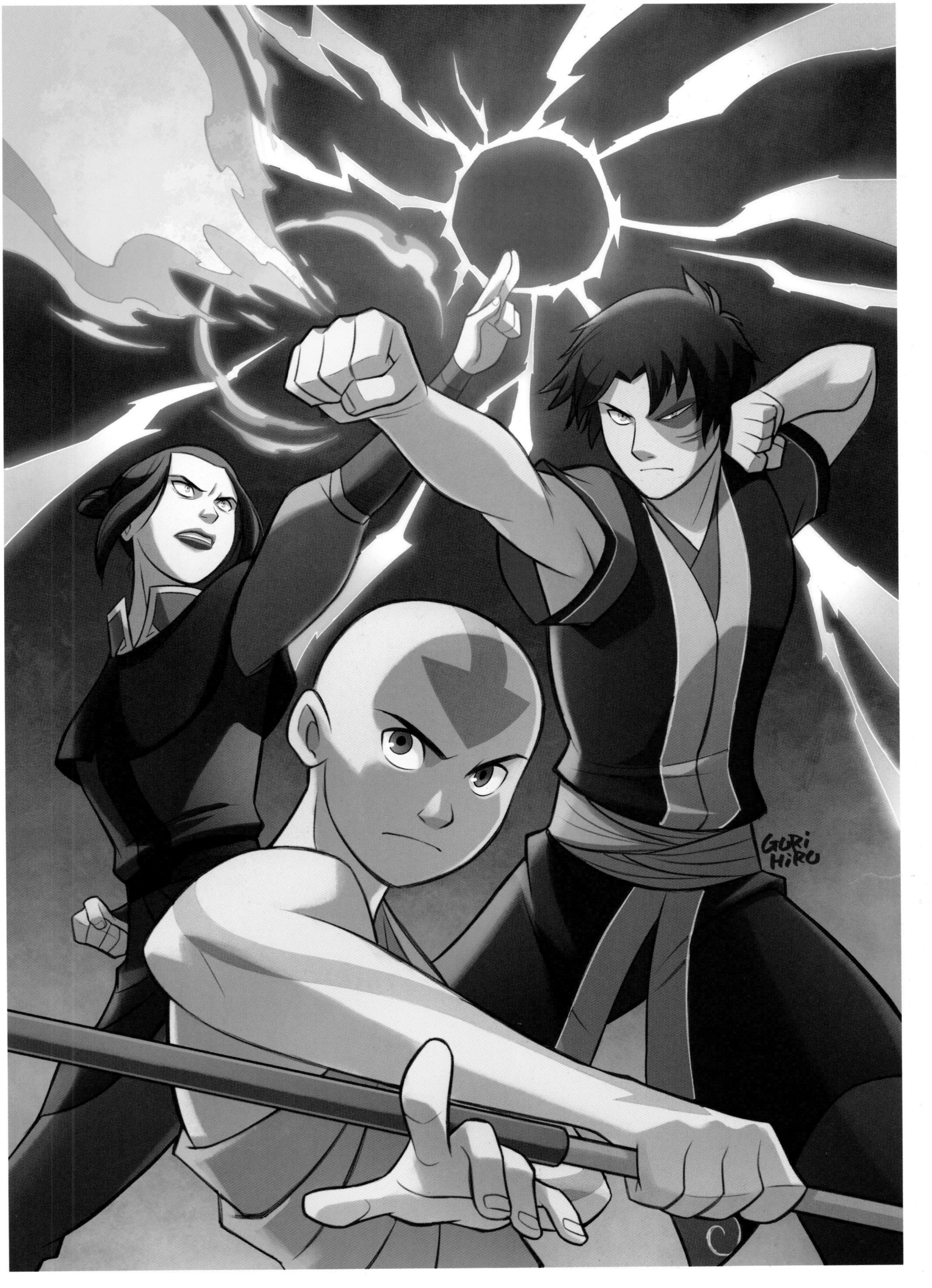
GURI
HIRU

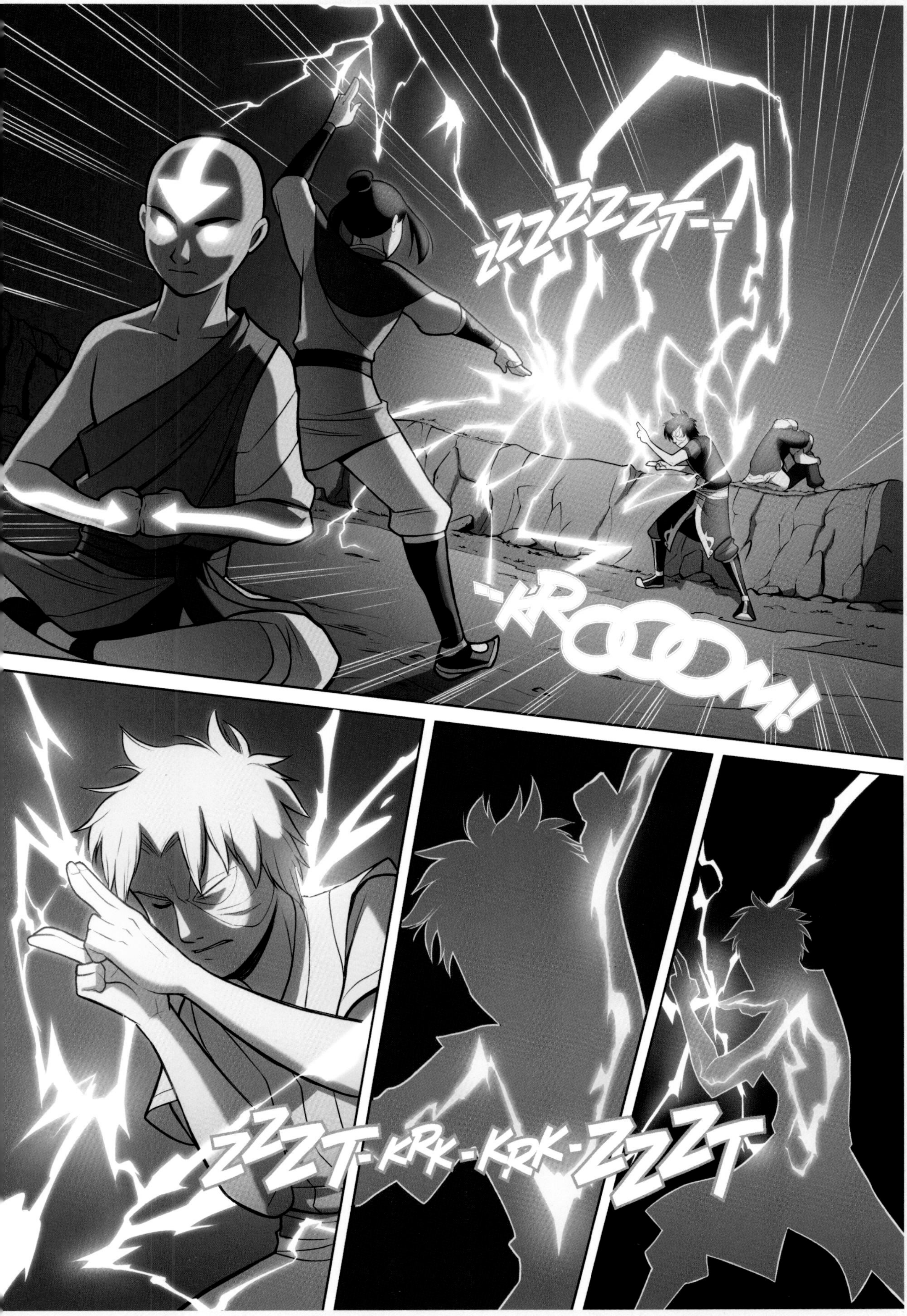
ZZZZZZZT--
-KROOOOM!
ZZZT-KRK-KRK-ZZZT

KRAKKA-BOOOM
DID YOU FORGET, AZULA? I KNOW HOW TO DEAL WITH YOUR LIGHTNING.
WHOA. I THINK I MIGHT BE SCARED OF YOU AGAIN.
MISU AND RAFA HAVE NOTHING TO DO WITH OUR MOTHER! HOW COULD YOU EVEN THINK --
BUT THAT'S EXACTLY WHAT SHE WANTS YOU TO BELIEVE! ZUZU, HOW COULD YOU BE SO NAIVE?!
YOU'RE RIGHT. I HAVE BEEN NAIVE.
TAKE HER DOWN.
GLADLY!
IT'S ABOUT TIME!

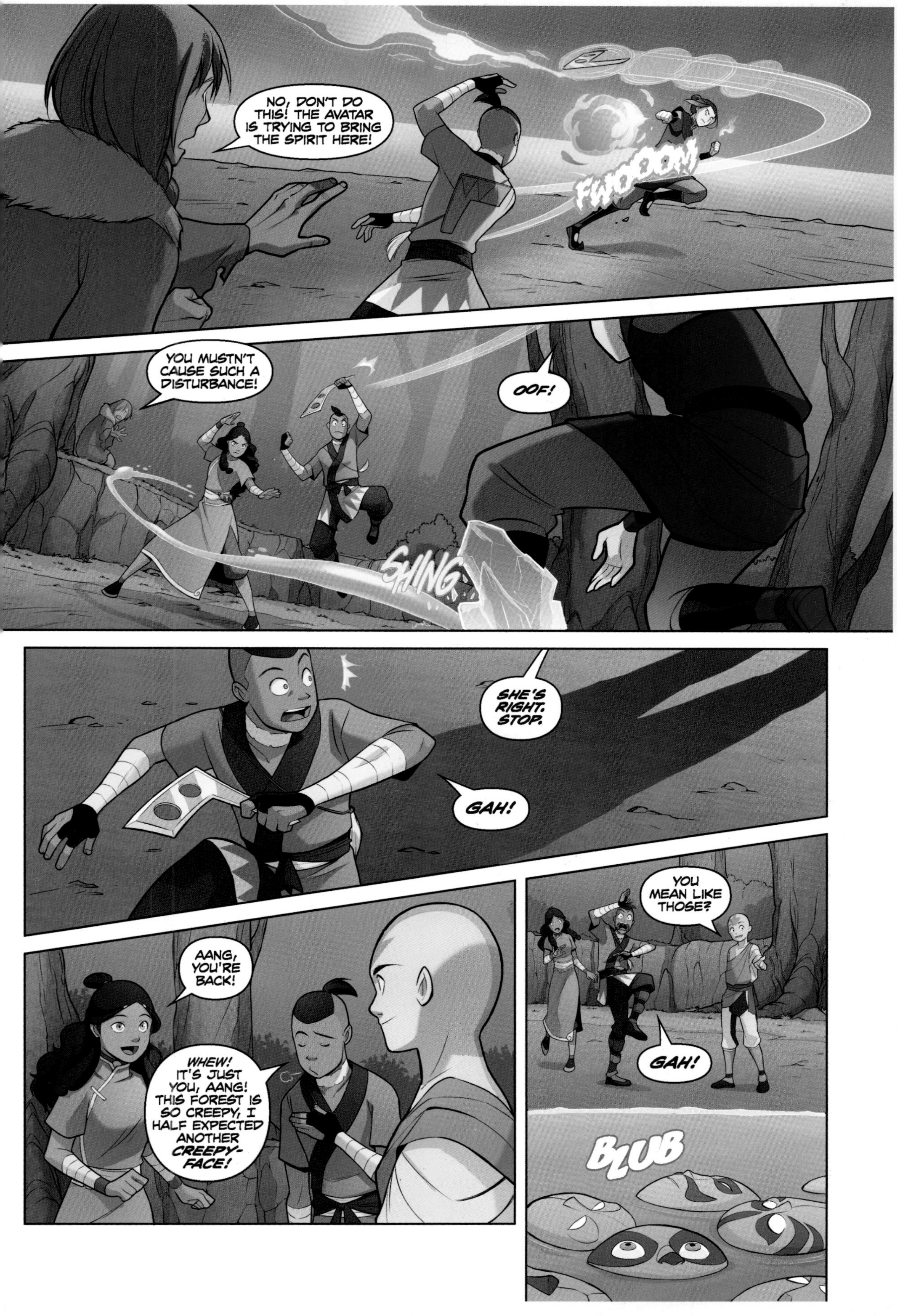
NO, DON'T DO THIS! THE AVATAR IS TRYING TO BRING THE SPIRIT HERE!
FWOOOM
YOU MUSTN'T CAUSE SUCH A DISTURBANCE!
OOF!
SHING
SHE'S RIGHT. STOP.
GAH!
AANG, YOU'RE BACK!
WHEW! IT'S JUST YOU, AANG! THIS FOREST IS SO CREEPY, I HALF EXPECTED ANOTHER CREEPY-FACE!
YOU MEAN LIKE THOSE?
GAH!
BLUB

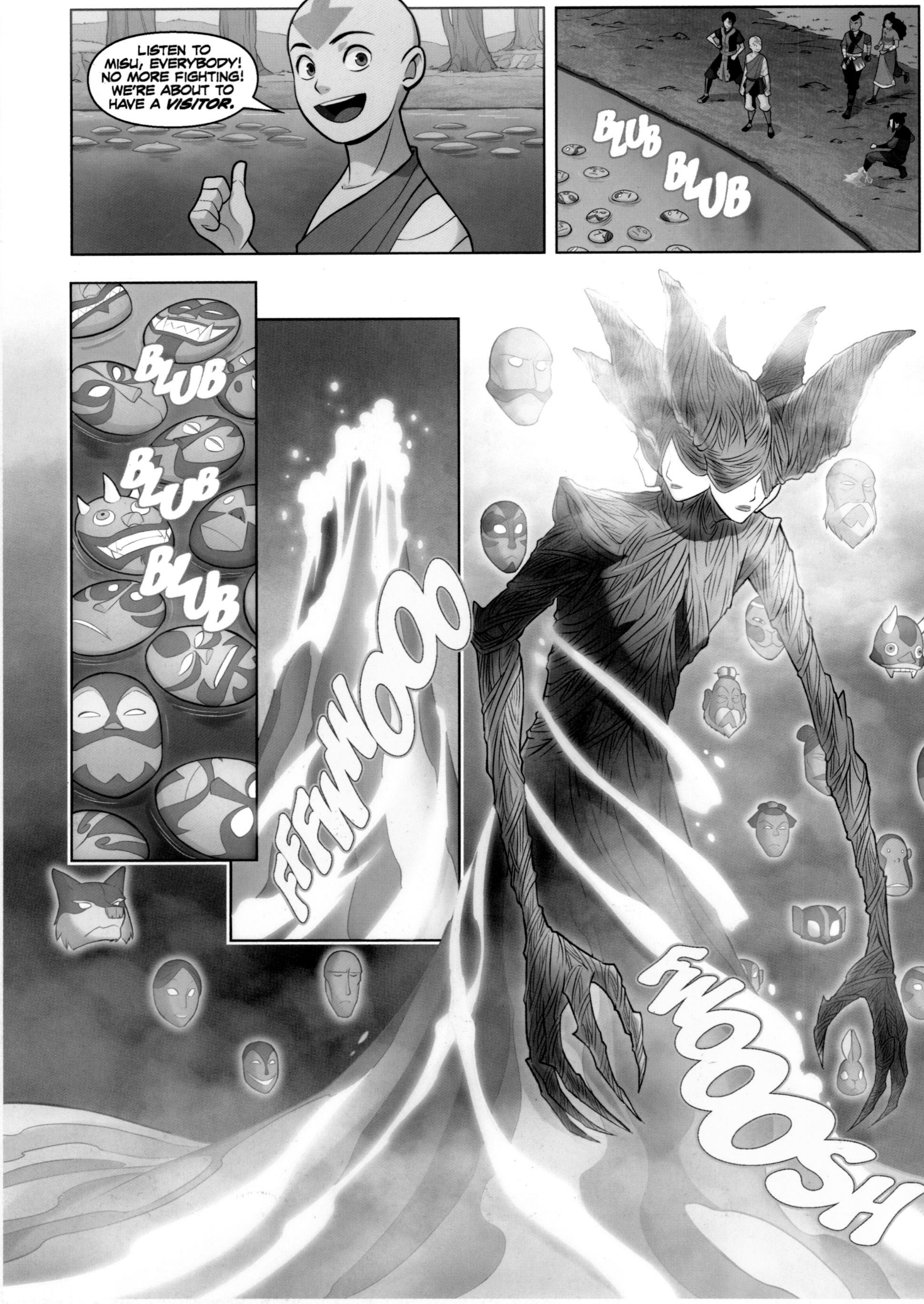
LISTEN TO MISU, EVERYBODY! NO MORE FIGHTING! WE'RE ABOUT TO HAVE A *VISITOR.*
BLUB BLUB
BLUB
BLUB
BLUB
FFFWOOOO
FWOOOSH

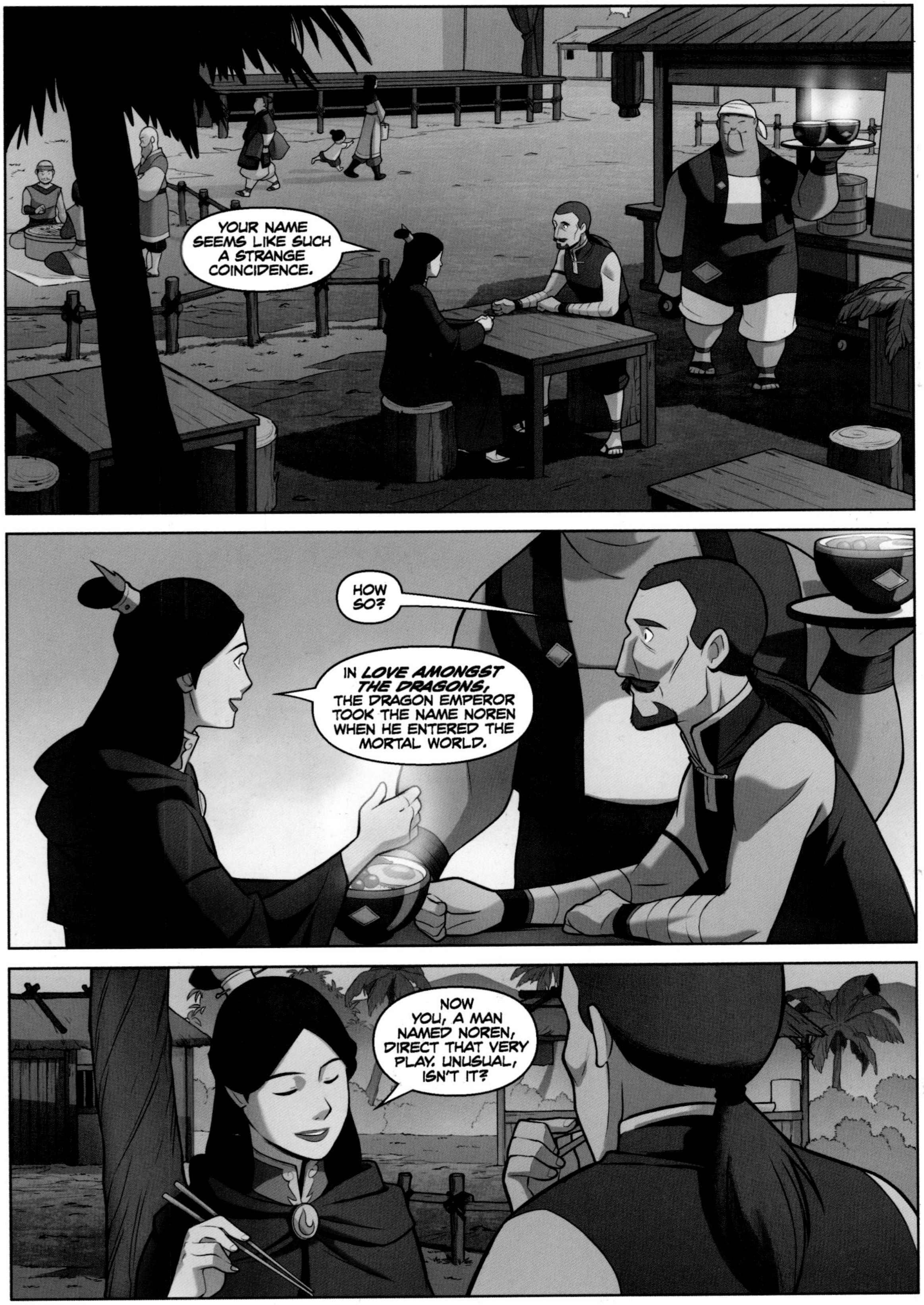
YOUR NAME SEEMS LIKE SUCH A STRANGE COINCIDENCE.
HOW SO?
IN *LOVE AMONGST THE DRAGONS,* THE DRAGON EMPEROR TOOK THE NAME NOREN WHEN HE ENTERED THE MORTAL WORLD.
NOW YOU, A MAN NAMED NOREN, DIRECT THAT VERY PLAY. UNUSUAL, ISN'T IT?

G: *The two are eating loco moco, a Hawaiian specialty.*

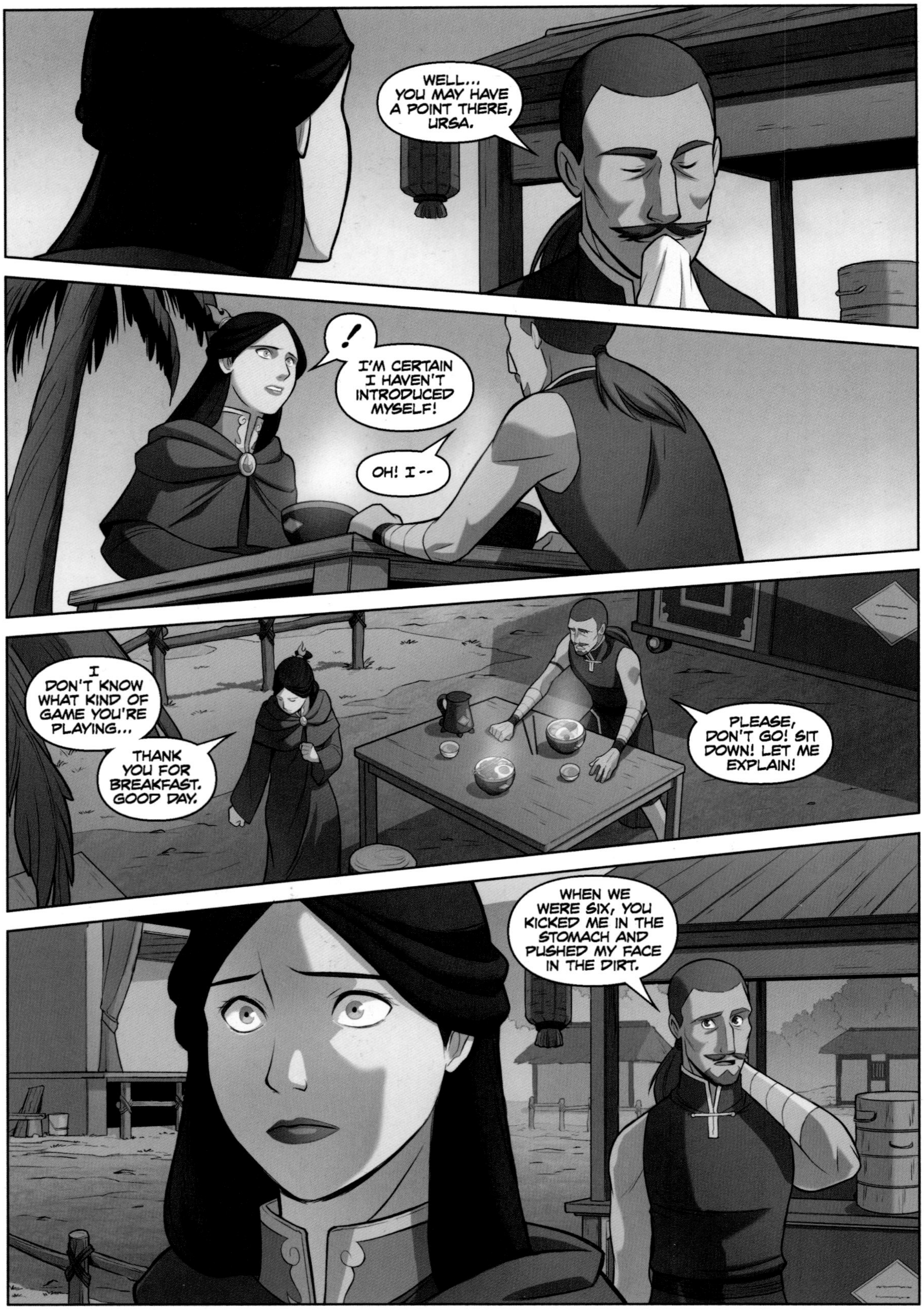
WELL... YOU MAY HAVE A POINT THERE, URSA.
!
I'M CERTAIN I HAVEN'T INTRODUCED MYSELF!
OH! I--
I DON'T KNOW WHAT KIND OF GAME YOU'RE PLAYING...
THANK YOU FOR BREAKFAST. GOOD DAY.
PLEASE, DON'T GO! SIT DOWN! LET ME EXPLAIN!
WHEN WE WERE SIX, YOU KICKED ME IN THE STOMACH AND PUSHED MY FACE IN THE DIRT.

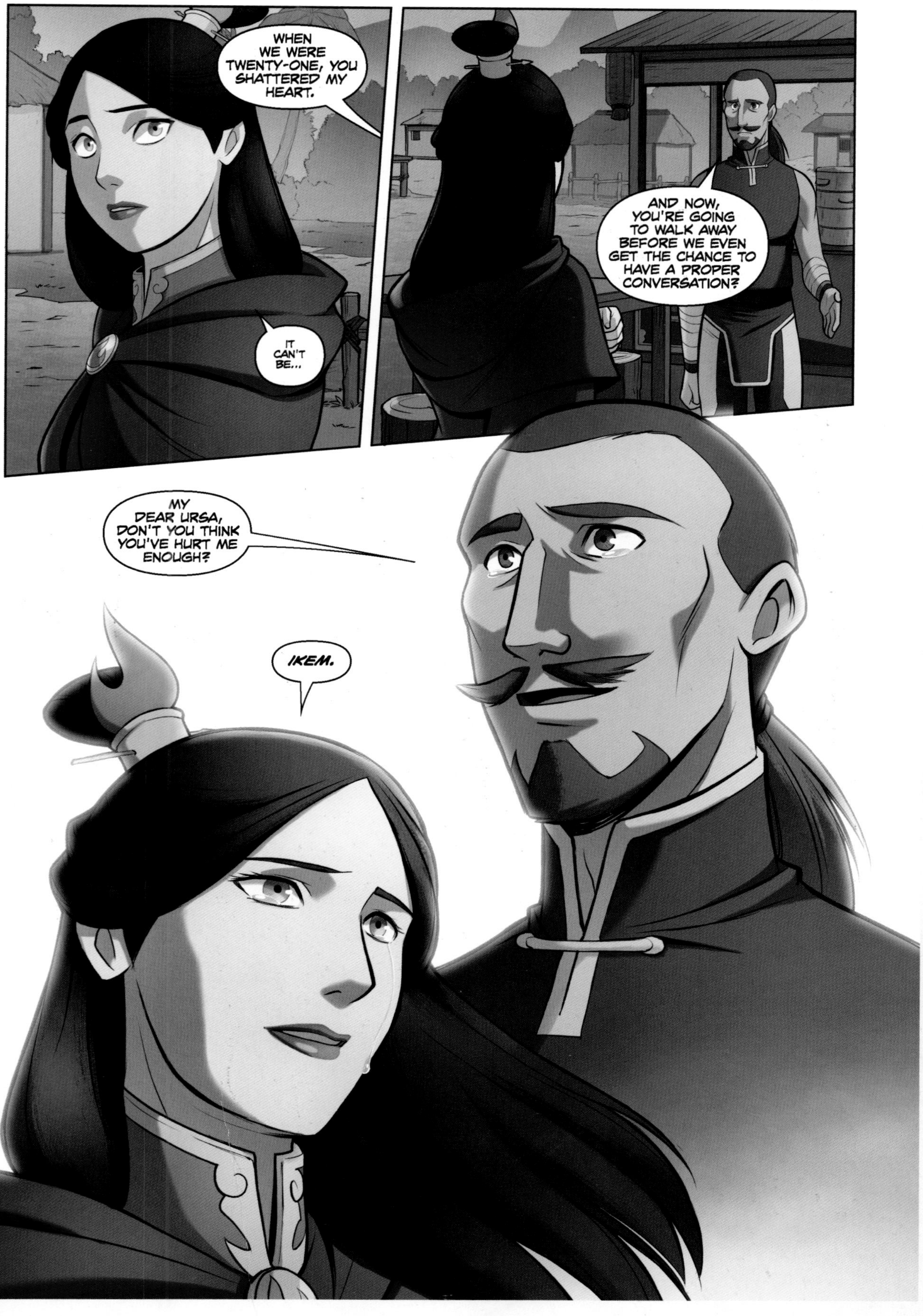
WHEN WE WERE TWENTY-ONE, YOU SHATTERED MY HEART.
IT CAN'T BE...
AND NOW, YOU'RE GOING TO WALK AWAY BEFORE WE EVEN GET THE CHANCE TO HAVE A PROPER CONVERSATION?
MY DEAR URSA, DON'T YOU THINK YOU'VE HURT ME ENOUGH?
IKEM.

GLY: *It took us a few rounds to get Mother of Faces right. I wanted Mother of Faces to be ancient and majestic and slightly terrifying, but I just wasn't sure how to get that across. I had her described as a Korean queen, but after Gurihiru's initial sketches, we quickly realized it just didn't work. Eventually, Gurihiru and Mike worked together to create the spirit that now appears in the book. They took inspiration from certain depictions of Guan Yin, the goddess of compassion.*

M: *Getting the right design for Mother of Faces took a few passes. We wanted her to feel primal, ancient, and mysterious. We sent Gurihiru photos of multi-headed Hindu goddesses for reference. I think she's a great addition to the pantheon of* Avatar *spirits.*

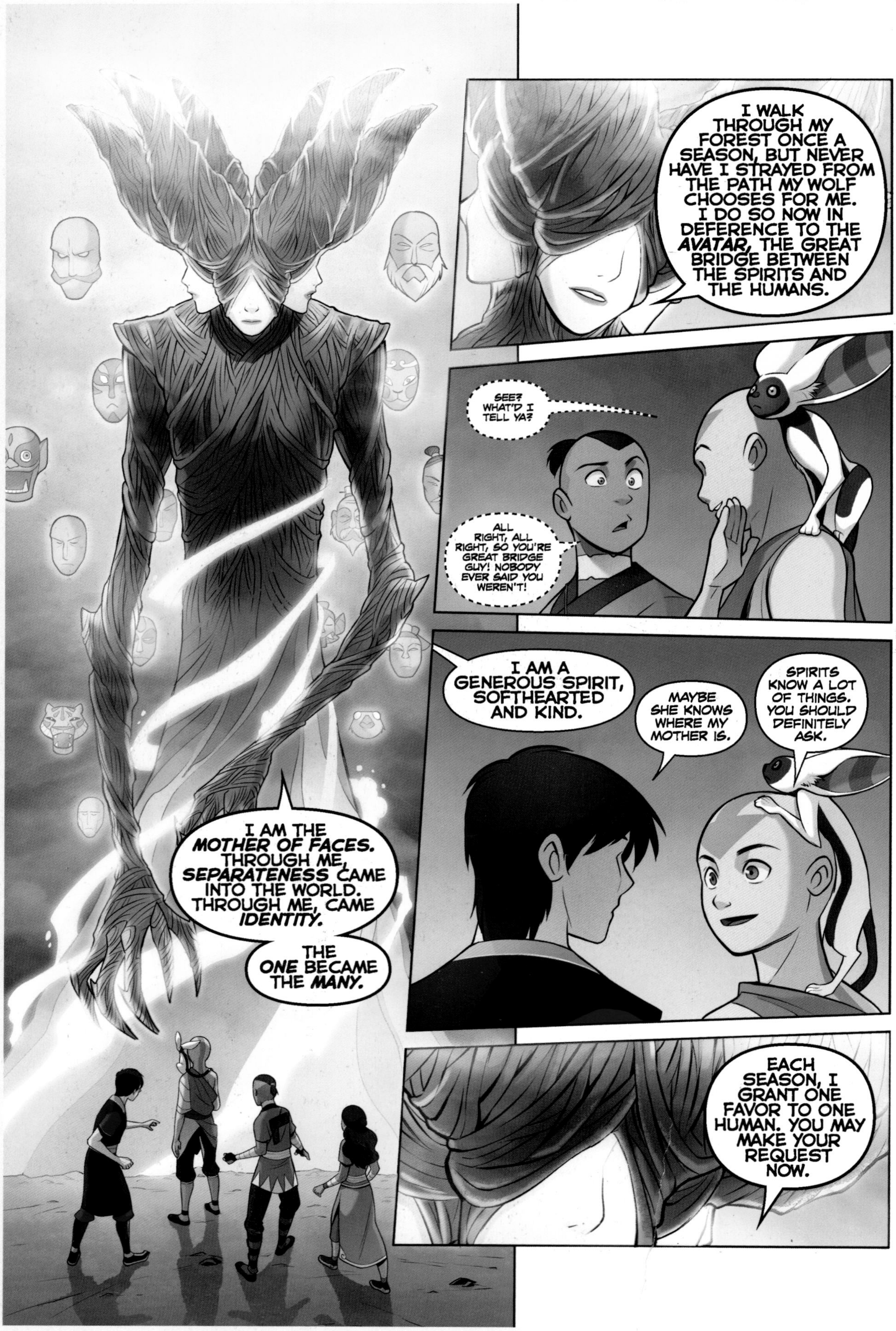
I AM THE MOTHER OF FACES. THROUGH ME, SEPARATENESS CAME INTO THE WORLD. THROUGH ME, CAME IDENTITY.
THE ONE BECAME THE MANY.
I WALK THROUGH MY FOREST ONCE A SEASON, BUT NEVER HAVE I STRAYED FROM THE PATH MY WOLF CHOOSES FOR ME. I DO SO NOW IN DEFERENCE TO THE AVATAR, THE GREAT BRIDGE BETWEEN THE SPIRITS AND THE HUMANS.
SEE? WHAT'D I TELL YA?
ALL RIGHT, ALL RIGHT, SO YOU'RE GREAT BRIDGE GUY! NOBODY EVER SAID YOU WEREN'T!
I AM A GENEROUS SPIRIT, SOFTHEARTED AND KIND.
MAYBE SHE KNOWS WHERE MY MOTHER IS.
SPIRITS KNOW A LOT OF THINGS. YOU SHOULD DEFINITELY ASK.
EACH SEASON, I GRANT ONE FAVOR TO ONE HUMAN. YOU MAY MAKE YOUR REQUEST NOW.

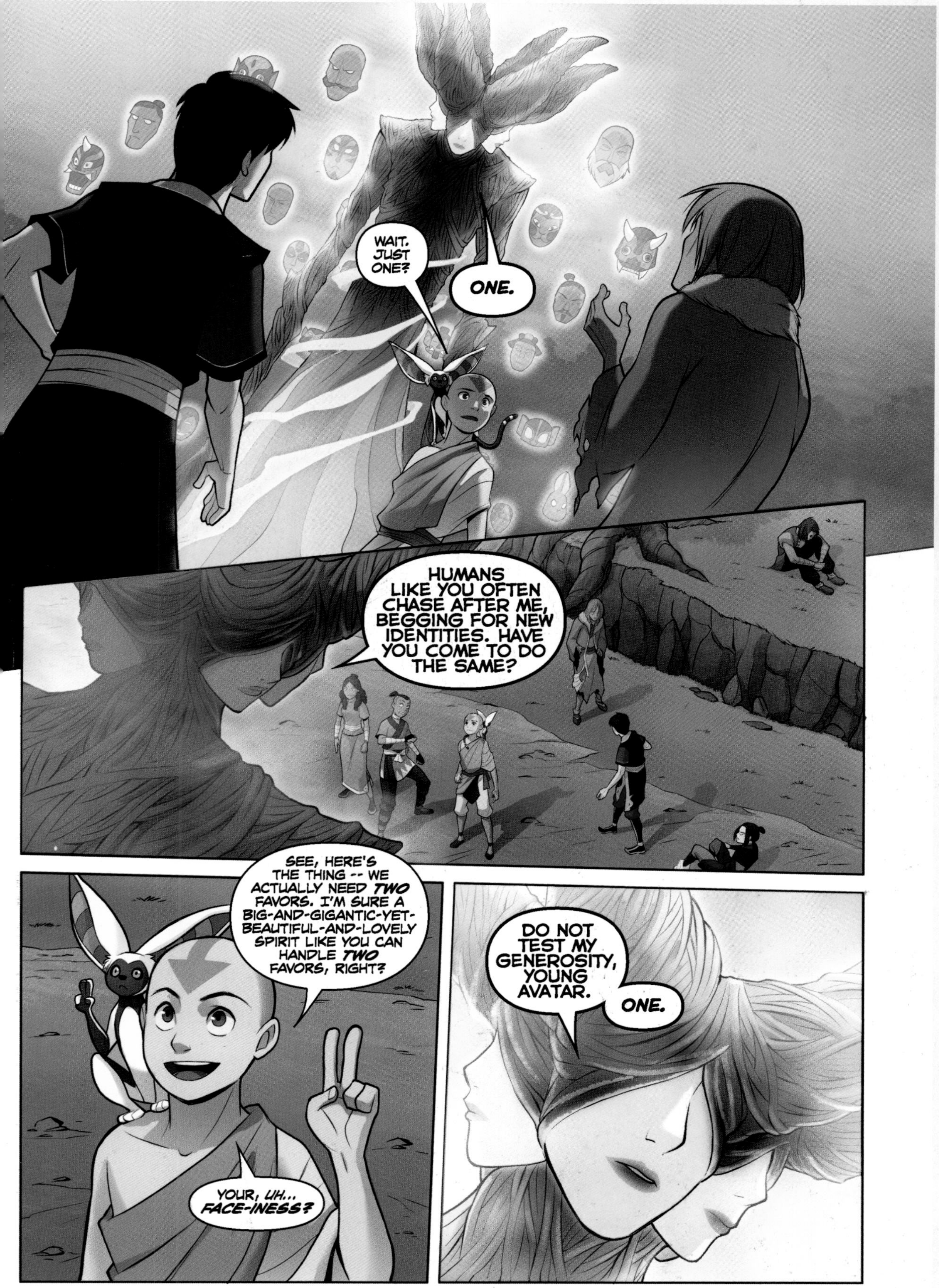
WAIT. JUST ONE?
ONE.
HUMANS LIKE YOU OFTEN CHASE AFTER ME, BEGGING FOR NEW IDENTITIES. HAVE YOU COME TO DO THE SAME?
SEE, HERE'S THE THING -- WE ACTUALLY NEED *TWO* FAVORS. I'M SURE A BIG-AND-GIGANTIC-YET-BEAUTIFUL-AND-LOVELY SPIRIT LIKE YOU CAN HANDLE *TWO* FAVORS, RIGHT?
YOUR, UH... *FACE-INESS?*
DO NOT TEST MY GENEROSITY, YOUNG AVATAR.
ONE.

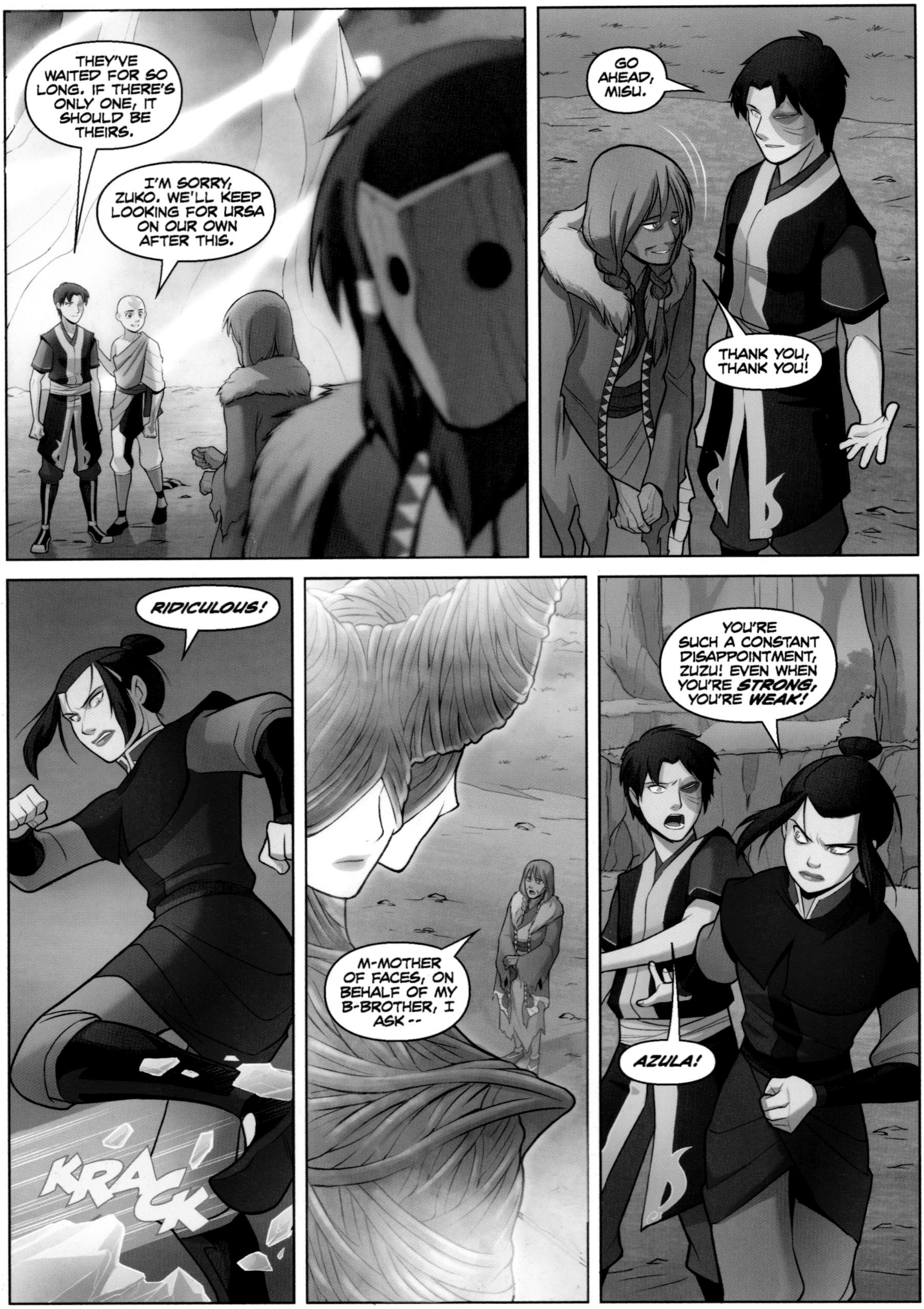
THEY'VE WAITED FOR SO LONG. IF THERE'S ONLY ONE, IT SHOULD BE THEIRS.
I'M SORRY, ZUKO. WE'LL KEEP LOOKING FOR URSA ON OUR OWN AFTER THIS.
GO AHEAD, MISU.
THANK YOU, THANK YOU!
RIDICULOUS!
KRACK
M-MOTHER OF FACES, ON BEHALF OF MY B-BROTHER, I ASK --
YOU'RE SUCH A CONSTANT DISAPPOINTMENT, ZUZU! EVEN WHEN YOU'RE STRONG, YOU'RE WEAK!
AZULA!

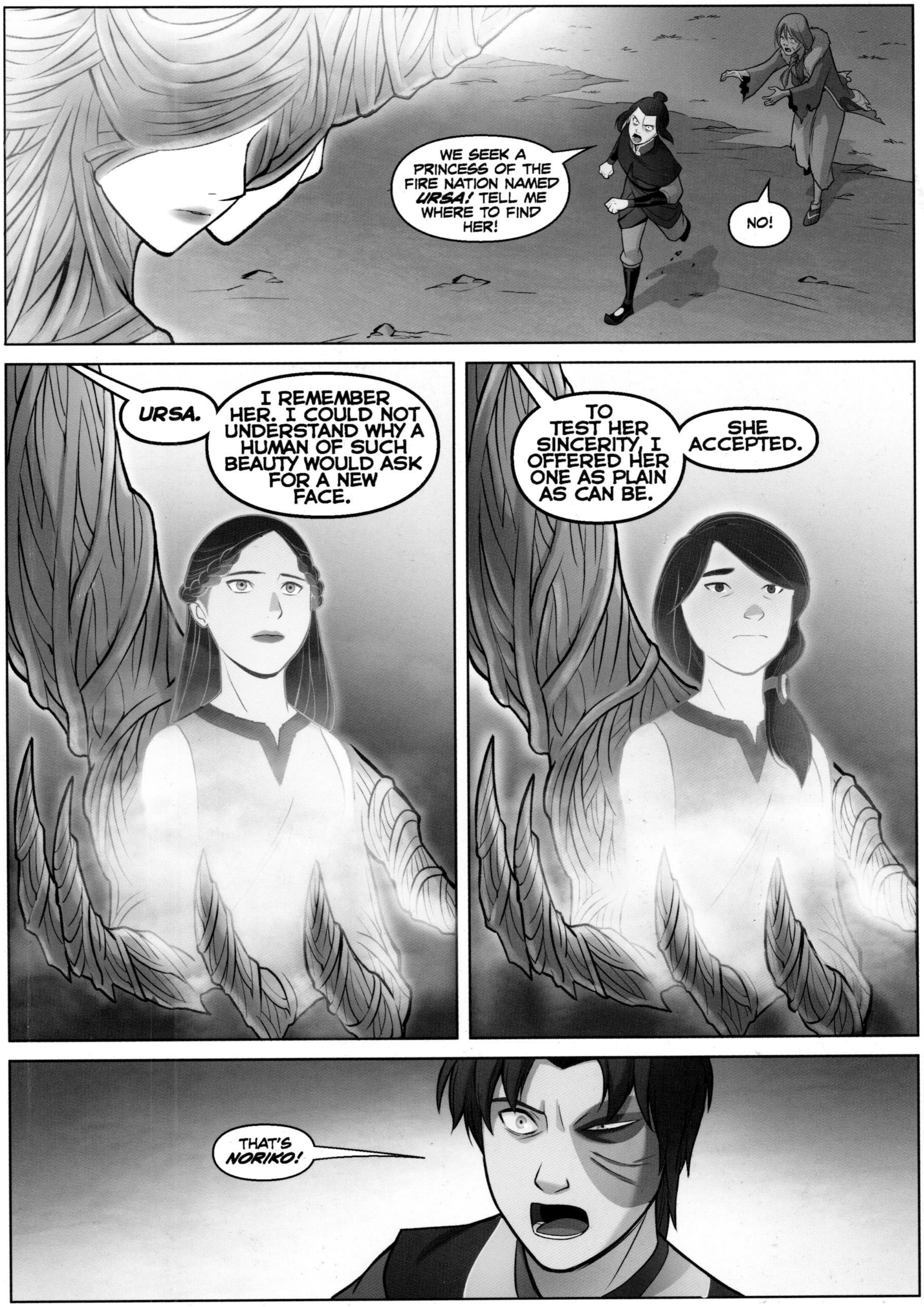
WE SEEK A PRINCESS OF THE FIRE NATION NAMED URSA! TELL ME WHERE TO FIND HER!
NO!
URSA.
I REMEMBER HER. I COULD NOT UNDERSTAND WHY A HUMAN OF SUCH BEAUTY WOULD ASK FOR A NEW FACE.
TO TEST HER SINCERITY, I OFFERED HER ONE AS PLAIN AS CAN BE.
SHE ACCEPTED.
THAT'S NORIKO!

AZULA, OUR MOTHER IS--

SHE'S GONE!

I KNOW EXACTLY WHERE SHE'S GOING -- BACK TO *HIRA'A*, BACK TO *NOREN'S* HOUSE!

WAIT!

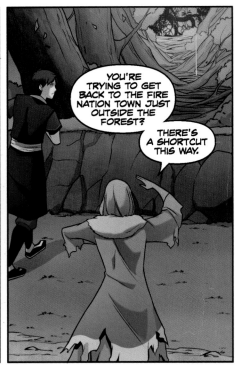

YOU'RE TRYING TO GET BACK TO THE FIRE NATION TOWN JUST OUTSIDE THE FOREST?

THERE'S A SHORTCUT THIS WAY.

THANK YOU.

YOU WERE KIND TO US.

I'M SORRY--

GO.

HOLD ON, ZUKO!

I KNOW SISTERS CAN BE A PAIN TO DEAL WITH, AND MINE'S NOT EVEN *CRAZY*. YOU'RE GONNA NEED BACKUP.

THANKS.

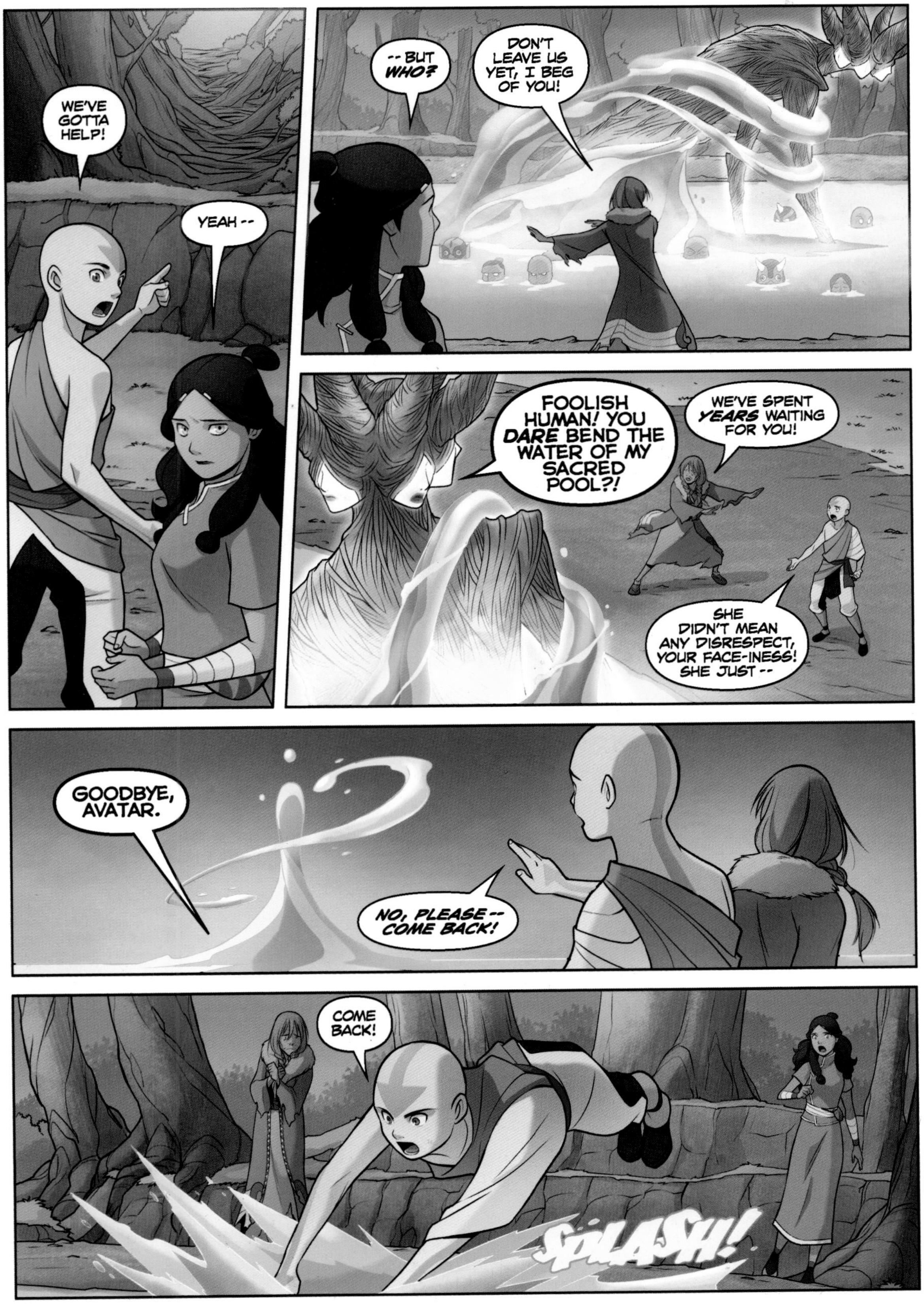
WE'VE GOTTA HELP!
YEAH --
-- BUT WHO?
DON'T LEAVE US YET, I BEG OF YOU!
FOOLISH HUMAN! YOU DARE BEND THE WATER OF MY SACRED POOL?!
WE'VE SPENT YEARS WAITING FOR YOU!
SHE DIDN'T MEAN ANY DISRESPECT, YOUR FACE-INESS! SHE JUST --
GOODBYE, AVATAR.
NO, PLEASE -- COME BACK!
COME BACK!
SPLASH!

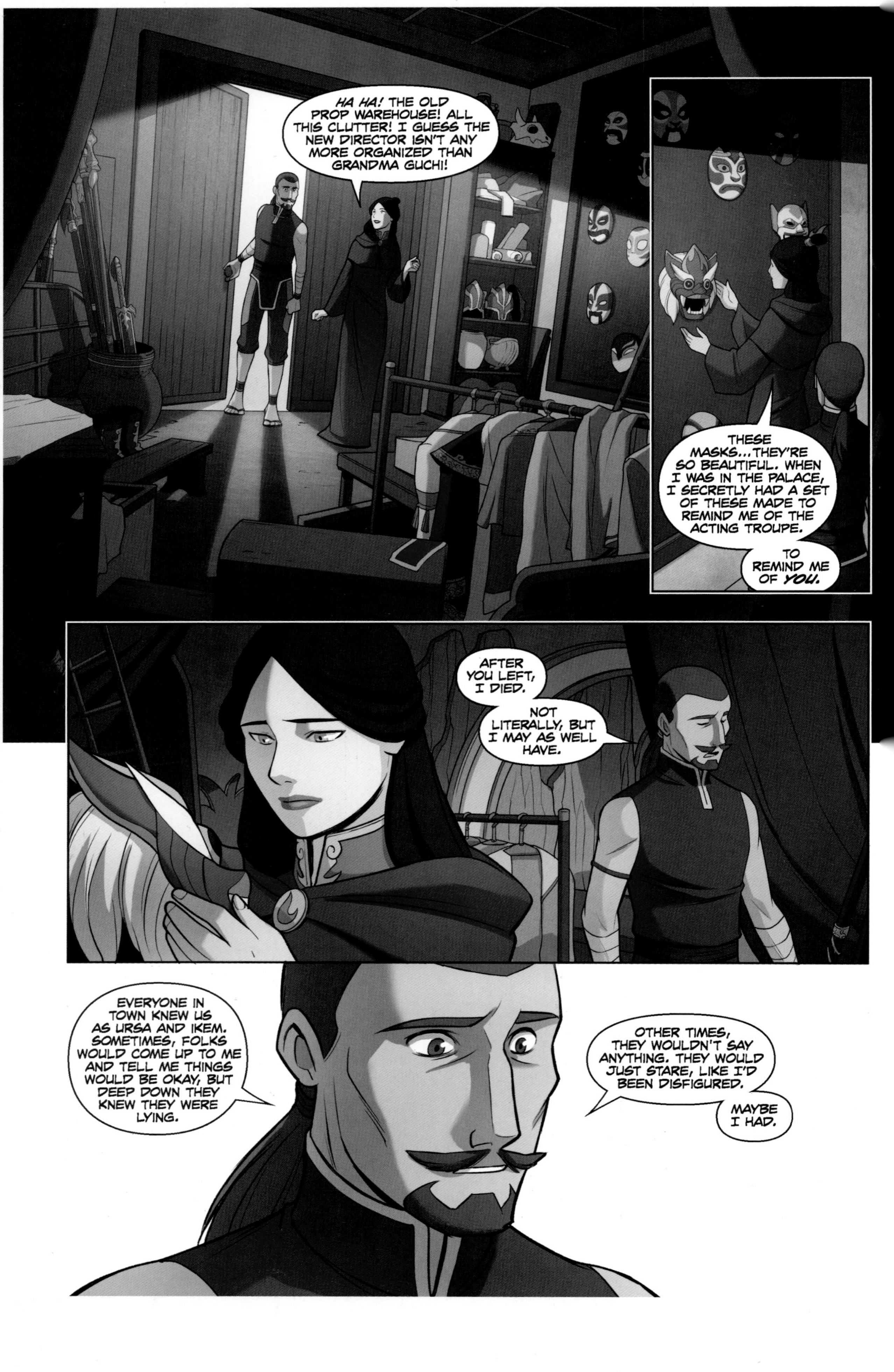
HA HA! THE OLD PROP WAREHOUSE! ALL THIS CLUTTER! I GUESS THE NEW DIRECTOR ISN'T ANY MORE ORGANIZED THAN GRANDMA GUCHI!
THESE MASKS... THEY'RE SO BEAUTIFUL. WHEN I WAS IN THE PALACE, I SECRETLY HAD A SET OF THESE MADE TO REMIND ME OF THE ACTING TROUPE.
TO REMIND ME OF YOU.
AFTER YOU LEFT, I DIED.
NOT LITERALLY, BUT I MAY AS WELL HAVE.
EVERYONE IN TOWN KNEW US AS URSA AND IKEM. SOMETIMES, FOLKS WOULD COME UP TO ME AND TELL ME THINGS WOULD BE OKAY, BUT DEEP DOWN THEY KNEW THEY WERE LYING.
OTHER TIMES, THEY WOULDN'T SAY ANYTHING. THEY WOULD JUST STARE, LIKE I'D BEEN DISFIGURED.
MAYBE I HAD.

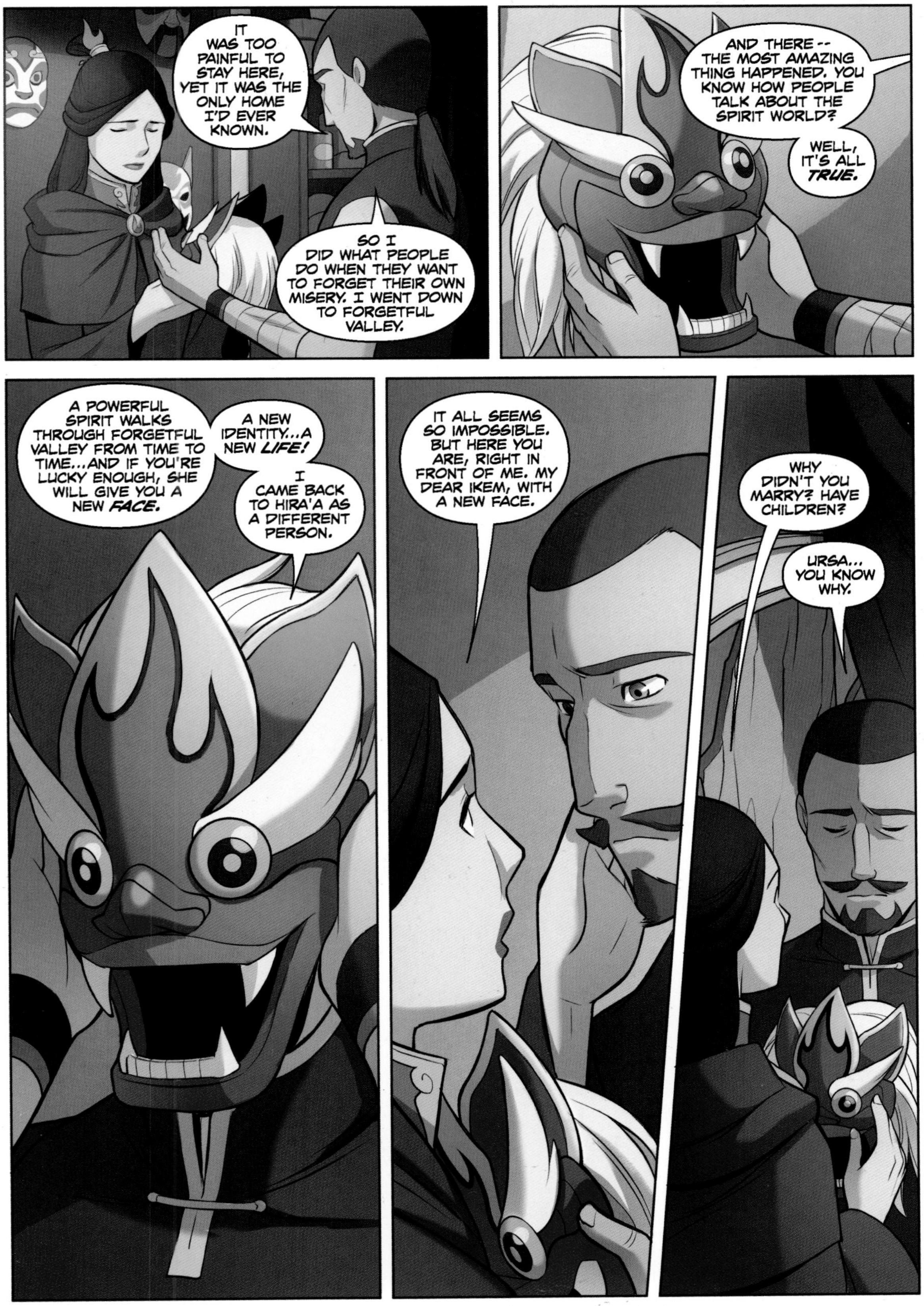
IT WAS TOO PAINFUL TO STAY HERE, YET IT WAS THE ONLY HOME I'D EVER KNOWN.
SO I DID WHAT PEOPLE DO WHEN THEY WANT TO FORGET THEIR OWN MISERY. I WENT DOWN TO FORGETFUL VALLEY.
AND THERE -- THE MOST AMAZING THING HAPPENED. YOU KNOW HOW PEOPLE TALK ABOUT THE SPIRIT WORLD?
WELL, IT'S ALL *TRUE.*
A POWERFUL SPIRIT WALKS THROUGH FORGETFUL VALLEY FROM TIME TO TIME...AND IF YOU'RE LUCKY ENOUGH, SHE WILL GIVE YOU A NEW *FACE.*
A NEW IDENTITY...A NEW *LIFE!*
I CAME BACK TO HIRA'A AS A DIFFERENT PERSON.
IT ALL SEEMS SO IMPOSSIBLE. BUT HERE YOU ARE, RIGHT IN FRONT OF ME. MY DEAR IKEM, WITH A NEW FACE.
WHY DIDN'T YOU MARRY? HAVE CHILDREN?
URSA... YOU KNOW WHY.

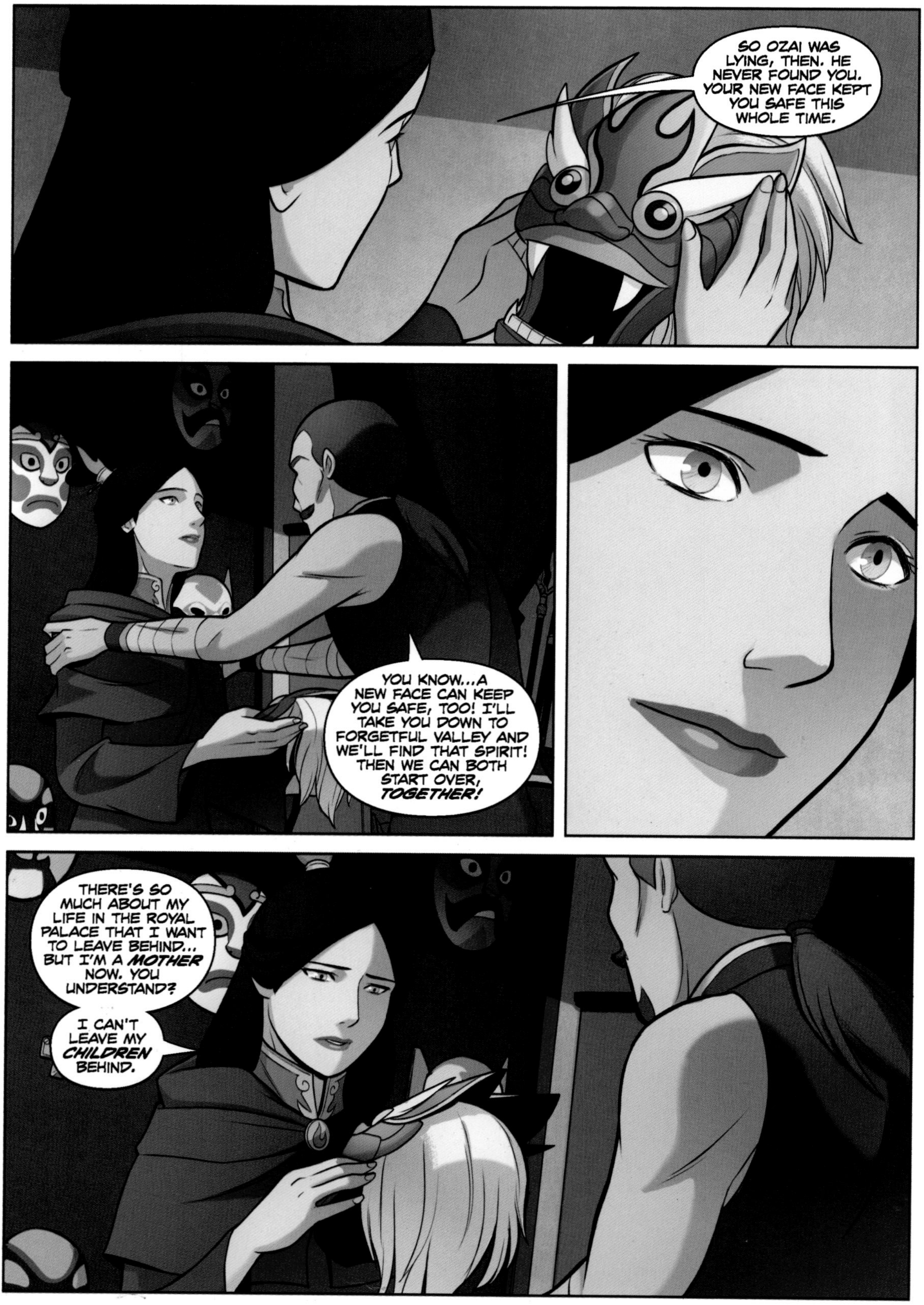
SO OZAI WAS LYING, THEN. HE NEVER FOUND YOU. YOUR NEW FACE KEPT YOU SAFE THIS WHOLE TIME.
YOU KNOW...A NEW FACE CAN KEEP YOU SAFE, TOO! I'LL TAKE YOU DOWN TO FORGETFUL VALLEY AND WE'LL FIND THAT SPIRIT! THEN WE CAN BOTH START OVER, *TOGETHER!*
THERE'S SO MUCH ABOUT MY LIFE IN THE ROYAL PALACE THAT I WANT TO LEAVE BEHIND... BUT I'M A *MOTHER* NOW. YOU UNDERSTAND?
I CAN'T LEAVE MY *CHILDREN* BEHIND.

M: *Gurihiru drew Ursa beautifully on this page and throughout the whole graphic novel. And the way Gene wrote her throughout the story really deepens her as a character.*

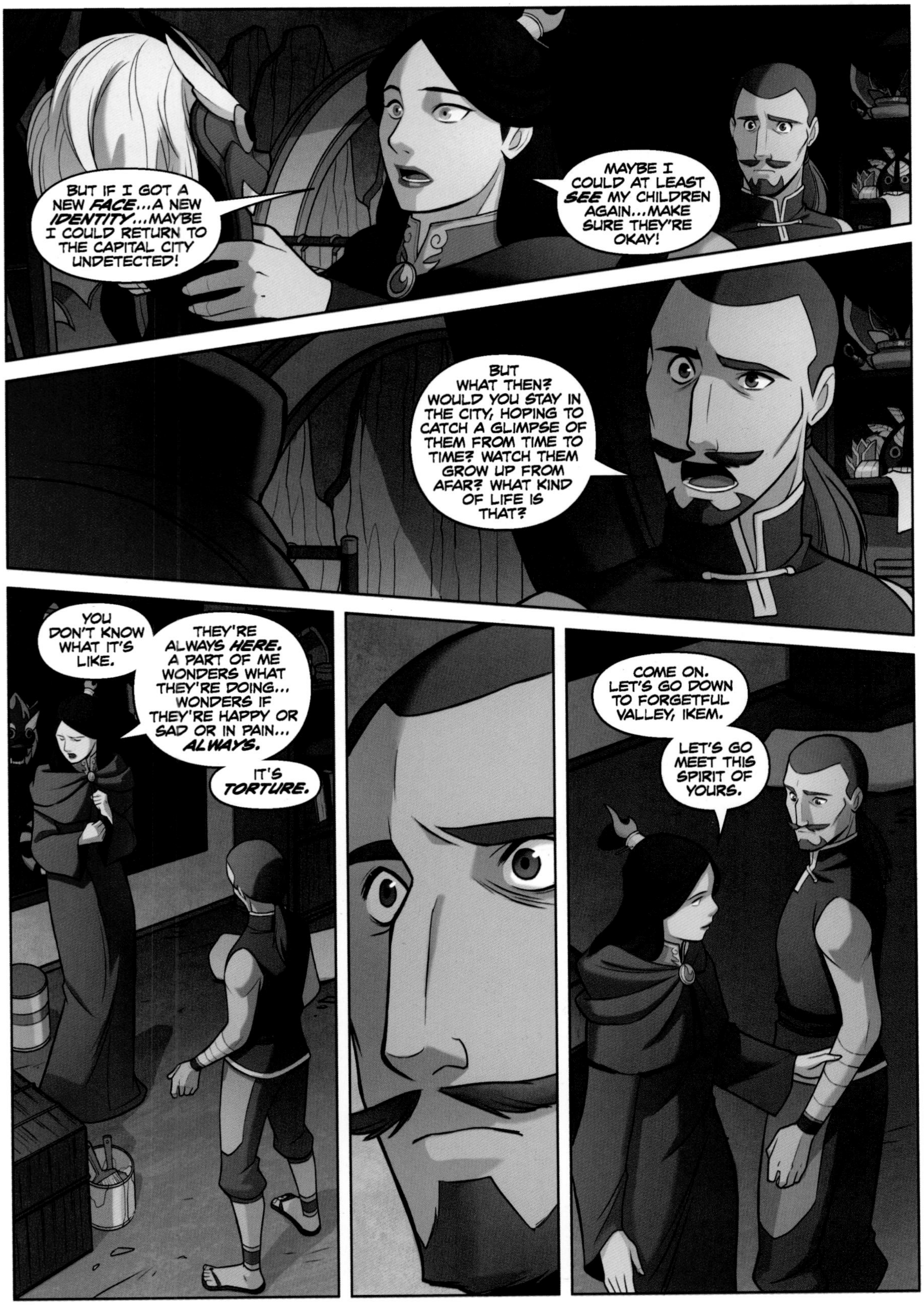
BUT IF I GOT A NEW FACE...A NEW IDENTITY...MAYBE I COULD RETURN TO THE CAPITAL CITY UNDETECTED!
MAYBE I COULD AT LEAST SEE MY CHILDREN AGAIN...MAKE SURE THEY'RE OKAY!
BUT WHAT THEN? WOULD YOU STAY IN THE CITY, HOPING TO CATCH A GLIMPSE OF THEM FROM TIME TO TIME? WATCH THEM GROW UP FROM AFAR? WHAT KIND OF LIFE IS THAT?
YOU DON'T KNOW WHAT IT'S LIKE.
THEY'RE ALWAYS HERE. A PART OF ME WONDERS WHAT THEY'RE DOING... WONDERS IF THEY'RE HAPPY OR SAD OR IN PAIN... ALWAYS.
IT'S TORTURE.
COME ON. LET'S GO DOWN TO FORGETFUL VALLEY, IKEM.
LET'S GO MEET THIS SPIRIT OF YOURS.

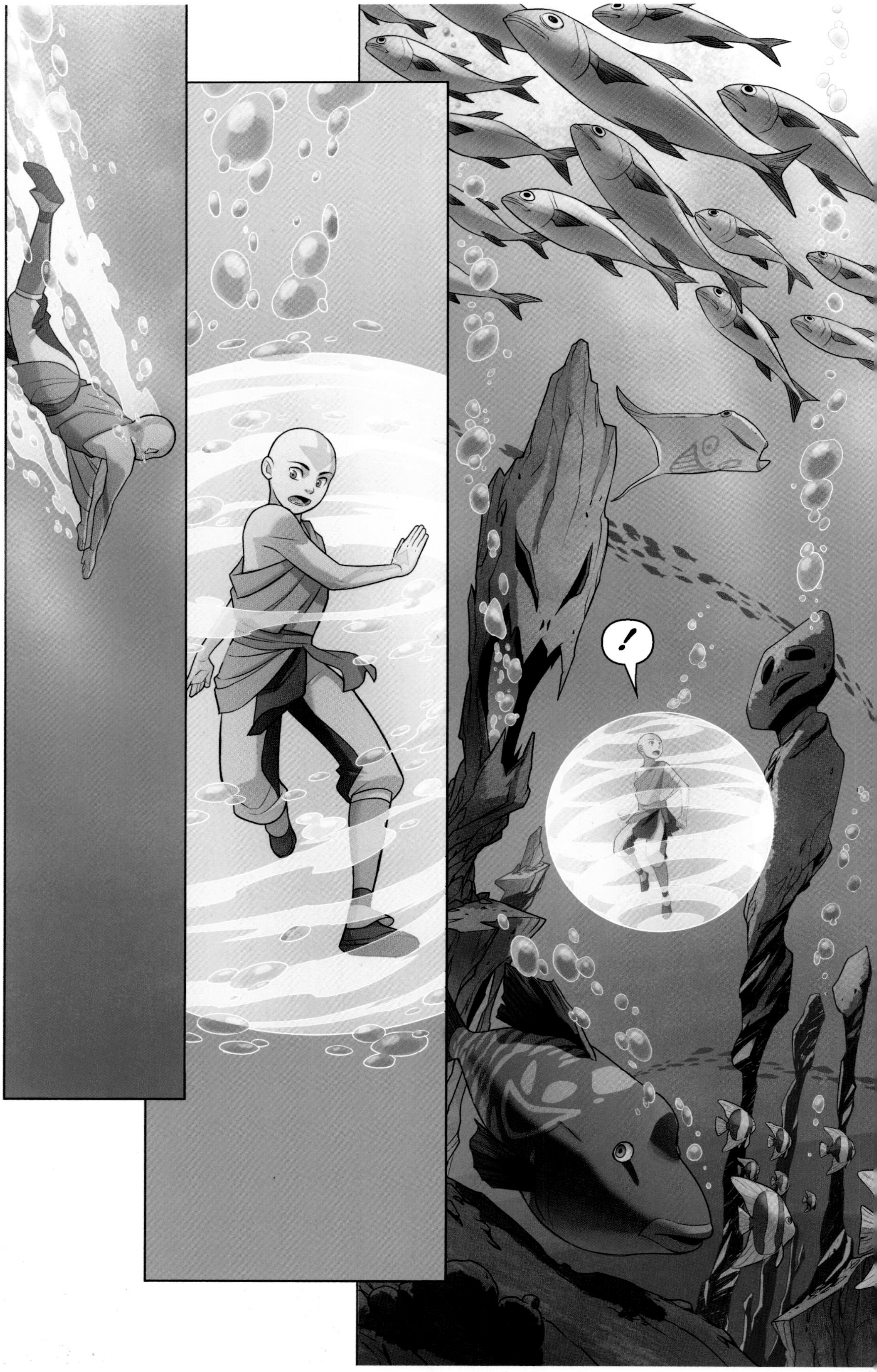
!

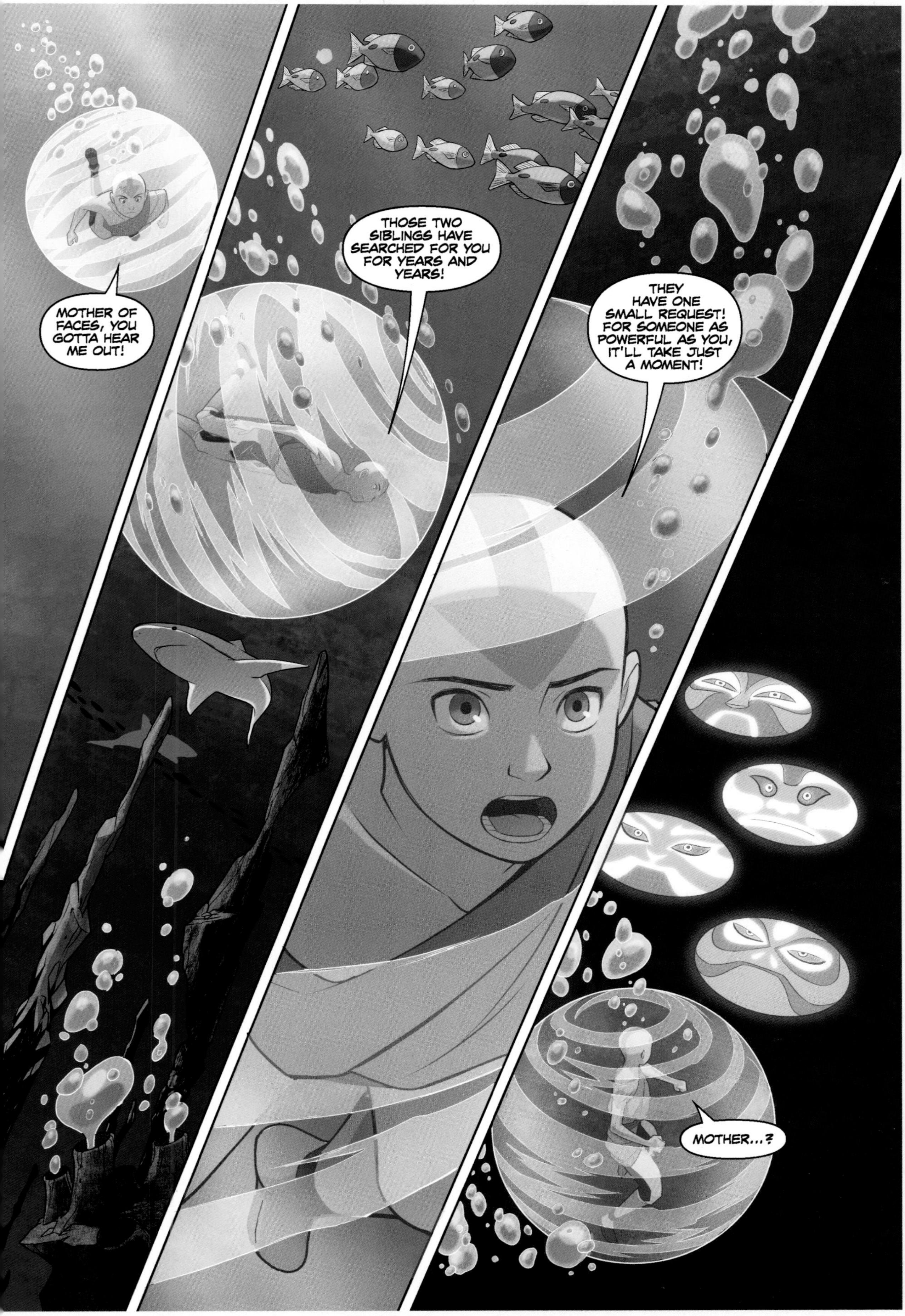
MOTHER OF FACES, YOU GOTTA HEAR ME OUT!
THOSE TWO SIBLINGS HAVE SEARCHED FOR YOU FOR YEARS AND YEARS!
THEY HAVE ONE SMALL REQUEST! FOR SOMEONE AS POWERFUL AS YOU, IT'LL TAKE JUST A MOMENT!
MOTHER...?

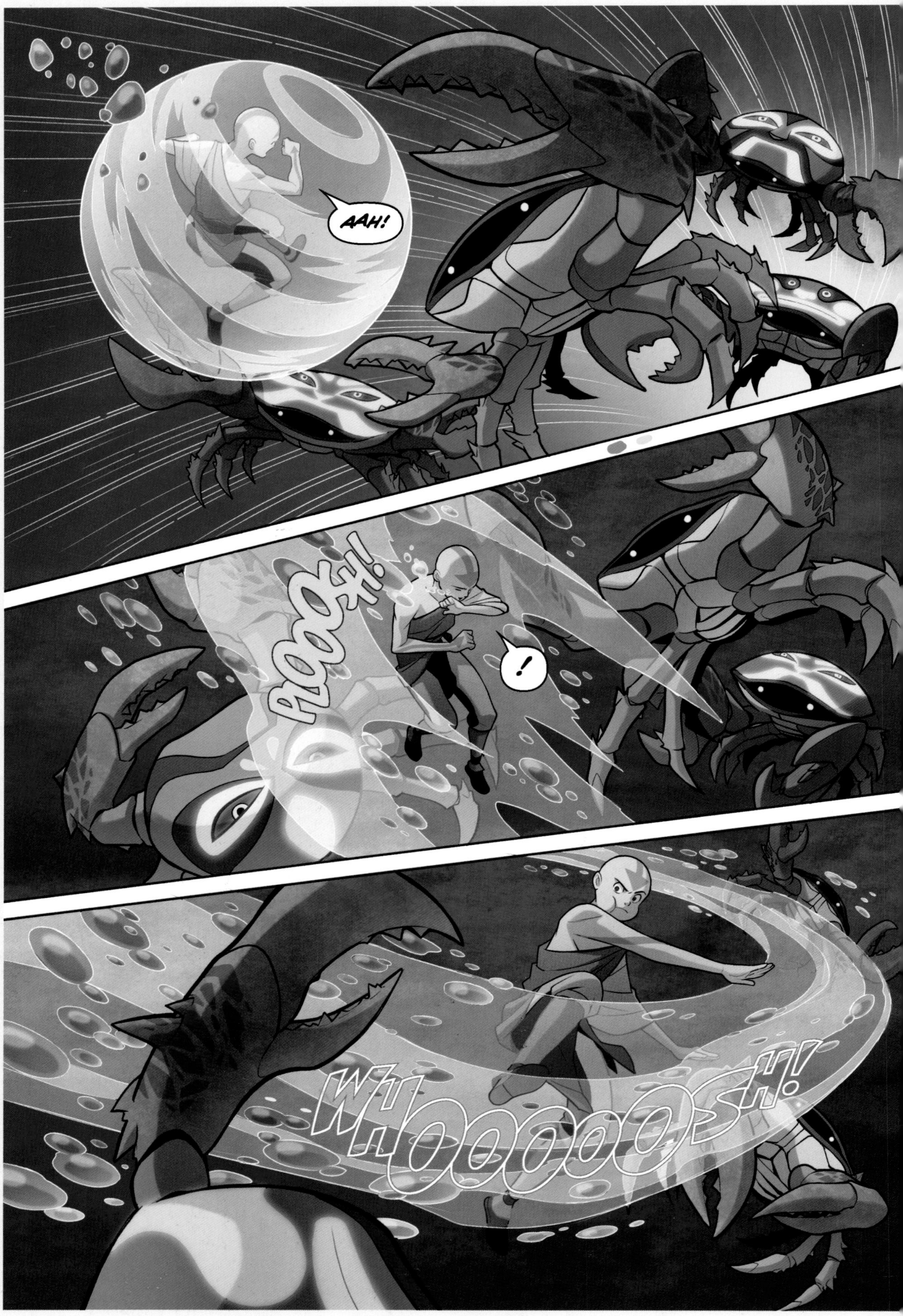
AAH!
PLOOOSH!
!
WHOOOOOOSH!

G: *The idea for the faces on the crabs' shells comes from Beijing opera.*

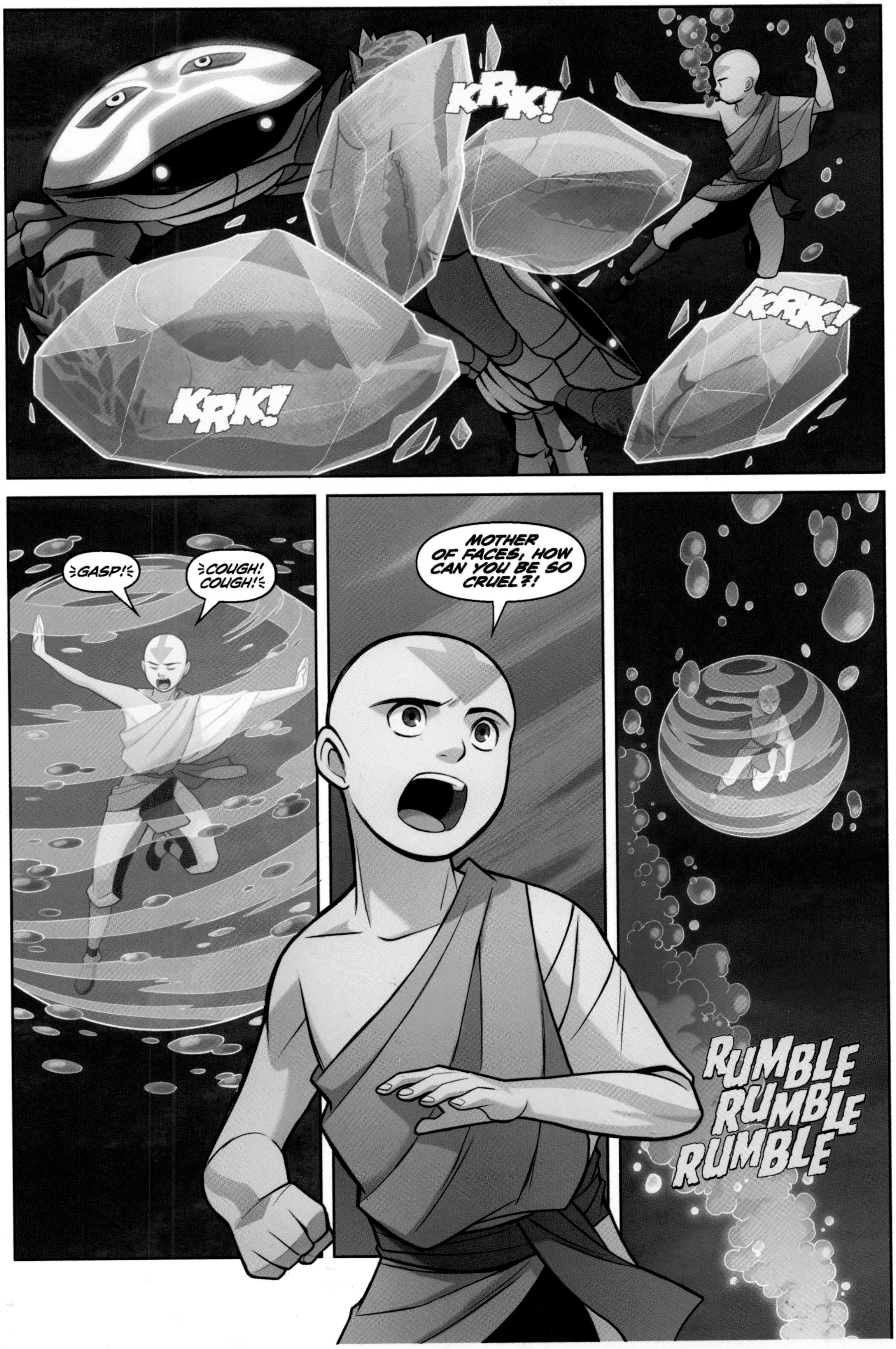
KRK!
KRK!
KRK!
GASP!
COUGH! COUGH!
MOTHER OF FACES, HOW CAN YOU BE SO CRUEL?!
RUMBLE RUMBLE RUMBLE

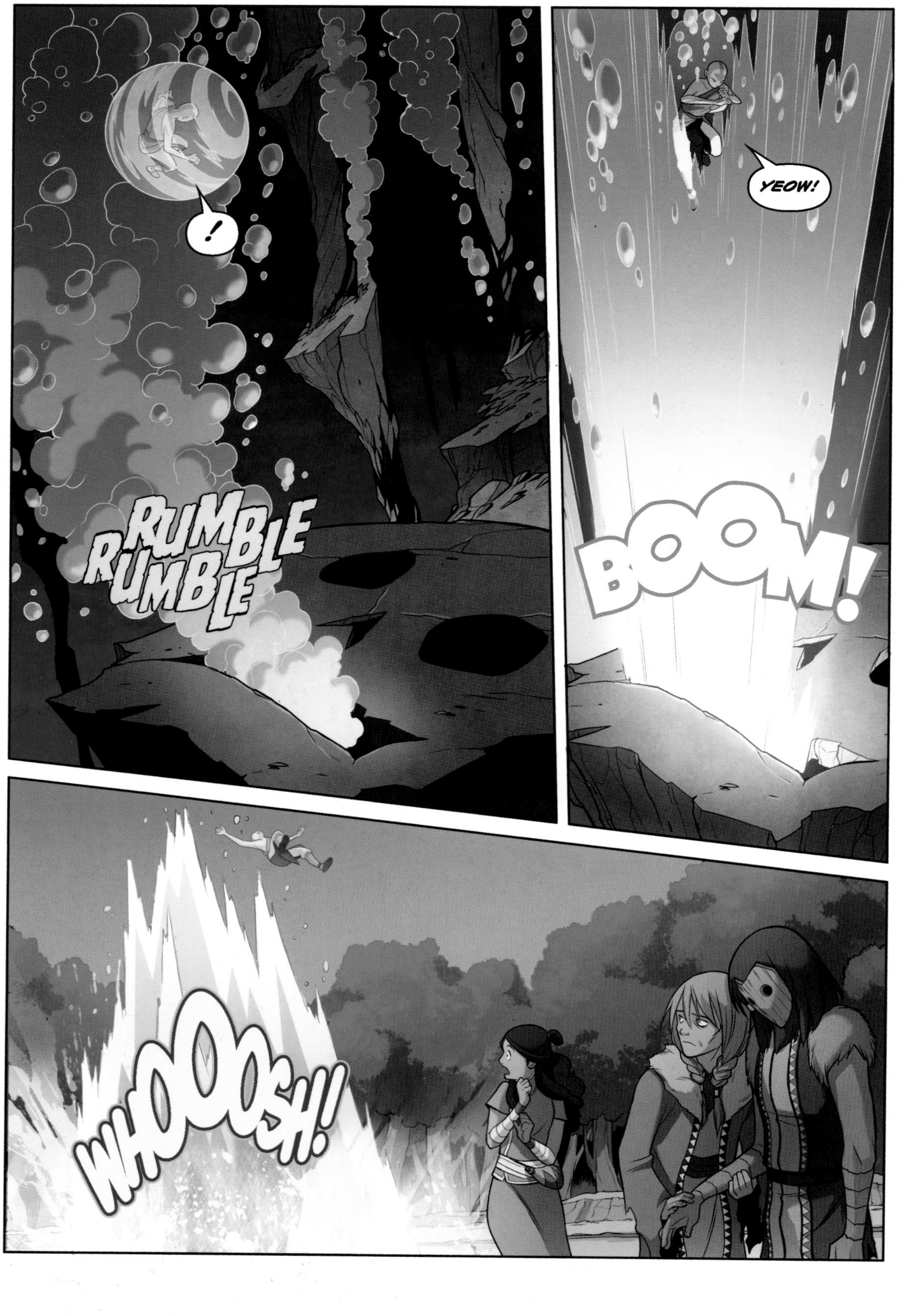
!
RUMBLE RUMBLE
YEOW!
BOOM!
WHOOOSH!

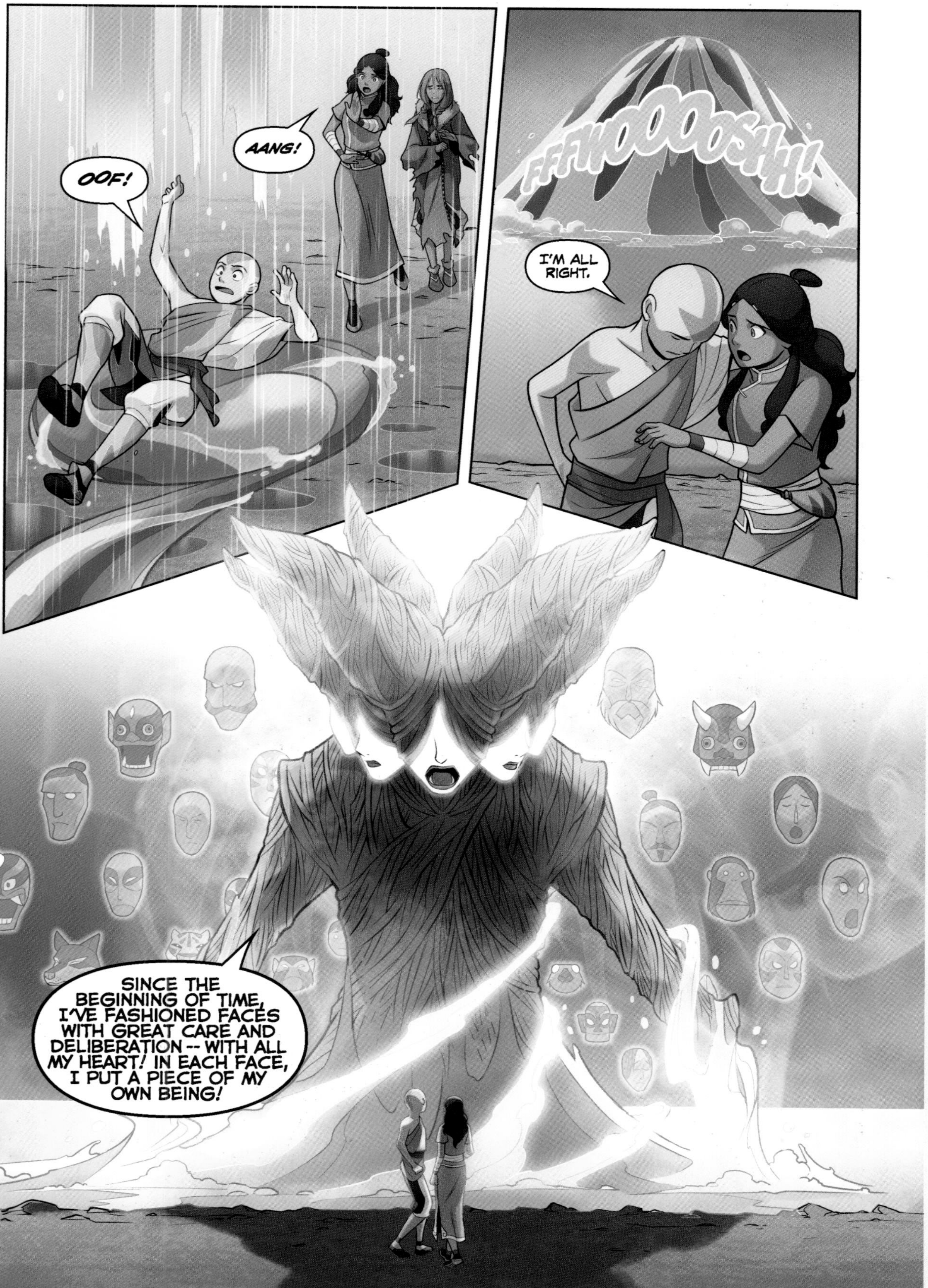
OOF!
AANG!
FFFWOOOOOSHH!
I'M ALL RIGHT.
SINCE THE BEGINNING OF TIME, I'VE FASHIONED FACES WITH GREAT CARE AND DELIBERATION -- WITH ALL MY HEART! IN EACH FACE, I PUT A PIECE OF MY OWN BEING!

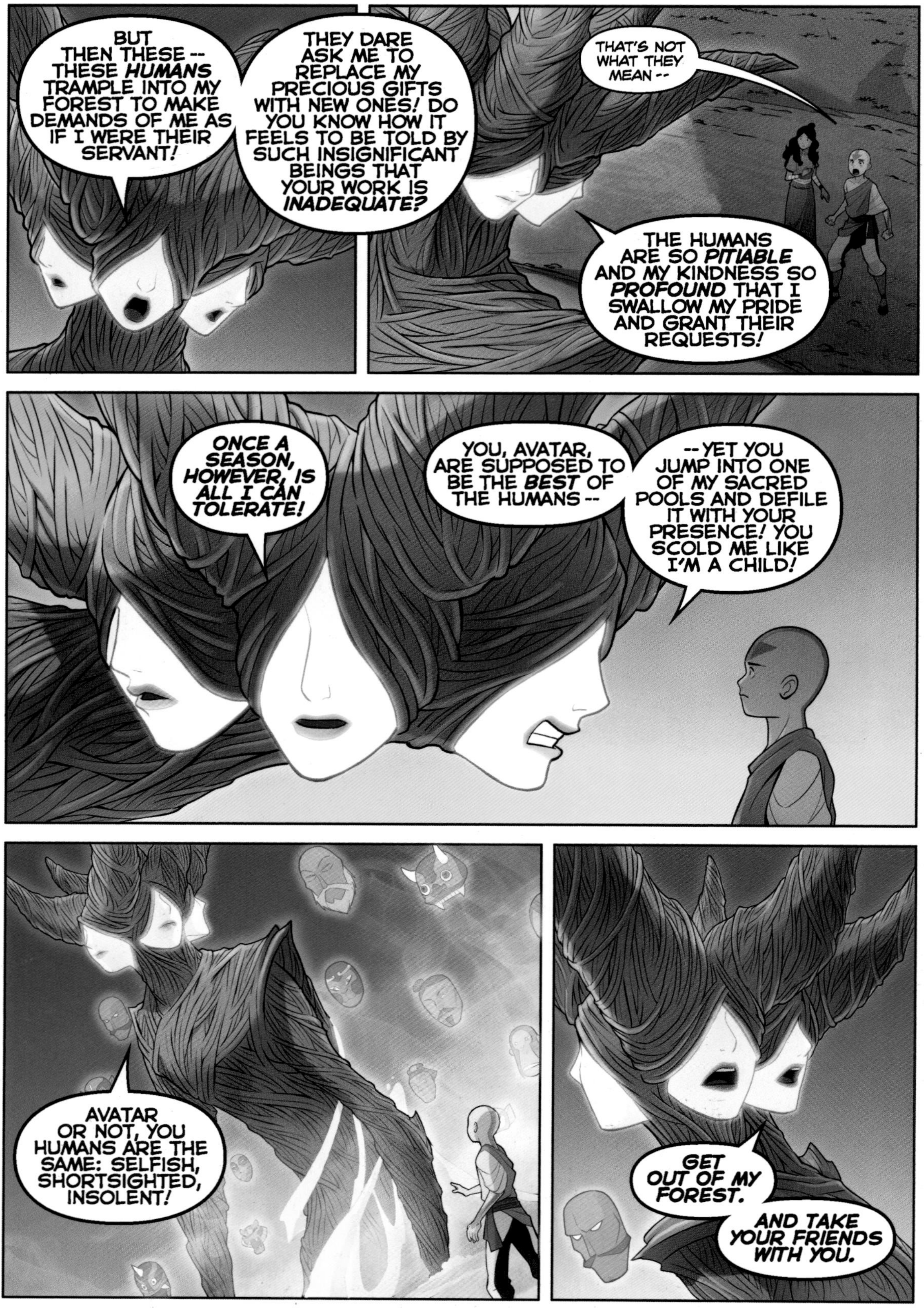
BUT THEN THESE -- THESE HUMANS TRAMPLE INTO MY FOREST TO MAKE DEMANDS OF ME AS IF I WERE THEIR SERVANT!
THEY DARE ASK ME TO REPLACE MY PRECIOUS GIFTS WITH NEW ONES! DO YOU KNOW HOW IT FEELS TO BE TOLD BY SUCH INSIGNIFICANT BEINGS THAT YOUR WORK IS INADEQUATE?
THAT'S NOT WHAT THEY MEAN --
THE HUMANS ARE SO PITIABLE AND MY KINDNESS SO PROFOUND THAT I SWALLOW MY PRIDE AND GRANT THEIR REQUESTS!
ONCE A SEASON, HOWEVER, IS ALL I CAN TOLERATE!
YOU, AVATAR, ARE SUPPOSED TO BE THE BEST OF THE HUMANS --
--YET YOU JUMP INTO ONE OF MY SACRED POOLS AND DEFILE IT WITH YOUR PRESENCE! YOU SCOLD ME LIKE I'M A CHILD!
AVATAR OR NOT, YOU HUMANS ARE THE SAME: SELFISH, SHORTSIGHTED, INSOLENT!
GET OUT OF MY FOREST.
AND TAKE YOUR FRIENDS WITH YOU.

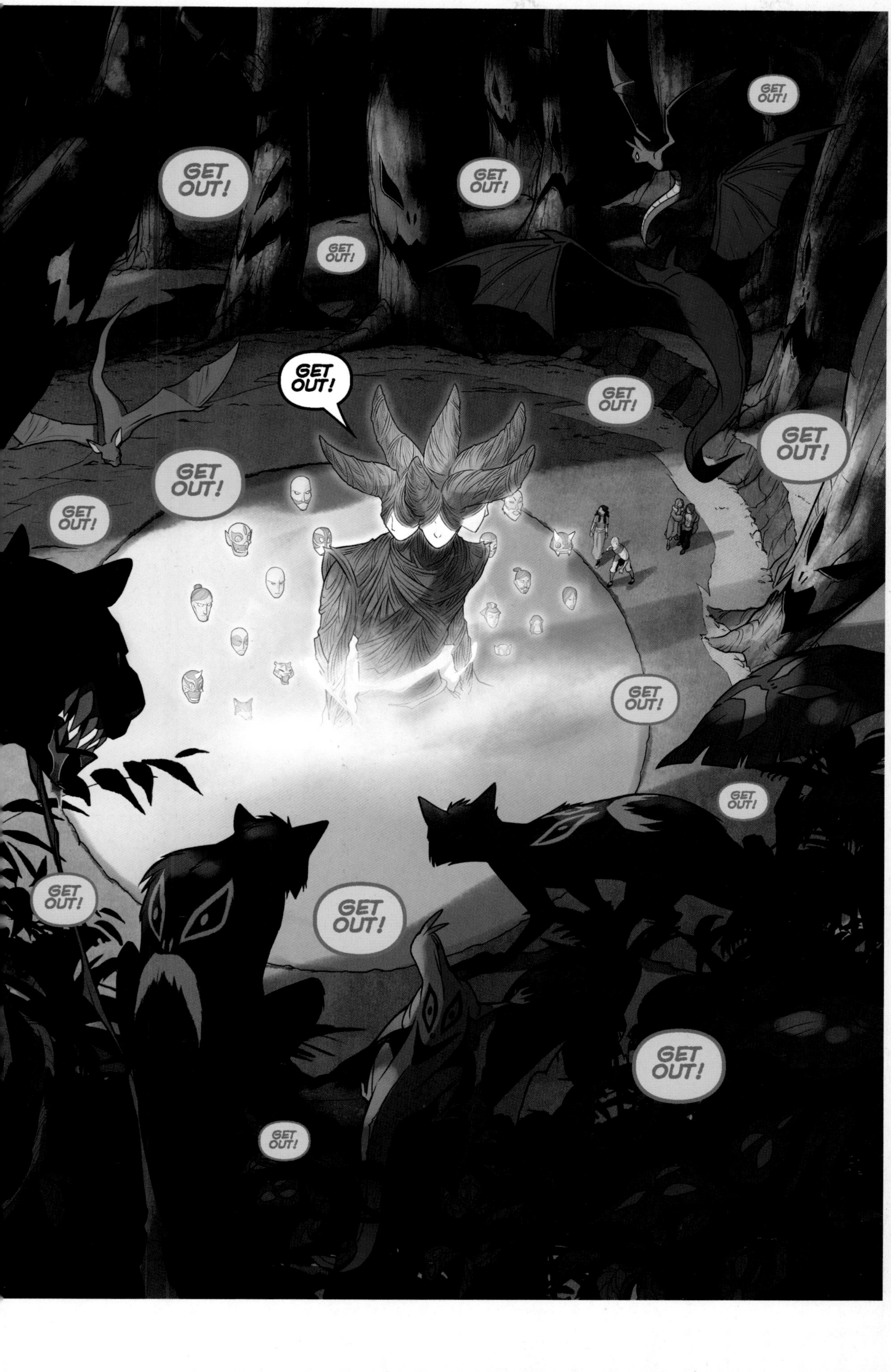
GET OUT!
GET OUT!
GET OUT!
GET OUT!
GET OUT!
GET OUT!
GET OUT!
GET OUT!
GET OUT!
GET OUT!
GET OUT!
GET OUT!
GET OUT!
GET OUT!
GET OUT!

G: *Since Mother of Faces does not have eyes or much facial expression, we expressed her emotions with color. Here, she is angry, resulting in a stronger red.*

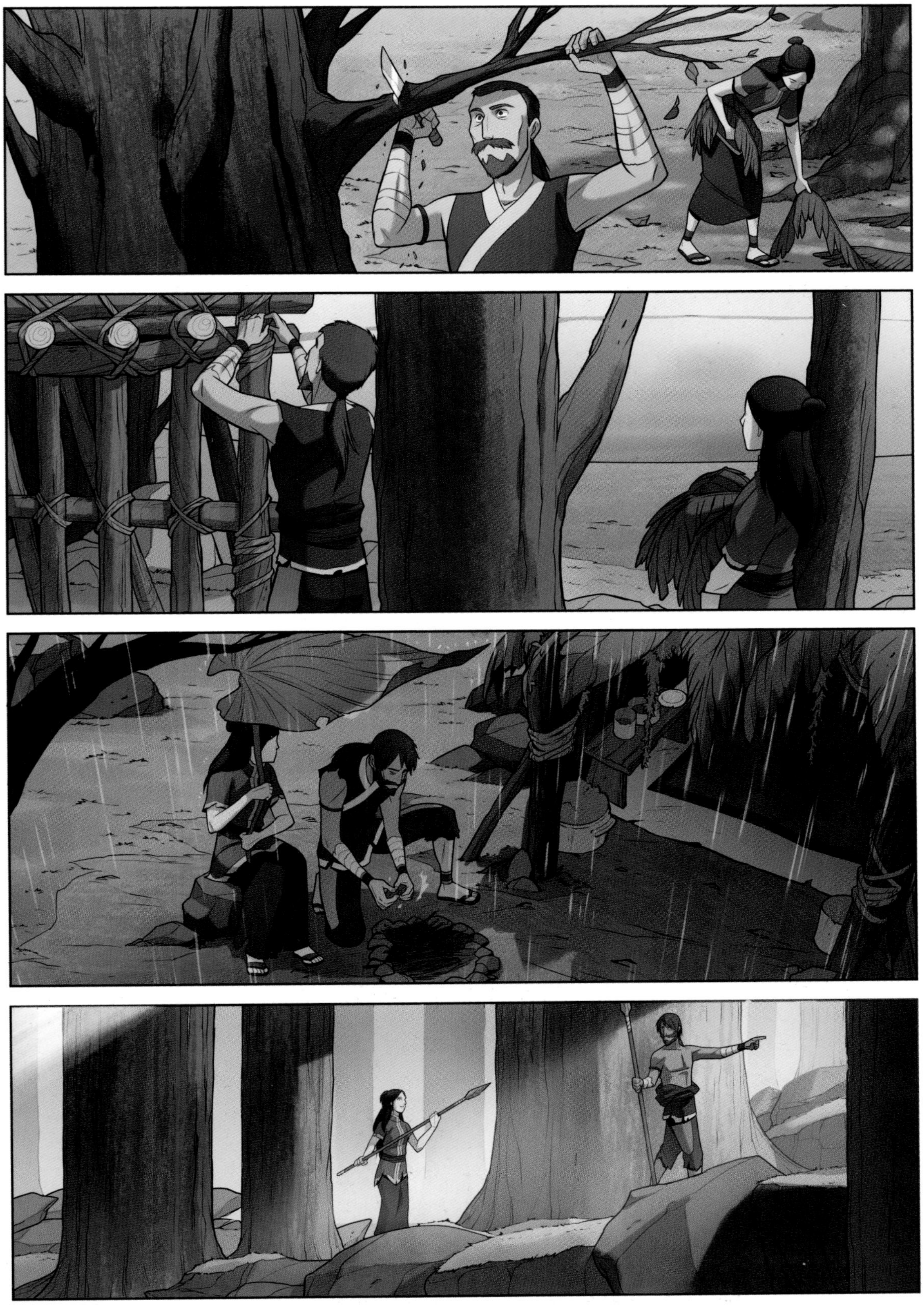

G: *We did this scene to contrast with part 1, where Ikem goes into the woods alone. But since he is with Ursa, nothing tragic happens.*

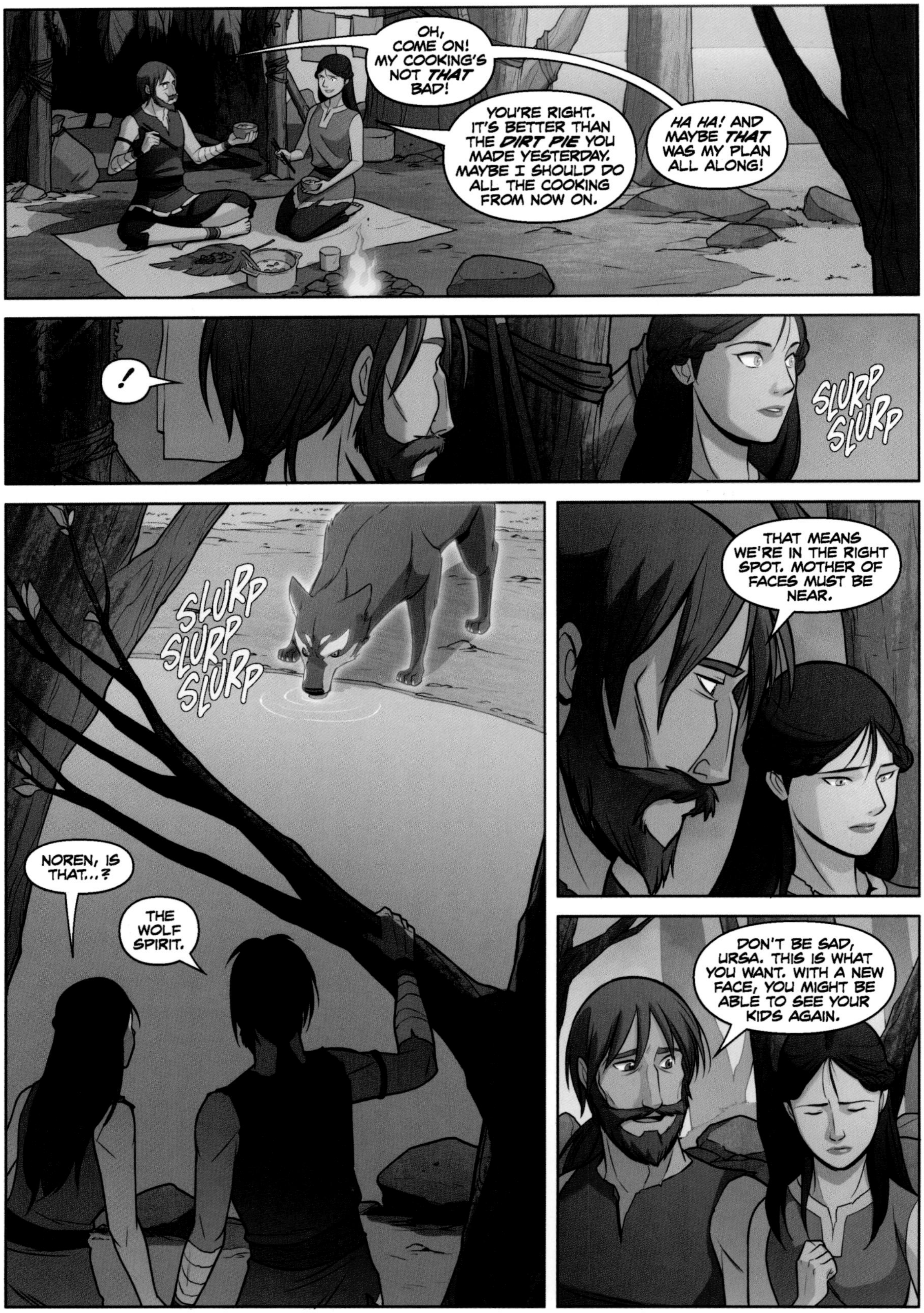
OH, COME ON! MY COOKING'S NOT THAT BAD!
YOU'RE RIGHT. IT'S BETTER THAN THE DIRT PIE YOU MADE YESTERDAY. MAYBE I SHOULD DO ALL THE COOKING FROM NOW ON.
HA HA! AND MAYBE THAT WAS MY PLAN ALL ALONG!
!
SLURP SLURP
SLURP SLURP SLURP
NOREN, IS THAT...?
THE WOLF SPIRIT.
THAT MEANS WE'RE IN THE RIGHT SPOT. MOTHER OF FACES MUST BE NEAR.
DON'T BE SAD, URSA. THIS IS WHAT YOU WANT. WITH A NEW FACE, YOU MIGHT BE ABLE TO SEE YOUR KIDS AGAIN.

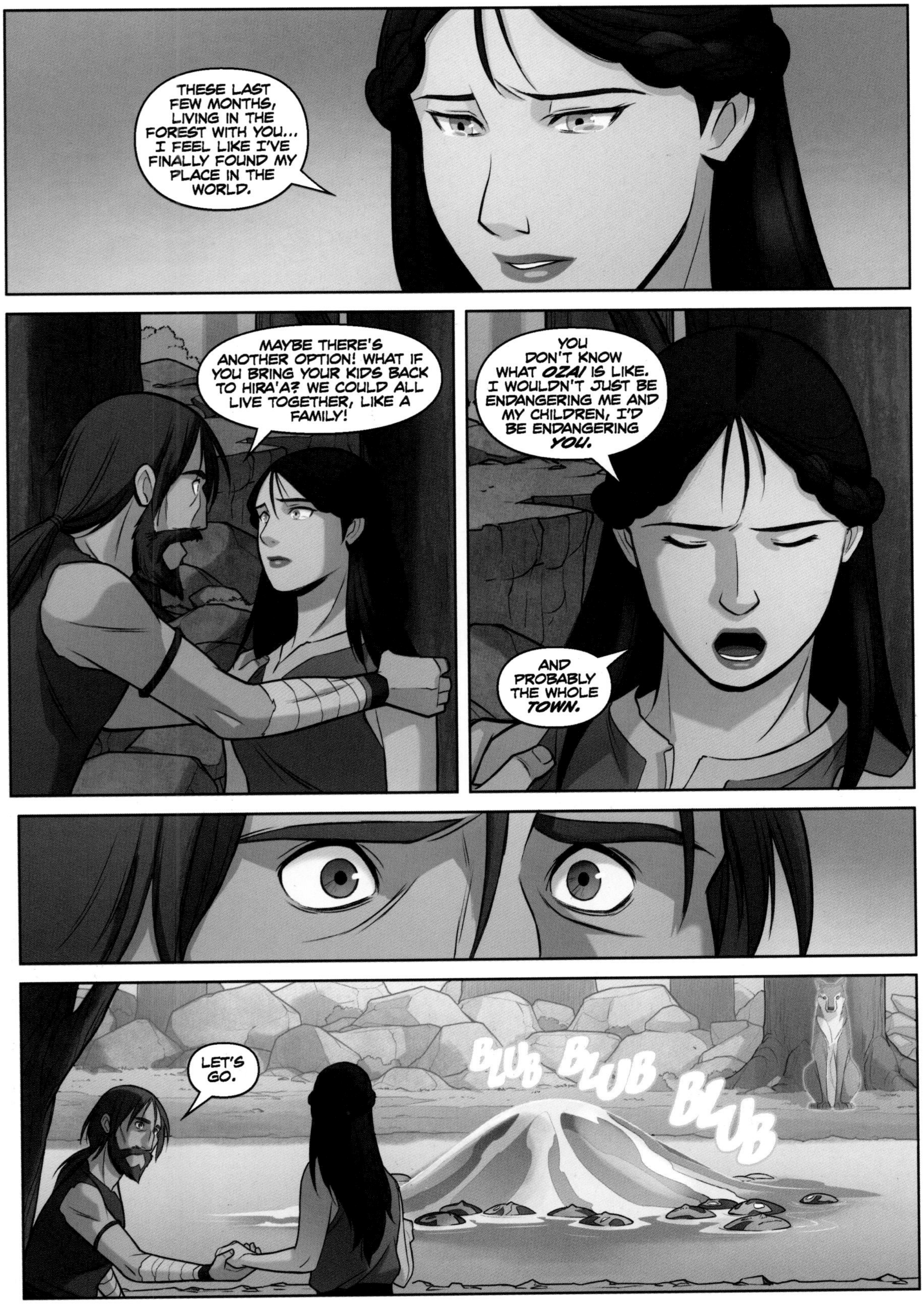
THESE LAST FEW MONTHS, LIVING IN THE FOREST WITH YOU... I FEEL LIKE I'VE FINALLY FOUND MY PLACE IN THE WORLD.
MAYBE THERE'S ANOTHER OPTION! WHAT IF YOU BRING YOUR KIDS BACK TO HIRA'A? WE COULD ALL LIVE TOGETHER, LIKE A FAMILY!
YOU DON'T KNOW WHAT OZAI IS LIKE. I WOULDN'T JUST BE ENDANGERING ME AND MY CHILDREN, I'D BE ENDANGERING YOU.
AND PROBABLY THE WHOLE TOWN.
LET'S GO.
BLUB BLUB BLUB

G: *To show the passage of time, we made Ursa's hairstyle the same as in her younger days.*

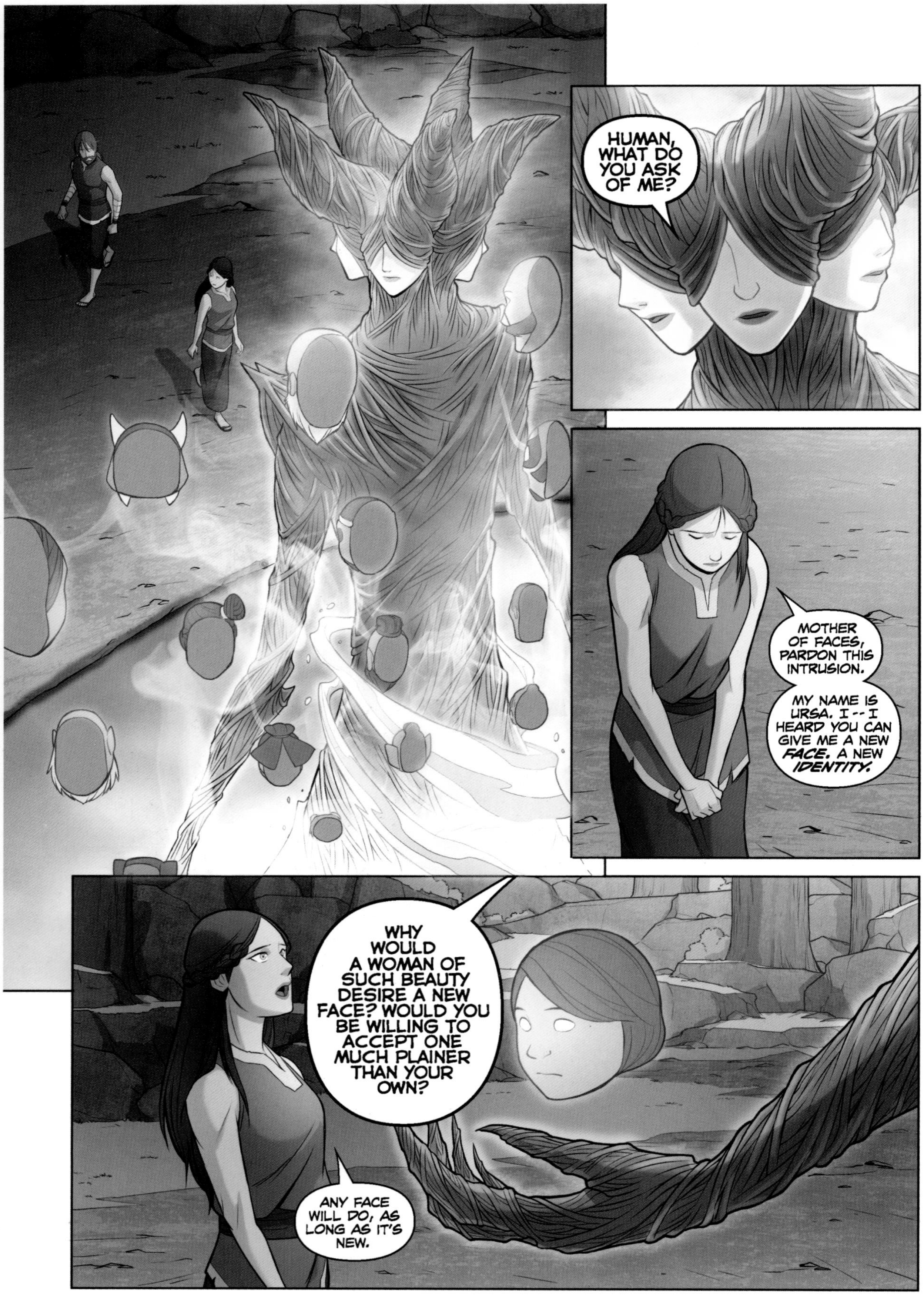
HUMAN, WHAT DO YOU ASK OF ME?
MOTHER OF FACES, PARDON THIS INTRUSION.
MY NAME IS URSA. I -- I HEARD YOU CAN GIVE ME A NEW *FACE*. A NEW *IDENTITY*.
WHY WOULD A WOMAN OF SUCH BEAUTY DESIRE A NEW FACE? WOULD YOU BE WILLING TO ACCEPT ONE MUCH PLAINER THAN YOUR OWN?
ANY FACE WILL DO, AS LONG AS IT'S NEW.

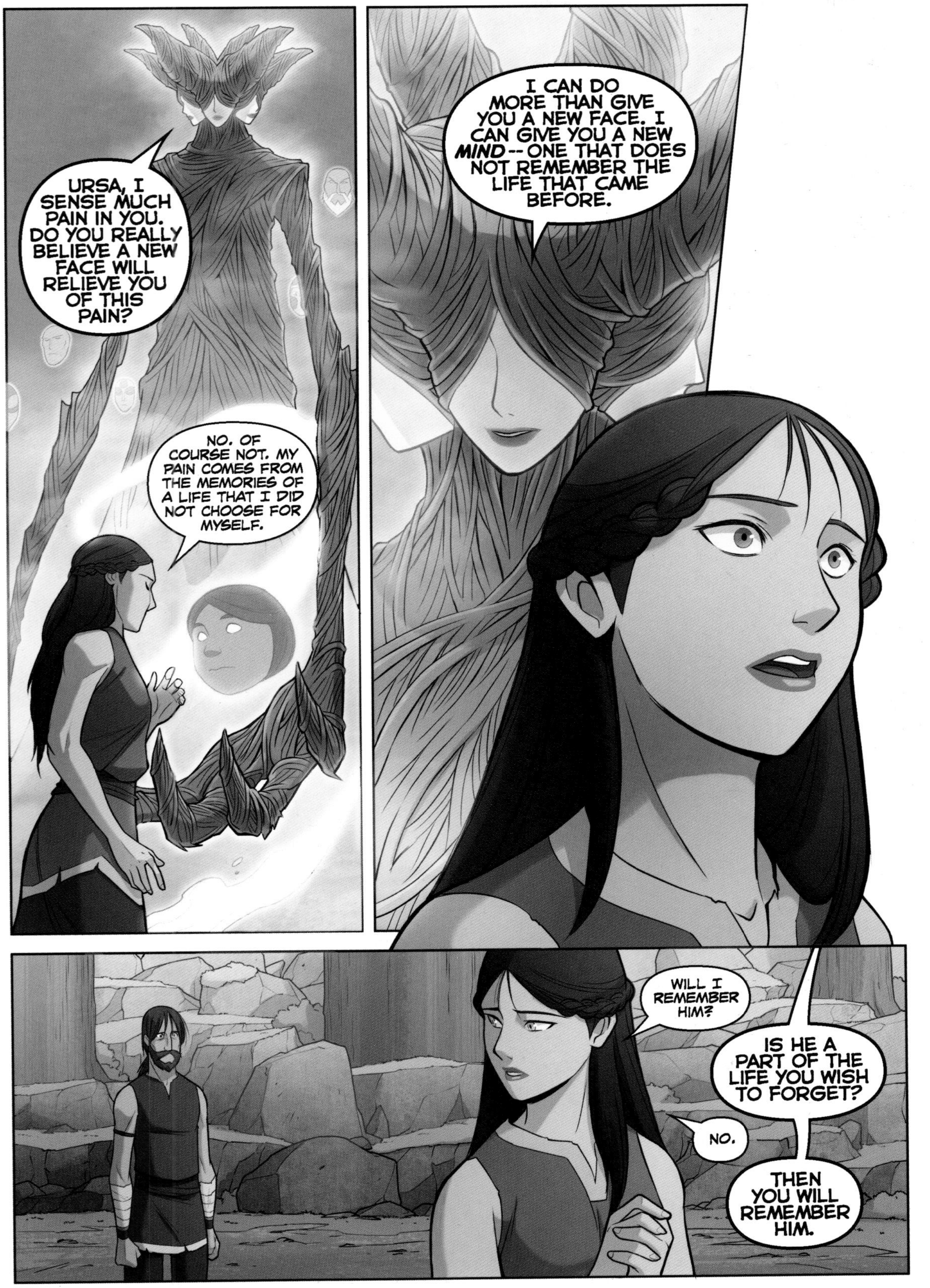
URSA, I SENSE MUCH PAIN IN YOU. DO YOU REALLY BELIEVE A NEW FACE WILL RELIEVE YOU OF THIS PAIN?
NO. OF COURSE NOT. MY PAIN COMES FROM THE MEMORIES OF A LIFE THAT I DID NOT CHOOSE FOR MYSELF.
I CAN DO MORE THAN GIVE YOU A NEW FACE. I CAN GIVE YOU A NEW *MIND*-- ONE THAT DOES NOT REMEMBER THE LIFE THAT CAME BEFORE.
WILL I REMEMBER HIM?
IS HE A PART OF THE LIFE YOU WISH TO FORGET?
NO.
THEN YOU WILL REMEMBER HIM.

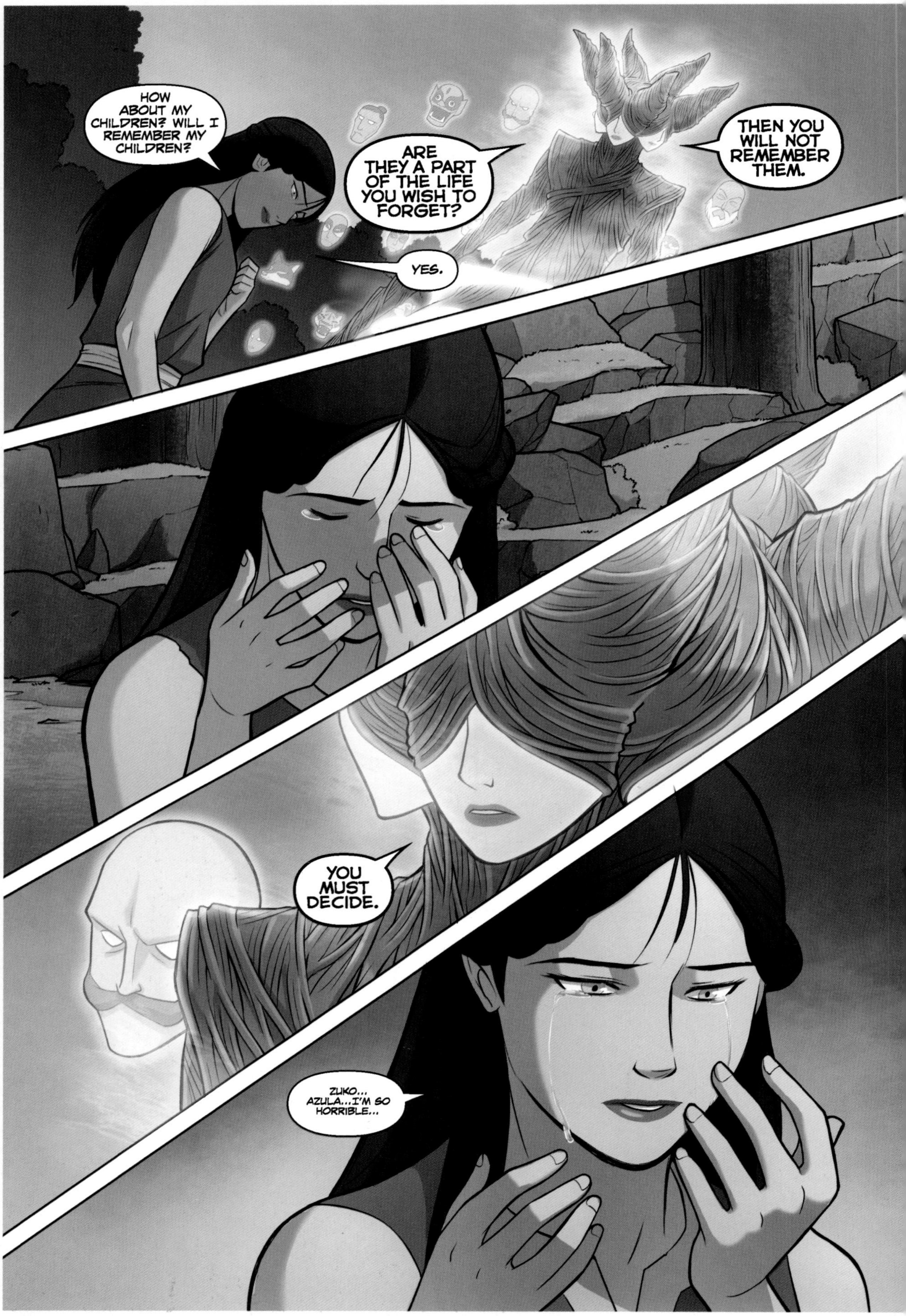
HOW ABOUT MY CHILDREN? WILL I REMEMBER MY CHILDREN?
ARE THEY A PART OF THE LIFE YOU WISH TO FORGET?
YES.
THEN YOU WILL NOT REMEMBER THEM.
YOU MUST DECIDE.
ZUKO... AZULA...I'M SO HORRIBLE...

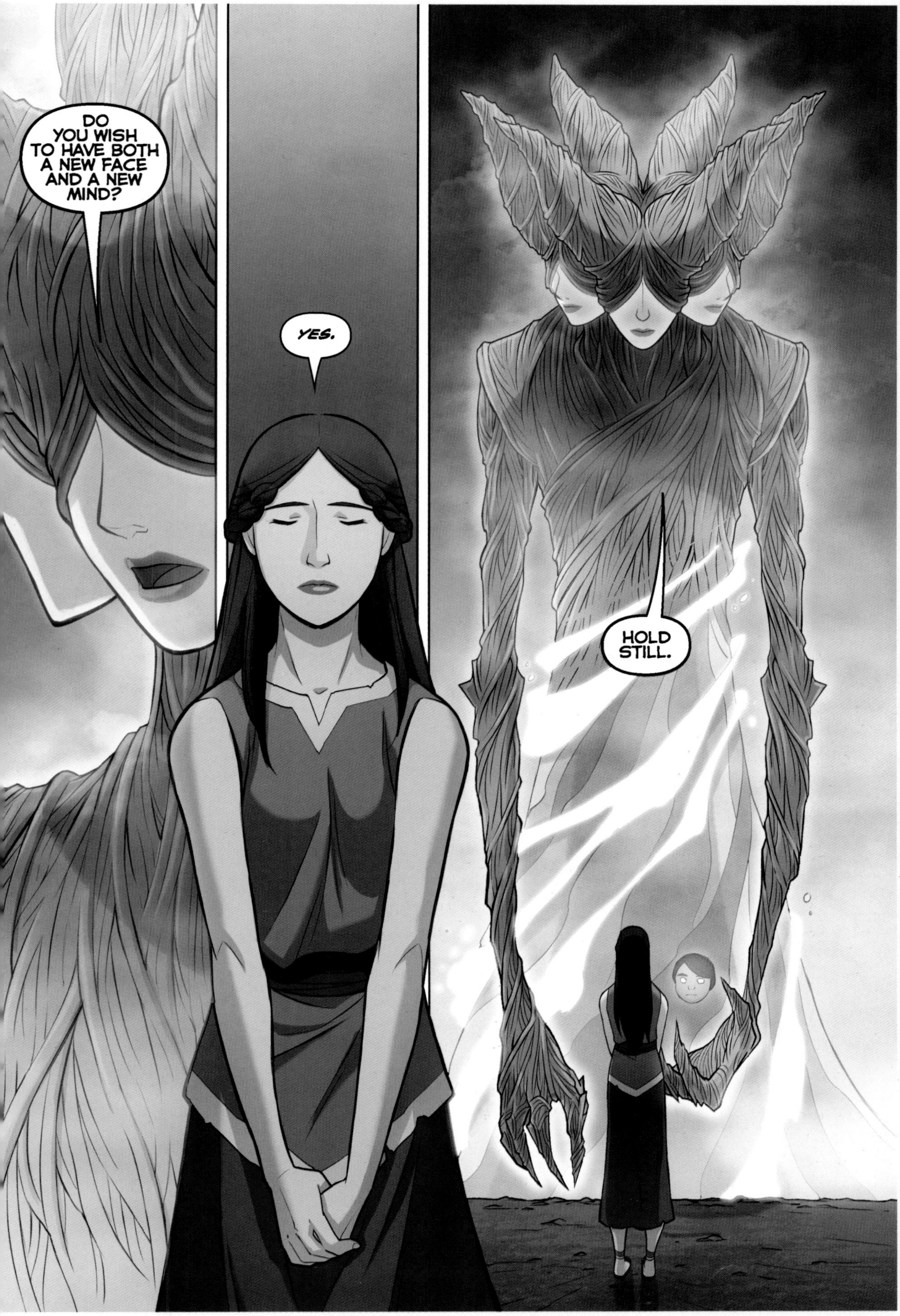
DO YOU WISH TO HAVE BOTH A NEW FACE AND A NEW MIND?
YES.
HOLD STILL.

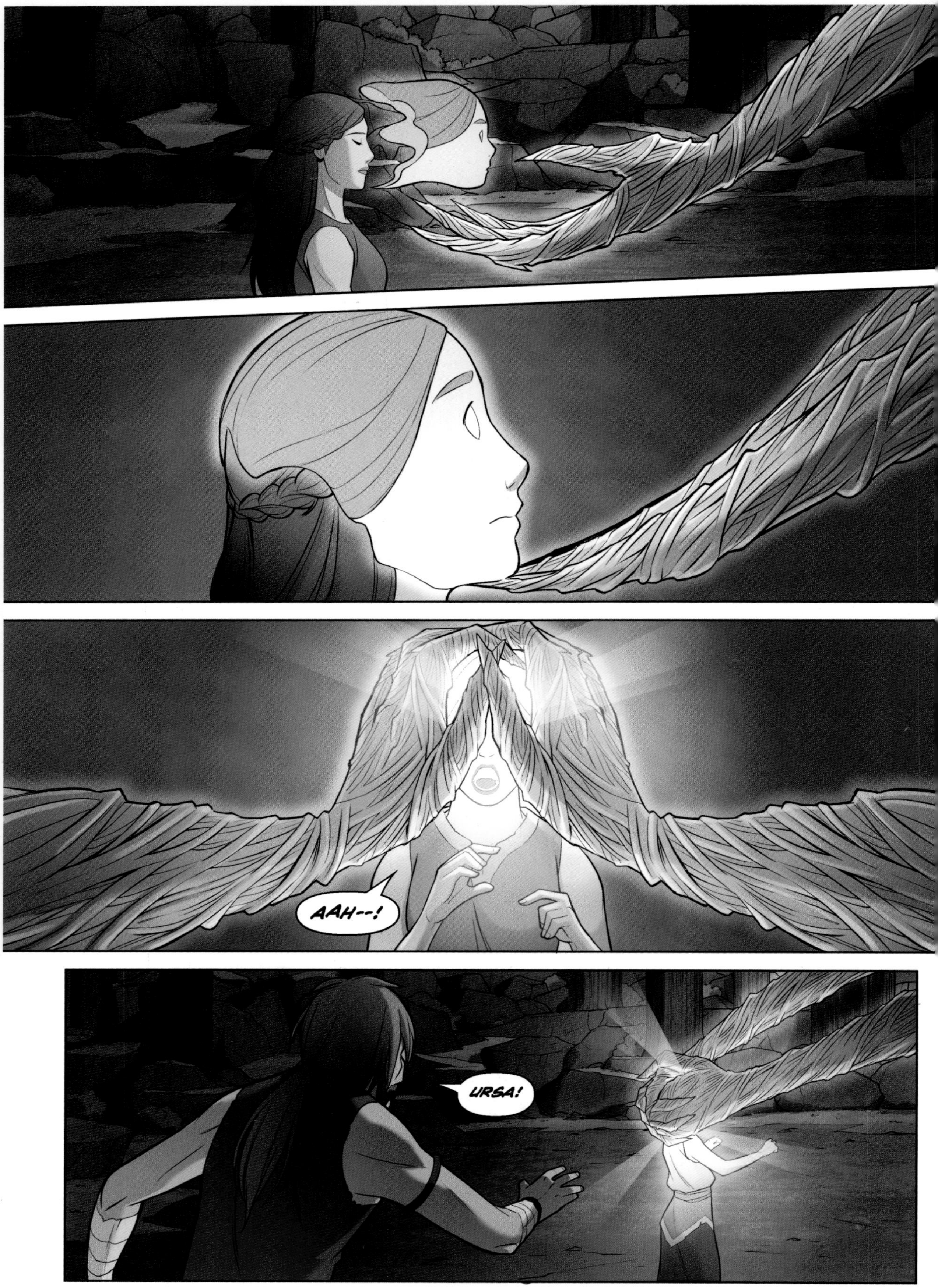
AAH--!
URSA!

M: *I remember when Gene first pitched me the idea of Mother of Faces. I was intrigued but a bit worried about her powers being a little too magical. Around the same time, Bryan, the writers, and I were developing more of the mythology around the spirits for book 2 of* Korra. *For one of the episodes, we came up with the idea that spirits can take over a human body for a short time, but at great peril to the human. I asked Gene to apply that concept to Mother of Faces, so by making physical contact with Ursa, she can alter her appearance. This is one example of how the work on the series influences what happens in the graphic novels.*

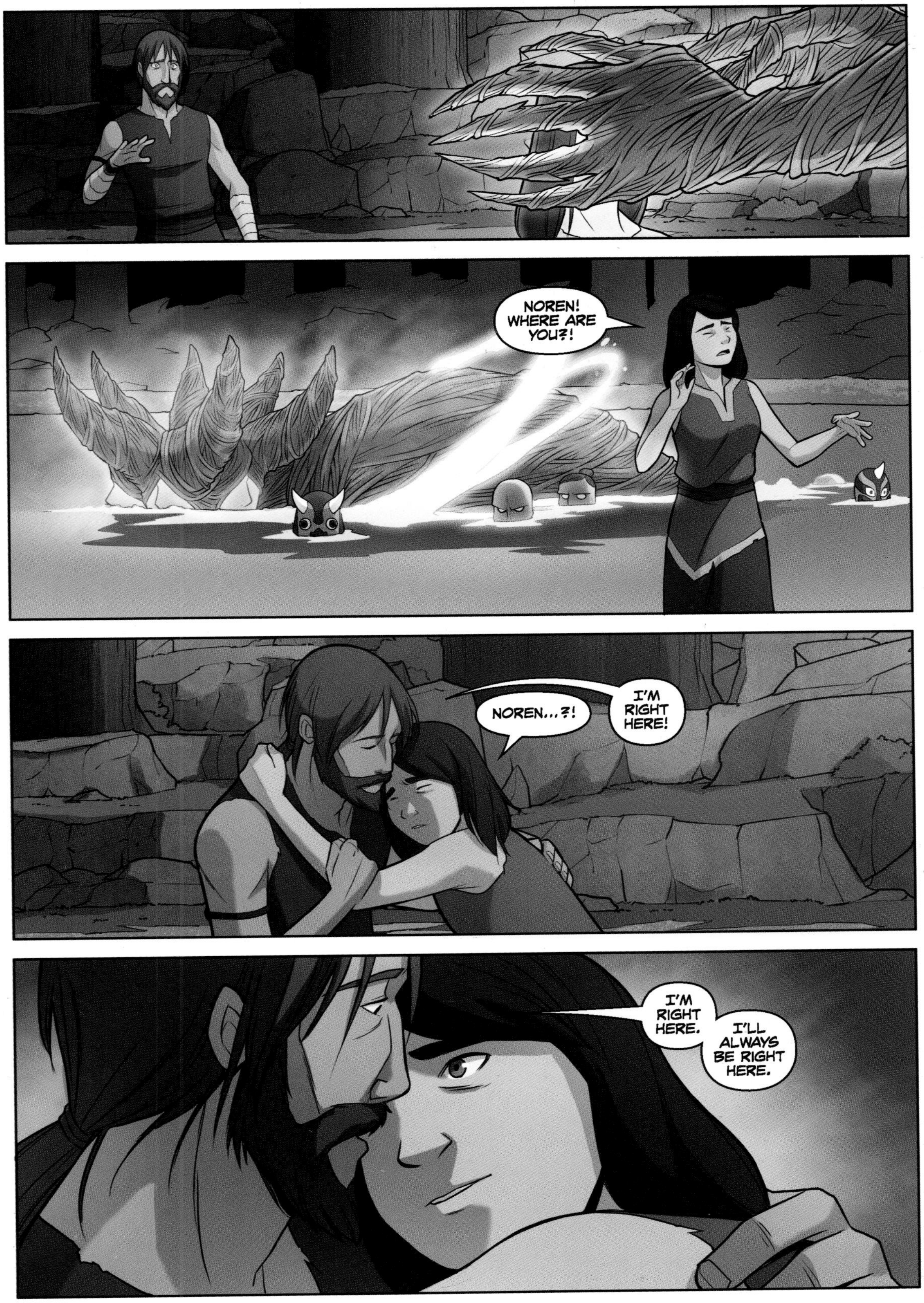
NOREN! WHERE ARE YOU?!
NOREN...?!
I'M RIGHT HERE!
I'M RIGHT HERE.
I'LL ALWAYS BE RIGHT HERE.

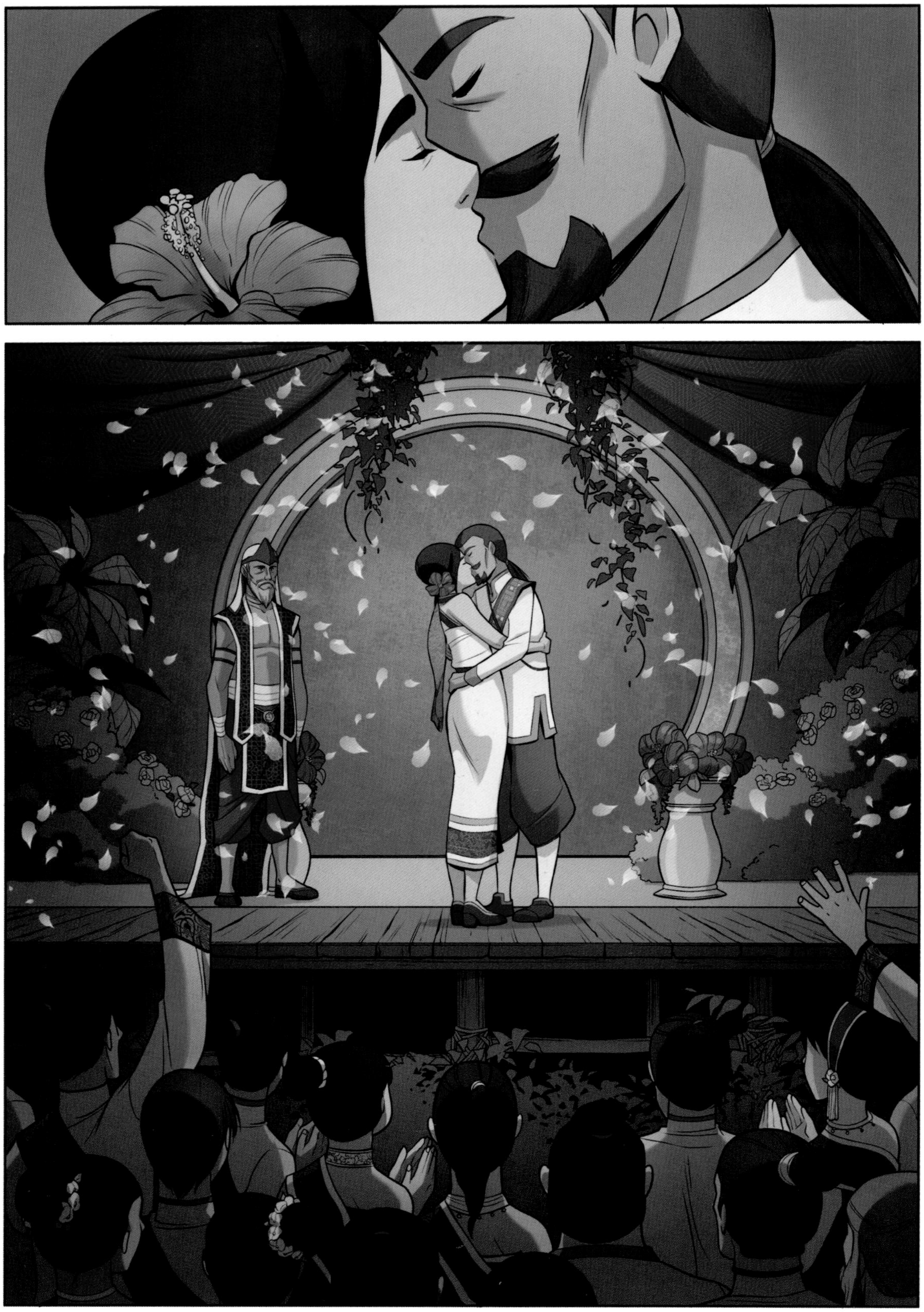

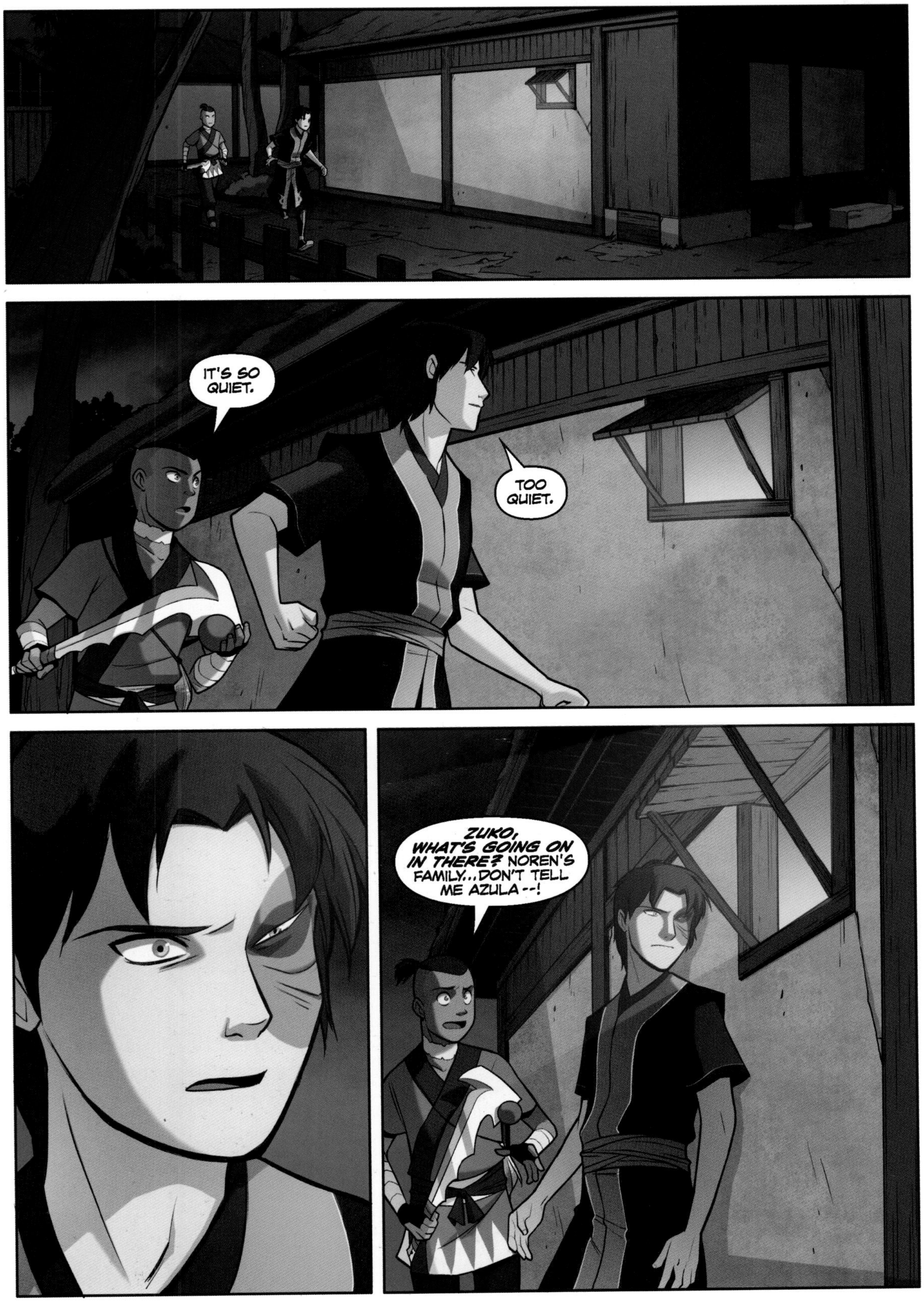
IT'S SO QUIET.
TOO QUIET.
ZUKO, WHAT'S GOING ON IN THERE? NOREN'S FAMILY...DON'T TELL ME AZULA--!

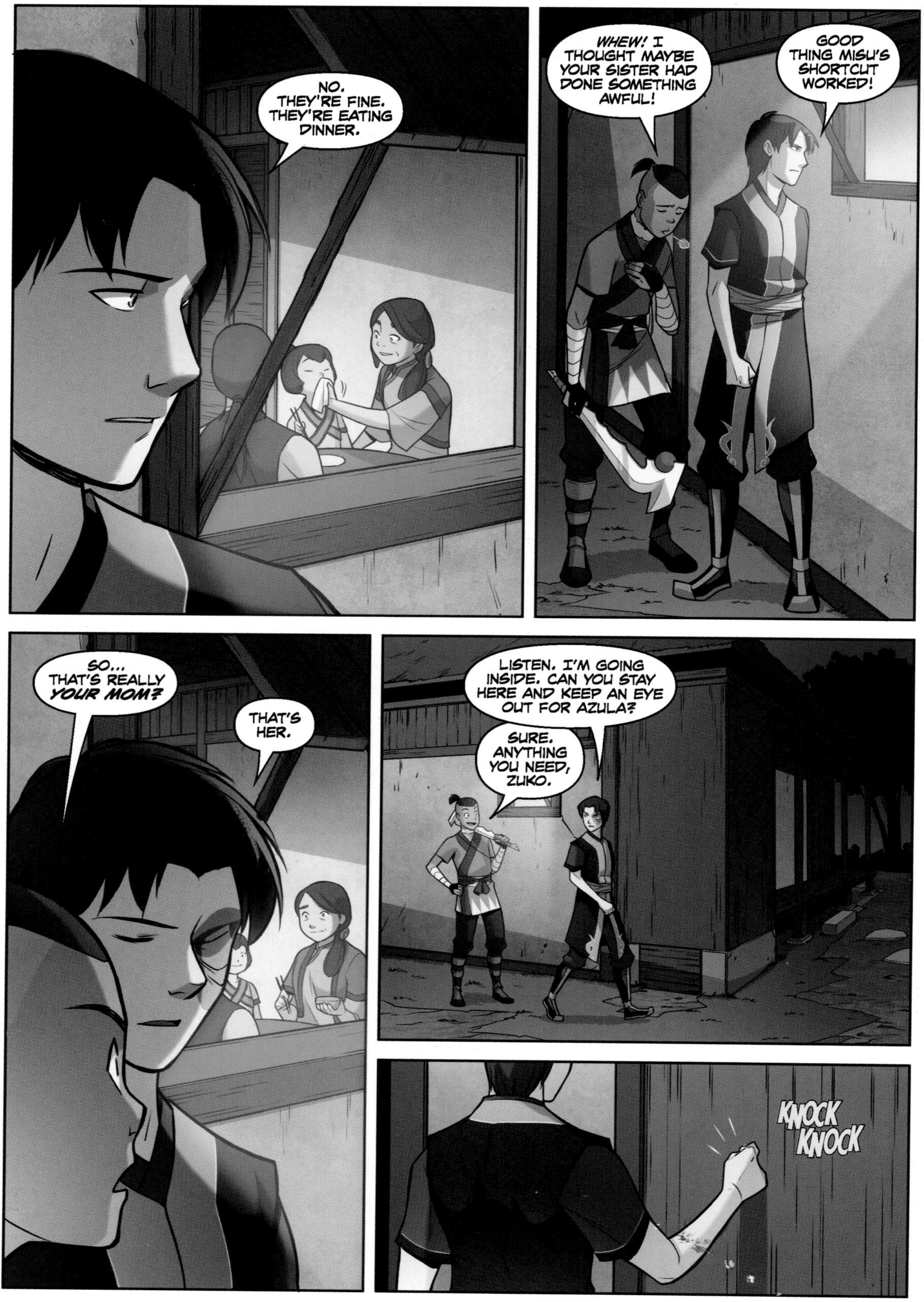
NO. THEY'RE FINE. THEY'RE EATING DINNER.
WHEW! I THOUGHT MAYBE YOUR SISTER HAD DONE SOMETHING AWFUL!
GOOD THING MISU'S SHORTCUT WORKED!
SO... THAT'S REALLY *YOUR MOM?*
THAT'S HER.
LISTEN. I'M GOING INSIDE. CAN YOU STAY HERE AND KEEP AN EYE OUT FOR AZULA?
SURE. ANYTHING YOU NEED, ZUKO.
KNOCK KNOCK

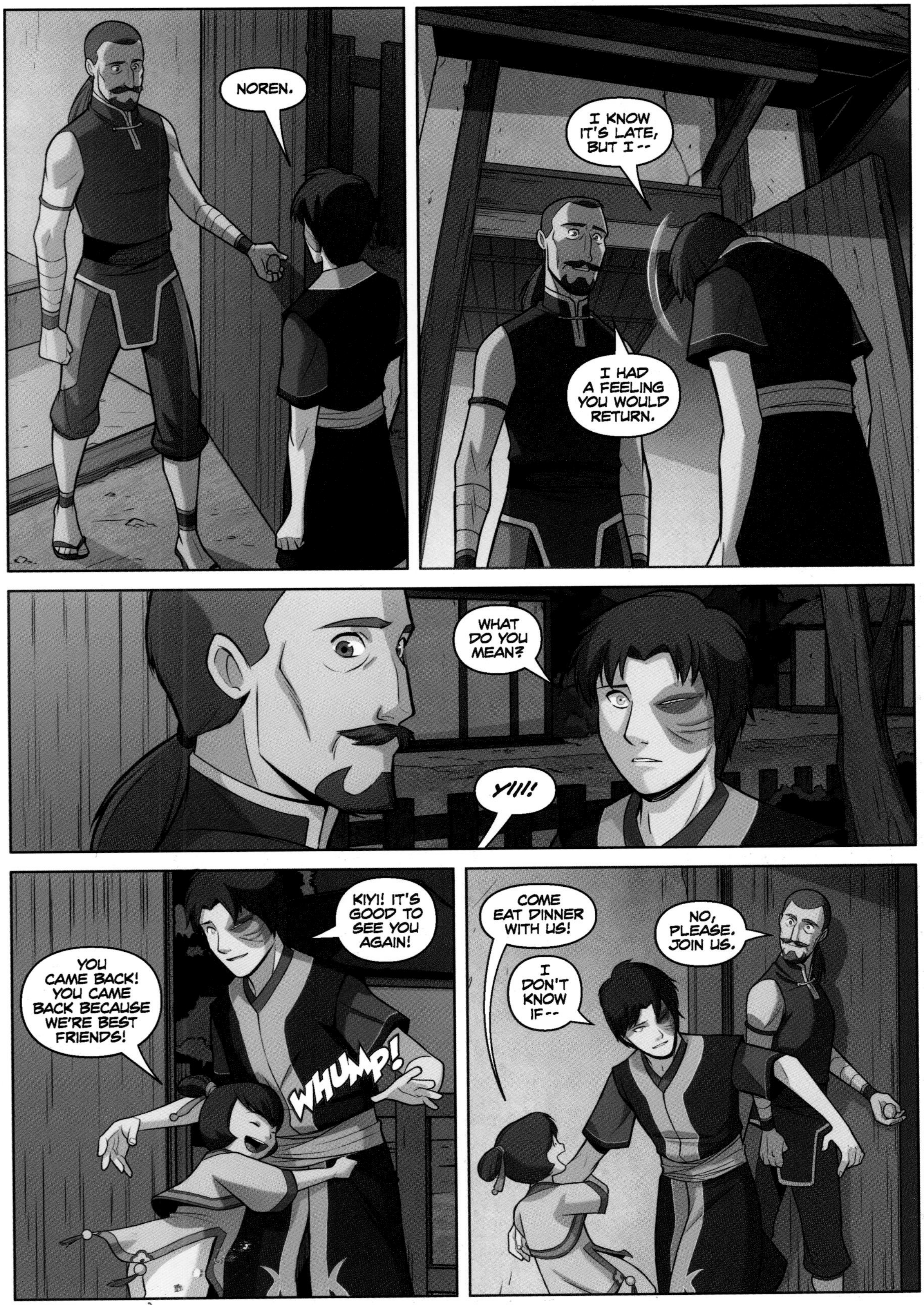
NOREN.
I KNOW IT'S LATE, BUT I--
I HAD A FEELING YOU WOULD RETURN.
WHAT DO YOU MEAN?
YIII!
KIYI! IT'S GOOD TO SEE YOU AGAIN!
YOU CAME BACK! YOU CAME BACK BECAUSE WE'RE BEST FRIENDS!
WHUMP!
COME EAT DINNER WITH US!
I DON'T KNOW IF--
NO, PLEASE. JOIN US.

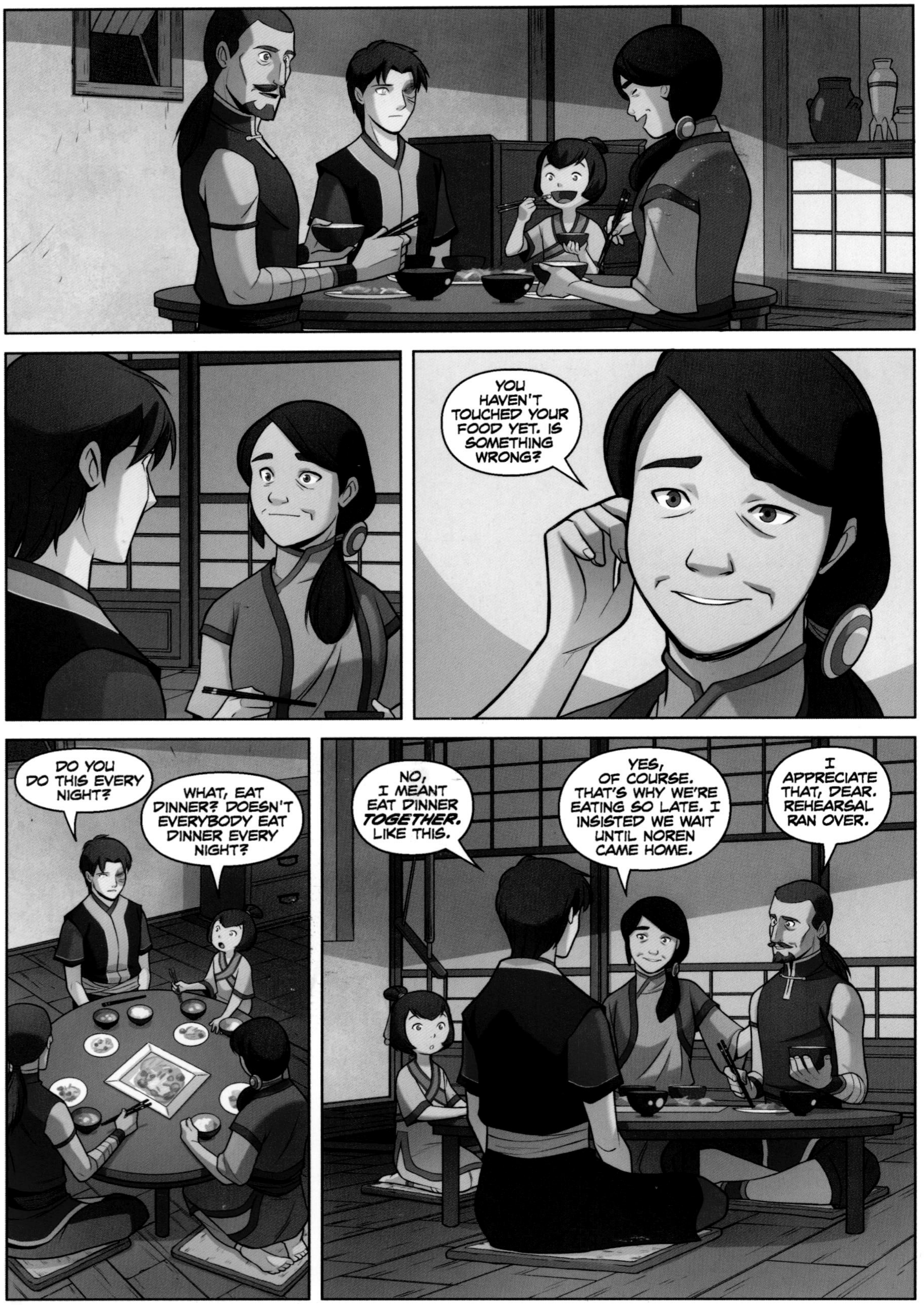
YOU HAVEN'T TOUCHED YOUR FOOD YET. IS SOMETHING WRONG?
DO YOU DO THIS EVERY NIGHT?
WHAT, EAT DINNER? DOESN'T EVERYBODY EAT DINNER EVERY NIGHT?
NO, I MEANT EAT DINNER *TOGETHER.* LIKE THIS.
YES, OF COURSE. THAT'S WHY WE'RE EATING SO LATE. I INSISTED WE WAIT UNTIL NOREN CAME HOME.
I APPRECIATE THAT, DEAR. REHEARSAL RAN OVER.

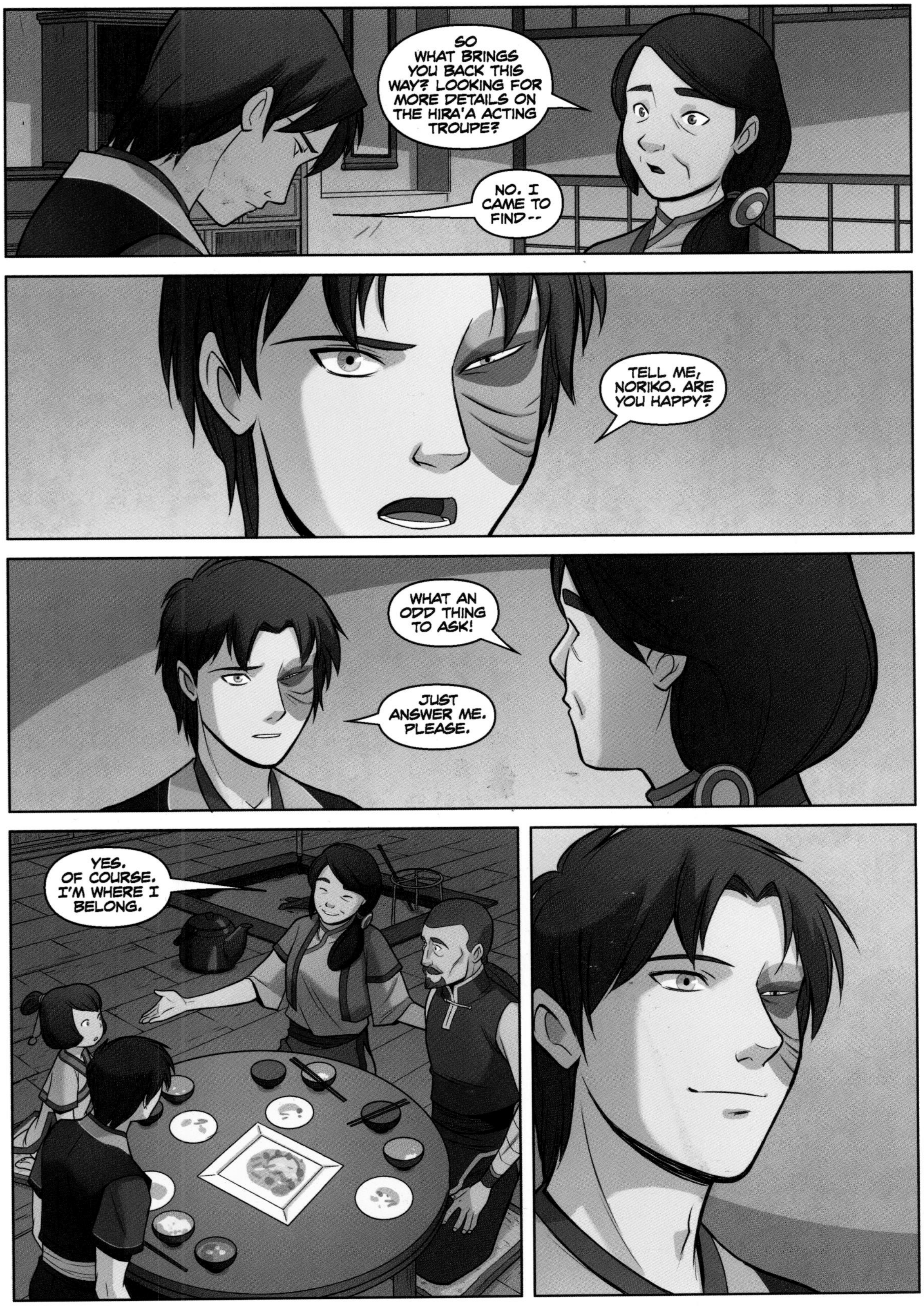
SO WHAT BRINGS YOU BACK THIS WAY? LOOKING FOR MORE DETAILS ON THE HIRA'A ACTING TROUPE?
NO. I CAME TO FIND--
TELL ME, NORIKO. ARE YOU HAPPY?
WHAT AN ODD THING TO ASK!
JUST ANSWER ME. PLEASE.
YES. OF COURSE. I'M WHERE I BELONG.

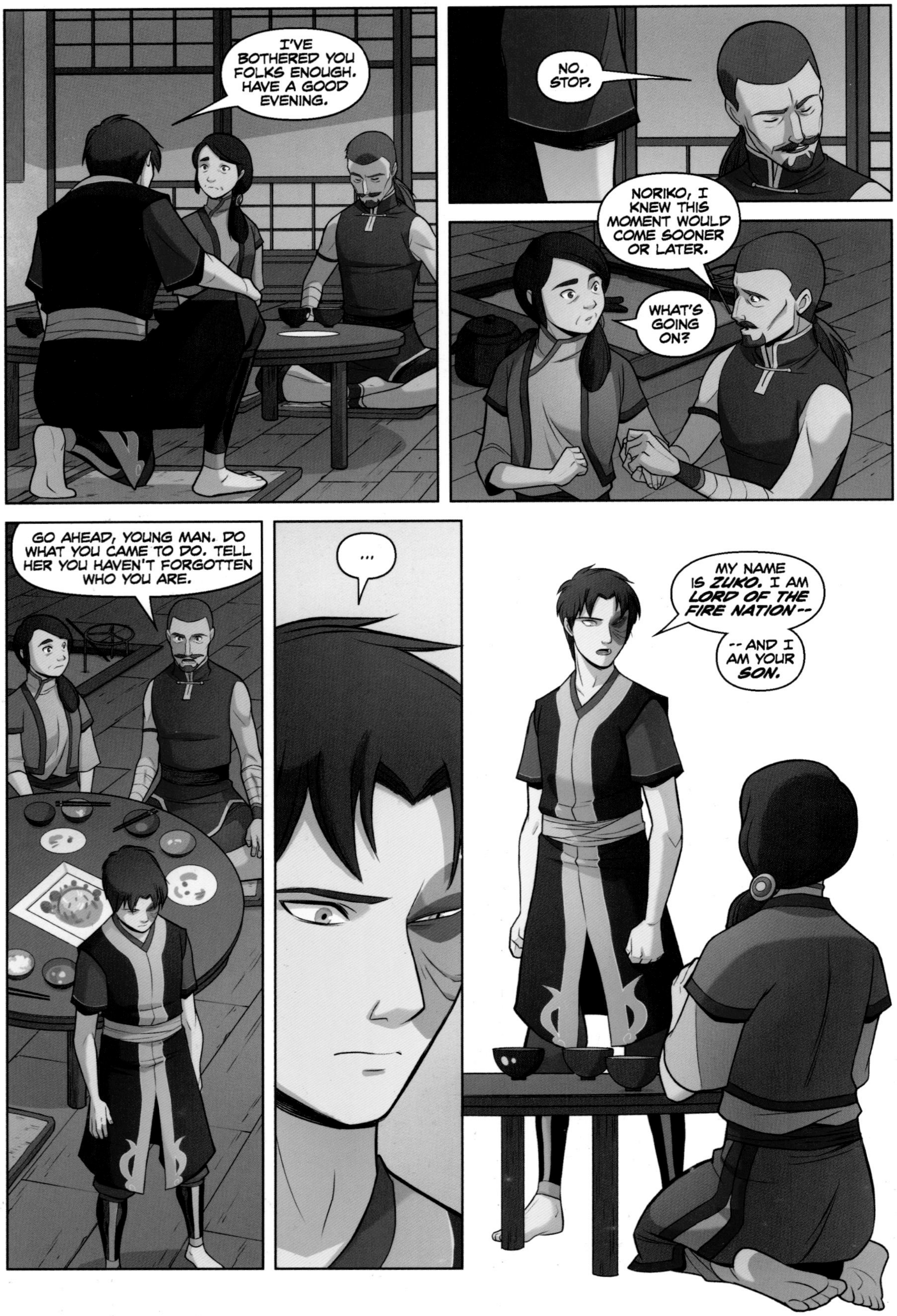
I'VE BOTHERED YOU FOLKS ENOUGH. HAVE A GOOD EVENING.
NO. STOP.
NORIKO, I KNEW THIS MOMENT WOULD COME SOONER OR LATER.
WHAT'S GOING ON?
GO AHEAD, YOUNG MAN. DO WHAT YOU CAME TO DO. TELL HER YOU HAVEN'T FORGOTTEN WHO YOU ARE.
...
MY NAME IS ZUKO. I AM LORD OF THE FIRE NATION--
--AND I AM YOUR SON.

G: *The script called for chairs and tables, but we changed them to a Japanese-style low table (*chabu-dai*) and cushions (*zabuton*).*

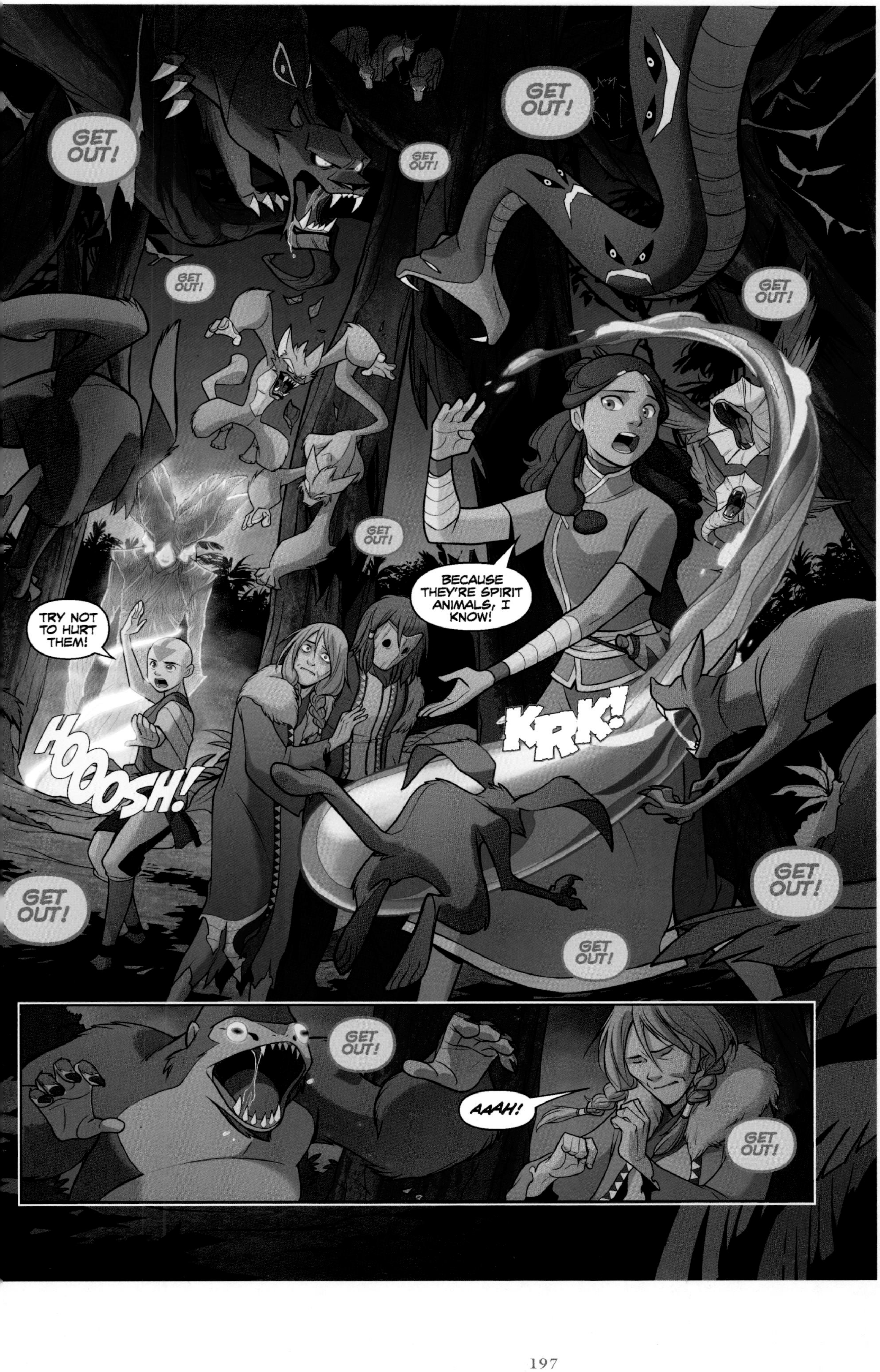
GET OUT!
GET OUT!
GET OUT!
GET OUT!
GET OUT!
GET OUT!
BECAUSE THEY'RE SPIRIT ANIMALS, I KNOW!
TRY NOT TO HURT THEM!
HOOOOSH!
KRK!
GET OUT!
GET OUT!
GET OUT!
GET OUT!
AAAH!
GET OUT!

SHING!
THANK YOU, KATARA!
WE WATERBENDERS HAVE TO LOOK OUT FOR EACH OTHER!
GET OUT!
GET OUT!
GET OUT!
GET OUT!
WE'VE GOTTA DO WHAT THEY SAY! LET'S GO!
NO.
GET OUT!
GET OUT!
MY BROTHER AND I AREN'T LEAVING THIS FOREST UNTIL WE HAVE WHAT WE CAME FOR!
YOU CAN COME BACK LATER! I'LL HELP YOU GET BACK! BUT THERE'S NO WAY THE THREE OF US CAN FIGHT OFF AN *ENTIRE FOREST!*
GET OUT!
GET OUT!
GET OUT!
GET OUT!

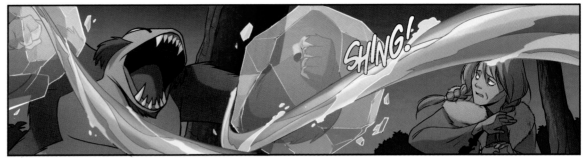

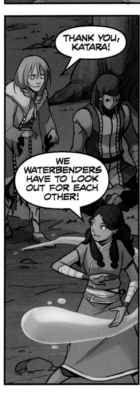

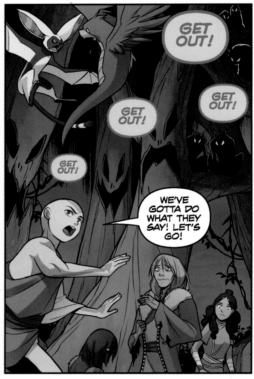

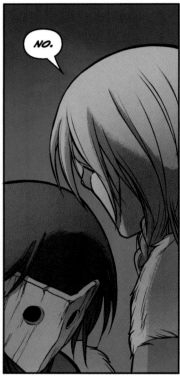

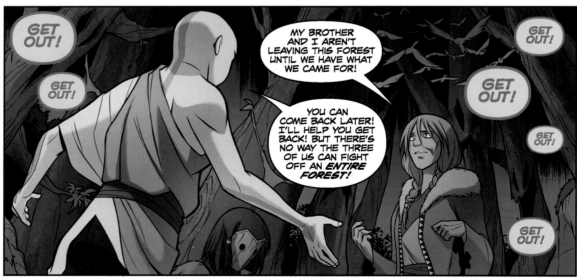

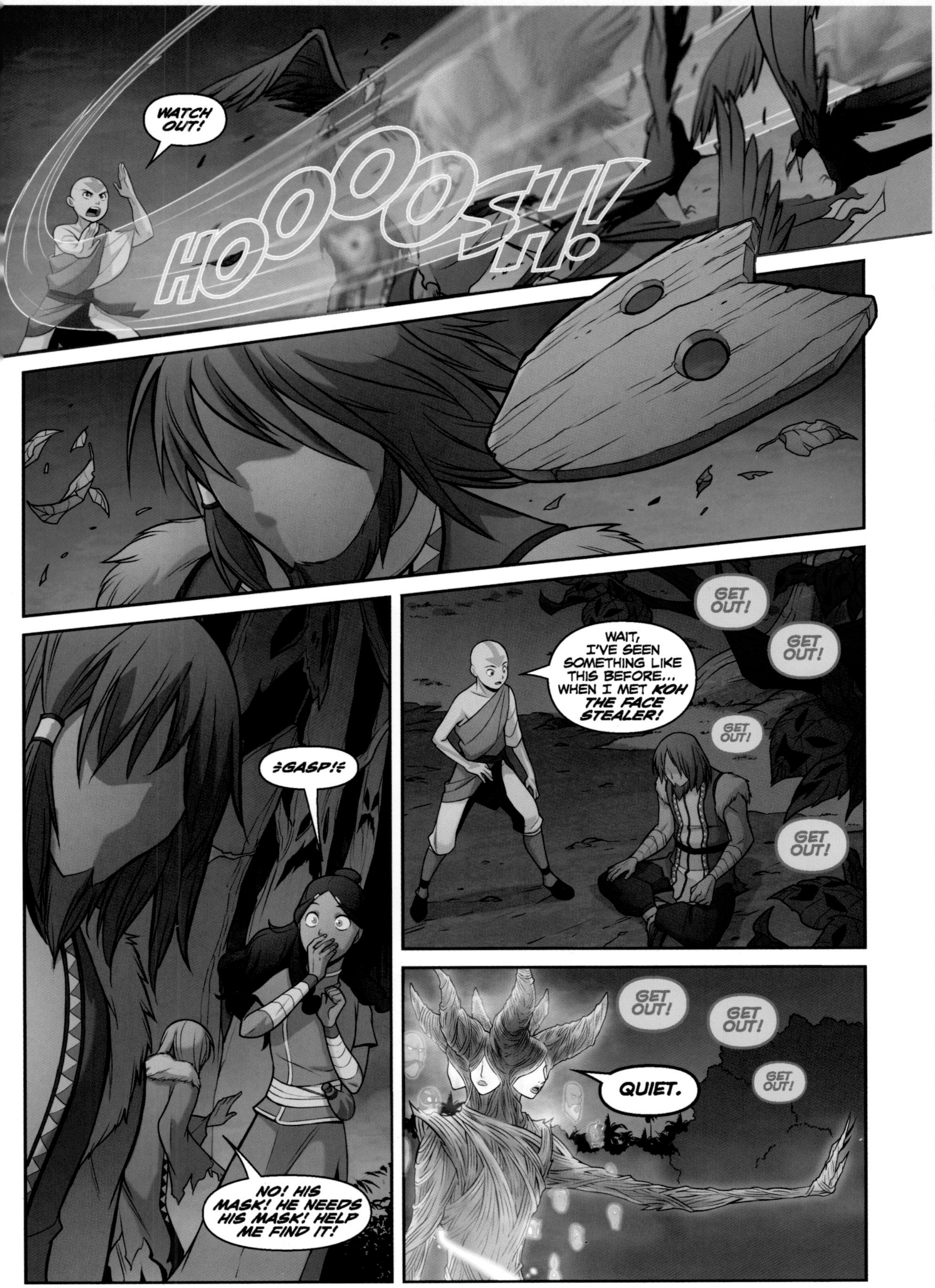
WATCH OUT!
HOOOOOSH!
ƎGASP!Ǝ
WAIT, I'VE SEEN SOMETHING LIKE THIS BEFORE... WHEN I MET KOH THE FACE STEALER!
GET OUT!
GET OUT!
GET OUT!
GET OUT!
NO! HIS MASK! HE NEEDS HIS MASK! HELP ME FIND IT!
GET OUT!
GET OUT!
QUIET.
GET OUT!

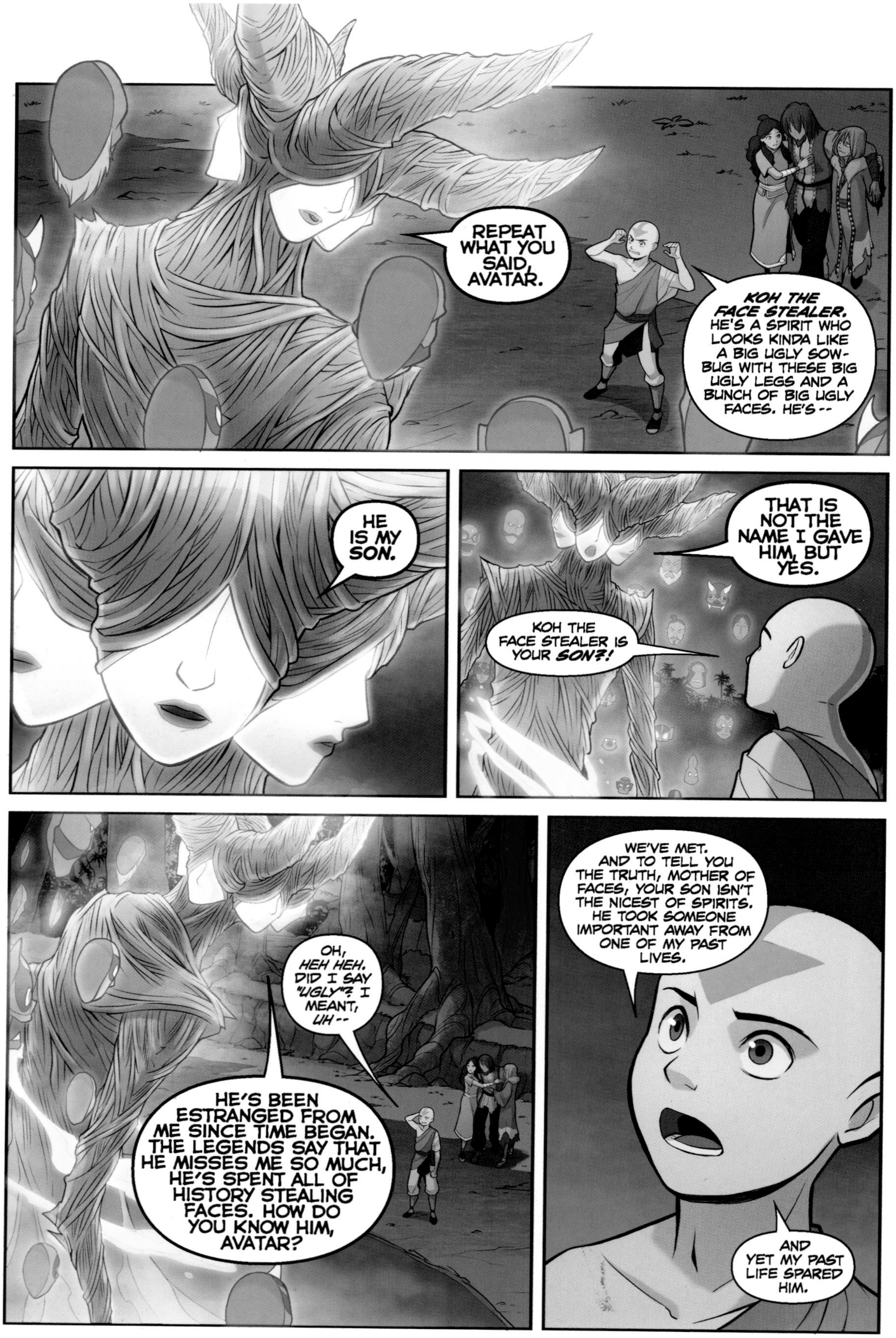
REPEAT WHAT YOU SAID, AVATAR.
KOH THE FACE STEALER. HE'S A SPIRIT WHO LOOKS KINDA LIKE A BIG UGLY SOW-BUG WITH THESE BIG UGLY LEGS AND A BUNCH OF BIG UGLY FACES. HE'S --
HE IS MY SON.
THAT IS NOT THE NAME I GAVE HIM, BUT YES.
KOH THE FACE STEALER IS YOUR SON?!
OH, HEH HEH. DID I SAY "UGLY"? I MEANT, UH --
HE'S BEEN ESTRANGED FROM ME SINCE TIME BEGAN. THE LEGENDS SAY THAT HE MISSES ME SO MUCH, HE'S SPENT ALL OF HISTORY STEALING FACES. HOW DO YOU KNOW HIM, AVATAR?
WE'VE MET. AND TO TELL YOU THE TRUTH, MOTHER OF FACES, YOUR SON ISN'T THE NICEST OF SPIRITS. HE TOOK SOMEONE IMPORTANT AWAY FROM ONE OF MY PAST LIVES.
AND YET MY PAST LIFE SPARED HIM.

GLY: *In my opinion, Koh the Face Stealer is one of the best villains ever created, in any fictional universe. Since we had this theme of faces running through* The Search, *I knew Koh had to show up, even if it was only a mention in dialogue.*

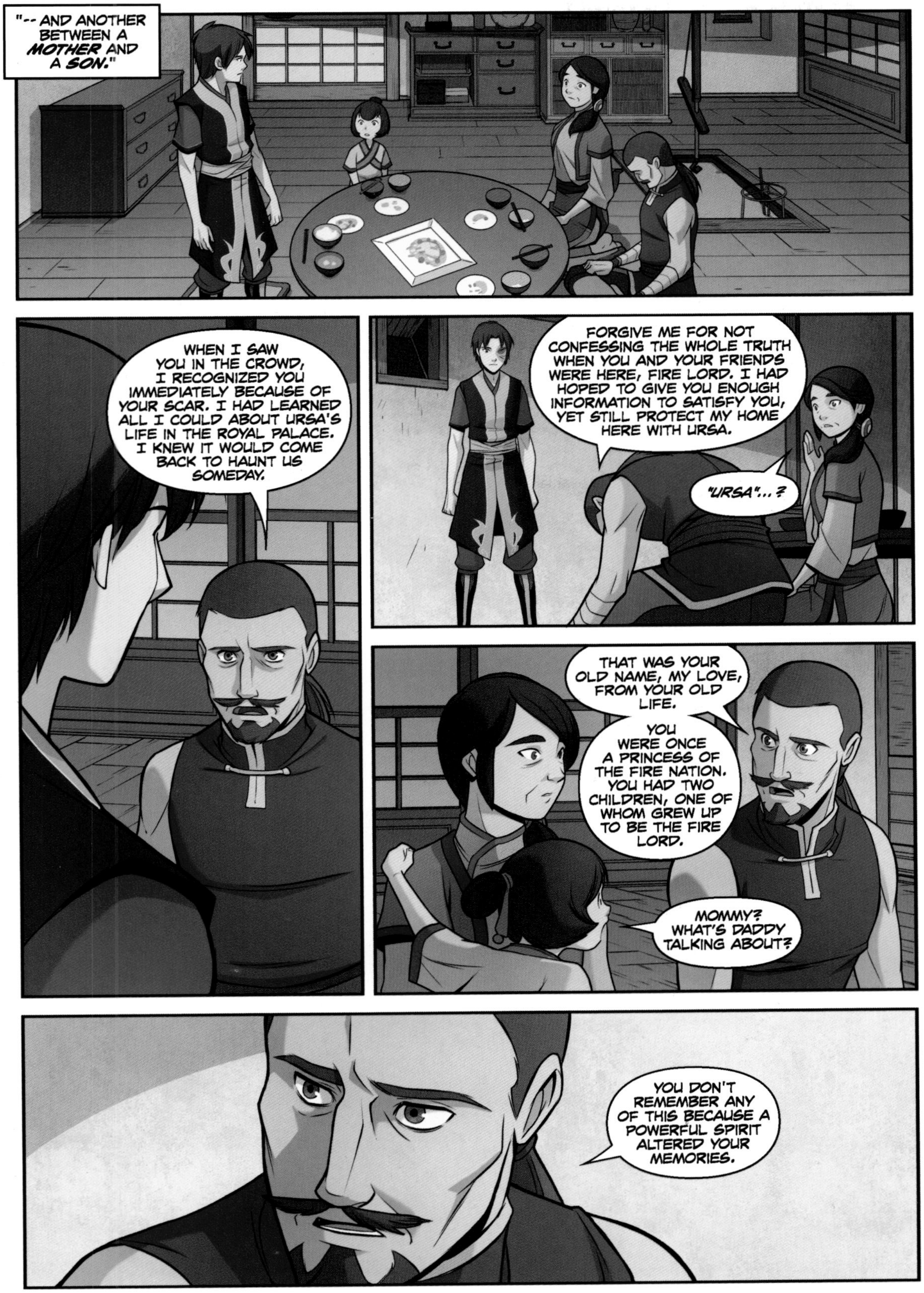
"-- AND ANOTHER BETWEEN A *MOTHER* AND A *SON*."
WHEN I SAW YOU IN THE CROWD, I RECOGNIZED YOU IMMEDIATELY BECAUSE OF YOUR SCAR. I HAD LEARNED ALL I COULD ABOUT URSA'S LIFE IN THE ROYAL PALACE. I KNEW IT WOULD COME BACK TO HAUNT US SOMEDAY.
FORGIVE ME FOR NOT CONFESSING THE WHOLE TRUTH WHEN YOU AND YOUR FRIENDS WERE HERE, FIRE LORD. I HAD HOPED TO GIVE YOU ENOUGH INFORMATION TO SATISFY YOU, YET STILL PROTECT MY HOME HERE WITH URSA.
"URSA"...?
THAT WAS YOUR OLD NAME, MY LOVE, FROM YOUR OLD LIFE.
YOU WERE ONCE A PRINCESS OF THE FIRE NATION. YOU HAD TWO CHILDREN, ONE OF WHOM GREW UP TO BE THE FIRE LORD.
MOMMY? WHAT'S DADDY TALKING ABOUT?
YOU DON'T REMEMBER ANY OF THIS BECAUSE A POWERFUL SPIRIT ALTERED YOUR MEMORIES.

M: *Although Bryan and I had never pinned down the exact details surrounding Ursa's whereabouts, I had always thought that amnesia would play a role in some way. I knew there had to be something big keeping Ursa from contacting Zuko all these years.*

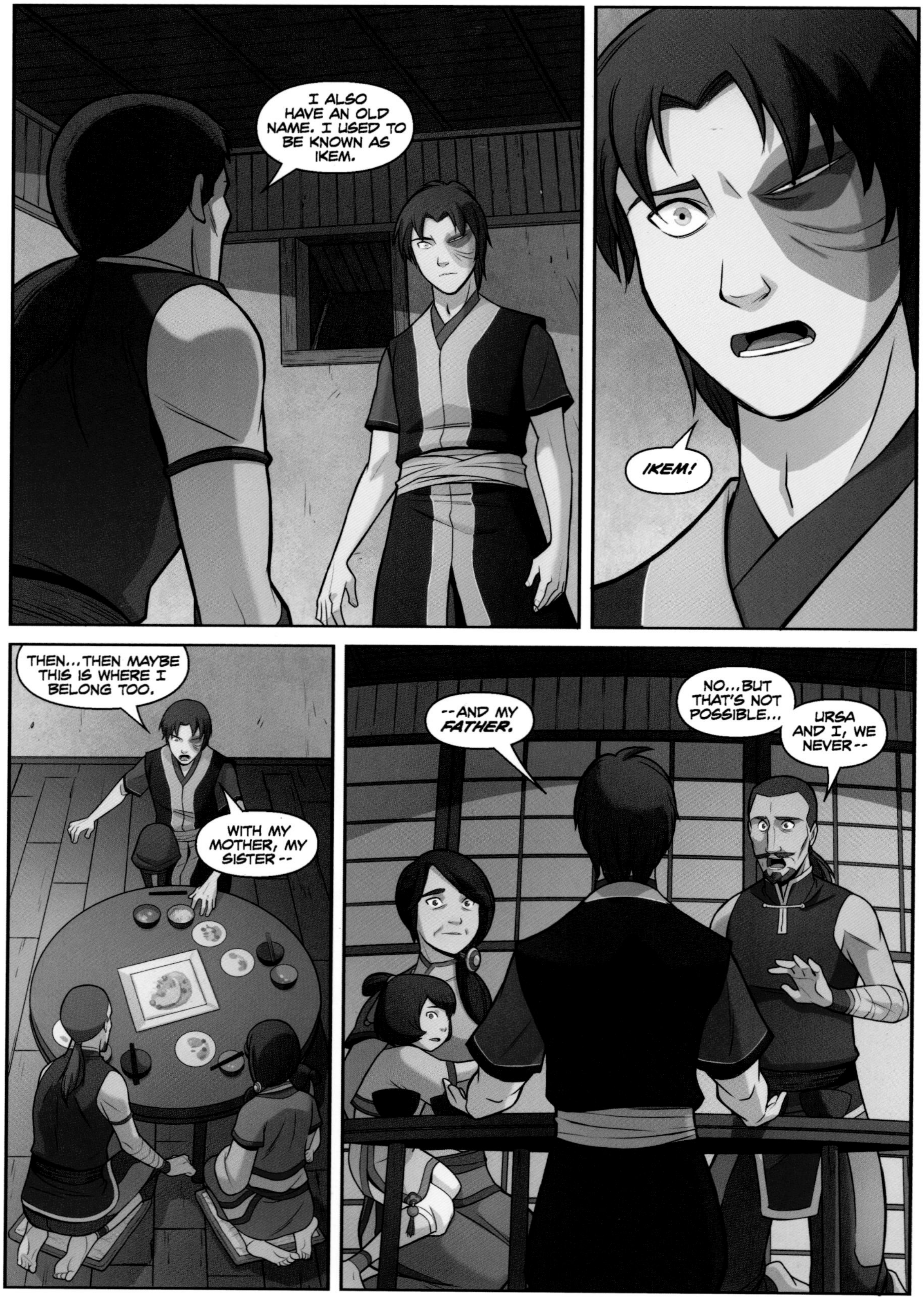
I ALSO HAVE AN OLD NAME. I USED TO BE KNOWN AS IKEM.
IKEM!
THEN...THEN MAYBE THIS IS WHERE I BELONG TOO.
WITH MY MOTHER, MY SISTER --
--AND MY FATHER.
NO...BUT THAT'S NOT POSSIBLE...
URSA AND I, WE NEVER --

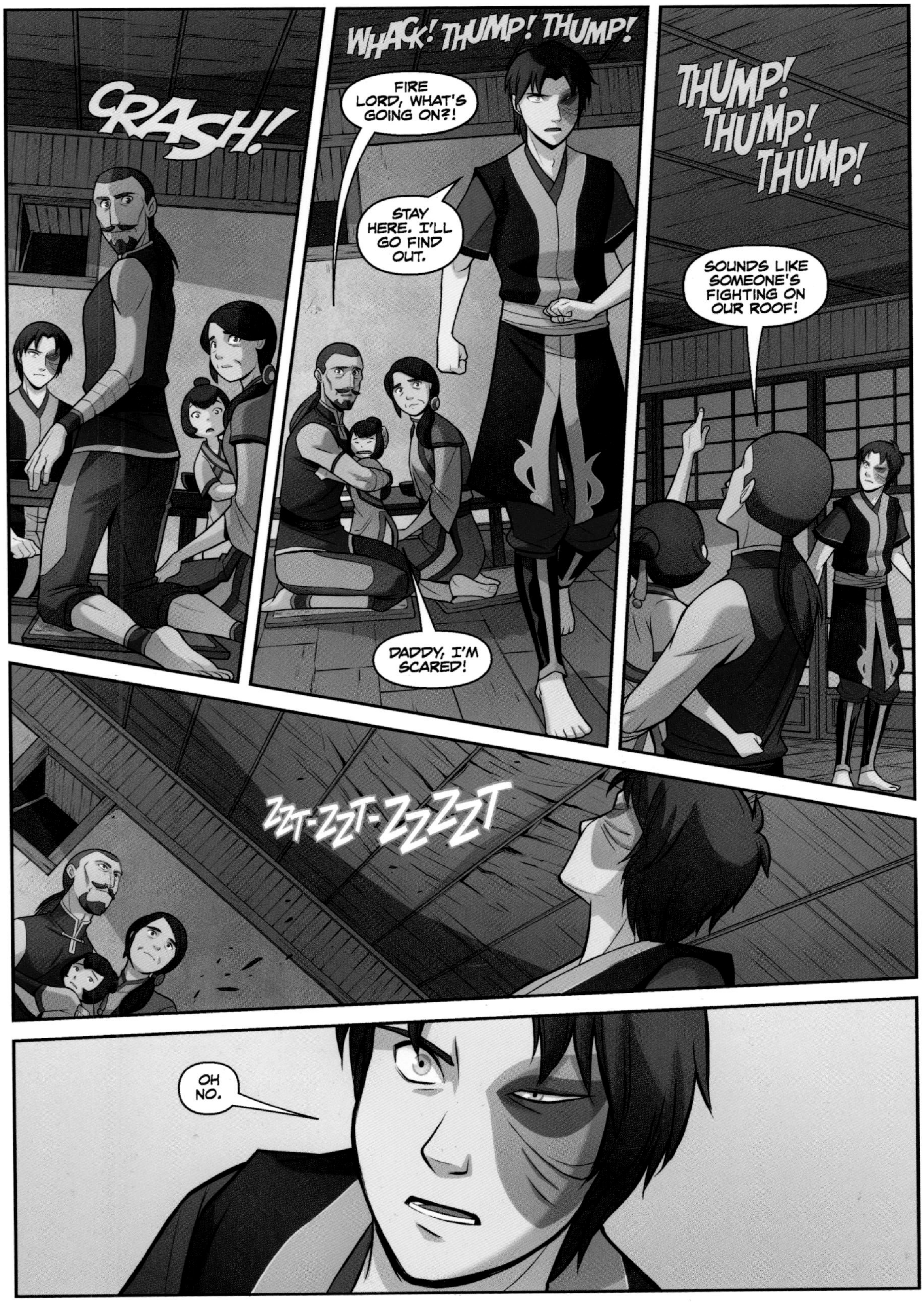
CRASH!
WHACK! THUMP! THUMP!
FIRE LORD, WHAT'S GOING ON?!
STAY HERE. I'LL GO FIND OUT.
DADDY, I'M SCARED!
THUMP! THUMP! THUMP!
SOUNDS LIKE SOMEONE'S FIGHTING ON OUR ROOF!
ZZT-ZZT-ZZZZT
OH NO.

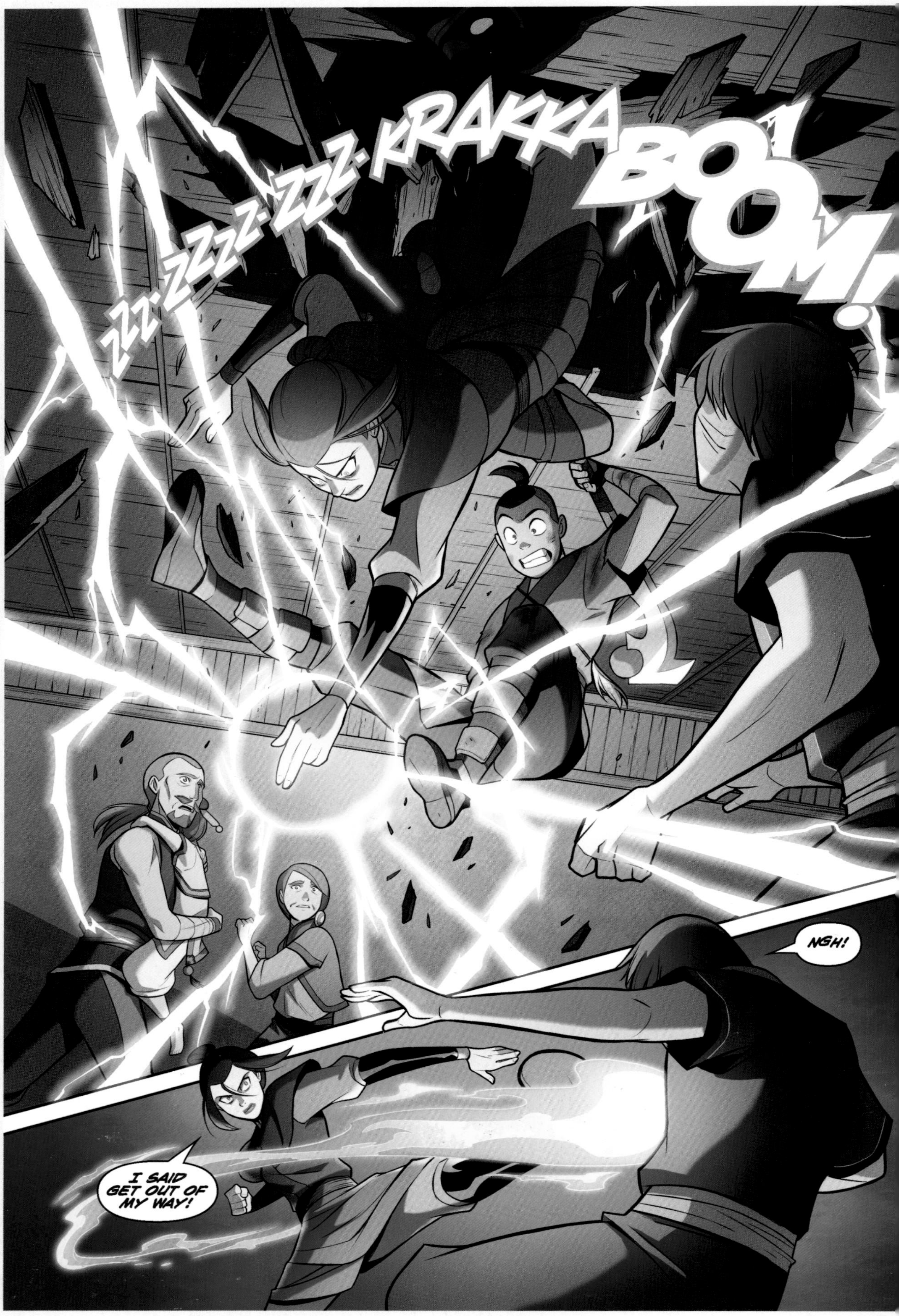
ZZZ-ZZZZZ-ZZZ-KRAKKA BOOM!
NGH!
I SAID GET OUT OF MY WAY!

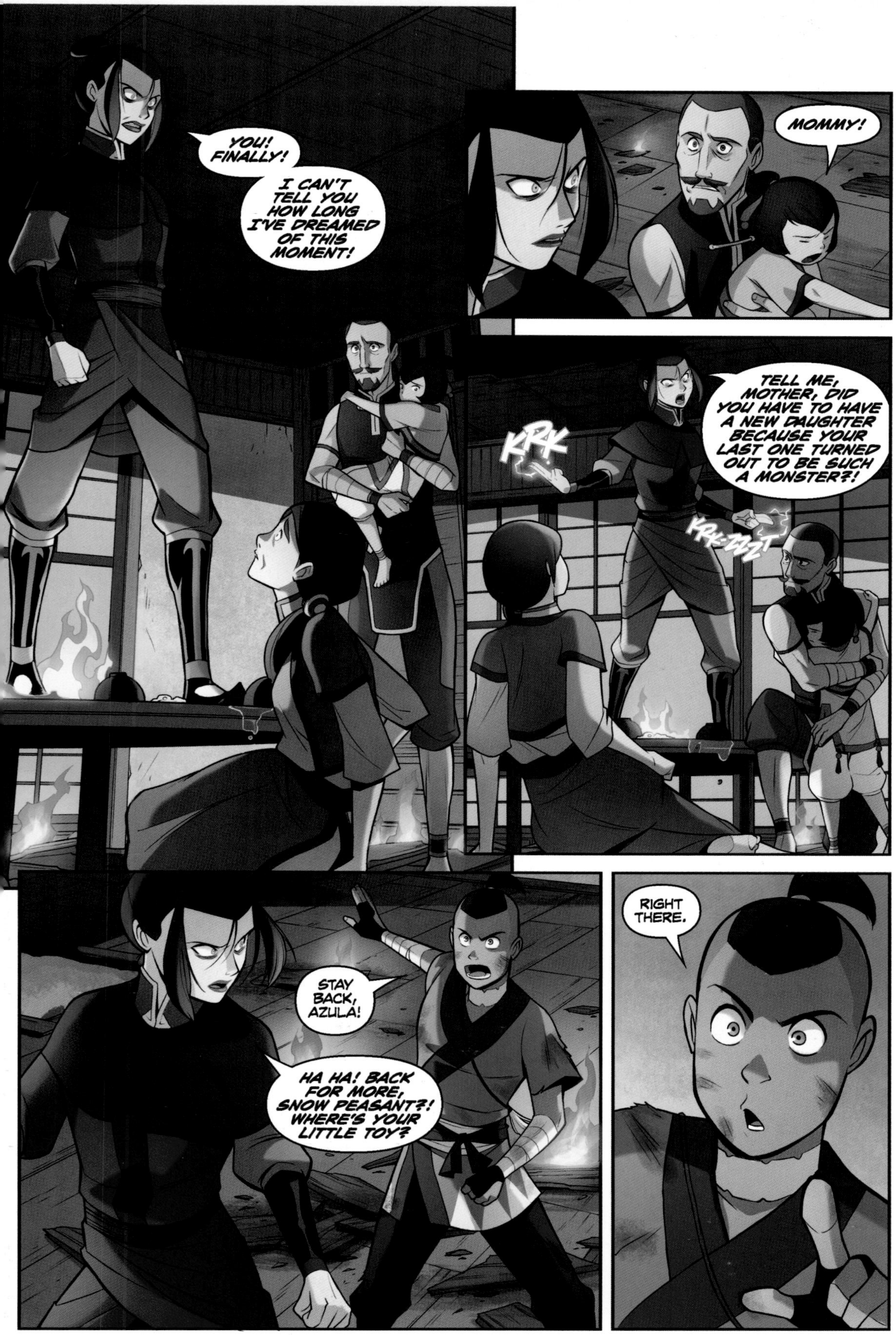
YOU! FINALLY!
I CAN'T TELL YOU HOW LONG I'VE DREAMED OF THIS MOMENT!
MOMMY!
TELL ME, MOTHER, DID YOU HAVE TO HAVE A NEW DAUGHTER BECAUSE YOUR LAST ONE TURNED OUT TO BE SUCH A MONSTER?!
KRK
KRK-ZZZT
STAY BACK, AZULA!
HA HA! BACK FOR MORE, SNOW PEASANT?! WHERE'S YOUR LITTLE TOY?
RIGHT THERE.

G: *In contrast to the warm colors before Azula arrives, we changed to colder colors here to show the tension after her appearance.*

GLY: *Sokka is to Team Avatar what Hawkeye is to the Avengers. He's a normal guy who hangs out with, and goes up against, the uberpowerful. Here, we show how he does it—with wit and cleverness.*

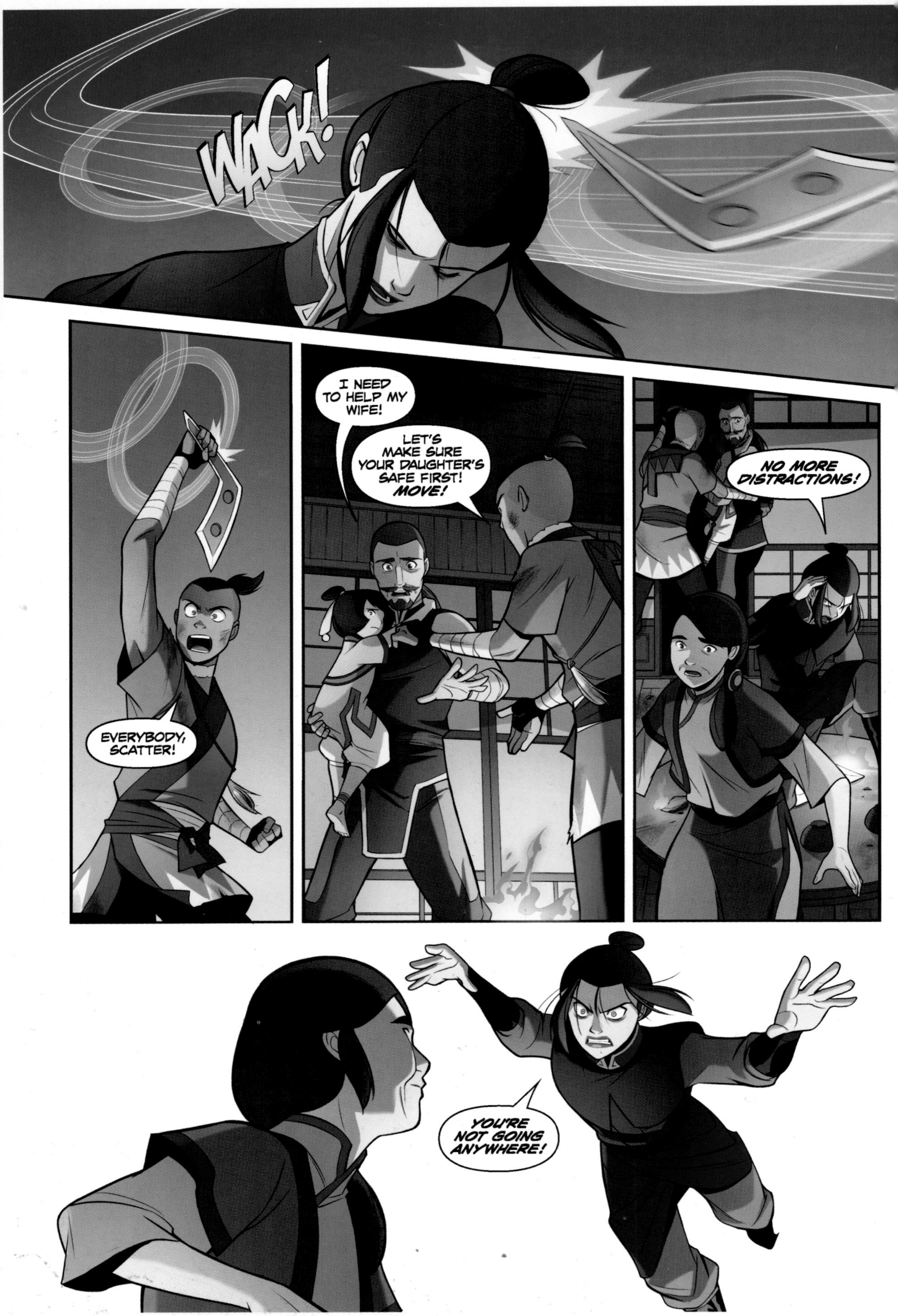
WACK!
EVERYBODY, SCATTER!
I NEED TO HELP MY WIFE!
LET'S MAKE SURE YOUR DAUGHTER'S SAFE FIRST! MOVE!
NO MORE DISTRACTIONS!
YOU'RE NOT GOING ANYWHERE!

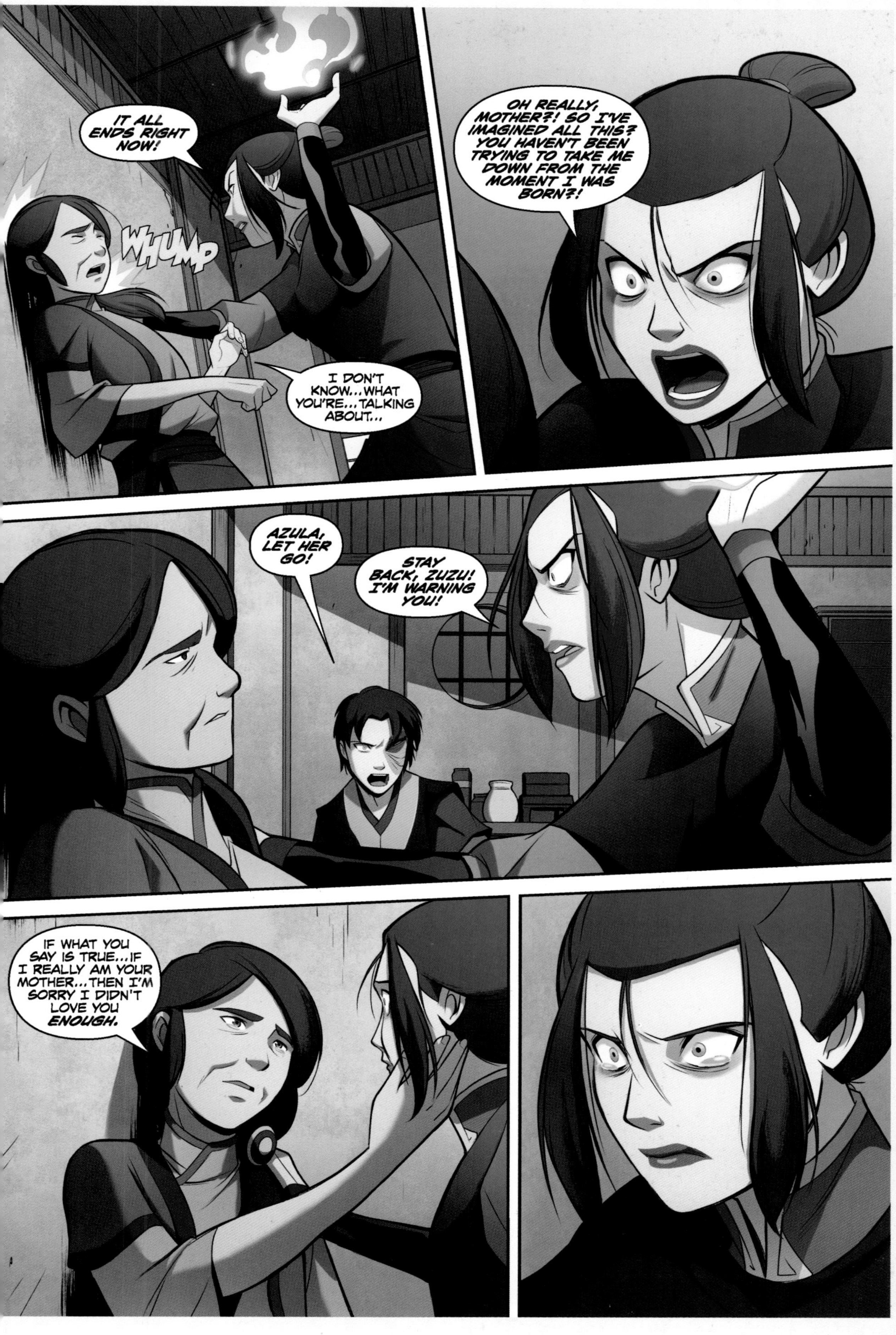
IT ALL ENDS RIGHT NOW!
WHUMP
I DON'T KNOW...WHAT YOU'RE...TALKING ABOUT...
OH REALLY, MOTHER?! SO I'VE IMAGINED ALL THIS? YOU HAVEN'T BEEN TRYING TO TAKE ME DOWN FROM THE MOMENT I WAS BORN?!
AZULA, LET HER GO!
STAY BACK, ZUZU! I'M WARNING YOU!
IF WHAT YOU SAY IS TRUE...IF I REALLY AM YOUR MOTHER...THEN I'M SORRY I DIDN'T LOVE YOU ENOUGH.

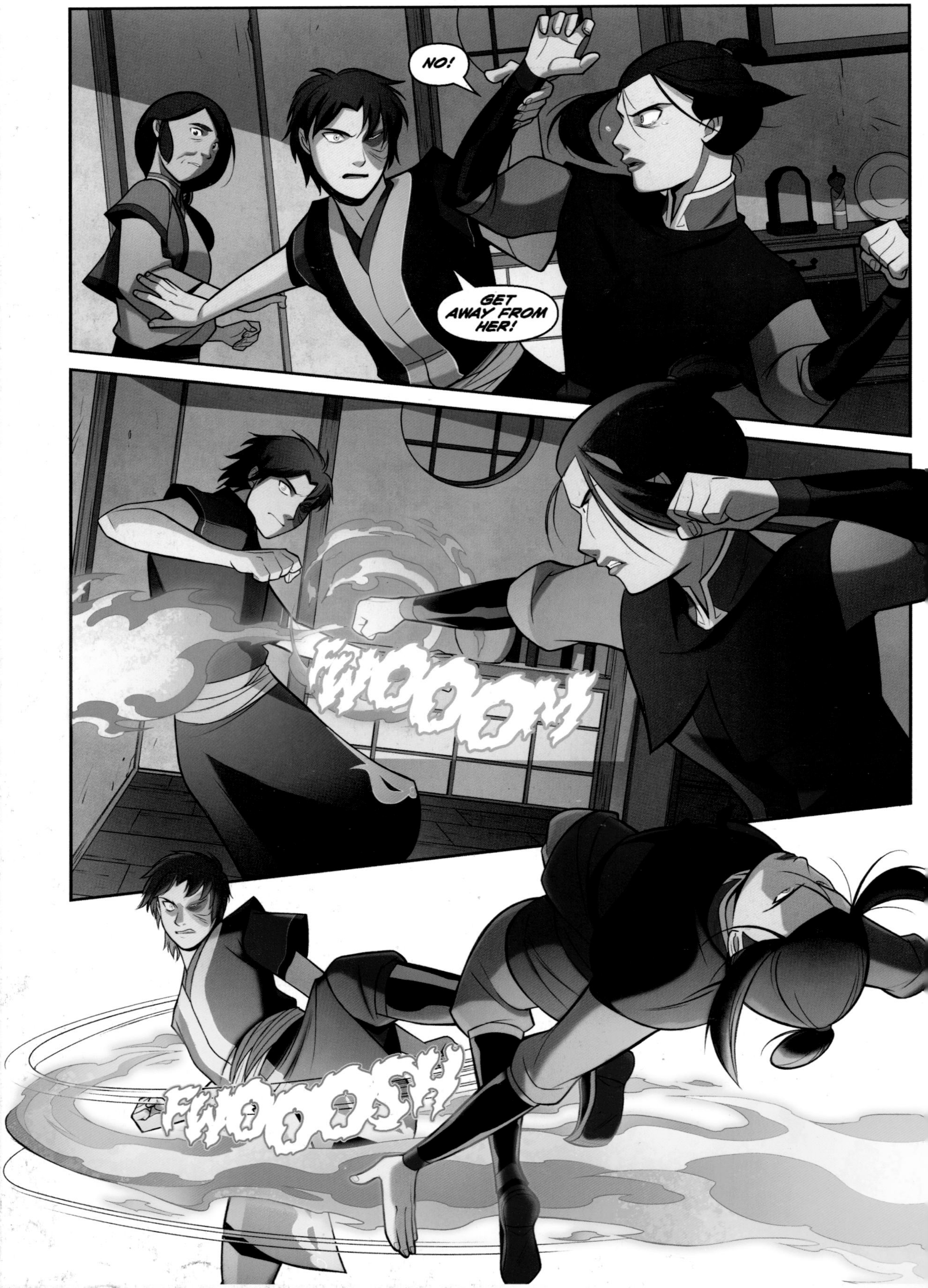
NO!
GET AWAY FROM HER!
FWOOOM
FWOOOSH

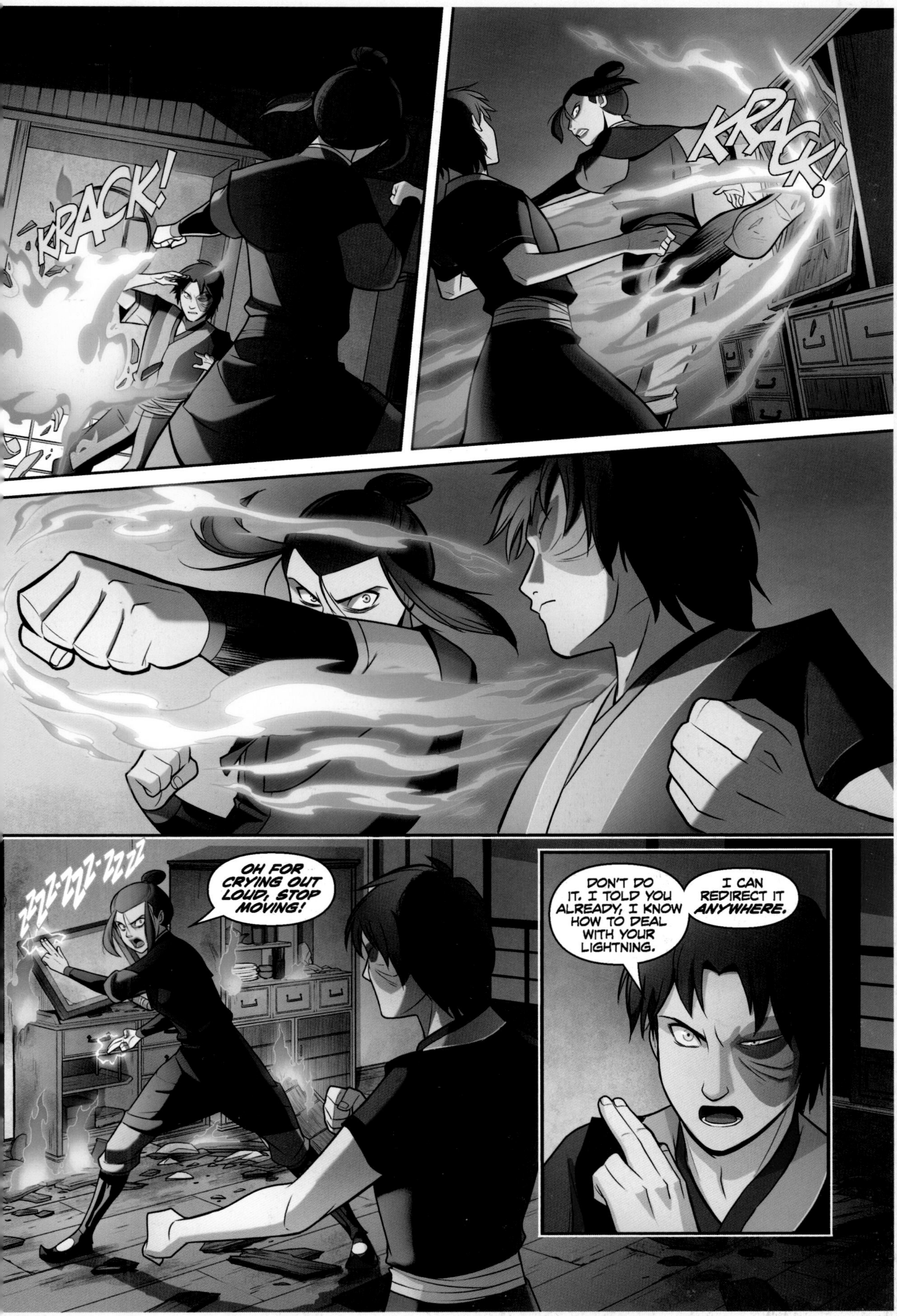
KRACK!
KRACK!
ZZZZ-ZZZ-ZZZ
OH FOR CRYING OUT LOUD, STOP MOVING!
DON'T DO IT. I TOLD YOU ALREADY, I KNOW HOW TO DEAL WITH YOUR LIGHTNING.
I CAN REDIRECT IT ANYWHERE.

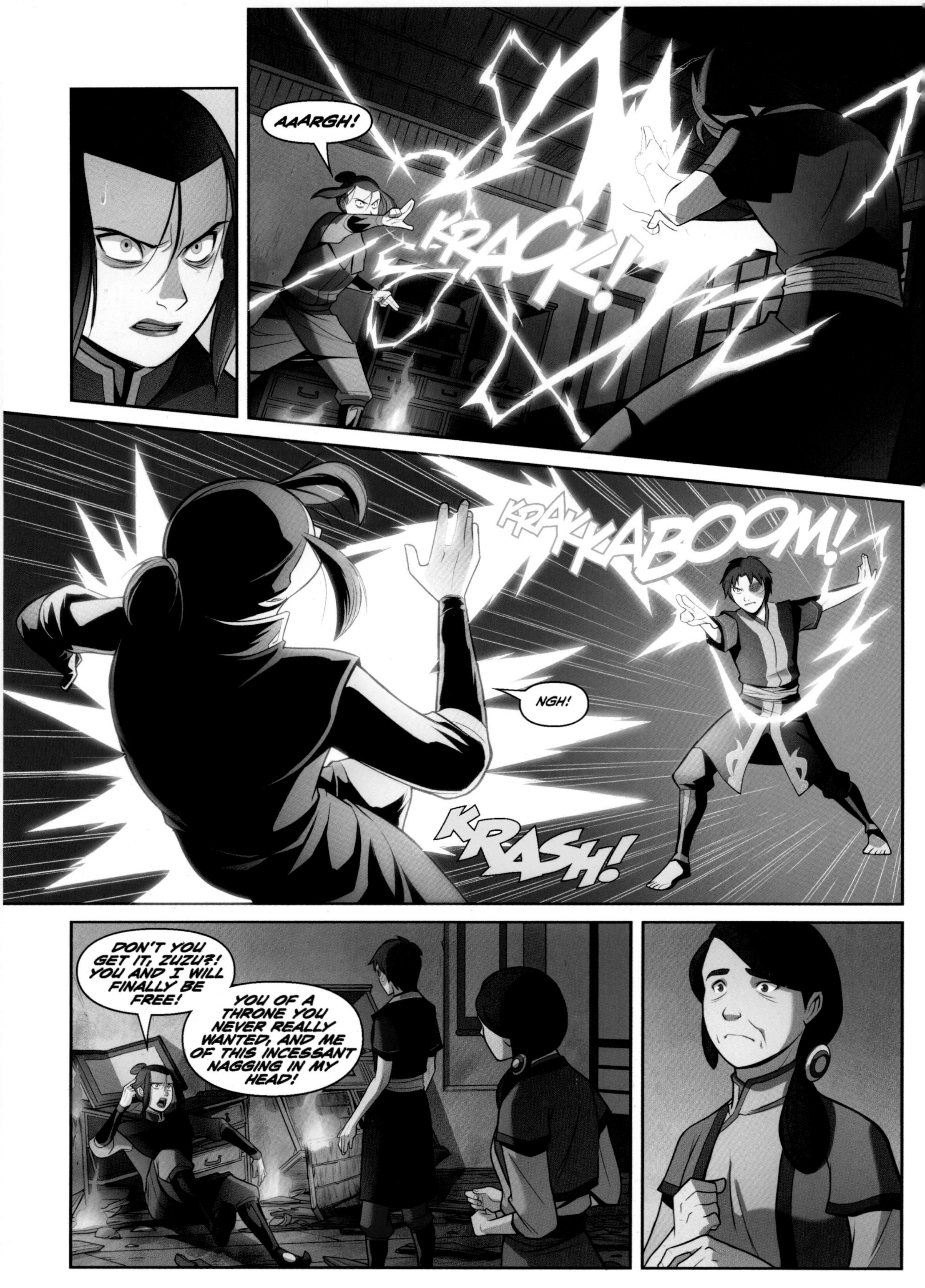
AAARGH!
KRACK!
KRAKKABOOM!
NGH!
KRASH!
DON'T YOU GET IT, ZUZU?! YOU AND I WILL FINALLY BE FREE!
YOU OF A THRONE YOU NEVER REALLY WANTED, AND ME OF THIS INCESSANT NAGGING IN MY HEAD!

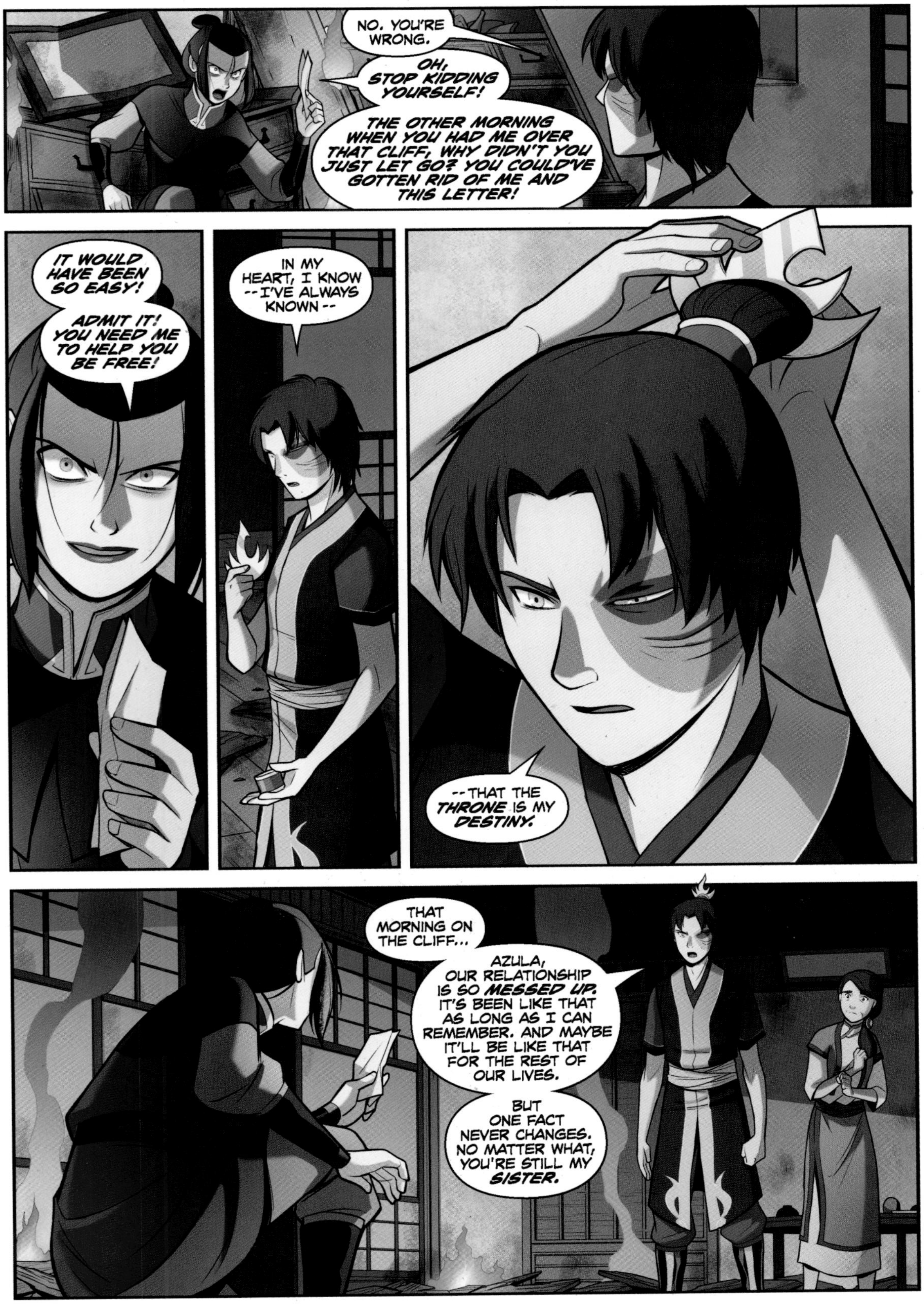
NO. YOU'RE WRONG.
OH, STOP KIDDING YOURSELF!
THE OTHER MORNING WHEN YOU HAD ME OVER THAT CLIFF, WHY DIDN'T YOU JUST LET GO? YOU COULD'VE GOTTEN RID OF ME AND THIS LETTER!
IT WOULD HAVE BEEN SO EASY!
ADMIT IT! YOU NEED ME TO HELP YOU BE FREE!
IN MY HEART, I KNOW --I'VE ALWAYS KNOWN--
--THAT THE THRONE IS MY DESTINY.
THAT MORNING ON THE CLIFF...
AZULA, OUR RELATIONSHIP IS SO MESSED UP. IT'S BEEN LIKE THAT AS LONG AS I CAN REMEMBER. AND MAYBE IT'LL BE LIKE THAT FOR THE REST OF OUR LIVES.
BUT ONE FACT NEVER CHANGES. NO MATTER WHAT, YOU'RE STILL MY SISTER.

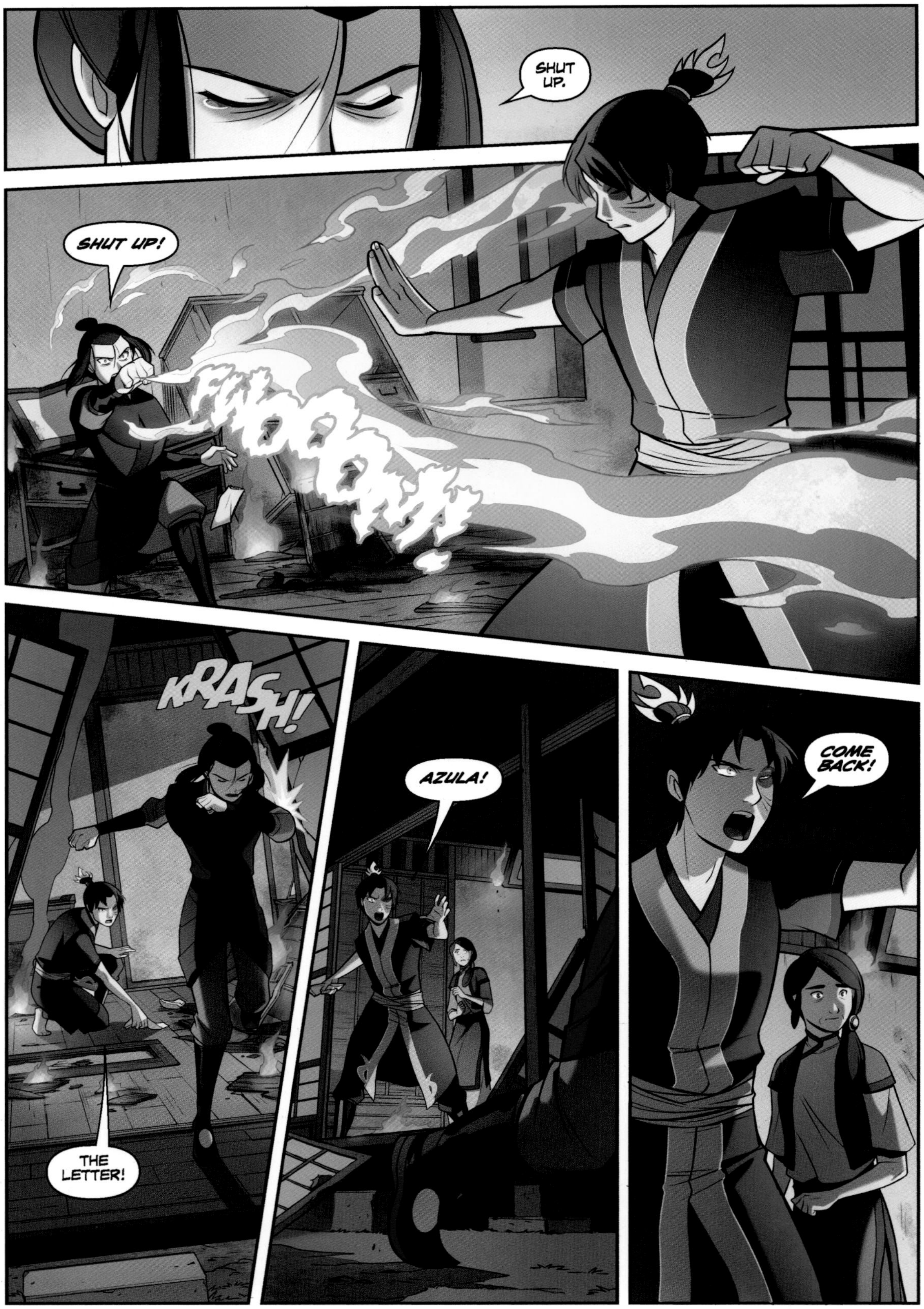
SHUT UP.
SHUT UP!
FWOOOOM!
KRASH!
THE LETTER!
AZULA!
COME BACK!

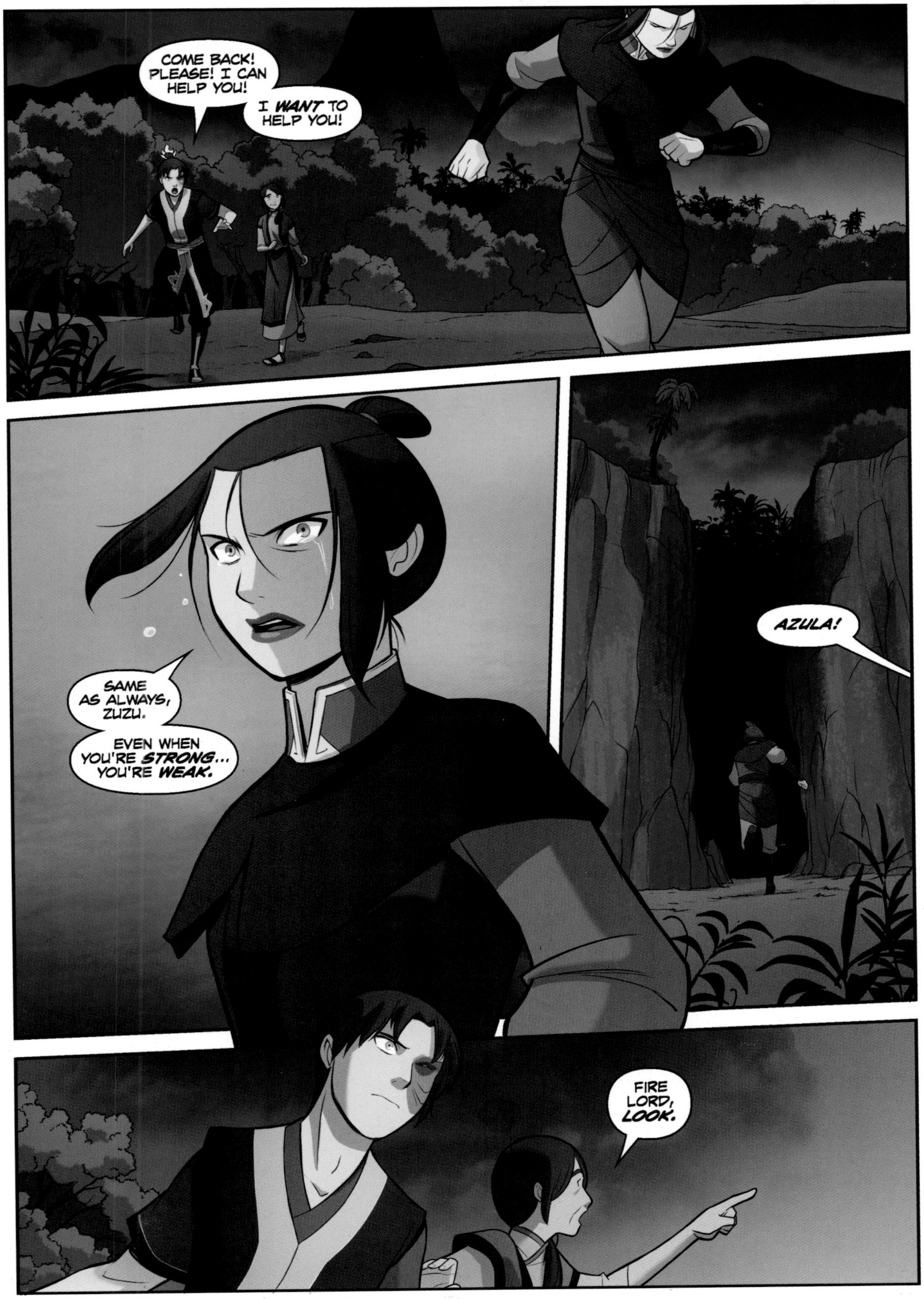
COME BACK! PLEASE! I CAN HELP YOU!
I WANT TO HELP YOU!
SAME AS ALWAYS, ZUZU.
EVEN WHEN YOU'RE STRONG... YOU'RE WEAK.
AZULA!
FIRE LORD, LOOK.

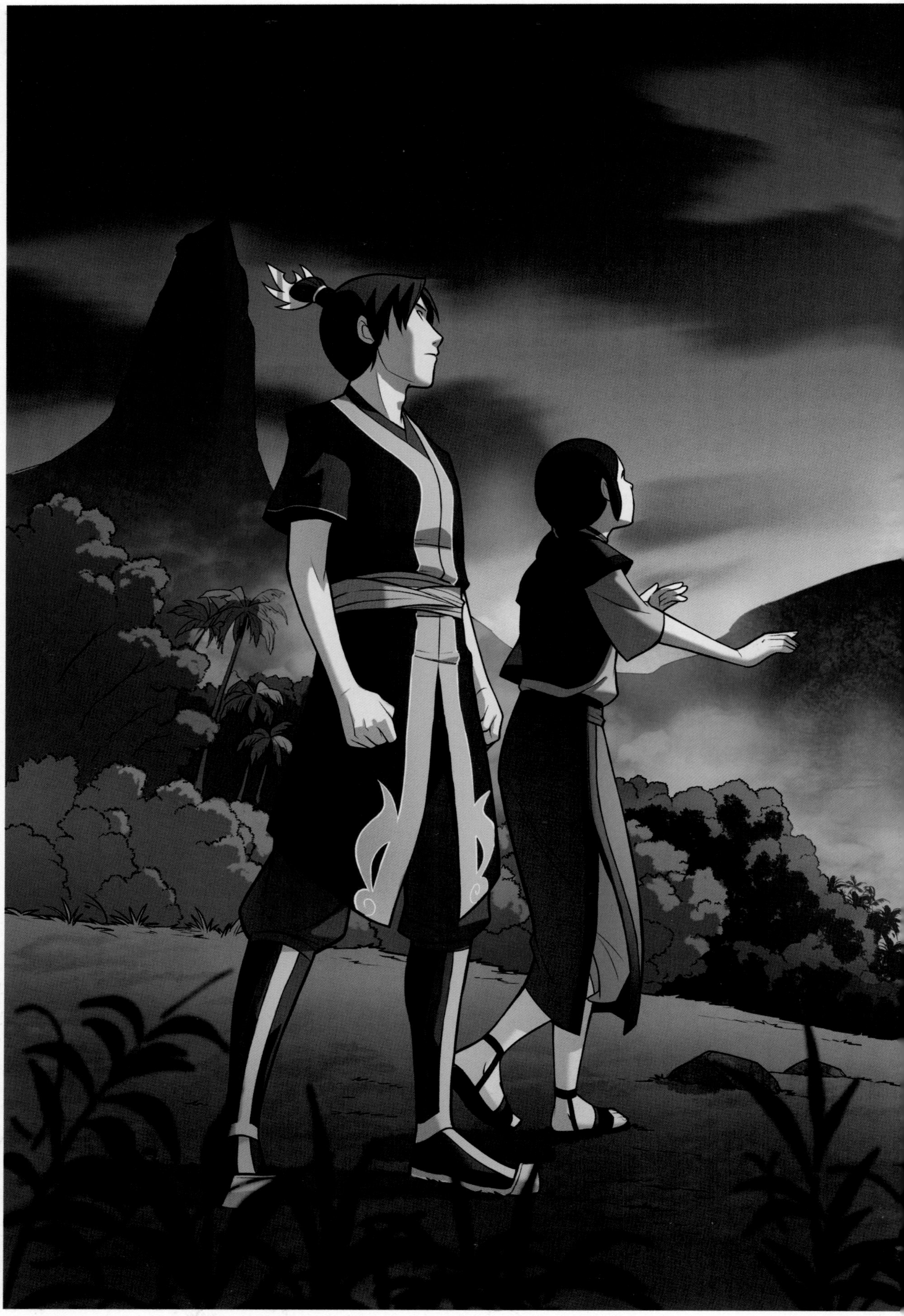

GLY: *It's no secret that the Avatarverse takes a lot of inspiration from the films of Studio Ghibli. That inspiration certainly shows up here.*

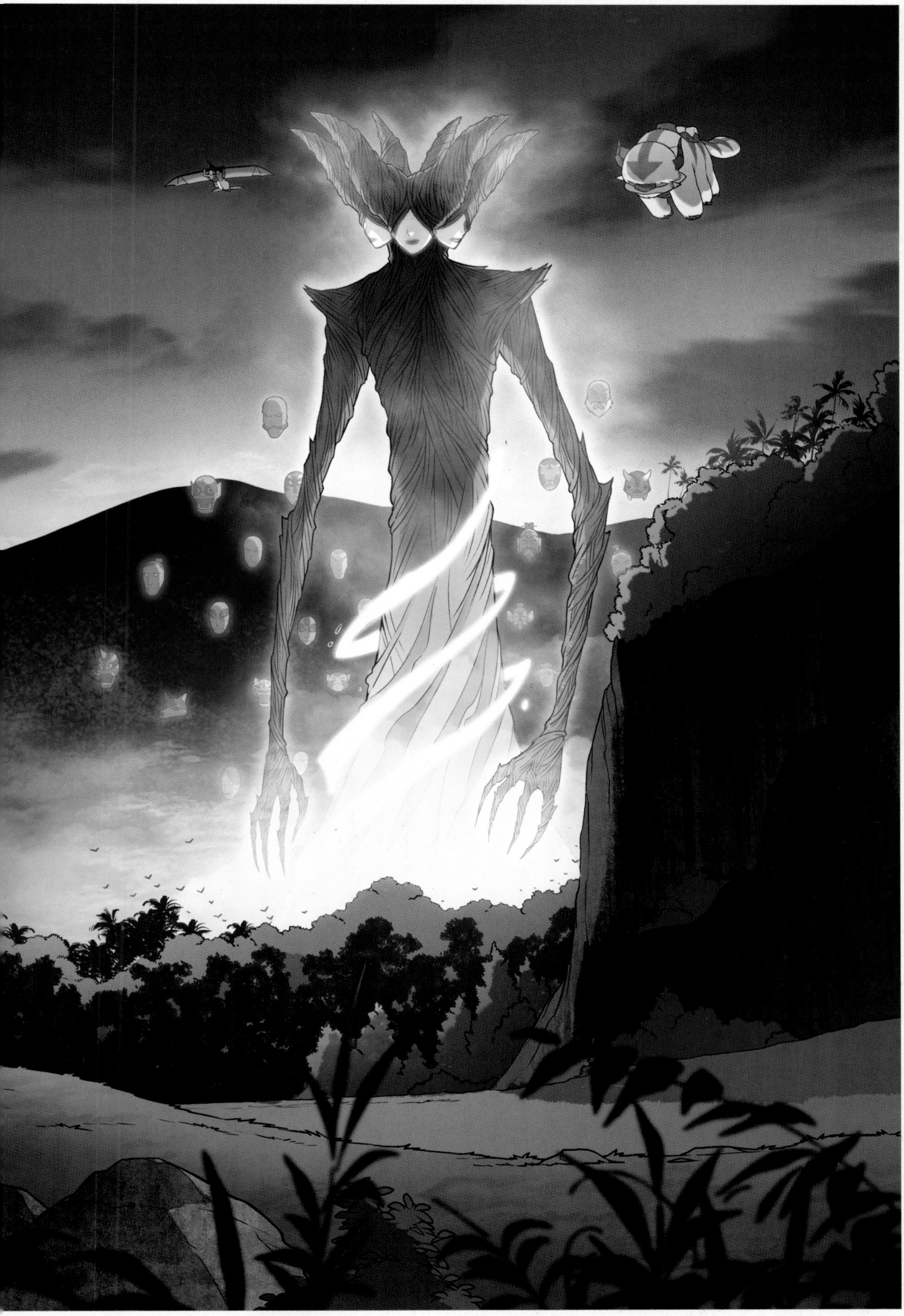

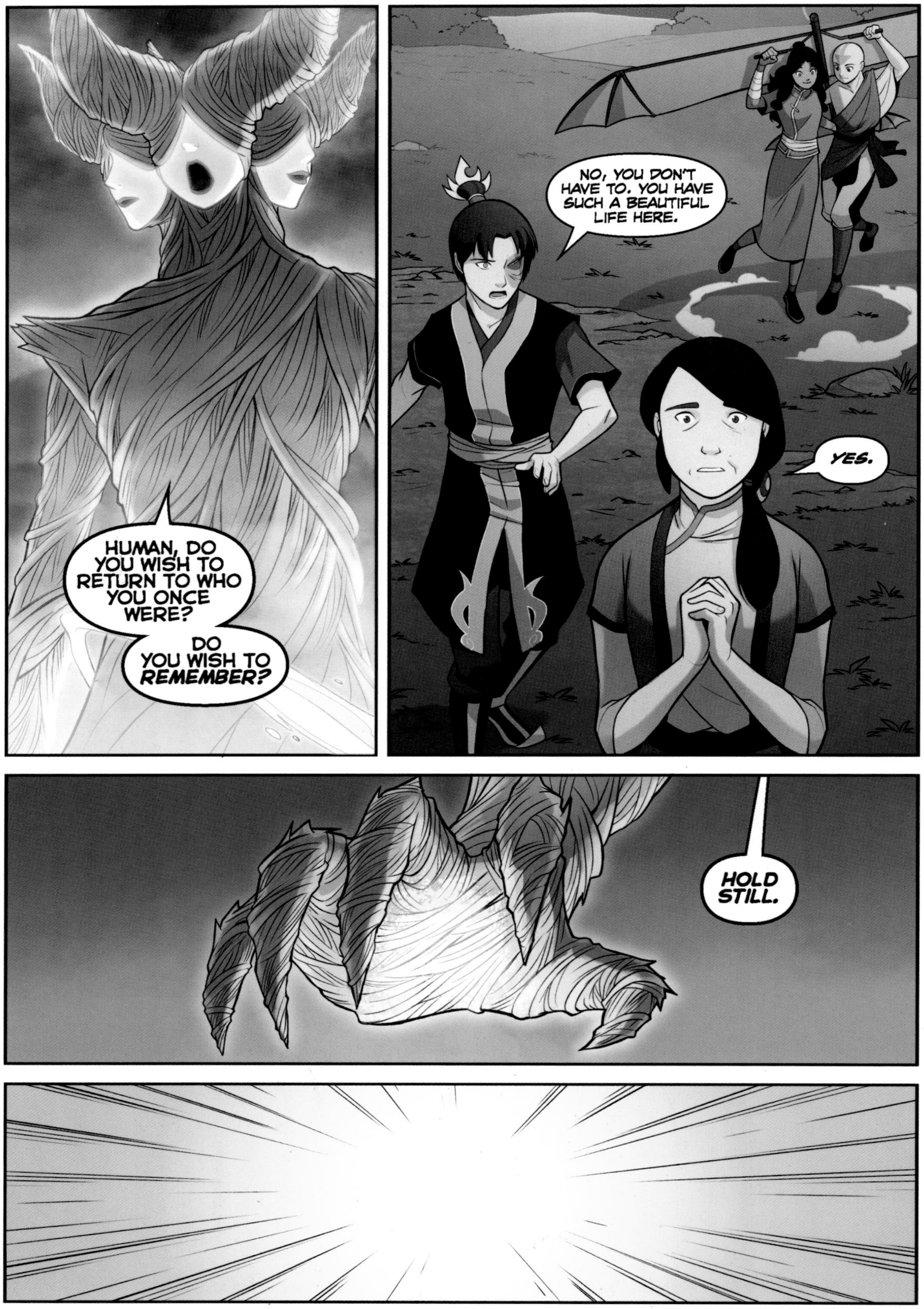
HUMAN, DO YOU WISH TO RETURN TO WHO YOU ONCE WERE?
DO YOU WISH TO *REMEMBER?*
NO, YOU DON'T HAVE TO. YOU HAVE SUCH A BEAUTIFUL LIFE HERE.
YES.
HOLD STILL.

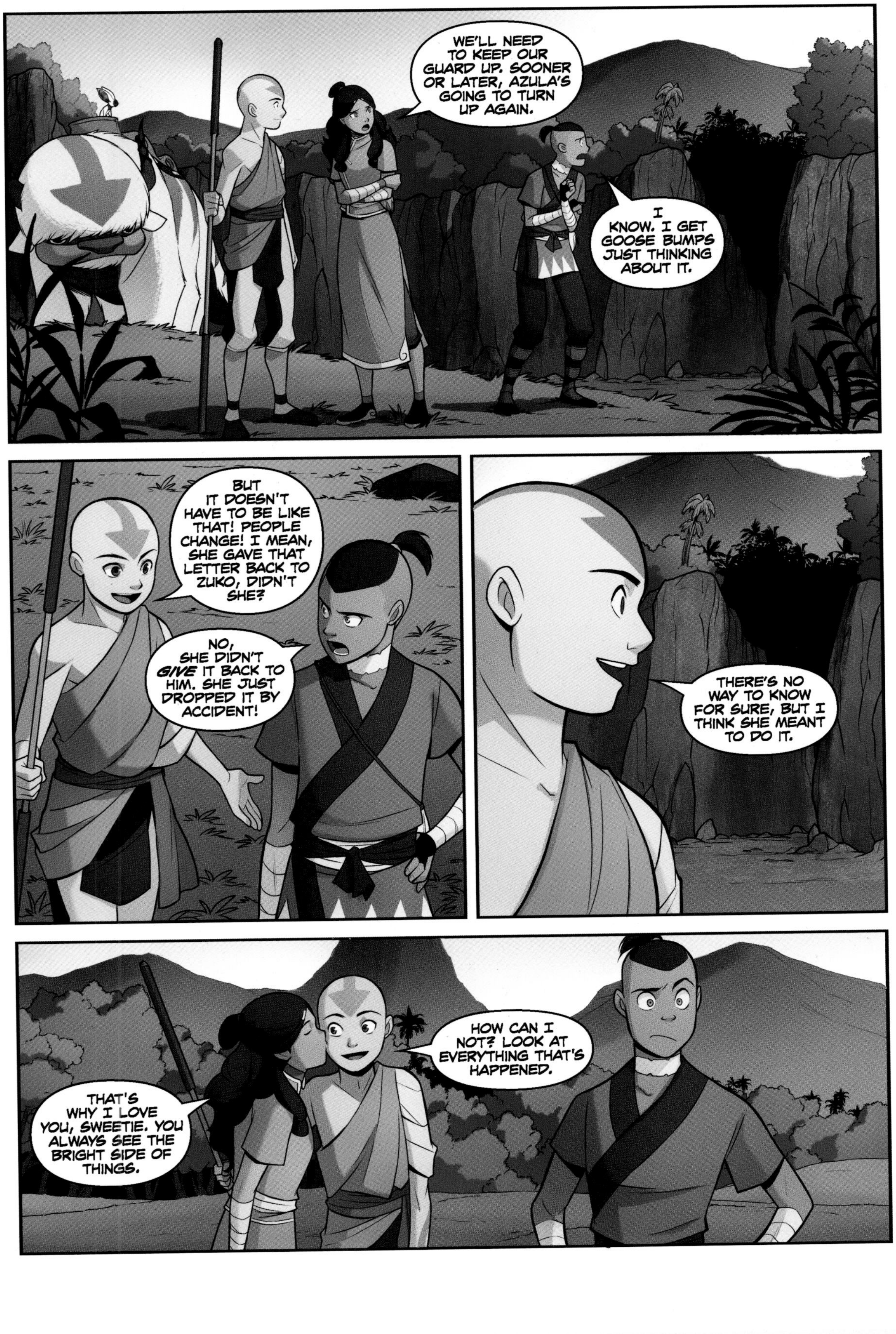
WE'LL NEED TO KEEP OUR GUARD UP. SOONER OR LATER, AZULA'S GOING TO TURN UP AGAIN.
I KNOW. I GET GOOSE BUMPS JUST THINKING ABOUT IT.
BUT IT DOESN'T HAVE TO BE LIKE THAT! PEOPLE CHANGE! I MEAN, SHE GAVE THAT LETTER BACK TO ZUKO, DIDN'T SHE?
NO, SHE DIDN'T *GIVE* IT BACK TO HIM. SHE JUST DROPPED IT BY ACCIDENT!
THERE'S NO WAY TO KNOW FOR SURE, BUT I THINK SHE MEANT TO DO IT.
THAT'S WHY I LOVE YOU, SWEETIE. YOU ALWAYS SEE THE BRIGHT SIDE OF THINGS.
HOW CAN I NOT? LOOK AT EVERYTHING THAT'S HAPPENED.

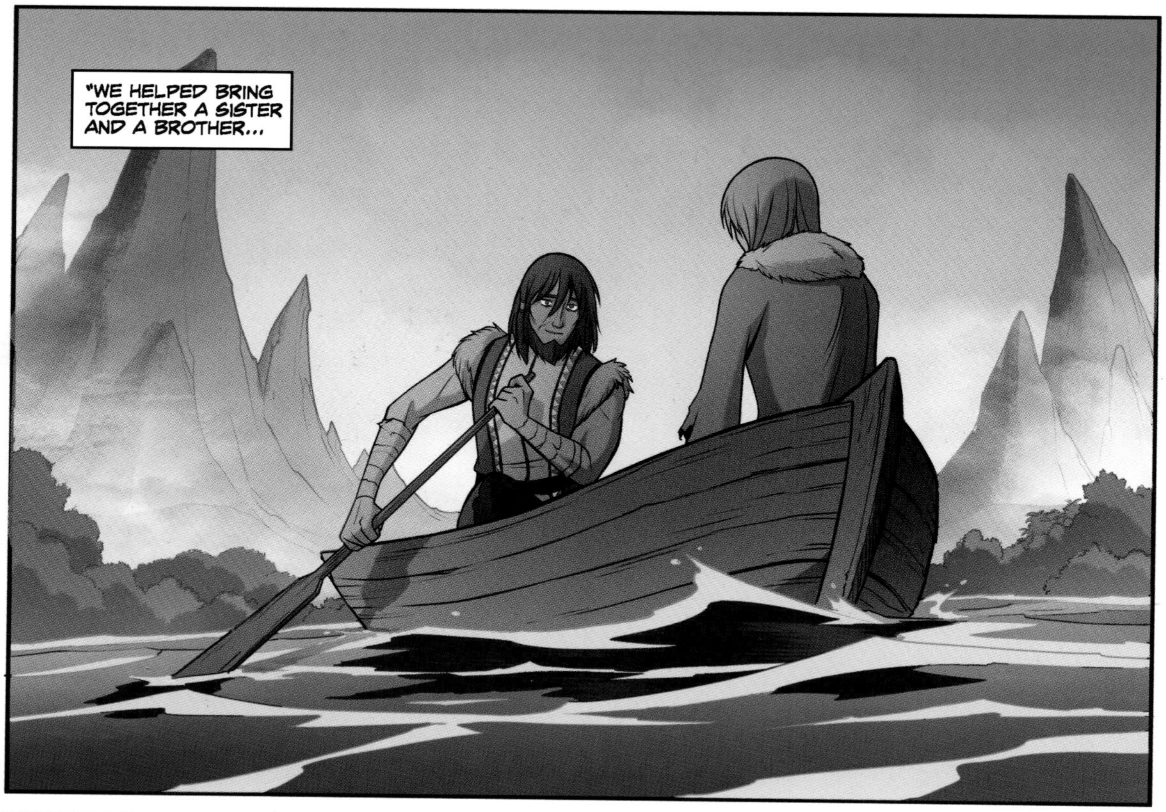
"WE HELPED BRING TOGETHER A SISTER AND A BROTHER...

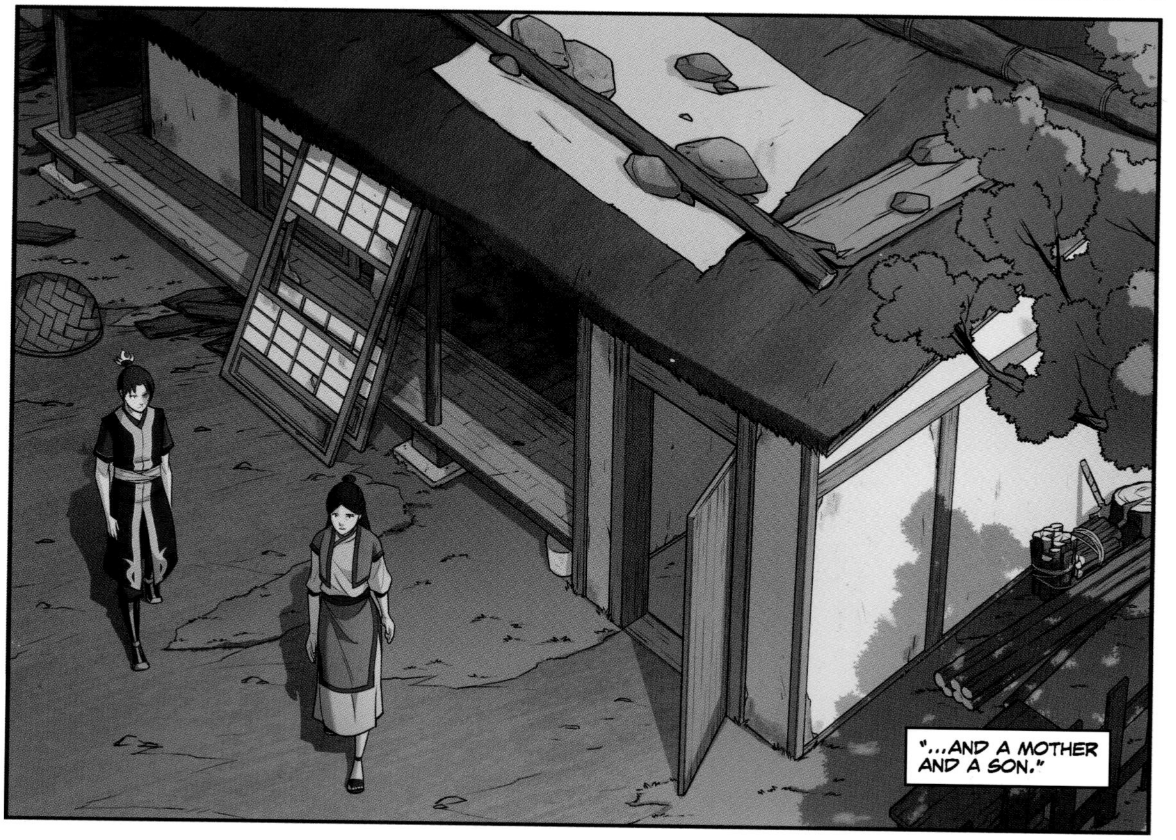
"...AND A MOTHER AND A SON."

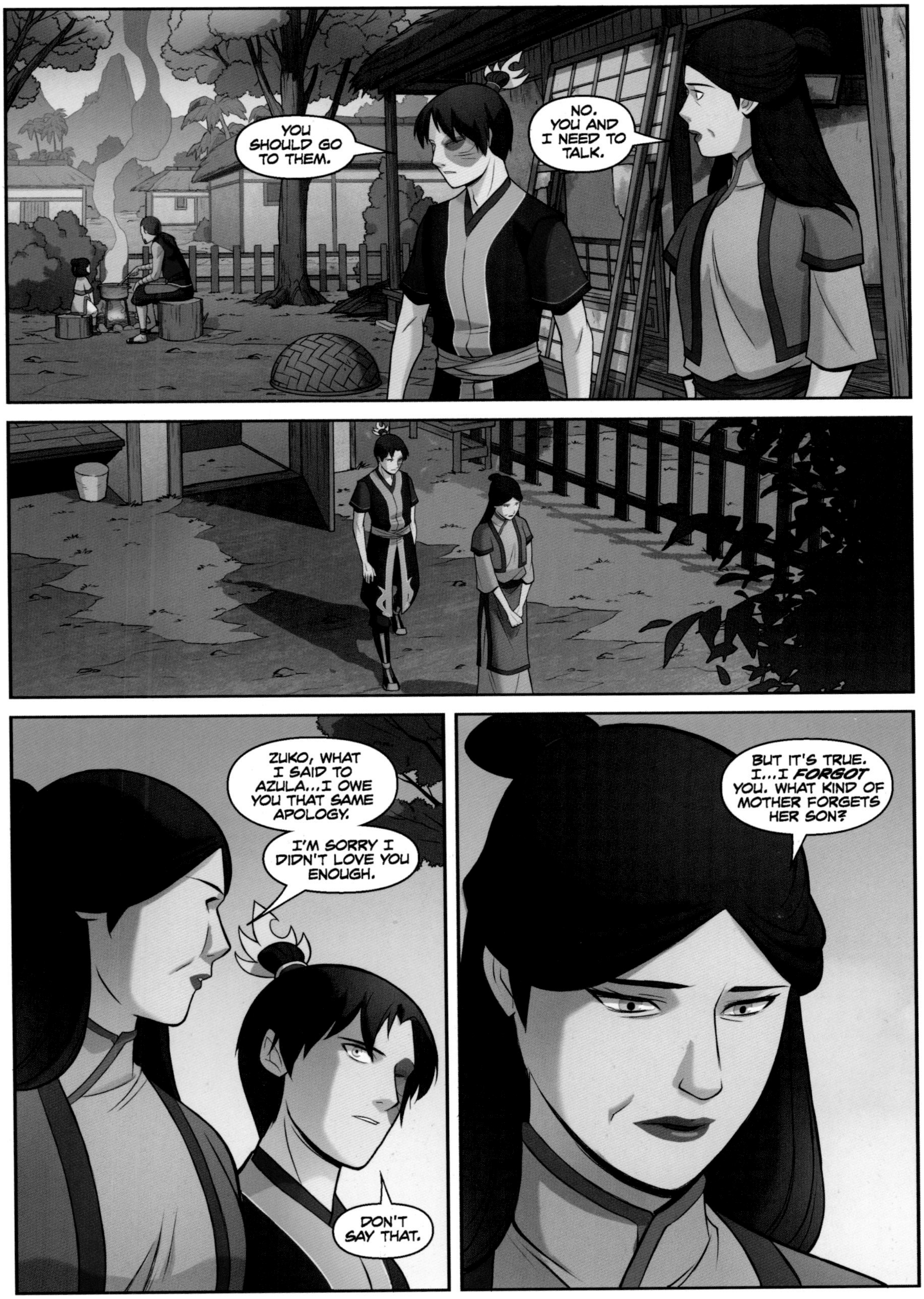
YOU SHOULD GO TO THEM.
NO. YOU AND I NEED TO TALK.
ZUKO, WHAT I SAID TO AZULA...I OWE YOU THAT SAME APOLOGY.
I'M SORRY I DIDN'T LOVE YOU ENOUGH.
DON'T SAY THAT.
BUT IT'S TRUE. I...I *FORGOT* YOU. WHAT KIND OF MOTHER FORGETS HER SON?

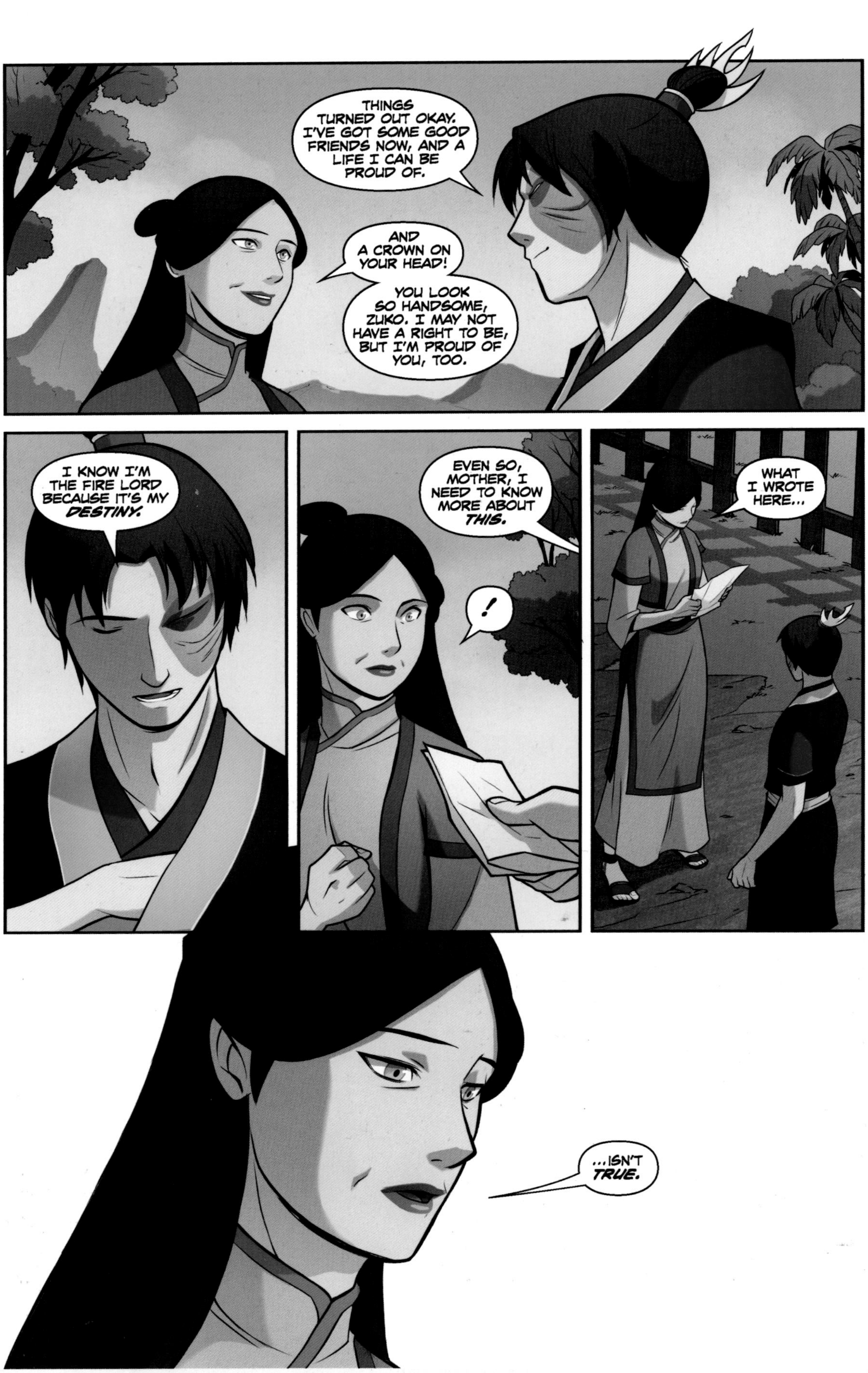
THINGS TURNED OUT OKAY. I'VE GOT SOME GOOD FRIENDS NOW, AND A LIFE I CAN BE PROUD OF.
AND A CROWN ON YOUR HEAD!
YOU LOOK SO HANDSOME, ZUKO. I MAY NOT HAVE A RIGHT TO BE, BUT I'M PROUD OF YOU, TOO.
I KNOW I'M THE FIRE LORD BECAUSE IT'S MY DESTINY.
EVEN SO, MOTHER, I NEED TO KNOW MORE ABOUT THIS.
!
WHAT I WROTE HERE...
...ISN'T TRUE.

M: I know people will be relieved to learn that Ozai is Zuko's real father after all. But I think calling Zuko's paternity into question was an important experience for his character to go through. Zuko's search for who he is and who he wants to become will be ongoing. Finding out what happened to his mother was an important step in his journey, but it's certainly not the end of their story.

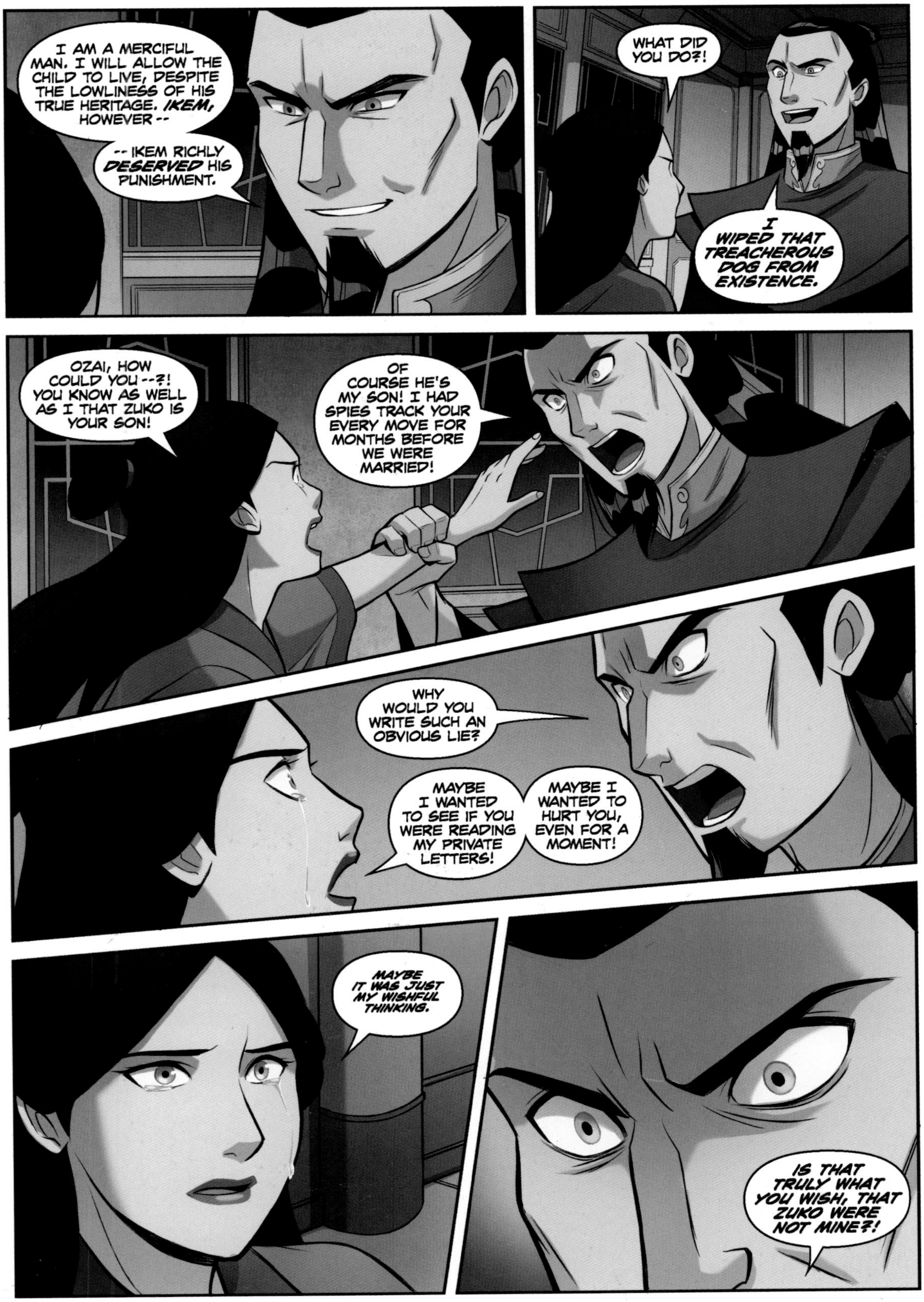
I AM A MERCIFUL MAN. I WILL ALLOW THE CHILD TO LIVE, DESPITE THE LOWLINESS OF HIS TRUE HERITAGE. IKEM, HOWEVER --
-- IKEM RICHLY DESERVED HIS PUNISHMENT.
WHAT DID YOU DO?!
I WIPED THAT TREACHEROUS DOG FROM EXISTENCE.
OZAI, HOW COULD YOU --?! YOU KNOW AS WELL AS I THAT ZUKO IS YOUR SON!
OF COURSE HE'S MY SON! I HAD SPIES TRACK YOUR EVERY MOVE FOR MONTHS BEFORE WE WERE MARRIED!
WHY WOULD YOU WRITE SUCH AN OBVIOUS LIE?
MAYBE I WANTED TO SEE IF YOU WERE READING MY PRIVATE LETTERS!
MAYBE I WANTED TO HURT YOU, EVEN FOR A MOMENT!
MAYBE IT WAS JUST MY WISHFUL THINKING.
IS THAT TRULY WHAT YOU WISH, THAT ZUKO WERE NOT MINE?!

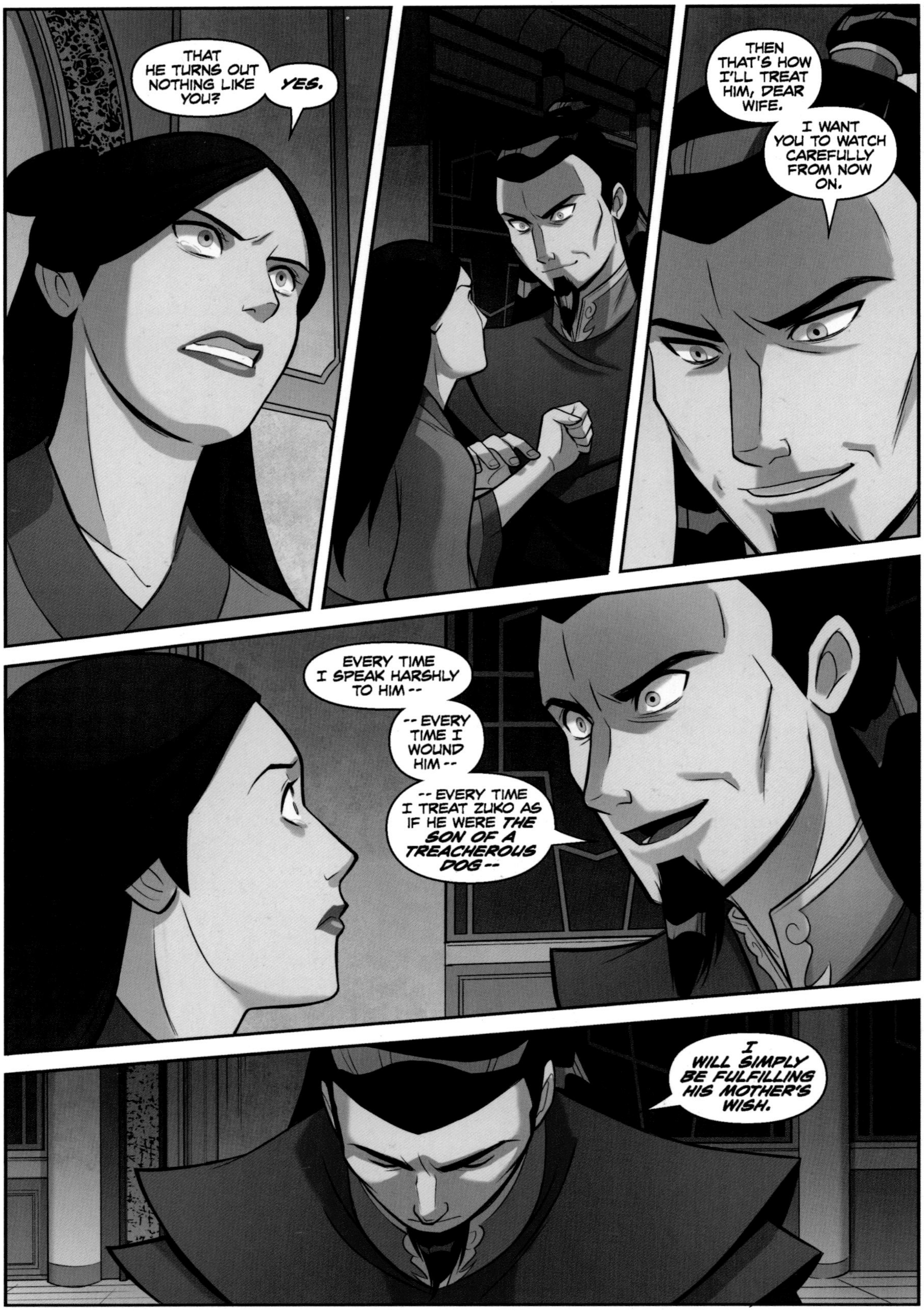
THAT HE TURNS OUT NOTHING LIKE YOU?
YES.
THEN THAT'S HOW I'LL TREAT HIM, DEAR WIFE.
I WANT YOU TO WATCH CAREFULLY FROM NOW ON.
EVERY TIME I SPEAK HARSHLY TO HIM --
-- EVERY TIME I WOUND HIM --
-- EVERY TIME I TREAT ZUKO AS IF HE WERE THE SON OF A TREACHEROUS DOG --
I WILL SIMPLY BE FULFILLING HIS MOTHER'S WISH.

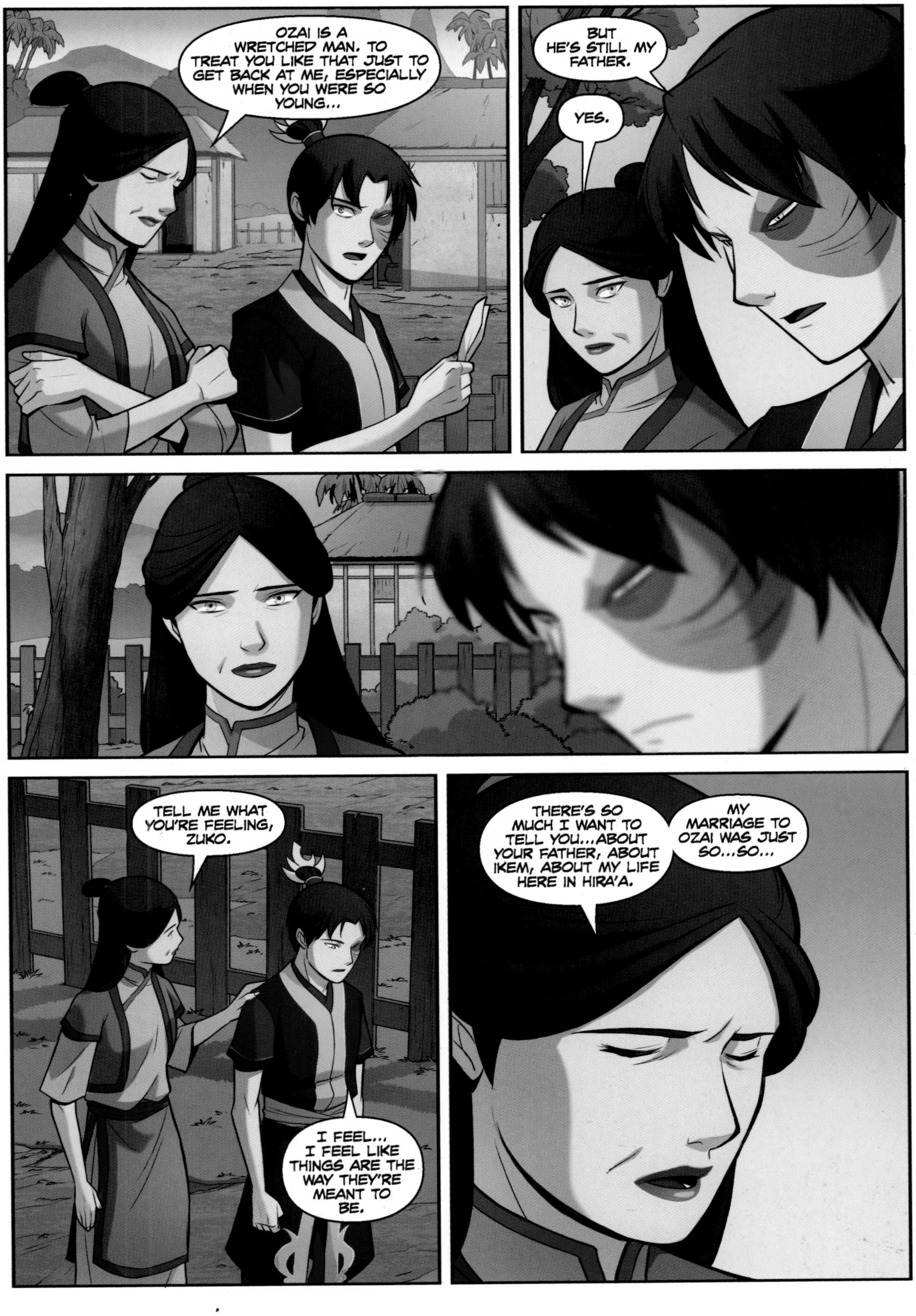
OZAI IS A WRETCHED MAN. TO TREAT YOU LIKE THAT JUST TO GET BACK AT ME, ESPECIALLY WHEN YOU WERE SO YOUNG...
BUT HE'S STILL MY FATHER.
YES.
TELL ME WHAT YOU'RE FEELING, ZUKO.
I FEEL... I FEEL LIKE THINGS ARE THE WAY THEY'RE MEANT TO BE.
THERE'S SO MUCH I WANT TO TELL YOU...ABOUT YOUR FATHER, ABOUT IKEM, ABOUT MY LIFE HERE IN HIRA'A.
MY MARRIAGE TO OZAI WAS JUST SO...SO...

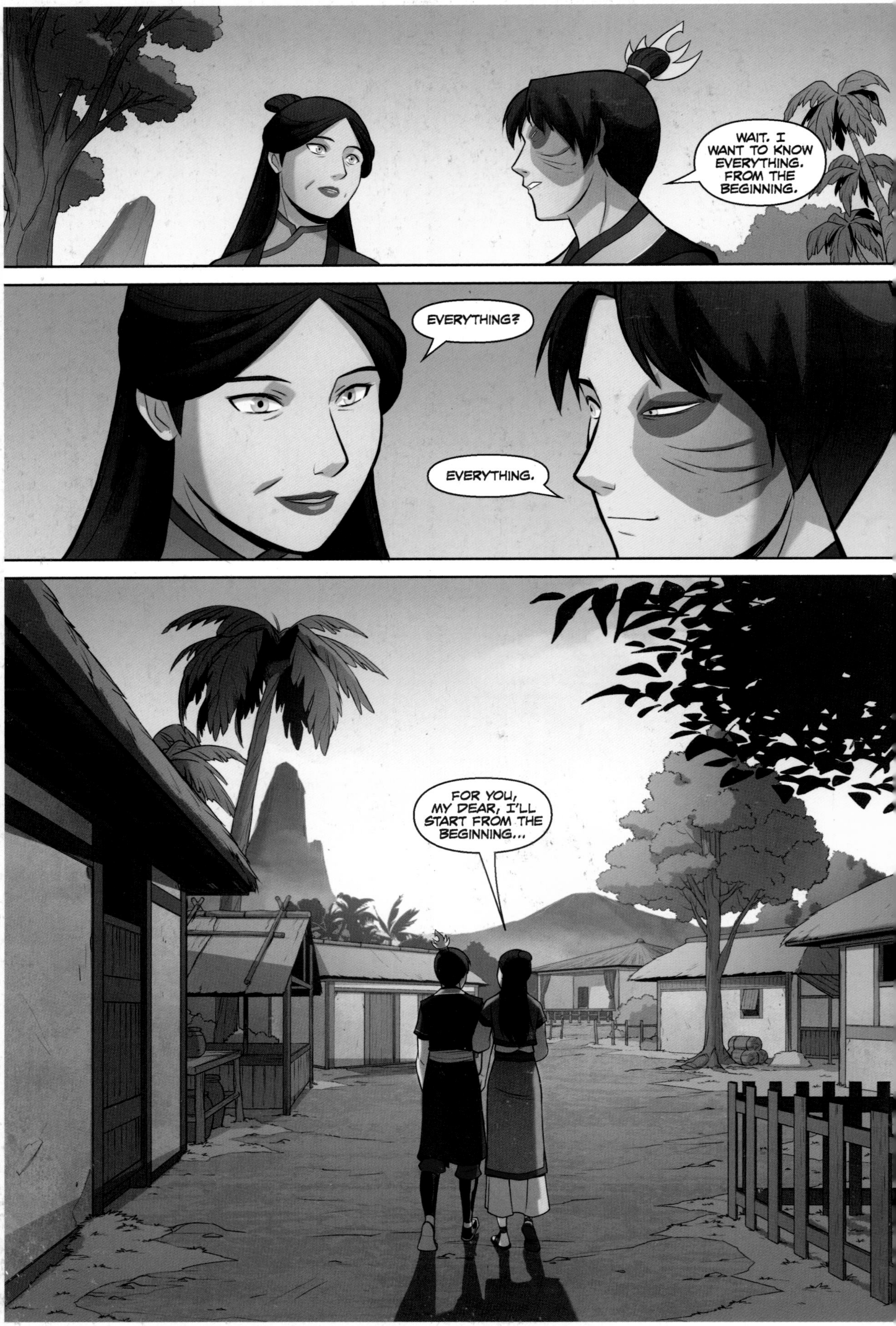
WAIT. I WANT TO KNOW EVERYTHING. FROM THE BEGINNING.
EVERYTHING?
EVERYTHING.
FOR YOU, MY DEAR, I'LL START FROM THE BEGINNING...

M: *When I first read the script, I got chills when I got to the end and realized it was Ursa and Zuko's conversation from the very first panel of the story, and we'd just been hearing Ursa tell her own backstory to her son. It's beautiful writing by Gene. Now when people ask, "What happened to Zuko's mom?" we can point them to this story.*

GLY: *In 2008, I watched the very last episode of* Avatar: The Last Airbender *with the eagerness of a true fan. Zuko asks Ozai what happened to his mom . . . and the scene cuts. I yelled curse words at my TV.*

Three years later, I'm working with Mike DiMartino and Bryan Konietzko on the story that explains what happened to Zuko's mom.

Sometimes, life is weird. Weird in a good, good way.

Artwork and captions by Gurihiru

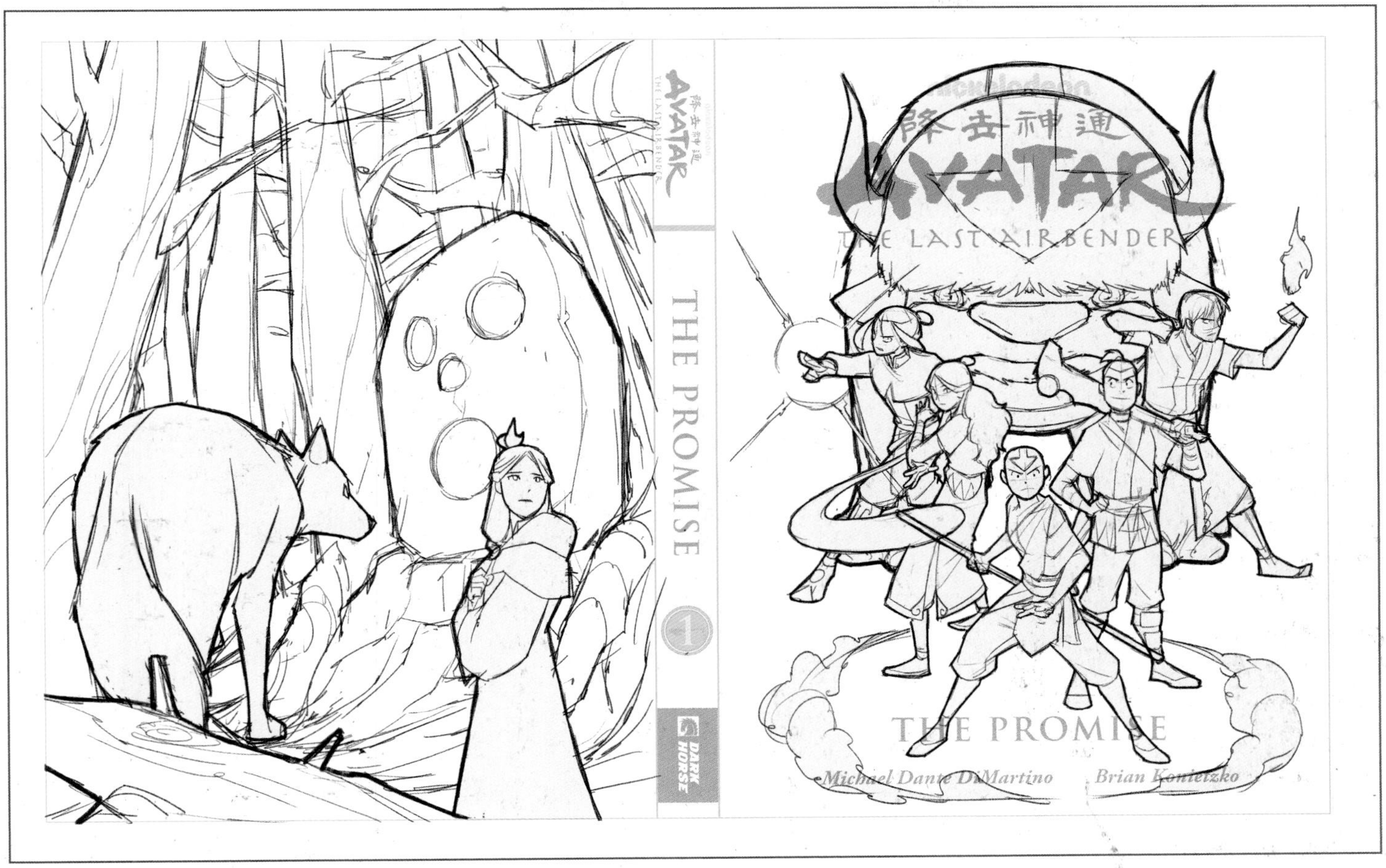
降去神通
AVATAR
THE LAST AIRBENDER
THE PROMISE
1
DARK HORSE
nickelodeon
降去神通
AVATAR
THE LAST AIRBENDER
THE PROMISE
Michael Dante DiMartino
Brian Konietzko

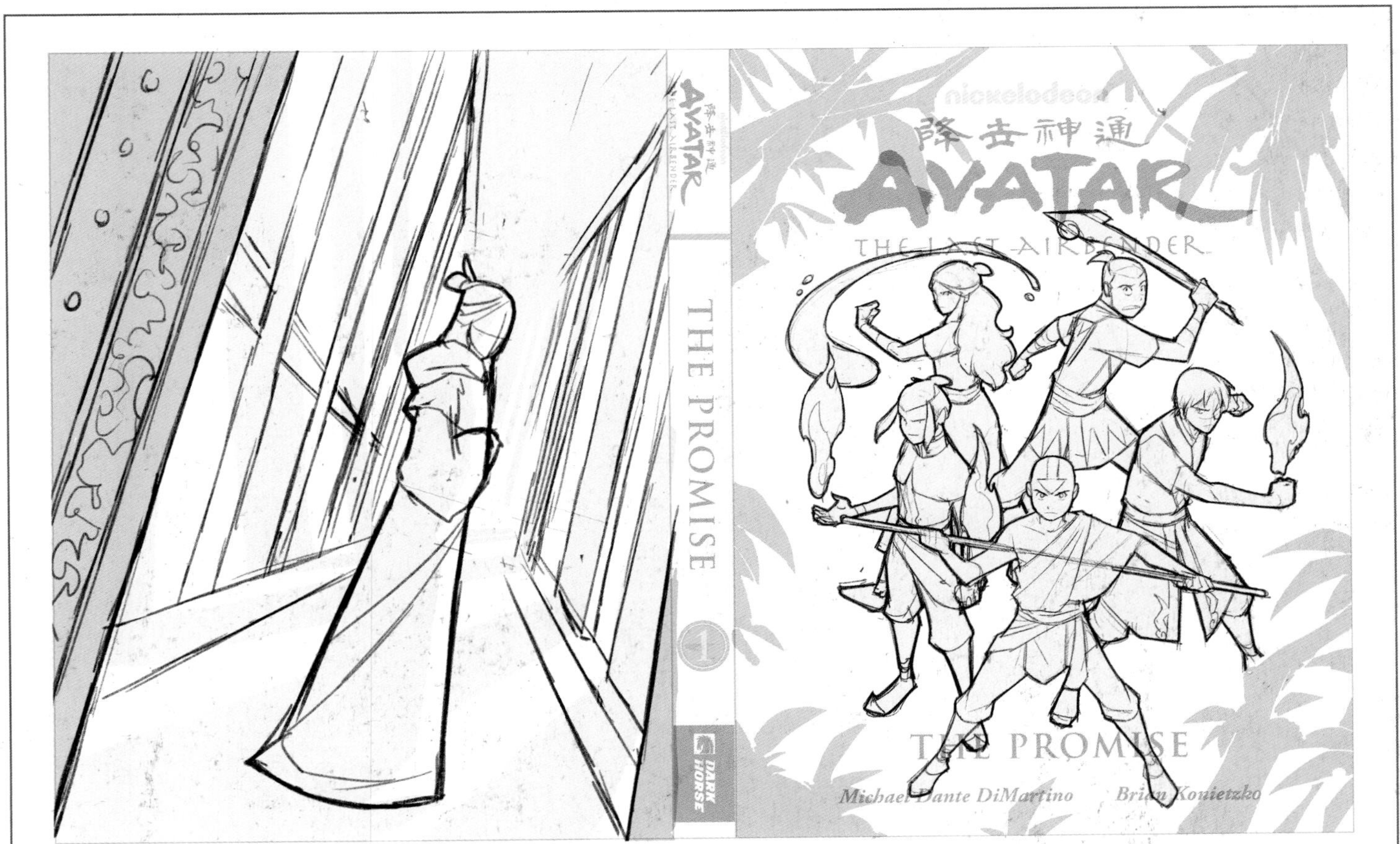
降去神通
AVATAR
THE LAST AIRBENDER
THE PROMISE
1
DARK HORSE
nickelodeon
降去神通
AVATAR
THE LAST AIRBENDER
THE PROMISE
Michael Dante DiMartino
Brian Konietzko

On the front cover, we show the ongoing story of Aang. The back cover depicts Ursa's history.

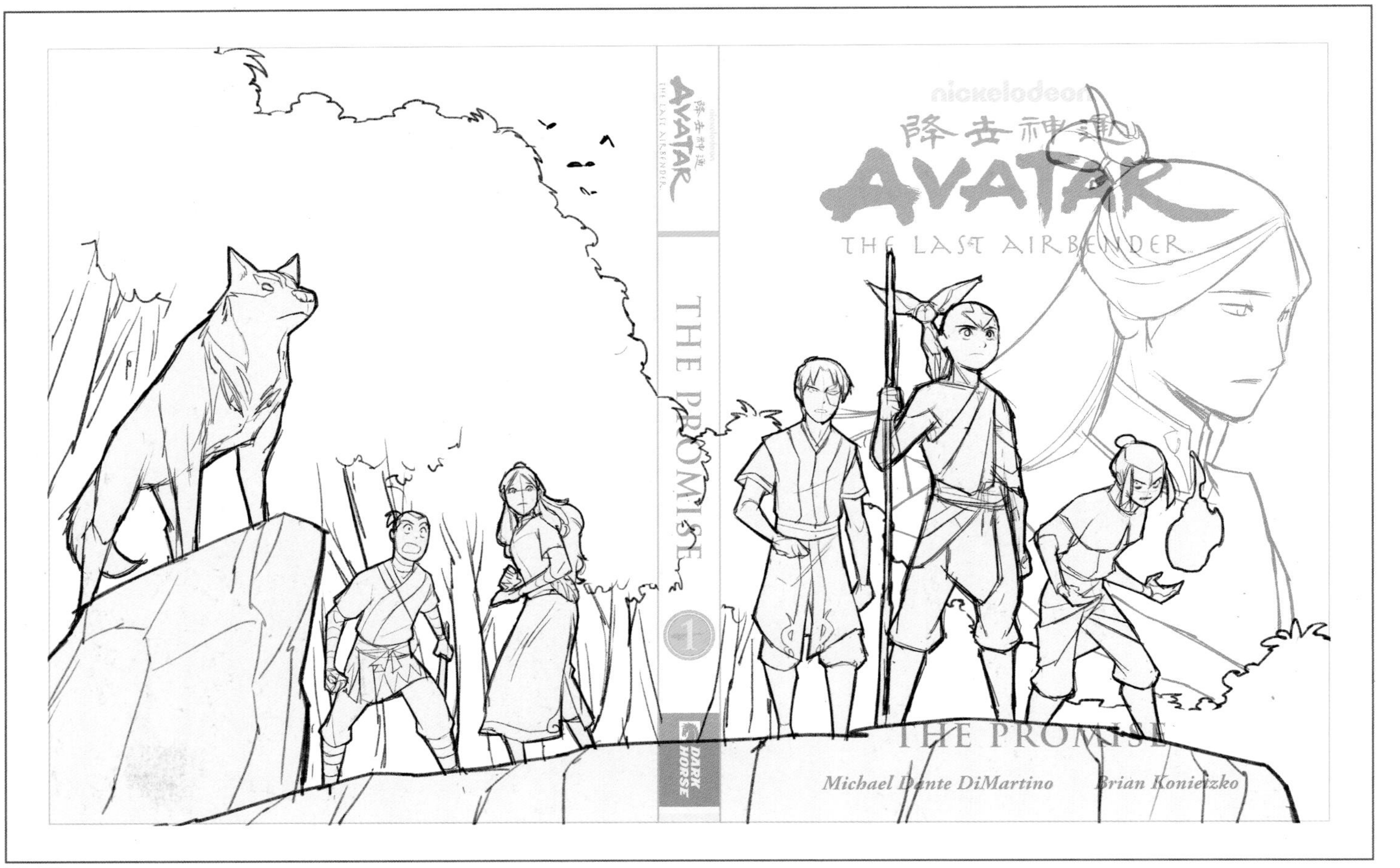
nickelodeon
降世神通
AVATAR
THE LAST AIRBENDER
THE PROMISE
1
DARK HORSE
THE PROMISE
Michael Dante DiMartino
Brian Konietzko

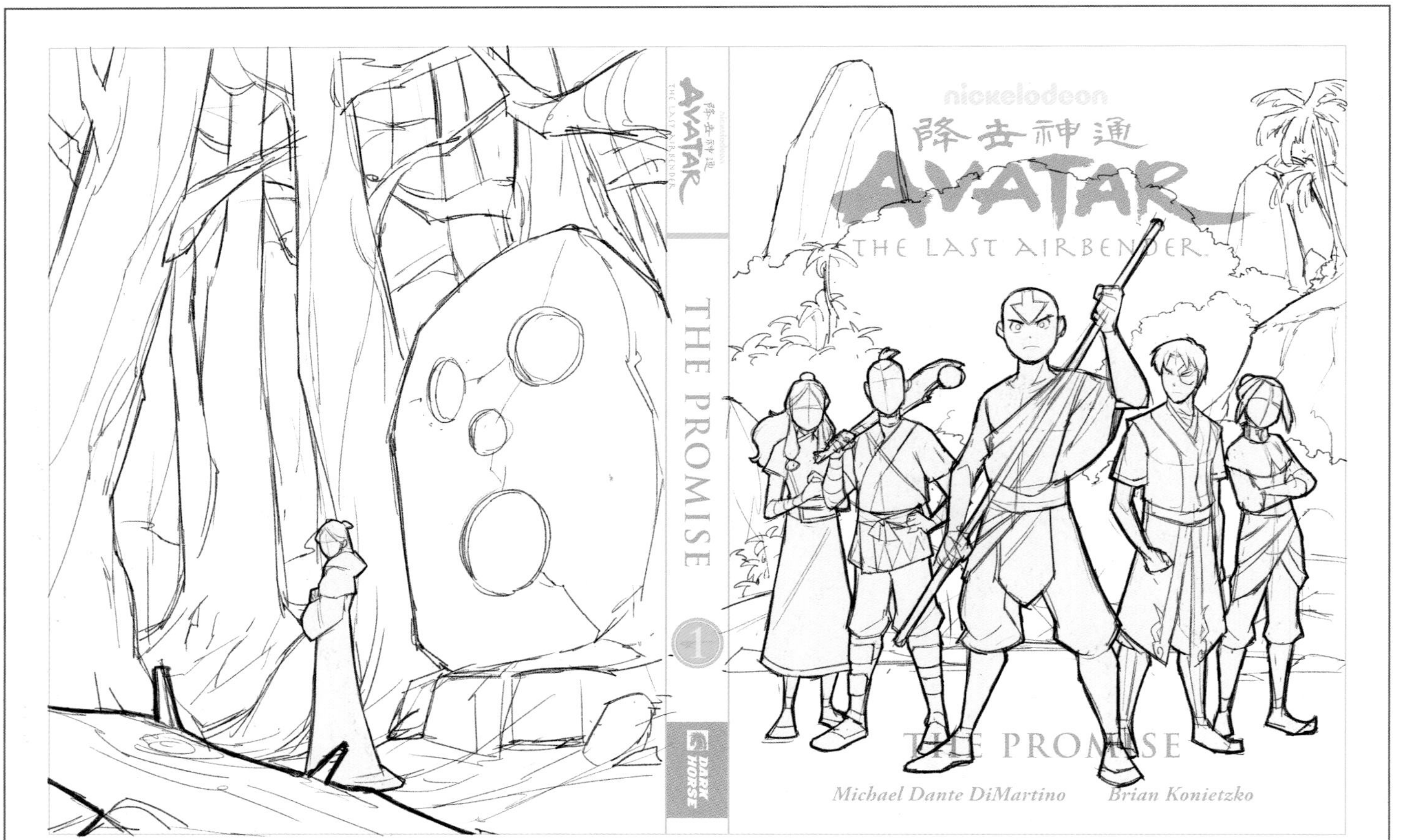
nickelodeon
降世神通
AVATAR
THE LAST AIRBENDER
THE PROMISE
1
DARK HORSE
THE PROMISE
Michael Dante DiMartino
Brian Konietzko

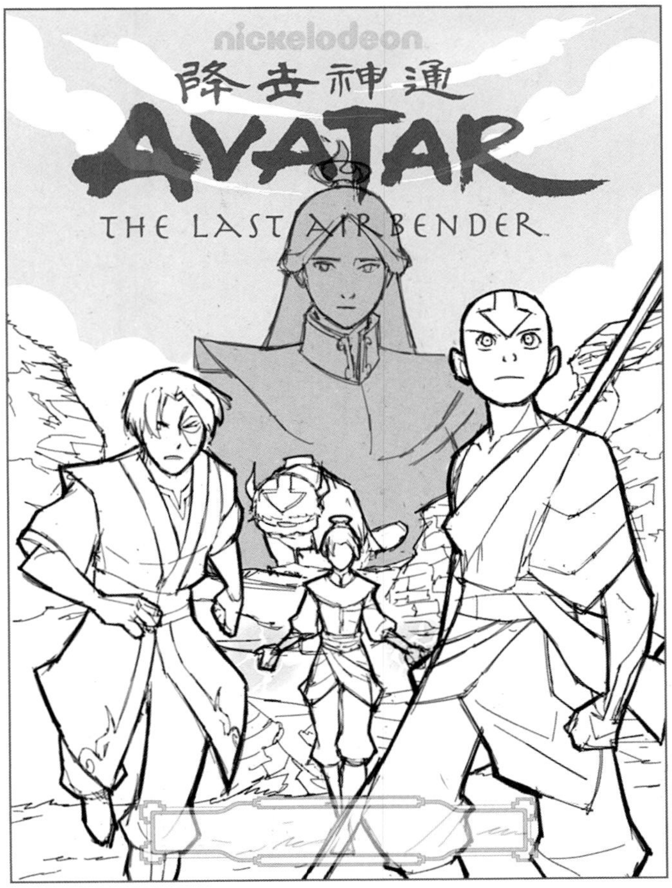
nickelodeon
降世神通
AVATAR
THE LAST AIRBENDER

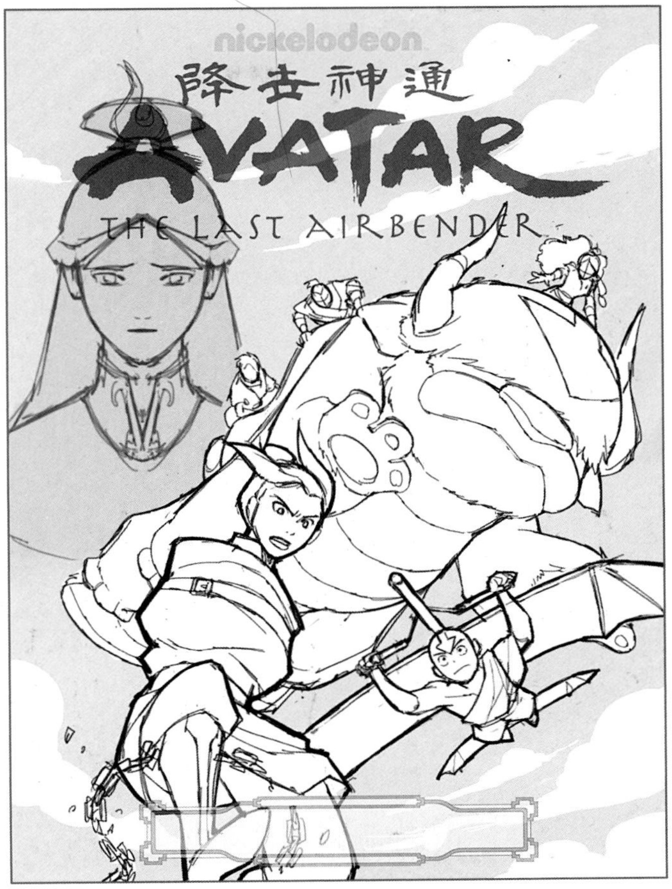
nickelodeon
降世神通
AVATAR
THE LAST AIRBENDER

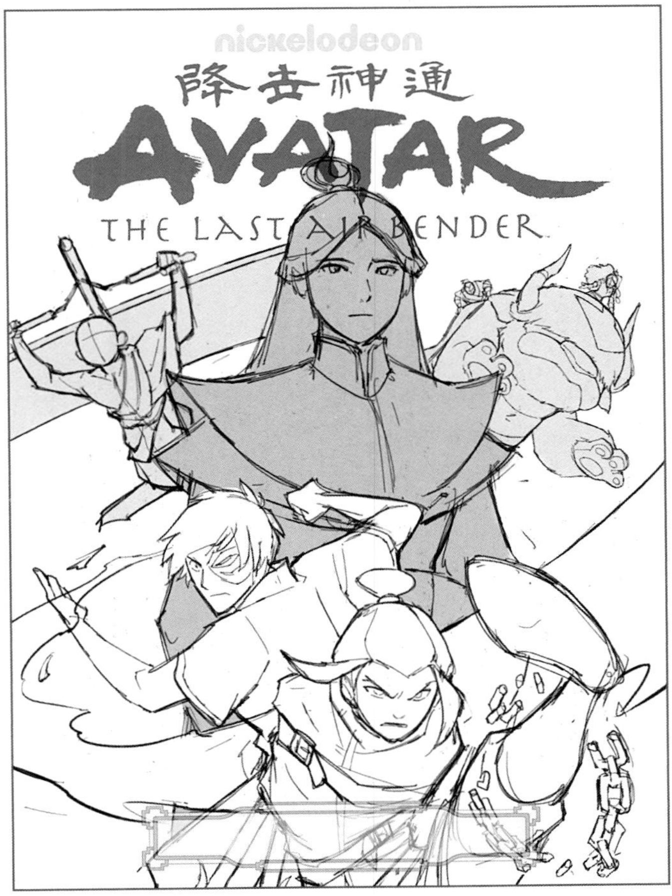
nickelodeon
降世神通
AVATAR
THE LAST AIRBENDER

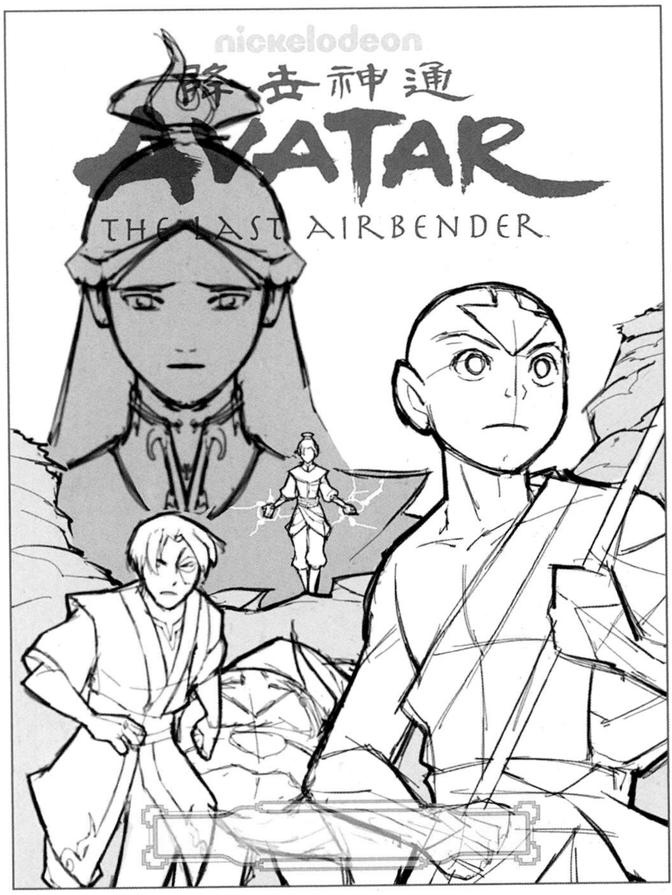
nickelodeon
降世神通
AVATAR
THE LAST AIRBENDER

We were asked to put Ursa on the cover for these sketches. Since Azula is at the core of the story, we had her appear, too.

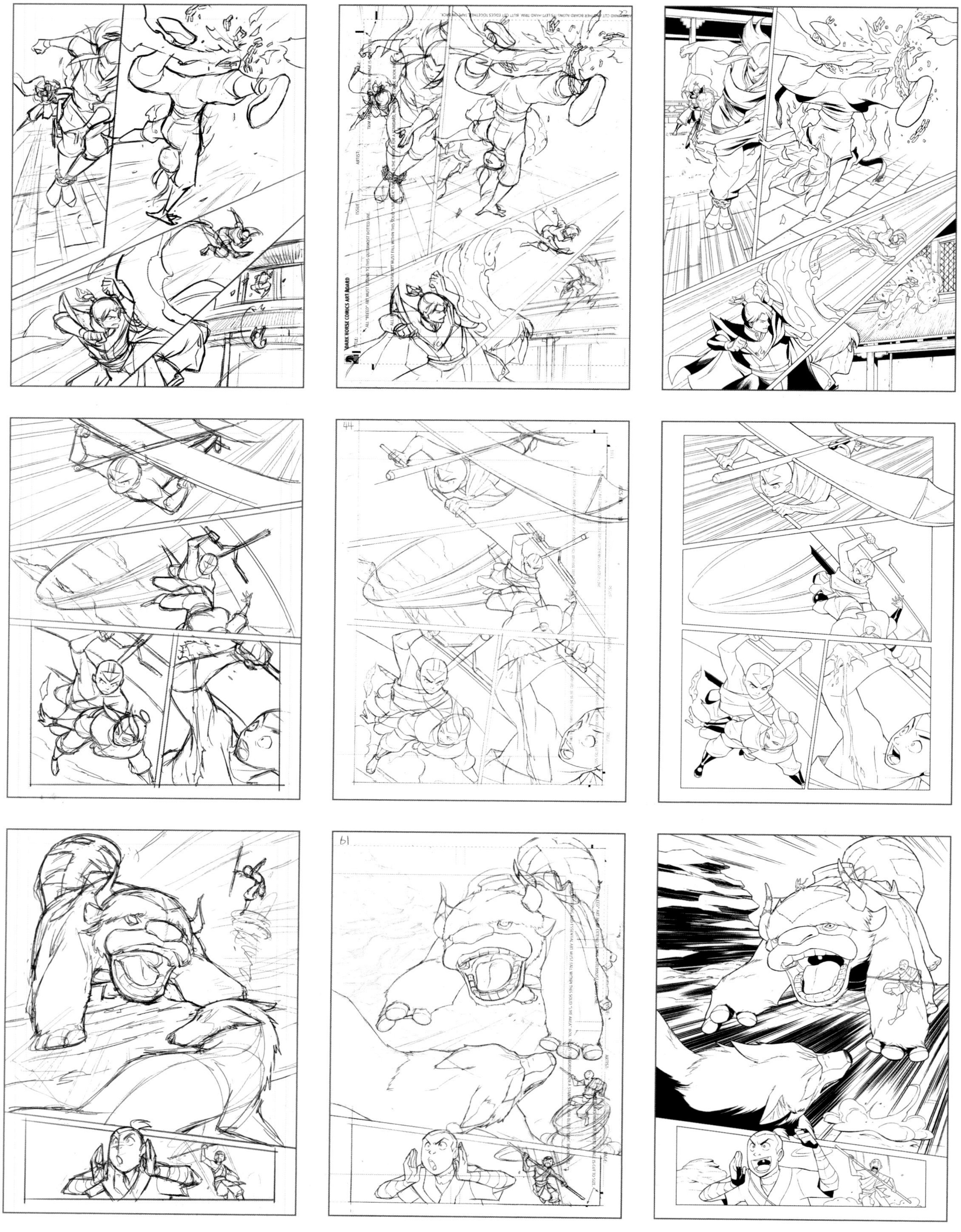

We always struggle with portraying action scenes. Unlike in animation, we have to show action in static images. We try to have the characters appear lively.

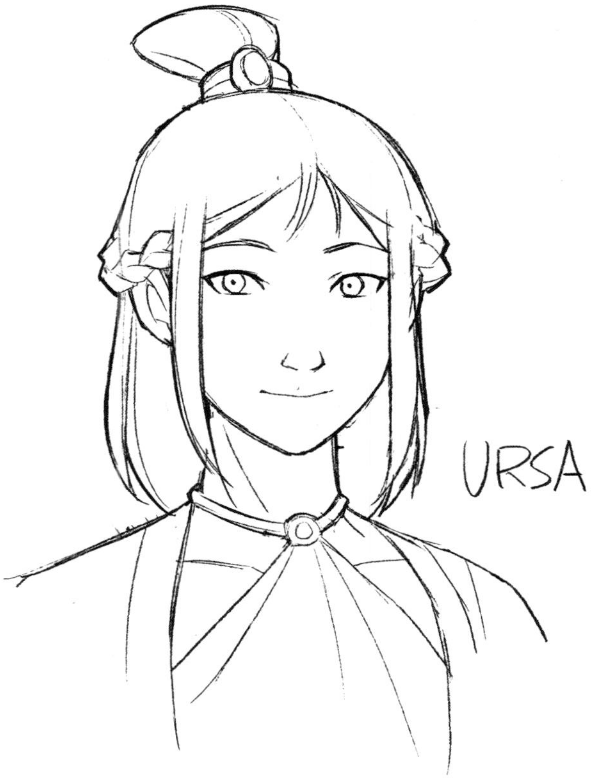
URSA

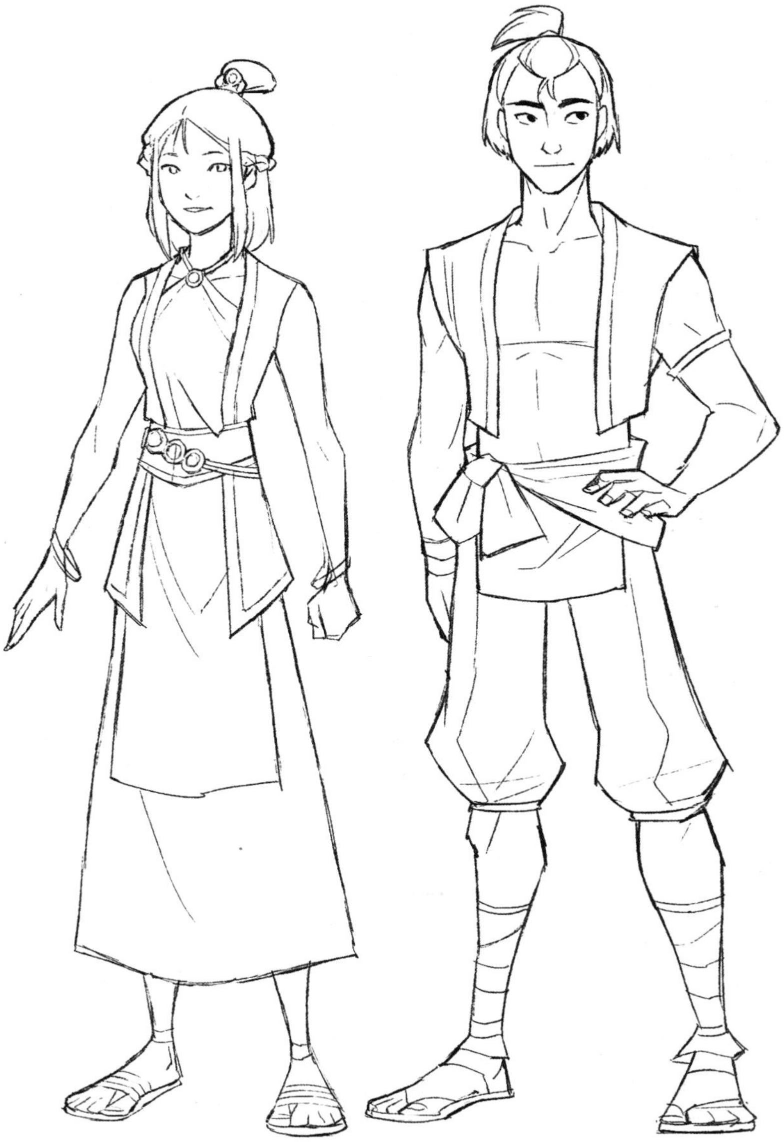

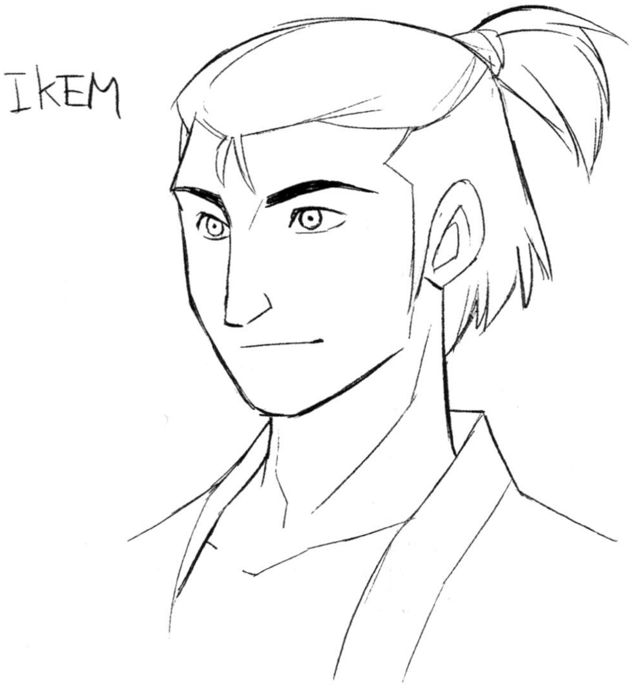
IKEM

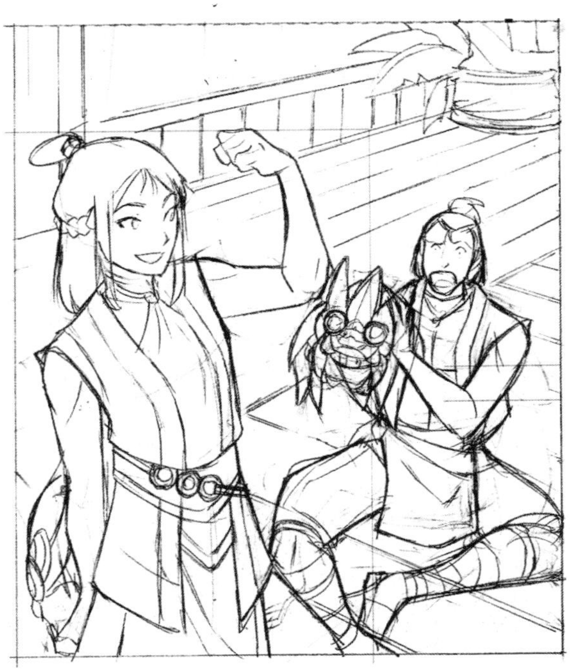

URSA AND IKEM

In the early stages, Ursa's hairstyle looked too much like Katara's, so we changed it considerably. We drew Ikem as handsome to distinguish him from Noren. Since Ursa and Ikem live in a warm area, the fabrics they wear are more sheer and show more bare skin.

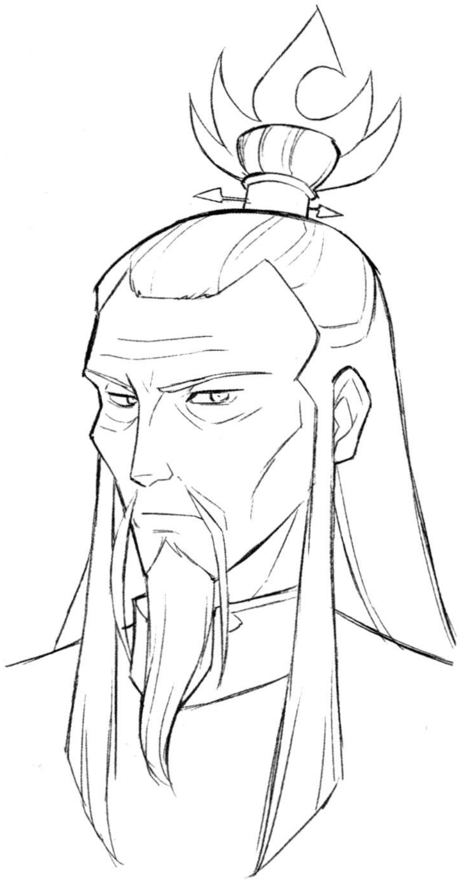

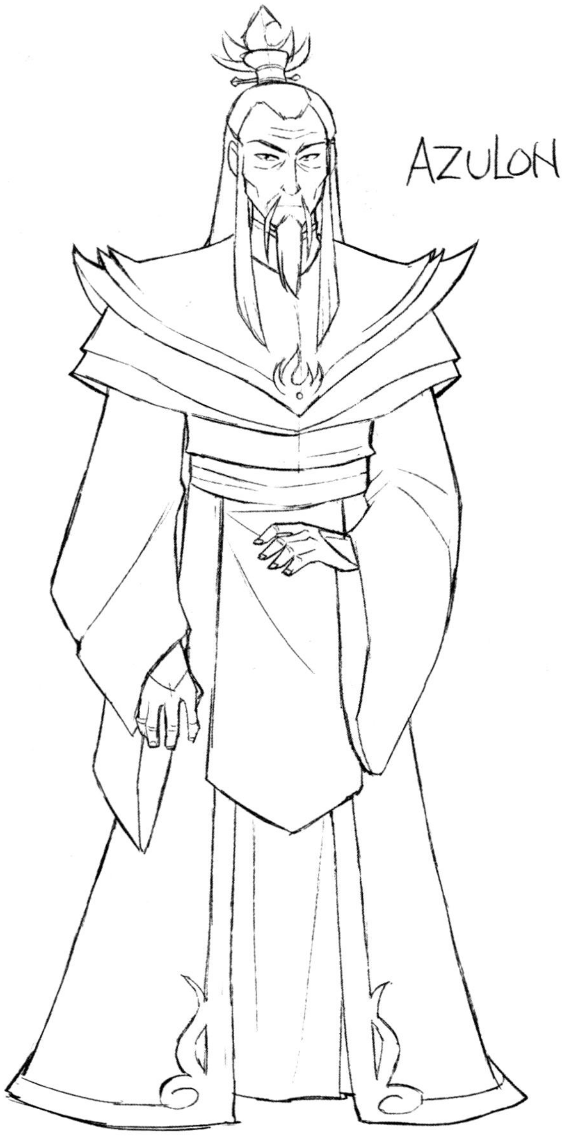
AZULON

AZULON

In the early designs, Azulon was younger, with shorter facial hair. But since he is eighty-five in The Search, *we made him look just a little younger than he is in the TV show.*

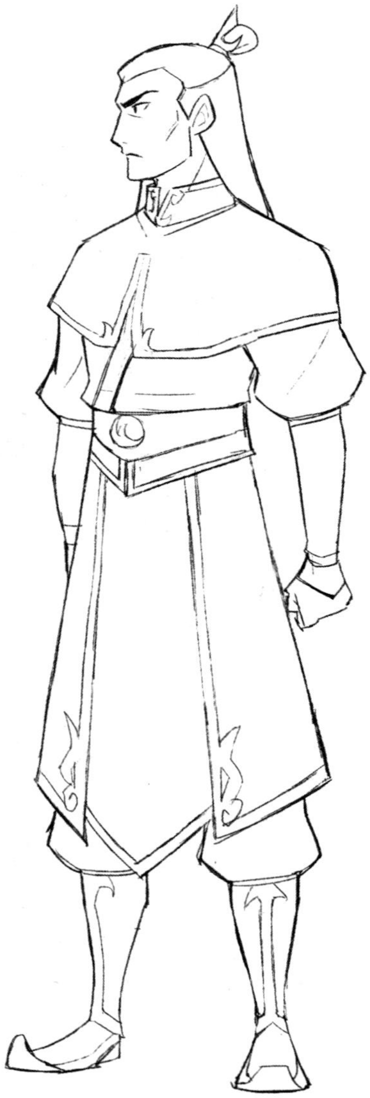

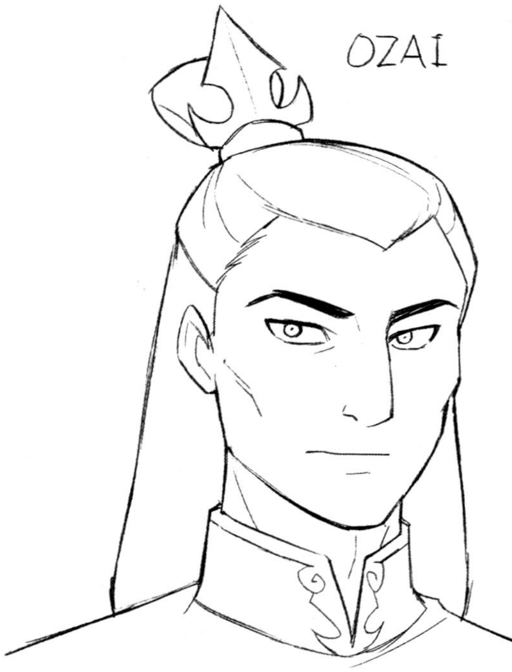
OZAI

OZAI

Ozai was younger and wore his hair bound up. Since Ozai was thirty and Ursa was twenty-one when they married, they appear similar to how they are on the show. We also decided to give Ozai a beard, though it's not in the sketch.

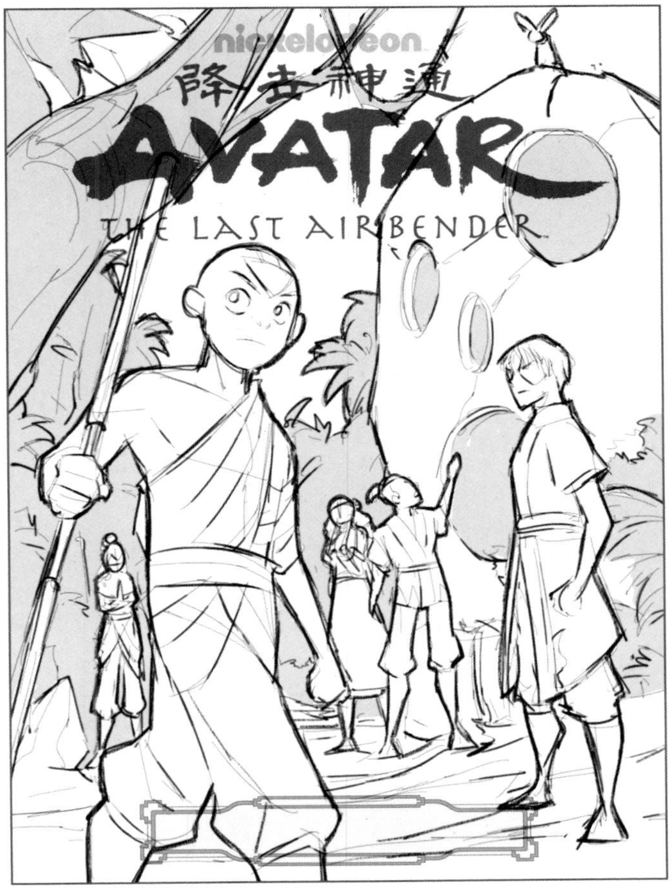
nickelodeon
降去神通
AVATAR
THE LAST AIRBENDER

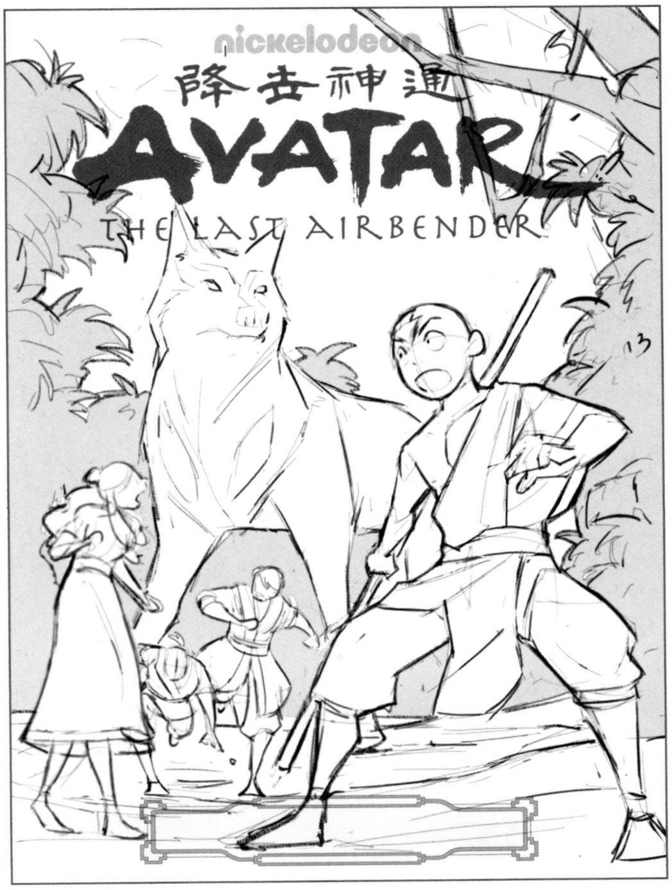
nickelodeon
降去神通
AVATAR
THE LAST AIRBENDER

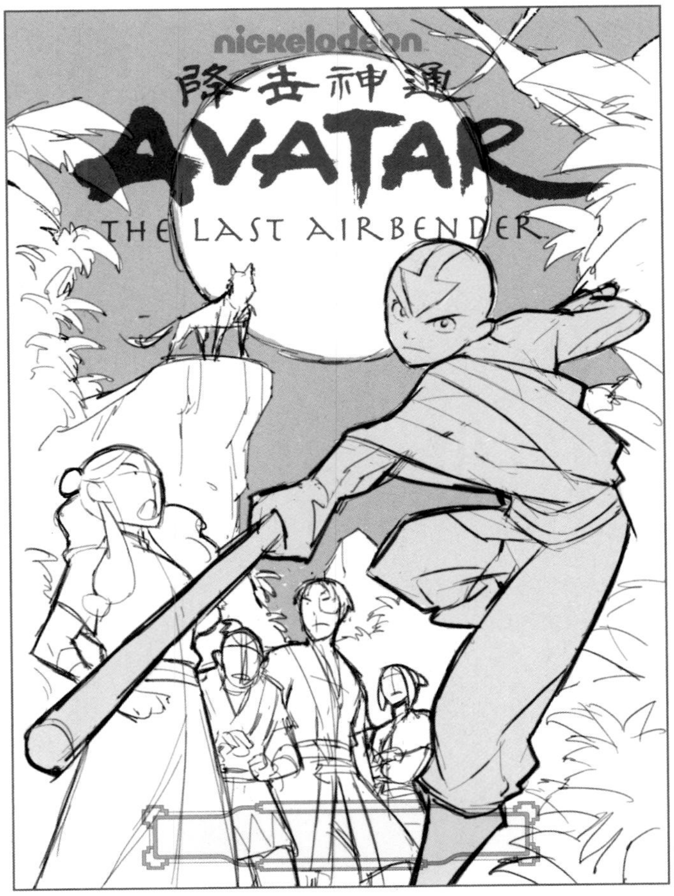
nickelodeon
降去神通
AVATAR
THE LAST AIRBENDER

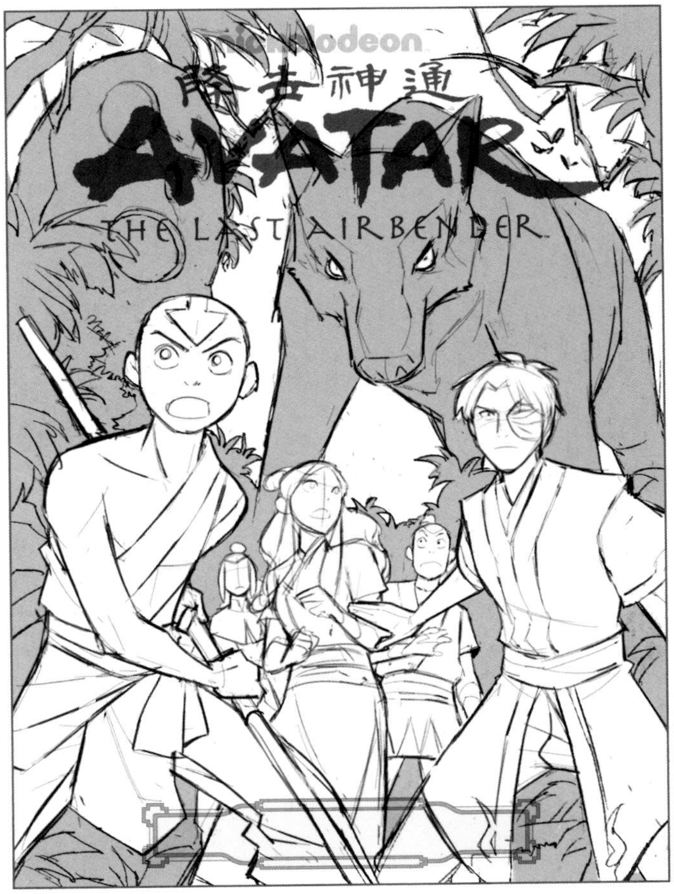
nickelodeon
降去神通
AVATAR
THE LAST AIRBENDER

We liked the one at the bottom left, but the ones we like best aren't always the ones chosen.

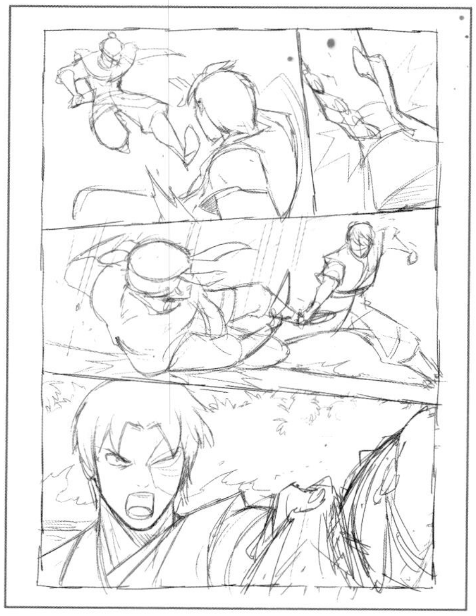
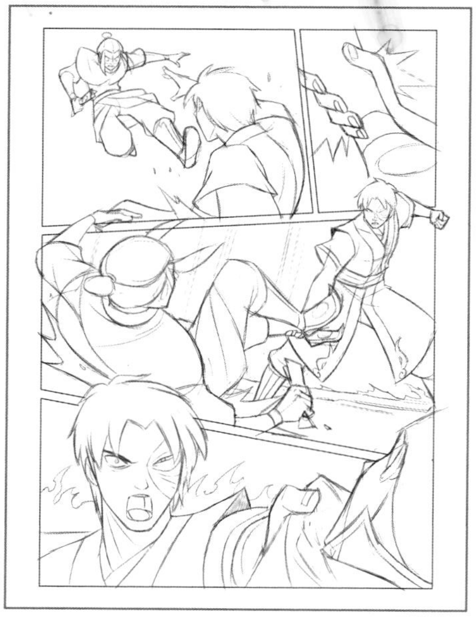
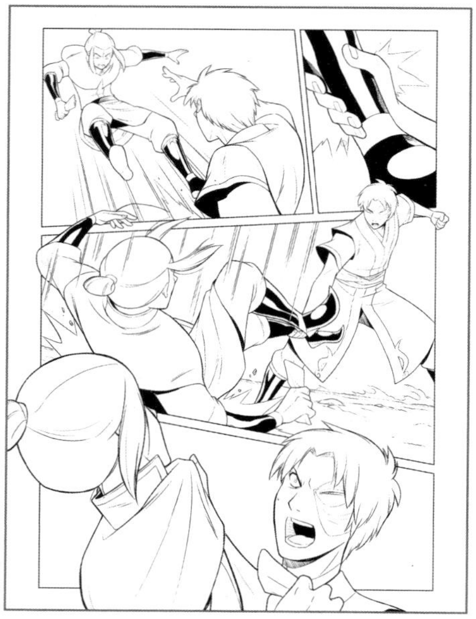
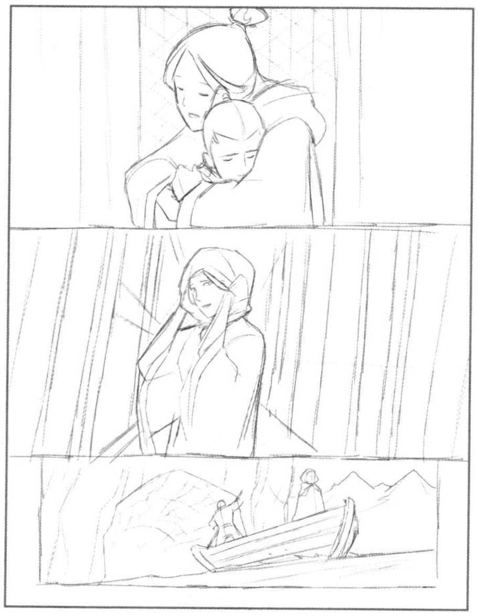
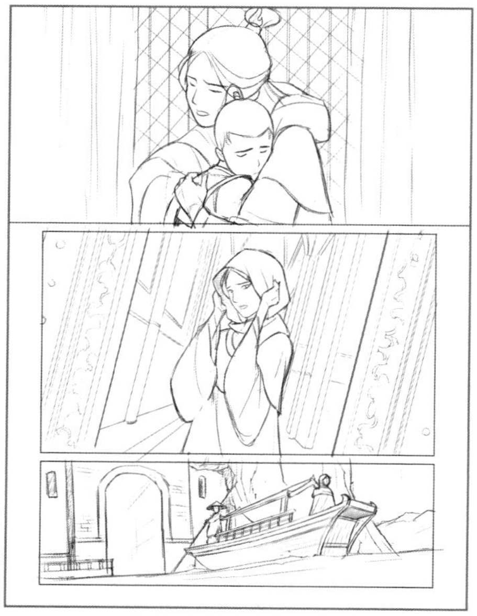
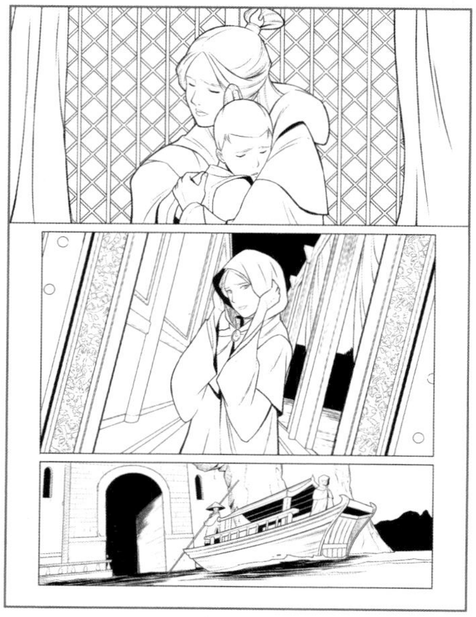
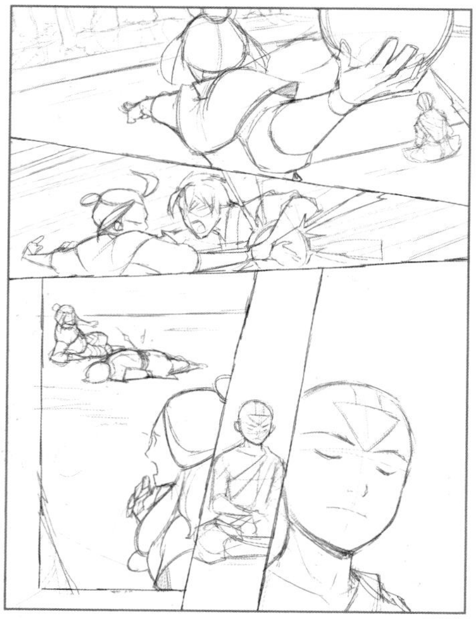
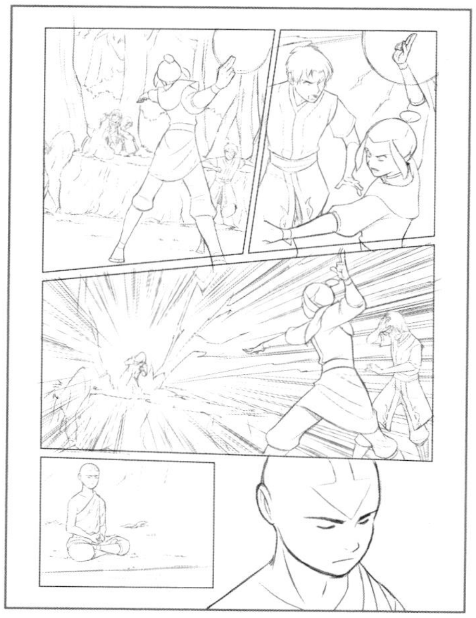
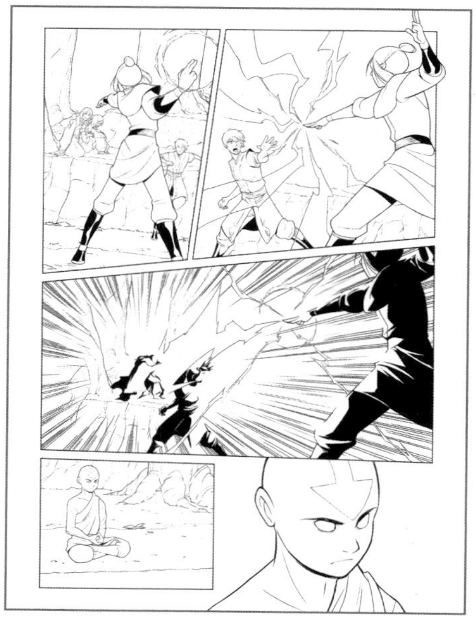

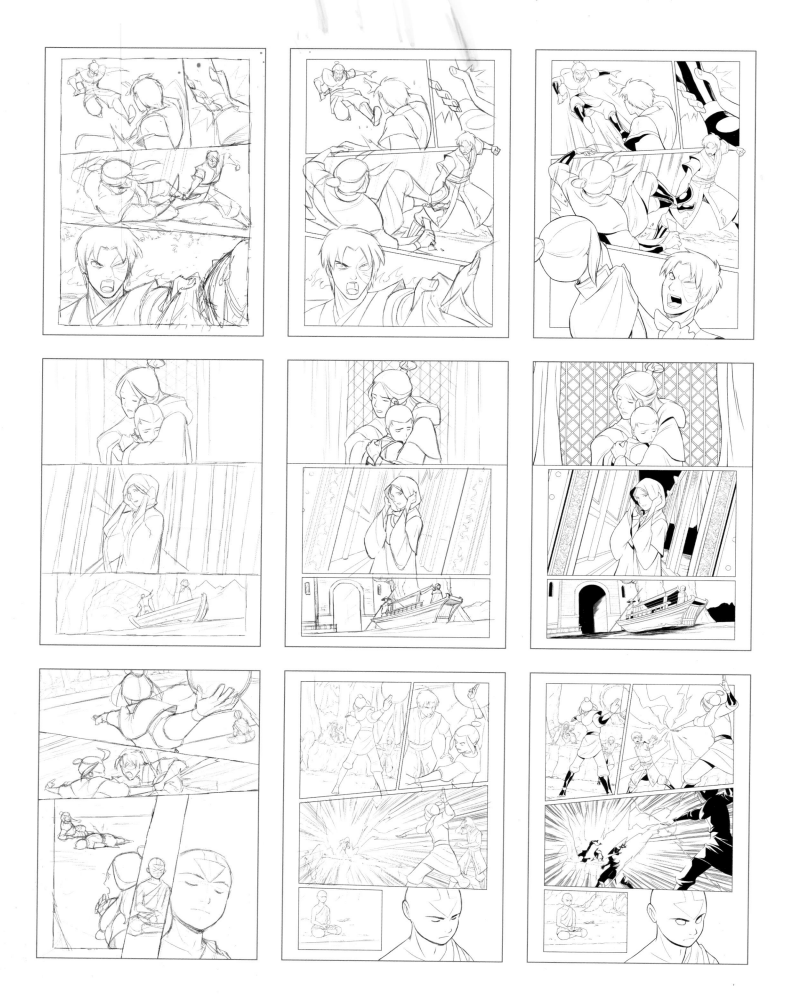

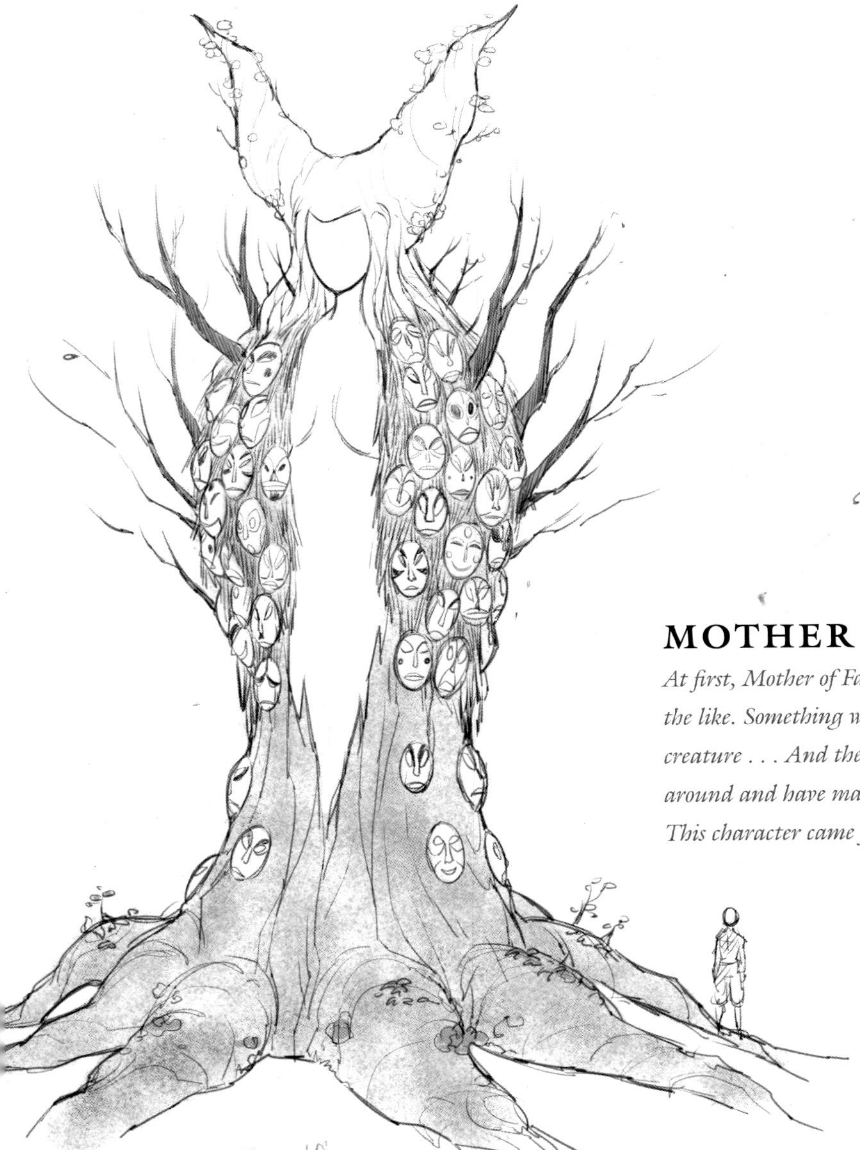

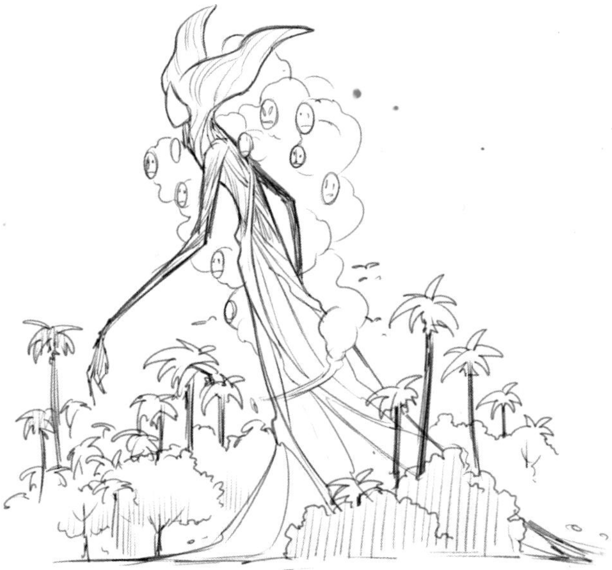

MOTHER OF FACES

At first, Mother of Faces was based on various motifs, such as animals, insects, plants, and the like. Something with four legs, but also a bit snake and spider, a little, scary-looking creature . . . And then, we settled on a type of giant tree. Since it was meant to walk around and have many faces, it eventually became a combination of plants and water. This character came from the ideas of many people.

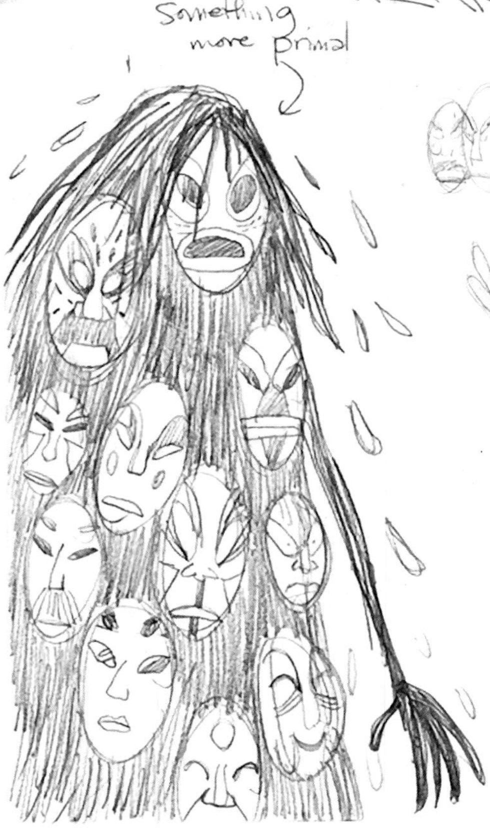
Something
more primal

Sketch by Gene Luen Yang

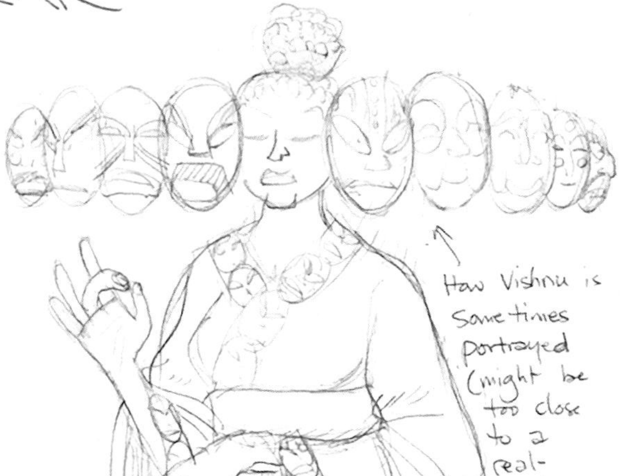
How Vishnu is
Sometimes
portrayed
(might be
too close
to a
real-
world
religion)

Sketch by Gene Luen Yang

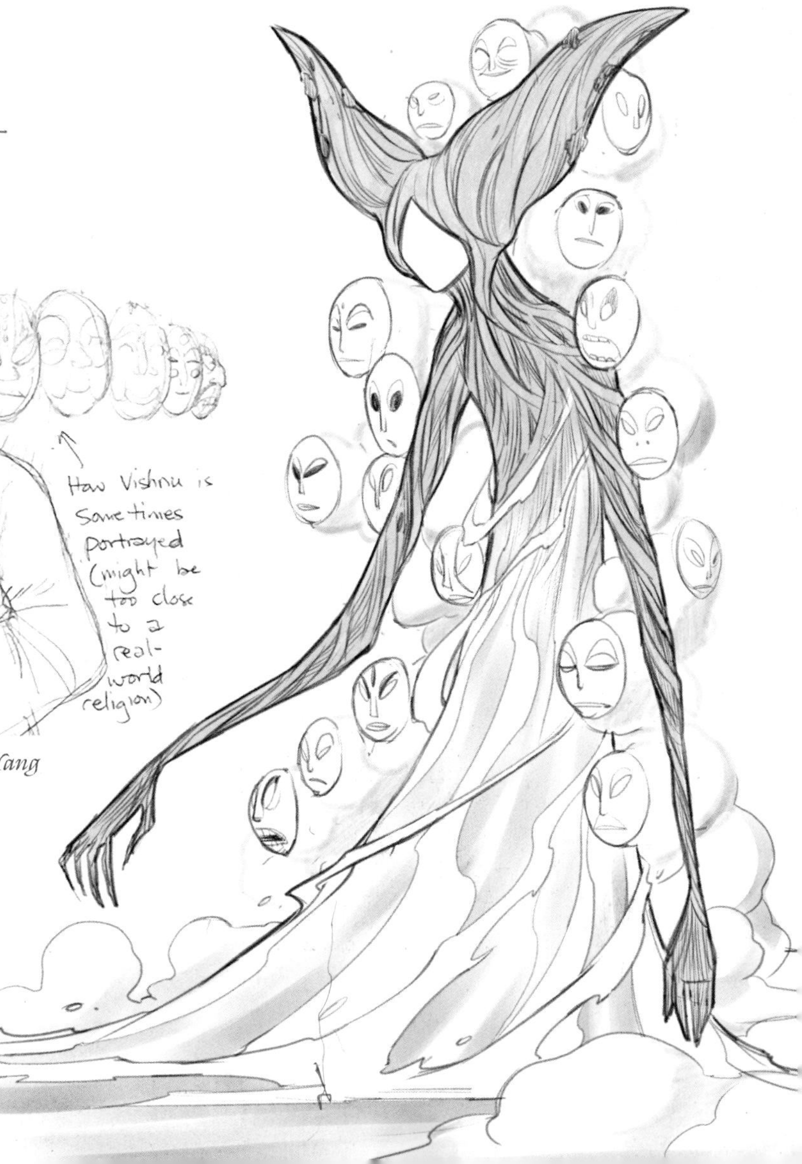

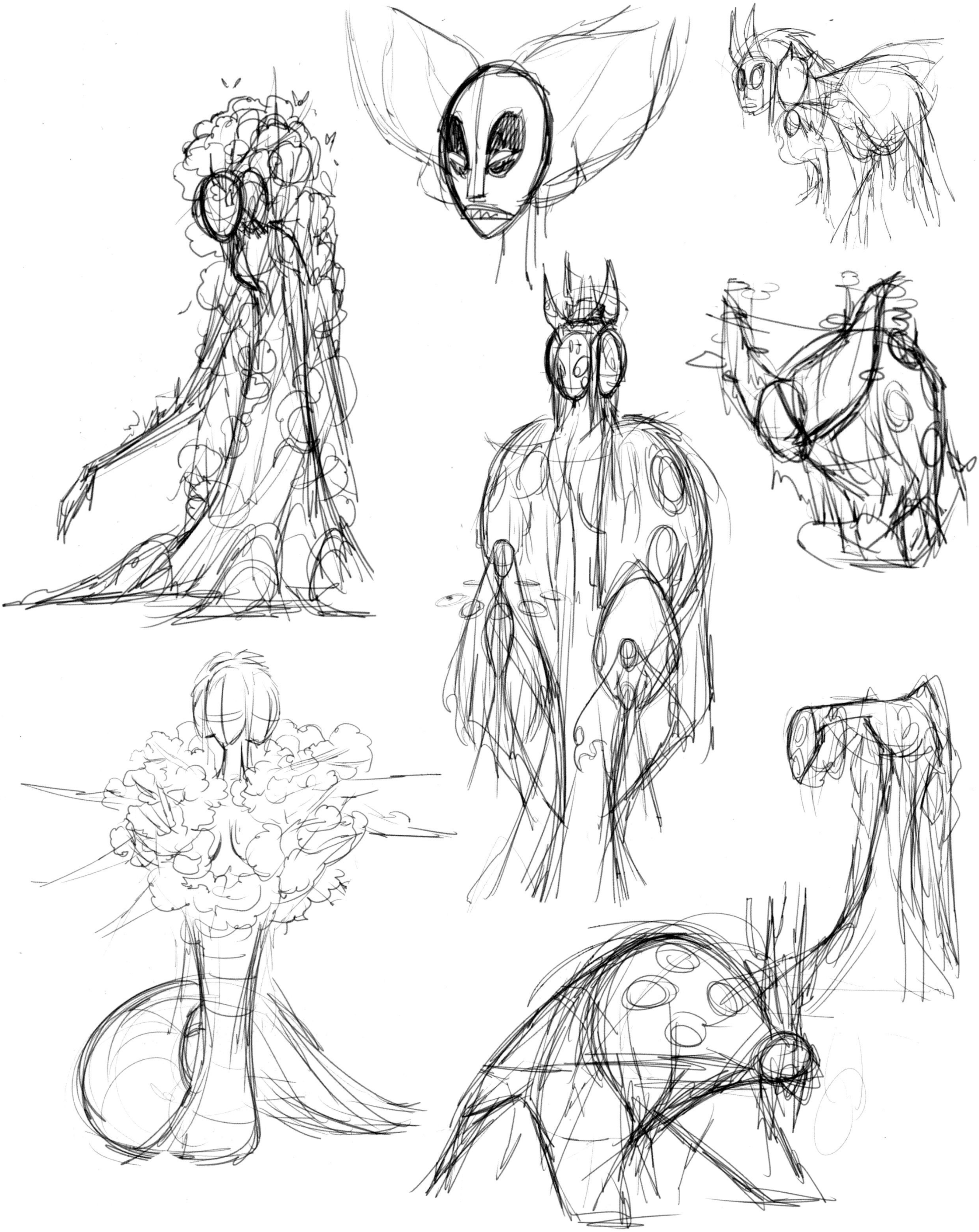

nickelodeon
降去神通
AVATAR
THE LAST AIRBENDER

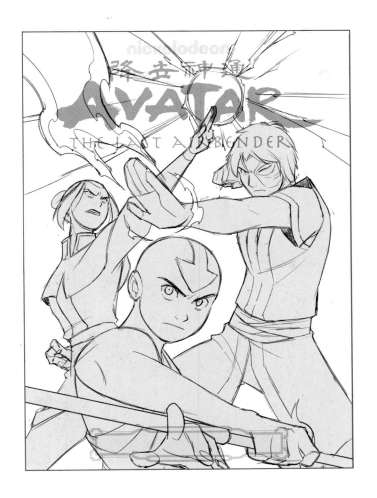

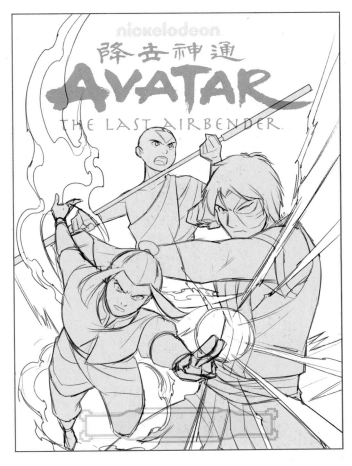

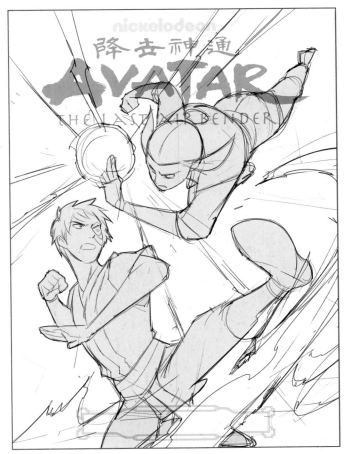

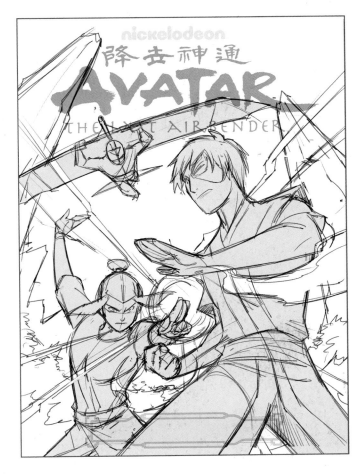

This is an image of Zuko and Azula. The one on the top left was chosen, and Bryan gave us helpful direction to get Zuko's bending pose just right.

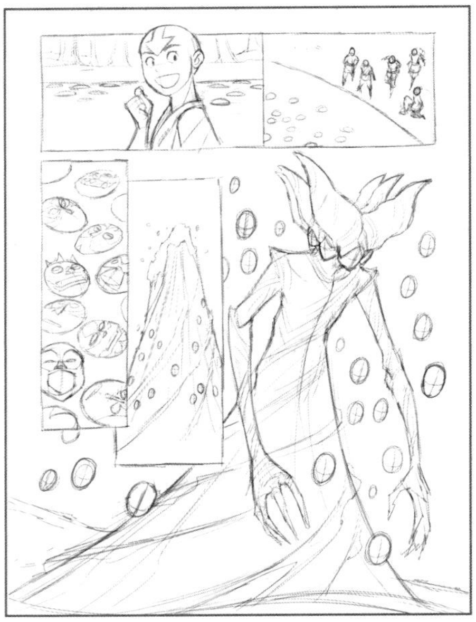
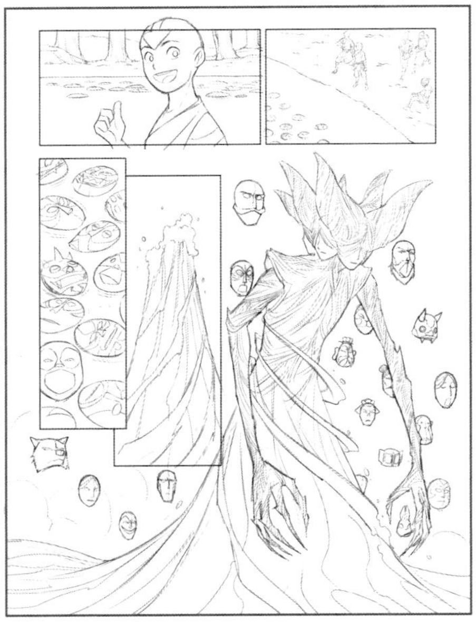
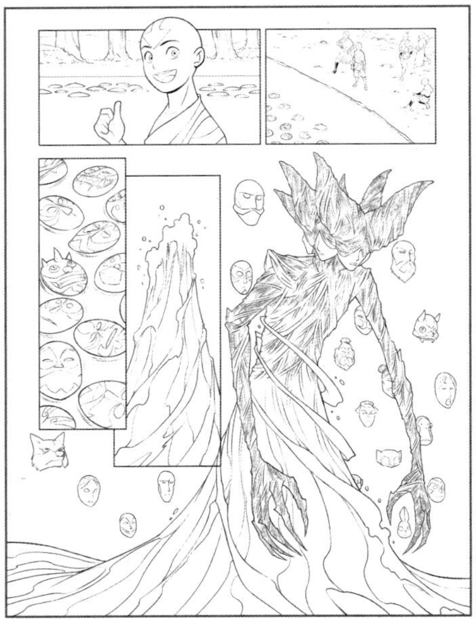
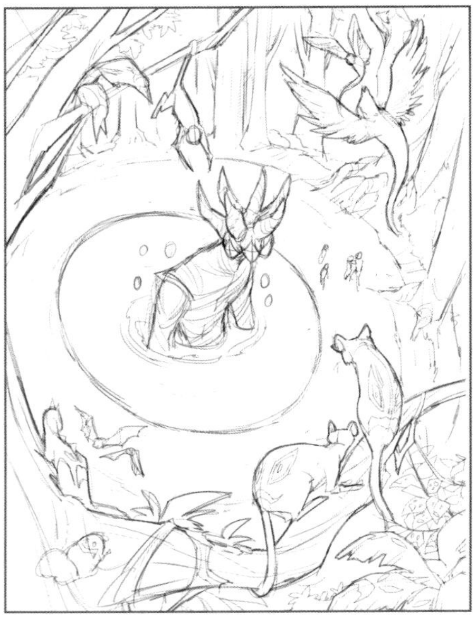
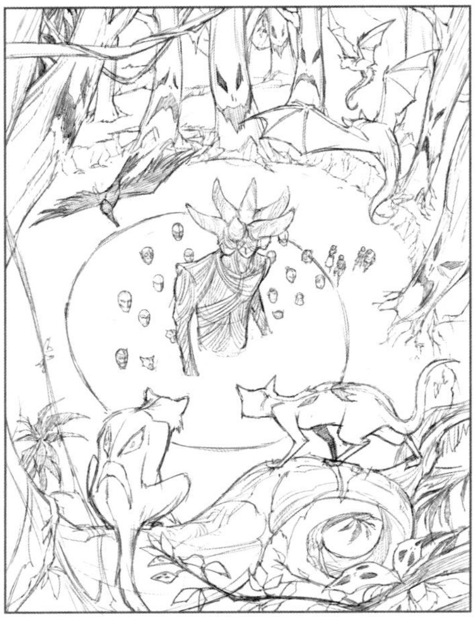
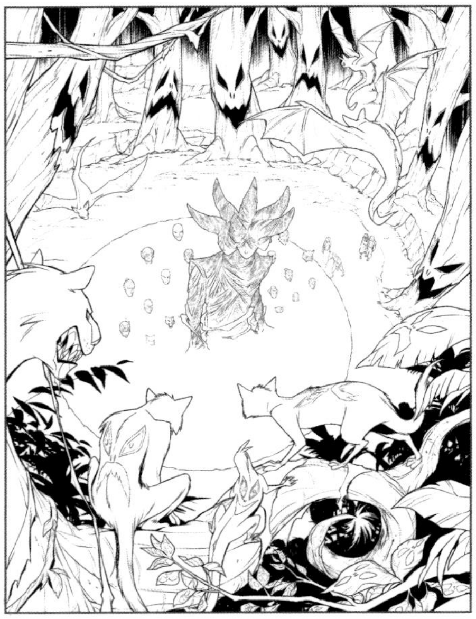
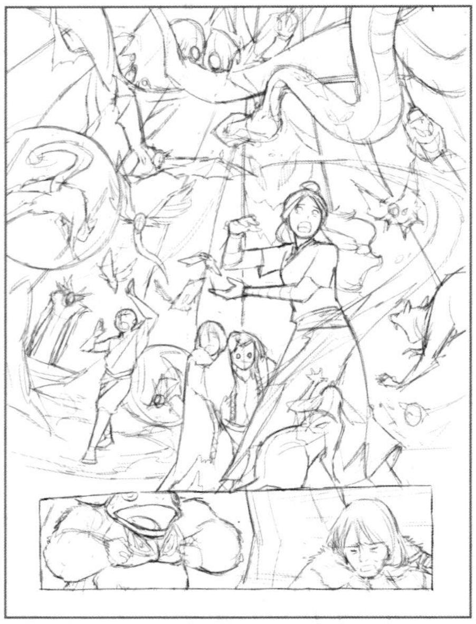
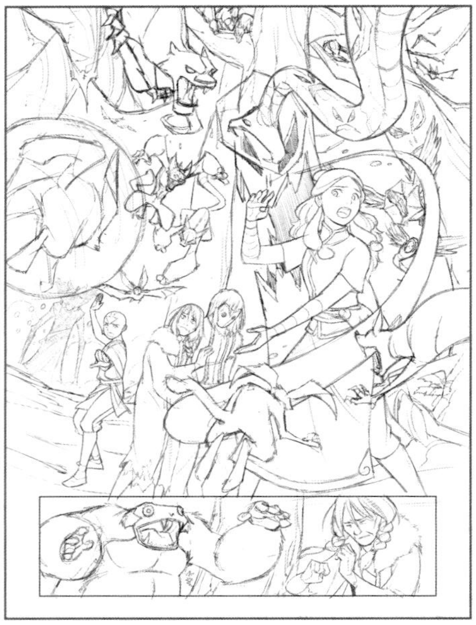
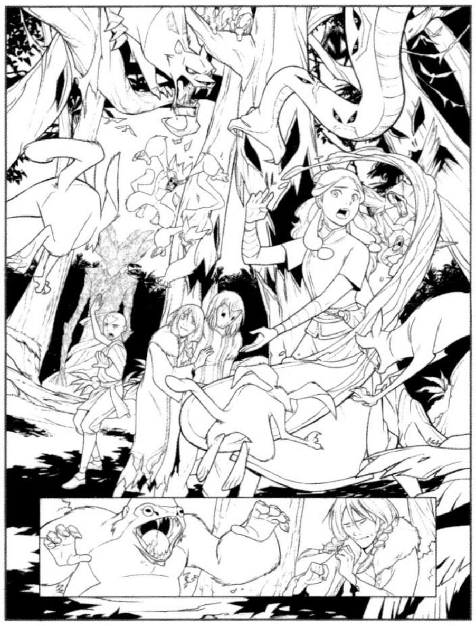

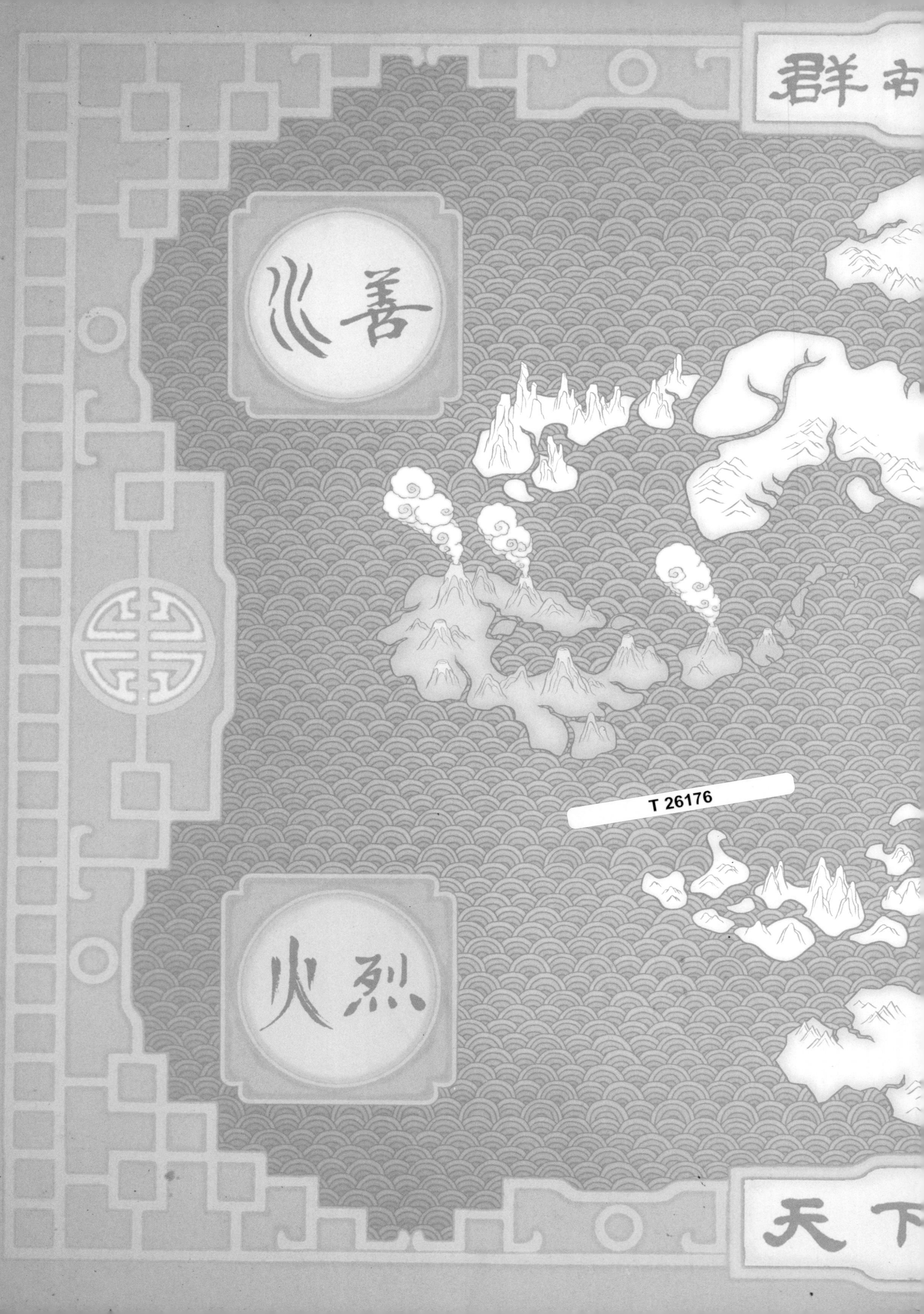
善
烈火
天下